FAITH

AND

COURAGE

COMMENTARY ON

ACTS

by
Derek Carlsen

Christian Liberty Press
Arlington Heights, Illinois

Christian Liberty Press

502 W. Euclid Avenue

Arlington Heights, Illinois 60004

www.christianlibertypress.com

Cover photo and design by Bob Fine

Layout and editing by Edward J. Shewan

Set in Minion

ISBN 1-930367-98-8

Printed in the United States of America

Preface

The Plowman Study Series

This Series has been produced with a view to helping people receive some devotional as well as doctrinal instruction. Neither of these two aspects of the Christian life should be separated from one another. We do not see this series as trying to fill the task of an exhaustive commentary that leaves no stone unturned. But, this does not mean *The Plowman Study Series* has taken short cuts with respect to hard study—it has not. We have labored to produce solid Biblical exposition, while at the same time being very aware of the audience that we are aiming at. We believe that there is a great need in our day for study helps that are simple but without being simplistic. Therefore, the language used in this series and the style of writing has been governed by the desire to produce a work that is easy to read and understand, but which also gives solid instruction in an atmosphere of devotion and challenge. We have taken the series' title from the period of the great Reformer, William Tyndale, who paid with his life (being executed in 1536) for giving his nation the Scriptures in a language that even a "plowman" could understand. He saw the great need for everyone (rather than just an elite few) to be able to understand God's truth for oneself and apply it to one's own life. Christianity is a way of life lived in submission to the Word of God. The teaching in the Scriptures is clear and relevant to everything we do here on earth. Our desire, as children of God, should be to exalt our God and Savior Jesus Christ, and His Kingdom by seeking to live by every Word that proceeds from His mouth. Our prayer is that these studies will help to foster a deep love for Christ and a desire to walk in His ways, for Jesus Himself said, "If you love Me, keep My commandments" (John 14:15).

To God alone be all glory, honor and power.

Dedicated to my parents,
Eric and Jeanette Carlsen,
for their self-sacrificial
support—without which
this project would not have
been possible.

Faith and Courage

Commentary on ACTS

Introduction

The title of this book, "Acts of the Apostles," was only added in the second century and is not really suitable because it does not cover all the acts that all the apostles did—only Peter and Paul are discussed in any detail. However, it is not solely about these two since we also read something about the ministries of Stephen, Philip, Barnabas, Silas, and Timothy.

The book is written by Luke and makes up the second volume of his writings (the first being the Gospel called Luke). Luke and Acts together, make up about one quarter of the NT, which is more than any other writer. Both books are addressed to the same person—Theophilus (whose name means, "loved of God" or "loving God" or "Friend of God"). Luke says in Acts 1:1 that in his former book (referring to the Gospel of Luke), he spoke of all the things Jesus began to do, and thus by implication, this next book (Acts) is a continuation of the ministry of Christ. Therefore, the best title for the book is probably, "*Christ's Continuing Work by His Spirit Through Members of the Early Church.*" It is not a comprehensive account of the early church since Luke records only the movements westward and northward from Jerusalem and briefly the movement eastwards into Asia and southwards into Africa (Acts 2:10; 8:27–39; 13:1; 18:24f.). Acts is the only book in the Bible that records the history of the early church, though it does not tell us everything that the Holy Spirit was doing in those days.

Acts was written after A.D. 62 (when Paul was released from prison, cf. Acts 28:30), and before the nineteenth of July A.D. 64 (when Nero began to persecute Christians after the fire of Rome). Acts 28 would not be historically true if the horrific persecutions that the Roman ruler Nero launched against the church were taking place or had already taken place (cf. 28:30, 31).

Luke emphasized the spread of the Gospel from Jerusalem, via Antioch to Rome telling us of its spread "to the ends of the earth" (1:8). The conclusion of Acts, after all the hindrances, persecutions, imprisonments and martyrdoms, is that the Gospel cannot be stopped. Christ's work will continue and success is assured (cf. 1:1, where Acts is the continuation of the work that Jesus began both to do and to teach, with 28:31, where it continued to flourish).

Luke's desire and purpose was to convince Theophilus that no one is able to stop the victorious march of Christ's Gospel. The book shows how the apostles exerted themselves to fulfill Jesus' mandate (Matt. 28:19), once they had received the necessary power (Acts 1:8; 2:4). In the Gospel of Luke, we are told that Jesus is the Messiah who was predicted in the Old Testament (OT). In Acts, we see how the Gospel advances into all the world and how the Name of Jesus is proclaimed to all the nations in an unstoppable victorious flow. Acts is a book on missions, evangelism and the early church's obedience to the Great Commission (Matt. 28:19). We must not think that Luke has just gathered together many different things that happened without any main purpose or flow to his book. The many different incidents that Luke records can only be understood correctly when they are understood in the light of Luke's overall message and one of his main purposes in writing was to show the spread of the Gospel, under the guidance and authority of the apostles, from Jerusalem to all nations. The NT church is a church of unity between Jews and Gentiles and such a change was brought about and confirmed by the Holy Spirit and the authority of the apostolic ministry. The book of Acts shows us how Jesus' promise/command (1:8) was fulfilled and all nations accepted as equal members in Christ's church.

We must not have a romantic picture of the early church as if it was without blemishes, for there were rivalries, hypocrisies, immoralities and heresies. Nevertheless, they had much that we should still try to copy, with perhaps, their great zeal and sacrifice for the work of the Kingdom standing out the most. May we be stirred up by their examples to live our whole lives to the glory of God and for the furtherance of His Kingdom. May we be consumed, despite our own many weaknesses, to fulfill our own special callings under God—doing everything for His glory and continuing the glorious advance of His Kingdom.

FAITH AND COURAGE

Acts 1:1

Theophilus must have been a significant person, since Luke writes two books to him (Luke 1:3; Acts 1:1), though little is known about him. There is much speculation about who he was, which is of no *real* value since it is only speculation. He was a Gentile and not a Jewish convert and it appears that he was converted by reading Luke's first book (the Gospel of Luke). When Luke says "all" that Jesus did, he does not mean that he has recorded everything Jesus did and said (John 21:25 tells us that it would not be possible to record all that Jesus did). Rather, Luke means *all* those things he had already told Theophilus about—the things recorded in the Gospel of Luke.

Luke is not making a distinction between the work that Jesus did and what the church is now doing, but rather, he is showing the two stages of Christ's ministry. In the first book (Luke) we learn about what Jesus *began* to do and teach, and now in this next book (Acts) we learn about all that Jesus *continued* to do and teach—especially through His apostles Peter and Paul. The ascension of Christ ended Luke's first book and begins his second one. Christ's earthly ministry ended with his ascension, but in Acts we see the ascension marks the beginning of His heavenly ministry. Luke tells us that Jesus' ministry on earth was only the beginning of His ministry, because He continues to minister from His throne in heaven, being active in the church through His Spirit (promising that He will be with us always, even to the ends of the age, cf. Matt. 28:20).

Our lives as Christians are to be lived with the reality of the power of the Holy Spirit dwelling within us and with the presence of Christ ever at our side. The King continues to work all things according His will and for the fullness of His Kingdom. Christ's ascension was the ultimate manifestation of His triumphant victory over all the powers of darkness. In Ephesians 4:10, we are told that Christ has ascended and now fills all things (a picture of the God/man), this tells us of His power, authority and control over all things—over Satan and over all his hosts. No matter what they plot and plan or how hard they fight against the church, they shall never bring their plans to pass. This is because Christ has dealt the death-blow and they are forever mortally wounded (1 John 3:8; Col. 2:15; Matt. 28:18). This Jesus of Nazareth, who was mighty in Deed and Word before God and all people in His earthly Life (Luke 24:19), continues to be mighty in Deed and Word after His ascension through the ministry of the Holy Spirit.

Acts 1:2

Luke begins Acts where his Gospel ended (with the ascension), however, Christ did not ascend until He had made provision for the care and maintenance of our salvation which is clearly seen by the amount of time Jesus spent instructing the apostles before His departure. This was an incredibly significant time because the NT church was going to be launched and then guided and taught by these men—they were going to be the foundation for the newly born church (Eph. 2:20). How could such a floundering, weak, "insignificant" group of people know that they were truly following the will of Christ? The Jewish religion was so powerful and corrupt, the ruling authority (the Roman Empire) was also very powerful and not sympathetic to this new religion. How could believers be sure in the light of so much opposition that they were following Christ? Jesus chose the apostles and taught them and imparted immense authority to them for this purpose of laying the foundation of the church. "The whole of the early church rested on their preaching and looked back to their testimony for authoritative guidance. The Christianity of the early church was the Christianity of the apostles" (Leon Morris).

How can we ever doubt that Christ is always careful to preserve and provide for us? Does not this show how graciously our needs are taken care of, before we even know they exist? These men did not take on such an office by their own authority. They were raised up by God for this special time in the history of the church. These men were chosen by Christ and instructed by Christ so that we can have confidence that their words are eternally Christ's Words and not the words of men. They had *divine* authority! Therefore, when they speak it is not man's voice, it is not merely Paul, or Peter or Luke, but God speaking, thus the whole world must listen.

None of the apostles, including Matthias (Acts 1:24) and Paul (Acts 9:15; 22:14, 15; Gal. 1:1), were self-appointed or appointed by any human agency. They were all specifically and personally chosen and appointed by Christ. The qualifications for an apostle were that they had to have been witnesses of the resurrected Lord (1 Cor. 15:7, 8; Acts 1:22; 26:16). There is no evidence that this condition was ever changed. Another distinguishing qualification was that an apostle had to have the signs of an apostle accompanying his ministry (Acts 2:43; 5:12; Rom. 15:17–19; 2 Cor. 12:12—signs, wonders, mighty deeds and also effective work among his own converts, 1 Cor. 9:1, 2). But as we have seen, there was also to be a direct call from God needed to make someone an apostle—no human authority could make someone an apostle. There is no evidence that these apostles appointed other apostles to follow after them. There is no Biblical evidence to show that they had the authority to do so. Our conclusion is to be that there is no longer any need for apostles since the foundation of the church has been laid and now we are responsible to build upon that foundation (Eph. 2:20), being totally submissive to apostolic teaching and authority (Acts 2:42; Rom. 6:17; 16:17; 2 Tim. 1:13; 3:10). Our highest authority is now the Bible, which contains the teachings of the apostles. It appears as if Paul referred to himself as the last person to have seen Christ (1 Cor. 15:8), thus there were no more apostles after Paul. (See comments on Acts 1:21–26; John 14:26; 16:13.)

Acts 1:3

There are more than ten recorded incidents where Jesus showed Himself to over 500 people (1 Cor. 15:6). This work that Jesus began to do during His earthly ministry was now continuing because He was alive. We see that Christ instructed the apostles for forty days in the things of the Kingdom of God.

The Kingdom of God is a major theme in the Gospels. The whole topic of the "Kingdom" is very large and cannot be dealt with here, however, we can touch on some of its aspects. The Kingdom is God's rule over all things (Ps. 103:19), including the hearts and lives of His people. The Christian way of life, initiated by God's will and grace in the believer by the new birth, is to manifest the character and will of God, i.e., manifest His Kingdom by doing His will. This means that the Kingdom is a manifestation of the character of the King. Regeneration is the starting place for the believer with respect to manifesting the Kingdom way of life. The Kingdom is the domain of The King, Jesus Christ, and to live in the Kingdom means to live under the reign of The King. The King, His Kingdom and His Law are inseparable (John 14:15—if you love me you will keep my commandments). To seek to live at any time by another law, i.e., by someone else's will, is to rebel against The King (Matt. 7:21–23). You cannot call Him Lord if you do not do God's will, and if you do not do God's will, you are lawless! (1 John 3:4). Thus to live by every Word that proceeds from the mouth of God is not only to live in the Kingdom, but also to manifest the Kingdom. To live under the Law-Word of God is the Kingdom (Your Kingdom come, Your will be done on earth as it is in heaven, Matt. 6:10).

The Kingdom of God, prophesied by Daniel (2:44; 7:13, 14) came with and through the activities of Christ's life, death and resurrection. Jesus announced the arrival of the Kingdom at the beginning of His ministry (Mark 1:14, 15), though the fullness of this Kingdom will only be realized at the final judgment.

The Kingdom message given to the apostles was to preach the good news of Christ's death and resurrection and make disciples of all nations—teaching them the full counsel of God so that whole nations would manifest the character of the Kingdom (Matt. 28:19). Christ's Kingdom is a Kingdom of power: He has broken the power of Satan; He entered Satan's house, bound him and then robbed him of his possessions (Matt. 12:29). Jesus said He saw Satan fall as lightning from heaven (Luke 10:18) and by this meant that Satan had yielded place to Him. Jesus has given His followers authority to oppose the forces of Satan and show forth the power and victory of God's Kingdom, manifesting the principles of righteousness, justice, love, mercy, and peace (see comments on John 12:31). We are to proclaim Christ's resurrection, the forgiveness of sins, eternal life and the authority of Christ over all things in heaven and on earth (John 20:23; Matt. 28:18). The Kingdom has come and will continue to grow, yet the glorious fulfillment of all things is still in the future. These are some of the aspects "pertaining to the Kingdom" that Jesus would have been teaching His disciples between His resurrection and ascension, though this would merely have been a continuation of what He had been teaching them before His crucifixion.

Acts 1:4, 5

Jesus ate with His disciples: this is proof that He was not a ghost, but a human being of flesh and bones—demonstrating the reality of the resurrection. He also promised them the Holy Spirit, who came only ten days after Jesus' ascension. They were told to wait in Jerusalem because this had been prophesied by Isaiah, "For out of Zion shall go forth the law, and the Word of the Lord from Jerusalem" (Isa. 2:3). This distinction between John's baptism and Christ's arises again in Acts so we will deal with it later. John's baptism was a sign pointing to the baptism they were here told to wait for.

Acts 1:6

Jerusalem probably brought to the minds of the disciples Psalms 48:2—it was the city of the Great King! It also probably brought to their minds the very exciting entry of Christ into Jerusalem on the donkey, when the whole city lined the streets and cheered Him as the expected King (Luke 19:38; John 12:12ff.). Thus in verse 6 they had a Jewish expectation of the Kingdom—they were looking for a political Messiah (John 6:14, 15; 18:33–36). It appears that they had not heard anything they had been taught over the previous three years. Calvin says there "were as many errors in this question as words." We see that Jesus rebuked the disciples on the road to Emmaus for thinking His Kingdom had this kind of emphasis (Luke 24:17–21, 25, 26). Their wrong expectations had been dashed by His death, but appear to have been revived by His resurrection. How often do not we do this? Our thinking is so fixed in one way that no matter what Jesus says we fail to realize what He means. In Mark 6:52 we are told that the disciples failed to understand the significance of the great miracle of the loaves and fish because their hearts were hardened.

Since 63 B.C., Israel had been under the dominion of Rome, however, the Israelites had not known real independence for more than 600 years. The disciples fully expected the restoration of their political sovereignty and were wondering if this was the time it was going to happen. It is extremely difficult to overcome wrong ideas and wrong teachings, even when very clear evidence is placed before our eyes. An important Kingdom characteristic is to be like little children. This does not mean we are to become immature, but rather that we are to have the humility which enables us to learn and change our ideas if necessary—humility and the ability to receive (i.e., conform to) the truth go together (Matt. 18:3–5).

Thus we see the importance of bowing to the Scriptures and not trusting anything we think unless there is clear support from the *whole* Bible. The whole Bible gives *one* system of theology and we can only understand anything in the light of that *one* system. Therefore, we need to understand the whole system in order to understand the smaller parts of the system. The disciples wanted to know if Israel would now be restored to its former glory and power as under David and Solomon. The emphasis of their question (which we can determine by the Lord's answer), was not on the role Israel would play, but on the timing of the Kingdom—was it going to be now?

Acts 1:7

Jesus answers that it is not their privilege to know such things; in other words, it has nothing to do with them! He does not say they are not allowed to know anything about *this* specific question, but that they were forbidden to inquire into times and seasons in general—there is no article (the) used here. Such inquisitive minds are a reflection of a deeper moral problem that people have. It in fact reveals their refusal to submit to every Word of God. God has set the limits and bounds of what we should and shouldn't know. Just as we refuse to obey and submit to His commands, we also refuse to submit to His limits. We feel we must know more, and we want to pursue many things that God has said are not lawful for us to know or seek after. This is because we do not want God to be the only source of law and we do not want God to be the only source of knowledge. We want to be free to do and know anything we feel is necessary. Calvin says the only way to become wise is to learn as much as Christ wants to teach us, and to be willingly ignorant of those things He hides from us. So when we are troubled with this foolish desire to know more than we ought, let us remember these words of Christ, "It is not for you to know!" "Therefore let us willingly remain enclosed within these bounds to which God has willed to confine us and as it were, to pen up our minds that they may not, through their very freedom to wander, go astray" (Calvin, *Institutes,* 1:14:1).

The godly person seeks to know *everything* that the Lord *has* revealed but he also does not want to go beyond what the Lord has revealed. There are many things that rest in God's secret power and counsel that we have not been given access to. According to the wisdom of God, there are many things we do not need to know. God has revealed everything we need to *know* and told us many things that we need *to do,* however, many people refuse to do what God has clearly told them to do, but still want to "know" more. If you cannot be faithful with the knowledge you have, why do you think you will be faithful with more knowledge? (Deut. 29:29). God has determined everything and nothing happens by chance since both the "times" (long periods of uncertain duration) and "seasons" (specific incidents. NIV, has "dates") are determined and set by Him.

Such curiosity arises when we are not doing what we should be doing (being idle), or if we do not trust the Lord (lack of faith). If we *faithfully* do what God has clearly told us to do, there will be no need, time or desire to have many curious little questions answered.

Acts 1:8

Power: means to be able, or to have the ability and power to do something. Many miraculous gifts were given at Pentecost, however, none of them are here spoken of. The central important thing for Christ was witnessing about Him. The power was primarily so that they would be effective witnesses (Matt. 28:19 has the same emphasis—all power is Mine, therefore witness about Me). This power is to manifest the Kingdom in our lives and proclaim it with the power of the Spirit (as Peter did, and his hearers were "cut to the heart," Acts 2:37).

The Kingdom of God, among other things, is the rule of God set up in the lives of God's people. To glorify the Lord is to manifest His righteousness by the way we live. The glory of God's Kingdom is seen when His people obey Him. This is possible when God regenerates our hearts by a sovereign act of His mercy and gives us the gift of faith (Eph. 2:8) so that we might believe in Him, and then empowers us by the Holy Spirit to walk in His ways. We are given the gift of the Spirit so that we might have the ability to face all things (Phil. 4:13—"I can do all things through Christ who strengthens me") and also fulfill the Great Commission of making all nations into disciples (Matt. 28:19). The Spirit is given so that there might be a victorious worldwide witness of Christ's authority over every aspect of life. "The kingdom means the subjection of all temporal affairs, of all ethical activities, of all spiritual experiences to a transcendent life-purpose in God" (Geerhardus Vos, *Redemptive History and Biblical Interpretation*, p. 311).

We are not to turn the Kingdom into some political savior (our hope is not in some political order), but nor must we deprive the Kingdom of its significance for all of life. It will have an effect on the lives of people on earth. It will have an effect upon God's people as they live and act in the social and political realm. Rome did not care what kind of god you worshipped in your heart, but they said, on earth, Caesar's word is law. They said, you can worship whom you want, as long as you obey Caesar in this realm (i.e., on earth). The early church said, "No! *Christ* is King of heaven *and* earth, and we are to live our lives on earth in obedience to His every Word." They were persecuted for this stand.

The disciples were not to go into the whole world and make predictions about when Christ would return, but were rather to teach the world everything Christ had said. Salvation and living by every Word of God is not for the Jews only but for the whole world. The book of Acts begins in Jerusalem and ends in Rome (the capital of the world in those days). The ends of the earth have been given to Christ (Ps. 2:8) and all authority has been given to Him (Matt. 28:19), thus we are to proclaim this to the whole world in the Power of the Spirit. The meaning of "ends of the earth" in Acts 1:8 and in Psalms 2:8 are the same—we are given the power to witness to the ends of the earth because the ends of the earth belong to the Lord. Jesus tells us that just as the Father sent Him, He is sending us (John 20:21).

Christ tells His confused followers that His Kingdom was over the whole world. Even the despised Samaritans were now to be part of it. There was no longer any separation between Israel and anyone else, for the middle wall of partition had been broken down (Eph. 2:14; Gal. 3:28; Col. 3:11). Thus, by the command of Christ it became lawful for the Gospel to be preached to us (the Gentiles).

Acts 1:9

Once again we see God ordering things for the sake of our own weakness—lest we should become doubtful. Jesus did not just disappear: after He had finished speaking to them He was slowly, deliberately and clearly lifted up in front of their eyes. Thus there was no reason to doubt where He had gone. The Man Christ Jesus had left them on the earth, and had gone to another place. We can be confident that although we never see Jesus on earth He is alive and seated at the right hand of God in the heavens. They watched Him ascend until He was taken from sight by the glory cloud of the Lord (the cloud in fact hides the full glory of the Lord from our view). Jesus will never stop having a real resurrection body, so the mystery continues with respect to the relationship between the human and divine natures—there is still only one Person we call Christ. Christ is now in heaven and worshipped by uncountable multitudes who say, "Worthy is the Lamb who was slain, to receive power and wealth and wisdom and might and honor and glory and blessing!" (Rev. 5:12).

We are told in Hebrews 1:3, that "[w]hen he had made purification for our sins, he sat down at the right hand of the Majesty on high." This is a dramatic way of showing that Christ had completed His work of redemption. The fact that He sat at the right hand of God means that all authority has been given to Him. (See 1 Pet. 3:22). Christ's ascension also has vital significance for our own lives. Our lives are united to Christ and what happens to Him, happens to us also. Ephesians 2:6 tells us that we are seated in heavenly places with Christ. Colossians 3:1 says since we are raised with Christ, we should seek those things that are from above. Christ was given power, glory and honor and we are not only His ambassadors but also joint heirs with Him. Since Christ has triumphed over all the powers of darkness, we too are able to destroy strongholds (2 Cor. 10:4). We are able to resist the Devil and make him flee from us (James 4:7). We are able to pray for anything in Jesus' name and the Father will give it to us (when we know the will of the Lord, then we can pray in His name). There appears to be a discrepancy between Luke 24:50–53 and this account in Acts, however, it is quite natural for Luke to emphasize some aspects at one time and leave out other aspects which were not necessary for his specific purposes at another time (even as we do when we report something—to emphasize one thing and not another does not necessarily mean that the report is distorted).

Acts 1:10, 11

The disciples were once again caught up with the secret mysteries of heaven. Christ had specifically given them commands and they were lost in the awesome experience. The angel's question is, "Why have you been standing looking up for so long?" The angels rebuked them by saying you do not demonstrate your love by gazing longingly up into the sky, but by instantly obeying His commands. They assure the disciples that Jesus will come again. Not too much can be forced upon the phrase "in the same way," since the whole of Scripture must form our understanding of the Second Coming. What we can determine is that this same personal Christ will return in power and glory.

The disciples had been commissioned to go to the ends of the earth and to disciple all the nations, teaching them everything that Jesus had instructed them—they had a task to do. They had seen Him go and were assured that He would come again, but the times were in God's hands and had nothing to do with the disciples—their responsibility was to go into the whole world. They were to be witnesses—proclaiming the full counsel of God to all the nations in the power of the Holy Spirit. Christ does not merely tell them to preach *to* all the nations, or to make disciples *in* all nations, but to make all the nations disciples. In Daniel 7, verses 13 and 14 tell us that after Christ had ascended to the Ancient of Days, "to Him was given dominion and glory and a kingdom, that all peoples, nations, and languages should serve Him." Christ's commission in Matthew 28:19, is that all nations will be discipled and come under Christ's universal Kingship (rule) with a view that they will willingly bow to and serve the Sovereign Creator and Lord of the universe.

Acts 1:12, 13

After the angels had spoken to the disciples they returned to Jerusalem, which was a Sabbath days journey—about one kilometer (this was not a law from God's Word, but a Jewish tradition that said on the Sabbath a person could only travel 2,000 paces from their house). There was an upper room where the apostles were staying which also appears to have been the meeting place for the believers in these early days. We are told very little about this upper room and it is pointless trying to speculate whether it was the same place where the Last Supper was held or some other room. It is not important. The important aspect for us is what the disciples were doing in this upper room.

Acts 1:14

Gathered in the upper room were all the remaining eleven apostles, together with some of the ladies—probably the ones that had followed Jesus from Galilee and had watched Him being crucified and buried (Matt. 27:55; Luke 23:55), and were also been witnesses of His resurrection (Luke 24:1). The only name among the ladies that is mentioned is that of Jesus' mother. She gave birth to Christ and was present at the birth of the New Testament (NT) Church (a truly wonderful honor to have this part to play in the plan of God, but it does not make her different from the rest of mankind). In fact, this is the last time the Scriptures mention her.

Roman Catholicism gives Mary a very high and important role to play in the operation of the church today, but if what they say is true, we should expect Mary to be a major figure in the life of the early church, but she is not. The Church of Rome teaches the "immaculate conception" and by this they mean that *Mary* was born without any sin and never sinned throughout her whole life. They teach that when she died she was raised on the third day (so her body never saw corruption) and was crowned Queen of Heaven and sits on a throne at the right hand of Christ. She now intercedes for millions of people who seek her assistance.

What do the Scriptures say about all of this? There is nothing in the Bible that says Mary was without sin. The only one who was without sin was Jesus Christ (Heb. 4:15; 2 Cor. 5:21). Mary needed a savior just like any other person and therefore, she called Jesus her savior (Luke 1:46, 47). The Scriptures tell us that all have sinned and come short of the glory of God (Rom. 3:23). This belief about Mary's body rising from the grave on the third day became a part of the teaching of Rome only in 1950—it was unknown in the early church! (This means that someone decided to make up this doctrine in the 1950s.) Mary cannot make intercession for us for two reasons: first, there is only one mediator between God and man and that is Christ (1 Tim. 2:5), and secondly, how can Mary listen to millions of prayers at the same time—unless she herself is God? Mary is blessed and favored (Luke 1:28, 30, 42), but this is for the role she had to play in relation to the Christ. In the same way John the Baptist was called the greatest prophet born among woman (Luke 7:28), because of his role in identifying the Messiah. How could Jesus have said what He said in (Mark 3:33–35), if Mary was so important?

We assume that the apostle's wives were included among these women in the upper room (Acts 1:14, cf. 1 Cor. 9:5). We are also told that Jesus' brothers were present and were now believers, though in John 7:5 we read that "even His brothers did not believe in Him." Jesus' eldest brother was James, and he became the most important and respected leader of the church in Jerusalem—he was most *probably* converted after Jesus' resurrection, for we are told in 1 Corinthians 15:7, that Jesus appeared to James after He rose from the dead. This is quite a turn around, since in Mark 3:21 (in the light of verse 31 most good commentators say this was his family) we see that His family came to restrain Him, thinking that He was crazy. The Scriptures tell us that the preaching of the cross is foolishness to those who do not believe, but to us who are saved it is the power of God (1 Cor. 1:18).

How can you explain Jesus' family's understanding of Him in Mark 3? What has happened between then and Acts 1? From thinking that He was a mad man, they have now come around to believe in Him as their Lord and Savior. He had lived with them for thirty years. We are told that Jesus lived an absolutely perfect life. He kept the law of God perfectly from the beginning of his life to the very end. He never sinned once in word or deed. He never had one wrong thought, never did one wrong thing to anyone—in or outside his family. Not only did He not do anything wrong, but He always acted in the best interests of the other person. Everything He ever did was for the best interests of the other person (Matt. 7:12, "whatsoever you want men to do to you, do also to them, for this is the Law and the Prophets," see too, Matt. 22:39). This is how Jesus lived His whole life. His family experienced this year after year after year. Then when He was thirty, and begins to preach about the Kingdom of God, His family is embarrassed by Him (John 7:3–5) and thinks He is crazy. Could Jesus have been a better example? The law is not just negative, it is positive too and this means that when the law says do not kill, it also means we are to protect innocent life and Jesus had fulfilled the law perfectly, doing everything right to every person all the time.

No matter what we hear, or see, if the Holy Spirit does not quicken our hearts first, we will never be able to believe in Christ. That is why Paul says we were *dead* in our sins before Christ made us alive (Eph. 2:1). Despite all that His brothers had seen, they refused to believe in Christ because they were dead in their sins.

All of them now believe and are continuing (sticking at it, persevering) with one accord in prayer and supplication. Everyone in this upper room was in one accord—having one mind or purpose. They all wanted the glory of the Lord, they all knew what Christ had promised, and with one united mind prayed for this. They had been told about the Kingdom; they had been instructed that they must be witnesses for Christ; they were commissioned to disciple all the nations; and they had been told by the Lord that in order to fulfill their responsibilities they would need the power of the Holy Spirit. Jesus had promised that He would give them this if they waited. Now they were waiting—not so they could make big names for themselves, or so they could impress people with their wisdom or power, but they waited because their hearts were consumed by the vision and purposes of God and they were united in their desire for the knowledge of the glory of the Lord to cover the earth as the waters cover the sea (Hab. 2:14). Jesus had promised that whatever they asked in His name the Father would give it to them. To pray in Jesus' name is not to put, "in Jesus' name" onto the end of our prayers, but it is to know the will of the Lord and to pray in line with that. This group of Christians knew the Lord's will and were constantly praying for it to come to pass—they were devoted. Does God need our prayers in order to be able to do anything? Are God's hands tied if we do not pray? Never! God needs no one in order to fulfill His will. So, why then should we pray?

God has ordained it so that we can have a part in His work. It is a mystery, but that does not mean it is not a real sharing in the purposes of God. What a privilege for us to be able to intercede, and pray for the manifestation of the will of God. We should not only obey the command of God to pray, but we should be amazed at being allowed to pray. This should encourage us to pray: the fact that God has said that we can come before His throne and have a real, though mysterious, part to play in His work. It is God's Kingdom; it is only through His Power that anything is achieved; He works everything according to His will; and yet He has said our part is not insignificant for He has made us heirs with Christ to the throne of God (we are to preach, but only God can open the hearts and eyes of those who hear us; dare we say preaching is therefore useless?).

Let us be encouraged that we need to pray, let us be encouraged that it is a wonderful privilege to pray. Let us find out how God says we are to glorify His name and then let us obey. May we be encouraged to pray.

Not only did these disciples of Christ pray, but also they *persevered*. They waited ten days. Jesus could have given the Holy Spirit in one day. The whole Christian life is one of perseverance. We must not become weary in well doing (2 Thes. 3:13) thus, we must not become wearied in prayer. We must persevere to the end (Phil. 3:12; 1 Cor. 9:24–27; 1 Tim. 6:12; 2 Tim. 4:7; Acts 20:24; Heb. 12:1, 3). Once we know the will of the Lord we must not give up. Prayer is ordained for our sakes not for God's sake. Prayer is an act of worship and it is through prayer that our hearts desire to seek, love and serve God. Prayer also helps us to be aware of what is going on in our own hearts. As we still our hearts in His presence and allow the light of the Spirit to search us, we are made aware of our sin and also strengthened to keep out of our lives all those things we would be ashamed of. Prayer helps us to be thankful for all that God does for us and gives to us, helping us to meditate more intently upon His grace, kindness and glory. Also, when we have prayed intently for something, we find great delight when God grants our requests. Prayer also keeps before our eyes God's providence—He is in complete control and nothing comes to pass except what He ordains (see *Faith and Reason*, chapters 4 to 6). Prayer is mysterious, powerful, and a glorious privilege which provides strength and vitality to our lives (the prayer of a righteous man is powerful and effective, Jam. 5:16) and yet we often think there is no need to pray.

Acts 1:15–20

In verses 18 and 19 we have an explanation of what happened to Judas. So let's look at these verses first. A field was bought with the money that Judas got for betraying Jesus. Judas gained a *field* for betraying the Lord! In Matthew 27:3ff., we have another account of Judas' death, but the differences between Matthew and Acts are nothing more than one writer giving more detail where another did not (there is no contradiction). When both accounts are put together we learn that Judas was upset after Jesus was killed, so he took the money back to the priests who refused to put it back into the temple treasury (since it was blood money—it had brought about the condemnation of Jesus). Judas did not want the money either, so he threw it down in the temple and went and hanged himself. Judas probably chose a place where a branch hung over a gully and tied one end of the rope to the branch and the other end round his neck, then jumped off the edge. This probably broke his neck and strangled him, but then the branch or rope couldn't take the weight and broke and thus he fell down splitting open his body so badly that all his insides gushed out (It is possible that his body hung by the neck for a day or two before the branch broke for then the body would probably have been more able to burst in this dramatic way. This is not important, only a thought). The priests, then took this money and bought a field in which to bury strangers and the whole of Jerusalem knew where the money came from to buy this field—blood money. The historical truth of Christ's death is clearly proven beyond a doubt by such a text. Every time a stranger was buried the whole of Jerusalem would have been confronted with the death of Christ. Everyone in Jerusalem knew this and none denied it.

Acts 1:15–17, 20

Peter addresses the disciples gathered in the upper room (there were about 120 people). Here we come across one of those teachings that people struggle with—God's sovereignty and human responsibility. Even though Judas was fulfilling prophecy, he had no excuse, because he was not being forced by the prophecy or God to do something he did not want to do. Rather, his wicked path was chosen by the evil in his own heart. God did not only foresee what would happen and record it in Scripture, but ordained every detail (we will deal with this more fully in 2:23).

Judas had been one of the Twelve and had fallen away. This was no surprise to Jesus, for He had already called him a devil in John 6:70—knowing what was in the heart of every man (John 2:24, 25). After the ascension, the disciples searched the Scriptures and, on the basis of the two Psalms which Peter quoted, made up the number of apostles to twelve again. Another probable reason for this was that the NT church was about to be born, taking over from OT Israel and thus they wanted a parallel between the twelve tribes of Israel and the Twelve apostles who would provide the foundational teaching of the church (Luke 22:28–30; the apostles would judge the twelve tribes which signifies a position of higher authority, see too Rev. 21:14).

Acts 1:21–26

In this section Peter mentions some of the requirements needed to be admitted to the apostleship:

An apostle had to be a witness of and thus proclaim the resurrection of Christ (Acts 4:33 and 13:30, 31). An apostle also had to have seen the resurrected Lord whom they were proclaiming (Acts 2:32; 3:15; 10:40–42). Thus Paul could later be made an apostle, because he saw the risen Lord (Acts 22:14; 26:16; 1 Cor. 9:1; 15:8). However, in order to be one of the twelve, there were stricter qualifications— they had to have been a close disciple of Jesus from the time of Christ's baptism until His ascension (Acts 1:21, 22). This was because of the importance of the task given to them (laying the foundation of he church), they needed to have been exposed fully to Christ's life and teachings. Thus we see that even Paul submits his teaching to the evaluation of the twelve, (see Gal. 1:18; 2:1, 2, especially verses 7–10). Finally we see that Christ alone could choose an apostle and in this case it was done by casting lots (Prov. 16:33), showing that even the apostles themselves did not have the authority to appoint more apostles (see also comments on Acts 1:2 above).

We can be instructed by how the apostles got their guidance: They found direction from the Scriptures (that Judas' office should be filled). They then used their knowledge of those around them to find men whose characters where worthy of such an office and then they prayed. This is how God guides us today: Scripture, common sense evaluation of the circumstances surrounding us (which is to be at all times under the authority of the Bible), and prayer. I do not believe that it is Biblical to cast lots to find out the Lord's will today, since we have the complete revelation God wanted to give us in the Scriptures and we also have the Holy Spirit who will guide us into all truth (there are no examples of casting lots after the coming of the Spirit). We also have access to God in prayer and we have Christ who said He will be with us always (Matt. 28:20).

Verse 25 tells us that Judas fell by transgression and went to the place where he belongs—that is the place of torment (Luke 16:28; Mark 14:21). This is *not* talking about falling away from salvation.

The first part of the verse shows that what is being talked about is the office of apostle—this is what Judas fell from. He was unfaithful to his calling.

The Lord chose Matthias and he becomes one of the Twelve, however nothing more is heard of this apostle. This has led some to say this incident was a mistake and the eleven apostles should have rather waited for Paul. The Scriptures clearly tell us that the Lord chose Mattias and as we saw in the beginning of Acts, the book does not claim to be an exhaustive record of everything that was done by the apostles and the early church. So it is foolish to say, because we have no record of what Mattias did, therefore he did nothing and was a failure.

Acts 2:1

Once again Luke does not go into detail about the place where this happened, but rather tells us about the disciples and what happened. They were all with one accord, having one purpose—which was to fulfill the purposes of God. In order to do this they needed the power of God, thus they were waiting all together for what Jesus had promised them. There were three major feasts celebrated in Israel each year (Passover, Pentecost, and Tabernacles).

Pentecost was called the "Feast of Weeks" in the OT (Ex. 34:22; Deut. 16:10) and took place seven weeks after Passover (a week of weeks after Passover). In Greek this feast took on the name of Pentecost (which means "fiftieth"), because it took place fifty days from the second day of Passover. This feast of weeks (or Pentecost) was the beginning of the harvest which was a time of great joy and celebration as the storehouses once again began to be filled. This was the beginning of the great harvest for when Peter later on stands up to preach, 3,000 people are saved, which was indeed the beginning of the great worldwide harvest of Christ. Jesus was crucified at Passover and ascended forty days after He rose from the grave—then ten days later the Holy Spirit was given to the Church. The most likely reason that the Holy Spirit was given during the Pentecost feast was because this feast was very well attended. There was a massive international crowd in Jerusalem, thus the birth of the NT church would be witnessed by many people and carried into many different countries fulfilling the prophecy of Isaiah that the Word of the Lord shall go out from Jerusalem (2:3). This was not the birth of the church, for "The church has been from the beginning of the world and will be to the end" (Belgic Confession, Article 28).

Acts 2:2, 3

Here we see the signs that accompanied the coming of the Spirit. Once again we see God's goodness to us. The power of the Holy Spirit and the Spirit is ability to accomplish God's will did not depend upon these signs. The signs were not absolutely necessary for what the Spirit had to do, but God saw that such signs (revealing the presence of God with His people) were necessary for the disciples and also for all who would follow after them. We are so stubborn and slow to believe God's Word and promises, that we need to have our senses involved. The Holy Spirit in abundant measure and power is now given to the church and the room where all the disciples are is filled with the sound of a mighty wind. There is no reason to believe that there was a mighty wind in the room, it was just something that sounded like a mighty wind. This noise suddenly came, not from something outside, but from heaven and filled the house. This pictures the power of God and shows that a significant supernatural event was taking place. This noise was not just heard inside the house, but was loud enough to attract the large crowd Peter would preach to.

Then we are told that the audible sign was followed by a visible one. Tongues of fire rested upon each one in the room. This fulfilled John the Baptist's prophecy found in Luke 3:16, that Jesus would baptise with the Holy Spirit and fire. I believe there are two aspects to the fire:

Firstly, for the child of God it speaks of purging us, that is getting rid of all that which is displeasing to the Lord. We are saved by Christ's work and nothing in ourselves, however we are also sanctified. We are changed more and more into the image of Christ which means getting rid of the rubbish in our lives. Both Ezekiel and Isaiah were purged by the fire of God (Ezk. 1:13; Isa. 6:7) and we are told that judgment must begin in the house of God (1 Pet. 4:17). To be cleansed by fire was an OT image (Num. 31:23).

Secondly, this fire represents God's wrath on those who do not believe. A clear picture of the judgment of God is seen in Matthew 3:12. The same Christ that brings life to some brings destruction to the rest. The same Word that is life eternal to some brings eternal death to the rest (John 12:48, "He who rejects Me, and does not receive My words, has that which judges him—the word that I have spoken will judge him in the last day"). The power and authority of Christ's Word is not only to save, but also to destroy. Christ's Word is a two edged sword and the same sword brings life to some and destruction to others. It has always been like this.

The promise of life to Adam and Eve (the Seed, is Christ)—meant destruction to the devil (Gen. 3:15).

The Word that brought life to Noah—brought destruction to the rebellious God rejecting world (Gen. 6).

The Word that saved Lot—destroyed Sodom (Gen. 19).

The path of life for Israel through the Red Sea—was the path of death for Egypt (Ex. 14:16, 17).

God is a consuming fire (Heb. 12:29) and it is only because we stand in Christ that we are not destroyed. What a wonderful honour it is to be able to come before the throne of God (this holy, unapproachable consuming fire) and say, "Father." Let us be amazed by what it means to be in Christ, but let us never forget who God is. God is not someone to play with. Here the disciples are surrounded by the real power and fire of God, yet they are not destroyed, nor are they even fearful because the blood of Christ has made full atonement for their sin. They can now be vessels in which the power of God can dwell and flow out from. We can boldly stand in the very presence of God. God's fire will purge His true children, but we can be confident that it will never destroy them.

Acts 2:4

They began to speak in other languages which were known languages (verses 6, 8, 11). This was not some silly babbling, but proper human languages. They had never learnt these foreign languages, but were enabled by the Spirit to speak them fluently in an instant. It was the Spirit that was giving them utterance. There is no basis to think that there is a difference between the tongues in Acts and Corinthians. The Scriptural evidence supports the fact that these were known languages, though the one speaking in tongues had never learnt that language.

The significance of this incident is related to Jesus' words in 1:8. A taste of what was to come: that every nation might be discipled and proclaim the wonders of God—each in their own language, yet united in the One Spirit and members of the One Body. Through the outpouring of the Holy Spirit the church was empowered to reproduce itself. Pentecost was also a clear picture of the enthronement and glorification of Jesus (John 7:39)—when Christ received all power, He then passed it on to His body. To confirm that Christ had given His disciples the authority to disciple all the nations, He gives them the ability to preach to the different nations in their own languages. This is not the complete reversal of Babel (when God made all the different languages in order to divide people into separate people groups in Gen. 11), but rather, shows that unity is to be found in Christ, not in a united language or humanistic "one world power" or force (like Babel). The Gospel unites all people in Christ, *without* destroying the different cultures and languages.

This is the official birth of the NT church and is part of the one work that Christ came to do. Christ's ascension was not the end of the saving ministry of Jesus. Jesus took on human flesh, lived our kind of life among us (John 1:14), died for our sins (John 1:29), rose from the grave (Acts 2:24), destroyed the power of the devil (Heb. 2:14), ascended into heaven and sat down at the right hand of God (Acts 2:33), then He sent His Spirit to His chosen ones so that they could all be one body and so that He could work out in them and through them (by the power of the Holy Spirit) the victory He had won (John 15:26; Matt. 28:18–21). The sending of the Holy Spirit was part of the whole package that makes up Jesus' saving ministry. Therefore, this event is not repeatable, just as Jesus' birth, death, resurrection and ascension are not repeatable acts. Everything, from Jesus' birth until the giving of the Holy Spirit, makes up the saving work of Christ and none of these things will ever be repeated, though the church will continue to receive spiritual vitality because of them. Pentecost was a once for all baptism of the church, and all Christians enter into these blessings when they believe in Christ.

There is no other sacrifice that needs to be made for us in order to make us cleaner. When we believe in Christ we are part of His one body. When we believe in Christ, all that He has done for us and given to us becomes ours, "For by one Spirit we were *all* baptized into one body … and have *all* been made to drink of one Spirit" (1 Cor. 12:13). This means that if we truly believe in Jesus Christ, then we *have* been baptized by the Holy Spirit. We all partake of the one

Spirit that was given to the church—when we believe we partake of all that Christ gained for us. God makes all true believers drink of this Spirit at conversion. There is no conversion unless we drink of this Spirit. God does not say, we can be converted and then later on, if we want to, we can receive the Holy Spirit. You cannot separate receiving Christ and receiving the Holy Spirit. The gift of the Spirit is nothing but the gift of Christ to His church. This is the final achievement of His work. Without this, the great victory of Christ's death and resurrection would be incomplete. The presence of Christ is with us through the Spirit (Christ's power, authority and victory). When we receive Christ we receive the Holy Spirit and it is impossible to receive Christ and not to receive the Holy Spirit (John 14:17, 18). We only know that Christ lives in us by the Spirit that He gives to us (1 John 3:24)—compare this with John 14:23; Rom. 8:16 and Rom. 8:9, 10 where the Spirit and Christ are equated, which means if we do not have the Spirit then we do not have Christ! Christ's ministry at the right hand of God and the ministry of the Spirit are one united work.

God was indeed doing a mighty new work. This outpouring was not only to empower the church for the work of the ministry, but these signs were also given to show the beginning of this new work. When God, through Moses, set up seventy elders to lead the twelve tribes of Israel (Num. 11:24–30), the Spirit was poured out upon the seventy in order to confirm that this was of God—and all the elders prophesied. Jesus purposely elected Twelve disciples, who He said had greater authority than the twelve tribes (Matt. 10:1; 19:28). Jesus was creating the new Israel of God—the Twelve apostles would replace the twelve tribes, and Christ's seventy (Luke 10:1) would replace the seventy elders of Israel. God had created a new Israel of God (Gal. 6:16—which can only refer to true NT believers, cf. Gal. 3:7, 9, 29).

This manifestation in Jerusalem, was a clear sign to all that the Presence and Glory of God had a new home in Christ's chosen community. This was a far greater manifestation than Moses' day, because One with far more glory than Moses had come (Heb. 3:3); He was far greater than Moses and was the One who Moses prophesied would come (Deut. 18:18). The other occasions in Acts where people receive the Holy Spirit (8:11–17; 10:44–47; 19:1–7) were to show that these groups were now accepted into the believing community. Thus those groups who were alien and even hostile to the

Old system, were now, through special signs, shown to be one with the true believers. After these incidents in Acts, there is no mention of anyone receiving the Holy Spirit by the laying on of the apostle's hands. Even through all of Paul's extensive missionary work, there is not one record of the Spirit descending as it did in these above accounts. The baptism of the Spirit then became a natural part of receiving Christ by faith—special signs were no longer needed, since it had now been made very clear to everyone that Christ was for the *whole* world.

Acts 2:5

The message of the Gospel was meant for the whole world (John 3:16), and provision had already been made by God for it to reach the whole world. He had brought people from every nation of the known world to Jerusalem—Luke is not exaggerating. Even Herod Agrippa said, "There is no people upon the habitable earth which have not some portion of you [Jews] among them" (*Josephus' Wars*, 2:16:4). These international witnesses were God-fearing Jews and proselytes.

Acts 2:6–11

This "noise" I believe, means both the sound in verse 2 and the noise of the disciples speaking in many different languages. The hearers were confused and amazed because those speaking all these different languages were simple people. Luke lists fifteen nations. The NT church is born when 120 people waiting in obedience to Christ's Words are filled with the Holy Spirit and almost immediately the witness of Christ floods into the whole world. The truth of God is no longer only to be found in Jerusalem—from now on the church is worldwide (John 4:21, 23).

Acts 2:12, 13

They were amazed and understood it not. Others mocked. Those who were amazed heard something they understood. Those who mocked understood nothing—these languages were foreign and therefore sounded like babbling.

I believe it was the local people who mocked. The foreigners were amazed. What the local people heard were unknown tongues. Paul tells us that this is a sign of the judgment of God on the unbeliever (1 Cor. 14:22). Those hard hearted Jews: who lived in Jerusalem and called for and witnessed the crucifixion of Christ; who rejected Him and would not repent, were under the judgment of God. This is a fulfilment of Isaiah 28:11, 12—God says, "If you will not hear my prophets when they speak to you in your own language, then there will come a time when I will speak to you in a language that you do not understand." This is the wrath of God on unbelief. God's nation was under His judgement. Because of their continued hardness of heart, God would speak to them in a way that they could not understand. Jesus did the same (Matt. 13:10, 11, 13). The judgment of God was about to fall upon Jerusalem (Matt. 21:41; Luke 19:41–44).

God had sent His people into captivity to foreign nations (e.g., Nebuchadnezzar, Jer. 35:15; 39:5, 6) when they rejected His Word and prophets. What would He do to them now that they had murdered His Son? He was going to utterly destroy them (Matt. 3:12; 21:41; 22:6, 7; 23:35–38, etc.). Israel in fact asked for God's fearful judgment to fall on them (Matt. 27:20–25) and it did, only about thirty five years later. Jerusalem was destroyed in A.D. 70. Here the condemned nation hears strange babbling and still, in rebellion to God's Word and despite the warnings from the prophets, continue to mock God's sign and warning.

Acts 2:14

Peter, together with the other apostles, came forward to explain what was happening. His standing up does not necessarily mean that all this had taken place while they were seated, for it could also mean that Peter and the eleven "took their stand." That is to say, they were standing for the light over against the darkness (the mockers) and standing as Christ's witnesses (1:8), making known the saving will of God. Peter speaks with the power of the Holy Spirit and the authority of God. He says there is absolutely no doubt as to what he is about to say and since it was God's truth, they had better listen to his words.

Acts 2:15

Peter hardly wastes time with the stupid accusation that the disciples were drunk. He says what you suppose is not based on fact and is nothing but a foolish irresponsible statement. We need to be slow to speak (James 1:19), especially when evaluating and passing judgment on people's characters and actions (it is not a small thing to break the Ninth Commandment, Ex. 20:16). Peter says it is only 9:00 a.m. and only the most hardened drinkers could possibly be drunk by this time in the morning. Moreover, his implication was that it is easy to identify hardened drinkers and there is not a great number of them, however, here there are at least 120 upstanding citizens who could not possibly all be drunk.

If we are going to allow the Scriptures to show us the meaning of Pentecost we will see that the importance of it is not found in the inner spiritual life of the disciples. The emphasis is not even on the *gift* of the Holy Spirit. No, what we see in the Bible as the focus is the preaching about Jesus Christ in power and authority. The purpose of Pentecost is so that the name of Christ might be exalted when the church is empowered to be effective *witnesses* for Him. The Spirit is poured out for the purpose of universal salvation— that all nations may be discipled and taught everything that Christ taught (Matt. 28:20). The speaking in other languages is a wonderful picture of God's launch of the worldwide message of salvation. The church's world mission is started by these disciples proclaiming the wonderful works of God in the world's languages. To be filled with the Holy Spirit is to want others to know about Christ (to be His witnesses).

Acts 2:16

Peter begins His sermon and explanation of what all this meant by quoting from the Scriptures. Even Peter, the apostle, finds clear solid Scripture to prove that this is in fact how the Holy Spirit does manifest Himself. We can only be sure that we are not being misled by the doctrine of demons and deceiving spirits if we rely upon the Bible to show us what is a true manifestation of the Holy Spirit and what is not (2 Thes. 2:9, 10; 1 Tim. 4:1). Peter says, *this* is *that—this* which you see manifested before your eyes is *that* which we find *written* in the Bible. If this is not how we determine a true from a false manifestation of the Holy Spirit, then we will find that whatever man's mind can dream up will be accepted as a real manifestation of the Spirit. Peter says these men are not drunk, but fulfilling a prophecy which had been given about 800 years before.

Acts 2:17, 18

Is Joel's prophecy with respect to the "pouring out of the Spirit" still waiting to be fulfilled in our days? Was what happened on the day of Pentecost just a little taste of what was going to come later on in history? No, Peter says that what was taking place was fulfilling Joel's prophecy (that was it, according to Peter). It was here that the Spirit was given in abundance to the NT church so that whoever enters into the church through faith in Christ, immediately becomes a partaker of this same gift—given once for all time.

It is very important that we have a Biblical understanding of the "last days," because many say it refers to the end of time. The most important time in the history of the universe was that period of time that focused on the life of Jesus Christ, whose life was lived out in fulfilment of divine prophecy. Jesus finished the work that accomplished God's plan of redemption (or salvation) for the world. All of Scripture has its focus on Christ. The OT looked forward to the coming Savior, while the NT testifies to His completed work (Luke 24:25–27; John 1:45; 5:39, 46; Acts 3:24; 10:43).

There are many OT references that talk of the Messiah coming in the "last days" (Gen. 49:1, 10; Isa. 2:2; Jer. 23:20; 30:24; Dan. 2:28; Hos. 3:4, 5; Mic. 4:1). These passages are not talking about Christ's second coming, but about when He would come to redeem (die for) His people. The period of the OT is often called the "former days" (Mal. 3:4; Mic. 7:14, 20) or the "days of old."

The "last days" began when the Son of man appeared (Heb. 1:2; 1 Pet. 1:20). He appeared in the last days to accomplish His work of redemption (Heb. 9:26). His work also included the pouring out of the Holy Spirit (Acts 2:17, cf. Isa. 32:14, 15; Zech. 12:10). The "ends of the age" came about during the ministry of the apostles (1 Cor. 10:11).

We must not confuse the "last days" with the "last day." The "last days" started with Christ's coming and referred to national Israel. This time of Christ's ministry and the apostolic ministry were the last days for Israel, though they were the early days for the NT church. It was a prophetic term proclaiming that the nation of Israel's position as God's special covenant people was about to end. These were warnings, written by the apostles to their own generation. John the Baptist, Christ and the apostles warned about the soon coming judgment upon national Israel (Matt. 3:7, 10; 22:6, 7; Matt. 24; Luke 19:41–44; Acts 2:20). Thus, the "last days" ended with the destruction of the rebellious covenant people of God (Israel), which included the destruction of the entire system of OT temple worship. The priesthood, temple, and animal sacrifices came to an end in A.D. 70, and have never been restored. The nation of Israel at this time were no longer merely disobedient children who could be reformed by a Father's discipline, but had become as the heathen—not only strangers to the Kingdom of God, but hostile to it and thus, they were cut off from their favoured position (Rom. 11:20). On the other hand the "last day" in Scripture refers the end of history (with the resurrection of the dead and final judgement, see John 6:39; 11:24; 12:48).

Thus when Peter, at Pentecost, says this will happen in the last days, we are not to think that there is something of what Joel promised that did not come at Pentecost, but is awaiting for some time in the future to be fulfilled. Everything that Joel promised was received on the day of Pentecost. The "last days" specifically refer to, and focus on, the whole of Christ's ministry (which included His sending the Holy Spirit).

The way we understand what is meant by the "great and notable day of the Lord" is by looking at the context of the sentence (e.g., Malachi 4:5; Acts 2:20). When God's judgment is talked about as a "dreadful" or "notable" day, we need to see if God, in the context, is referring to a *specific* people, city or nation, or whether it is a *general* prediction. If it is general, then it refers to the final day of judgment (when all such nations, etc., will be judged), however, if God is talking to a specific nation, then it refers to God's wrath that is about to fall upon those particular people. It means their day of judgment is not awaiting that final day, but will take place in history. In a sense, nations can only be judged on earth, while individuals can be judged on earth and on that final day—ultimately sin is personal. It is individuals who will be in hell because of their own personal rebellion against God, even if they stand before God as a "nation" (Matt. 25:32ff.). Rebellious nations are made up of rebellious individuals.

This pouring out of the Spirit is upon the whole Messianic era which stretches from the first to the second coming of Christ— which is not just a small sprinkling, but more like a heavy thunderstorm. The Spirit is *abundantly* given to Christ's church. The giving of the Spirit will not be taken back and it is given to the universal church, including all different nations and people groups. This pouring out talks of great plenty, whereas in the OT there was not such an abundant giving of the Holy Spirit. In the NT there is a greater abundance of the Holy Spirit for a greater number of people. This event at Pentecost was not just a sign or shadow of something else, for with the coming of Christ, this promise finds its reality or fullness. Pentecost was the actual pouring out of the rivers of life, and the effect of this will continue to grow, bringing health and restoration to everything it touches, covering the whole earth (Ezek. 47:1–12; Hab. 2:14).

All flesh: does not mean every person no matter what their spiritual condition is like (the Spirit is only given to those who receive the Son by faith), rather, it means all different classes and types of people—it is not reserved for certain types of people in society, i.e., for those having a special social distinction, gender or position. This is for everyone, men, women, children and slaves (Gal. 3:28). The Gospel is, as Acts clearly emphasises (1:8; 8:5, 27; 10), for all nations and peoples, not just for the Jews (Gal. 3:14; Eph. 2:13ff.; 3:6; Col. 3:11).

They shall all be prophets. Visions and dreams were the ordinary ways that God revealed Himself to His prophets (Num. 12:6). What is meant here by prophecy is that wonderful and amazing gift of understanding the mysteries of the Kingdom of God. This was the special privilege of the prophets in the OT, but now in the Kingdom of Christ, even the lowest person will have a deep relationship with God, (compare this with 1 Sam. 7:8; Ex. 19:21, 24; 20:19). We are not to think that "prophet" is used here as it is used in the OT, for here it means God's excellent gift of understanding (Calvin). Under the New Covenant, all believers, without distinction receive spiritual wisdom (John 6:45; 1 John 2:20, 27) and know God in an intimate way (John 14:23; Rom. 8:15; Gal. 4:6, 7). All believers are now able to speak about the mysteries of God's Kingdom and make known His majesty, glory and salvation. Moses longed for such an abundant out-pouring of God's Spirit (Num. 11:29, cf. 1 Chron. 25:3). "Every man shall no longer teach his neighbour; because they shall all know me, from the least unto the greatest" (Jer. 31:34; Heb. 8:11). All who believe would be intimate friends of God and acquainted with His secrets and counsel (cf. Gen. 20:7 with James 2:23, see too Matt. 13:52). The major emphasis in OT prophecy was not predicting future events, but making known the great truths of the faith, calling on people to have hope in God and calling them back to God's eternal standard of right and wrong. For the most part, prophets brought people's attention back to that which God had *already* revealed.

Acts 2:19–21

We saw in 2:3, that Jesus baptises in the Holy Spirit and fire: where great blessings are poured out upon the righteous, but the wrath of God is poured upon the disobedient (Matt. 3:11, 12). The same word that brings life also brings death to the rebellious (John 12:48). Now we see this same picture about the work of Christ repeated—the wonderful blessing of the gift of the Holy Spirit on the one hand and then on the other the terrifying judgment of God. God's judgment was coming upon the Jewish nation (Jesus had clearly talked about it in His ministry, Matt. 21:41; 24; Luke 19:41–44; 23:29).

The terms used here are familiar OT prophetic pictures (Isa. 13:10; 34:4, 5; Ezek. 32:7, 8; Joel 2:10), where the prophets used such language to talk of God's judgment upon a once great civilisation or people. The moon being turned into blood and the sun into darkness tells of the destruction of Israel's civil and religious government and the putting out of all their lights (so to speak). Just as the first part of Joel's prophecy was a message telling them that the fullness of the Spirit had come, so the second part pronounces the judgment of God on the nation. The changes that were coming upon this people were as great as would be the effects in nature if the sun was put out. This great and notable day of the Lord refers to the judgment of God particularly on Israel, but that same judgment continues down through history upon all those who reject the Messiah until the day of final judgement.

God is the eternal judge who judges today. We must not forget this. The nation of Israel had for the most part rejected their savior and had Him murdered. They now mocked the tongues and Peter says, "O you blind fools, how is it you still cannot see? You mock at the very thing that foretells of your destruction and judgement!" The land of Israel was about to lose its favoured purpose and function in the plan of God. Their significance as the special nation of God was going to be forever gone—a terrifying judgment of God upon a rebellious and hard hearted people (there would be a remnant out of the nation that would be saved, Rom. 11). Israel has been rejected so that the Gospel might come to us, but this should make us fearful and not slothful (Rom. 11:19, 20). May we be encouraged to persevere in fervent prayer and devotion to the Lord and to His whole counsel. True faith manifests itself in every area of life.

But whoever calls upon the name of the Lord will be saved: God always displays His mercy, even in His judgment (Hab. 3:2). The prophet does not leave them without hope in the midst of their misery. History tells us that at the destruction of Jerusalem more than one million people perished, yet not one Christian was killed (those who believed in Christ for salvation also believed His Words and He had warned of Jerusalem's coming destruction in Matt. 24). God's salvation is comprehensive and has significance for all of life. In the midst of such spiritual and physical darkness which hung over this nation, Peter presents the glorious light of salvation in Christ. This should encourage everyone to call upon the Lord. The Gospel message is for all people and it is only stubborn unbelief that keeps anyone from sharing in its glorious fullness.

Peter rebukes the fools, showing that what they were calling drunkenness, was the coming of the Holy Spirit, promised by God hundreds of years earlier through His prophet Joel. Peter also quotes from the same prophet to show God's righteous judgment coming upon all those who reject God and His Word. Thus, Peter turns the thoughts of his audience upon themselves, inquiring about their own salvation. He says the judgment of God rests upon you, but whoever calls upon the name of the *Lord* will be saved. Therefore, the natural question in everyone's minds would have been, "Who is this *Lord* Peter is talking about?"

Acts 2:22

By saying, "Men of Israel," Peter is reminding them that they are the chosen people of God. He reminds them of the covenant and appeals to them to now act in a way that is worthy of this high privilege. Peter speaks with God's authority and is not ashamed of his message, saying, "Hear my words!." This probably also reveals the heart of someone who is a true witness for Christ—speaking with compassion and an earnest desire for the sinner's salvation (please, listen to me). They do not realize what a wonderful mercy it is to hear these words of salvation, so Peter is anxious that they listen to him carefully.

The emphasis of Pentecost, according to Peter, is not Old Testament prophecy, or the speaking in other languages, but Jesus Christ (He is what all this was about). What Peter says next is important and teaches us much. The translation should be "Jesus the Nazarene." When Peter denied the Lord, it was because a little servant girl had asked him if he was with Jesus the Nazarene (Matt. 26:71). Jesus came from a little village called Nazareth. It was a town held in very low regard by the Jews (in fact it was despised). When Philip told Nathanael that he had found the one that Moses and the prophets wrote about: Jesus who came from Nazareth, Nathanael said, "Can anything good come out of Nazareth?" (John 1:46).

Matthew in his Gospel said, Jesus shall be called a Nazarene and this would fulfill what the prophets said about him (Matt. 2:23). Now there is no OT prophet that says this. However, Matthew does not say a prophet, but the prophets. This speaks of a prophetic understanding of the Messiah rather than a specific prediction. This understanding is what Isaiah had when he talked about the Messiah saying, "He was despised and rejected by men ... he was despised and we esteemed him not" (Isa. 53:3). Paul tells us that he preaches Christ crucified, which is a stumbling block to the Jews and foolishness to the Gentiles (1 Cor. 1:23). Jesus said that if you were ashamed of Him, He would be ashamed of you (Mark 8:38).

Peter not only says that the *Lord* they must believe in to be saved is Jesus, but he uses the very term that is despised—the hated name, Nazarene. Peter was not about to apologise for who Jesus was. He was not ashamed of the offence of the cross. Paul said the same: "For I am not ashamed of the Gospel of Christ, for it is the power of God to salvation for everyone who believes" (Rom. 1:16, also 2 Tim. 1:12). Peter refused to remove the offence that the Jews had with respect to Jesus. He had once denied that he was associated with the Nazarene, but now he was standing boldly and unashamedly with the only savior. He did not care what the world thought, he was not afraid or embarrassed by those who laughed and made fun of who Jesus was, for God has chosen the foolish things of this world to put to shame the wise (1 Cor. 1:27), moreover, Christ alone has the words of eternal life (John 6:68).

Neither must we apologise for the message of Christ. We must not be ashamed of what God has said and what He has told us to teach all men and nations. Let God be found true and every man a liar (Rom. 3:4). We are not to change the message or try to remove from the message that which will offend the unbeliever. When Paul preached to the Greeks who loved to hear new things and talk about philosophy, he did not hide what was offensive to these people. He told them that Christ rose from the dead (according to these Greeks, the resurrection was an impossible and foolish idea), when Paul said this they mocked him and many no longer wanted to listen to him (Acts 17:32). Our responsibility is to preach the full counsel of God and not to think large crowds are the most important thing.

Peter says, "Do you want to be saved from the wrath of God? Then believe on the *Lord*—Jesus the Nazarene!"

The religious leaders had condemned Jesus to death, saying he was an evil dangerous person, however, Peter says this Man was approved of God—God had sent Him and also clearly shown that He was approved by God (what He did was proof that He was from God). And what was this clear proof? Miracles, wonders and signs—these were to show the Jews that Jesus was from God (God was using Jesus to do these things). Jesus Himself pointed to His works as proof of His Divine mission (John 14:11), because they prove that Jesus is who He claimed to be (see also John 9:31–33; 10:37, 38; 11:42; 20:31). These wonders and signs that Jesus did *then*, continue to be valid proof *today* of who Jesus is. John tells us that the things that Jesus had already done were sufficient proof for us to believe in Him—we do not need more and more signs in our day to prove who Jesus is again and again (John 20:31). What Jesus did was clear proof that He was God both for His own generation and for every generation after that.

Peter goes on to say that all of this was not done in some corner. Peter did not have to explain who Jesus the Nazarene was, or tell them what kind of miracles He had done, because Jesus had done these things right among all the people in the nation. Peter says you already know all of this. The Jews had seen Jesus' works, but had still rejected Him as their Messiah. The reason they had rejected the Messiah was not because His works were not clear, but because they hated Him and they hated God (John 15:24, 25).

Acts 2:23

Peter says, "Him," or "this one," meaning the one whom God had chosen, called, sent and shown to be His own through mighty miracles—this is the one they murdered!

Peter also deals with something that could be confusing: how could the Messiah, the one who came to save others, die? If He could not save Himself, then how could they be confident that He was able to save them? (Mark 15:30, 31). Peter says the only reason that this could happen to Christ was because it was ordained by God. Nothing could have happened to Jesus if it was not God's purpose. Jesus said the same to Pilate (John 19:10, 11). It was God who had purposed to save those who were His (John 6:65; 10:14; 17:6, 9), through the death of His Son, at the hands of wicked men.

Having been determined: shows that this was something that was fixed and ordered back in eternity. The Lamb was slain from the foundation of the world (Rev. 13:8; 17:8; 1 Pet. 1:20). The reason God's foreknowledge is so sure is because He ordains whatsoever comes to pass. Everything is ordered and settled by God's will and therefore, God knows everything. To have foreknowledge of something, means that particular event is fixed and certain. The Jews took Christ and because they were not allowed under Roman rule to execute anyone, they got the Romans to do it. They gave their Messiah over to the Gentiles to be killed. There is no crime to compare with this crime. This is the Messiah that the nation of Israel had looked for and longed for from the beginning of her existence. Abraham, the first Jew and father of the nation, had longed for the coming of the Messiah (John 8:56). Moses, and all the prophets spoke about this Messiah and longed for His coming. Every woman in Israel longed to give birth to the Messiah. The Messiah had finally come and John (the greatest OT prophet Luke 7:28), went before Him and told the people who Jesus was, saying, "Behold the Lamb of God who takes away the sins of the world" (John 1:29).

We see that God, in many different ways, had made it abundantly clear that Christ was the Messiah (see too, Matt. 3:17; Luke 9:35; Act. 2:22). These people, who prided themselves in being called Israel, and prided themselves that they were Abraham's descendants (Luke 3:8), and prided themselves that they had the law and the prophets (John 5:39), murdered the very one that their whole existence pointed to. The only reason that God had chosen Israel and preserved them was so that the Messiah could be born in Israel. The Jews despised the Gentiles calling them unclean and lawless, yet they took their Messiah, the hope of the nation and surrendered Him to the Gentiles to be killed. The Jews basically forced the Gentiles to kill their Messiah. When Pilate said I can find no fault in this man, they said it does not matter, just kill Him! (Luke 23:15–23; Matt. 27:23, 24). We see, however, in Acts 4:27 that the Gentiles were as guilty as the Jews for this crime against Christ.

Peter says, you people have done this wicked thing. You are guilty of His murder. Yes it was ordained by the eternal counsel of God, however, your wicked wills freely chose to do this evil deed. Peter points to their personal guilt before God.

The sinner is in rebellion against God, he hates God and suppresses the truth of God that is clearly set before his eyes (Rom. 1:18f.). It is wrong for Christians to try and make unbelievers feel good about themselves with the hope that then they might want to hear about Jesus. The sinner who feels good about himself, has no need of a savior. We need to point to their guilt and God's condemnation resting upon them before we offer them a Savior.

When God ordains something it does not mean man's actions are innocent. There was never a more wicked crime than this one of murdering the Son of God, and yet it was ordained by God from eternity. God in no way is tainted with this sin, for He did not sin. The sin was committed by these men and it was sinful because they were not forced by God to do what they did. What they did they freely willed to do. When we talk of man's free will we must define what we mean. When we ask if man has free will we are asking if man is *able* to do something.

The Scriptures teach that when man does something, he is not forced to do it. God predestines whatever happens in this world, however, He never forces anyone to sin. God does not force people against their desire or will. Whatever they do they do freely. Another aspect, however, must be included in order to complete the whole picture, namely, people's choices are governed by their inner character or nature. A person is only free to choose (or able to choose) what he desires and therefore, he cannot just choose anything. A person's inner character (the condition of his heart) determines what he is able to choose.

A tree is known by its fruits. The fruit a tree produces is determined by the character of that tree (Luke 6:43–45). People can do whatever they desire, but what they desire is determined by their character. If their character is evil, they will have desires that are evil and they will freely do what is evil. The choices that a man makes are his own choices, he is not forced to act against his will, but his choices reflect his inner character. The sinner is not free to choose between good and evil in a moral sense. He is not able to act in a way that is not sinful, because he is a slave to sin (Rom. 6:17). It is because the unregenerate man is a slave to sin that he freely chooses to sin, however, the truth is, he can only choose to sin: he can only ever act in a sinful way. It makes no difference whether such a person chooses to rob a bank or to play soccer with his son—both are sinful choices. The reason they are both sinful, is because such a person does not do everything to the glory of God or give thanks to God (1 Cor. 10:31; Col. 3:17; 1 Pet. 4:11).

Such a person is only able to choose to sin. This is all his inner character can do. He hates God and suppresses the clear revelation of God that is in him and around him (Rom. 1:18–20). He is a rebel in his mind towards God (Rom. 8:7; Col. 1:21). Such a person is not able to choose to love God. His will cannot freely choose to love God while all the time he hates Him. The sinner is in bondage to Satan, he is a slave to sin and he loves to sin (Rom. 1:32). According to God, such a person is as good as dead with respect to his ability to choose what is good (Eph. 2:1, 5). He needs to be quickened or made alive by God before he is able to choose what is right. His inner character needs to be changed, by the grace and power of the Holy Spirit, before he can produce good fruit. It is God who has to first make us alive before we can act in the right way or choose what is right.

Every detail of Christ's death was planned by God. If this event of extreme wickedness was predestined by God and fixed by His eternal counsel, then every event that led to it was also ordained by God. If God ordained such a murderous event, making it part of His wise counsel and then tells us that His eternally determined purposes do not destroy human freedom and responsibility, then it should not be difficult for us to accept that all events are under His control and are planned by Him for His wise purposes. Why do we say there is a contradiction where God says there is no contradiction? This same truth is repeated in Acts 4:28—God ordained Christ's murder, yet the Jews (and Gentiles) were charged with the guilt of the murder (Acts 2:23; 3:15; 4:10; 5:30; 10:39).

In the same way, Judas was ordained by God to betray the Lord (David had prophesied about it, Acts 1:16). Judas' actions were as fixed as Jesus' death. Every part of what happened was set by God's will in eternity, however, Judas was not forced to act against his will. He freely betrayed Christ. Despite all the ministry and teaching he had received from Christ, despite all the miracles (so many that all the books in the world in John's day couldn't contain them, John 21:25), despite such a clear manifestation of the glorious power, love and grace of God, Judas chose evil. He chose what was evil because he was acting in accordance to his inner character. He could not decide to choose the good, despite all the light he had received because he was in bondage to Satan and a slave to sin. Judas couldn't choose not to betray Christ, however, he was not forced to choose to betray Christ. He freely chose to betray Jesus and was able to do it because he was guided by his inner nature, however, he was not free (or able) to choose to do what was right and not betray Jesus. Did Judas have a free will? Yes! His will was free to act according to his inner nature which was in bondage to sin. Those who say Judas was free to act and choose to do good or evil are not being guided by the revelation of God, but by their own wisdom. (Phil. 2:13, and see comments on John 3:16 to see how this applies to salvation).

If the Jews couldn't escape the condemnation of God for their actions, even though what they did was ordained by God, then no sinner can. Despite God's ordering of all things down to the smallest details of life (e.g., the hairs on our head are all ordained by God and even sparrows only fall by God's will, Matt. 10:29, 30), this can never be an excuse for sin. It is nothing but stupidity to demand to know all the mysteries of God. Such stupidity is nothing but an attempt to throw God off His throne and climb onto the throne of Heaven ourselves (this is what Satan wanted to do!). To demand a full explanation from God as to how this can be, is really to challenge the justice of God and call God to give an account of Himself. But God does not have to explain or give account of His actions to anyone. We have to give an account of ourselves to Him—it is Satan who tries to reverse the situation, making God accountable to the creature. Superiors demand explanations from inferiors and we are infinitely inferior to God. Our wisdom is in bringing all our thoughts into line with God's revelation, not in demanding God to restrict Himself to our limitations.

Acts 2:24

a). God had handed Christ over to evil men. b). These evil men took Him and they killed Him. c). Then God raised Christ from the dead.

This is the first preaching of the resurrection by the apostles. The resurrection of Christ was also part of the eternal plan of God and predicted by Scripture. God was in complete control and everything was taking place just as He had said: the apostasy of Judas (1:16), the out pouring of the Holy Spirit (2:16–21), and the resurrection of Christ (2:24ff.). God had given Christ up to be killed and now it is God who raises Him from the dead. The reason that Jesus could be raised from the dead, was because the pains of death (or as some translations have it, the agony of death), had been destroyed by Christ. Now the pains of death can refer to both the torments that Christ suffered in death and also the chains or cords that bind you in the tomb (i.e., in the realm of the dead). Christ destroyed both the terror of death and the power of the grave.

We need to realize that the terror of death was more than just the physical suffering that Christ endured in His body. Christ not only suffered agony in the physical qualities of His being (His body), but also suffered torment in the spiritual qualities of His being (His soul). [It is very important to realize that a person's being is *one*—this includes everything that makes up who he is. However, this one being has different qualities. There are the physical qualities that are usually called the "body" and there are the spiritual qualities that are usually called the "soul." We must not think that people are made up of two "substances" and that we have a spirit living inside a physical body. It is wrong to think that we are two different substances that are somehow joined together. People are a unity, and all of our different qualities make us one being or person. People are not made up of a soul and a body, but rather we are to think of ourselves as one being, having body like qualities and soul like qualities. For an understanding of how this applies to death, see comments on John 11:25, 26].

When Jesus was facing the cross, was He merely thinking about the pain His body was about to suffer? Was it the thought of this physical pain that caused Him so much anguish? When Christ groaned in secret, unseen by any one else, was He merely afraid of the physical pain and suffering He was about to endure? (Luke 22:44). Was

Christ less brave than the many examples of martyrs who confidently and calmly faced death—some singing hymns while the
flames slowly burnt them alive? Is Christ's example inferior to those
who faced physical death with joy and exaltation? Was Christ pleading with His Father that He might not have to suffer the physical
pain on the cross (Luke 22:42)? Was Christ so weak that at the pros-
pect of dying, He needed an angel to appear from Heaven and
strengthen Him (Luke 22:43)? Surely it is obvious that there was
more going on than just physical death. Christ could not be so terrified of normal death that it forced His sweat to become *like* drops
of blood (Luke 22:44) and an angel was required to revive Him. He
told His disciples that He was exceedingly sorrowful and troubled
(Matt. 26:38; Mark 14:33, 34 and see comments on John 12:27).

Jesus Christ was not going to merely die as God the Son, but as our
substitute. He was taking our place and about to pay our debt to
God. He was about to take our sins upon Himself and suffer for
these sins. He was about to be accounted a sinner and to be punished as sinners should be punished. Our sins began to be laid upon
Him in the garden where He was being made a curse. As Isaiah said,
"The Lord has laid on Him the iniquity of us all" and "It pleased the
Lord to crush Him and put Him to grief" (Isa. 53:6, 10). This
extreme agony that Christ was feeling was not fear of physical
death, but the real terror of feeling God's wrath against sin—
against Him! Christ never actually became a sinner. Our sin was
laid upon Him, but it never became part of Him. Christ was made
sin, for our sakes (2 Cor. 5:21).

Christ suffered *all* the punishments that were due to us. He truly
experienced the divine wrath and vengeance that God pours out
upon sin. He became a curse for us (Gal. 3:13), and therefore,
endured the whole of the curse that God's law demands should fall
upon sinners. This curse and judgment has reference to body and
soul (the whole person). Christ endured all the punishment that we
should have received and that includes the torments of hell and the
agony of separation from God (Mark 15:34).

However, all of Christ's suffering was completed on the cross. When
Jesus said "It is finished" (John 19:30), it was finished! Redemption
had been accomplished: there was nothing left to do. Justice had
been fully satisfied and there was nothing more to be done in order
to pay for our sins—it had been paid in full. Thus Jesus could say to

the thief next to Him, "Today, you shall be with Me in paradise" (Luke 23:43). When Jesus said to God, "Father, into Your hands I commend My spirit" (Luke 23:46), that is exactly what happened— the suffering was over, the price had been paid in full. Christ suffered the torments of hell while on earth and never went to the actual place where the lost are kept.

The resurrection of Christ out of the tomb is proof that our penalty has been paid in full (1 Cor. 15:17). We no longer stand under the curse of the law, because the curse of the law has been removed. The law is not a curse and the law has not been removed, but the curse of God that rests upon those who break the law has been removed (Gal. 3:13). It has been removed not because God has changed the standard of the law, but because God has poured out His wrath upon disobedience. He has judged our sinful actions by laying them on Christ and then pouring out His wrath upon Jesus—who had had no sin. He was judged for our sin, but since He had no personal sin, death could not hold Him.

The power of the devil over people is their fear of death (Heb. 2:14, 15). Now death has been destroyed. Death has been swallowed up in victory (1 Cor. 15:54)—by the victory of Christ the curse has been swallowed up. By the cross Christ disarmed the power of Satan and clearly showed His complete victory over him (Col. 2:14, 15). Christ has not only tied up the strong man, but has robbed him (Matt. 12:29). The purpose that Jesus came was to destroy the works of the Devil (1 John 3:8). This He has done by bearing the full wrath of God for those who believe in Him. Christ destroyed the agony of death. He destroyed the power of Satan (we are now told to resist the Devil, James 4:7; 1 Pet. 5:9). He set us free from the bondage of death, fear and sin—Oh death where is your victory, O grave where is your sting? (1 Cor. 15:55).

How can I be sure that this victory is real? Look at Christ: did He not rise from the grave? The resurrection proves that the power of death is forever broken. If the power of death is broken it means that the power of sin is broken and if the power of sin is broken, it means that the power of the Devil is destroyed. Do you see the glory of the resurrection. Oh, Satan, what a blunder! Oh, powers of darkness, what a mistake! Oh, rulers of Israel, what blindness! Through your wicked murdering of the Son of God you destroyed your own power, setting the captives free.

Christ was innocent of any personal sin. The evil powers murdered the perfect God-man and thus were unable to hold Him, but not only were they unable to hold Him, through His suffering a way of salvation was opened up for God's people. Christ's death appeased God's wrath and satisfied His justice in a way that God can sincerely offer salvation to all people. Those obstacles facing every sinner, arising from their guilt and the law, are ready to be taken out of the way (see comments on John 3:16). When people believe in Christ, the curse and wrath of God hanging over their heads are removed (having been paid in full by Christ), thus, freeing them from the bondage of the Devil (Acts 26:18). They are then released into the liberty of the sons of God. Not only are they set free from fear, but they are sent forth into the world in the power of the Holy Spirit to proclaim this liberty to all captives (Luke 4:18, 19; Matt. 28:18, 19).

Not only has Satan's power been destroyed, but those who go forth in the Name of the Lord have God's full backing and blessing in order to fulfill their task of discipling the nations (they are heirs to the throne of God and receive the backing of heirs, Rom. 8:17; Gal. 4:7). With such backing from God, the gates of hell cannot prevent them from fulfilling their mission (Matt. 16:18)—the defeated powers of darkness will not be able to hold out against the advancing church. The forces of evil couldn't hold Christ; they cannot regain the power they lost at Calvary; they will never repair the devastation Christ caused them; and they will never be able to hold back Christ's empowered, ever increasing witnesses (see comments on John 12:31).

Acts 2:25–31

Peter says, I am not making this up and it is neither impossible nor unheard of that someone should rise from the dead, for it was prophesied in the Scriptures. Peter's authority for saying this was not himself, but, once again, the Word of God (as in 2:16). This time he quotes Psalms 16:8–11. Peter says it is obvious that David was not talking about himself in these verses, since David is still in his grave. Rather, David was speaking prophetically about Christ's resurrection. Peter explains that David, with prophetic insight, clearly saw the resurrection of Christ. If the Messiah was going to be resurrected then it meant that the Messiah was going to have to die first. Paul explains the meaning of these verses in the same way (Acts 13:35–37). The term, "You will not leave my soul in Hades" is to be understood to mean that "You will not leave me among the dead." Some translations say you will not leave me in the grave. David's hope was for a descendent to sit upon his throne *forever*— which could only refer to the Messiah. David, aware of this promise from God, saw it pointing to the Messianic Kingdom. The authority and extent of the Messiah's Kingdom in David's understanding can be seen in Psalm 2 and Psalm 22—a comprehensive and universal reign.

Acts 2:32

Peter has quoted from the Psalms (Ps. 16) explaining that David was not talking about himself, but about one who was still to come—the Messiah. This was a prophecy of the Messiah's resurrection that had now been fulfilled in Christ. The one whom David talked about, has been raised from the dead. Peter says, this Jesus whom you all knew (2:22), He has been raised from the dead, for He is the Messiah. The Man whom you crucified, has been raised by God. Peter adds that they were all witnesses—there were many people who had seen Jesus after He rose from the dead: over 500 believers in all (1 Cor. 15:6). The whole city of Jerusalem knew of Christ's death (Luke 24:18; Acts 2:23) and many more besides (cf. Acts 10:36, 37). The fact that Jesus was no longer in His tomb was also very common knowledge (Matt. 28:11–15). Peter's listeners knew about Jesus' death. They also knew that He had been executed for being the King of the Jews (John 19:19–22) and they knew that this Jesus was no longer in His grave. Peter had already said that the works that Jesus had done were clear proof that He was the Messiah (Acts 2:22). David's prophecy was proof that the Messiah would in fact die, and also rise from the dead. There were more than 500 people who personally saw Christ after He rose from the dead— which easily refuted the testimony of a few guards who had been bribed (Matt. 28:12, 13) to lie about what they knew to be true (Matt. 28:3, 4).

Acts 2:33

Peter goes on to explain the whereabouts of this Jesus now. The reason no one else is able to see Him is because He has been taken to heaven. He has not only been taken to heaven, but God has given Him the place of highest honour and power. Christ's ascension resulted in Him receiving power and authority over all things both in heaven and in earth. The prophet Daniel saw all of this, at least 560 years before it happened (Dan. 7:13, 14). What Daniel saw was the Messiah going up to (not coming down from) the Ancient of Days (that is God). This refers to the ascension of Christ and not His Second Coming. The clouds of heaven, refer to the glory of the Lord (Ex. 40:34, 35) and speak of Deity. That this cloud in Daniel was the same cloud that was seen by the disciples at Christ's ascension (Acts 1:9) is a possibility. God's glory cloud brings revelation (Ex. 19:9; 33:9; Matt. 17:5) or judgment (Isa. 19:1). What Daniel saw was the Messiah presented to God in order to receive His prize. Psalm 2:8 tells us what the Messiah would ask for, and here we see Him receiving that which is rightfully His (Dan. 7:14).

After Christ's comprehensive victory on the cross where the powers of the enemy were defeated, the Father granted Christ all authority in heaven and on earth. This prophecy of Daniel refers to Christ's ascension and was fulfilled when Christ ascended. What Daniel said the Messiah would receive, is exactly that which Christ said He had received (Matt. 28:18)—the similarity cannot be denied between these two verses. Jesus said all authority in heaven and earth was now His and this included His authority over all the nations who were to be brought into obedience to Him and to live by every Word from His mouth (Matt. 28:19). What Daniel said the Messiah was to receive, He has received, and this is not only according to Matthew 28:18, but is also seen in 1 Peter 3:22 and Ephesians 1:20–22.

Now to get back to Acts 2:33: The right hand of the throne of God is the place of universal rule and authority. Christ made Himself nothing by becoming a man (Phil. 2:7), and endured complete humiliation on the cross and in the grave (Phil. 2:8), but now He is crowned with glory and honour (Heb. 2:9). Just as when the victorious warrior returned from battle and gave gifts to his friends and subjects (1 Sam. 30:26), so too we see Christ giving gifts to His subjects (Isa. 53:12; Eph. 4:7–12). Peter says, do you want proof that Christ has all authority, do you want proof that He has already received that position of complete Lord over heaven and earth (Dan. 7:14; Matt. 28:18ff.; Eph. 1:20–22; 1 Pet. 3:22)? Then this, which you are witnessing, is proof! This manifestation of the Holy Spirit and incredible gift from Christ is a direct result of His absolute victory over the forces of darkness and of His exaltation to the position of supreme power. The people had asked in Acts 2:12,

"Whatever does this mean?" Peter has now explained its meaning. We could not have these gifts if the victory had not been secured. Christ is the King and has been given all power.

We couldn't have had such gifts if Christ had not been glorified (John 7:39). The victory has not only been completed, but also secured and Christ has been glorified, therefore, we have been empowered to disciple whole people groups and every part of their culture and life—not only individuals, but whole cultures/nations (Matt. 28:19). *This* (Pentecost) is proof of *that* (Christ's supreme authority now). What a terrifying task Matt. 28:19 would have been if Christ had not also provided the power of the Holy Spirit to accomplish the work that He had given the church to do.

Those who reduce the discipling of the nations to merely discipling individuals within nations are in rebellion to the Lord's clear revelation. Just as Israel rebelled against God and refused to conquer the Land of Canaan because they found the task too terrifying, so too it is rebellion today to say, "No Lord, the task you have given us in Matthew 28:19 is impossible." God had promised to provide the power and the victory for the task He had given to the new nation of Israel (Ex. 23:20, 23), however, Israel rebelled against God's commands (Num. 14:1–4; Deut. 1:21, 26, 28–33) and in rebelling against these commands denied His protection and His power. They denied His sovereign control and thus rejected the idea that He was able to manifest His purposes and victory on the earth. They believed that He was God in heaven, but on earth it was a different story—the giants were just too big for God (so Israel thought). Their failure and rebellion arose from not trusting God's Word and not living by faith in His promises. For most of these people, the situation surrounding them was just too much for God to handle. The world was a hopeless mess, God could do nothing, so they wanted to just get out of there. They ignored the fact that they were called by God for a purpose—God's purpose and Kingdom. God wanted to work through their faithful obedience to His Words. They reduced God's power and purposes to the limits of their own power and abilities—what they couldn't do, God couldn't do.

When we reduce the extent of our responsibilities found in Matthew 28:19, we not only deny the victory of Christ, but also deny His power and turn His glorification into some small worthless celebration in heaven. A church with these views, rejects its calling, rebels against the command of God and ends up living for itself (its own comfort, plans and security, rather than for Christ's Kingdom).

Acts 2:34, 35

Peter once again goes to Scripture in order to support what he is teaching. He quotes David again, but this time from Psalms 110. David not only prophesied about Christ's resurrection (Acts 2:31), but also about His exaltation (2:34). This cannot be referring to David, for God is speaking to someone greater than David (Matt. 22:42–46), and David did not rise from the dead and ascend into heaven.

Long ago, God had ordained that Christ should be raised to the highest place of honour. The significant thing is what God says to David's Lord—"Sit at my right hand." Hebrews 1:13 tells us that God has only ever said this to Jesus, who in His human nature has now been exalted and rules with supreme power. When a ruler conquered another ruler he would place his foot upon the defeated ruler's neck to show his victory (cf. Josh. 10:24, 25). Peter says the words of Psalm 110 find their fulfilment in the exaltation of Christ.

Christ will remain seated at the right hand of God, until all His enemies are completely subdued. He is not going to leave that position and come back in order to subdue all of His enemies. Christ's reign and power shall flow from this position (seated in heaven at God's right hand), until the last enemy is destroyed. Christ is ruling now and His sovereign power will continue to bring all things into subjection to Himself. The power of God, working through the Son, is accomplishing this work. The glorious privilege, is that Christ has made us co-workers in this plan. It is only through the power of God and through the authority that Christ earned and received that God's enemies are destroyed, however, in God's mysterious providence, we have a part to play. Whatever we do is accomplished by the power of the Holy Spirit (Acts 1:8) and flows out of Christ's authority and position in heaven. When Christ comes the next time, history will end (1 Cor. 15:23, 24): for He must reign *until* all His enemies are put under His feet (verse 25)—this means He must reign from His seat at the right hand of God. Christ stays at the right hand of God, reigning over all things and bringing all His enemies into subjection and placing them under His feet until the last enemy is destroyed or brought to nothing—this last enemy is death (verse 26).

Acts 2:36

Peter says, "House of Israel, there is nowhere to run to. There is no escaping from the evidence and there is absolutely no getting away from the evidence that has been laid before your eyes. Assuredly therefore, let it be known"—there is no room for disputing or arguing and there is nothing left to say. The only possible conclusion is that Jesus is the Messiah. This Jesus whom they had despised and murdered is not only their sovereign King, but He has been raised from the dead and now has all power in heaven and on earth. This realization brings terror to the hearts of those listening to Peter. The one they fought against, is their Lord! The one they crucified is not only their Messiah, but also their God—Peter here makes Christ equal with God. The last word in Peter's sermon in the Greek is the word "crucified"—that is the thought that is left ringing in the ears of the audience. Peter says, "God has made Him both Lord and Christ; this Jesus whom you *crucified!*" Jesus had often told His disciples, not to say who He was until after His resurrection (Matt. 16:20; 17:9). Now that He had been raised from the dead, ascended to the place of absolute authority and power and had given His followers the gift of the Holy Spirit—well now His name was to be proclaimed from the house tops. Everyone was to be told that He was both Lord and Christ and everyone, everywhere, was to repent and believe in His Name (Acts 17:30).

Acts 2:37

What would have caused the most trouble to Christ's disciples with respect to the Great Commission? If the world rejected Christ, how would it listen to them? How could they be expected to disciple *all* the nations, when Christ's very own people had not only rejected His teachings, but had murdered Him? Jesus had told them to wait for the Holy Spirit before they set out to fulfill their task, for it was only with the Spirit is power and enabling that they could accomplish this massive calling.

Jesus had told His disciples that when the Holy Spirit came He would convict the world of sin, righteousness and judgment (John 16:8). The specific sin that people are convicted of is that they do not believe in Jesus (verse 9). The conviction of righteousness is related to Christ's ascension (verse 10) and all that that means (see Acts 2:33 above).

Peter's speech was very well argued and left his hearers with nowhere to hide. However, good speeches, in and of themselves, can do nothing to change people's hearts. The Holy Spirit, who was present in super abundance, was doing His work on the crowd (John 16:8) and therefore, these people felt crushed and their hearts were deeply convicted about their sin. The conviction was so intense it felt as if a spear had been pushed right through them (they were so troubled and disturbed about what Peter had said that it was like experiencing great pain). The Holy Spirit had opened their eyes to see that they had murdered their Messiah, and King and God. Their behavior had been nothing but high treason against the Holy One of Heaven. The realization of their sin and guilt and the size of the crime that they had committed, left them terrified and helpless. They did not know how they could get out of this horrible situation that they had put themselves in.

The Word of God together with the working of the Holy Spirit had done its job (Heb. 4:12). By the question they ask the disciples, we see an acknowledgement of their guilt, and a recognition of their helpless situation, thus they cast themselves on the mercy of God. They did not flee from the conviction of the Holy Spirit as Judas had done (Matt. 27:3–5), but rather fled to God's messengers and asked for God's answer to their situation. Sorrow must lead to repentance, not self-pity (2 Cor. 7:9, 10).

Acts 2:38

Was Peter a better preacher than Jesus had been? Did Peter say something different to Jesus? Could these people understand Peter better than they could have understood Christ? We must say no to all of these questions. It is the Holy Spirit who brings people to salvation by working in their hearts with the Word that is preached (1 Cor. 1:21). Salvation is God's work. But, you might say, did not these people ask Peter what *they* must do, and did not Peter say *you* must repent? Yes, this is true, however, the Scriptures show us that there are a number of different steps involved when a person is redeemed (saved).

In Romans 8:30 we see that those whom God has predestined unto salvation, are first called, then justified, and then glorified. This is still not the whole detailed picture, but only a broad summary of the actual steps in our redemption. It must be pointed out that this "call" spoken of in Romans 8:30 is not the same as the general call found in Matthew 22:14, where many are called, but few are chosen. The "calling" in Romans 8:30 is a specific calling by which God's predestined plan is worked out in the lives of His elect. It is this same calling that calls us into fellowship with God's Son (1 Cor. 1:9) and by which we are called to be saints (Rom. 1:6,7; Eph. 4:1; 2 Tim. 1:9). For those who are saved, their calling is an outworking of the eternal purposes of God. When God's eternal purpose of redemption is *applied* to someone's life, the call of God is the first thing that takes place (in the eternal plan of God, His counsel and predestination obviously come before that point in time when people are actually called, Eph. 1:5, 11; Rom. 8:28, 29; 2 Thes. 2:13).

The fact that those whom God calls, *are* justified (Rom. 8:30), means that God supplies that which is necessary in order to accomplish His purposes. Jesus said people only come to Him if God draws them (John 6:44, 65). The reason we cannot come to Christ on our own accord is because we are dead in our sins (Eph. 2:1, 5) and in bondage to the principles of Satan's kingdom (Col. 1:13, see *Faith and Reason*, chapters 3 and 4). Therefore, when God calls those who hate Him (Rom. 8:7; Col. 1:21), He also changes their hearts so that they are able to believe and respond to Him. We know from Romans 1:18–21 that God's truth is clearly seen by the unbeliever and yet he stubbornly refuses to bow to God. That is why God's answer for man's problem is to give us a new heart and a new spirit (Ezk. 36:25, 26; cf. Acts 3:26). Thus, when people are born again, it is due to God's will (John 1:13). Jeremiah tells us that when God gives His people a new heart *then* they will turn to Him with their whole heart (24:7). God has to first make us alive and only then are we able to believe. God first calls us and then quickens us (i.e., makes us alive or regenerates us) which enables us to exercise the gift of faith (Eph. 2:8) and believe in Christ.

Faith and repentance go hand in hand. You cannot have one without the other (faith means to believe in God's mercy found in Christ, and repentance means to turn from sin). When we have faith in Christ it is in order to be saved from our sins, thus we turn from our sins to Christ (faith and repentance). When we turn from our sins it is because we are placing our faith in God's mercy (repentance and faith). Despite the fact that both faith and repentance are gifts from God (Eph. 2:8; 2 Tim. 2:25), we still have to exercise them. Faith and repentance are things we have to do and God holds us accountable for not believing and not repenting (John 5:45–47; 11:26; Luke 13:3; Rev. 2:22). However, it must never be forgotten, that in order for us to exercise our faith and repent, God has to first make us alive from the dead. Our wills need to act, but it is only by God's grace that they are able to act in the right way.

The Holy Spirit used Peter's sermon to pierce the hearts of those in the crowd and it was not wrong for them to ask what they should do. There was something that they had to do—repent. Peter says when they turn from their rebellion against God and live by His Words, believing in the completed work of Christ, only then will they be justified (that is, moved from under the wrath of God and placed under His favour). We must accept the clear teaching of Scripture on this whole process that leads to justification, bowing to the sovereignty of God and to His wisdom (see *Faith and Reason*, chapter 6). This process of salvation is in this order: call, regeneration, faith and repentance, justification.

Peter tells them to repent and be baptized. Baptism has two messages: the first and most important one is a message from God to us and then of less importance it is our message telling others that we serve Christ.

Firstly: baptism is God confirming the promise of salvation to us. God has said in His Word that if we believe in Him we will be saved and this is a promise that cannot be moved. However, due to our weakness and blindness, God saw that it was necessary for us to have this sign of baptism in order to strengthen us. Thus in His mercy, God not only gives us a promise in His Word that is perfectly trustworthy, but then adds a sign to confirm this promise He has already given. Baptism is effective when you have faith in the power of Christ to cleanse you from guilt and sin. When we believe in that which baptism signifies (the cleansing power of the blood of Christ), our faith is strengthened. Our troubled hearts and consciences need this double assurance. Baptism brings assurance that our sins are forgiven—it is a seal and confirmation of God's promise to forgive sins and break the power of sin. The value of baptism is only found when we, by faith, take hold of that which it promises (see comments on Acts 22:16). We need to raise our eyes above the outward form and focus on the mysteries it speaks about—the cleansing from sin and freedom from the death of the flesh. Baptism speaks of God removing the guilt of sin and breaking the power of sin over us.

Secondly: baptism is also a testimony of our relationship with Christ. It tells others whose disciples we are—we are Christ's disciples and follow His teachings. Thus to be baptized in the name of Jesus, means to submit to His authority, to live by all that He commanded and taught, to rely upon His merit and to serve only Him (see comments on Acts 16:15).

Peter tells the crowd that if they have faith in Christ they can be assured that they are both forgiven and set free from the bondage of sin. The only remedy for their pierced hearts was to cast themselves upon the mercy of God. Baptism is the seal of God whereby He would confirm to these crushed hearts that their wickedness and sin against Christ was no longer hanging over their heads (2 Cor. 5:19). Baptism is not necessary for salvation, however it is necessary for the Christian life of submission and obedience to every Word of God.

Peter says, "And you will receive the gift (singular) of the Holy Spirit." This does not mean that you have to be baptized with water before you can receive the gift of the Spirit. This is the receiving of the Holy Spirit Himself—the receiving of His indwelling power, which takes place at conversion. It is the gift of grace and salvation that enters the hearts of those who are saved.

The glory of God descended on the church at Pentecost, as it had descended on the tabernacle and temple in the OT (Ex. 40:34; 2 Chron. 5:13, 14), showing where God dwelt. The church is now God's holy place—His dwelling place on earth. When we receive Christ, we receive the Holy Spirit and it is impossible to receive Christ and not to receive the Holy Spirit. We only know that Christ lives in us by the Spirit that He gives to us (1 John 3:24). In John 14:16–18; Romans 8:9, 10, 14, 16; and 2 Timothy 1:14, we see that the work of Christ and that of the Holy Spirit are inseparable, which means if we do not have the Spirit then we do not have Christ—we are not saved. If we are saved it is because Christ lives in us (John 6:56; 14:23; 15:4–7) and He lives in us by His Spirit (John 7:39; 16:7; 2 Cor. 3:14, 16,17). We become members of Christ's body (1 Cor.12:12) by being baptized into it by the Holy Spirit (verse 13). To receive the gift of the Holy Spirit, means to receive the indwelling power of the Holy Spirit. The Spirit is received with the forgiveness of sins (Acts 2:38; Titus 3:5; 1 Cor.6:11,19; Eph.1:13,14).

Peter said to the crowd, that if they repented and were baptized, then they *would* receive the gift of the Spirit; this is because if they repented they would be saved—if you are saved you receive the Spirit. There is no evidence to show that these converts spoke in tongues or that the apostles laid their hands on them in order to receive the Spirit. Therefore, we assume that speaking in tongues and laying on of hands are not requirements for receiving the Spirit or showing that one has received the Spirit. The Scriptures tell us that it is the fruit of the Spirit that provides us with proof that we have the Spirit—that is have Christ (see, Matt. 7:18; 12:33–37; Gal. 5:22–25).

Acts 2:39

Promise: refers to the gift of the Holy Spirit which Joel prophesied would be given to the New Covenant church (2:16). Peter holds out the promise of the Holy Spirit as the motivating incentive for repentance and baptism—when you repent this amazing gift will be yours. The promised gift is for all those whom God will call, since all whom God calls are brought into fellowship with Christ through faith. It is God's *specific call* that has with it the power to achieve its goals and is to be distinguished from His general call (see 2:38 above). Peter says the Holy Spirit is for all who are called.

The church received this promise on the day of Pentecost and Peter says to the crowd, that this out-pouring of the Holy Spirit is for everyone (who believes). Such a gift was not just for the apostles and Jesus' close disciples, but was meant for all those who would believe in His name—even those who had murdered Christ could receive the Spirit. As we saw in 2:17, 18, the Spirit was for all classes of people—sons, daughters, servants and now Peter clearly includes Gentiles ("to all who are afar off," cf. Eph. 2:11, 13, 17). God had promised through Isaiah, saying, "I will pour My Spirit on your descendants and My blessing on your offspring" (Isa. 44:3, see too 59:21).

We see the glory of the New Covenant where God gives the Spirit to all of His chosen (those who believe because they have been called). There is no longer a small group who receive a special position in

God's Kingdom and are able to taste of the deep things of God. The fullness of God's revelation is now available to everyone who believes (who calls on the name of the Lord, Acts 2:21).

Acts 2:40

With many other words Peter exhorted the crowd: now whether this means he continued after this speech to tell them many other things, or whether it means the speech we have in Acts is merely a summary of what Peter actually said, we cannot be sure. All we do know for sure is that we do not have a record of everything Peter said. He said many things in his attempt to win these people. Peter's example of being a witness for Christ includes trying to persuade people with arguments, solemn exhortations and commands. He kept on urging them to be saved from their perverse generation (1 Pet. 3:15). Peter fully instructed them as to what they should believe and what they should do. He exhorted them to be separated from their present generation who were on a path to utter and eternal destruction—rather, he was offering a way to be saved from the doom awaiting that generation.

Wicked generation: referred to the whole of the unbelieving nation of the Jews with the corrupt controlling religious rulers at the top (Sanhedrin). The power, influence and control that these religious leaders had over the people was immense. We can see the control and influence that they were able to exert when Jesus was condemned. Shortly before He was condemned to die, a great multitude praised Him as the Messiah and the whole city of Jerusalem was moved (Matt. 21:8–11), yet the chief priests got the multitude at Jesus' trial to call for His death and ask for the release of a murderer (Mark 15:11–15; Matt. 27:20, 24, 25).

We can see the wickedness and perverseness of these religious leaders by Jesus' own words of condemnation pronounced upon them (Matt. 23). Jesus said to the scribes and Pharisees that after they have finished teaching someone they turn that person into twice as much a son of hell as themselves (Matt. 23:15). They were wicked, wicked people with perverted ideas, but worse still, they had tremendous influence, power and control over the lives of the people and therefore the people were also a perverse generation. The whole of Jewish life was influenced by their religion and it was a serious thing to be out of favor with the religious authorities (John 9:20–23).

John the Baptist came preaching and calling on people to repent, for the judgment of God was about to fall upon that generation (Matt. 3:10, 12). He also condemned the religious leaders (Matt. 3:7) and exhorted the whole nation to repent. Jesus pointed out the intense struggle and conflict that was involved when one repented and believed in Him, because it was no small thing to turn your back on that perverse generation and follow Christ. He says in Matthew 11:12, "And from the days of John the Baptist until now the kingdom of heaven suffers violence and the violent take it by force." This is *not* talking about guns and physical force, but is presenting a picture of what is entailed in entering the Kingdom of heaven. You have to get out of the clutches of the perverse generation—out of their control, influence and manipulation. This is not easy, but rather is such an intense struggle that it can be called *violent* (cf. Matt. 10:21, 34). There has to be earnest, intense determination with a total casting off of the old life and all of its influences. Zeal and determination are characteristics of those who are born again and are made new creatures in Christ. These characteristics of zeal and determination to receive all that God has promised are clearly seen in Jacob. Jacob knew what was his and struggled to obtain the fullness of what God had promised to bless him with (Gen. 32:24–30)—he wrestled with God the whole night and said, "I will not let you go unless you bless me" (verse 26).

The world is at enmity with God and seeks to exist in complete contradiction to everything God says and does (see *Faith and Reason*, chapters 3 and 4). That is why there is such a radical difference between the kingdom of darkness and the Kingdom of light—they are exact opposites. Peter says, be saved from this perversity! God had said the same through Isaiah, "Come out from among them and be separate, says the Lord. Do not touch what is unclean and I will receive you" (2 Cor. 6:17; Isa. 52:11).

Often we do not realize the complete change that is required when we come into God's Kingdom. We are told that friendship with the world is enmity with God. Whoever therefore wants to be a friend with the world makes himself an enemy of God (James 4:4, see too Rom. 8:7; Col .1:21). What exists in this world are two whole systems of thinking and living—one is in obedience to God and the other is in rebellion to Him (these are the only two options the Bible recognises). God is a jealous God who demands absolute obedience. We either humbly submit to His every Word or we proudly rebel against Him and follow some other word, living by some other standard.

Our own generation and times are as perverse and as rebellious as that one Peter was talking about. The basic similarity between the two is their refusal to humble themselves under the hand of God and live their lives by every Word that proceeds from His mouth (Matt. 4:4). This is where we have to be aware of the "violence" required to enter the Kingdom in our day (Matt. 11:12). Our minds are to be renewed by the Word of God (Rom. 12:2)—knowing what He has said and bringing every thought into captivity to the obedience of Christ (2 Cor. 10:5).

Everything in the world opposes the way God would have us to live. The whole mindset is anti-God: from education to media outlets—television, cable, satellite, radio, newspapers, books, magazines, and government publications—everything. Even Christians and churches are often in opposition to God, because they fail to bring *every* thought, belief and action into submission to Christ. Everything we do and think, at every moment, is to be brought into obedience to Jesus. This is what Revelation 13:16 is talking about: those who have the beast's mark on their forehead and hand are those people whose actions and thinking are completely controlled by the beast's ways, whereas, God requires us to be totally controlled by His Word in all of our thinking and actions (Deut. 6:4–9). Many Christians in our day continue to live in rebellion against God's comprehensive instructions for all of life. They think that Revelation 13:16 is still way off in the future and they say, we definitely will not compromise when that day arrives and the beast demands that we live by his commands. However, in not living by every Word from the mouth of God, they are already living by another standard and the mark of the beast is written over their whole body and life.

We also need to heed Peter's words and be saved from our perverse generation. Firstly, by believing in the Lord Jesus Christ and then secondly, by the power of the Holy Spirit, we need to work out our salvation with fear and trembling, bringing every thought into line with Christ and living by every Word that proceeds from God's mouth (Phil. 2:12; 2 Cor. 10:5; Matt. 4:4). If we do not do this we will never know what it is to live in the Kingdom of God as we ought to.

Acts 2:41

3,000 of the crowd received Peter's words and were baptized. The word *baptized* incorporates the whole salvation process of believing, being baptized, and receiving the Holy Spirit. Many, however, hardened their hearts even more and walked away from the words of life. These same words from Peter led either to blessing or increased condemnation—there can never be a neutral response to the Gospel. The Word of God always demands submissive obedience and we have to respond one way or another. The only two possibilities are obedience or rebellion! Prior to Pentecost, the number of believers in Jerusalem was about 120. It is probably safe to say that more people came to true faith in Christ after Peter's first sermon than had believed throughout the whole ministry of Jesus. This growth of the early church continued at a remarkable rate so that a conservative estimate says there were about 20,000 Christians in Jerusalem at the time of the persecutions in Acts 8:1. For this remarkable growth of the church in Jerusalem see Acts 2:41, 47; 4:4; 5:14; 6:1, 7.

Jesus had said that His disciples would do greater works than He because He was going to the Father (John 14:12–18). For the significance of what it meant for Him to go to the Father see Acts 2:33. Thus the power of the Holy Spirit had been given to the church by Christ so that the great commission could be fulfilled (John 16:7; Matt. 28:19) and here we see the effectiveness of the Holy Spirit working through the preaching of the apostle. Our hope for success must rest in the power of the Holy Spirit who works mightily in people's hearts when the Word of God is preached simply and purely. We do not need fancy programs, buildings and shows in order to fulfill the great commission. What we need is pure doctrine and the power of the Spirit, so that people's faith does not rest in the wisdom of men, but in the power of God (1 Cor. 2:5). Even when people come to faith in Christ through our witnessing, we must never forget that it has nothing to do with us: primarily it is God's work, but there have also been others before us who have will not in this work (John 4:37, 38; 1 Cor. 3:5–9).

Baptism does not need to follow extensive instruction and examinations, however, the person being baptized needs an understanding of a basic statement of faith (enough to make an acceptable profession of faith) and be able to explain the Biblical promises sig-

nified in baptism. As we have seen already, baptism is primarily
God's message to the sinner of the cleansing and acceptance available through faith in Christ (2:38 above). Baptism is not primarily
the sinner's message of repentance to God and therefore he does
not need extensive classes and instruction before he can be baptized. This group of 3,000 was sufficiently instructed in only one
long lecture (the fact that they were devout Jews might account a
little for the fact that they needed only one lecture), and the reason
being, baptism is for the benefit of the sinner, so that he might have
full assurance of forgiveness. Thus, for a person to know that he is a
sinner in need of a savior, and for him to be able to explain the basic
beliefs of the Christian religion and the promises signified by baptism, is all we should require before baptizing him. This confirmation of assurance is vital for the believer's heart, for the *Holy Spirit*
increases the faith of the one who is baptized by enabling them to
understand God's promises signified in baptism. They receive
grace, are built up, strengthened and encouraged through receiving
this sign of the cleansing power of Christ who alone can take away
sin. We need to be aware that there is a blessing received in baptism
that is not received in the preached Word alone. 3,000 souls were
baptized and added to the church that day.

Acts 2:42

The new converts were persevering in the apostle's teaching. This
means more than merely personal attendance, but includes sticking
close to the side of something or someone. Now what they were
persevering in was not a certain set of beliefs. The apostles' teaching
or doctrine does not refer to the actual truth that was taught, but to
the new converts' practice of diligently attending the lectures
(teachings), which the apostles were giving. They persevered by
faithfully attending all the teachings—as a result they received a
solid Biblical understanding that was true to apostolic truth. The
emphasis is that the converts were diligently coming to the lectures.
They hungered to be instructed in the pure Word of God.

The new converts' perseverance was not just with attending the lectures, but also with respect to communion (fellowship), breaking of
bread and common prayer. Their fellowship was with the apostles
and with one another—reflecting a very close intimacy one with
another. It obviously also referred to their new and deep fellowship
with the Lord (1 John 1:3; 2 Cor.13:14). A true oneness was mani-

fested by them in all that they did; loving others as themselves (Matt.7:12; 22:39; Gal. 5:14). This was an ability to give and receive, and to seek someone else's benefit before their own. The emphasis here is upon their singleness of heart, mind and purpose.

The "breaking of bread" in this verse, does not refer to the Lord's Supper, but continues to explain the extent of this intimate oneness. In Luke's Gospel, we do not see that the Lord institutes the Supper as something that was to be continued (I am not saying that it is impossible that Jesus could have done this, but rather that we have no record that this was done). This is important in the sense that Luke wrote both his books to Theophilus (Acts 1:1) and in neither book is Theophilus told that the Supper had become a permanent aspect of the life of the church. Thus, "breaking the bread" in verse 42 would not automatically bring to his mind the Lord's Supper as we understand it today. I think commentators have read the Lord's Supper into this verse. If Theophilus did wonder what the term "breaking of bread" meant in verse 42, then surely verse 46 would have lead him to conclude that this term referred to normal meals? Moreover, if Theophilus, wanting to understand this term "breaking bread," turned to Luke 24:30, 35 he would have concluded that Luke used the term to refer to a normal meal, for there is no way that the Lord was about to celebrate the Lord's Supper with the disciples from Emmaus (common meals had played an important part in Christ's ministry before His crucifixion, cf. Matt. 9:10, 11; 11:19; Mark 2:15; Luke 15:1, 2). In Acts 20:7, 11 there is nothing to force him to think that it is talking about anything other than a Sunday evening meal, which was delayed by a long lecture. And Acts 27:35 is definitely *not* a celebration of the Lord's Supper! This was among a group of unbelievers and verse 36 shows they were in need of food.

It is reasonable, therefore, to assume that Luke would have made a clear distinction between these different uses of "breaking bread" (if they really were different) and also given some kind of explanation to Theophilus if he was talking about this very important and divinely instituted sacrament of the Lord's Supper in Acts 2:42. However, we find no such thing and it is only by importing our own ideas into these verses that we can see the Lord's Supper there.

I do not see this verse (42) as outlining a worship service. The whole section (42–47) is a record of the infant church and not a pattern of conduct we ought to try to implement. What we need to imitate is the zeal, devotion, commitment to sound teaching, concern for one another, and singleness of purpose that the infant church had. We should desire to have hearts like them, rather than seek to imitate their actions in exactly the same way.

There were times of prayer in the temple, however, the prayer here (42) is better understood as flowing out of the small individual gatherings of believers. This was not some big, church organized, prayer meeting, but was part of their lives. Prayer was a natural outflow of their fellowship and being together in each other's houses. Prayer is a crucial and vital aspect of the life of the church, however, it is necessary to explain the different ways we are to understand the word *church*.

The word church can be used in the sense of the "institution" (the place where believers come to hear the Word preached, the place where the body gathers for worship and instruction), or it can be used to refer to the whole body of believers who are the church. Thus, on Monday morning the church goes out into all areas of life and should spread the fragrance of Christ everywhere. Thus the word church is used in a specific (the institution) and a general (all believers) sense and unless we make this distinction then we will become confused and misled. We will expect the institution to do the work that the whole body should be doing. The institution is to equip the body to do the work God has given the church to do. The problem is we want the institution to do everything and think that it alone is called to do the work of Christ's church. God's rule and Kingdom are over all things and it is the church (which means the whole body of believers) that is to fulfill the work of the ministry—going forth in the power of the Holy Spirit into all of life and bringing all things into obedience to Christ's Word (2 Cor. 10:5; Luke 24:47, 48; John 20:21).

Many times our understanding of the ministry of the church is limited to what the institutional church does or does not do. Thus, if the institutional church has no prayer meetings or does not organize any fellowship meetings or does not organize any "love feasts" then the body does not do any of these things. What we fail to realize is that the whole body of the church in Acts 2:42ff. was doing the work of the ministry. All these things were coming naturally to them and flowed out of true conversion and good teaching. They realised that they had a calling under God that entailed more than just going to the institutional church meetings on Sunday and doing a few gardening jobs around the church building. Thus prayer, fellowship and meals were things that naturally flowed out of their new life.

The work of the ministry is far, far, greater than what the institutional church can possibly do on its own. And its responsibility is not to control and oversee every activity done by the whole body of believers. The whole body of believers receive their instruction from those within the institutional church whom God has gifted and given authority for this task, but then the believers are to go out to do the work of the ministry. In our day we limit the ministry of the church to that of the institutional church and all the believers (who make up the whole body of Christ's church) have to fulfill their "ministries" within the narrow confines of the institutional church. This greatly retards the ministry of Christ's church to the whole world.

The institutional church has authority to oversee the preaching and teaching of the Word and administration of the sacraments, for these are the tools that are needed in order to equip the whole body of Christ for the work of the ministry (Eph. 4:11–16). However, we need to realize that the ministry of the church is to cover the whole of God's Kingdom—and He reigns over all things. Therefore, the church's work is not to be restricted to, or completely controlled and organized by the institutional church. The work of the Kingdom is *not* to be limited to the work of the institutional church, whose task from God is to preserve true doctrine and impart this to all believers, showing them how to rightly divide the Word of truth. The body needs to be thoroughly equipped for the work of the ministry (2 Tim. 3:17) and shown how to live by every Word that proceeds from the mouth of God. They need to be able to apply God's Word to all of life, earnestly praying for and working toward that day when the knowledge of the glory of the Lord will fill the earth as the waters cover the sea (Hab. 2:14).

Acts 2:43

The apostle's teaching was authenticated (confirmed) by miracles. Paul's proof of his authority as an apostle was that he had performed miracles (2 Cor. 12:12; cf. Heb. 2:1–4). The words of the apostles therefore carried divine authority and these words have been preserved by God for us in the Bible and thus continue to have divine authority. It is not necessary to have these words confirmed again and again by more and more miracles. They have God's authority and were confirmed by miracles once, which is enough. Our responsibility is to live by these words. We are to love the Lord with our whole being (heart, soul, mind and strength) and we do this by obeying all of Christ's Words (John 14:10; 1 John 2:3–5; 5:2, 3; Rev. 22:14). Thus, we are to be consumed in our seeking to know His will and do it, by His grace. This alone is what should consume us! To seek for miracles is to be side-tracked and taken down a dead-end path that only leads us away from what we should be doing. The purpose for these miracles was to show the authority of the apostles' teaching—who taught us what Christ and the Holy Spirit had taught them (John 14:26; 16:13, 14; Matt. 28:19, 20). We now have this teaching in the Scriptures and it is this teaching that is of vital importance for our ministry in the Kingdom.

Acts 2:44, 45

There are only two classes of people—believers and unbelievers. All those who believed were together. This does not mean that they were all living in one place, for the numbers of believers were just too great. This, as I have mentioned in verse 42 refers to the unity of feeling, purpose and affection one to another that was manifested in the infant church. This led them to hold all things in common and when the need arose someone would sell what they had and meet that need. The question is, should this be our example today?

What we need to imitate is the infant church's heart of generosity and concern for the body. But this does not mean that we must imitate everything that they did. The principles to notice are their desire to meet *real needs*. We too need to be sensitive to the *real* needs around us, however, many think that it refers to every need. This is not so.

First: this meeting the needs of others flowed out of close intimate fellowship. This was not merely giving to complete strangers (cf. Acts 3:6), but to those whose characters and lives were known. There are many people in this world that are just lazy and deceptive. The Scriptures speak strongly about laziness (Prov. 6:6–11; 10:4, 5; 12:24; 13:4; 19:15; 20:4, 13; 21:25, 26; 24:30–34). We are not to think that the NT is a time where laziness is no longer a sin (1 Thes. 4:11, 12; 2 Thes. 3:10–12). Even Jesus' disciples had a wrong understanding in this area. They thought that any extra money should be given to the poor—Jesus rebuked them for this (Matt. 26:7–11, see too comments on John 12:8). Our understanding of the needs of the poor are to be seen in the light of all the above verses.

Second: it was not compulsory. Some still had houses (verse 46; cf. 5:4). When someone saw a need and felt they would like to help, they sold something and helped to meet that need. All this help was purely voluntary, i.e., real charity.

Thirdly: this was a unique situation. There were many visitors in Jerusalem who had been converted and in order to be instructed by the apostles, had extended their stay which created real needs (it is quite understandable that such people could have run out of money). But, where else could they have gone in order to be instructed in these early days of the church? Thus they had to remain in Jerusalem. These happenings were totally unexpected and therefore these converts were totally unprepared for an extended stay. It is only in the very early stages of the church (Acts 2 and 4) that this kind of behavior is recorded.

Fourthly: John the Baptist had prophesied about the soon destruction of the nation (Matt. 3:10, 12; cf. Mal. 3:2; 4:1, 3, 6). Jesus had prophesied about the destruction of Jerusalem (Matt. 23:35—24:34). Peter had said, "Be saved from this perverse generation" (Acts 2:40). Surely with clear, specific and repeated prophecies about the destruction of the city they were living in, this would not have been ignored by the apostles in their daily instruction of the people. Thus all of these believers were aware of Jerusalem's soon coming destruction and the fact that when it came, they would have to flee and leave everything behind (Matt. 24:16–18). They would not even be able to take a cloak, never mind fixed property, therefore, it was wise to sell while they could and use this money for a worthy cause.

Fifthly: if this part, of everyone owning nothing, was meant to be copied, why not the rest? What if the whole body of Christ continued, every day in nothing but continual worship and fellowship, with no one doing any work? If we were to copy their example exactly we would end up as the lazy man in Proverbs.

Therefore, we conclude that this is not to be something that we try to copy in our own day. Socialism does not work, because at the bottom it does not take into account the depravity of man's heart (see further comments on Acts 4:32ff.).

Acts 2:46

This was a unique time in the history of the NT church. What they were doing daily is not a realistic picture of the Christian's responsibilities. As we saw in the previous verse, there are biblical principles behind their actions and these should be part of our lives, however, we are not to copy the details of how these principles were manifested in their situation. The church should not try to have daily meals together, thinking that this will produce revival and true spirituality. The essence here was not the meals but that which caused the meals to happen, namely, being in one accord. This is what we should seek to imitate within our church and relationships. The infant church's oneness of heart manifested itself in daily meals, etc. This is how their oneness was expressed in those unique times and circumstances, but that does not mean it is the only way that oneness of heart is manifested and expressed.

We need to be wise and relevant to our own times and circumstances and see how best to show forth the same spirit seen in Acts 2. The principles are always eternal, however, the specific manifestation of the principle will vary from culture to culture and age to age. For example: having a railing around the roof (Deut. 22:8) has an eternal principle of protecting life, whereas the specific manifestation was relevant to that culture where they did lots of entertaining on their roofs. We will fulfill this principle in different ways in our own day, i.e. putting fences around swimming pools, so that children cannotfall in and drown, manifests the principle of preserving life. Also, putting fences around playgrounds so that the children do not run onto the road, etc. We need to be warned though, that where God *has* given us specific detailed instructions about what we should do, then we are to fulfill these and not to try to manipulate them by saying these are not for our own culture and time: for example, trying to do away with the death penalty for murders. God's Word clearly tells us that murderers should be executed. So too should convicted rapists, homosexuals, kidnappers, etc. (Gen. 9:5, 6; Deut. 22:25; Lev. 20:13; Deut. 24:7).

Thus, there is no sure basis for thinking we are to have meals every day in each other's houses and in the same way we should not hope that the temple will someday be restored so that we might copy the early church perfectly and go and worship in the temple. The early Christians were in one accord both in their public worship and in their private lives—this is what we ought to learn from them and seek to imitate.

The OT way of worship ended with Christ: the temple, the priesthood, sacrifices, feast days (all the ceremonial laws), came to an end. Thus, the apostles and the early Christians would not have participated in the daily animal sacrifices that were done in the temple and nor would they have looked to the OT priesthood to assist them in anyway. So there was a radical break in some ways, however, in other ways there was a slow transition or change where the old system overlapped the new one. The early Christians still worshipped and prayed in the temple—they still used that facility although it was passing away and would be totally destroyed, never to be restored. One cannot imagine that the Christians went up to the temple to receive instruction from those who were dead in trespasses and sin (the old priesthood). There were some aspects to the old order that they could have participated in without compromising their new faith in Jesus—this was acceptable during this transitional period. They also must have used the facility for their own teachings, worship and prayer (since it was able to accommodate many people at one time, whereas in the houses only small groups could gather). The temple was also a good place to evangelise, since many Jews gathered there every day. Nevertheless, their presence in the temple, was an overlapping of the Old and New orders. There was not a radical break in absolutely every way.

There are important principles to learn through this. Christianity is both revolutionary (see Acts 2:40 above) and not revolutionary and we need wisdom to know which one is required when. At times we see a sudden and sharp break with the past, but at other times we also see a slow moving away from the past. This can be seen in the ministry of John the Baptist who called for a complete and sudden break with the religious order of his day—to repent, believe in and follow the One who was coming, yet he still continued to minister even after Jesus had arrived. There was a period of ministry where they both overlapped, however, the one was increasing and the other was decreasing (John 3:26,30).

We must never compromise the fundamentals of the Christian faith, but there are times when, with wisdom, for the sake of furthering the Kingdom, we should be sensitive to the need for gradual change, being sensitive to deep cultural convictions (cf. Acts 16:3 with Gal. 2:3). There are some circumstances when a complete sharp break with the past will do more harm than good. Maturity is knowing the difference between a fundamental of the Christian faith and something that is indifferent or can be slowly changed without compromising our crucial beliefs (e.g., Acts 18:18; 21:18–25). Sometimes it is obvious that radical over-night breaks are quite impossible (2 Kin. 5:18, 19)—though we must always be careful to make sure we are not contradicting God's clear Word with respect to salvation! There can never be any compromise in this area—ever!

Breaking bread from house to house: is having normal meals in one another's homes, showing us the close unity among the believers (see comments on 2:42). The way they ate their meals tells us much about Christianity. They did it in gladness and simplicity of heart. The emphasis in this whole section (verses 42–47) is upon the unity, harmony, sincerity and joy of those in the infant NT church.

The singleness of heart was due to a number of things: They were totally focused on Christ; worshipping Him and doing His will; having one aim, purpose and motive. But at the base of this was an attitude of humility within their own hearts. There was no one trying to manipulate or control anyone else, but rather each esteemed everyone else better than themselves (Rom. 12:10; Phil. 2:3; 1 Pet. 5:5). Nor did they allow their different characters to get in the way and cause unnecessary problems. No one was putting stumbling stones on the path to cause offence and disruption—the surface was smooth and flat and humility has a major part to play in creating this kind of a situation among brethren (Eph. 4:2, 3; Rom. 15:5, 6).

This gladness in eating is a beautiful picture and gives us a proper Biblical understanding of life. Life on this earth is a wonderful gift from God and has been made for us to enjoy. It is not to be seen as something to endure while we wait for heaven. The only way that we can be truly glad in all that we do in this life is if we are in Christ. When God approves of us then we are able to be joyful in the simple things of life (Ecc. 2:24–26; 3:13; 5:18–20; 9:7; Deut. 12:7). We must not only be contented with what we have, but must rejoice in it (Phil. 4:4; 1 Thes. 5:16). Eating and drinking talks of companionship, rejoicing and fullness (satisfaction). There was a time in the OT when God's money (tithe) was to be used to buy whatever you wanted to eat and drink and you were to have a joyous celebration and feast with your family (Deut. 14:26).

God is sovereign over all things. Nothing can happen without His permission. Thus we can rest in Him and pursue our earthly responsibilities, and enjoy our earthly pleasures as coming from His hand—enjoying them for His glory. We are to enjoy the blessings that come from God! Work is a blessing. Food and drink are also blessings. Health and the ability to earn wealth are blessings. Our possessions and our families are to be blessings. Our giftings and callings are a blessing. Our joy is not only to be *in* our hearts, but is to be manifested in the way we walk and live and in everything we do. Many think that they can have joy in their hearts without manifesting this in their waLuke In Ecclesiastes11:9, cheerfulness is not just allowed, but it is commanded and makes up an essential part of what a Christian should be. The difficulties of life, the foolishness of the world and hard and disappointing experiences can vex us and thus we can lose our joy (Ecc. 11:10). If people have taken advantage of us in the past, we must first of all accept it from the hand of God, knowing that all things work together for good to those who love God (Rom. 8:28), second, we must learn form the experience and become wiser, thirdly, we must know that God will deal with all unsettled accounts—perfect justice will be dealt out. Sometimes this is carried out here on earth, but definitely on that final day everything will be made right. Thus we need not worry and be bitter about anything. We are to live unto the Lord with sincerity, being joyful and wise, and we must not let our hearts get vexed by the evil in this world and the sinfulness of people. Justice is God's department (Rom. 12:19), our responsibility is to walk before Him in faithfulness, doing all He has told us—that includes rejoicing. Thus, we must not let the sinful actions of others make us sin (cause us to walk without joy). When David had Uriah murdered (2 Sam. 11 and 12:9), he had sinned against both Uriah and Bathsheba, however, when he confessed to God, he said, "Against You and You only have I sinned" (Ps. 51:4). Therefore, those who sin against us sin against God and God will not leave one sin unpaid for. They will receive God's chastisement which will lead to repentance or they will receive His eternal damnation. "Judgment is Mine," says the Lord, "I *will* repay!" (Heb. 10:30). As for the pure in heart, they alone are able to rejoice. The joy of the Lord is our strength (Neh. 8:10).

The early church had this kind of gladness because they were accepted by God. They were not trying to earn acceptance. They were justified and living by faith and thus, all that they did was approved by God (we are not talking about sinful behavior here). The Christian is not striving for acceptance and approval before God, he is already completely accepted in Christ. Thus our lives should consist of thankfulness and true joy. Even the most basic everyday things, like eating a meal are opportunities to manifest this glorious new position in life—oneness with God through Christ, resulting in deep, sincere, overwhelming joy. Therefore, we are not to strive after some formula or appearance of unity or "joy" (i.e., insisting upon daily meals together), but rather we are to have the real thing—real joy, which is a consequence of true faith in Christ and sound apostolic teaching or understanding of who we are in Christ.

Acts 2:47

Praising God was just a natural expression that flowed from their hearts as a result of this amazing blessing they had been given through Christ. Their whole life was one of praise to God. The next phrase could mean either that they had favor with all the people or that the believers had goodwill towards all the people. Most commentators go with the first option, saying the Christians found favor with all the unbelievers in Jerusalem. There is some merit for the second option though, however, Acts 4:13 adds weight to the first option and we probably should interpret 2:47 in this way. I am, however, unable to make a definite choice between the two options at this time. The Lord daily added saved people to the church. Salvation is the Lord's work and this wonderful miracle was taking place *daily*. The believers own godly way of life was used by the Lord as a means of drawing people to Himself. The infant church's unity, love, humility, self–denial, consistent Christian witness, zeal and devotion to the Lord were powerful tools in the hands of the Holy Spirit. Such behavior will draw many people to ask about the reason for the hope that is in you. It will make them open to hear what the church has to say, thus giving opportunity for them to come under the preaching of the Word. When we believe, we are saved and become part of the eternal body of Christ, His church.

Acts 3:1

Many think that Peter and John were going up to participate in the daily temple sacrifices. There was a lamb sacrificed in the morning and the evening every day (Ex. 29:39ff.) which was a constant reminder to the nation of their need for innocent blood to cleanse their sins—pointing to the Lamb of God who would take away the sin of the world. It would be very strange if the apostles joined in with these since they preached forgiveness of sins in the name of Christ (2:38; 3:18, 19). The fact that Peter so strongly preached that the Messiah had come and that this Jesus was the Messiah would be undermined if he participated in sacrifices that looked forward to the Messiah who was still to come (these sacrifices pointed to His coming). I am following Calvin who said that it cannot be true that the apostles went up to the temple to pray according to the rite of the ceremonial law. It makes good sense to go to the temple at the time of prayer, since many people went up at this time—making it an ideal opportunity for evangelism (see 2:46 above). Though we must also remember that there was not an immediate break with every aspect of the old system and it appears that there were still some aspects of the old order that the apostles could freely participate in without compromising the truth—prayer was one of these (see comments on 2:46 above and 21:17–26).

Acts 3:2, 3

This man had been like this for over forty years (4:22). He did not know who Peter and John were, but merely begged from them as he did from everyone who entered the temple.

Acts 3:4

Peter and John both firmly fixed their eyes upon him. The reason Peter told him to look at them was so that the glory would go to Jesus and not be explained away as something amazing that God had done. The Jews would have been quick to avoid any connection between this miracle and Jesus the Nazarene. They had rejected the miracles done by Jesus, seeking to kill Him for them (John 11:45ff.; Matt. 28:2–4, 11–15), thus, Peter and John wanted there to be no doubt as to the source of this miracle. The religious leaders were in rebellion against Christ. They hated Him because He showed their deeds were evil (John 7:7). Wanting to continue in their sin and rebellion they needed to get rid of the light, thus if they could, they would deny the connection between this man's healing and Christ.

Acts 3:5

The furthest thing from this man's mind was being healed—he was expecting some money. He had been in this condition for all these years so that God might be glorified (John 9:3). God is the sovereign Lord of all things and works out every detail according to His plan and for His glory (Matt. 10:29, 30)—Matthew shows us that God is indeed in control of the *smallest* details (see too, Acts 15:18; Isa. 46:10; and *Faith and Reason*, chapter 6). The Holy Spirit was guiding Peter and John and it was God's purposes to heal this particular man, therefore, even though he was not looking for healing at that particular moment, and had no faith when he saw Peter and John, God brought him into a position to receive his healing. It was the Lord who was moving Peter and John to heal him, though they had seen this man many times before—since he was laid at the temple gate daily and they went up to the temple often (Acts 2:46).

Acts 3:6

Peter never said anything to awaken faith in the cripple nor did he even tell him to have faith. Peter did not explain to the man what he meant by saying, "What I have I give to you." The beggar was probably expectant, but that is far different from having faith. Peter, speaking at the prompting of the Holy Spirit and in His authority, commands the man to rise in the name of Jesus. With this command in Christ's name comes all that was necessary for the accomplishment of the task. The Word spoken by Peter was powerful and able to bring about the very thing commanded. Peter did not *offer* the cripple something. The accomplishment of the command did not depend upon anything in the cripple. Peter's Words did not just create a force that hovered around the cripple waiting for him to reach out and take hold of it before it became effective. He was not healed because he had faith to be healed. The power of God came upon him in such a way that in an instant his limbs were not only healed, but he was also able to walk and leap perfectly (there are two amazing miracles here). This result did not in any way rest upon the cripple's understanding, faith or will with respect to being healed—it was a sovereign act of God for His own ends that later brought the man to a knowledge of Christ through faith. The power of the Word has within itself what is necessary to accomplish what it needs to do. He was not healed because of his faith, but because God moved upon him.

There are no formulas that "make" God respond. The Bible teaches us what God expects of us. We are then responsible to live in obedience to all of God's commands. God has given certain promises to us of what we can expect to receive when we obey His every Word, but these are never to be seen as absolute formulas. For example, God has said if we believe in Him and walk in all His ways then our children will also be blessed by Him—yet salvation is still God's sovereign act and *ultimately* has nothing to do with what we or our children do. We are responsible before God to believe and obey all His commands, and our children are responsible to believe, yet only God can grant faith that enables us to believe (Eph.2:8). From beginning to end, salvation is a gift from God and not earned in any way, either by the child or the parent. To try to discover formulas is to try to play God ourselves and to try to control and manipulate the True God by our wills. We are called to a life of submissive obedience and trust in the goodness of God. Our belief in God's rewards is a position of faith not of magic formulas (Heb. 11:1, 6). We are weak and slow to believe, thus God gave us physical signs demonstrating His power and ability to make all things whole and confirming His promises in His Word to do this. He not only has the power to heal bodies, but to cleanse from sin too (Matt. 9:4–6).

Acts 3:7–11

The fact that Peter helped the man had nothing to do with the miracle. He was healed the instant Peter uttered the words. Peter lifted him up by the hand, probably in order to show the cripple that he was now healed, or else he might have sat for the rest of the day unaware of what had taken place. It was all of God and it was done in an instant. Thus we see that the miracle was not only to give strength to previously weak limbs, but that this man was also able to jump around. The fact that he walked in an instant is as remarkable as his being healed in an instant. His response was one of joy and praise to God. He kept leaping and jumping and praising God for such a wonderful and gracious gift. In Isaiah 35:6 it says that when the Messiah comes, then the lame will leap like a deer. How is it that we do not realize the greatness of this same gift that God has given to us. This man was overjoyed with such a simple thing—

something we do not even think twice about (walking and jumping). In Him we live and move and have our being—everything we have from God is a gracious, wonderful gift. Like we saw in 2:46, where we are to have joy over a simple meal, so too, we ought to realize the abundance of God's mercies that are given to us every moment. What is the greatest blessing about being alive? The chance we have to glorify God and enjoy Him and all things.

Everyone in the temple recognised this man as the one who lay at the gate every day for many, many years. They now saw him leaping and praising God and twice we read that they were filled with amazement and they ran to gather around the apostles in a large open space where people often gathered for instruction (Solomon's porch). It is important to realize that when the Power of God manifests itself, it leaves people amazed and often bewildered, thus instruction or doctrine is needed in order to understand what is happening (see also 2:12)—we must not interpret such situations by our own understanding and wisdom, but look to God and His Word to explain them for us.

Acts 3:12

This situation required an explanation and Peter was once again ready to give it. What the apostles did, had its source in God and did not come from them. It was not by their power or because of their godliness that this miracle was done. Peter rebukes the people for taking glory away from God. It is a great evil to attribute to the ability of men that which is wholly from God. To even give a fraction of the glory to men is to steal from the full glory due to God. Peter quickly directs all attention away from the apostles. Both this miracle and the outpouring of the Spirit at Pentecost were manifestations of the power of the exalted Christ and Peter does not lose the opportunity given to him to present the claims of Christ.

Acts 3:13

Peter is making it absolutely clear from the beginning that this is not something new and different from what God has done with the nation of Israel in the past. Peter ties in this incident and what he is about to say, with the very heart and beginning of Israel's religious beliefs and experience. What Peter was about to say was in line with the promises made to Abraham, Isaac and Jacob. God had promised Abraham that through his Seed all the nations of the earth would be blessed (Gen. 12:3; 18:18; 22:18). This is talking of the Savior who was to come (Gal. 3:16). Thus what these people are told is that Peter's preaching in Christ's Name, is not only directly in line with the religion of Israel, but is the fulfilment of it (Luke 24:44). Peter ties everything in with Abraham and Moses (there are no bigger names in the history of Israel than these two).

What Peter says is the same thing that God said to Moses (Ex. 3:6, 16), thus he is standing on the foundation of that revelation Israel received from God. The God Peter is speaking about is the One and Only True God and it is this God who has glorified His Servant Jesus. By talking about Jesus as God's Servant, Peter would bring to the minds of the Jews the prophecies in Isaiah that talked of the suffering and glory of the Lord's servant (Isa. 52:13—53:12). Jesus was God's Servant (Matt. 12:18) and He took on this position in order to obtain our salvation. Therefore, He suffered, but He has now been raised and lifted up and highly exalted (see Acts 2:33). This glorification refers to the resurrection and exaltation to the right hand of God.

Peter now gets very personal and specific, pointing to their great sin and wickedness. He does not tell them how nice it would feel if they believed in Jesus, or that He has such a wonderful plan for their lives if only they will allow Him to do it. No, he goes to the heart of the problem—mankind's sin and rebellion against God. Peter does not try to make these people feel good about themselves, but rather crushes their self confidence and exposes the wickedness of their hearts (see *Faith and Reason,* chapters 3 and 4).

They denied and rejected their Messiah. They not only denied Him before Pilate (a Gentile), but forced this Gentile to kill Him. Even Pilate had been more "just" than them, since he had wanted to release Jesus, finding no fault in Him. These Jews demanded that this pagan judge murder the Seed of Abraham, the hope of Israel. Pilate wanted to release Jesus, however, the Jews demanded His death. And how did they get Pilate to conform? The same way that people do today—disruption and riot (Matt. 27:24). This idea has taken hold of the whole world today. Many want to create a better world through chaos—they want to destroy and break down in order to go forward. This same philosophy is found in both the highly educated and in those who are not educated. In fact the universities are often the worst places for believing this philosophy. If people are not satisfied in their nation, job, etc., they say we want something better now, and if we cannot have it right now then we will destroy what there is. It is very easy to destroy, but it is difficult to build. It is easy to destroy a family, friendship, relationship, nation, city, etc.

The Jews, through their rebellion against God and their commitment to this philosophy of chaos, forced Pilate to execute Jesus. Reason and justice mean nothing to a frenzied mob. Often mobs in the name of "justice" will destroy, injure and even kill other innocent people who have nothing to do with their grievances. Pilate, aware of what problems could be caused by a violent mob, is prepared to deny justice. He is prepared to put to death an innocent man in order to keep his position in Jerusalem secure. This is wickedness!

Peter is pointing accusingly at the Jews, saying, "Look what you have done!" People need to be made aware of their sin. The greatest sin is refusing to believe in the name of Jesus. All other sins flow out of this rejection of the Only Savior and Lord, Jesus Christ. There is no neutral response to Christ. We either call on Him to save us or we join in with this mob and cry out for His murder. We either ask Him for life or we ask Pilate to kill Him, thus whoever does not believe in Jesus stands as guilty as this mob and Peter's words should echo in their ears; "You have delivered up and denied the Christ, the Savior of the world".

Acts 3:14

At Pentecost (Acts 2:27), Peter had quoted from Psalms 16:10, where the Messiah is called the "Holy One" (see too, Isa. 41:14). The prophets had also called the Messiah the "Righteous One" or the "Just," as some translations have it (Isa. 53:11; Jer. 33:15; Zech. 9:9). The Sanhedrin had charged Jesus with blasphemy (Matt. 26:65) and this, they said, was the reason that He ought to be put to death. If a prophet claimed to speak in the name of the Lord, and what he said did not come to pass, he was to be put to death (Deut. 18:20). All revelation from God, reveals His holiness and glory, because it is a revelation of Himself and therefore, to claim to be revealing His glory when you are not, is a serious offence. The law and the prophets revealed the holiness of God, therefore, when Jesus claimed to be God, He was claiming to be a perfect revelation of God's holiness (Hebrews 1:3 says this is what Jesus was—the perfect revelation of God). The religious leaders and the nation of Israel, claimed to be obeying God's revelation and thought of themselves as protectors of God's holiness and righteousness, but Peter says *they* actually put to death the "Holy One" and the "Righteous One." Their utter and complete rebellion against God and His truth, resulted in utter self-deception. Peter here tells the crowd that the One they had denied and condemned was God's complete and perfect revelation of Himself—perfect Holiness and Righteousness.

Peter continues to bring forward His evidence. The people had had their day with Christ, but the tables had now turned and it was they who were being examined by the Supreme Judge. This was true Justice, unlike the Jews who had lied and brought forth false evidence in order to condemn Christ (Matt. 26:59–61; Mark 14:55–57; Luke 23:2). Not only did they condemn the perfect Holy and Righteous One, but they asked for a murderer to be set free instead. Peter points to their double crime: they condemned the innocent and set the guilty free—preferring a murderer to their Messiah (Luke 23:18, 19)—being murderers themselves they felt more at home with Barabbas than with Jesus.

Acts 3:15

Peter does not let up on pointing out their terrible sin. He says, Pilate did not kill Jesus, but you killed Him—the Prince of life. They had forced Pilate to release Barabbas, a murderer, and to murder Jesus, the Prince of life. Jesus is the source of life, He is the author of life (John 1:4, 9; 1 John 5:11) and therefore, they were unable to be rid of Him. Actually, the reason Peter was standing and preaching to them was because the One they had murdered, had been raised from the dead. Peter once again shows the two sides of this incident—they murdered Him, and God raised Him (see 2:23, 24). This is an often repeated combination throughout Acts—you killed Him, God raised Him and we are witnesses of this (2:23, 24; 5:30–32; 10:39–41; 13:28–31). The Jews had murdered Jesus hoping to escape from His light which exposed their sin (John 3:19, 20; 7:7). Just when they thought that they had escaped from His searching light and could get back to their good old comfortable man-made religion, they are told that this Jesus is alive. Not only is He alive, but the conviction that they had felt when He was on earth is greatly multiplied (John 16:8–11). Through the Holy Spirit, who had entered into the fullness of His ministry, working through

Christ's servants, Christ and the light of His Word were going to shine into every dark corner in the whole world (Matt. 28:19, 20).

Acts 3:16

The name of Jesus is not a magic word or formula that brings healing. Jesus' name is a revelation of who He is and stands for the fullness of who He is. Thus the name of Jesus presents before our eyes all that He is; all His power and authority—all His resurrected glory. It is faith in this name that has made this cripple whole. We see too that this faith comes through Christ or is brought about by Christ. This faith that is in Christ's name is also from Christ, so that all the glory might be His. It was not the cripple who had the faith to be healed, but rather Peter and John had received faith to believe that God would heal the man (Matt. 17:20). It is not an absolute rule that the one being healed has to have faith *before* they will be healed. In this story, it seems more than likely that the man did not have faith before he was healed, because the way the story is told leaves no reasonable time for the man to have come to a realization of what was happening. In a similar way Jesus also healed a man without apparently first drawing out his faith (John 5:6–8).

The general principle in Scripture appears to be that the one being healed ought to have faith (Matt. 8:13; Mark 9:23; 11:24), but how does this become an absolute law? In the same way, God has ordained to save people through the preached Word (Rom. 10:14, 15; 1 Cor. 1:21), but does this make it an absolute law, so that people only believe in Christ through listening to a preacher? Cannot someone believe in Christ by personally reading about Him? Indeed he can! Christ is moved by faith and pity, but either way it is for His own glory. In this case Christ's pity and power were communicated through the faith of Peter and John, resulting in healing for the cripple and glory for God. It *is* an absolute law that in order to be *saved* you have to have faith (Eph. 2:8), however, there is no such law that says every person that is healed had faith in Christ.

Acts 3:17

It is very strange that most commentators think that what Peter is talking about here is the same as the sin referred to in Numbers 15:22–31 and Leviticus 4:1–4. Peter is not in any way letting up on his condemnation of the crowd's wickedness. The whole law of God as found in the OT was both demanding and difficult to keep properly, however, it was sinful not to keep it perfectly. There were just so many things to remember that it was impossible not to sin with respect to all these requirements, therefore, God made the provision of Numbers 15 and Leviticus 4. When all these details were not fulfilled properly as a result of forgetfulness, there was a particular offering to be made. However, when someone purposefully raised his hand against God, such sacrifices could not be made for that person. The man in Numbers 15:35 was put to death because he consciously acted in violation of a clear requirement. He did not merely forget one small detail from among many small details. The same Hebrew word is also used to make the moral distinction between murdering someone and killing someone by accident (Num. 35:15ff.). These offerings (Num.15) for forgetful sin cannot be equated with the sinner's stubborn, wicked rebellion against the clear revelation of God in and around him (see *Faith and Reason*, chapters 3 and 4).

Peter says the leaders and the people acted in the same way—ignorantly. This ignorance was not because the revelation was not clear. All the Scriptures clearly spoke about Christ (John 1:45; Luke 24:27), thus it was their rebellion against God and His Word that led to this ignorance (Luke 16:31; John 5:46, 47). Tied into this ignorant condition is a wilful blindness. In Ephesians 4:18 Paul tells us how a person arrives at being ignorant. He says their hearts were darkened and they were separated from God (Rom. 1:21 tells us that this darkness is a result of rebellion against what one knows to be true). The reason their hearts were darkened and they were separated from God was because of ignorance, and this ignorance arose from hardness of heart—a stubborn rebellion against the light of God that is clearly set before their eyes (this agrees with Stephen's evaluation of the same people, cf. Acts 7:51–53). Their wickedness was deliberately active (Acts 3:36—God was clearly reaching out to them). Therefore, when Peter says they were ignorant he implies all of the above—he is increasing their condemnation *not* reducing it. The hope of relief is not given in this verse, but comes in the next one.

It is necessary at this point to briefly discuss the difference between what has been said above and the struggle that the Christian has with sin. Nowhere does the Bible allow the Christian to play down the seriousness of sin, but rather he is exhorted to a life of holiness and perfection (Heb. 12:14; Matt. 5:48; 2 Cor. 13:11). However, the

Spirit helps us in our weakness (Rom. 8:26) and Christ warned us
that the spirit is willing, but the flesh is weak (Matt. 26:41). In
Hebrews 4:15 we see that we have a High Priest who is made in our
likeness and thus can sympathise with our weaknesses. Paul in
Romans 7:14–25 talks of the real struggle that exists in the believer's
heart, because we are never totally freed from sin in this life. In one
sense the Christian life consists of striving, struggling, conflict and
stumbling (1 Cor. 9:27; 2 Tim. 2:3; Matt. 10:34; Rom. 8:36; 2 Cor.
4:7–12; 1 John 1:8). Thus we need to be aware of the seriousness of
remaining sin within the believer's life, however we also need to be
aware of the compassion of our High Priest. His compassion does
not lead us to a lax view about sin, but to greater sorrow for the sin
we do. Yes, sin remains and we find ourselves doing that which we
know we ought not to do, but when we do sin there is a heart-felt
sorrow for our actions. In a sense we sin "against our will" (Gal.
5:17), however, in saying this, our personal guilt for what we do is
in no way lessened. What we need to understand is the constant
struggle within the believer as he grows in grace and sanctification—this is a lifelong battle. The Christian falls, gets up and continues to struggle and overcomes and falls, though he never thinks
lightly of any sin he commits. The reason he continues is because he
hates sin, he hates the sins he does, he loves the holiness of God and
strives to walk in that holiness, yet the sole foundation that enables
him to continue is the compassionate understanding of his High
Priest and the Holy Spirit dwelling in his heart. It is because he
despises his sin that the believer flees to Christ and he flees to Christ
because he is confident that Christ will assist him in his weakness. It
is this confidence in Christ that enables him to come boldly unto
the throne of grace (Heb. 4:16).

Our sin and weakness ought to drive us to Christ, not to hopelessness. The realization of how much we need Christ and how helpless
we are in ourselves (for everything) is not just to be something we
hold to in our minds; it is the very life blood and heart beat of our
existence. Without Him we are doomed to failure. From the beginning to the end of our lives we are completely dependent upon Him
and His enabling. In our struggles we need to hold onto Christ as a
drowning man grabs onto a lifeline—a *realization* of desperate,
total dependence. This total dependence upon Christ is necessary
for the whole of our life, no matter what we are doing.

Acts 3:18

All that God had spoken about through the prophets with respect
to the sufferings of the Messiah, had not only been fulfilled, but had
been fulfilled in *this* way. What way is this? God's purposes had
been fulfilled through their wickedness, which is a repeat of Peter's
point in his Pentecost sermon (2:23)—man's wickedness and God's
eternal plan are inseparable from one another. Peter was not trying
to give them hope by saying their actions were not as bad as they
might have been (for indeed they couldn't have been more sinful),
but instead, their hope was to be in the fact that God's eternal plan
(Rev. 13:8; Matt. 25:34) had been to provide a way of salvation. The
guilty could obtain salvation through the shed blood of an innocent
substitute (this is what the whole of the sacrificial system was
speaking about). God had fulfilled, through Christ, what He had
been saying for centuries. Here we see the wisdom of God, who
used man's wickedness in His plan to remove man's wickedness.

Acts 3:19, 20

Peter calls upon his hearers to repent of their sins, which in the context refers to their terrible wickedness and guilt with respect to the
crucifixion of Christ (though it would also include all their sins).
"Repentance" means to forsake your evil ways, to hate sin and follow Christ's teachings. While "turning to God" is the same as having faith in God or believing in Him—faith and repentance cannot
be separated (see Acts 2:38). Peter says when they repent and
believe, then their sins will be wiped away. This is a complete and
thorough cleansing of all their sins, which is God's doing. Their
horrible wickedness had not frustrated God's plans, and nor had it
cut them off from His mercy—what boundless love and grace there
is in the heart of our sovereign God!

Peter calls on the crowd to repent so that they might be forgiven
and so that times of refreshing might come from the presence of the
Lord. These people were standing under the wrath and condemnation of God—His eternal judgment and the soon coming destruction of Jerusalem (in A.D. 70). Peter talks of the real relief they will
feel when their sin, guilt and the terror of judgment are removed
from their consciences and they taste of the sweetness of God's
goodness and mercy (Ps. 34:8; 1 Pet. 2:3). This offer of refreshing is
in the very immediate future if they repent, and not something that
is thousands of years away. Peter promises them rest, relief and

refreshment which is a real part of forgiveness. Sin is a burden and a weight, but when it is washed away, we receive the joy of salvation (Ps. 51:12; Jer. 31:12; 1 Pet. 1:8). The favor of the king and of God is likened to the spring rains that refresh the earth and people (Prov. 16:15; Hos. 6:3). The Great Shepherd feeds and refreshes His sheep even in the presence of their enemies (Ps. 23:5). Thus, refreshing from the presence of the Lord is very much a part of the Christian's life—flowing naturally to all who have found favor in God's sight (this favor is found only in Christ's completed work).

Peter tells them that another reason or motive for repenting was so that God could send Jesus to them. This was something that was on offer the moment they repented. The context and flow of the passage clearly support this understanding. Some argue that since the Scriptures nowhere say God sends Christ to people, this must refer to the Second coming. However, the Scriptures nowhere talk of God sending Christ with respect to the Second coming either.

In the context, Peter connects repentance with the forgiveness of sin, times of refreshing, and the sending of Jesus. All of these are a direct consequence of the repenting, therefore, if it is argued that this promise of sending Christ was thousands of years in the future (i.e., the Second Coming), then how can we be sure that our sins are forgiven now? Maybe sins will be forgiven only at the Second Coming too? It appears to make no sense that Peter would say to those listening to him, that if they repented right then, God would send Christ into the world in a few thousand years. Rather, Peter was presenting Christ to them the moment they repented. In Acts 3:26, Peter tells his audience that God, after raising Christ from the grave, sent Him to those in Jerusalem, before sending Him to anyone else. Jesus Himself had promised His disciples that He would come to them even after He had gone to be with the Father (John 14:18). Christ comes to live with us when we believe (John 14:23, see too the discussion on Acts 2:38). When the Spirit comes to dwell in the believer, then Christ also dwells with us (Rom. 8:9, 10)—Christ comes to His people in salvation, dwelling in those who have faith in Him.

These Jews had rejected, despised and killed the Messiah when He was on earth, yet Peter said this same Messiah would come to them when they believed—they still had an opportunity to receive their Messiah, for it was not too late. Peter was not offering them a new religion, but that which the prophets had already spoken about. He was not offering them some strange Messiah, but the very Messiah that had been ordained by God from the beginning. The One who had been foreordained to suffer at the hands of wicked men and in that way, to provide salvation for those who believe.

Acts 3:21

Peter had spoken about Christ remaining in heaven until all His enemies were made His footstool (Acts 2:34, 35). He now repeats the same thing. Christ will remain in heaven until things have been restored to the degree that had been foretold by the prophets since time began. Restoration is a process that takes place in history. It is a progressive movement towards God's predetermined end or climax (1 Cor. 15:25; Ps. 110:1). The whole purpose of the Messianic Kingdom was one of restoration, starting with John the Baptist (Matt. 17:11) and flowing through Christ's ministry, death, resurrection and exaltation to the position of supreme power at God's right hand (Matt. 28:18; Acts 2:33). Christ came to take away sin (Matt. 1:21; John 1:29); remove the curse; destroy the devil (Heb. 2:14); free us from sin and death (Rom. 8:2; 1 Cor. 15:22); destroy Satan's works (1 John 3:8) and the strength of his hosts (Col. 2:15), thus saving the whole world (John 3:17; 4:42). Christ's redemption is as broad as the effects of sin and it touches and reforms all of life. Christ's work is able to counter the whole of the curse in the whole of life and is far greater than the curse.

Christ did not go to the right hand of God and receive all power in heaven and earth so that He could sit there with all this power waiting for 2 or 3 thousand years before He used it. Jesus said to His disciples that the reason they should go into all the world was because all authority *was* His (Matt. 28:18). This meant that it was available for their benefit right then (in A.D. 33). The restoration was to begin with the apostles, for they were to teach all nations everything Christ had said (Matt. 28:20). Jesus is not waiting in heaven until some future date when the time to begin restoring arrives. Many people think that it is only when Christ returns that the restoration will begin, that is, they think Christ is coming back in order to begin the restoration. However, Peter is saying that Christ will remain in heaven, *until* those days arrive when *all things* will have been restored. This is not talking about absolute and complete perfection, for that only comes with the Second Coming. Rather, the restoration Peter is talking about is the one all the prophets spoke about (Acts 3:24).

The Kingdom came with Christ (Matt. 4:17; Mark 1:15) and continues to grow until it fills the whole earth (Matt. 13:31–33; Dan. 2:35) and *then* Christ returns (1 Cor. 15:24, 25). Christ returns when all His enemies have been put under His feet or to put it another way, Christ remains in heaven until all things have been restored. Peter said Jesus would be sent to them when they believed, but he quickly clarifies what this means. It does not mean Christ's Second Coming, for Peter immediately says, this Christ who will be sent to you *when* you repent, remains in heaven throughout the whole period of restoration. Peter distinguishes between Christ coming to believers in salvation and His Second Coming.

Peter then continues to speak about these times of the restoration of all things (the niv Bible is a poor translation at this point). This restoration God had spoken about through His prophets from the earliest days. Everything that the prophets predicted (e.g., Hab. 2:14; Isa. 11:9; 65:17–25, etc.), flows out of Christ's completed work and exaltation at God's right hand. This restoration arises from the spread of Kingdom teaching, resulting in the reign of the Kingdom of Heaven in all areas of life (the starting place of restoration being the triumph of the Gospel in people's hearts through the power of Christ and the ministry of the Holy Spirit). Peter says, "I am but telling you what has been prophesied from the beginning with respect to God's glorious plan. The work the Scriptures said the Messiah would do, is the work that is being completed by Jesus Christ." It was this Jesus who had been the focus of every prophet from the beginning of time!

Acts 3:22

Peter now begins to show the vast amount of biblical authority that supports what he is saying. He starts with Moses' prophecy about Christ which is recorded in Deuteronomy 18:15–20 (God had called Moses a prophet, Deut. 18:18). As we have already seen, Peter's ultimate authority is the Scripture (see, Acts 1:20; 2:16, 25, 34). Peter does not decide for himself who Christ is or what He is like, for it is God's Word alone that can do this (see comments on John 7:40–44). Moses was rightly regarded by the Jews as the chief teacher in the OT and therefore, Peter is wanting to show that he was not in revolt against Moses. He wants to prove to his hearers that this Jesus is the Messiah. The Jews appear to have been some-what unclear about the exact meaning of Moses' prophecy—some seeing it as referring to the Messiah, others as referring to someone who would appear at the same time as the Messiah. (cf. John 1:21, 25; 6:14; 7:40; Acts 7:37). The understanding that Moses was speaking about the Messiah appears to have been a realization that developed over time. The term is thought to have also included all those who would come in Christ's name and testify about Him.

In the context, Moses was saying God would provide a succession of prophets to speak to His people. God would continue to speak to His people in this way when Moses was gone. And the way the prophets resembled Moses was in their authority and responsibility to declare the Word of God. Israel was not to listen to diviners (Deut. 18:14), but to live by God's Word that would come through the true prophet. These prophets were ordained by God to teach His people until the ultimate Prophet came and revealed all things (Heb. 1:1, 2; John 4:25). Christ is the source of all truth and thus, God said we are to "Hear Him" (Matt. 17:5). Christ is far greater than Moses, as the book of Hebrews clearly points out (Heb. 3:5, 6).

Acts 3:23

Peter quotes Moses' prophecy in order to underline the seriousness of not repenting. God's Word is not to be despised, for God will have no mercy on such a person. Jesus is the only revealer of truth, He is the only light and the only way to get to God (John 8:12; 14:6), and therefore it is utter foolishness to reject Him and His Words—for this will mean sure death. To reject the Messiah will result in being totally cut off from God and His people (Acts 4:12). This is a solemn warning about the severe penalty that will fall upon those who continue in stubborn, wilful, rebellion against the only True God and Savior of the world. Such people refuse to bow to His revelation, choosing rather to live by their own standards for they desperately want to decide for themselves what is good and evil (see *Faith and Reason*, chapters 1 to 3).

Acts 3:24

Peter emphasises the fact that all the OT prophets spoke with one united voice. They had one message, one vision and one longing desire—Christ and His Kingdom. Peter's hearers were living in these very days that were spoken of by all the OT prophets. This was still at the beginning of the Messianic age, however, the prophets had not only spoken about these early days, but had also told of the glorious growth of the Kingdom that would continue to increase until Christ returned; they spoke of the whole age of the Messiah (from His first to His second coming); they spoke about the times of refreshing and of the times of the restoration of all things, thus those who claim to be devout followers of God and to believe Moses and the prophets, should submit to Christ and His Words.

Acts 3:25

Sons: talks of a special relationship and standing that these people had with respect to the prophet's message. They were not real sons, nor were they prophets themselves, but rather, heirs of what the prophets spoke about (heirs of those promises made by God through the prophets). These Jews not only received everything that the fathers had stood for, but were the ones who were to carry on with that same message and hope. All that the prophets spoke of had been passed onto them and therefore, to be true to the whole prophetic message, they had to receive, hold onto and run with it. What the prophets had seen in the distant future about the Messiah had been fulfilled and what they had seen about His Kingdom, was now unfolding before the eyes of Peter's hearers. Peter is reminding them of their tremendous privilege of being part of the covenant. He is reminding them of their responsibility that arises out of their privileged position.

This is New Testament teaching being given by Peter and not some out of date OT teaching. These people are not born again; they do not yet believe in the Messiah, Jesus Christ, and yet, Peter says they have a special relationship to the prophets and a special relationship to the covenant. They were members of that special community which God had set apart as His own, thus, they stood in a privileged position, even though they were not believers.

People can be part of the covenant community which means they have a different relationship with God than those who are not part of the covenant community (i.e., Gentiles). It also means they have a special relationship towards the promises and blessings of God, and yet they are not believers. The grace of God is extended in a special way to those who are born into the covenant community. Thus, even though those born into the covenant community will not all be saved automatically, we must not deny the clear Biblical teaching that these people and their children have a different relationship towards the covenant than those who have no connection to the covenant. It is a special blessing and privilege to be part of that community that receives teaching from the mouth of God (Amos 2:11; Rom. 3:2; Acts 3:22 above) and has God's special sign upon it (circumcision in the OT and baptism in the NT). It must be remembered that persistent rebellion will result in being removed from the privileges and blessings of the covenant community.

The covenant was made with Abraham and thus extended to all his descendants (of whom these hearers were a part). The great blessings of God are not tied to Abraham's many descendants, but are found only in the one Seed—Christ (Gal. 3:16; cf. Gen. 12:3; 22:18; 26:4). It is only as we stand united to Christ that we share in these blessings promised to Abraham. All the nations of the earth have the opportunity to receive these blessings, however, they are only received when the nations stand united to Christ—thus living by every word that comes from His mouth. Our blessings are in proportion to our being joined to "The Seed," Jesus Christ. We are blessed and become a blessing when we are united to Jesus. With the appearing of "The Seed," all that which had been promised, was now actually present.

Acts 3:26

To raise up: does not refer to the resurrection, but rather to God's equipping and appointing of Christ for this work of blessing the nations. God had ordained Christ for this service and supplied everything that was necessary to fulfill this task—He had been raised up by God for the express purpose of fulfilling God's decrees (cf. verse 22). God had sent Jesus to the Jews first, thus Peter's hearers should have confidence that God was truly offering them salvation. God's purpose in raising up Christ was to first save the Jews, though after their rejection of this offer, the apostles would turn to the Gentiles (Acts 13:46). The glorious promise of salvation was always for all the nations, however it was to be sent first to Israel (Rom. 1:16).

The whole world sits under the wrath and judgment of God and therefore, the single most important blessing is deliverance from God's anger—which is obtained only in Christ. This blessing that Peter is talking about is the forgiveness of sin, for both repentance and salvation originate in Christ. The blessing is that Christ would turn them from their evil ways. The greatest blessing that anyone could ever receive is to be turned from their wickedness and thus moved from the kingdom of darkness into the Kingdom of light (Col. 1:13). This is a personal turning that takes place in individuals and is not something done as a group (even when whole groups do repent, it is because each individual has personally repented). When Christ turns us, then we are able to turn. We have to repent, but are unable to do so until Christ first quickens us (Jer. 31:18; Lam. 5:21; Acts 2:38; 5:31; John 6:65).

When Christ saves in this way it is not so that these people may then sin without fear. Christ's sovereign act of salvation does not only mean a person's sins are wiped away, but that he is also made a new creation. This is what the new birth is all about. When Christ moves to save us, He also changes our inner nature so that we are no longer in bondage to sin, but have a nature that loves righteousness and hates sin (this does not mean the person is now perfect, for we do still struggle with sin until we are glorified, see comments on Acts 3:17).

Acts 4:1

We see three groups of people coming upon the apostles. The priests were organized into twenty four groups who served in the temple on a rotation basis (cf. Luke 1:8). The priests and Levites were the ones who offered the morning and evening sacrifices. The captain of the temple was the person who was in charge of those who maintained order in the temple and was thought to be second in authority to the High Priest. And the Sadducees were members of the Sanhedrin who were very wealthy and had ingratiated themselves with the Roman authorities in their desire for power. Their desire to hold onto their positions of authority was greater than their desire for truth. The High Priest, Caiaphas, was a Sadducee (John 11:49, 50). The Sadducees were not looking for the Messiah and they did not believe in angels, spirits, demons or the resurrection of the dead (teaching that a person's soul died with their body, see Acts 23:8). The Sadducees only accepted the first five books of Moses as authoritative.

Acts 4:2

We were told in Acts 2:46 that the Christians were in the temple daily and the implication is that here as well, the apostles taught them daily. Now these Jewish leaders had reached the end of their "patience." They had become extremely angry due to the continual preaching and teaching of the apostles and decided, enough was enough: it was time for this "heretical nonsense" to stop! According to the Sadducees, the apostles were untrained men (4:13) and therefore unqualified to teach the people (see comments on John 7:15). Besides this fact, they were teaching things that were extremely offensive to the Sadducees, namely, about Jesus and the resurrection. They had despised Jesus, clashed with His teachings, been embarrassed by Him publicly, thus hated Him and plotted to murder Him. Jesus had already told them that the reason they thought there was no resurrection was because they did not understand the Scriptures (Matt. 22:29–33). Jesus quoted from the Pentateuch (Ex. 3:6, 15)—that portion of Scripture the Sadducees accepted as authoritative. Peter and John were not only teaching about Jesus, but also saying that He had been raised from the dead. This meant the Sadducees' arch enemy had been right and they were wrong. They despised both Christ and the teaching that people rise from the dead, and thus decided to put an end to this kind of teaching. Caiaphas, the Sadducee and High Priest at the time, was at the fore-front of this persecution unleashed against Christ and His followers (Matt. 26:57–66; Acts 5:17f.; 7:1; 8:3; 9:1f.).

Acts 4:3

They were locked up until the next day when they could be tried for heresy.

Acts 4:4

The actions of the Sadducees couldn't stop many from turning to the Lord. This verse appears to say that many believed so that the number of men who had now believed since Pentecost was 5,000 (this is excluding woman and children). Persecution cannot stop the truth. Communist Russia, China and Cuba (to mention only a few) have all tried to suppress the preaching of Christ and all have failed, even though they used cruel tortures and punishments. It is God who is the author of salvation and it is God who is building His church, therefore who can stop Him? (Ps. 115:3; 135:6).

Acts 4:5, 6

The Jewish leaders' extreme concern over this situation is demonstrated by the speed with which they assembled the Sanhedrin and
also by the fact that all the most powerful leaders were present.
These top officials had been the ones who condemned Jesus and
now they treated it with utmost urgency that they put an end to His
name being revived. The high priest was the most powerful member of the Sanhedrin and Caiaphas was the leader at this time, however, we are here told that Annas was the high priest. The reason for
this confusion in the Jewish system was because of the intervention
of the Roman authorities who controlled the appointment of the
high priests. According to the Jewish law, a high priest was in this
position for life and could only be removed by God (i.e., by death).
However, Rome, for their own political ends had deposed Annas
and the Jewish historian Josephus says five of Annas' sons, including his son-in-law Caiaphas, were high priests at one time. There
were sometimes a number of people living who had all been high
priest at one time. This was something unheard of for the Jews. The
Roman governors who appointed the high priest were often bribed,
so this became a position that could be bought. Thus this office was
dominated by a small group of wealthy families. Therefore,
although Caiaphas held the position according to Rome, Annas still
had immense authority in the eyes of the Jews and in the actual
running of affairs. Due to his influence and seniority, Luke names
him as the high priest. Therefore it is quite easy for there to be two
high priests at the same time (cf. John 18:12, 13).

The rulers: probably refers to this high priestly line (family), for they
carried much power and influence (Mark 14:53). Thus the Sadducees were the ones who had the greatest influence in the Sanhedrin
and they hated Jesus and teachings about the resurrection. *The
elders*: were heads of families who were mature and respected and
thus called to a position of leadership—these were the real representatives of the nation of Israel (Ex. 3:16). *The scribes*: were mostly
made up of the Pharisee party and were the ones who preserved,
transcribed and expounded the law (they were the nation's spiritual
guides).

Not much is known about John and Alexander, though they were
obviously influential names in Luke's day.

Acts 4:7

Peter and John were brought into this imposing group of leaders—
the same group that had used false witnesses in order to condemn
Jesus to death. Both Peter and John had been very close by when
Jesus was tried (John 18:15, 16; Luke 22:60–62) and they would
have recognised many of the men who were now going to pass
judgment on them. The most obvious thing would have been for
Peter and John to think that they would receive the same treatment
that Jesus had received (John 21:18, 19; 15:20). There was no reason
for Peter and John to think that they would receive any better treatment than their Master received—they were in a very real sense,
facing death.

The Jewish leaders were not asking *what* had been done, but rather,
how it had been done. Jesus had been condemned by this very
council as a blasphemer (Matt. 26:65), therefore, for anyone to do
anything in His Name would make them guilty with Christ. The
Pharisees had accused Jesus of doing His miracles by the power of
demons (Matt. 12:24). The Sadducees did not believe in such a
spiritual realm, however, in order to get the Pharisees' support in
the Sanhedrin they worded their question in such a way that it
might appear that they were implying that Peter and John were
using demonic power to work miracles. This question was filled
with scorn and contempt; "What power do people *like* you use?"

Acts 4:8

Peter had been terrified and denied Jesus when a little servant girl
had asked him if he had been with Jesus (John 18:17). Now, Peter
stood before the most powerful Jewish leaders in the land—men
who had nothing but hatred and contempt for Jesus and anyone
who taught in His name. These were evil murderers who would
stop at nothing to get rid of the truth of God. The Sanhedrin had
put Peter and John on trial, however, we see that in the power of the
Holy Spirit, Peter is a completely changed man from that dreadful
night when he denied the Lord. He now speaks in the name of God
and therefore, puts the whole Jewish council on trial and finds
them guilty. Jesus had promised this kind of boldness to His disciples (Matt. 10:19, 20).

Acts 4:9

The Sanhedrin had not mentioned the healing of the lame man specifically, but had only said, "this thing." Peter corrects this and clearly states the "crime" he and John were being charged with, namely, for healing a lame man. The word "if" here implies that it is really amazing that any kind of charge could be brought against them for what they had done for this poor man. He is saying, "How can we be judged for this good work?" Peter asks if things have deteriorated to such a degree that people in Israel are now judged for their good deeds and acts of mercy? However, if their crime was healing a helpless man, then Peter wants there to be no doubt about just how the healing came about. He wants there to be no doubt as to whose power performed this marvellous miracle (see comments on Acts 3:4). The Sanhedrin called this glorious manifestation of the exalted Christ, offensive and wicked, instead of glorifying Him with worship, rejoicing and thanksgiving (see Titus 1:15, 16).

Acts 4:10

Jesus did not do anything in some dark corner away from the light (John 18:20, 21), thus in the same way, Peter wants this to be made know to the whole nation—for all to see. What Peter was about to say was not just for the Sanhedrin, but for all people to hear. Peter once again uses the authoritative words, "let it be known to you" (cf. Acts 2:14, 36).

Peter, standing before this fierce, murderous council, boldly proclaims the Name of Jesus. He does not fear what men might do to him. The truth burns in his heart and is more important to him than life in this world. It is utter foolishness to deny the source of life in an attempt to hold onto our earthly life. The Sanhedrin were the ones who were deceived and living a lie. They were the ones who were filled with the fear of death, not the apostles (Heb. 2:14). Jesus alone has all power, authority, and glory (Matt. 28:18). It is in His name alone that people can be saved (Acts 4:12). The victory is His, and we have been created and saved for His glory. His Words alone are truth, and He alone is the eternal God who holds all things together by His powerful Word (Heb. 1:3). Man is but a vapour which quickly disappears and yet we so often fear the faces of men; we fear their power and influence. We fear what they might think of us and do to us. Peter understands who God is and thus even the most powerful men in the nation were nothing but dust in the balances and a drop in the bucket in comparison to the Lord of the universe (Isa. 40:15).

The Jewish council, in the name of preserving the truth, were suppressing the truth. They were spiritually blind and in bondage to sin (Matt. 15:12–14). They couldn't see the Kingdom of God (John 3:3); they did not believe in Christ (John 5:46, 47); refused to obey Him, and therefore, knew nothing about truth or freedom (John 8:32).

Peter is not ashamed of who Christ is and thus uses His full title. This council that had condemned Jesus to death is now charged with His murder. The apostles put the Sanhedrin on trial and find them guilty. Once again Peter points out the wicked actions of men and the glorious actions of God—you put Him to death, but God has raised Him (2:23, 24; 3:14, 15). Peter says they were fighting against God and sows the seed that would later cause the wisest Jewish leaders to doubt their own position, realising that they were not absolutely sure anymore (Acts 5:38, 39). This is not what the Sanhedrin had anticipated. They had brought two ignorant Galilean fishermen before them in order to stop them from teaching heresy, however, this powerful and proud Sanhedrin has been put on trial and found guilty of murder and rebellion against God. These men who prided themselves in the fact that they were Abraham's seed and therefore had eternal life, were being told that they needed to repent in order to be saved—they did not have salvation, but were in need of salvation. They needed to believe that Jesus Christ the Nazarene, was both Lord and Savior. They needed to bow to His authority and believe that God had raised Him from the dead. Proof for Christ's resurrection was the healed cripple standing in their midst. It was the power of the risen Lord that made this man whole (or saved him). These religious leaders were already aware that Christ had risen from the grave (Matt. 28:2–4,11–13), and the proof is now multiplied. It was only by wilful blindness and suppression of the truth that they could continue in their stubborn unbelief (Ps. 86:5).

Acts 4:11

Peter continues his condemnation of these leaders. This is the seventh time since the beginning of Acts that Peter refers to Scripture as the basis or authority for what he is saying (Acts 1:16, 20; 2:16, 25, 34; 3:22). He is preaching in the power and anointing of the

Holy Spirit and clearly demonstrates what true NT preaching should be like—expounding the written Word in the power of the Holy Spirit (John 16:13, 14; 1 Cor. 2:4, 5). The work of the Holy Spirit is to enable us to understand the Written Word, expound it, and apply it to our own lives and situations.

Peter quotes Ps. 118:22, saying this verse is a prophecy about Christ and these Jewish leaders. They were supposed to be the builders of the nation and yet they had cast away, as worthless, the most important and vital part of the building that they were to build. The corner stone was the stone that set all the angles and measurements for the entire building and was the main support for the whole structure. Without the proper corner stone a proper structure couldn't be built. Peter says to these proud leaders that they should have been resting on Christ, and getting their direction from Him and building everything upon Him, however, they had not only failed to recognise who He was, but had spent all their time plotting to murder Him (John 11:53). Yet despite the rebellion and blindness of these builders, despite man's rejection of this chief stone, God had exalted it and placed it in its rightful place (cf. Eph. 2:20; Isa. 28:16; Rom. 9:33; 1 Pet. 2:4, 6–8; 1 Cor. 3:11). Does the truth so burn in our hearts, so that we will declare it with humble boldness no matter who is opposing it? We are to testify to the truth, and this truth is Christ and His teachings (Matt. 28:20).

Acts 4:12

These builders had made a grave mistake, for they had tried to destroy the only source of salvation there is. On a human level, they had cut themselves and the whole nation off from any chance of salvation. No matter how religious someone is or a nation is; no matter how many times a day they pray; or how many services they have; or how much charity work they do; if they do not fully embrace Jesus Christ and trust completely in Him and Him alone for their salvation, they are going to hell. There is absolutely no other name by which to be saved, and that name is Jesus, and nothing else. Peter here even offers the Gospel to these hard hearted, rebellious, murdering leaders—they too can be saved in Jesus' Name. Peter, in answering the question put to him about how the cripple was physically healed, moves to complete spiritual healing. Jesus not only has the power to heal bodies, but He alone has the power to cleanse from sin (Luke 5:20–24). Peter and John had been brought before this company in order to be condemned for preaching in the name of Jesus, however, Peter tells his accusers that they will be eternally condemned unless they whole-heartedly believe in this very name. Salvation is in the name of Jesus alone, it is never Jesus and something else. Only Jesus and all of Jesus is the only way in heaven and on earth by which people can be delivered from the just judgment of God that rests upon them.

Acts 4:13

Peter's powerful preaching convicts the hearts of these leaders, however, this does not lead to repentance on their part, though it does silence them. We too need to be prepared to give an answer to all people for the hope that we have (1 Pet. 3:15) and this answer, even if it does not result in repentance, should be good enough to silence the arguments of the rebellious. This "boldness" that the apostles manifested was not just courage to say what they had said, but included great ability in public speaking. These simple fishermen from Galilee had received no training from the recognised teachers of the day (either theological training or public speaking), and yet Peter's ability to interpret and quote Scripture and his ability to speak to these highly educated men and impress them, confused the Sanhedrin. These educated leaders were staring in amazement at what they were experiencing—Peter's accent would have pointed to the fact that he was from the uneducated class. The way he dressed would have confirmed that he was from the low class. He did not even come from an important town. He had had no recognised training and no experience as a speaker, and yet he is not just giving a good talk, but a powerfully stunning one. Therefore, we are told that they marvelled—they were amazed and unable to come up with an explanation for how this could be so.

As these rulers of the Jews contemplated this dilemma (that such untrained men could speak as if they had been highly trained), they recognised the connection between the apostle's and Jesus' preaching (Matt. 7:29; Mark 1:22; John 7:15, 46). The Jewish leaders probably felt the same conviction in their hearts that they had felt when Jesus spoke (it was the same Word and Spirit coming from Peter that had come from Christ).

We too should preach the full counsel of God, not apologising for any aspect of God's revelation (His sovereignty, predestination, election, unmerited favour, law, hell, etc.). Our hope for success should not be based upon enticing people to come and listen to our message (1 Cor. 2:4). We should not think that we have to imitate the way the world gets people to listen to what they have to say. We preach the Word of the living God and it is His Word that is powerful and able to pierce to the depths of the sinner's heart (Heb. 4:11, 12). The sinner needs to be made aware of his sin and his need for Christ. The danger he is in needs to be emphasised, not ignored. Much of the preaching in our day leaves unbelievers thinking that for the most part their lives are quite fine, though things would be better for them if they decided to add Jesus to their already pretty good lives. This is not how Jesus or Peter preached!

Acts 4:14

The evidence is overwhelming and beyond question. Both the message and the evidence stun the audience and prevent them from asking more questions. They had no reply to what Peter had said. There was just an embarrassed silence (cf. Luke 21:14, 15). They couldn't deny the charges and facts that Peter had placed before them (murder, rejecting God's corner stone and that salvation was only found in Christ), yet they refused to repent. Christ's own Words about these leaders were very accurate (cf. Matt. 23:13, 24, 27–31).

Acts 4:15, 16

The confusion of these leaders is seen by the fact that they removed the apostles from the room in order to try and save the situation. To bring these men before such a powerful gathering of leaders and then to let them go without a charge was embarrassing. Once again we see how the rebellious in heart easily ignore or explain a sign in another way. They admit that an amazing sign had been done, though they refuse to accept its true meaning. Although they would have loved to punish the apostles, they were afraid of the people, thus they find themselves in a very difficult position and probably discussed this in private for a long time. Even though these leaders cannotdeny the miracle, they refuse to give it its true meaning— that Jesus Christ has been raised from the dead and exalted to the right hand of God where He received all power in heaven and on earth. This notable sign was clear proof of this fact!

Acts 4:17

The Sanhedrin, in their private discussions say they cannot deny the miracle, *but* they still need to stop the spread of Jesus' Name. Peter had clearly told them that the miracle had been done in Jesus' Name (verse 10). These leaders cannotdeny the miracle or argue against the connection Peter makes between the healing and Jesus, however, they are determined to bring an end to the Name of Jesus. The Jews believed that the miracle was a real miracle, yet they still rejected Christ. This is because the miracle was a sign of who Jesus really was (the supreme Lord of the universe) and they wouldn't bow to His Lordship. They were in rebellion to God and no sign was going to convert them. Believing a miracle is far from true conversion (see my comments on John 2:23–25). The Sanhedrin was very anxious to stop the spread of this new religion, and wanted the apostles to stop promoting and relying upon this Name. The Sanhedrin thus clearly reject Peter's call for repentance and offer of salvation (verse 12).

Acts 4:18

The council tells the apostles that under no circumstances are they allowed to mention the Name of Jesus. Christ had commissioned His apostles to be His witnesses (Acts 1:8), but the Sanhedrin says no, you are not allowed to be witnesses for Him. We get this same thing in our day because people do not want to bow to Christ as the absolute and only Lord of all things. What happens in our day, even within the church, is that Christ can be Lord within the four walls of the church building, however, Jesus is not allowed to be Lord in the rest of the world. Thus, we are not allowed to speak in Jesus' Name outside of the church building. We can only tell people that they must believe that Jesus can save them from their sin, but as far as telling them how to live in every area of life, there we are told, Jesus has no authority. We must not speak about Jesus' teachings with respect to the political realm. We must not speak about Jesus' teachings with respect to education, business, money, taxation, war, international relations between countries, etc. Jesus told His followers to teach the nations everything that He had commanded, for He was Lord of all things (Matt. 28:18–20). We are told today, not to speak in Jesus' Name in relation to all things. Jesus is not relevant to much that goes on in the world—so we are led to believe. However, Christ has redeemed the world and everything in it and God's

Kingdom is relevant to all things. Christ is Lord of all things and thus, all things need to be brought into obedience to Him (2 Cor.10:5). The church is to be the light of the world (Matt. 5:14) and God has placed members of the church in all areas of life and they are responsible to make the Name and message of Jesus known in these areas. All areas of life are to hear what Jesus has commanded—our courts or justice system, immigration laws, customs, government, what is taught in the schools and universities and all areas of business. All of these areas belong to Christ, but we are threatened in our day not to speak in the Name of Jesus in these areas of life. Whom should we obey?

Acts 4:19

Jesus had said go and teach in My Name (Matt. 28:19). The Sanhedrin said, "Do not speak in this Name." Peter and John both responded, "You are not our highest authority—God and His Word are." Therefore, when there is a disagreement between what Jesus claims authority over and what the rulers claim to have authority over, then it is obvious to Peter and John that they should obey God. The apostles say it should be obvious to anyone as to who should be obeyed in this situation. Peter and John say to the highest authority in the Jewish nation, that they will gladly obey a ruling that is not in contradiction to God's Word, however, they will not, under any circumstances, obey what contradicts His Word. The apostles say they have decided to obey God rather than men and are prepared to suffer the consequences. Now these leaders must decide whom they are going to obey. To obey the counsel of ungodly men, no matter who they are or how much power and respect the world has for them, is to become part of their rebellion against God (see also the comments on Acts 5:29ff.). The apostles had been bold in their first statements, even when they knew the danger they were facing. Their boldness is not reduced even when this fearsome group of religious leaders threatens them. The Sanhedrin, commanded them not to speak in Jesus' Name—there was no higher authority in the Jewish nation other than God. To disobey their command was no small undertaking.

Acts 4:20

In this verse the apostles very clearly proclaim that they definitely were going to speak again in Jesus' Name. No government, church, or person has the right to control our consciences. We are account-able before God for what we believe and therefore, what we believe should be shaped by God alone. This does not mean that people cannot teach us anything, but it does mean that no person or organisation can *force* you to believe anything. Every individual has the right to private judgment and submission to his own con-science. In our own day there is much talk about "rights," but free-dom of conscience is not among them. There is talk about rights, which are no rights at all, and these are used to suppress people's true rights (e.g., there is the so called "right" of all children to get an education, but this is done to suppress the true right of the individ-ual to be guided by his own conscience as to what he should learn. Instead, the government decides what everyone has to learn and then forces it into everyone's minds—this is not a right, but oppres-sion!).

These Jewish leaders had been told that there was salvation in no other name, but they still said do not speak in the Name of Jesus. They wanted to destroy man's only hope of salvation and remove grace from the earth. Tyrants always act in this way. *In the name of protecting the people,* they destroy the people. The tyrant always has comforting words, saying, trust in me because I am doing this for your own good. The fool believes these words, and only finds out when it is too late, that together with the fancy words a spear was being pushed through his heart. If there is no liberty of conscience then there can be no liberty!

The apostles ask how they can be expected to be silent about the things they know are true. If we really have the truth, it will burn in our hearts and we will not be able to hide it. This does not mean that there is no self control and wisdom about when to speak and when to keep silent.

Acts 4:21, 22

These leaders were unable to do with the apostles what they would have liked to do. They could find no reason to punish Peter and John, but we must not think that these men were acting according to justice—they did not release the apostles because there was no evidence. This was not the reason for releasing them, but rather, they were released because the people would have risen up against the leaders if they had punished Peter and John. No case, reason or argument was given why the apostles should not speak in Jesus'

Name. There was no just reason for their judgement, so all they could do was threaten. A threat implies there is some crime that deserves punishment, however, if there was some basis then the apostles *would* have been punished. The Sanhedrin did not want the nation of Israel to realize that they were unjust, so, out of view of the people, they threaten the apostles again. These leaders knew what everyone was saying about the healing of the crippled man—they were all glorifying God. The Jewish authorities were trying to stop the spread of Christianity by silencing the leaders and teachers of this "new" religion. A time was coming when even the ordinary person who believed in this Name would be under threat (Acts 8:1, 3).

We must not think that this passage is only talking to these Jewish leaders. The emphasis is not on believing in miracles or believing in Jesus, but rather it is on obeying God and living by every Word that comes from His mouth. The early church would later be persecuted by both the nation of Rome and the Jews. Rome did not care who a person worshipped, just as long as Caesar was called Lord on earth—(i.e., just as long as the Roman government was treated as the highest authority when it came to matters of how to live in this world). The early church refused to bow to any word except God's. They said Jesus Christ is Lord in heaven above and on earth beneath and therefore we must obey God rather than men. Judge what is the right thing to do—is it better to obey God or man? Choose you this day whom you will serve. Christ is Lord of all of life and His Word and redemption is for all of life. The fall came about because Adam and Eve rejected a law that was very much a part of their earthly existence. We are to obey every Word of God and God's Word addresses everything.

Acts 4:23

We see here that true believers are really one—they went to their own. We do not know who this included and practically it probably couldn't refer to all the believers. It might have referred to that group that included the apostles (1:13–15), though we cannotbe sure. Peter and John did not take the threats from the Sanhedrin lightly. They realised the seriousness of clashing with this powerful religious body. They knew how much influence these leaders had (they had "persuaded" the people in Jerusalem to change their minds about Jesus, cf. Matt. 21:8–11; 27:20). These leaders were influential with the Roman authorities, and therefore, their threats were very real and disturbing. Peter and John realised that they were walking in complete opposition to these leaders and that it was going to be a difficult road. They wouldn't have doubted who would be victorious, however, the clash and the persecution they had been threatened with was something they knew they had to go through and it would not be pleasant.

John Wyclif translated the phrase, "*all that* the chief priests and elders had said to them," as "*how great things …,*" which appears to be closer to the meaning of the Greek. The Sanhedrin had indeed made some terrifying threats. As terrifying as any that could be made in our day by some tyrant who rejects the fact that Christ is Lord over all of life, yet these great threats couldn't frighten the apostles into compromising the truth.

Despite what the Jewish leaders could do to their bodies, Peter, John and the other believers know what God requires of them and therefore, realising their own weakness in the situation, flee to God in prayer. What God has clearly told them to do, they have been threatened not to do, thus they seek from God the power and grace to faithfully do what He commanded.

Acts 4:24

The power of the Sanhedrin and the might of the Roman Empire were both going to try to destroy this tiny group of Christians. The most powerful human authorities possible were about to work with all their might to crush the church. These Christians, aware of what they were up against, started their prayer with the fact that God was the Creator of all things. They did not all pray at the same time, but were all so united with one desire and mind that the inspired prayer of the one was the prayer of them all.

The word used for Lord, is the one that is used to refer to someone who has absolute authority and power. God is the Sovereign ruler over everything that He has made. The Christians refer here to the Lord's unchallenged power. He made all things and thus, everything is in His hands and He has complete control at all times to do whatever His will has determined. This means that man's will can never resist God's Sovereign will and control—for even one moment. It is the providence of God that orders every detail in life and not the ideas and plans of rebellious people. The Christians reassure themselves with these facts (see *Faith and Reason*, chapter 6).

God's eternal decree had set that the full counsel of God, which is the only standard for all of life, should be proclaimed to every nation (Matt. 28:20), thus, no amount of human opposition could change it. For us to conform our behavior to the will of the rebellious, is to join in with their rebellion.

These believers realize that they are in a battle unto death and therefore, they prepare and strengthen themselves by prayer. We need to stand together and encourage one another to have full confidence in the victory that is ours. May the Lord open our eyes to see the reality of His Kingdom rule over all people, nations and things. It is our responsibility and calling to know His truth, proclaim His truth, and bring every thought into line with His truth—this is the only way to maintain life, health and strength.

Seeing God as Creator and in control of all things, including the rebellious, is a sure comfort for us when we become fearful about the mad ravings of God's enemies. Those who hate God can shout and scream all they want, but only what God has decreed will come to pass (Eph. 1:11). Unbelievers cannot argue against the truth of the Christian message, and so what they often do is use other means to escape from it (i.e., by threats and violence), however, nothing can happen to God's children except what He has ordained and no one can take our lives unless it is according to His will. What creature can resist the power of our God who spoke and the worlds came into being? God has a right to do with us as He pleases—our responsibility is to live faithfully according to the revelation He has given to us, trusting in His sovereign power. "Though He slay me, yet will I trust Him" (Job 13:15). God is able to deliver us from any evil, but even if He does not we mustn't compromise the truth or deny His Name (Dan. 3:17, 18).

What is there to fear? For to me, to live is Christ, and to die is gain (Phil. 1:21). Death has no power over the Christian (1 Cor. 15:54–57), for through it we receive something more than we now have (even if we cannotsee this, it is true and we need to bring our thoughts into line with the Scriptures). Tribulations and sufferings for the Lord's sake are opportunities to glorify God and receive blessings from Him (Matt. 5:11, 12; Acts 5:41; Rom. 5:3–5; 8:35–39; 2 Cor. 12:10; Col. 1:24; Jam. 1:2; 1 Pet. 1:6; 4:13–16).

Remembering God's Creative power when we pray, not only helps calm our fears when we are faced by a strong enemy, but it also helps us pray with confidence that God is able to help. We need to pray in faith, believing in God's willingness to help and ability to do even above what we are able to imagine (Eph. 3:20). We need to believe that God not only hears prayers, but answers them. Often we do not see past the actual words we pray or the prayer meeting itself, thinking that the fullness of the meaning of prayer is completed when the last word is said—we do not actually believe that anything will come of it. Faith is having sure confidence in that which we have not seen (Heb. 11:1). Our sure confidence is in God's promises—He is our Rock, Foundation, Fortress and Salvation (Ps. 18:2, 31; 62:2). He is a very present help in time of need (Ps. 46:1), He is our shepherd and protector and nothing is able to separate us from the love of God (Ps. 23; Rom. 8:35). Nothing can pluck us from His hand (John 10:28). Our greatest desire should be to be found in Christ and nothing can be compared to this (Phil. 3:8, 9). Our minds need to be renewed in this area, so that we realize that true life is not measured by what is around us, or by what we have and what we can do, but it is found in Christ and His truth. God says we are prospering and have abundant life when we faithfully stand on the side of and proclaim His Righteousness. When we live by every Word of God, He comes and makes His home with us and His fullness is our fullness (John 14:23). Living in obedient submission is proof that we really know God and to really know God is to know true life—eternal life (John 17:3). May our minds be renewed so that we see things as God sees them. It is God's absolute, sovereign will that we must believe in, submit to, and trust in. He is in control and what He does is best—we might not understand all the details, but we are to trust that all things do work together for our good when we love Christ and do what He has said (Rom. 8:28; Heb. 11:1).

Acts 4:25, 26

God's sovereign control is not just over some spiritual realm, but over every aspect of life. This is clearly demonstrated by the words of David (the eighth prophecy or OT passage of Scripture expounded so far in Acts). In this life, it is earthly kings who are most able to do exactly as they please. Kings (and rulers), of all people, are the ones who have the power and resources to most effectively oppose the purposes of God on earth if they want to (or so one might think). David, inspired by the Holy Spirit, shows that even if many nations and kings join together in an attempt to stop God's purposes, all their attempts will be useless. The enemies of God thought they were victorious when they crucified Christ. They thought they were able to stop the spread of Christ's Name by threats and imprisonments, but all these attempts were futile or worthless. In fact they were worse than useless for they advanced the purposes of God. What God's enemies thought would bring an end to the influence of Christ's teaching, greatly multiplied this influence. Christ did not only rise from the dead, but received all authority in heaven and in earth and was exalted to the right hand of God and it is now Christ's power and control from this position that spreads His Name and glory (see comments on Acts 2:33). The enemies of God's church cannot stop the victorious forward movement of God's Kingdom (see comments on John 12:31–33).

When we proclaim the truth about all things and shine the light of God's Word into every part of life, bringing every thought into obedience to Christ, then those who hate the light will rage against us. The truth is, if we shine the full light of God into all of life, we *will* suffer persecution (2 Tim. 3:12), however, when people rage against us, they rage against God. They are opposing the Lord of Creation and this is the most worthless thing a person can try to do. God is the Creator and controller of all things thus, even those on earth who have the most power (e.g., kings), are unable to hinder Him in any way.

David, who wrote these words experienced this opposition to God's will. God had made David king, yet many opposed Him and tried to remove him from this position. But even if the whole world was to gather together to resist the will of God, it will never succeed—even for one moment! God will always be in control and because David believed this, he could go forth as a youth against Goliath and he could bravely go out against all the Lord's enemies, knowing that they were fighting against God and that he was fighting for God (1 Sam. 17:45).

What David is talking about goes far beyond himself and points to the Messiah. Even though David clearly knew what it was like to be opposed by the ungodly, the power, authority and dominion of the one he is writing about can only refer to the Messiah and not to himself. It was not something strange that there was such opposition to the Messiah, for it was prophesied hundreds of years before Christ came. This Psalm was recognised by the Jews as a Messianic Psalm even before Christ came. David said the world and all its rulers would resist the light.

Ultimately it is not our battle, it is God's. Our responsibility is to be found faithfully believing in, doing and proclaiming the full counsel of God (Luke 12:42, 43). God is the God of truth and His truth is the only thing He will support. If we proclaim error, or live in a way that is not pure, then God will resist us. The reason we are to bring every thought into obedience to Christ is so that we might glorify His Name and so that we do not find our goals, etc., being opposed by God. We need to know and make known the full counsel of God, however, this is offensive to the natural man and to those Christians who will not have their minds renewed by the Word and the Spirit (Rom. 12:2).

This "imagining" of the nations is a purposeful, deliberate, meditating upon how to destroy the light. We have many modern day examples where nations commit themselves with determined effort to destroy the church of God (Rome did that with the early church). Yet even this whole-hearted commitment and effort, comprising of time and resources, is futile. It is not only futile in the sense that they cannotsucceed, but the futility is also in the sense that it leads to their own destruction. The Roman Empire purposed to destroy the church, yet succeeded only in destroying themselves. God does and will reign over all people and nations, either in grace or in judgment (Ps. 2:9)—but there is never any doubt as to Who is in complete control.

Acts 4:27

Herod Antipas is the Herod meant here ("Herod" was a family name and this family ruled under Rome in Palestine during the period 37 B.C. to A.D. 100). Antipas was one of the sons of Herod the Great. When Herod the Great died, his territory was divided between 3 of his sons. Herod Antipas became tetrarch (which means a ruler over a section of a Roman province) over Galilee and Perea (a stretch of land running down the east side of the Jordan River, between the Sea of Galilee and the Dead Sea). The Herods identified themselves with the Jews and shared in their religious worship and spent much money and effort in restoring the Temple in Jerusalem. However they would just as easily build temples to pagan gods in other regions. They were politicians who knew how to keep their hold on power. Herod Antipas kept on very good terms with the Romans, for his authority was based upon their granting it or withdrawing it. The Scriptures talk of Herod as the king (Matt. 14:9; Mark 6:14, 22, 25–27). He was a native to the area and had received his position by natural descent (though with Roman acceptance). The reason he was in Jerusalem at the Passover, when Jesus was arrested (Luke 23:7), was to participate in the Jewish festival and worship. Antipas had no authority in Jerusalem or Judea. The Romans often allowed the native rulers to stay in power when they conquered a territory—as long as these rulers served the interests of Rome and Antipas did this very well.

Rome ruled over this whole region and much more and they made new boundaries according to how they drew the lines for their provinces. Judea did not fall under Herod's (Antipas) authority, but under another man appointed by Rome. At the time of Christ the name of the ruler over Judea was Pontius Pilate. So although Israel originally covered all this area, we must not think of the old boundary lines when we are trying to understand the different political officials in the NT. Matthew 2 talks of Herod the Great, who was Antipas' father. He ruled over a larger area and divided this up between three of his sons when he died. The area of Judea fell to his son Archelaus (Matt. 2:22), however Rome removed him from this position when it seemed that the people would revolt against him. This area was then governed by procurators who were appointed by Rome. The procurator of Judea at the time of Jesus was Pilate. Later, Judea was given to another Herod, King Agrippa, whom we read about in Acts 12. It is his son Agrippa II that we read about in Acts 25:13 and 26:32. Thus we must not confuse Herod the Great, Antipas, Agrippa I or Agrippa II, in the Gospels and Acts. Rome was over all these areas, though different people had authority in different areas and at different times. Under the Roman governors of Judea, the High Priests had much power and became the absolute representative and spokesman for the Jewish nation.

Now with this brief background we are better able to understand verse 27.

Psalm 2 had just been quoted and now they are showing the evidence that justifies them in applying this to the actual circumstances surrounding Jesus—truly this was fulfilled in Christ. To make matters worse, this terrible thing happened in this very city of Jerusalem. Who could have ever imagined that there would come a day in God's chosen city, where the Jews and pagans, together with the king of the Jews and the pagan leader would conspire to murder the Jewish Messiah. The Jews despised the Gentiles and to think that they would unite together with the Gentiles against their Messiah is nothing but amazing. This had been prophesied hundreds of years before it took place, and now it had been fulfilled right upon the holy hill of Zion. It is noteworthy that Herod and Pilate hated each other until they were united or brought together through the arrest and trial of Christ (Luke 23:12). The common ground between all pagans is that they hate the light and often they will put aside all other differences and unite so as to suppress the truth of the Gospel and the Name of Christ.

These rebellious Jews and Gentiles had come together in order to make an assault upon God's Holy Servant. Everyone is included in the crime of plotting to murder Christ—Herod, representing the Jewish leadership in this context and Pilate representing the Gentile leadership, together with the Jewish people and the Gentile people. The two main groups in the world were the Gentiles and the Jews and thus the nations are represented by them. The nations had united against Christ—both Jews and Gentiles.

Their gross wickedness is seen in the fact that they not only rose up against an innocent (holy) person, but also rose up against a God appointed office of authority—Christ was holy in the sense that He was set apart and consecrated to the service of God. All these people had declared war on the throne of Heaven. The Christians here encourage themselves by remembering that the rebellious' battle was with God, for God had anointed the one they murdered. Jesus was anointed by God after His baptism by John (Matt. 3:16; Luke 4:18; Acts 10:38; Isa. 11:2).

Calling Jesus "Servant" probably refers to the Suffering Servant prophecies in Isaiah (52:13–15; 53:1–12). The Christians were not to think that a suffering Messiah was contradictory to the Biblical picture of the Messiah—the prophets had clearly spoken about this.

Acts 4:28

What we saw in Acts 2:23 is repeated again. There is an inseparable connection between God's sovereign will and man's sinful rebellion. We see that God uses means to carry out His decrees without polluting Himself. God's sovereignty and human responsibility are assumed in Scripture without apology. Christ's suffering happened according to the definite (predestined) plan of God, yet the responsibility is placed completely upon those who conspired and killed Him. This verse is talking about predestination, which means to choose beforehand or to foreordain, or predetermine in an exact way that which would come to pass. These Jews and Gentiles did exactly what God's power (or hand) and will planned beforehand to happen—they were merely carrying out His will.

The wicked did not get together and say, "Well what has God foreordained? Oh, the death of Christ, well then we had better do that!" No, they were brought together by their sin and rebellion against God. God did not force them to do what they did, they freely chose what they would do, guided by their own corruption, yet what they did was ordained by God. If we do not like what Scripture clearly teaches then we must be honest and say, "God, I reject your explanation and prefer my own explanation." We should not pretend that we are following Scripture and then follow our own minds. We must not pretend that Scripture is our only sure foundation and then build another foundation by making our minds the final authority for all that we think and believe.

The wicked were motivated by a specific evil purpose: which was to destroy the truth, exalt Satan's power and eternally bind man in his bondage to sin and death. They had evil motives and an evil goal (this is what was behind their actions even if they said something different and did not fully understand the consequences). The Scriptures tell us that these goals were empty and worthless because they could never be achieved. However, God made these things serve His purposes which were to establish the truth, destroy Satan's power and eternally loose man from his bondage to sin and death (see comments on John 12:38–40).

What the evil people did was not just foreseen by God, but foreordained by Him, yet despite being foreordained, these wicked people were not forced in any way to carry out God's will—they willingly chose to do what they did. The Providence of God is not just that

God sees (foreknows) everything, but that God acts to bring about what He has planned. Not one single thing (small or big), happens without God specifically ordaining it to happen. Every detail is planned and controlled by God (see *Faith and Reason*, chapter 6). This includes control over the general things like seasons, day and night, feeding the animals (Ps. 147:9), etc., as well as control of the detailed specifics (Matt. 10:29).

Nothing happens according to some impersonal law in the universe (something outside of God). Rather, everything happens according to the will, plan and governing of our personal God. But this does not mean that we know or understand God's plan for all things, for much of what happens lies hidden in God's secret will and thus we will not be able to know how many things could be "for the good" (Rom. 8:28). If God does not choose to reveal the eternal significance of things to us we will not know why many things happen. We wouldn't have known the significance of Christ's death if God had not revealed it to us. We would have thought about it as a dreadful and unfortunate loss (Luke 24:20, 21), whereas it was God's way of securing an eternal and glorious victory by destroying the power of Satan, sin and death (Heb. 2:14, 15; Col. 2:14, 15; 1 John 3:8).

Christ's terrible death and suffering was God's way of delivering us from eternal damnation and uniting us to God in true fellowship. We do not know the eternal purposes of all things and therefore, can never know the reasons or significance of many things that happen. It is by faith that we believe God orders every detail and not because our minds are able to look into the workings and explain and understand why everything happens as it does.

Although evil people act in opposition to God and attempt to over-throw God's purposes, this will never happen, because what they are doing is actually acting in complete accordance with what God has eternally ordained and thus, their actions are fulfilling God's secret plans (this is what Acts 4:28 is teaching). There was no greater sin ever committed than the murder of the Son of God, yet every detail was brought about by God's own hand in accordance with His will. We cannot escape from this teaching that is found in the Bible, nor can we understand it completely, however, we must let the Bible determine how we are to think about these things. Unfortunately, many people today, call anything that their own minds cannot understand, unlawful—this reduces God to the size of man's mind. Either Scripture alone tells us what is possible and what isn't or we have to depend upon our minds to do this. It was a capital offence to demand to look into that which God had not revealed (cf. Deut. 18:10–12, fortune telling). This clearly shows man's limitations and also that there are secrets that are not lawful for people to know about—we are to live by faith at all times and that means trusting God, even when He sees fit not to reveal or explain certain things (Deut. 29:29).

The Christians in Acts 4:28 are encouraging themselves by recognising that although evil people joined forces to overthrow God's light, they could not do it because what they were doing was predestined by God to further His Kingdom. Wickedness can never triumph over good, thus the Christians were comforted that no threats against them could be fulfilled unless it was according to God's will and if they were persecuted they would still rejoice because it meant that God's Kingdom would be furthered through it (Acts 5:41). Whether they suffered or not would be in accordance with the will of God and would advance God's purposes and destroy Satan's purposes.

It is not God's foreknowledge that is referred to in this passage as some try to maintain, saying, God foresaw this evil and then used it for His own purposes. Luke tells us that it was God's hand that *determined* these things before they happened. God knew what would happen because He had fixed things to happen as they did. God's foreknowledge was based upon His decree and His decree was the only sure basis that things *would* work out as they did.

Acts 4:29

These believers, having reviewed in their prayer what had happened, now come to their request. They obviously were concerned for their personal safety, however, their desire was not merely for their own safety. They said, "Lord, in the light of all these threatenings upon our lives, give us boldness to fulfill our calling to be your witnesses." Their greatest desire was to proclaim the full counsel of Christ to all people (Matt. 28:20). No matter how powerful the people were who opposed them, they would not keep silent about the truth—we are to love the truth and God's purposes and Kingdom more than anything else—more even than our own lives (Matt. 10:28; Rom. 8:35–39; 1 Pet. 3:14; Prov. 29:25). In our days too, there are powerful people, both within the church and the state, that do not want to hear the full counsel of God. These people want to continue in their positions of privilege and authority and therefore, will use all their influence to silence those who will shine the light of truth upon their errors.

Christ's disciples here in Acts are probably asking that God would watch to make sure that the threats made against them did not happen, however, their primary reason for wanting protection was so that they might boldly proclaim the truth committed to them. They humbly call themselves, servants (literally slaves), and thus see it as their duty to proclaim the full counsel of their Master, though they look to Him to supply the gift of boldness to do this. If we do not have the boldness of the Spirit we will never be able to be true to all that God has revealed. We will compromise the truth by speaking about only those areas that are acceptable in our own day—and there are many areas today that the world wants us to remain silent about. It is the Word of God alone that is able to bring about change and therefore our primary desire should be to boldly proclaim the *whole* truth of God.

These servants of the Lord, in verses 25,26 had just quoted Psalms 2:1, 2, therefore, it is possible that this Psalm is still in their minds. God merely laughs at the plans of the wicked kings of the earth who try to stand in His way (Ps. 2:4). Such a picture of God's almighty power and sovereign control greatly encouraged the disciples to trust in the protection of the Lord: if God was for them who could be against them? (Rom. 8:31; Heb. 13:6; Isa. 8:10; Jer. 20:11). The only fear believers should have is a reverent fear for God (Mal. 4:2; Heb. 10:31; 12:28, 29; 1 Pet. 2:17).

Acts 4:30

In the OT, one of the most basic and important reasons for miracles, was to prove that the one who performed them was a specially approved messenger from God. It was crucial for Moses to receive miraculous confirmation from God before men so that they might know that he spoke with the authority of God (Ex. 4:1–9). Signs and wonders in the OT were God's stamp of approval that the one performing the work was to be received as God's inspired messenger. Elijah understood the purpose of signs (1 Kings 18:36). The miracles were to get the people to believe that the revelation that came through the miracle performer was of God. Ps. 74:9 shows that when there was no sign it meant that there was no prophet or revelation from God. The sign was to confirm the authority of the prophet so that the people would obey the revelation that came through him.

In the NT, the apostle John tells us that the miracles performed by Jesus, which he records in his Gospel, were recorded so that people would believe in Christ's authority and Word (John 20:30, 31)—thus believing in the Messiah. Jesus Himself said that we ought to believe Him because of the signs that He had done (John 5:36; 10:37, 38)—to believe in Him is the only way to be saved. Nicodemus concluded that Jesus was a teacher come from God on the basis of the signs He had done (John 3:2). Peter in his Pentecost sermon proved that Jesus was approved of God by pointing to Jesus' miracles (Acts 2:22).

The apostles had the authority to perform miracles for the purpose of proving that the apostolic message was from God (2 Cor. 12:12; Gal. 3:5; Rom. 15:18, 19). The apostles' role in the history of the church was unique and not to be repeated. They brought eternally binding, absolutely perfect revelation from God. They were entrusted with the continuation of revelation and their most important task, together with Christ, was to be the rock, foundation and pillars of the church (Matt. 16:18; Gal.2:9; Eph. 2:20; Rev. 21:14). To this revelation the church is bound for all time. It is upon this revelation that the church is built. Signs were used to confirm and seal the authority of this revelation. Every person other than an apostle, who received the gift to work miracles (only two are mentioned in Acts: Stephen and Philip, cf. 6:5, 6, 8; 8:1–4), received this gift only from the hands of the apostles, yet these miracle workers were unable to pass on this gift to others—this too was meant to underline the apostles' authority. The Biblical testimony with respect to the purpose for signs and wonders was so that the church would perceive and receive the new revelation God was giving to them. Revelation is now complete and we surely do not need more and more confirmations from God that the revelation we now have is true—we are to live by faith not sight. The Christian's absolute authority is to be the Word of God and the Word alone. If anything is added to this we will open the door for deception and destruction. If there is not one absolute unchanging authority then there is no absolute authority for life. We are to have faith in God's Word—which is complete and has been confirmed as the Word of God by many signs in the early church. Our responsibility is to submit totally to this authority and build according to it.

The completed Bible had not yet been given to the church. There was still much revelation that God wanted to give to His church. Some things from the old order were to be changed, but these had originally been give by God. Only God could change His previous revelation and therefore only God could show where such changes were to be made and He did this through the authority He had imparted to the early church by the apostolic tradition. Such authority was powerful and unique and came to an end once the NT was completed, therefore, nothing is to be added to this or subtracted from it. Miracles are not a regular part of the Christian life and should not be chased after (see comments on Acts 5:15). God is sovereign and works according to His own secret will and is accountable to no man, thus we are not to say God cannot do miraculous things in our day—He does. This is the exception, however, and not the normal way. There does not appear to be the same authority to heal today as there was in the NT. This is not just due to "unbelief," since many in our day strongly believe that the same miracles can be done today if we just have faith and ask, yet an honest evaluation shows the opposite.

In the light of this we can better understand the request made by the Christians in Acts 4:30. These believers were coming with a "new" message. They were rejected by the powerful leaders of the then established religious authorities of Israel. The most hostile opponents to the early church were the Jewish religious leaders who had much influence among all the people. Therefore, the prayer is made that when they go out to proclaim this "new" doctrine, God would confirm the truth of their message by miracles.

Far from discouraging us, the threats of God's enemies should drive us to prayer and to seeking the Lord, which should make us more determined to speak the full counsel of God.

Acts 4:31

God now shows that He had heard their prayer and granted their request by shaking the place where they were praying. One wonders if those who insist that signs and wonders are to be chased after in our day also look for this sign of a shaking building at the end of their prayer meetings as proof that God has heard them. The Scriptures clearly teach that the presence and power of God will be with us and that He does answer our prayers. There is no evidence that this sign of shaking is to be a necessary part of our prayer meetings. They were filled with the Holy Spirit which meant that God was answering their prayer and equipping them to fulfill their calling— to speak the Word with boldness. God's purpose in all this is seen in Acts 5:19, 20. The apostles had been preaching boldly all the time, but now after these new serious threats, they fled to God that they might be empowered to continue speaking boldly.

They went forth without any fear of the Sanhedrin and obeyed God rather than men. God was their Lord and the Lord of the whole world. The Lord of heaven and earth expects complete obedience from all people and His Word is to be the only true standard for all of life. We too ought to speak the full counsel of God with boldness and leave the consequences to God. We are not to decide what we will speak about by first asking if people will like our message. We are to be true to the full revelation of God, and then we are responsible to speak it all, not fearing the faces of men who hate the truth. All who live godly in Christ Jesus will suffer persecution (2 Tim. 3:12). If they persecuted Christ they will also persecute us (John 15:20). If they rejected His message they will reject ours too, however we are responsible to bring the full light of God upon the whole of life. Let us realize our need for prayer and our dependence upon the enabling of the Holy Spirit in order to fulfill our task, but may we never take our lead from what the world wants to hear. If we let the popular ideas of our age determine what we should and shouldn't speak about, we will not be bringing God's Word to the world. All of life is to be lived unto the Lord (as revealed in the Scriptures) and thus wherever we find ourselves we are to depend totally upon the provision of the Lord. We are to rely upon His grace and power to help us live to His glory in our families, work places and personal lives. We are to look to Him at all times, for it is in Him that we live and move and have our being and it is only by His power and enabling that we are able to glorify Him as we ought to.

God has placed us in our different positions and callings in life. There is nothing that happens by chance. Everything fits into the whole eternal plan of God and we are to glorify God where we are, though we can only do this when we depend totally upon His provision found in the Word and the Spirit.

Acts 4:32

This section (4:32, 34–37), is a repeat of (2:44, 45), with the addition of some details. Both these sections refer to the early stages in the history of the Early Church, which is covered in the first seven chapters of Acts. We are told what these early Christians did in Jerusalem before the persecutions scattered them far and wide (8:1). Once again, we must not interpret these verses as supporting compulsory communism, and laying down rules to follow, but rather, they describe the actions of the first believers and must be understood in the light of other verses on the same subject (e.g., 5:4; 12:12, where Christians still owned property). This section reveals what was really in the hearts of these Christians—immense devotion, love and gratefulness to God for what He had done for them. What is in someone's heart is manifested by his actions (Matt. 12:33), and generosity is not a fruit that can be easily imitated (cf. Acts 5:3). These passages show us the radical change that takes place in a person's heart when they are converted. The unconverted cannot understand such self-sacrificing, free-will generosity (their cheap imitation of this is forced sharing, i.e., communism).

These Christians did not deny the right to own property, but practised the *voluntary* sharing of what they owned—this distinction must not be overlooked. This free-will supplying the needs of others flowed from their oneness of heart and mind. Such care for others is part of the law's summary (Matt. 22:39, 40). In the context of speaking about collecting an offering for the poverty-stricken saints, Paul mentions Christ making Himself poor for our sakes (2 Cor. 8:9). Thus, our self-sacrificing love is to be motivated by the example of Christ and also by our gratitude for what He has done for us. Paul makes it very clear that there can be no forcing of people to share (2 Cor. 8:7, 8), though sharing is inseparable from the Christian life (1 Tim. 6:17–19). The righteous man shows mercy and gives (Ps. 37:21) and he gives because this a manifestation of a heart transformed by the grace of God. It is a sign of the redeemed person's appreciation for being set free from a life of hopeless spiritual poverty (1 John 3:17; Matt. 25:40; Prov. 19:17). Sharing of possessions is only one aspect of loving your neighbour as yourself, but as we know, the whole of God's law is to be obeyed at all times by all people. This means that while those who are rich are to be aware of the *real* needs of the poor (Deut. 15:7, 11), the poor also have to love the rich in obedience to God's law; they are not to covet or steal

from the rich (Ex. 20:15, 17). The poor are also to realize that God
has placed them in their situation (Prov. 22:2; Matt. 10:29, 30; John
12:8; Jam. 2:5) and that they are to learn to be content with what
they have. This does not mean that the poor have to remain poor
for ever, but they ought not to grumble about it or try to get out by
unlawful means (Phil. 4:11; 1 Tim. 6:8; Heb. 13:5). Many times we
see that those who are rich are as guilty of the sins of grumbling and
discontentment with what they have. It is a Godly desire to want to
advance oneself and one's family, but the only way to do this is by
lawful means—lawful and unlawful are defined by God's Word. A
covetous person will not be concerned about equal justice in a
nation if he is actually gaining through unbiblical state laws. The
covetous person is not prepared to exercise discipline and do diligent hard work in order to advance himself. Such a person, being
discontented with what he has, sets his eyes upon the possessions of
those who have more than himself and tries to advance by unlawfully taking from them—usually with the help of government legislation (e.g., excessive taxation).

This universal bondage to covetousness is clearly seen by the laws in
almost every nation, which unlawfully (in violation of God's Word)
takes excessive amounts from those who have more, and gives to
those who do not have as much (though much is wasted and stolen
on the way from the one group to the other). God's law alone can
determine what is just and unjust—in *every* area of life. Thus, when
the *state* makes laws that are not equally fair for all people, and even
if covetousness prevents most people from saying these laws are
unjust, it does not make these laws and practices just—they are still
sinful in the eyes of God. Covetousness does not stop merely with
desire, but leads to actions and the covetous person will either act
personally to advance himself unlawfully, or he will "ask" the state
(i.e., by votes) to unlawfully take from those with more and give to
him. These verses in Acts cannot be used to justify a nation's laws
that forcefully take someone's possessions—even if they intend to
give it to poorer people. "You shall not steal" is a law that applies as
much to the government as it does to the individual. All charity
should be voluntary and Acts clearly teaches voluntary giving to
those who *deserve* it.

The foundation for this generous activity was unity in Christ. All
the believers had one purpose and desire—the glory of Christ and
His Kingdom. This love for Christ and for what belonged to Christ

manifested itself by outward actions. No one thought that their own possessions were to be used only for themselves, but were to be used for the whole united body, as need arose. The unity was not based upon equal possessions, but upon equality in Christ: equal commitment to Christ; equal desire for eternal life; equal desire to be faithful to the will of the Lord; equally self-sacrificing lifestyles; equal comfort from the Holy Spirit; all having the *necessities* of life (not the equality of all things). All these thousands of believers had one heart or mind, and acted as one body—this is indeed a very strong statement showing the unity that existed among these first believers.

Acts 4:33

The apostles focused their attention upon their calling (1:8) and preached with great power. This great power would have included the work of the Holy Spirit in anointing the apostle's message, confirming it with signs and convicting the hearts of those who heard them (cf. 1 Cor. 2:4). The apostles proclaimed the whole of the "new religion" without shame or fear and in wilful disregard of the Sanhedrin's threats (4:18, 21). It seems best to understand the phrase, "witnessed to the resurrection of Christ," as a summary of their whole message—the resurrection being the foundation of all Christian doctrines: it is the final step that secures our redemption; it clearly shows the deity of Christ; that His work completely satisfied the demands of God's righteousness; that He has been exalted above all things; has received all power; rules over all nations; and is head of the church (Acts 2:33; 5:31; Phil. 2:9; Heb. 2:9; Isa. 52:13; Dan. 7:14; Matt. 28:18).

Great grace was upon them all: this refers to all the Christians and not just the apostles. God's abundant grace resulted in these Christians being totally focused upon the things of God's Kingdom, which in turn was the basis for them all being of one mind and will, which was then manifested in real care and provision for those who did not have enough to meet their basic needs. Thus, the church's care for the whole body (verse 34ff.), both came from and manifested the grace of God. Some think that Acts 2:47 is the idea repeated here, namely that the Christians found great favor in the eyes of those outside the church. The context here however, does not speak about those without the church, but rather tells of the amazing generosity and self-sacrificial care within the church—this manifestation of Christian love was a result of the abundant grace which God had poured upon the Jerusalem church. Such behavior would have had an effect upon those outside the church, but Luke does not tell us about it here.

Acts 4:34, 35

The fact that there was no needy person among them, was proof that great grace was upon them. Christianity is very practical and relevant to this life; causing those who had much, to share with those who had nothing. This verse does not imply that everyone had exactly the same (i.e., equally wealthy), but that there was no one who lacked those things that were *essential* for life. The niv tries to bring out the sense of the Greek when it says the wealthy from "time to time" sold possessions in order to meet the needs of the poor. It was not a once off event, where all the rich sold all they had and brought all the proceeds to the apostles. Rather, this selling of property was an on going practice—as real needs arose, someone who was able, helped meet the need (they *continued* to sell and *continued* to bring and *continued* to place the money at the apostle's feet).

The early church had a central fund that was controlled by the apostles and was used to help those believers who had nothing. It was the real needs of the poor that were met out of this fund, and not their every desire (though we must add that the desire of these poor believers, at this time, was not covetousness but only what was needful for life—they too had great grace and were not seeking more than they needed). You have to twist this text in order to arrive at the conclusion that everything was sold and equally divided between everyone (covetousness makes one see this here). The apostles gave only *to such* as had genuine needs. The believers held their property in common in the sense that if a genuine need arose, they would use what they had to meet that need. These verses do not teach the abolishing of private ownership, or that you are a better Christian if you own nothing. Peter clearly shows that there was nothing wrong with having property or money (Acts 5:4). It is also important to note that the poor who were helped had one heart and soul for the things of the Kingdom of God and were not seeking their own benefit (Phil. 2:21, for further comments on helping the poor see John 12:8).

There is nothing in these verses that can support the state being involved in helping the poor by taking from those who have. The state is to be a minister of justice, not grace and if these terms are confused, then the whole Christian faith will be confused. While God will look unfavourably upon those who do not help the deserving poor, this does not mean that the state has a right to intervene in making sure that charity is carried out. There is nothing voluntary about the state taking taxes from people for this purpose. Once the state says people *have* to pay a tax that will be used for the poor, this is forcing people to give to the poor. This is an unbiblical concept and therefore must not be made to look like something that will be pleasing to God. The state does not have the God given authority to be involved in charity and therefore only increases the problem by getting involved. Most of the money collected for the poor never gets to the poor, because it is used up in administration and more is lost through bad administration. Moreover, the whole process of forced charity cannot be blessed by God since it is done in rebellion to His revelation. When people deny the Biblical account of God, man, sin and law, then they will live their lives in rebellion to Him. To try to help the poor by rebelling against God is a worthless exercise. God called King Saul's taking 10 percent of the peoples' income oppressive (1 Sam. 8:15). What does He think about nations today that take more than 40 percent or even 60 percent? State enforced "charity" removes the God ordained responsibilities from both the "giver" and the poor (see comments on Acts 2:44, 45). A just judge must not be partial to the rich or the poor (Ex. 23:3; Lev. 19:15). Every thought about every aspect of our lives needs to be submitted to Christ and everything must be done according to His Word (Matt. 4:4; 2 Cor. 10:5).

Acts 4:36

Luke now introduces someone who turns out to be an extremely significant figure in the book of Acts and was highly respected by the apostles. By the time Luke wrote Acts, this person had come to be called Barnabas due to his special gifting of exhortation, persuasion, encouragement, comfort and instruction. He was a very gifted and anointed teacher/preacher and his name can mean either "Son of encouragement" or "Son of prophecy/exhortation." His ministry of encouragement can be seen in both his words and actions. God revealed much to Barnabas and enabled him to communicate and apply this revelation—it is only as we bring God's pure Word to people and show how it applies to their lives that we are able to encourage them. Bringing our own wisdom to people and saying "nice" things to them that are not based upon the full counsel of God does not make us "sons of encouragement," but "sons of stumbling." Barnabas was a man of great gifting, full of the Holy Spirit and faith (Acts 11:24). He was very influential in getting Paul accepted and involved in missionary work (Acts 9:27; 11:22–25), and was totally given to the Kingdom of God, not seeking his own comfort or advancement, but rather labouring at his own expense (1 Cor. 9:6).

Acts 4:37

Total sacrifice is the first account we have of Barnabas and this was something that characterised the whole of his life. He sold a field that he owned and brought *all* the proceeds to the apostles, to be used for the needs of the early church. Our calling in the Kingdom is to selfless, unceasing labor for God's glory and the furtherance of His Kingdom—this is our primary purpose and all other things are secondary (Matt. 6:33). The example of the apostles' was the same as this (2 Cor. 6:3–10).

Acts 5:1

The Pharisees placed the emphasis of their religion on outward appearances. Many today also think that all God wants is an outward show of commitment to Him. The whole of the Bible reveals that God wants us to love Him with our whole being (heart, mind, soul and strength). Here, in the beginning of the NT church, we see, in the strongest way possible, how God hates an outward appearance of religion that has no internal reality (see comments on John 8:2–11). Christianity includes everything—every thought, motive, desire, goal and action (Matt. 5:28; 22:37). Christ is Lord over all: His rules are over all and are to be taught to all (Matt. 28:20). Christ is the one standard for every thought (2 Cor. 10:5) and action (Matt. 4:4; Col. 3:17; Jam. 1:25; 1 John 3:18).

When outward show is emphasised at the expense of inward devotion, it is a rebellious attempt to hide from the light of God—all of life is to glorify God in the way God has said. Outward show delights in the praise of men while disregarding the praise of God (Matt. 6:2). There are always attempts to copy the real thing. In

Barnabas we saw real Christian self-sacrifice and love. Now we see a cheap imitation. This story is recorded for our instruction (Rom. 15:4; 1 Cor. 10:11). Ananias and Sapphira conspired *together* to do this wicked deed.

Acts 5:2–4

They wanted the praise without the sacrifice. Their desire was not motivated by a heart of compassion to meet the needs of the poor, but by a love for the praises of men. Their goal was not to sacrifice much so as to benefit the body of Christ and glorify His Name, but to sacrifice a little in order to puff up their own self images and glorify their own names (Jam. 3:14–17). To place high value in the praises of men, while living in total disregard of God, is nothing but blind foolishness. We too need to be warned; we might easily fool people by our actions, but it is impossible to fool God (Prov. 16:2; Heb. 4:12).

The sin here, was lying about what was done. Peter clearly shows in verse 4 that before they sold the land and even after it was sold, they could do whatever they wanted with their possessions. There was no compulsory sharing in the NT church. All the sharing that took place was voluntary, and it was voluntary because it was lawful to own property and still be a Christian. If it was unlawful to own property, or if you were less of a Christian if you did own property, then the sharing of your things wouldn't have been voluntary, and thus one couldn't have received praise for disposing of your possessions—since it was what Christians *ought* to have done (Ananias and Sapphira were looking for that praise which came from voluntary self-sacrifice). Peter's words would be misleading if everyone was expected to sell everything—that is, if the "church" automatically owned everything and thus it was the responsibility of those with possessions to sell as quickly as possible, bringing the money to the apostles. Peter clearly tells Ananias that the property was rightfully his before he sold it and the money was rightfully his after he sold the property.

Peter tells Ananias how wicked his actions were by saying, "Satan has filled your heart." Satan tempts and discomforts people with persecution and trials, but there is never an excuse for giving into temptation, no matter in what form it comes (1 Cor. 10:13). Satan had complete control over Ananias, resulting in his wilful blindness and wilful rebellion against God. This conspiracy was done under the complete control of Satan, yet, the action was presented to the apostles as a manifestation of hearts completely surrendered and dedicated to God. Such behavior arises from the idea that either God does not exist or, as it appears here, that one is able to fool God (Prov. 15:3). Peter equates the Holy Spirit with God, saying, "You lied to the Holy Spirit which is the same as lying to God."

Acts 5:5–11

The first sin we are told of within the NT church is the love for man's praise and the love of money. This incident is proof, both then and for all time, that God will not tolerate hypocrisy (John 12:43; 1 Tim. 6:10).

This judgment was from God and He is the same yesterday, today and tomorrow (Heb. 13:8; James 1:17; Mal. 3:6). We must not be fooled, God is not mocked (Gal. 6:7). When God does not immediately judge, this does not mean He has not seen what took place, but rather that He is mercifully giving us opportunity to repent (Rom. 2:4). Great fear should characterise all true believers, for although God is merciful He is also a consuming fire (Heb. 10:31; 12:29; Deut. 4:24). The Spirit had clearly and powerfully manifested His presence through the apostles and yet Ananias and Sapphira thought that they were able to deceive them, the church and God. These two people, with Satan ruling their hearts, came forward saying, "God is moving upon us to do this thing—this is a manifestation of the grace and glory of God working in our lives." Such wicked deception received its just reward!

God's judgment is always just and He has the right to carry it out according to His will. Those who say this was harsh are using a human standard to condemn God. Such people do not understand how wicked hypocrisy is—probably because their own hypocrisy is very much before their eyes. Nor do they realize how much God hates hypocrisy (Rom. 12:9; Matt. 22:18; 23:13–15, 23, 25, 27, 33; 24:51). To call God harsh or unjust is a severe accusation and reveals much about what is in the heart of the one who makes the accusation.

Christianity is simple: we are to love God with all our heart, soul mind and strength and love our neighbour as ourselves and the reason we do this is for the glory of God and the advancing of His Kingdom. We are to pray that God would help us to discern our own motives and the reasons for doing what we do, that He might keep us true to Him and keep our hearts single for His glory. Hypocrites like Ananias and Sapphira are after *personal* gain and many hypocrites in our day run to this passage and try to enforce total sharing and complete equality upon all believers. Yet such people fail to see the fearful message of the passage, namely, that God hates hypocrisy! Those who want to force all believers to live in this way today are often envious that others have more than they have and their motive for "serving" God or "believing" in Christ is controlled by their greater desire to advance themselves in this life rather than His Kingdom—they name the name of Christ to see what riches it might bring them.

Acts 5:12

The Lord once again confirms the authority and message of the apostles by working many miracles through their hands. The apostles had prayed for God to do this (4:30). This manifestation was a powerful testimony to the nation of Israel (both the people and the religious leaders) that the apostles were bringing God's message and thus they were to be obeyed (see comments on Acts 4:30; 5:15). It also confirmed the fact that the Messiah had come and that the restoration of all things was now underway (3:21). The regular practice of all the believers was to meet in Solomon's Porch. This was their habitual practice—coming together for worship, prayer, teaching and exhortation.

Acts 5:13

Great fear was upon all the unbelievers because of the power of God resting upon the apostles. The death of Ananias and Sapphira together with the abundance of miracles meant that the unbelievers had great reverence for the apostles and the believers. The distinction is between the believers and unbelievers. The all, refers to believers and the *rest*, refers to unbelievers (see 2:12, 13 where there is a distinction made between *all* and *others*, see too Rom. 11:7). The believers were united together with one heart, but the unbelievers feared to be united to this body—even by appearance. We are told in John 2:23–25, that many people believed in Christ and followed Him, yet these were not true believers (see comments on John's Gospel). John the Baptist's disciples complained to John saying that everyone was going to Jesus, but John says, these are not true believers (John 3:26, 32. See too John 6:26, 27). At this time in the Jerusalem church, no one dared join with the believers unless true conversion had taken place. The unbelievers appear to have watched from a distance, holding the believers in high regard, but not blurring the distinction between the two groups.

Acts 5:14

This fear among the unbelievers, resulting in them keeping their distance, did not mean that no more people came to believe in Christ. Salvation is totally God's doing and this is what we are to always remember. The church's responsibility is to proclaim the full counsel of God and it is God who will add the numbers. When churches are tempted to tickle ears (2 Tim. 4:3), then there will be many people in the congregation who join themselves to the church for their own benefit. Such people are not seeking forgiveness for their rebellion against God, but have some other reason for joining themselves to a church. If the Word of God is not preached in its fullness then these unbelievers will become a permanent part of the institutional church. If, however, the Word is preached in the power of the Spirit, making known the whole counsel of God, then such people will either be saved or be offended and leave (John 6:66). All over the world there are examples of churches that have stopped preaching the full counsel of God and as a result these churches are full of unbelievers who end up controlling the church.

When people rely upon their own ideas, strengths, and abilities to bring people into the church, they usually compromise the Truth found in the Bible for the sake of keeping many people in the church. To such ministers, success is not determined by how well the congregation understands and applies the Word of God to themselves and every area of life, but by how full the church is on a Sunday morning.

In the Jerusalem church, no one apologised for what happened to Ananias and Sapphira and no one tried to water down the truth about sin, righteousness and judgement. The apostles preached the full counsel of God fearlessly. The believers wholeheartedly joined themselves to the apostles' teaching and lived in obedience to it. No one was trying to *entice* people to join the church, they preached the truth and lived the truth, and God added the numbers. Luke tells us that multitudes of both men and women were added. It seems as if Luke has stopped counting now—the numbers joining were too big. God adds mightily to a pure church: pure in Word and deed.

Acts 5:15

These multitudes, which Luke cannot even number, returned to their homes, found family and friends who were sick and carried them onto the main street and laid them by the side of the road. There were too many people for the apostles to individually touch, however the power of God was with the apostles in such great abundance that we are told even the shadow of Peter touching someone was enough to heal them. *All* the apostles were working these mighty miracles (5:12). These sick people were probably placed on the main street that led to the Temple and thus when the apostles went up to the Temple they would heal everyone they came across. The faith of the believers led them to bring all these people who needed healing. It was God who was doing the healing through the apostles and He was doing it for His purposes of establishing the NT church by confirming the authority of the apostles in a truly remarkable way. It is clear when we read the rest of the NT, that this was a unique time in the lives of the apostles—never again do we see such power manifested in this way. Healings continued to be done from time to time, but we also see occasions where healings were not granted (2 Cor. 12:7–9; Gal. 4:13; 1 Tim. 5:23; 2 Tim. 4:20; and Phil. 2:26, 27, where the distress about Epaphroditus, was due to the fact that there was no absolute guarantee that he would be healed). To think that the manifestation of healing in the book of Acts is something for all time is to misunderstand the significance and importance of the healings in Acts.

Acts 5:16

As you might expect, word of this amazing manifestation of God's power quickly spread to neighbouring cities and these other cities also brought multitudes of sick people and those oppressed by unclean spirits—and every single one of them, without exception, was healed (some good commentators believe that almost everyone from these surrounding cities were coming up to Jerusalem). These mighty miracles were clear proof that Christ had conquered the powers of darkness; that He had risen from the dead and had ascended to the right hand of God (Acts 2:33, 36); it was clear proof that Christ's claim that He had received all authority in heaven and earth was a reality (Matt. 28:18); it was clear proof that the apostles were indeed sent from God and proclaimed the Words of God and thus, were not to be rejected. This meant that Jesus Christ was not an impostor and deceiver of the people, but the Messiah and therefore, the religious leaders and the nation of Israel were guilty of the murder of God's Son.

Acts 5:17

The High Priest was filled with anger or passion, probably because the apostles were still preaching in the Name of Jesus and also because of the immense number of people coming under their influence. He probably felt that he had tolerated this disruption for long enough and had in fact been far too soft with the apostles, thus he makes a move to silence them. What the High Priest and the Sadducees felt was zeal or passion for their false beliefs (which the teaching of the apostles was destroying), together with great jealousy that the apostles were having such a great impact on the nation. These religious leaders, who were extremely proud about who they were and what they stood for, had never had anything like the response that these simple Galileans were having and therefore, their party spirit and envy motivated them to silence the "opposition." When the Spirit of God moves mightily, the powers of darkness react in a desperate attempt to hold onto what they think is theirs. They will seek to oppose the work of God in many different ways; usually by coming against the leaders God has greatly anointed and is using in a powerful way against Satan's Kingdom. The sad thing is, many times Satan uses those within the church, who are full of jealousy and false doctrine, to oppose God's true servants.

The High Priest and his close companions were afraid that if everyone followed the teaching of the apostles then their positions of authority, power and wealth would be threatened. These leaders were not concerned about the truth of God, but about their own positions of privilege that they had created. It is indeed a terrifying thing to see such blindness manifesting itself, especially in the lives of those who are supposed to preserve the truth of God among the Lord's people. Unless we bow completely to the Word of God and allow the Holy Spirit to help us understand the whole message of the Bible, then we too will be led into such blind foolishness.

Acts 5:18

In one swoop, all the apostles are arrested and put into the holding prison. It was the community or public holding place. Prison in the Bible, was not a place of punishment, but merely a secure place where people were kept until their trial. The idea that prison is a place where criminals should "pay" for their crimes is a modern humanistic (unbiblical) idea. The most basic principle in the Biblical idea of justice, is restitution (Ex. 22). This means when something is stolen or destroyed, either what was taken has to be restored to the rightful owner, or an equivalent value given to him, plus a fine equal to what was stolen has to be paid to the rightful owner (paying a fine to the state in such cases does not make sense, other than showing that the state thinks itself to be god, i.e., an offence against anyone, is an offence against the "god state"). Biblical justice demands the death sentence for capital offences and restitution made for all other offences. Habitual criminals faced the threat of execution (this is clear from the fact that if a grown son faced execution due to habitual rebellion, then how much more did not a habitual criminal face the same end. This is not talking about a small child but someone mature in years who refused to change his ways of drunkenness and violent abuse of his parents, see Deut. 21:18–21; Ex. 21:15, 17; Lev. 20:9; Matt. 15:4). Every area of life needs to be brought into line with God's mind, including prison, crime, punishment, politics, taxation, etc.

The entire leadership of the NT church was arrested for teaching about Christ and held in prison over-night so that they could be brought to trial the following day.

Acts 5:19

This miraculous manifestation was once again for the purposes of God. The freedom of the apostles was not the goal, since they were commanded to go back to the temple where they were arrested again. We must not think that God must or will always deliver us from death or difficult situations. Our faith is to rest in God and His will for us, not in our circumstances or personal expectations. True faith is to trust in our sovereign Lord even when we do not understand why certain things are happening (Job 13:15). This was another sign by which God confirmed the apostle's authority and thus the message that they brought. The faith of the Christians would be strengthened and the condemnation of those who rejected their message would be increased. What we have here is a clash between the leaders of the old order and the leaders of the new order and God confirms His support for the leaders of the new order. God had sent the apostles to preach His Word; the highest authority in the nation of Israel says they are not allowed to preach and physically restrains them; God then clearly passes judgment upon the situation—showing us that the apostles had His authority to preach and no one was able to hinder the preaching of the Gospel since it was God's will. We see too a wonderful manifestation of the power of God's messengers, the angels, who are always working on our behalf in accordance with God's commands (see comments on John 1:33). The Sadducees, we must remember, denied the existence of angels (Acts 23:8), so this was particularly embarrassing for them.

Acts 5:20

These religious leaders had forbidden the apostles to preach in the Name of Jesus, however, here God instructs them through the angel to preach the full message of salvation. The Sadducees denied the resurrection, yet for the apostles this was the foundation of their hope for eternal life and they are instructed to continue speaking as they had done before. Jesus had said to His disciples when He sent them out, that if they were persecuted in one city to go to the next (Matt. 10:23), however, here the angel has a specific command that they should not leave Jerusalem, but stay there and preach. Our contentment ought to be found in doing God's will and we should not allow ourselves to be discouraged. Our responsibility is to faithfully do God's will and leave the results to Him.

The arrest of the twelve apostles would have been common knowledge to all the people in Jerusalem. It is also likely that everyone knew that the Sanhedrin had ordered their arrest and was going to put them on trial in the morning. The public jail would have been well known to everyone in the city and they would have known that it was very secure. Thus it is easy to see the powerful witness it would have been to the whole city, when first thing in the morning, the twelve were back in their usual place, fearlessly preaching the very same doctrine. They were the ones who had the words of eternal life and God had placed the responsibility of making known the riches of God's grace and nurturing the infant church upon their shoulders. If they did not preach and teach, then there would be no one to do it. The apostles, totally committed to the glory of God and the furtherance of His Kingdom, instantly obeyed God's will without regard for their own comfort or lives—in this they were imitating their Master (cf. Matt. 26:39, 42; John 4:34; 5:30; 6:38; Heb. 10:7; 1 Pet. 4:1, 2, 17, 19).

Acts 5:21

All the elders and judges of Israel were gathered very early in the morning. Some think that there were as many as 116 judges called together for this meeting. These leaders felt the seriousness of the threat brought about through the apostles and thus they gathered this large company so that they could once and for all put an end to this "new religion" (it is clear what their intention was from the very beginning, see 5:33). The whole of Israel's eldership, which included all the wisest and most respected people in the nation, were now set to confront the entire leadership of the NT church. The way to overturn this teaching that had filled Jerusalem, these Jews thought, was to have it openly condemned by this massive delegation. Who in Israel would be able to argue with such a body of elders? The Jews had managed to give the appearance of a God honouring legal hearing, but that's all it was—an appearance, for the heart of it was rotten rebellion against God. The plan was perfect; they would just go through the motions and by lunch time the name "Jesus of Nazareth" would finally be put to rest. There was never an intention of a fair trial, but rather a plan to make sure that the apostles were put to death. The counsel was set and waiting for the apostles to be brought—they had all the power and they were in complete control; or were they? (Ps. 2:1–4).

Acts 5:22–24

Verses 22 and 23 need no comment other than it must have been extremely embarrassing for these "mighty" leaders to be stood up in this way. In verse 24 we are told that the leaders were completely embarrassed and confused and did not know what to say or think. They did not know how such a thing could happen and they were certainly worried about what effect this incident would have upon the growth of this teaching. They must have wondered, how they would ever be able to stop these men. These leaders continued to suppress the truth in unrighteousness. The unbeliever suppresses, distorts, reinterprets and ignores the truth in order to protect his own false beliefs and continue in his rebellion against the authority of God. The unbeliever knows the truth, however he will rather deceive himself than submit to the truth (see *Faith and Reason,* chapter 4). Thus, these Jewish leaders continue to stubbornly deny something that is very obvious to the rest of the people in Jerusalem—that God is confirming the message of the apostles and exposing the foolish behavior of the Sanhedrin.

Acts 5:25, 26

On finding out that the apostles were not hiding like some terrified criminals in an unknown hideout, but were in fact preaching not far from where the Jewish leaders were gathered, a delegation was sent to bring the apostles to the trial. This delegation, realising how highly the people regarded the apostles were quite fearful for their lives. Instead of taking hold of the apostles and dragging them roughly like some common criminals, this delegation did not touch or abuse them in any way, lest the people interpreted their actions as a blasphemous assault upon God and stoned them.

Acts 5:27, 28

Having been brought before the judges, the High Priest starts to question them, however, it is very noticeable that he does not even ask them how they had escaped from the prison. It is obvious that he feared the answer he would get from the twelve to this kind of a question so he acts as if nothing out of the ordinary has happened so far that day. Rather, his concern is with the apostle's rebellion against the strict commands of the Sanhedrin. The apostle's greatest enemy testifies to the success of their efforts—"they had filled Jerusalem with their teaching." It was the chief priests who had convinced the people to ask for Jesus' death (Matt. 27:20) and they were so sure that Jesus was not innocent that they said, if He happens to be innocent, then let His blood be upon our heads (Matt. 27:25). It is very possible that the High Priest once again evaluates the situation correctly (cf. John 11:49–51), namely, that the Sanhedrin was losing control for there appeared to be nothing they could do to stop the apostles and all of Jerusalem was coming under the influence of this new teaching. To make matters worse, if more and more people believed in the teaching of the apostles, then the people would in turn hate the chief priests, for it was the chief priests who got them to deny Christ. It was obvious to the High Priest that if the people followed the teaching of the apostles, then they would blame the Sanhedrin for the death of Christ (and rightly so for they had clearly and openly worked for His death). The High Priest was not trying to deny his involvement in the death of Christ, but he was desperate to prevent the people from believing that Jesus was innocent. It is very possible that the High Priest and these leaders could see that their positions of power, privilege and authority that they were so desperate to hold on to, were in fact slipping away.

No humanistic power, no matter how strong and determined, can resist the flow of God's power and truth. The gates of hell will not be able to withstand the work of the Spirit through the people of God (Matt. 16:18). No matter how weak and insignificant God's children might appear to be in comparison to those who hate the truth, the fact is, God's enemies are dust in the balances (i.e., insignificant) when compared to God (Isa. 40:15; Ps. 2:4). We need to believe in the victory of Christ and realize how great our God is and go forth in the power of the Holy Spirit, boldly declaring the *full counsel* of God.

Acts 5:29

Peter once again speaks on behalf of all the apostles and the answer is like that given in 4:19, 20. Christ is the Lord of all of life and expects us to obey Him in all of life (living by every Word that comes from the mouth of God and bringing every thought captive to Christ, Matt. 4:4; 2 Cor. 10:5). These words from Peter are the necessary balance to those verses that tell us to submit to human authorities (Rom. 13:1ff.; Titus 3:1; 1 Pet. 2:13ff.). All authority comes from the Lord, however God does not give honour and power to people so that they can then use it to fight against the Kingdom of God. Thus, anyone in a position of authority (father, pastor, teacher, leaders in government, etc.) who commands anything that is against the Word of God, no longer has God's backing with respect to that command. That is why Paul tells us that if we resist *lawful* authority we resist God (Rom. 13:2). It is foolishness to think that Paul was saying that if you resist a wicked law made by some government then you are resisting the command of God (see *Muse Time*, occasional papers 3 and 5, for a brief look at Romans 13 and the state).

God expects obedience to His Word, not just from the common person, but also from kings and national rulers. Proverbs. 16:12

tells us that it is an abomination for kings to commit wickedness, and Psalms. 119:53 tells us that wickedness is forsaking God's law. God is to be feared by all people and rulers, because He is the King over all the earth (Ps. 47:2). The king of Babylon was condemned for his pride (Isa. 14:9). Egypt was judged for not worshipping God and for its ungodly rulers (Isa. 19:1, 13, 14). The king of Tyre was also condemned by God for his pride (Ezek. 28:1–10), and the king of Assyria for his arrogance (Isa. 10:12). Another king of Babylon, Belshazzar, was also judged for his pride, which like all pride, is manifested by rebellion against God (Dan. 5:22–28). The prophet Amos singled out the rulers of Damascus for their brutality and passed God's judgment on them (Amos 1:4), also pronouncing God's judgment upon other nations and their rulers (Amos 1 and 2). It is clear from these passages that God expects obedience from all rulers, since He has placed them in their positions of authority. God gives rulers authority for the purpose of serving Him and advancing His Kingdom. They are to do this by walking in obedience to Him and making laws that bring glory to Him (Ps. 2:10–12). We are expected by God to obey those rules that do not break the commandments of God. As soon as anyone in authority makes a law that violates the Word of God they no longer have God's authority in that area and therefore, to disobey that particular law is *not* disobedience to God, rather, to obey that law would be to join with those rulers in their rebellion against God.

Peter tells these leaders that their command not to preach in the Name of Jesus violates Christ's command and therefore, to obey them would be disobeying God. Although Peter recognised that these rulers had received their authority to rule from God, at this point they were in rebellion against God and so did not have God's authority in this matter, thus, in *dis*obeying them, the apostles were *obeying* God. Therefore, we learn that the Biblical teaching with respect to all human authorities is that if an authority misuses its God given power and commands what He forbids, or forbids what He commands, then the Christian's obligation is to disregard that command in order to obey God. Peter says in such situations it is absolutely necessary that we obey God and not man—God's authority is always primary and God has spoken about all of life!

Acts 5:30

The High Priest had accused the apostles of trying to bring the
blood of Jesus upon the heads of the Jewish leaders (5:28). Peter's
careful response shows that what the apostles were teaching was
right in line with all those godly Jews that the whole nation referred
to as "the fathers." This term ties the apostles in with Moses who
traced the nation's beginning back to Abraham, Isaac and Jacob
(Ex. 3:15). Peter points out that all the godly fathers of Israel longed
for the Messiah and thus to be one with the fathers, these leaders
ought to share in that same hope—which had been fulfilled in
Christ. Peter is saying to this group, that Abraham's God, and
Moses' God and Israel's God, is the One who raised up Jesus from
the grave. Peter says there is no getting away from the fact that our
God has raised Jesus from the dead and there was no getting away
from the fact that these leaders were guilty of the killing of the Messiah. Peter fearlessly says, "What do you mean we are trying to bring
the blood of Jesus upon you? It was you who murdered Him and
there is no way that you can get away from the fact that His innocent blood rests upon your hands." Peter tells this court that they
were in rebellion against God (in murdering Jesus), yet God had
reversed their actions by raising Jesus from the grave. Peter is here
forcing the High Priest and his group, the Sadducees, to face the
reality that there was not only a resurrection (Acts 23:8), but that
Jesus had been raised.

These Jewish leaders had desired for a long time to put Jesus to
death and had plotted for many hours about the best way this could
be done (Matt. 12:14; 26:3, 4; 27:1; Mark 3:6; Luke 6:11; John 5:18;
7:1, 19, 25; 11:53). They had to do this in a sly way because they
feared the people (Matt. 21:46; 26:5; Mark 11:18; 12:12; Luke 20:19;
22:2). They needed to come up with some plan by which they could
kill Jesus without offending the people.

Their plan was to arrest Jesus and get the Sanhedrin to condemn
Him while the city slept (Mark 14:55; Luke 22:53, 56–60; John 18:3)
and then very early in the morning hand Him over to the Romans
to sentence Him to death (John 18:28). Thus by the time the city
realised what was happening, Jesus was in the hands of the Romans
and the Sanhedrin was in control (Matt. 27:20; John 18:28–30),
putting the emphasis on the "charges" that Christ was in revolt

against the authority of Rome and not on the fact that it was a purely Jewish religious matter (Luke 23:2, 5; John 19:12, 13, 15).

The Romans had not arrested Jesus and according to their law He had done nothing wrong, so Pilate wanted nothing to do with this Jewish problem (Luke 23:4, 14, 15, 20; John 18:38), however, he made a tactical error. He thought he could please everyone: he found Jesus innocent, yet in order to please the religious leaders and the crowds, he was prepared to pretend that Jesus was guilty (Mark 15:15; Luke 23:16; John 19:1, cf. verse 4), and then he could later release this "guilty" man since it was the Passover (Matt. 27:17, 20; John 18:39). However, he had not anticipated the rejection of his plan by the crowds (Matt. 27:20, 21) and wanting to avoid a riot (Matt. 27:24) he acted in violation of his God-given responsibility to judge with righteous judgment and handed over an innocent man to be crucified.

The second part of the Sanhedrin's plan was to make sure Jesus was crucified (John 18:31, 32), for the law of God said that he who hangs on a tree is cursed of God (Deut. 21:23; Gal. 3:13). These leaders thought that they could use God for their wickedness and in this way shut the mouths of those who supported Jesus. Once Jesus had hung on a cross, they hoped it would make no difference debating whether He was guilty or innocent. The cross would have the final word and the cross was enough to prove that He was cursed by God. They thought that by pointing to the fact that Jesus died on a cross, there was no way that He could have been a prophet and certainly He couldn't have been the Messiah, for why would God curse His holy servant? The Jewish nation said that Jesus ought to be cursed by God when they all cried out, "Crucify Him!"

Acts 5:31

Peter does not deny that Jesus was cursed by God (for this is the heart of the Gospel, Gal. 3:13; 1 Pet. 2:24), yet he shows that while the Jews thought they had disgraced Jesus, God exalted Him to the place of supreme power and authority. It was due to Christ's willingness to be disgraced that God granted such honour to Him (Phil. 2:8, 9). The Sanhedrin believed that if Jesus was cursed by God then He would be forever rejected by God, however, Peter says this has rather led to His eternal exaltation by God. This exaltation refers to Christ's human nature which will be forever united with the divine nature—Christ's divine nature could not be exalted more than it already was.

Pilate knew the reason that Christ was handed over to him—envy (Matt. 27:18). He knew Jesus was innocent, yet he was manipulated into denying his God-given responsibility of judging with righteous judgement. However, he made it very clear that he was giving an innocent man to them for them to crucify (Matt. 27:24; Luke 23:24)—the crucifixion was their doing.

The High Priest had complained to the apostles saying he was offended, since through the apostle's preaching the people might start believing that Jesus was innocent and lay the blood of Christ upon the Sanhedrin (see comments on Acts 5:28). Peter's answer is that it was God who has clearly demonstrated that Jesus was innocent—not only of the "crime" the Sanhedrin had charged Him with, but that He was completely without sin (the proof of this being that He had been raised from the dead, Acts 2:24). Peter says, "God raised Jesus from the grave, thus it is *God* who is accusing you of shedding innocent blood, not us".

The very one whom the Sanhedrin had crucified has not only been raised from the dead, but exalted to share in all the power and dignity of the throne of God. Christ has been given all rule and authority over all things (see 2:33 and John 3:35). God has made Jesus, both Leader and Savior and from this position of supreme authority, Jesus gives repentance and forgiveness of sins (both of these are gifts, cf. 3:26). God has entrusted all power to Christ (Matt. 28:18) so that He can bring people to repentance (John 17:2)—forgiving sins is a divine right (Isa. 43:25; Dan. 9:9; Mark 2:7). The whole work of salvation is a gift of grace; Christ alone has the power to forgive people's sins and Christ alone has the power to produce repentance within a person's heart (see John 6:51 where Christ is the bread and also gives the bread of life). Christ is the Author of salvation and He gives repentance, which is something beyond man's ability to do for himself. When a person repents, that person's will is involved in turning to God, however, the Scriptures plainly show that unless God first gives us a heart of flesh we will not repent (Ezk. 11:19, 20; 36:25, 26; see comments on Acts 2:38). As soon as repentance is worked in someone's heart, God in heaven declares them justified, pronouncing them free from the penalties or consequences of their sin. These two stages (repentance and justification) always are found together, though they only happen in this order. As soon as the sinner repents, his release from judgment is announced in heaven (Luke 15:7, 10). When Christ gives repentance to someone, He also gives them perseverance, so that they might continue to the end (John 10:29, 30; Eph. 1:5, 13, 14; 1 John 2:19; Jude 1, 24, 25)—repentance is never given without perseverance. Peter offers the Gospel to those who wickedly planned and brought about the crucifixion of God's Son, the Prince and Author of salvation. God will receive all those who repent, no matter how great their sin.

Acts 5:32

The apostles were both eye witnesses of these things and the ones entrusted by God to declare them before all people, thus if they did not do this, they would be resisting God (cf. Jer. 20:9; 1 Cor. 9:16). It seems best to regard the witness of the Holy Spirit here, not as the inward witness that each believer has (Rom. 8:16), but rather as the powerful manifestation of signs and wonders that confirmed the apostle's message. These signs and wonders were so plentiful, and done so openly, that there could be no doubt about the authority and truth of the apostles' teaching. It was nothing but stubborn, wilful, blind rebellion on the part of these leaders who hardened their hearts and refused to repent.

Acts 5:33

Peter's words did not produce repentance and a humble submission to God's judgment of them (cf. 2:37), but rather the exact opposite—a violet outburst. Peter was grinding his foot into a sensitive wound, and their reaction was like that which we would expect from a lion if we squeezed its wounded paw. This response from the council is what happens when the light of God's Word shines brightly into consciences that are rebelliously trying to hold down the truth in unrighteousness (Rom. 1:18). The truth, to such people, chokes their nostrils with the stench of death (2 Cor. 2:16), and they writhe in agony like some creature trying to escape from the fire it has fallen into. The only way for them to escape from this pain is to repent of their sin and rebellion against God, but they refuse to do this and thus their solution, from the beginning, has been to stop the light shining—which is impossible, because it is God's will that this light shines, and who can resist Him? (Isa.

14:27; Hab. 2:14; Mark 16:15, cf. Col. 1:23). These leaders, who had already set their hearts on killing the apostles (even before the Twelve were brought before them), were now even more determined that this is what they should do after Peter had finished speaking. They were so worked up they were almost out of control.

Acts 5:34

Only the most respected and learned leader of the day was able to calm their fury—Gamaliel was his name. He was of the Pharisee party (if you remember, there were two main groups in the Jewish leadership). The Sadducee party, which included the High Priests, were the most powerful group at this time, however, the reason for their power was because they were extremely rich and influential and not because they had the popular support of the people.

The group that was held in high esteem by the people were the Pharisees and Gamaliel was the most respected Pharisee—both his grandfather (Hillel) and his father (Simeon) had been very influential teachers of the Jewish law. Gamaliel is the teacher who instructed the apostle Paul (Acts 22:3). There is no proof that Gamaliel was a friend of the Christian religion, though he was known for his moderation and here we see an example of his moderation. The council was about to kill the apostles, but Gamaliel says this is not the right thing to do (Paul did not follow his teacher's example, when later he violently persecuted the church, Acts 8:1–3; 9:1, 13, 21; 22:4, 19; 26:10, 11; Gal.1:13). Gamaliel asks that the apostles be removed from the meeting for a little while so that he could address the council, probably not wanting to encourage the apostles by what he had to say. We can appreciate what kind of respect and weight Gamaliel's words carried when we see the outcome of his speech—completely changing the minds of those who moments before were ready to kill the apostles.

Acts 5:35

It is difficult to tell what Gamaliel's real motive was for saying what he said. Was he trying to score points for the Pharisees over the Sadducees? We do know that his advice was according to his moderate and "compassionate" approach to life. He had worked for moderate changes to be introduced into the Jewish way of life—he relaxed the strict regulations with respect to Sabbath travelling and introduced laws to help bring a hint of protection to divorced women. He was also open to non-Jewish scholarship, and allowed his followers to be exposed to its thinking as well. What he advised the council was in line with his view and approach to life.

He says, "Beware, for you could be in error." What he is really implying is that they have no real basis for killing the apostles and it is merely an emotional outburst (we do not know if Gamaliel himself saw his statement in this way, but this definitely was the implication of his words), and therefore, they were about to endanger themselves. He obviously meant that since they were acting as judges of Israel ("men of Israel"), they were accountable to God and could come under His judgment if they gave a wrong judgement. He also might have been referring to the physical danger they would be placing themselves in by offending the people (nation). Fear for your own well-being usually makes you listen and reconsider your course of action.

Acts 5:36

Gamaliel then lays a foundation for the advice he's about to give: he cites *similar* examples to the one they were now facing—examples that were known to all those listening to him. He first talks of a Theudas (which was a common name). The Jewish historian Josephus also talks about a Theudas, a different man, who came after the one Gamaliel talked about and so these two Theudases must not be confused with each other.

Acts 5:37

It is likely that this census was taken in A.D. 6, which involved more than just counting the people, but also included paying a tax to the Roman government. There were apparently riots protesting against the census and Judas excited a revolt by saying the Jews were cowards if they paid the tax. The Romans were merciless in putting down the rebellion, killing Judas in the process. This census was not the one referred to in Luke 2:2.

The common point in both these examples which Gamaliel referred to, was that shortly after the leader of the movement was killed, the followers were scattered and came to nothing. Gamaliel's implication was that Jesus, the leader of this group, was dead and so why should the Sanhedrin endanger their own lives by chasing after his followers—who would probably be dispersed anyway.

Acts 5:38, 39

These leaders had all rejected the wisdom of God (1 Cor. 1:24, 30) and thus they now call foolishness wisdom (1 Cor. 1:20). This is an example of the wisdom of the greatest and most respected mind in Israel, which also convinces all the elders, leaders and wise men. Yet, what he said was real folly (1 Cor. 1:19). This is the result when people reject the Word of God as their absolute authority and rely upon their own understanding and insight.

These are the very same men that condemned Jesus to death for being a blasphemer (Mark 14:63, 64). The apostles were teaching that Jesus had been raised from the dead by the God of Israel, who had also exalted Him to the place of highest authority. The apostles were teaching that the only way to be saved from one's sins was by believing in and obeying Jesus the Nazarene (Acts 2:22, 32, 33, 38). Gamaliel, referring to this teaching then says, "If this is of men." Was there now some doubt that Jesus' claims were wrong? Was there no way to be absolutely sure whether what the apostles said was true or false? Gamaliel was actually saying that the Jews did not have a clear revelation from God and therefore were not in a position to be dogmatic about any belief. There was enough doubt in their minds to think that this movement, just might be of God and if this was so, then they could be fighting against God. The only real certainty they could have, according to Gamaliel, was the test of time (yet he conveniently forgot to specify just how much time). According to this kind of reasoning, almost every religion in existence today might just be the right one, for only if it passes away will we know for sure that it is not of God. Gamaliel says the only option open to them is to wait and see. God used this foolish counsel to save the lives of the apostles, yet this does not change the fact that it was foolish advice.

Without realising it, Gamaliel had basically condemned the Sanhedrin for executing Christ. He was saying that there was no way that they could be sure whether Jesus' teachings were from men or from God. In a sense he said to them, "Hey, you messed up with the trial of Jesus, so do not make another mistake with the trial of His disciples!"

On this basis there is nothing that can be judged, since there is no sure standard by which to evaluate anything. There are many people in the church today who have the same opinion that Gamaliel had, believing that we are unable to be absolutely sure about many things in life. They do not believe that God has given us a comprehensive revelation that enables us to be equipped for every area of life. Even with respect to those areas they believe God has spoken about, they still say you cannot be completely sure that you are right. Thinking themselves to be wise they become fools (Rom. 1:22), for if we have no absolutely sure Word from God, then we have no Word from Him.

Acts 5:40

We are told that the council agreed with Gamaliel and decided not to execute the apostles. But there must have been much going on in the mind of the High Priest and his close followers—I would suggest more than merely the doubt presented by Gamaliel. There were other political considerations that arose in the light of what Gamaliel said that probably influenced their decision. The Sadducees (the High Priest and the majority in the council) had realised the great threat these apostles were to their positions of power. Thus, they had called this massive council together in order to put to death these "false" teachers. They were aware of how much respect the people in Jerusalem had for the apostles, so they gathered all the elders in Israel in order to condemn the apostles, with the hope that this would prevent any uprising from the people when the apostles were put to death. After Gamaliel's speech, the Sadducees realised that if the apostles were killed there would be an uprising, since they did not have the support of the Pharisees, who would all definitely follow Gamaliel's advice, and moreover, the people had great respect for the Pharisees' opinions.

The fact that they had the apostles beaten with rods means that they did not agree completely with what Gamaliel said, i.e., that this movement might be of God. For if they truly believed this and were going to wait and see if this group would continue before they decided whether it was of God or not, then they wouldn't have passed judgment (by beating these fellow Jews, they were saying, "You are guilty!"). What were they guilty of? If blasphemy, then they should have been executed, but if not blasphemy, then what? It was obvious that they were beaten for speaking in the Name of Jesus, for they then commanded the apostles not to speak in His Name. But why were they not allowed to speak in the Name of Jesus? Was it because Jesus was a blasphemer? If Jesus was a blasphemer, how did they know this? If Jesus was a blasphemer, then why did not they execute those who were continuing His blasphemy? If Jesus was not a blasphemer, then why did they murder Him? This "wise" group of elders was nothing but a confused mess. Thus, I believe that their agreeing with Gamaliel, was purely a political thing—they believed that the apostles were a threat to them while they were alive, but to kill them would threaten their positions even more at the present time. So they agreed that it was best not to kill the Twelve, but still treated them as guilty. It is only by completely relying upon the Word of God that we can be saved from such foolishness in our thinking.

Acts 5:41

To be beaten by rods was meant to bring disgrace upon a person, yet these men went out rejoicing that they had been counted worthy to be disgraced for Christ. They rejoiced that they were treated in the way Christ was treated (Matt. 5:11, 12). It was an honour for them to share in the fellowship of Christ's sufferings (Phil. 3:10; Col. 1;24; 2 Tim. 3:12; 1 Pet. 4:13). If we share in His shame and suffering we will share in His glory too.

Acts 5:42

They went away and continued just as before. The apostles had already explained that they would obey God and not these rulers (5:29) and we see that they fearlessly continued with the task given to them by Christ—not just in homes, but openly, before the eyes of the whole city, in the temple. The victory is Christ's and the battle is Christ's, all we have to do is live faithfully in the light of God's revelation, spreading the fragrance of His grace wherever we go (2 Cor. 2:14; Matt. 5:13–16).

Acts 6:1

In those early days of powerful, fearless preaching, which God confirmed by numerous signs and wonders, many more people were added to the church. However, with this increase in numbers, an administrative problem developed. This problem was not due to deliberate neglect, but arose because the church had become too big for the existing leadership to do everything (some commentators believe that there was at least twenty to twenty five thousand believers at this time in Jerusalem).

The Hellenists and the Hebrews were both Jews, though there was a distinction between them because they spoke different languages and had different cultures. The Hellenists, or Greek-speaking Jews, not only spoke Greek as their main language, but had embraced the Greek culture too (their culture would now have been a mixture of Greek and Hebrew cultures). Whereas, the Hebrews spoke Aramaic and Hebrew and had a strict Hebrew culture. They were both Christians and they were both Jews, however their languages and cultures were very different. It is noteworthy that there was no deliberate neglect implied in the verse, yet the neglect turns out to be only towards *one* group. We have no reason to believe that there had been a drastic change in the early church from the oneness and unity of Acts 2:44–47 and 4:32, yet the neglect is only with one group, nevertheless, this neglect was not deliberate. There is an important lesson to learn from this situation, namely, despite the oneness and unity in the Lord; the singleness of heart and mind; despite the equality in Christ and the Kingdom, we can not get away from the real differences that arise from language and culture.

The fact that there are different cultures is not evil, for they were made by God for His purposes. The glory of the Gospel is that all different cultures are united in Christ (Gal. 3:28; Col. 3:11), and thus all those who believe in Christ are brothers and sisters (see comments on Acts 2:4). All Christians ought to have one united desire and goal; they ought to treat each other as equals and be willing to help and relate as one body. However, the differences between cultures are not to be despised and they are not to be destroyed—for they cannot be. As a result of the different cultures there will be a natural distinction between cultural groups and these differences will lead to a different emphasis upon where and with whom you most commonly relate. It was because of this different *emphasis* upon relating that the widows in one group were neglected. There were different cultural groups among the Christians, which meant that every believer was not relating *equally* with every other believer, but rather the *emphasis* of the relating was more in language and cultural groups. However, this did not mean that the oneness and unity spoken about earlier in Acts had been broken.

We should not seek to make the whole world one culture. The different cultures are a healthy part of the Kingdom of God. What we need to do as Christians is make sure our culture is brought into line with the Word of God. We need to respect other cultures to the degree that they manifest the wisdom of God; and we ought to relate freely and openly with Christians from other cultures. We must realise, however, that even if all cultures were brought into line with the Word of God, they would still be very different from each other. The beliefs of a people are reflected in their culture (showing what people believe about God, man, sin, right and wrong, the future, etc.), but there will be many other things that are neither right or wrong in and of themselves that will vary from culture to culture (e.g., sounds/music, tastes, dress, language, etc.). We are not to evaluate one culture by another culture to determine which one is better. There are better and worse cultures, though a culture is good to the degree that it comes into line with the Word of God and to the degree that it rejects the Word of God, it is wicked. We all have a responsibility to be renewed in our own thinking and then also to renew our cultures. Every aspect of life is to glorify God, thus every aspect of our culture is to be brought into line with God's Word.

Acts 6:2

There is a real problem and the apostles act quickly to deal with the complaint. They look to the *body* to meet the need. Just as Moses needed to appoint helpers for the work (Ex. 18:13–26), so too the apostles realize that they are unable to cope with the demands of the growing church unless they have some help. This is not the apostle's problem, but a problem for the whole body of Christ, thus the body is called together and the apostles say what should be done. Their reasoning was not that the job of overseeing the task of helping to feed the widows was below their dignity. Rather, they recognised that God gives different gifts to His body and that they had been called to peach and teach the Word. Thus, for them, there was nothing more important than teaching the Word and to neglect their responsibilities would have been a serious mistake. It would not be right for them to stop teaching and see to the needs of the widows. This did not mean that the needs of the widows were unimportant, or even less important than preaching the Word. In God's kingdom, every calling and all work is equally glorifying to Him and we need to be faithful to the calling of God upon our lives—whatever that might be. All Christians should be servants and there ought to be no task that we feel is too low for us to do

(Christ washed His disciples' feet, which was the task of the lowest servant in a household, and we should have this same attitude, John 13:5). However, if any task gets in the way of your primary calling, then you ought not to do that task, for the simple reason that in doing it, you will neglect what you ought to be doing.

Acts 6:3

The apostles acknowledge the importance of the need by giving authority to some men to oversee this matter. These men were drawn from those who had been instructed by the Word of God and whose lives were full of Christian fruit—they were chosen by the believers. The apostles then imparted authority to the seven men who were selected by the Christian community. Seven were chosen, because that is how many the apostles calculated would be needed to fulfill the task. These men had to have good reputations, be filled with the Holy Spirit and be wise—needing to know how to apply the Word of God to real life situations and problems. The indication from the verse is that these men were given places of authority to oversee the task of distributing to the needs of the widows, which means there were others involved in the whole ministry, but these seven were in charge. Though their primary calling was not to preach, they still needed to be filled with the Holy Spirit in order to carry out their task. In 1 Timothy 5:3–16 we see Paul's instructions about which widows ought to be helped: those who really needed daily support and had a history of Christian service for others; others should be supported by their children and grandchildren; younger widows should marry again, etc.

Acts 6:4

Christ's departing command was that the whole counsel of God should be taught to every nation in the world (Matt. 28:19, 20). Pastors are called by God to make known His whole counsel to a group of people somewhere in the world and their success can be measured by how well this has been done (do their people know the whole counsel?). When a pastor and thus, the body of Christ, neglects some aspect of this whole counsel they fall short of Christ's command. To the degree that those teachers, ordained by God and recognised by the people, fail in expounding the whole of God's Word, to that degree the whole body of Christ fails in its calling—thus to that degree the Kingdom of God is not manifested by the body of Christ as it ought to be (when the pastor does not faithfully fulfill his responsibilities, all those under his care will fall short of their responsibilities).

We see in these first chapters of Acts two of the most common ways that this failure (of not preaching the full counsel of God) can creep into the church: when leaders (pastors and teachers), are fearful to preach the full counsel of God, or when they are distracted from doing this—either way the full counsel is not communicated to the people. Pastors are ministers of the Word of God and the people will not know the full counsel of God unless they are taught by the pastors—if the pastor fails, the people fail and if the people fail, the ministry fails (Eph. 4:11–13). The apostles realised this fact and therefore had to be ruthless with anything that would distract them from their primary calling. They realised that the power was not in themselves and their wisdom, but from the Holy Spirit working through the Word of God (1 Cor. 2:4, 5; Rom. 10:17). The apostles were not fearful of preaching the full counsel or distracted from doing this, yet the same cannot be said for most ministers of the Word today.

The apostles realised how much time and effort it required to minister the Word properly. The *apostles* said that they were unable to merely throw together some thoughts in order to teach the Word of God. What was needed was much prayer and time to search the Scriptures and wrestle with the text. The apostles realised how vital this ministry was to the body and therefore refused to compromise in their preparation—in this way the foundation for true reformation was laid. You cannot nurture a successful army or athlete on a watered down soup made from vegetable scraps. They will not die, but neither will they be effective in their tasks. This is one of the primary reasons why the body of Christ is so weak, anaemic and ineffective in our days—their diet is so pathetic! Some ministers are just too lazy to prepare properly, but many have been deceived into being distracted from their primary calling, feeling that there are a hundred and one other things that are more important than prayerful, dedicated preparation of the Word of God.

To prepare properly is hard, time consuming work, but a minister has been called by God to feed His troops with solid food. It is nothing but shameful for ministers to be distracted from their God given priorities and it is nothing but disastrous for the flock. If the *apostles* needed time to prepare in order to discharge their duty—how much more do not pastors today?

The work of ministering to the widows was an excellent ministry and Luke uses the same word to refer to that ministry as he does to refer to the ministry of the apostles. Thus my concern is not with lazy ministers, but with those who are hard working and doing many things, yet are being distracted from proper preparation. You cannot give solid teaching about God with good application for today without thorough preparation. This is how God has ordained it to be. Preaching and teaching are spiritual supernatural works, however, the labor required from ministers is a necessary and real part of this supernatural work.

It is not easy to week after week prepare for hours at a time in order to deliver a 45 minute message. This has to be done with faith, for the fruit of such work is not immediate, but often takes years before it is seen. But that does not mean nothing is happening each week: it is just not easy to see. The minister is primarily God's servant, and he is to equip the people of God, but if he is distracted from this he fails God and the people. The way to do this, according to the apostolic understanding, was by prayer and diligent time con-suming preparation. Today, many pastors think that they are wiser than the apostles and thus spend their time on many little, time consuming programmes and functions, that they hope will achieve the same end—such men are deceived. Some pastors also let them-selves be forced by the immature expectations of people, to get involved in things that distract them from their primary calling (Gal. 1:10). It is not difficult to discern the difference between watery scrap soup and roast beef. Jesus is looking for faithful ser-vants who will be found doing what they ought to be doing when He comes (Matt. 24:45–51). If a minister is not doing this he is not faithful, but either lazy or deceived (James 3:1).

Finally we need to realize that every Christian can be distracted from their calling. All callings are of equal importance in God's Kingdom and everyone faces the same danger of being distracted. Even when we are distracted by "good" things, we are still guilty of failing the Lord. Husbands and wives can be distracted from their responsibilities to each other. Parents can be distracted from their responsibilities to their children and on it goes. Every person has been given priorities by God and is responsible to fulfill those.

Time is limited—there is not enough time to fulfill our responsibilities and also have much time to do other things. We are on this earth for God and His Kingdom, not for ourselves or our pleasure (in fact, real pleasure is found in faithfully doing His will). We are not to live unto ourselves. Our priorities are to be God's priorities and that will take up almost all the time there is—everything else that you might want to do fits in after this (remembering that whatever we do is to be done to the glory of God). There is time for recreation and doing something that we enjoy, e.g., a hobby. But how much time can we spend upon these other things? Well, that depends how much time is left when we have finished our priorities—it is simple.

Acts 6:5

The apostles did not rule with an iron fist. What the apostles suggested as the solution was well pleasing to the people who then chose seven men with the necessary qualifications. The fact that all seven men had Greek names does not mean that they were all from the Hellenist community. Many strict Hebrews also had Greek names (two of the apostles who definitely were Hebrews had Greek names, namely, Andrew and Philip). Thus it is nothing but speculation to say how many were from either group. Of the seven men chosen to fulfill this task, Stephen and Philip turn out to be the most significant in the book of Acts, however, Acts is not an exhaustive record of the early church and so we must not think that if Acts does not record the activities of a person its because they did not do anything. It is very safe to conclude that there were many people who did many wonderful things in those days who are not mentioned in Acts.

Some people receive recognition and others don't, but we should never do something in order to gain the praise and recognition of people. Rather, whatever we do should be done only for the glory of God and the advancing of His Name. Whether we are recognised or not by people should make no difference to us, for our sole desire and motive for what we do should be to advance the Kingdom of God. We need to ask God to burn the reality of His Kingdom deep into our consciousness, and give us sure confidence that what we do in the Name of the Lord by faith, has real eternal significance with respect to God's unfolding purposes. We should not set as the goal and purpose of our life that which has no eternal value, but seek at all times to accelerate the growth of God's Kingdom. Our desire should not be for fame, but to be found faithfully doing the will of the Father, even if no one else notices our efforts—to God alone be all the glory!

Acts 6:6

The people then bring the seven chosen men to the apostles whereupon the apostles lay hands on them giving them authority to perform their task of overseeing the ministry of feeding the widows. There is no indication whether this was a permanent office or a temporary one; e.g., Paul and Barnabas were set apart for a certain missionary task with a specific, though temporary, goal (Acts 13:3). In the same way, these seven who were already filled with the Holy Spirit might have been appointed to carry out some specific need which the apostles had no time to do, and thus they could be seen as the apostle's assistants. The word deacon is not used here with respect to these seven men and the qualifications are not the same as those we find later with respect to deacons (Acts 6:3, cf. 1 Tim. 3:8–13). Traditionally, most commentators have traced the beginning of the deacon's office to this passage, though in my opinion it is difficult to be sure that this was the beginning. It is possible that these men functioned more like elders than deacons.

The laying on of hands is a symbolic act which imparts the authority and privileges that accompany the office. The seven were taken out of the huge group of disciples or believers. Up until now there were two groups mentioned in Acts: the apostles and those who believed (disciples). A new office is created, though this new office was not to the teaching/preaching ministry or else it would contradict the apostles' desire to preach and not be distracted (verse 4). If the seven could do both, why couldn't the apostles? I believe the principle we learn from this is that the preparation for preaching the Word should not be interfered with by anything and it is the responsibility of the whole church to guard the ministry of the Word.

Acts 6:7

The effect of the Gospel message became more and more noticeable as it had greater and greater influence upon the people of Jerusalem. There was continual growth, probably spurred on by the dedication of the apostles to their ministry and the dedication of the "seven" to their ministry. When everyone in the body of Christ is doing what they ought to be doing the Lord usually adds to the church.

The power of the Holy Spirit working through the Word of God is seen by the fact that a great many priests came to be obedient to the faith, that is, to submit to the whole counsel of God as explained by the apostles (cf. John 12:42, 43). This should encourage us that even the hardest hearts and most intelligent minds are not beyond the power of God's grace. We must remember that it is the Word and Spirit that converts people, not our wisdom.

Acts 6:8

Stephen is the first non-apostle to do such signs and wonders—though the apostles had laid their hands upon him. He was full of grace and power which refers to the special gifting of God that flowed through his life—gracious wisdom together with the convicting power of the Holy Spirit.

Acts 6:9

Stephen's activities brought him into contact with the Hellenist Jews who had rejected Christ. The "Freedmen" were the descendants of those Jews who had been taken as slaves to Rome and then been given pardon and enabled to return to Jerusalem as free men. It was nothing but the goodness of God that had brought about their return. The others were Jews who had been scattered as a result of the different upheavals in Israel, but had since returned to settle in Jerusalem (some might have been visiting too). God had graciously made a way for them to return from distant lands in order to hear about the Messiah, and what do they do?—resent God's messenger. This was a common weakness throughout Israel's history (Matt. 23:30, 34–36) and continues among most people today.

The seven were not preachers or teachers in any official capacity (Philip does later become an evangelist, but that is a different office to what he was appointed to here, see Acts 21:8) and yet immediately after Stephen is set apart for the ministration of the widows, Luke tells us of his healing ministry and his great wisdom concerning the things of God. In the context, this must have been taking place while he was overseeing the ministry of the tables and could be done without neglecting his office. His official office in the church was to oversee the feeding of the widows, and whatever else he did was in his capacity as a believer, though we see a special gifting of God given to him (1 Cor. 12:4–11). Every believer who is "qualified" is allowed to speak about the mysteries of God and of their hope in Christ. By qualified I do not mean "ordained" to some office within the church, but that the person is born again, and knows the Word of God, i.e., has been prepared/trained to give an answer (1 Pet. 3:15; 1 Cor. 2:12–16). The believer who shares the Gospel with someone else has to be properly equipped. It is the responsibility of pastors and teachers to impress upon believers the seriousness of sharing only the truth and also of equipping them for this task.

Acts 6:10

Stephen was equipped to share with those who did not believe, but we see too in his ability, a fulfilment of Christ's promise (Luke 21:15). This promise was not just for the apostles, but for all His disciples who were about to enter into the persecutions that Jesus had talked about (Matt. 24; Mark 13:5ff.; Luke 21). Here we see the wisdom of man up against the wisdom of God—they could not resist the wisdom of God's Spirit in Stephen. We need to realize that Christianity is not only true in the "spiritual realm," but is the only philosophy that is able to work in this life—it alone is totally logical and rational (1 Cor. 1:19, 20).

Acts 6:11

Even in our day the unbeliever prides himself in his own wisdom—in his logical and reasoning powers, which often serves as his god. Therefore, when their "god" is shown to be inadequate, they have to resort to other means to "win" the argument—violence, deceit and murder. The unbeliever has no sure foundation and therefore, when his "sacred" beliefs are shown to be nonsense, he reacts against that which is exposing his foolishness (he has to put out the light). He is a fool for his rebellion against God, and he knows he is a fool, however, he reacts violently when this fact is spelt out to him. The unbeliever has to react in a desperate and frantic way to defend his beliefs—*he* made them and therefore, *he* has to defend them. The Christian on the other hand stands upon the Word of God. It is God's truth and it is God who watches over His truth. We do not need to react to any situation. What we need to do is respond in accordance with the Word of God. When people act in violation of the Word of God, when their behavior is out of line with the truth (in whatever way), we as Christians must learn to *respond* with the truth. Since we stand upon the eternal truth of God we can speak with authority (thus we need to know His Word) without reacting. We are to shine the light of God's Word at all times in all situations, but we must *respond* with the light, not *react*. We need to mature in this area, so that we can respond with the truth no matter what circumstance we find ourselves in. Stephen is a wonderful example of this even when those opposing him were reacting with violence. Even while he is being stoned we see him *respond* according to the truth (Acts 7:59, 60, cf. Phil. 1:21; 2 Cor. 5:8). We must not apologise for the truth or feel shy about it, but rather, respond graciously with the truth at all times and in accordance with it.

Blasphemy was a capital crime and therefore in order for these people to silence Stephen they seek his death—even if they have to lie to accomplish it. Self-deception is frightening: how can you lie in order to get someone put to death in the Name of God, who is ultimate truth?

Acts 6:12

We see a different approach taken by these Jews against Stephen than that taken against Peter, John and the apostles. Here they get the *people* on their side. When the Sadducees wanted to put the apostles to death, they did not have the support of the people and were afraid of their reactions, since the people held the apostles in high regard. With Stephen, these Hellenists manage to influence the minds of the masses and convince them that Stephen's words were heretical blasphemy. There was nothing more sacred to the Jews than God and Moses and to blaspheme against them was a serious offence (and rightly so), however, the charges against Stephen were false. It is easy to distort what someone is trying to say and misquote their statements. Thus, they were able to drag him away as a common criminal (cf. 5:26). When these men failed in debate, then they made up lies in order to make it appear that they were doing things legally. We can see corrupt people in every nation using the "legal" means to further their ends and achieve their goals. This is nothing but a manifestation of the rebellion in the hearts of people, for they have the works of the law written on their hearts (Rom. 2:15). Their self-deception is very real—they cannot escape from their realization that there needs to be a just trial, however they are quite willing to manipulate the system in order to get what they want. This is nothing but a show to keep the fools in the nation believing that all things are going along well.

Whatever a person relies upon or looks to as their ultimate authority, this is their god. In our day the state (or government) claims to be the only ultimate authority for all things. They are the ones who decide upon what is right and wrong in every situation. They are not accountable to anyone but themselves. Most people have been deceived by the propaganda that the state pushes through the television, newspapers and books and now see the state as the final authority in life. It is believed that the government will provide the solutions to all the problems and unless we have the opinion of the government on any given matter we cannot be sure what is the right course to take. Christians have forgotten the fact that Christ is Lord of heaven and earth and the government is to be a servant of Christ and a servant of the people. Yet today, politicians are full of their own self-importance and enjoy the power they have given to themselves and use it for their own ambitions. Politics is a religion—a religion of power and domination and fools continue to look to these people to sort out the problems of the world. The politicians' promises are the same the world over: "We will sort out all your problems and make this world a paradise, if you just give us more power and more money".

Such politicians have made themselves and their systems into gods and thus they resent the fact that they ought to be accountable to the Creator of the universe. They see themselves as gods on earth and thus they want to be treated as gods: they want to have the power, privilege and worship that gods have—however, there is only one True God on this earth and that is Jesus Christ who rules by His Word (Rev. 1:16; 2:16; Eph. 6:17). To reject His Word is to reject His rule. The modern world is captivated by a view of life that is politically centred, not Christ centred—this has become so embedded in the mindset of modern people that it is held to with religious zeal.

Christ will not bow to anyone and the modern state refuses to bow to Christ. There can be no compromise from either side and people have to whole-heartedly decide for one or the other—only one can be ultimate and the other has to submit to it, and this submission is in every respect. This is no game. Christ's agenda is total conquest—every knee will bow to Him and every tongue will confess that He is Lord of heaven and earth. According to Christ, the state is *His* servant and is meant to strive to live in obedience to His Word, which means limiting itself to the boundaries that God has set for the state and then in those limited areas where God has given the state authority, to advance Christ's Kingdom. The modern state however, if it allows a place for God, uses God for their ends, making Him subject to their authority.

The Christian does not believe in salvation by politics, but salvation through faith in Christ. The Christian also believes that Christ is Lord over all things and that His Word is to be submitted to in all areas. The King has a Kingdom and laws and He expects complete obedience to all His will—and if we love Him we will obey Him in all of life, seeking to make known the wisdom of God wherever we go. We are to be light and salt, which means making known who the King is and making known His will for all things (Matt. 28:20).

Christianity is a system of belief. It is a complete system of belief, that is, it touches every aspect of life on earth. Christianity is not a belief about a small area of life (a religious aspect of life), saying all other areas of life are not directly related to this. We are to have the mind of Christ, which means thinking about all things in the way God thinks about them. This clearly shows that Christianity has its own distinctive beliefs about all things and these beliefs, in order to be Christian, have to be related to Christ. There is only one source for everything we believe and that is the Word of God. God expects complete obedience to His Word. It is laziness or rebellion that makes Christians try to reduce the extent of Christ's Kingdom. This battle is total war and each side is aiming at complete conquest. There are no neutral areas. When we deny this full extent to Christ's Kingdom and therefore His right to exercise His will in all areas we are joining with the enemy and fighting against Christ.

Acts 6:13, 14

These Jews knew that a person's ideas arise from his whole system of belief (or worldview, see *Faith and Reason*, chapter 1)—they realised that there was total war between these two systems (theirs' and Stephen's). There was no conflict between Moses and Christ, but

between the Jews' self-made religion and Christ (Moses was standing with Christ). These men were in rebellion against God and His
law. They hated the Messiah, who was clearly revealed throughout
all the law and the prophets (Luke 24:27; John 1:45; 5:46; Acts 3:24;
10:43). They hated Christ because they hated God and knowing
that they were in rebellion against God's clear revelation, they had
made a religious system suitable to their consciences (something
that wouldn't convict them of their sin and rebellion). Stephen's
blasphemy was not against Moses and the temple, but against their
own beliefs—which they had exalted to the place of supreme
authority. These Jews realised that there could be no compromise,
for only one system could survive. Each system was totally opposed
to the other and sought to destroy the other. If you do not realize
that this is the nature of the battle you will be deceived by the
enemy. Your guard will be down and you will not realize the
destruction he is causing. If you do not have the courage for this
type of conflict, pray that the Lord will give you the necessary courage. This same conflict we see with Stephen, is an on-going battle
throughout the history of the church. Christians have fallen asleep
to the fact that Christianity is a whole view of life (it covers everything) and there are no neutral areas. If Christians are not thinking
like Christ about any area, then they are thinking like the enemies
of Christ in that area. Do not be fooled, Christianity is not some
side show where we go for entertainment—we are called into the
fiercest battle there is and we are called to fight with the armies of
heaven. It is a battle and it is only when we compromise God's truth
that we are able to forget the fierceness of the struggle—for then we
are not resisting and driving back the enemy or feeling his attacks,
but marching with him and conforming our thinking to the world
around us.

Stephen was only following the teaching of Christ who had not only
said the centrality of Jerusalem was ended (John 4:21, 23), but that
the temple in Jerusalem would be destroyed (Matt. 24:2). All the
ceremonial aspects to the Mosaic law were only shadows that
pointed to the reality that was coming—this reality was Christ and
now He had come. The temple curtain had been torn in two, showing that those things were no longer to be observed (Matt. 27:51).
The temple pointed to Christ, not to itself. The temple and all the
ceremonies that Moses instituted only had value because they were
shadows of Christ. To deny Christ and keep the shadows was mad-

ness. Christ said that He did not come to destroy the law or the prophets, but to fulfill them (Matt. 5:17). Christ came to uphold the law and confirm its validity down to the finest detail (both the moral and ceremonial law). All the ceremonial aspects like the blood of bulls and goats, the feasts, priesthood, etc., have all been fulfilled by Christ. All these things are realised in Him, for He has always been the centre and focus of all things. Jerusalem was the centre for blood sacrifice, however, this was no longer necessary since Christ's one sacrifice had made atonement for all time (Heb. 9:14, 26). We must no longer hang onto the shadows of the ceremonies—the reality is with us and lives in us and we meet, live and worship in Him!

Instead of taking Christ's Words about the destruction of the temple as a warning of God's judgment upon their rebellion, these leaders silence the prophet—just as they had done throughout their history.

Acts 6:15

Stephen's message had been confirmed by God with many mighty miracles. He was now filled with the Spirit in a mighty way as he was about to bring his defence (just as Jesus had promised). This powerful presence of the Spirit upon Stephen made his face shine like an angel, however I think there was another message in this radiance for the Sanhedrin: When Moses had received the law from God, God had underlined Moses' authority by making his face shine (Ex. 34:29f.), thus showing the people that Moses had been with God and that he therefore brought the Word of God. Stephen had been accused of blaspheming Moses, yet God makes his face shine like Moses' face did. Luke is not saying that Stephen was calm—no, his face shone with the glory of an angel's face, yet the hearts of these Jews were hard and they refused to see the parallel.

Acts 7:1

The High Priest, as the chief leader and chief magistrate in the nation, was acting as president of this whole counsel and thus asks Stephen if these charges are true. Stephen's response was not to try to get himself out of "trouble," but rather to give an apology or defence for the Christian religion (1 Pet. 3:15). Christ's teachings were not blasphemy, but showed the only pure and acceptable worship of God. Stephen proves this from the authority of the OT by citing Israel's history from Abraham to Solomon. These Jews had come to equate their present set up of worship as the one and only way to worship God. They believed you could only ever worship God in the Jerusalem temple and according to the ceremonies Moses had instituted. Stephen shows that these conclusions find no support from the Scriptures. It must be pointed out that at this time in the history of Israel only blood sacrifice was restricted to Jerusalem. *Worship* was never restricted to only one place. Stephen also shows that the outward organisation and manifestation of the church had been through many changes and that the present structures and forms had only come into existence in Solomon's time. Thus, for thousands of years (from the birth of the church, until Solomon) the church of God had met all the essential conditions for true worship, yet this worship was quite different from how the Jews worshipped in Stephen's day. In the past, true worship had not been confined to Jerusalem and God's presence had not been restricted to the temple. Stephen points this out to the council and adds that Solomon's temple was never intended to be permanent (Acts 7:48–50), thus proving it was never God's intention that the focus of worship would be fixed to one place on earth for all time (John 4:21). God's presence was not restricted to one place, for He has always dwelt with His people wherever they worshipped.

Stephen also shows how Israel from the very beginning had always rebelled against God and rejected His messengers (saviors)—culminating in their rejection of the Messiah (cf. Matt. 21:33–41). Stephen clearly demonstrates that in the past history of the nation, God had always acted in ways very differently from the normal expectations and thoughts of men and thus had often been misunderstood and opposed by Israel. The service and worship of God was a gradual unfolding revelation that was always moving towards the coming of Christ.

Stephen was definitely not trying to set himself free, for it would have been difficult to come up with a speech that would be more offensive than this one in the eyes of those who were judging him. He was a preacher and a prophet and the truth of God was more important to him than anything else. Christianity itself was under attack and thus he refused to compromise the truth—defending his position from Scripture.

Acts 7:2

Stephen respectfully addresses the whole crowd with its different
groups, asking for their attention, though he speaks with authority,
saying, "Listen." He then shows his deep reverence for God, referring to the self-revelation of the eternal God when he says, "The
God of glory." This refers to the character and attributes of God
that He has seen fit to reveal to us. Abraham had first lived in a
place called Ur and then he had moved to Haran. When God spoke
to Abraham in Genesis 12:1, he was living in Haran. Thus, many
say Stephen makes an error by saying that God called Abraham in
Ur, before he came to Haran. However, Stephen is not quoting
Genesis 12:1, but giving divine revelation about something that is
clearly implied in the Bible, namely, that it was God who brought
Abraham from Ur to Haran in the first place (Gen. 15:7; Neh. 9:7)
and therefore it was quite natural to believe that God merely
repeated and confirmed His call in Haran (Gen. 12:1). We are told
that Abraham and his family were on their way to Canaan when
they left Ur, which also lends support to the fact that they were
moving under divine direction. It was not uncommon for God to
repeat His divine communications to His servants (e.g., Gen. 12:3;
18:18; 22:18). In this recounting of the nation's history, Stephen is
beginning to show the outward changes that the church had gone
through from the beginning. In a sense he is saying to his accusers
that their sole reason for charging him with blasphemy was because
he had spoken about changes in the present way of worship, yet
God had constantly changed the outward form of worship (these
were not changes made according to man's own desires or knowledge, but changes in accordance with God's authoritative revelation).

Acts 7:3

Stephen points out that Abraham was called in Ur and thus his life
of faith started then and being in relationship with the true God
(with a faith strong enough to forsake all) he moves to Haran. Is it
possible to have faith in God and not worship Him? No. So, Abraham had worshipped God in Ur, on the way from Ur to Haran, and
then in Haran where he had settled for some years. God expected
His church to continue worshipping Him, even though His call was
to move to *whatever* land He would show them (Heb.11:8). There
was no definite land named to Abraham at this time and there was

much uncertainty with respect to the specifics, which magnifies the great faith Abraham had in God—this was real worship, and it made no difference whether Abraham was in Ur, Haran or in an unknown location. We do not need to know all the details of everything along the path that God calls us to walk upon, nor do we need to know what the consequences might be for walking in obedience; all these things are in God's hands—we are to trust Him and faithfully walk in His light (Ps. 119:105; 1 John 1:7).

Acts 7:4

Stephen now talks about the call that came to Abraham while he was at Haran. His stay in Haran was only temporary and when his father (Terah) died, he left. Some people get into all kinds of difficulty over this verse, for Genesis 11:26 *appears* to say that Abraham was born when Terah was seventy years old, but Terah died in his 205th year (Gen. 11:32). In Genesis 12:4 we are told that Abraham was seventy-five years old when he left Haran *after* his father's death. However, if we add 70 + 75 = 145. Thus people find a fault with the Scriptures where it says Terah was 205 years old when he died. The solution to this problem is in realising that Abraham is mentioned first in Genesis 11:26, not because he was the first born but because he became the father of the Jewish nation. Moses places his name first, since he had greater dignity than the others. We do not believe that all three sons were born in Terah's seventieth year or that Abraham was the first born.

We see that Nahor (Abraham's brother) had a *granddaughter* named Rebecca who was married to Isaac (Abraham's son, cf. Gen. 24:24), which also supports our belief that Nahor was older than Abraham and the names of Terah's sons are arranged according to importance, not age. Again, in Genesis 11:29, we are told that Nahor (second named son in the list of Gen. 11:26) married the daughter of Haran, which means that although Haran is named last, he probably was the eldest. To support this interpretation further, we are told in Genesis 5:32 that the sons of Noah were Shem, Ham and Japheth. However, it seems probable that Japheth was the eldest (cf. Gen. 10:21). In Genesis 9:24 we are told that Ham is the youngest, yet in 5:32 he is mentioned second. This clearly shows that the order the names are given in does not necessarily mean that was the order they were born and therefore, we should find fault with our understanding rather than rashly say the fault is in the Scriptures.

So the solution to the "problem" is to realize that Terah was seventy years old when he *began* to have his sons (Gen. 11:26) and that Abraham was born when he was 130 years old (Abraham being the youngest of the three). Abraham is named first due to his distinguished position of being the father of God's covenant people. The only objection to this is that some people feel Abraham wouldn't have been shocked to have a child at 100 (Gen. 17:17), if Abraham was born when his father was 130 years old. But does it mean that if a father is very fit, healthy and active into old age, that his son will necessarily be the same? Surely not! In Genesis 17:17 Abraham is not comparing God's Word with his own father's ability to produce children at 130 years of age, but rather, Abraham is overjoyed in worshipful amazement (due to his strong faith), that his and Sarah's relationship, which had been *fruitless* for such a long time, was now going to bear fruit—and that in old age. Romans 4:19 does say that his body was as good as dead and that Abraham was aware of this, though this did not hinder his faith. Rather, Abraham, being aware of his own situation, is amazed at God's goodness and believes the Word of God despite his and Sarah's weaknesses (it is interesting to note that Abraham goes on to father a number of children after this, Gen. 25:2f.).

Acts 7:5

Abraham was brought to this very land, Stephen says to his hearers (end of verse 4), yet he received not even a foot of inheritance. Abraham had massive promises from God, but he had absolutely nothing to touch and see with his physical senses. God had said that He would give Abraham the land for his children after him, yet Abraham did not have any land from God and he did not have a child. Abraham did buy a small piece of land for a burial place, but this was not in the first few years of his stay (Gen. 23:9–17). He had no children and he had nothing to give them even if he did have a child. Abraham followed God without knowing where he was going and then when he got there, he still had nothing physical to show for it. Even after Abraham arrived in Canaan, he still had no land of his own, yet God had promised it to him for an inheritance and this *promise* was enough for Abraham. To him, whatever God said was just as real as if he actually had all the land and many children.

This is amazing obedience and faith, showing complete trust in God and a total denial of himself, his will and his desires. Abraham was prepared to leave behind everything that people believe brings most comfort and security in this life and to continue faithfully following the will of God even though what God had promised took a long time to come. Abraham did not become self-centred or bitter saying, "Look what I have left for You God, yet You still haven't given me anything worthwhile." Isn't this the real life of faith that God would have us to copy (I am not talking about rushing off to unknown parts of the world without any money). What we ought to copy is Abraham's complete trust and dependence upon God and His Word (Heb. 10:35–38). What assurance do we have other than the providence of God—God's will is the best and what is happening is God's will? We are to be faithful to His Word, continuing without discouragement even when there is no immediate evidence of His promised benefits. The Word of God was Abraham's sure confidence. We too have the Word of God in the Scriptures and we should not question this Word. It is not having many physical things that keeps us strong in faith and hope, but the Word of God. Our strength is obtained from the Word, for it alone is immovable and sure for all times. Our flesh and our minds demand something more certain than the Word of God and we are constantly tempted to demand a form of assurance from God according to our own human wisdom. This is not how we ought to act! The Word of God is our assurance and strong confidence (Rom. 1:17). We are to walk by faith, not by sight, knowing that it is the Word and not our feelings, own ideas, desires, wisdom or understanding that can help us stand both now and always.

Acts 7:6

We have seen Abraham's immense faith. He followed the Lord and forsook everything He knew and moved to an unknown and unspecified land. Then even when Abraham was wandering in this foreign land, he still had no land and no descendants, yet he trusted God's promises. There was nothing physical for Abraham to hold onto and receive reassurance from—all that he had was the Word of God. As if this was not already hard enough, God then said to Abraham, who still had no descendants, "Even when you eventually do get descendants, they are going to be strangers and foreigners (that is have no land of their own) for 400 years and besides this they will be enslaved and wickedly treated as well." So not only would Abraham receive nothing physical, but neither would his descendants for 400 years. Yet Abraham and his descendants still believed that God would fulfill His promise (Heb. 11:13).

Do we have such a trust in God's Word that we will live in a certain way, enduring hardship and sacrifice for the Kingdom of God, knowing that the fruit of our labor will only be seen hundreds of years after we have gone? So often our faith is dependant upon what we can see with our physical eyes. If we can see a solution, or some fruit, then we have confidence in God's Word, but there is nothing more sure than God's Word.

Stephen talks about a time of 400 years, though he is talking about Abraham's descendants enduring a period of being strangers and suffering persecution that lasted for this length of time. There is no way to force this text to say that the enslavement in Egypt lasted 400 years. He is showing how long Abraham's descendants would still be without a land of their own (strangers in other people's lands) and included in this time of being strangers there would be a time when they would also be treated wickedly. This Stephen takes from Genesis 15:13. In Exodus 12:40 we are told that the children of Israel were strangers for 430 years. Both the above verses (in Exodus and Genesis), appear to say that the children of Israel will be slaves in Egypt for at least 400 years (the one says, 430 years). However, Paul in Galatians helps to clarify this for us. He says in Galatians 3:16, 17 that from the promise to the giving of the law was a period of 430 years. Now the promise is the promise given to Abraham in Ur (Acts 7:2, 3), and the giving of the law was on Mt. Sinai, which happened shortly after the Israelites were set free from their enslavement in Egypt. Therefore, this 430 years refers to the whole period from when God called Abraham until Moses gave the law on Sinai. During this whole time, God's covenant people were merely strangers—it includes their nomadic stay in Canaan and their slavery in Egypt. The reason some passages talk of 400 years and others talk of 430 years is not to be attributed to "rounding off." Abraham had Isaac thirty years after leaving Ur, and therefore, Stephen is talking about what happened to Abraham's *descendants*—which started with Isaac. Thus the other thirty years refers to Abraham's life before Isaac was born. We know that Abraham was seventy-five when he left Haran (Gen. 12:4). Twenty five-years later Isaac was born (when Abraham was 100, Gen. 21:5). Abraham, after having received the promise from God in Ur, left Ur and spent five years in Haran before God told him to move on (Gen. 12:1, cf. Acts 7:2, 3). This gives us thirty years before the birth of Isaac (Abraham was called when he was seventy years old). Stephen and Paul both confirm these calculations: Stephen talks of the period from Isaac until the Exodus (400 years) and Paul talks of the period from when the promise was given to Abraham in Ur until the Exodus (430 years). Therefore, this period of time (either from Abraham's call, or from the birth of Isaac), refers to the whole time that Israel were strangers without a land and not to a 400 year period of enslavement in Egypt (they were probably slaves in Egypt for about 115 years. My calculations for this will have to be shown when we do the book of Exodus, see comments on Gal. 3:17).

Acts 7:7

God would judge that nation that made slaves out of Abraham's children. The reality of ultimate perfect justice must always be before our eyes. No wrong is going to be left undone. If it is not made right in time then it will be done at the end of time—perfect justice will be measured out. This ought to stop us from having bitterness and resentment, which only destroys the person who has it. There can be no justification for ungodly behavior at any time, thus it is foolishness to think that if you have been ill treated by someone else then your responsibility to act righteously is gone. When people act in an ungodly way towards us we still have to act in a godly way towards those who ill treated us, and thus it goes without saying that we have to act in a godly way to those who did not mistreat us—despite being wounded by the ill treatment we received. Many today are bitter against everyone and they justify it by pointing to bad experiences in the past at the hands of some people or person. We are to always act in the light of Scripture and fulfill our responsibilities in every situation in which we find ourselves (Deut. 32:43; Rom. 12:17–21).

Stephen says, the children of Israel would then come out of Egypt (whom God would severely judge for their wickedness against His people), and worship in the Promised Land. Israel's ability to worship God and God's close relationship with His people came long before the temple and that way of relating to God prescribed in the ceremonial law—God's grace and favor was not tied to ceremonies. God had been truly worshipped in Ur, then on route to Haran; in

Haran and on route to Canaan; in Canaan and on route to Egypt; in Egypt and on route back to Canaan—and all this without the ceremonies of Moses. God is committed to His holy people, not to some "holy" location in the earth. It would have been foolish for God's people to claim that any one of these stages was the ultimate unchanging one and close themselves off to God's continuing revelation. The Jews despised the Samaritans because they rejected God's further revelation as to how people were to relate to Him. The Samaritans claimed Abraham and Isaac as their examples and thus rejected Jerusalem and its temple (see comments on John 4:9, 20). The Jews were now doing this very same thing: on their own authority they were claiming that one of the stepping stones in God's unfolding plan (sacrifices in the temple in Jerusalem) was the only way to worship.

While the OT expected a certain kind of worship and way of relating to God at different historical times, it was also clearly looking forward to God's ultimate goal and thus God, by His divine revelation, was always moving His church towards that goal. Therefore, to exalt one of the steps along this road as the "all time binding way to do things" is extremely foolish. Just because the people of God did something in a certain way at some point in their history, does not mean that God has made that the normal way of doing things for all time. God's revelation (now preserved for us in the Scriptures) indicates what was merely a steppingstone and what was the ultimate goal and the ultimate goal alone is binding for all time. Even in our own day we must not try and keep alive some "childhood" aspects of the early church's history, when the Scriptures show that these were not to be for all time and when clear historical proof shows that such things have ceased to be a *normal* part of the church's life—even among those who sincerely seek them (cf. 1 Cor. 13:8–13). Stephen says to his hearers, that since there is a long history of change moving towards a specific goal, they shouldn't presume that one particular historical example is the ultimate goal. The fact that the ceremonial law of Moses and the temple in Jerusalem were in the Bible was not enough to justify their claim that upon that basis, it should be a constant part of their walk with God. God is unchanging, however, His revelation of His purposes and ultimate goal was growing and unfolding and the steps along the way were designed by Him to lead us into the fullness of His revelation. Childhood is a process moving towards the goal of adulthood.

Those who desire to recapture their childhood, reject the maturity
and responsibility of adulthood and thus fail to understand and fulfill their calling under God.

Acts 7:8

Abraham had been worshipping God and walking before Him in
righteousness for twenty nine-years *before* he received the sign of
the covenant (Gen. 17:24; Rom. 4:10–12; cf. Acts 7:6 above). All the
children of Abraham (the patriarchs of the nation of Israel) were all
born into a covenantal relationship that had not existed when
Abraham was first called, though Abraham was still said to be the
friend of God (Isa. 41:8; Jam. 2:23). Abraham had been called, and
to both him and his seed God had promised a land and redemption, before he was even circumcised. If righteousness was even
before circumcision, then how foolish was not it for these Jews to
think that righteousness could only come through the temple and
the ceremonies of Moses? Stephen's point is that the outward forms
of how to worship God had gone through repeated changes—
changes as radical as those Stephen preached about in Christ's
Name (i.e., the end of the ceremonial law and temple). The sign was
to confirm the promise and all those who shared in the privileges of
the covenant were commanded to receive the sign. To be in the covenant, meant to share in all the blessings, promises and responsibilities of the covenant (their responsibilities were to walk in
obedience to God's Word, Gen. 17:1). God had eternally committed
Himself to His people, not to some place. It was God's covenant
that was to provide Israel's security and continuity throughout
time, not the temple and those ceremonies that went with the temple. The covenant came before and was greater than the temple and
the ceremonies of Moses. The temple and the ceremonies were only
shadows pointing to the reality that was still to come, and that reality was Christ—The Promise.

Acts 7:9

Joseph's brothers were filled with envy or jealousy after he shared
his dreams with them (Gen. 37:9, 11 cf. 42:6, 9). Although Jacob
rebuked Joseph for his dream (which suggested that even Joseph's
parents would bow down to him Gen. 37:9, 10), he still kept these
things in his heart (verse 11). Thus it appears that both Jacob and
Joseph's brothers believed that there was some truth to these

dreams. The brothers could not accept the fact that God would raise Joseph up and exalt him in this way. God raises up righteous people for the benefit of His Kingdom, and those within the Kingdom and therefore to envy such people is foolishness. Stephen shows how the very fathers of the nation of Israel rebelled against the one that God was going to use to save their lives. He says God's saviors and deliverers were always rejected by the Jews, thus showing a pattern that would end in the rejection of the one and only true Savior, Jesus Christ. All those who came before Jesus were shadows and signs that pointed to Him. This constant rejection by the Jews of these signs should have warned later generations not to behave in the same godless ways. These Jews to whom Stephen was talking, looked back on how Joseph's brothers treated him and shook their heads in amazement at such wickedness, however they had acted in an even worse way towards Christ. The patriarchs had sold their own brother into the hands of unbelieving foreigners, yet this generation had handed their Messiah over to the Gentiles to be killed. It is easy to look at the sins of other people and other generations, while being blind to our own wickedness. The fact is, many people often point to the sins of others in order to suppress the knowledge of their own sins.

The patriarchs (fathers of the Jewish nation) had sought to destroy Joseph and who he was going to be. The envious person will try to destroy someone who is better than himself, even when he will gain nothing by doing this—he just hates anyone who has more than him or is greater than him. Despite the actions of the brothers, Stephen says, "But God was with Joseph." In other words the patriarchs were fighting against God!—these religious leaders were already aware of such a possibility in connection with their actions against Christ and His followers (Acts 5:39). If God was with Joseph, how much more was not He with Christ?

Acts 7:10

Stephen jumps quickly to Joseph's exaltation, and leaves out his long hard struggles along the way. The last sentence in Psalms 105:18 should be translated, "into iron came his soul," meaning Joseph experienced intense, intimate physical and spiritual suffering, bringing much hurt and sorrow to every aspect of his being. Joseph's sufferings were not only physical, but spiritual and emotional also. Imagine how he would have been tormented by the

rejection of his brothers and the terror of being sold into slavery
(Gen. 42:21), being torn away from his father, the false accusations
about attempted rape that he couldn't disprove (Gen. 39:10–14),
the fact that Potiphar, whom he had served so faithfully, treated
him so badly in the end (Gen. 39:3, 4, 20). There was also loneliness
and dashed hopes to go along with the physical pain which was
inflicted upon him (he was physically hurt by the slave traders and
by the jailers when he was first put into prison—attempted rape
was a serious crime for a foreigner to be charged with and he would
have been treated accordingly; it was no holiday!). Yet because God
was with him he did not give up, nor was he eaten up with resentment, nor did he stop being faithful wherever he found himself. In
every situation he served others to the best of his ability. This all
lasted for thirteen long years (it seams probable that Joseph was still
seventeen when sold as a slave, Gen. 37:2, cf. Gen. 41:46). The
whole thing was God's doing and God, in due time, made him ruler
over Egypt and Pharaoh's house (Gen. 41:40, 41). Only Pharaoh
himself had more authority than Joseph. Not only was Joseph the
supreme controller of the royal household, i.e., the highest official
in Pharaoh's palace, but he was a parental advisor to Pharaoh, that
is, his chief advisor, and ruler over all the land (Gen. 45:8). God
opened the heart and eyes of Pharaoh to recognise the gifting that
He had given to Joseph. God gives gifts to and exalts people so that
He might fulfill His own purposes. These gifts are given to His
whole church, though the way God distributes them among people
is not on the basis of equality—not everyone is equally gifted. Yet,
no matter how great or small the gift is, it is to be used for the Kingdom of God. God blesses His church through these giftings and we
ought to recognise and receive these from the hand of God. To be
threatened by someone else's greater gifting or be jealous about it is
foolishness, for everyone's gifts (no matter how great or small) are
God's gift to the whole church and are to be received with thanksgiving. When people are envious or jealous about someone's gifting, then they cannot receive from that person and thus foolishly
deprive themselves of much that God has graciously given to His
church (actually they are rejecting God's gift).

God was with His servant in a mighty way and Joseph called upon
and relied upon the Lord, drawing his strength from that very real
relationship he had with God—and this was all done in Egypt, far
from the Promised Land, without a temple and without Moses' law.

God had given Joseph all this authority in the land of Egypt in order to preserve the children of Israel.

Acts 7:11

Despite the great wickedness of the patriarchs, we see God's mercy in using their evil deed for good and preserving their lives. Peter said the same thing about Christ; that God used the evil deed of the Jews to bring salvation to the nation (Acts 2:23; 4:10–12; 5:30, 31; Gen. 50:19, 20). Joseph was going to be the source of their survival and well being, yet they despised, hated and rejected him—this is the same way that Christ had been treated.

Acts 7:12–14

God Himself drove the children of Israel out of that land which He had promised to them as an inheritance and brought them into Egypt—God's ways are not our ways (Rom. 11:33). Our responsibility is to live faithfully in accordance with God's Word at all times, wherever we find ourselves. God has told us what we need to know (how to live before God and men), but He has not revealed all the reasons for the details along the way (i.e., why certain things happen as they do). This is God's secret counsel and we are not to demand to know why God does things in certain ways when He has seen fit not to tell us. This wonderful inheritance that God had promised to Abraham, was unable to support seventy-five people. Why did God send His people away from the land of promise for such a long time and why did Joseph have to endure such hardship? God's ways are not our ways.

When Joseph revealed himself to his brothers it was twenty-two years after they had sold him into slavery (Gen. 37:2, cf. 41:46, 53, cf. 45:6). Even after all these years, they were still burdened by guilt and shame for what they had done to their brother (42:21, 22). The modern world tries to deny the existence of guilt and sin, but this is something that they cannot escape from and therefore they try in many different ways to free themselves from this burden. Guilt is real and it arises from rebellion against God and His Word, which causes separation from God. The *only* way to put this right is to seeking forgiveness in the Name of Christ through faith. God told Jacob that it was His will for him to go down into Egypt (Gen. 46:3), yet He had forbidden Isaac to do this (Gen. 26:2). It was in Egypt that God's promise to make his descendants like the dust was fulfilled (Gen. 28:14, 15). Seventy five relatives went with Jacob into Egypt and in just over 200 years there was an immense multitude (Ex. 1:7; 12:37)—there could have been as many as two million people who left at the Exodus.

Now in the OT we are told of sixty-six people from Jacob's loins going into Egypt and other calculations talk of seventy (Gen. 46:26, 27; Ex. 1:5; Deut. 10:22). The Greek translation of the Hebrew Scriptures, called the Septuagint, says seventy-five in Genesis and Exodus. It is claimed on this basis that Stephen quotes from the Septuagint. How can we justify the Septuagint making these alterations of the Hebrew text? How can we then support the idea that Stephen under the inspiration of the Holy Spirit quotes the Septuagint? This would imply that the Hebrew Scriptures were in error at this point. Stephen is not quoting any text, but speaking from a deep knowledge of the Scriptures and with the guidance of the Holy Spirit mentions the number of *relatives* that went *with* Jacob into Egypt (Joseph was already there). Genesis 46:26 talks of those who came from the loins of Jacob and excluded his son's wives—making a total of sixty-six. Stephen now includes the wives that went down and this brings the number to seventy-five. We are not told the specific details of which wives went down and it is not impossible that some stayed behind (e.g., Simeon appears to have had a Canaanite wife as well as another wife, cf. Gen. 46:10). Stephen specifically says seventy-five relatives went with Jacob and this does not have to be confirmed by other verses before we accept it as true. Since it does not necessarily contradict any OT text, we ought to bow to the inspiration of the Holy Spirit, realising how limited our understanding is.

Acts 7:15

Not only Jacob, but all the patriarchs died in Egypt—without a land, temple or the Mosaic law! The whole foundation of the Jewish religion did not have these things for 430 years, so how can Stephen be charged with blasphemy since he said that these things were passing away? Even though the law came after 430 years, the land only came much later and the temple in Jerusalem later still.

Acts 7:16

There is much confusion with respect to this verse. The reason being that Stephen says Abraham bought some land in Shechem, whereas in Genesis 33:19 we are told that Jacob bought some land in Shechem. Jacob was buried in a cave of Machpelah at Hebron which Abraham bought (Gen. 49:30; 50:13). While Joseph was buried in Shechem in a plot of ground which Jacob had bought (Joshua 24:32). Thus either Stephen or the OT Scriptures are mistaken in the eyes of most commentators. But, why couldn't Abraham have bought some land in Shechem which we are not told about? We know he was in Shechem (Gen. 12:6, 7)—it was in Shechem that God promised to give Canaan to Abraham's descendants and Abraham built an altar there.

Jacob's burial was a massive ceremony and well known to everyone (Gen. 50:1–13). Joseph's final resting place was also well known by all since he had made the Israelites swear an oath to bury him in the Promised Land (Gen. 50:25; Joshua 24:32). Stephen would never have made such a blunder and his hearers definitely wouldn't have let him get away with it if he did. Rather, in this very brief historical survey, Stephen ignores the two well know facts about where Jacob and Joseph were buried and concentrates on the other patriarchs. The OT is completely silent about the final resting place of these men. The only reference in all of Scripture about where these patriarchs were buried comes from Stephen. They were buried in Shechem, not where Joseph was buried (on the piece of land bought by Jacob), but on the piece of land bought by Abraham. Just as the OT does not tell us about where the patriarchs were buried, why couldn't it also have been silent about this piece of land that Abraham bought? Why do commentators accept Stephen's words that the patriarchs were buried in Shechem, but then refuse to accept his explanation that they were buried on some land bought by Abraham? There is no textual proof to suggest that Stephen originally said Jacob and then later on some scribe, by mistake, wrote Abraham. No, Stephen speaking under the inspiration of the Holy Spirit reveals something that we would not have known by just reading the OT Scriptures. Rather than altering the text of Scripture, we should alter our own understanding and way of looking at these verses. Once again we need to defend the inspiration of the Bible and thus the absolute authority it speaks with—if we do not stand here, there will be nowhere to stand!

Acts 7:17

Stephen had been accused of speaking blasphemous words against
God and Moses. He thus spends the most time in his speech on he
life of Moses, showing great reverence for both Moses and Moses'
God. The promise to Abraham was to multiply his descendants and
give him a land, thus God began to greatly increase the Israelites.
This was amazing growth, but not impossible for God to do.

Acts 7:18, 19

This growth was noticeable to others and when Pharaoh noticed it
he became alarmed. The reason Joseph had been exalted to such a
position of authority was because the Pharaoh of his day had recognised God's hand upon him. This new Pharaoh is either ignorant of
this past history or else is deliberately fighting against the knowledge of it. From when this Pharaoh started his persecution of the
Jews, it was only a little over a hundred years before the mighty
Egyptian nation was brought to its knees (after the entire Egyptian
army was destroyed in the Exodus, see Ex. 14:27, 28).

To forget the goodness of God is to invite ruin upon yourself. This
is the same for individuals and nations—God has not changed.
Although God is merciful and long suffering we must not think
that because God does not judge immediately then He will not
judge. Wickedness will bring a nation to shame, but very few
believe this in our day. Wickedness does not just refer to murder,
theft, adultery, etc., but includes living as though God does not
exist: despising His law and rejecting His providence over all things.

This Pharaoh "who knew not Joseph" tried to reduce the number of
Jews by forcing them to do extremely hard labour, but this did not
work because it was God who was increasing their numbers. When
this failed, he told the midwives to kill the baby boys at birth (Ex.
1:15, 16) and when this also failed, he ordered all the new born
males to be thrown into the Nile river (Ex. 1:22). The reason Pharaoh did not just kick the Israelites out of the land and be rid of
them, was because he wanted to use them as slave workers. Surely it
seemed as though the Jews were finished as a nation once Pharaoh
set his heart to destroy them. We must always be mindful that our
lives and destinies are in the hand of God and that His promises
will be fulfilled—we need to learn how to rest with patient trust in
the providence of God. God's ways are not our ways and many

things will happen in a way that we will not understand, however, everything works together for our good (Rom. 8:28) and the advancing of God's Kingdom.

Acts 7:20

Moses was born in the midst of these dangerously critical times and we can understand this verse better when we take notice of the word in verse 19 that tells us the way Pharaoh dealt with the people. He was crafty or subtle. He sought to conquer them by subtle devices, or take advantage of them in a cunning way with cunning words. It could also quite possibly mean to deceive by persuading with sweet talk (as one Greek-Lexicon puts it). It is very possible that Pharaoh was not excessively harsh in the way he got the Hebrews to throw their baby sons into the river. The Hebrews were pressurised to do this, but not in a ruthless way (not like Herod's killing of the children when Jesus was an infant, Matt. 2:16f.). Rather, Pharaoh convinced the Hebrews that it would be in the best interests of the whole family if they got rid of new born boys on their own. It seems likely that the Hebrews were submitting to this decree from Pharaoh, for in Exodus 2:2 we are told that Moses' mother did not throw him into the river because of his great beauty. Three times in Scripture the exceptional beauty of Moses is mentioned (Ex. 2:2; Acts 7:20; Heb. 11:23). This beauty stopped Moses' parents from throwing him into the Nile to drown. Their faith (Heb. 11:23), which was very weak and only lasted three months, followed after they had been captured by his beauty. God used the physical beauty of Moses to preserve his life and strengthen the weak faith of his parents for a season.

Acts 7:21

Eventually the faith of Moses' parents fails and they cast him out and there is no excuse for their behaviour, however, in this way God brought Moses into the very same house as Pharaoh. Pharaoh was afraid that the Jews would help to bring about the downfall of Egypt by joining with an enemy. God organises it so Pharaoh ends up raising the man whom God would use to destroy the nation of Egypt—God makes fun of the wicked!

Acts 7:22

Moses was well educated and God's perspective was that he was mighty in word and deed. Moses' own perspective was that he was slow of speech and tongue (Ex. 4:10). It is one thing to have a humble opinion of your own abilities, however, this should never lead us to resist the will of God for us. Moses used his own low opinion of himself to refuse to do God's will and this made God angry (Ex. 4:14).

Acts 7:23

After forty years, the Spirit of God moved upon Moses to identify himself with his brethren. It was only by the grace of God that Moses could have given up what he had and rather identified himself with the Israelites (Heb. 11:24–27). The word "visit" here means to help someone in need with the purpose of assisting or relieving, rather than taking a casual trip to say, "Hi" (this is how it is used in the NT in all except one place, cf. Luke 1:68, 78; 7:16; Acts 15:14; Heb .2:6; Matt. 25:36, 43; Jam. 1:27). It was God's working in his heart which made him concerned about his brethren and led him to be their protector. As Hebrews 11:24–27 shows, Moses' loyalties lay with the Israelites—he was a man with a mission, and very aware of God's calling upon his life.

Acts 7:24

What are we to make of Moses' actions? Was this murder? Was it uncontrolled anger? Was Moses presuming to be someone he wasn't? Was he running ahead of God? Were these the actions of an immature man? Was this just stupid? A careful reading of the text will show that *none* of these is correct.

The word translated "avenged" is only used in this form six times in the NT and each time it is referring to God's justice and judgment (e.g., Luke 18:7, 8; 2 Cor. 7:11; 2 Thes. 1:8; 1 Pet. 2:14). It means to do justice to an injured and oppressed person, or to maintain the rights of the oppressed. The Holy Spirit, speaking through Stephen, tells us that Moses vindicated (did justice to) the oppressed Israelite. How did he maintain the rights of the oppressed man? By killing the Egyptian! The words in this verse do not lend support to the idea that Moses was a murderer, but rather that he had been ordained by God to be a judge and deliverer of Israel, comparable to Samson, Deborah, Ehud, Barak and Gideon (see the book of Judges). He was a judge, with special God given authority to do what he did. This was not taking the law into his own hands, nor are his actions to be confused with the modern heretical "Liberation Theology" teachings. Moses had the authority and courage to strike down the Egyptian because God had called him to this task.

Acts 7:25

This verse shows that Moses' actions were not a result of uncontrolled anger or doing something without thinking. The word "supposed" or "thought" is in the imperfect tense which speaks of continuous or repeated action in the past. Therefore, this supposing by Moses that his brethren understood what God was doing through him, was something he constantly thought about before this incident of killing the Egyptian. Moses believed (for some time), that his brethren knew that God was delivering Israel through his hand. "Was giving deliverance/salvation" is in the present tense and the implication is that Moses believed the Israelites knew that he would deliver them from their oppression and that by this action of killing the Egyptian, they would have realised that this deliverance had started. Moses' killing of the Egyptian was God beginning to deliver Israel. Moses had known for some time that God would deliver Israel by his hand, and Moses was under the impression, also for some time, that the Israelites knew this.

There is no evidence in Scripture to support the idea that Moses had prematurely entered his calling. The children of Israel rejected God's deliverer, even as they rejected Christ. This is Stephen's point! The Israelites in Egypt were in bondage, just as the Jews were in bondage to sin and Rome in Stephen's day, however, just as Moses, God's deliverer, was rejected, so Christ, God's deliverer, was also rejected.

The offer of deliverance from Egypt was a real offer. The fact that Israel did not move out of Egypt at this time does not prove that it was not the right time. In the same way, when Israel refused to enter into the Promised Land through unbelief, it did not mean that the offer was not real (Num. 14:3,6–9, 22, 23). Moses is nowhere condemned for killing the Egyptian, whereas the Israelites of his day are seen to be at fault, for we are told that they did not understand. The reason for not leaving then (forty00 years before they did) was due to their own envy and stubbornness.

Acts 7:26

This can either mean that Moses appeared suddenly or that he appeared in his official office as God's appointed deliverer. In this incident we see that the Jews did not just refuse to recognise Moses as God's judge, but wickedly rejected him and in doing this, despised the grace of God. These were two Hebrews who were fighting and the text seems to say that Moses authoritatively commanded them to be a peace with one another, rather than suggesting that they shouldn't fight. He spoke with the authority of his office that had been given to him by God. Moses calls on them to justify or account for their foolish behaviour—"Why do you wrong one another?"

Acts 7:27

It appears that Moses physically restrained the man who was abusing his neighbour. This man then thrust Moses away, both physically and verbally. Moses' office and authority are rejected with contempt (scorn). Although one man speaks to him in this way, the fact that the rest of the nation remained silent and did not rebuke this foolish person proves that he spoke for the whole nation. The whole nation is charged in verse 35 with the rejection of Moses and the whole nation (not Moses) remained in Egypt for another forty years of slavery. The words used in this rejection show that the Jews did not see Moses as just some interfering onlooker, but realised that Moses had assumed a position of authority and had intervened from this authoritative position, speaking as their judge. They did not reject his advice, but his *office*—his position of authority which they saw as self-imposed. This was a costly mistake, because God had raised up Moses for such as time, and such stubbornness made them wait another forty years before God moved again to deliver them. We must never think that because God is sovereign our actions are meaningless. We are responsible at all times to walk in obedience to the Word of God and there are consequences attached to all our actions—which either receive God's blessing or judgement. We do not know God's secret will or plans, but we do know our responsibilities and thus we are to do what we know, rather than wonder about what we do not know (Deut. 29:29).

Acts 7:28

According to Stephen, the Hebrews knew about the incident (of killing the Egyptian). This should have made them realize that Moses was acting under God's authority, instead they use the incident as a basis for rejecting him. The startling thing was *not* that other Hebrews knew about the killing of the Egyptian, for such an incident would naturally have spread amongst the oppressed slaves. The thing that disturbed Moses was that the Hebrews were prepared to use this knowledge as a weapon against him. Moses was a highly educated, mature statesman. He had an intimate and comprehensive understanding about Pharaoh, Egyptian politics, military capabilities and the official policy towards the slaves. Moses was not a fool who wanted to die. He was not trying to single-handedly overthrow the might of Egypt.

When Moses openly showed his commitment to the slaves, he showed in a very clear way (as we are told in Heb. 11:24f.), that he had turned his back on his amazingly privileged position, closing the door very firmly to his future in Egyptian politics and Egyptian privileges. It is not impossible that Moses might have become the next Pharaoh of Egypt. All this the Hebrews should have realised! The slaves were no match for the Egyptian army, thus Moses was not trying to get out of Egypt in either his own strength or the strength of the slaves. It should have been obvious that this high ranking "Egyptian" was being moved by God and he would only have exposed himself in such a bold way, if God's deliverance had arrived—this is Stephen's point!.

What did these slaves have to gain in spreading the news about killing the Egyptian in the way that they did? Moses was shocked that this man knew about what he had done, probably because this was in another area of the huge slave camp. Moses concluded that if this news had already spread so quickly, then even Pharaoh would know about it (Ex. 2:14). Moses realised that the Jews despised him and that they were using this information to destroy him. Even if the Jews did not realize that their deliverance had begun, what justifiable reason was there for them to despise Moses? What could they possibly have gained by hurtfully spreading what Moses had done?

Moses was a Hebrew in a powerful political position—quite possibly the next Pharaoh. He was not only in an influential position, but mature enough to make a difference (forty years old). He was the only person in a position to realistically change the harsh Egyptian policy towards the Hebrews. Moses had not only shown himself to be on the Hebrews' side, but totally committed to helping them. The Hebrews should have been laying down their lives to protect such a man, yet instead, they are trying to bring harm upon him. This does not make sense, but then sin never does make sense—it is utter foolishness! These Hebrews were in rebellion against God and under His wrath. The only explanation for this behavior towards Moses, is envy. Envious people seek to destroy, hurt or bring down those who are better than themselves in some way. The envious person is not necessarily trying to advance themselves when they destroy someone else—their reward is seeing the downfall of the one they envy.

Stephen had just said that the other "savior," Joseph, had been envied by his brothers (Acts 7:9). The Hebrews' "savior" in Egypt, Moses, was also envied by the Jews and thus rejected. We are told that the ultimate Savior, Jesus Christ, was rejected and murdered because of envy (Matt. 27:18). "Envy rots the bones" (Prov. 14:30). "Wrath is cruel, and anger is outrageous; but who can stand before envy?" (Prov. 27:4). I think Stephen is making a very pointed accusation against those he is speaking to. They were no different from their fathers who envied and rejected Joseph and Moses and preferred worshipping idols to serving the true God (Ezk. 20:7, 8).

Acts 7:29

Moses flees from Egypt, leaving behind all his riches and comfort, though he had already forsaken all of this when God moved upon him to visit his brethren (verse 23). This was not a judgment on Moses—he was no worse off now than he would have been if Israel had followed him. He was no worse off now than he was when Israel did follow him forty years later. Moses was a stranger in the land of Midian, but this was no different than the kind of life that Abraham, Isaac and Jacob had lived. Moses in fact came into contact with a good family. He had a job, a wife, children and freedom. On the other hand, the Hebrews who stayed in Egypt had another forty years of severe bondage and slavery (oppressed by both Pharaoh and their own idolatry, Ezk. 20:5ff.). They had rejected God's deliverer and this became a characteristic of the nation of Israel throughout her history—not recognising, but rejecting the ones God kept sending to them.

Stephen was giving a very clear warning to these religious leaders, saying, even Moses (the greatest figure in the OT) was rejected by the nation of Israel, thus they had better make sure that they do not do the same thing and reject the one God had raised up to be their deliverer and Savior. The generation that rejected Moses, died in Egypt. How much worse wouldn't it be for those who rejected Christ? (Matt. 23:37–39).

In my opinion, Hebrew 11:27 refers to this time when Moses left Egypt. Others believe that it refers to the Exodus because it says that Moses *feared* that Pharaoh knew about what he had done and they say, fear is incompatible with faith (Ex. 2:14,1 5). However, Exodus does not say Moses left because he feared Pharaoh and I believe the writer of Hebrews is making it clear that Moses was not motivated by fear when he left Egypt to dwell in Midian, but rather by faith. The New English Bible's translation of Hebrew 11:27 says, "By faith he left Egypt, and not because he feared the king's anger".

Moses had been called by God and anointed by the Spirit for the task of delivering Israel. This resulted in identifying himself with the despised slaves, rejecting the privileges of Egypt and killing the Egyptian. Yet when Israel rejected God's deliverance, Moses did not try and manufacture something himself, but had the faith to wait upon the timing of God. There is no Scriptural basis for thinking that it is always sinful to suddenly fear when you are confronted with a terrible situation. If a gun is suddenly stuck in your face or if the kgb suddenly arrived at your door, there is nothing sinful about the fear that will more than likely grip your heart in such circumstances. However, when this fear blocks your trust in the providence of God and your life becomes governed by it rather than by faith, then this becomes sinful. Moses was suddenly gripped with fear when this accusation was sprung upon him, yet it was not fear that caused him to leave Egypt, but faith—he trusted that God would preserve his life and bring about the fulfilment of that calling God had placed upon his life. He also believed that God would shortly fulfill His promises to Abraham. God was in complete control and Moses left everything in God's hands, knowing that faithful was He who called him, who would also bring it to pass (1 Thes. 5:24).

Acts 7:30

It was God's plan to let forty years go past. When Moses was eighty
years old God appeared to him in the wilderness of Mount Sinai
(Horeb and Sinai appear to be terms that are interchangeable, cf.
Ex. 3:1). This revelation of God as a flame of fire in a bush was
brought about by a manifestation of the angel of the Lord, who is
not a created being, but rather the Second Person of the Trinity.
This angel says He is God (Ex. 3:6, cf. verse 4). Moses was afraid to
look upon God (the flame) and due to the presence of God (in the
flame of fire) the place was said to be holy (verse 5). A distinction is
made between God and the one who speaks from the burning
bush, yet the one who speaks, speaks with the voice of the Lord
(Acts 7:31), He claims to be God (verse 32), and is called *the Lord*
(verse 33). This angel speaks and acts like God and yet is clearly distinguished as a different person. Appearances of the angel of the
Lord are mentioned many times in the OT (e.g., Ex. 23:20, 21;
Num. 22:31; Josh. 5:14f.) and these can only be understood when
we see them as manifestations of Christ before He became a man
(John 1:1, 2, 14).

Acts 7:31

Moses, drawn by his curiosity towards the burning bush, was then
addressed by God. He did not see God or see any form of God. He
saw the fire and heard God's voice. Nor did Moses decide on his
own what the meaning of the burning bush was—its meaning was
explained to him by God.

Acts 7:32

God addresses Moses by His covenant name and shows that this
revelation to Moses is a continuation of God's one covenant of
redemption promised to Abraham. The revelation Moses was
about to receive was based upon what had gone before and the reason for the deliverance of Israel from Egypt rested upon God's
faithfulness to His promises to Abraham, Isaac and Jacob. God does
not keep changing His mind, but rather God gives more and more
revelation (unfolding His one plan) and the new revelation can
only be understood as it is seen in the light of what had been given
earlier. The faithful covenant-keeping God who watches over His
Word was the one who was speaking to Moses. God had promised
to make Abraham's offspring into a great multitude. He had prom-

ised to give them a land. He had promised to deliver them from Egypt. The fact that God used this title for Himself spoke also of the reality of eternal life with Him, for He was not claiming to be the God of those who were dead and no longer existed—God who had been the God of these patriarchs while they walked on earth, still calls Himself their God after their death. God was still in a covenant relationship with the patriarchs, but how could this be if they no longer existed? Death in this life is not the end. An eternal, personal relationship exists between God and His children and what we experience on earth is but a taste of that glorious relationship we will forever have with the Lord (this was Jesus' point in Matt. 22:32). God had not forgotten Abraham, nor was He unaware of the suffering Israel was going through in Egypt.

This fear that Moses had, was good and healthy and ought to char-acterise our relationship with the Lord. God was being gracious to Moses in giving him this sign of the fire in the bush. Its purpose was to prepare Moses for the task that lay ahead for which he needed much reverence for God and boldness to stand for the truth of God (cf. Ex. 20:20).

Acts 7:33

This verse is central to Stephen's argument in defence of the Chris-tian faith, namely, there was holy ground outside Israel. This is added to Stephen's previous observations that God revealed Him-self to Abraham in Mesopotamia and watched over and exalted Joseph in Egypt—places all far from Jerusalem and the holy land. This piece of ground in Sinai, was holy ground since God was revealing Himself there (i.e., His presence was made known). There is no place on earth that is holy in and of itself. The Jews Stephen was speaking to believed that Jerusalem had now become holy in and of itself. They refused to obey God, but gloried in His temple.

The full revelation of God has now come, as bright as the noon-day. This is because Christ has fully revealed the Father to us. God's presence is everywhere, thus in one sense all the ground in the whole world is holy, and belongs to the Lord—this means God is to be reverenced, feared and obeyed wherever we are. Removing one's shoes was an outward sign of reverence based upon the awareness of one's own personal defilement and fearful realization of one's complete unworthiness to stand in the presence of such a holy God. This same understanding should always be part of out thinking when we look at ourselves. The only reason we are accepted is because we stand before God in Christ Jesus. We have His merit and His merit alone and thus we can confidently come into the presence of God. We should ever be mindful of the God before whom we stand, for too often we forget His power and holiness. Putting off of the shoes symbolised man's complete unworthiness before God (in every aspect of his being). All of our thoughts and actions are unworthy and we need to acknowledge this and then draw all our wisdom from God's revelation—the Scriptures alone being the final authority showing what is and isn't of God.

We do not need to take our shoes off, but we need to live in such a way that manifests what the taking off of the shoes symbolised. Are we walking around in this world confident about our own ideas or do we strip ourselves naked of our own wisdom and live by every Word from the mouth of God? Do we at all times bring every thought into obedience to Christ's revelation? Do we acknowledge the unworthiness of our whole being and therefore cast ourselves completely upon the mercy and wisdom of God? We are not just meant to "take our shoes off" when we attend a worship service or a Bible study, but we are to walk at all times with the awareness that we are in the presence of the Lord and thus we are always on holy ground. Not to live in this way is to invite the displeasure of God. Removing of the shoes symbolised the putting away all impurity— the feet are particularly exposed to such things (cf. John 13:10). What is impurity? It is walking contrary to the revelation of God— which means walking in rebellion to the revelation of God. To walk in holiness means bringing our thinking into line with God's mind all day long. It is only by knowing the Scriptures that we can be sure that we are doing this and not following our own ideas and traditions.

Acts 7:34

Stephen is exalting Moses in these verses. Moses was specifically chosen by God for the purpose of delivering His people. God had chosen Moses for the task, God was sending Moses and God was going to deliver His people. Stephen had been accused of blaspheming against Moses, but we see nothing but a very high view of Moses' authority in Stephen's words. Human terms are used for our own benefit—God came down and saw. It is not necessary for God to do anything in order to find out what is happening (Ps. 139:1–

12), but such language makes us more aware of God's direct involvement (something we should be conscious of but due to our weakness, we often forget or ignore this fact). We are not only told of God's knowledge of all things and His compassion, but also of His desire and power to act on behalf of His people. God was not just going to sit on the sideline and shout encouragement to Moses, rather, He was going to be the one doing the delivering. We need to become more conscious about God's direct involvement in our own lives and in all things—it is God who is working in us both to will and to do of His good pleasure (Phil. 2:13). It is in Him that we live and move and have our being (Acts 17:28). The victory is His and we are on His side.

Acts 7:35

Here Stephen confirms what he was saying in verse 25: that Moses was their deliverer back then and Israel rejected him (which led to them being in slavery for another forty years). Stephens's main point though, in this verse, is to show his high regard for Moses and also to show how his own generation had rejected Christ in the way that Moses was rejected by his generation. This was just another way of saying what Jesus Himself had said to the Jews, that if they really believed Moses they would have believed in Him (John 5:46). Just as Joseph's brothers had rejected him as their ruler and yet God had appointed him to his position of authority, so too, Israel had rejected Moses even though God had appointed him to be their ruler and deliverer. As we have noted already, the parallel between Moses and Christ is very obvious. The Jewish nation's greatest longing was for a deliverer or redeemer (Luke 24:21). Israel longed for this in Egypt, and the Jews in Stephens' day longed for it, however, both rejected their God appointed redeemers. The apostles had said the very same thing to the council in Acts 5:30, 31. There is no getting away from the centrality of Christ and submission to Him and His teachings.

Acts 7:36

Stephen says, proof that Moses was God's appointed leader and redeemer is found in the wonders and signs that were done through him (see Ex. 4:1 cf. verses 3, 5). This leader that Israel rejected, accomplished the task he was sent to do, namely, to deliver Israel from her bondage. The signs that Moses did, covered a significant period of time—for more than forty years and were truly amazing (all the mighty signs in Egypt, the passage through the Red Sea, Egypt's destruction in the Sea and the numerous other signs throughout the wilderness wanderings). Despite all of this, Israel still stubbornly resisted and even rejected Moses. Stephen's parallel is once again Christ, whose mighty signs showed that God had indeed sent Him to redeem His people (Acts 2:22). There could be no getting away from the fact that God had sent Moses and nor could the Jews in Stephen's day deny the reality of the mighty deeds that Jesus had done—which as we have seen, were proof that God had sent Him to redeem Israel. These leaders were not ignorant of the mighty works done by Jesus (John 11:45–47; 15:24; Matt. 9:34; 12:24ff.), but their hatred for God and their rebellion against Him caused them to suppress the truth.

The mighty works of God need to be interpreted by God. God, through Moses, interpreted the signs that were done in Egypt, or else Israel wouldn't have understood their meaning. If we do not have God's explanation of something then we can make up many different meanings for it. Peter also explained the meaning of the manifestation of the Spirit by divine revelation (Acts 2:16). All mighty works and signs must find their explanations from divine revelation (Scripture) and not from our own subjective desires and ideas.

Acts 7:37

The primary way that God made known His will to Israel was through His prophets. Jesus Christ was the ultimate revelation of God and His will. Moses never claimed to have given the final revelation of God and His will, rather Moses spoke of another prophet who would come after him (Deut. 18:15) whom the Jews were looking for as the ultimate prophet (John 6:14; 7:40). Moses had said that they must listen to this prophet. God, speaking from heaven at the transfiguration said listen to Christ (Mark 9:7; Matt. 17:5). These Jewish leaders were accusing Stephen of blaspheming Moses and the law, however Moses had said listen to Christ, thus these leaders were in rebellion against Moses since they refused to listen to Jesus. Stephen was preaching in the name of Jesus, and teaching only that which Jesus had taught, yet they refused to listen to him. Although they said they were trying to defend Moses and his teachings, they in fact never believed Moses, for if they had

believed Moses they would have believed Christ (John 5:45–47).
Stephen was saying, that as Israel in the days of old rejected Moses,
so too they reject him when they reject Christ whom he clearly
spoke about. The fact that Moses pointed to another teacher shows
that he was aware that he had not said the last word—God's full
revelation had not yet been given. Thus it was foolish for these Jewish leaders to be offended by the changes brought about through
Christ. When the reality came, it was to be expected that the shadows and signs that pointed to it would have served their purpose.
Christ was not opposed to Moses, any more than an object is
opposed to its shadow. There are differences between an object and
its shadow, but you cannot separate them. A shadow presents a true
picture of its object, though not a full picture. The temple and the
ceremonial law of Moses pointed to Christ and so with the arrival
of the Messiah, these necessarily fell away. What they represented
did not fall away, for they represented Christ and His work of
redemption. Stephen says, how foolish you are to say Moses is your
only teacher, when Moses himself said another prophet was coming
who would say more than Moses had said. The fact that Moses said,
"Hear Him," meant that this coming prophet would say things that
Moses never said—bringing greater revelation. The religious leaders were using Moses against Stephen, yet it was Moses who supported Stephen. It was the religious leaders, not Stephen, who were
dishonouring Moses, for *they* rejected the One Moses predicted
would come.

Acts 7:38

God's people are here called the church in the wilderness. The word
"church" in the NT is used for any assembly of people, whether religious or political. Here it is obviously the religious gathering of
God's children that is meant. That same Angel that spoke to Moses
from the burning bush (see verse 30 above) was with him in the
wilderness and it was Moses who was the mediator between the
Angel and the people. It was the Angel who was guiding and
instructing the children of Israel, but this was done through Moses
(Ex. 23:20; Num. 20:16). As we have seen, this Angel was Christ and
as Christ was with the OT church, so He is with the NT church. He
is still the only guide, teacher, savior, and defender of His church,
though we now all have direct access to Christ and through Him,

access to the throne of God. We need no mediator other than Christ (1 Tim. 2:5).

Living oracles: we learn that fullness of life is found in obeying the Word of God (Deut. 30:19–20; 32:46–47). The Words of the living God are themselves life-giving (Rom. 7:10, 12, 14; 1 Pet. 1:23; Matt. 19:17). The problem is not with the law, but with sinful people who oppose the law. Such Words did not originate with Moses, but with God. Moses was merely the one who received them from God and was commissioned to pass them on to God's people. The Jews were said to have had a privileged position because they had received the living oracles of God (Rom. 3:2). These oracles had come to them through the hand of Moses.

The Jews prided themselves in the fact that they were the ones who had the truth—and they had received it in the wilderness, far away from Jerusalem and the temple. Stephen's high regard for Moses is clearly seen when he says, Moses' words are the very Words of God, thus how could his accusers say that he was opposing Moses? It was not possible for Stephen to give Moses greater respect than this.

Christ is the living heart of the law. It is only in Christ that the law can be said to be living. To deny the essence of the law (Christ) leaves you with a dead letter that brings death. It is only when we believe in Christ and are made new creatures by the power of God that our position with respect to the law is changed. The law then stops being a weight of condemnation hanging over us and becomes our wisdom and light for a blessed life.

Acts 7:39

Despite priding themselves in these great privileges that God had given to them (the living Word and the many miraculous signs of God's power), the Jews in the wilderness rebelled against God and therefore, rejected Moses. Despite the bitter memory of slavery and oppression that was very fresh in their minds, they still longed to return to Egypt. They felt it was better to be an Egyptian slave than the Lord's freeman. These Jews were not wanting to be treated badly again, but longed for the pagan, idolatrous way of life that they had become accustomed to in Egypt. If we are not guided totally by the Word of God, then we will allow that which we are familiar with to be our guide—and what we are familiar with is rebellion against God (see *Faith and Reason*, chapters 3 and 4). The

Jews did not want God to be their guide and provider. They did not want God's Word to be their standard for all things. They hated God's will for them so much that their hearts turned back to Egypt, preferring Pharaoh's future for them, rather than the future God had promised and was working out for them. In our day people still prefer the bondage of sin and the bondage of oppressive governments to the law of God (see *Muse Time*, paper 15). For many people God's law is an evil thing to be avoided at all costs! They comfort themselves by saying that they like God, but then they "create" Him after their own image and decide on their own authority what is and isn't God's will. To do this is to reject God and to turn back into the pits of bondage and death. Everyone wants the blessings of God, but they want them on their own terms. They want the many benefits that come from the law of God, but *they* want to decide what that law should be like.

The children of God in the wilderness continued to "thrust away" Moses, even after all the amazing signs and wonders that had been performed through his hands (all the signs in Egypt, the Red Sea crossing, the daily provision of manna and the provision of water, the cloud during the day to protect them from the sun and the pillar of fire at night, etc.). Despite all of this, they thrust him away, just as that first Israelite had done (Acts 7:27).

Acts 7:40, 41

The Israelites wanted the benefits that God alone could give, however they wanted the final say about God's character and law—they wanted to be in control in this very important area. These people did not want to submit completely to God's revelation for their lives and all things. The Jews in Stephen's day also wanted God's benefits, but on their own terms. They rejected the clear revelation of God from Moses and from Christ, yet they were accusing Stephen of blasphemy.

Stephen shows in these two verses that Israel wanted to determine on her own how to worship God and the way of relating to Him. Their thinking was that whatever *they* thought about God, or whatever *they* did in His name, should make Him grateful: they were doing Him a favour. In this way, they could be in control—which is the ultimate desire of the sinful heart.

The children of Israel were delivered out of Egypt by a manifestation of God's power and might (Ps. 105:23–45; 78:12–16, 43–51). They crossed the Red Sea, which once again was an awesome manifestation of God's grace, strength and judgement. They saw the whole Egyptian army destroyed before their eyes (Ex. 14:22–31; Ps. 78:53). These people all saw the great works of God and feared His name. God gave them food and drink and preserved them from their enemies (Ex. 16–18). God descended upon Mount Sinai in awesome power (Ex. 19:16–18) and all the people saw this glorious, terrifying manifestation (Ex. 20:18).

Moses then went up into this thick cloud on Mount Sinai to speak with the Lord. However, he was up on the mountain a long time and the people feared that Moses had died in the midst of God's terrifying power. The children of Israel, who could still see the presence of the Lord upon the mountain, decided to make some images of *this* God who had brought them out of Egypt (Ex. 32:1). By making these golden idols they were not looking to serve another god, but the same God whom they had been following (Ex. 32:4). What they wanted was something to look at when they worshipped, and something to go in front of them when they moved to a different location. They wanted to picture God and thus they chose an animal to represent His power and strength—which they had witnessed. The image of a bull was, they thought, a good and fitting symbol of God's strength and they believed they were honouring Him. This, however, was not only an insult to the Lord, but it also deceived and corrupted the people (Ex. 32:7, see too, *Faith and Reason,* chapter 5).

Very few people will blatantly condemn God. Most people retain (according to their own standards) some sort of respect for God, and by this they believe that they have done what is required of them. However, the Lord demands complete obedience to every Word that proceeds from His mouth and nothing less will satisfy Him.

The same struggle, seen in the days of Moses, and in the days of Stephen, continues in our day—who is going to be the source of our law and thus lord of everything we do and think? Is it going to be God and His Word, or is it going to be man's own ideas, traditions and wisdom? In other words, is man going to submit to the true God, or is he going to make a god after his own image? This battle will continue to the end of time. We need to open our hearts to God's Word and Spirit so that we might only live according to His Word.

Acts 7:42

Even at the height of the miraculous beginnings of the nation's history (the abundance of signs and wonders, and manifestations of the power of God) even here there was persistent foolish rebellion against the truth. The presence of God with His people couldn't have been clearer, yet their hearts resisted what they knew to be true. Stephen shows that Israel had always been bound in superstition, rebellion and will worship, refusing to follow the Lord according to His revelation. As a result of this persistent, foolish hatred of God (despite God's abundant favor and goodness that had been showered upon them), He turned away from them and thus became their enemy. When the restraining power and grace of God are removed from a nation or individual, they are then controlled by their natural corruption. Any act of righteousness, no matter how small, comes only from the grace of God and when this grace is removed, people are then controlled completely by their sinful natures (see *Faith and Reason*, chapters 3 and 4). When God "gives people up," He does not merely allow them to do evil things, but condemns and judges them by giving them up to blindness and perverse actions (cf. Rom. 1:24, 26, 28). God actively hands such people over to their wicked lusts (see comments on John 7:33, 34).

Such a horrifying situation does not happen in an instant and thus it should be a warning to our hearts to be true to the whole counsel of God. We must not be fooled into the belief that as long as we *mostly* follow the revelation of God, then those "small" areas where we still want to live by our own standards, will not affect us. Rebellion and unbelief do not stand still—they are never satisfied with only a little. If we do not deal ruthlessly with all that which would oppose the Word and will of God (Matt. 5:29, 30) then it is like putting a fire within our pocket and thinking that we will not get burned (Prov. 6:27). Error and truth cannot remain in the same place—they are at war with one another and each one seeks the complete destruction of the other. To consciously hold to that which you know to be against the revelation of God (no matter how small), means that self-deception is *already* at work in your thinking. You are thinking that God's law and will for us are not where true liberty is found and thus you refuse to submit to Him. If you do not deal with such a situation by the grace of God, you will be carried away and entangled by much superstitious foolishness—this is how God judges those who refuse to obey His Word (2 Thes. 2:11, 12 see too Ezk. 20:24, 25).

Such verses ought to produce Godly fear in us (Luke 12:4, 5; 2 Cor. 7:1; Phil. 2:12), which in turn should show us how desperately dependant we are upon the Lord for His grace and enabling in order to walk in obedience. This realization should cause us to cast ourselves upon Him for He is the only source for our wisdom and ability—He supplies the knowledge "how to" and the strength "to do." We need to look to God's Word alone with the help of the Spirit to lead us into all truth. We ought to be aware of our stubbornness in refusing to submit to the *whole* counsel of God. We need to allow the Word and the Spirit to search our hearts and show us where we are living in rebellion and self-deception. We need to be constantly washed by the reading and hearing of the Word and constantly renewed in our minds (Rom. 12:2) so that we might truly love the Lord with all our heart, soul, mind and strength (Mark 12:29, 30). The wise listen to the warnings of the Lord and respond to His correction, but fools take no notice, and being filled with pride and stubbornness, rush on to destruction (Prov. 5:11–14; 10:17; 12:1; 13:1; 15:5).

God here gave His people over to the worship of heavenly bodies, since they refused to bring their thoughts about Him into line with His revelation. As we saw above (40, 41), they did not want another God, but wanted to worship the true God in their own way. Stephen quotes from Amos (5:25–27), possibly with Jeremiah also in mind (25:9–12). Although the people did offer sacrifices in the wilderness, their hearts were not sincere, and they were in rebellion against the law of God, therefore, these sacrifices were not to the Lord, but to idols. Stephen says the idolatry and rebellion of Israel started from the very beginning (Ezk. 20:5–26; Jer. 11:7, 8). The people of Judah were conquered by the king of Babylon and taken as captives into Babylon because of this kind of rebellion (2 Kings 24:10–16; Hab. 1:6), yet this rebellion had continued even after they returned from Babylon. There was one common thread that united Israel from its beginning—rebellion against God's revelation.

Acts 7:43

Moses would not have tolerated open, blatant worship of Moloch any more than he tolerated the worship of the golden calf (Ex. 32:19, 25–29). The people would certainly not have been allowed to worship their idols in the tabernacle of God, nor is God's tabernacle here being called the tabernacle of Moloch (the true tabernacle is spoken of highly in verse 44). It seems best to understand this to mean that the people continued to secretly carry little tabernacles for their idols among their own private possessions. The worship of small shrines was a common practice in these lands—even in NT times (Acts 19:24, 27). Moloch was the Ammonite God (1 Kings 11:7—king Solomon built altars to this god). It was a huge brass image with outstretched arms and the people would heat this image and then worship by throwing children onto the glowing arms to be burned to death. Although the children of Israel were not worshipping Moloch like this in the wilderness, they were still worshipping this god. However, later on, even though this was forbidden in the law of Moses (Lev. 18:21; 20:2–5), Israel did worship Moloch by burning their children (2 Kings 21:6; 2 Chron. 28:3; Ezk. 16:20, 21). Yet even this horrific rebellion of these kings had not reached full maturity—Israel's rebellion would get worse (cf. 44). This emphasises the point made above, that sin does not stand still, but becomes more and more consistent with itself (i.e., more and more sinful). Persistent sin will brand (or burn) the conscience so that it becomes completely insensitive to sin (1 Tim. 4:2).

When we see wicked deeds, we are often shocked and wonder how a person could bring himself to do such things. We must not underestimate the fact that sin, if not dealt with, will mature over time. Many people who might have been horrified by some activity in the past, later find themselves freely doing that very thing and no longer being horrified by it. Why? Because sin has taken its natural course and matured. Every individual and nation either moves towards righteousness or it moves towards unrighteousness—all are going to mature in one way or the other. Jesus said, "If you are not for Him, then you are against Him" (Matt. 12:30); there can be no standing still! We either increase in our rebellion or in our obedience. To resist the truth is to choose the path of rebellion and to continue to rebel will mature and strengthen your rebellion. Thus, to harden one's heart against the conviction of the Word and Spirit is a serious thing to do (Heb. 3:15; 4:7, see too comments on John 12:40).

The rest of this verse (Acts 7:43) tells us more about the images that Israel secretly carried with them. I do not believe that these are names of other gods, but rather *descriptions* of the images of Moloch that they carried. Just as the true and living God had a tabernacle, so too did the false gods. However, when the true God's presence was in the tabernacle there was great glory and bright light/fire (Ex. 40:34, 35, compare this with Solomon's temple in 1 Kings 8:10, 11). Thus, while one could imitate the tabernacle of the Lord, it was impossible to imitate the supernatural glory of God that filled His tabernacle. However, the pagans always tried to create an atmosphere of "glory" by making their idols with shining metals and stones (gold and silver and precious stones). Stephen had already said in verse 42 that the Israelites were worshipping the stars and planets in the heavens and in this verse he is not signalling out which of these he means. Rather, he is exposing the foolishness of the man made "glory" that these images had. He says, "The *star* (i.e., glory, brightness) of your god, [the] *remphan* (i.e., burning, fire, light) of your images, which YOU MADE to worship." They not only had to make and carry their god, but they had to make his artificial glory also (the Greek translation of the OT and Stephen's quotation of Amos 5:26 are both in agreement with the Hebrew Scriptures. We no longer have definite proof about the meaning of the Greek word "remphan" and thus we must not think it is a change made to the Hebrew text, but find its meaning from the Hebrew. See Parkhurst's Hebrew Lexicon, cf. Keil and Delitze on Amos and Lenski on Acts). For this foolish stubborn rebellion, God said He would carry them beyond Babylon. In Amos the prophet said that God would carry them beyond Damascus—this happened to the 10 northern tribes of Israel (2 Kings 17:23), but then 100 years later, He carried the southern tribes of Judah to Babylon (2 Kings 24:10ff.). Stephen here reminds them of the more recent judgment on Judah.

Acts 7:44

The children of Israel in the wilderness worshipped this artificial glory of gold and precious stones, while the true glory of God in the tabernacle was in their midst—how foolish can people get? Stephen's point throughout his whole speech is to always draw the parallel with Christ. The generation that Stephen was speaking to, also despised the true glory of God that was in their midst and pre-ferred their own man-made religion and worship. The flesh of Christ became the Temple of God on earth (John 1:14; 2:19) and the glory of the Lord filled this tabernacle as in the days of old. John says, "We beheld His glory" (John 1:14). The nation of Israel, how-ever, preferred to worship the image of God made in their own minds, rather than the clearest manifestation of God that had been given to man—the Person of Jesus Christ who walked and taught in their midst (Col. 2:9; John 8:19; 14:7). If the actions of the children of Israel in the wilderness were madness, how much worse were not the actions of those who set their hearts on destroying the true glory of God so that they could continue to worship the false man-made "glory" that they loved so much? The Israelites in the wilder-ness, despite their rebellion and foolishness, never reached the level where they waged war on the tabernacle of God that was with them, yet Stephen's generation did (John 1:14 cf. 5:18). The Israel-ites in the wilderness rebelled against the tabernacle that pictured Christ, whereas Stephen's accusers destroyed The True Tabernacle. As the tabernacle in the wilderness was a witness against that rebel-lious generation, Christ was an even greater witness against those who rejected Him—for He was greater than the temple (Matt. 12:6). Who would have thought that this "childish" hanging onto some images in the wilderness while following the true God would eventually mature to the stage where the children of God would murder the Messiah? Sin will mature!

Acts 7:45

Israel had the tabernacle with them wherever they went in their wil-derness wanderings. When they stopped in a place, they would put it up and when they moved on, it would be taken down and carried with them. It was not only a clear sign of the very real presence of God with them all the time, but was also a picture of God's constant desire and provision for their salvation and prosperity. These things were forever before the eyes of the Israelites in the wilderness, yet they refused to submit to the covenant God had made with them—loving instead, to worship their worthless idols (Acts 7:39–43).

The tabernacle, which Moses had made according to the exact requirements of God, was passed onto the next generation (the first generation that came out of Egypt, died in the wilderness because of their rebellion, nevertheless, God's presence was still with them as they wandered around the wilderness). This next generation, under the leadership of Joshua, inherited the tabernacle of God, and with the tabernacle leading them, went into the land that was possessed by the Gentiles. God did not only give Israel some land, but He gave them land that was possessed by other nations, meaning these nations were *dis*possessed as Israel inherited it. These other nations were all idol worshipers, and Israel, with the tabernacle of the True God leading them, cast these people out of their lands (defeating them and their idols), yet Israel continued to be dedicated to their secret idols.

The Jews saw Stephen's doctrine about the destruction of the temple as the destruction of God, but it is heathen gods that are restricted to manifesting themselves only in their temples. Stephen has made it very clear that the True God is in no way restricted to this—He had revealed Himself, without a temple in many places, e.g., Ur, Haran, Egypt, Midian (burning bush), and the wilderness. The Jews had so united the Jerusalem temple and God that they now believed that if the temple disappeared then God would be gone too. However, Stephen's point was that even when God used the tabernacle as a place where He revealed Himself, this was first done in the wilderness. For thirty-eight years, the tabernacle did not even cross into the Promised Land and even when it eventually did cross over, it had no *fixed* resting place. Stephen says, based upon the Scriptural evidence, there was no basis for the Jews to demand that the Jerusalem temple was forever going to be the center of religious life and the only place where God could or would reveal Himself—this was presumption and madness.

From Moses to David God dwelt with His people in a movable tent, which was taken from place to place. For *hundreds of years* the tabernacle, which was not based in Jerusalem was all that Israel had. It was with this tabernacle that God conquered the pagan nations and then gave Israel complete victory and dominion over their enemies in David's time. These Jews that had put Stephen on trial, acted as though the God of heaven and earth would cease to exist if the Jerusalem temple was destroyed. What they were trying desperately to defend, however, was their man-made image and worship of God. They were not defending the Triune God of the universe, but an idol fashioned according to their own liking.

Acts 7:46, 47

Was God desperately in need of a temple in order to be propped up as God? Was the temple crucial to His plans and His sovereign rule? Was it impossible to relate to, serve and worship God without the temple? Such things were implied in the attitude of these Jewish leaders.

Stephen says, "Why do not we look at the facts"! David was loved by God and greatly blessed by Him. David also had a very strong desire to build the Lord a wonderful temple (1 Kings 8:18, 19; Ps. 132:1–5), yet the Lord was not in a desperate need for a temple or else He would have made this known (2 Sam. 7:6, 7). Thus, it was delayed by God until king Solomon's time—clearly showing that the temple was not essential (it was David though, who collected much of the material and received the plans for it from God, 1 Kings 7:51; 1 Chron. 22; 28:11—29:5).

Acts 7:48–50

Even Solomon himself, who constructed the most glorious temple in the history of the nation of Israel, openly declared after completing the building that God does not dwell in man-made temples (1 Kings 8:27). God not only said this through Solomon, but also through Isaiah, whom Stephen now quotes. Isaiah, speaking more than 250 years after Solomon clearly shows that God did not always intend to have a temple in Jerusalem. Isaiah 66:2 tell us that it was God's intention to dwell in human hearts (cf. 57:15) and that the ceremonial laws, which God Himself had instituted for a season, would be changed by God Himself. The destruction of the temple would be God's doing, however this would not mean the end of the worship of God. The prophet says to follow the old rituals after their change (Heb. 7:27; 9:12, 26; 10:9, 10) would be as offensive to God as idolatry (Isa. 66:3). Stephen is now showing the Biblical support for his position. He is not condemning earthly temples in and of themselves, but condemning the idea that God can be restricted to and satisfied with them for all time—God dwells in heaven and on earth. God cannot be limited in any way and He is everywhere at the same time—the whole world is His temple. The Jews had come to place an unbiblical significance upon the temple and come to think that it was the permanent home of God. God had promised to always be with His people and wherever they are,

He will be. Despite this, Stephen was accused of blasphemy for saying the Jerusalem temple was not essential.

The temple and tabernacle were only ever meant to be signs and were given because of man's weakness—the sign confirmed the promise of God that He would be with His people. God could never be worshipped by the sign in and of itself. The temple, no less than all the ceremonies, pointed to a spiritual reality and it was only as the people entered into that spiritual reality by faith that their physical ceremonies had any worth with God (it is the same with baptism and the Lord's Supper). God has never been pleased with the physical worship of ceremonies, temples, objects and bloody sacrifices (Heb. 10:6). It was always the spiritual significance that was of utmost importance. The Jews had turned these things into the ultimate goal, whereas God gave these things to help direct them *towards* the ultimate goal. The ultimate goal was that the heart with pure faith might ascend into heaven in true spiritual worship of Christ. However, instead of rising up to worship in spirit and in truth, the Jews brought God down and bound Him to these signs. In doing this their concept of God was perverted and remade by their own minds and thus they were worshipping a man-made image and not the true God. These people exalted their own will-worship to such a high degree that they arrogantly boasted about and prided themselves in their childish activities, making themselves superior to everyone who did not join in with their "little games." The true worshipers, who are heard by God in His heavenly temple are the ones who lift their hearts by faith and spiritually feast upon Christ in heaven (this was true even in the OT, cf. John 8:56). To think that God is restricted to some physical location or to think that we have truly worshipped Him by merely going through some ceremony or ritual, is to be greatly deceived. God has always wanted true worshipers to worship Him in spirit and in truth (John 4:23).

Stephen condemns the Jewish idea that God could be tied down and restricted to one place. God had said through the prophet, "Where will my resting place be?," meaning His presence couldn't be localised and no building could control His activity. Even the heaven is not a home for God, but only a throne and the earth which is insignificant in comparison to heaven, is only a footstool. Neither heaven nor earth can contain God, for they were made by Him. If God does have a home on earth, it is with His true worshipers (John 14:23). When we forget the infinite greatness of God, our thoughts about Him will be shaped by man's imagination, whose goal in limiting God, is to control Him. When we allow man's mind to determine what is and isn't possible for God and make all of God's activities submit to man's ability to understand them, then we are limiting God and making a god after our own image. Grand buildings and ceremonies might impress foolish people, but they are offensive to God when the hearts of the worshipers are not humble and broken before Him, submitting completely to His Word. Man's greatest problem is his desire to determine by himself what is right and wrong for every area of life. He is constantly bringing all things into line with his own heart, rather than into line with God's Word.

God desires a true meaningful relationship with our whole being. His love for us is total and He wants us to love Him with all our heart, soul, mind and strength (Mark 12:30). God wants us and not what we have—He made everything and needs nothing. He wants us and not some cold ritual. The essence of God is relationship and thus to seek to worship Him without a real living relationship is madness. A relationship with God is based upon loving, obedient submission to His every Word, for it is His Word alone that tells us how to relate—to Him and to others around us (Matt. 22:37–40). Only a broken, devoted heart can obey God (John 14:15, 23; 1 John 2:3–5; 3:22, 24; 5:3; 2 John 6) and thus love Him.

Acts 7:51

Stephen has proven his case, as we saw above. He had been charged with blasphemy and disregarding the law of Moses. Stephen had been preaching the message of Christ. To charge him was to charge the Christian religion, therefore, he set out to defend the doctrines of Christ from these false accusations. He clearly showed that the ceremonial law and the temple were aspects of God's revelation that were going to pass away with the coming of the Messiah. He proved this by referring to Solomon and Isaiah who spoke of these exact changes (he could have quoted from other prophets to prove the same point).

Stephen had also shown that despite the great privileges that God had given to Israel, they had constantly been unfaithful. Therefore, the removal of the temple in Jerusalem was also a sign of God's judgment upon a rebellious generation. Stephen had pointed out the rebellion of previous generations (his hearers would have agreed with him on this), but then he said those listening to him were even worse rebels than the older generations who had rebelled against Joseph and Moses. His hearers quickly believed God's evaluation of previous generations, however, stubbornly suppressed God's evaluation of themselves. Isn't this what we see all the time: individuals, politicians, reporters, etc., all shouting loudly about the sins of others, while at the same time stubbornly refusing to admit to their own many sins? When the Scriptures talk of having a soft heart and a humble heart this does not mean that we are to have hearts that never ever sin—that is impossible (1 John 1:8–10). A person who has a soft heart does not want to sin and strives not to, however, when he does sin, he humbly bow to the authority of the Word of God and repents, crying out to God for forgiveness and the grace to bring his thoughts and actions into line with the mind of Christ (2 Cor. 10:5). David understood the need for a contrite heart—a heart that felt deep sorrow for personal sin (Ps. 51:17).

The whole of Stephen's speech had been leading towards this one inescapable point—that those who had put him on trial were no different than their forefathers whom God had repeatedly called *stiff-necked* and *uncircumcised in heart* (Ex. 32:9; 33:3, 5; Lev. 26:41; Jer. 9:26, etc.). Such terms likened the nation to a rebellious, disobedient ox that refused to take the yoke and was therefore useless to its master—no work could be done with an ox that stubbornly refused to bend, bow or submit to the authority of its master.

Uncircumcised heart and ears: this spoke of their impurity, insensitivity and resistance towards God and His Word. Such an accusation was extremely disturbing to a Jew. Circumcision was a sign in which the Jews prided themselves, for it was a sign that they were God's special children. It spoke of their unique relationship with the God of heaven and their separation from all other nations. By calling them uncircumcised, Stephen was saying that they were no longer God's special children, but had been completely cut off from the blessings and privileges of the covenant. Israel paid no more attention to God's Word than the heathens did (cf. Jer. 9:26) and were now even worse off than the Gentiles whom they despised so much, for rebellious children receive greater judgment for rejecting their greater privileges—their behavior was nothing but treason to the Most High God.

All the outward signs of the OT were meaningless unless the worshipers entered into the spiritual reality of these things by faith (cf. Rom. 2:28, 29; Gal. 3:7). Christ was the realization of all these things, so to reject Christ did not mean that these people just had not yet made the connection between the OT signs and Christ. They were not true worshipers who merely made a little mistake by not recognising Christ, but rather, had been living lives of rebellion against God and His Word for a long time before this. The sacrifices, ceremonies and signs they were participating in were being done in rebellion to Christ, before Christ even came. If these people had been worshipping in spirit and in truth, as they should have been doing, then they would have recognised Christ immediately. However, they were dead to the spiritual meaning of the signs and therefore, they were dead to the reality (Christ) too (cf. John 5:46— to believe in the law was to believe in Christ. To reject the law is to reject Christ). These leaders were in rebellion against the *signs* and therefore were in rebellion against the *reality* too.

Stephen makes it very clear that their rejection of Christ was not a matter of ignorance, but deliberate resistance to the Holy Spirit. This means that it was clear what God's Word said; it was clear who Christ was; it was clear that they were rebelling against God, yet they continued in their foolishness. The Holy Spirit does not work in an uncertain or unclear manner. When a person resists the Holy Spirit, they are resisting the truth and they are resisting the truth while knowing it is the truth, not as just another idea that they haven't realised is the truth. They know the truth and it is the truth that they specifically hate (Rom. 1:18–22; John 3:20, see too *Faith and Reason*, chapters 1 to 6). All through Israel's history the Spirit of God was reaching out to the Jews. Christ also testifies to this constant reaching out on the part of the Triune God (Matt. 23:37). Stephen says to his generation that they were as guilty as their fathers. He says the nation has one consistent characteristic common to every generation—rebellion against God and resistance to the Spirit.

Acts 7:52

Israel resisted the very clear prophetic Word and not some secret uncertain revelation. Their resistance was not due to ignorance but to willful rebellion against what they knew to be true. Stephen removes all grounds for a plea of ignorance from Israel. When

Israel rejected a prophet, they were rejecting the Holy Spirit who spoke through that prophet. Every single prophet that God sent to His children was persecuted (cf. Matt. 23:29–32). Stephen says, just name one prophet that was not persecuted! The prophets' greatest honor was due to the fact that they spoke about the coming Messiah. Stephen appears to say that this glorious announcement was the cause of the prophet's persecution. They spoke of the "Just One" meaning that His life would be lived in perfect obedience to the law of God—there would be no fault in Him whatsoever. The rebellion of these previous generations, however, was nothing in comparison to Stephen's accusers, for they had not only betrayed, but also murdered the "Just One." When the Sanhedrin had hired Judas to betray Jesus (Luke 22:2–6), they become His betrayers. When they forced Pilate to kill Christ (Luke 23:13–18, 24), they became His murderers. The supreme leaders and judges of the nation conspired to murder the Righteous One.

The Jews, throughout their history, killed the people that brought them the good news about their deliverance and salvation, refusing to be guided by divine revelation. They wanted to put out their source of light (John 1:9–11), thus destroying their source of hope and life. Then this final generation received the ultimate manifestation of God's light, love, grace and mercy and they rejected Him with violent hatred—sin does not make sense! Sin is rebellion against God's will and Word which is the height of foolishness, so how can it make sense?

Acts 7:53

What was the greatest privilege in being a Jew according to Paul? The most important thing in the mind of Paul was that they had received the oracles of God (Rom. 3:1, 2; 9:4). To receive God's special revelation was indeed a most wonderful blessing. The law of God is glorious and is a real treasure to those who have spiritual eyes (Rom. 7:12; 2:18; Ps. 119:97, 98, 99, 104, 105, etc.). The greatest advantage that the Jews had over the other nations was being in possession of this special revelation from God. This revelation was ultimately meant to be a blessing to the whole world (Gen. 12:3; Deut. 4:6–8), nevertheless, in the early stages of God's plan of redemption the Jews were the ones who were meant to receive extensive advantage from it. They were given divine wisdom showing them how to live in all of life and they were also given wonderful promises and a certain hope about the coming Messiah and His Kingdom. The Jews, of all the peoples in the world, were the ones equipped to recognise the Messiah when He appeared. The knowledge of God's gracious salvation was given to them—this is the most glorious piece of information available to sinful people. It contains, not only God's desire to save us from the penalty of sin, but also His intention to deliver us from our bondage to sin and unite us in perfect relationship with Himself. Knowledge that God has made a way for us to escape from His just judgment is the sweetest news this world will ever know. The proclamation of the message of good tidings is a treasure, second to none (Rom. 10:15).

God had used His heavenly messengers, the angels, to reveal His law to the nation of Israel through His chosen servants like Abraham, Moses, Joshua, Isaiah, Ezekiel, Daniel, Zechariah, etc. Israel had revealed to them God's divine standard of right and wrong, the only way of salvation and assurance of God's sovereign control and victorious reign over all things—they were not groping around in the dark trying to discover these things.

Stephen says to these leaders of the Jewish nation, "You, the very people who had all this divine revelation, have rebelled against it. You had all this light delivered to you in a most stunning way (through angels) and yet you have not walked in obedience to it." The very ones who were given the light of God, betrayed and murdered the True Light of the world! Stephen's whole speech supports this final statement. There is no escape for his accusers and they have only two options before them: either repent and submit to the Lordship of Christ, or continue to suppress the light of God.

Acts 7:54

The anger of the crowd would probably have been steadily building throughout the whole speech, however, the abrupt, clear, pointed and "insulting" conclusion was more than these men could bear. The searching light of God was shining deeply into their hearts and what it revealed produced tremendous agony for these rebellious leaders. This gnashing on Stephen with their teeth, speaks of uncontrolled rage in response to intense pain and can be likened to either the bellowing, groaning and roaring of animals, or to the deep cry of a wounded soldier caught in the pain and terror of death. One translator put it this way: "their hearts *burst* with rage." What brought about such an intense eruption?

Hypocrisy, rebellion and suppression of the truth are activities that demand much effort, resulting in much turmoil in the inner person. The unbeliever cannot escape from the knowledge of God and thus he is very aware of his rebellion, which means he is aware of the wrath and judgment of God hanging over him. The fear of judgment has to be suppressed, which requires much effort and it is never successful. The discomfort and turmoil that results from this situation together with a proud unbending heart is the cause of such violent emotion when confronted with the bold proclamation of the full counsel of God (Heb. 4:12). Preaching of the Word of God in the power of the Holy Spirit exposes the condition of the human heart and shines deep into the depths of our innermost being, showing all the hidden motives and thoughts. When there is long term hypocrisy and suppression of the truth together with a very hard heart that refuses to repent, there is only one way to deal with this intense pain—uncontrolled anger and destruction of the person who is causing the pain.

Guilt is a terrible thing to carry and can only be dealt with in the way God has said: by repentance and faith in Christ's atonement. People who refuse this way of escape are controlled by their guilt, however, they deny that it is a consequence of their own wilful sins, and blame it upon something outside of themselves. The more guilt is denied, the more the internal pressure and turmoil from guilt increases. These men refused to be held responsible for their sin and guilt and therefore blamed Stephen for the internal pain they were experiencing. They said the source of their problem was something outside of themselves (Stephen), thus in order to ease their pain they would have to silence the one "causing" their discomfort.

Old Simeon prophesied over baby Jesus, saying that through Him the "thoughts of many hearts will be revealed" (Luke 2:35). The light of Christ's Word bursts the hearts of hypocrites and rebels, and this can lead to angry and even violent reactions. When faced with the possibility of a similar response, we have to ask ourselves whether we fear God or man? Do we make known the whole truth or do we change our message, fearing what people might do and say in response to the full light of God's Word? (cf. Acts 20:27).

These religious leaders were seeking justification—but in man's way. They wanted to cover or work off the guilt that they felt, and what better way than to do something for God. This was "works salvation'—where God owes people something because of what they do for Him. These men tried to convince themselves of their own self-righteousness by calling Stephen a blasphemer and getting rid of him for God. Their mindset was that if they pointed out someone else's "sin," then they couldn't possibly be guilty of the same sin: they hoped, by killing Stephen, not only to make atonement for themselves, but also to prove their own innocence.

Acts 7:55, 56

What Stephen now sees is a gracious revelation from God, and by the Spirit is enabled to look into heaven. What he was greeted with was a very real manifestation of the glory of God. We are not told that he saw God, but just His glory. Stephen's eyes were opened and enabled to perceive in a very real way the reality of the spiritual realm. He was completely captivated by this revelation so that it appears as if he was almost completely unaware of what was happening in the natural realm. All Stephen's judges merely saw him and did not share in the glorious vision that he could see. Luke names Jesus and then quotes Stephen who calls Him the Son of Man (from Dan. 7:13). Jesus used this term for Himself at His own trial. The emphasis of this title is upon the sovereignty of Christ and speaks of His absolute power and dominion over all things. The great commission (Matt. 28:18–20) is based upon the dominion and authority that the Son of Man received in accordance with Daniel's prophecy (7:13, 14, see comments on Acts 2:33). Christ has defeated the powers of darkness and now has all authority in heaven and in earth—Satan has been crushed, we are not waiting for this to happen (Col. 2:15; Heb. 2:14; 1 John 3:8).

When Jesus was on trial He said that He was the Son of Man and that the religious leaders would see Him sitting at the right hand of power and coming on the clouds of heaven (Matt. 26:64; Mark 14:62). The clouds often symbolise the majesty or glory of God and/or divine judgment (Ex. 19:9; 33:9; 34:5; Ps. 18:10–14; Ezk. 30:3–5; Lam. 2:1; Isa. 19:1). Christ was telling those who were judging Him that they would know that He was the Lord of glory when He returned to judge that generation. Remember, it was this generation that prayed for Christ's blood to be placed upon their heads (Matt. 27:25). That generation indeed received everything that they asked for in A.D. 70 when Rome destroyed Jerusalem. Josephus, the

Jewish historian, recorded the horror and suffering that was experienced at that time. Josephus tells us that the famine was so terrible in the city of Jerusalem (for the Roman soldiers had surrounded it and stopped any supplies going in) that people were eating what animals wouldn't. There were thieves and thugs within the city, stealing whatever they could find and tormenting everyone. What little food people might have had was stolen by these rogues. Some people even ate their children. Others who tried to sneak out of the city to find food were caught by the Romans and severely beaten and tortured and then crucified. At least 500 Jews a day were being crucified by the Romans. This was the judgment that the Jews asked to be upon their own heads and it was the judgment that Jesus was talking about when He said to those judging Him, " *You* will see the Son of Man coming on the clouds of heaven".

Stephen confirms that Jesus was in fact at the right hand of God—a place of supreme power and authority. He saw Jesus standing and not sitting (cf. Ps. 110:1). I believe that this has two messages: one for the believers and one for the unbelievers. Everything Christ ever does or says, has this same result, bringing blessing to those who believe and judgment upon those who rebel. The power and authority of Christ's Words and actions are not only to save, but also to destroy. Christ always operates with a two edged sword and the same sword brings life to some and destruction to others (see comments on Acts 2:2f.).

Stephen, about to become the first Christian martyr, sees Christ ready to receive him and pronounce, "Well done, good and faithful servant." Stephen had fearlessly proclaimed the name of Christ before a violent mob, and thus we see Christ acknowledging him before God and the hosts of heaven (Luke 12:8). However, there is another message in the fact that Christ is *standing*, and this message is for the rebellious leaders—it is the same message that Jesus had given to them: "Judgment is upon you!" The Scriptures often talk of God arising to judge His enemies (Isa. 14:22; Ps. 3:7; 7:6). We know that all judgment has been committed into the hand of Jesus (John 5:22, 27ff.). This judgment includes the final judgement, but also includes the judgment of God's enemies in history (see comments on John 5:28, 29).

Thus the standing of Christ includes His intercession for and receiving of Stephen, as well as His judgment upon God's enemies.

Due to the mercy of God, these rebels are once again warned about the terrible wrath of God that was hanging above their heads—Christ had arisen, the judgment was coming soon.

Acts 7:57, 58

By placing Jesus at the right hand of God, Stephen was claiming divinity for Him. Christ had also claimed divinity for Himself, but did not receive such a violent reaction—screaming, blocking their ears and rushing upon Him (Matt. 26:65). This was not an out of control mob, but an angry religious mob. They took Stephen out of the city, according to the law (Lev. 24:14; Num. 15:35) and had witnesses cast the first stones, according to the law (Deut. 17:7). I believe that this strong reaction from the religious leaders was not merely because Stephen had made Christ God, but more so because they had clearly understood that Stephen had just pronounced the soon destruction of the *temple.*

Stephen's accusers had brought him to trial because he taught that the temple would be destroyed by Christ, which meant that the ceremonies of Moses would also be changed (Acts 6:14). The High Priest then asked Stephen if these charges were true (7:1). Stephen then went on to defend his position and finally ends off by saying, "Indeed, Jesus Christ, who has all power and authority given to Him by God, has arisen and is ready to destroy this temple." Jesus had told these same leaders that they would see Him coming on the clouds (i.e., in judgement). Stephen says, he can see Jesus standing (i.e., ready to judge).

We know that the Jews did not have authority to put people to death. Rome, who ruled the Jewish nation at this time, were the only ones who could execute anyone (John 18:31). If, in the stoning of Stephen the Jews had taken the law into their own hands, Rome would not have looked lightly upon such rebellion against their laws (they wouldn't have been upset over Stephen's death, but over the fact that the Jewish leadership had disregarded Roman law)—yet we find no repercussions for this execution. There is not sufficient proof to prove that Rome was having political problems at this time (as some have argued) and therefore, hardly noticed Stephen's execution. The fact is, Rome *had* granted the Jews full authority to execute for one type of offence, namely, for any attack upon the temple—whether in word or deed. In cases of blasphemy against the temple, the Jews could immediately carry out the sentence and did not need the governor's permission—they already had Roman authorization and this is why the Roman authorities did not react to the execution of Stephen. His murder was in line with Roman law, however, in complete rebellion against God's law and name.

This is our first introduction to Saul (the Apostle Paul) before his conversion. Saul, coming from the tribe of Benjamin, was most probably named after Israel's first king (Rom. 11:1; Acts 13:21). Saul was probably about thirty years old at this time and that the garments were laid by his feet, most likely points to the fact that he was already a person of authority and standing in the Jewish community. It does not seem likely that he was still studying under Gamaliel at this time and he was certainly not following the moderate approach of his teacher (cf. comments on Acts 5:34ff.), for Saul becomes a very fierce persecutor of the church (8:1ff.).

Acts 7:59

Luke now tells us a little more about the stoning of Stephen. He contrasts in a very strong way, the actions of the Jews with the actions of Stephen. We are not only told about Stephen's actions, but also of his firm belief and conviction. The words used here show that the Jews were repeatedly throwing stones against Stephen's body despite the fact that he was praying and calling upon the name of the Lord. The Jews' stubborn rebellion and hatred of God meant that they felt nothing to repeatedly cast stones at Stephen while he prayed. His calmness and godly response of devotion to God's will in the midst of terrifying circumstances probably increased the Jews' hatred for him. Thus on the one hand the hardness of the Jews is seen (they continued to cast stones, even while Stephen was calling out to the Lord), while on the other hand, the devotion of Stephen shines brightly for all to see.

Stephen not only prays while boulders fly past his head and crash into his body, but he firmly and immovably believes and trusts in the goodness of God's providence in the midst of this horror. The huge rocks that were crushing his bones and internal organs did not in any way cause him to doubt this truth. His faith couldn't be shaken because no matter what this screaming, violent mob believed, thought or did, it had no influence upon what Stephen knew to be true. Truth is eternal and immovable, whereas man's "wisdom" that flows out of his rebellion is not only constantly changing but has no content or foundation and thus cannot provide any real security or assurance. The unbeliever rejects the only sure foundation of God and His Word and tries to build a structure not only upon lies, but out of lies—which is as hopeless as trying to make a container out of water, upon water, in order to store water. Stephen believed the truth and was standing firmly upon the truth and therefore, was not affected in the slightest by this hatred against him. Blessed is the man who trusts in the Lord (Ps. 34:8). The Psalmist understood this when he pictured a situation of greatest instability and turmoil, where the very foundations of the earth were shaking and the mountains crumbling. There is nowhere to run to and hide in such a situation, yet he says, even here the Lord is our refuge (Ps. 46:1–3, 7 see too 62:2, etc.). Such upheaval also refers to the strife and turmoil in the world brought about by man's wickedness, which Stephen was surely facing. No matter who despised him and no matter what they tried to do to him, he knew the truth and fearlessly held to it.

Whenever we stand up against the lies of Satan and oppose the thinking of the world we will be despised, hated and persecuted. The earth is the Lord's and everything in it (Ps. 24:1) and thus everything is to bring glory to Him. There are only two options open to us: we are either for Christ or we are against Him (Luke 11:23). We either do everything in obedience to the Word of God (Matt. 4:4), bringing every thought into obedience to Christ (2 Cor. 10:5) or else we act and think in the way the world thinks. The worldly or sinful mind is hostile to God and refuses to submit to His law (Rom. 8:7). To be friends with the world means we have hatred towards God and become His enemies (Jam. 4:4). In this world we have only truth and error and nothing in-between. Our actions and thoughts are either submissive and God-glorifying or else they are rebellious and God-despising. God's Word needs to take root in our hearts so that we do not look for the praises and acceptance of the world or first seek its confirmation before we are prepared to stand upon and boldly proclaim God's truth. We have been called to be salt and light (Matt. 5:13, 14) and this is what we have to be despite the hatred and suffering that might come our way as a result of this. It is a blessed thing to be persecuted for righteousness sake (Matt. 5:10). If we are persecuted for Christ's sake we will be blessed by Him and should rejoice in the fact that we were found worthy to suffer (Acts 5:41; 1 Pet. 4:12–16). If we are killed for our testimony of the truth we enter into a more blessed situation—eternal life (Phil. 1:21, 23).

Stephen's understanding of and trust in the truth was very real (you cannot pretend in such terrifying situations). He prayed to Jesus even though Jesus had taught His disciples to pray to the Father (Matt. 6:9). It is by calling upon the name of Christ that we are saved (Rom. 8:9; 10:13, see too 1 Cor. 1:2; Acts 9:14; 22:16). Paul prayed to Christ for healing (2 Cor.12:7–9). When Jesus died He had said, "Father into your hands I commit my spirit" (Luke 23:46, cf. Ps. 31:5). Stephen now prays this same prayer to Jesus. Once again we are shown the perfect equality between the Father and the Son. It is not wrong to pray to any member of the Trinity (Father, Son or Holy Spirit), since each one is in and of themselves, completely God. The emphasis, however, is that the Father is usually addressed in prayer—this was Christ's teaching and example. There are occasional prayers addressed to Christ, though we find no examples of prayers addressed to the Holy Spirit. It is the Holy Spirit who births prayer in our hearts and enables us to pray. Our prayers, made in the name of Christ, have to go through Christ and be brought by Him to the Father (John 16:23; 1 Tim. 2:5; Heb. 9:24; 1 John 2:1). Christ intercedes for us and the Holy Spirit also intercedes (Rom. 8:26, 27). Prayer constantly makes us aware of the triune God. Each Person within the trinity is equally God, yet there is an inter-relationship between Father, Son and Holy Spirit that to pray to one of them, necessarily includes and involves all the others. A true picture of God constantly keeps our minds focused upon the "threeness" and oneness of God.

Stephen asked Jesus to receive his spirit, i.e., his person. There is more to us than the physical dimension (Matt. 10:28). We need to be reminded about this, since we are often more aware of the physical aspect of our being than the spiritual aspect. Our real essence and person lives on when the physical aspect of our being dies, though we do not become ghost-like beings, but assume some sort of body structure appropriate for where we are (see comments on John 11:25, 26). When we die our person goes straight to Christ—this indeed is a great comfort and joy for us. Unbelievers, when they die, do not wander around either, but are held by God in a place of torment, from which they cannot escape (Luke 16:19–31).

Acts 7:60

Stephen, wanting to die in an attitude of prayer, knelt down. He was not praying with a hope that his executioners would hear what he was saying and not kill him, but rather it was a natural outflow of a godly heart (Matt. 5:43, 44). Stephen, as Christ, was not caught up in self-pity and hatred, but rather was completely focused on others. He knew he was saved by the grace of God alone (Eph. 2:8, 9) and thus prayed for the eternal welfare of those who were murdering him. His prayer was not that when these men stood before the judgment seat of Christ they wouldn't be charged with this particular sin. The only way that these men could not be charged with this sin, would be if they repented and were found standing in the righteousness of Christ on the day of judgment. His prayer was for their conversion, not that God would pervert His justice by ignoring this particular sin. This sin of stoning Stephen was the fruit of their rebellion against God. Stephen prays that their rebellion would not remain with them for long. In the case of Paul we see that God indeed honored Stephen's prayer.

Having said this, he fell asleep. In the midst of this violent, terrifying experience, Luke draws attention to the calmness of Stephen by using the gentle term of sleep for the death of his body. Remember, Stephen's spirit or person had been committed to Christ. Sleep refers to his death from an earthly perspective. Believers do not die, but *live* with Christ until the final day when they receive their eternal resurrection bodies (John 5:28, 29, see comments on verse 59 above).

Stephen had absolute trust in God's providence and thus could willingly and peacefully submit to this cruel death. He did not question God and ask Him where He was, or why He allowed such a terrifying and painful thing to happen. God's ways are not our ways (Isa. 55:8, 9). He is sovereign, He is loving and good and thus we ought to imitate Stephen as we tread the path of this life (for Stephen imitated Christ). We are to proclaim the truth and love our enemies by responding to them at all times in accordance with the Word of God, not fearing what men might do to us. We exist to glorify God's Kingdom and Name. May nothing distract us from this high calling and may we be found faithfully doing the Father's will until we breathe our last breath.

Acts 8:1

Saul (Paul) was always a sharp thinker and understood the issues clearly. Both before his conversion and then afterwards we see that he rejected the idea of compromise. He knew that everyone's way of thinking was a complete system and to break it at one point would be to break the whole system. Saul realized that there could be no peace between the old order and this new teaching of having faith in Christ—this was a struggle unto death. These two different worldviews could not tolerate one another. Jesus claimed absolute obedience to His every Word and complete commitment to His cause—thus if you are not totally for Him then you are against Him (Luke 11:23). Saul's teacher, Gamaliel, had failed to realize the seriousness of Christ's claims and thus was prepared to compromise with the new faith (Acts 5:34–39), stating that it might just be true. Although Gamaliel rejected the teaching about Christ, he had not realized that by allowing even a slight possibility of its truth, meant the destruction of his religious position. Saul, on the other hand, saw this clearly.

Rebellion against God touches every area of life because His Word touches every area of life, thus there can never be a uniting between those who obey Christ and those who reject Him. The foundation, goal and motive for the unbeliever's thoughts and actions will always be completely opposed to the Christian's position. Everywhere, whether in the social realm, family, economics, politics, military, or education there is either submission to God's ways and purposes or hatred of God's ways and purposes. The unbeliever cannot and will not submit himself to the truth of God's Word. He cannot do anything but act with enmity and hatred against God's truth (Rom. 8:7), therefore, the believer should not be deceived into thinking that it is possible for such a person to adopt a neutral position towards true knowledge and godliness—you either love it or hate it. We are told in Colossians 1:21 that unbelievers are alienated and enemies in their minds against God. *Do we believe this?* Or do we overturn it, thinking that some unbelievers are not opposed to God's truth?

It is important to realize that the 'gentle' soft-spoken Gamaliel (cf. Acts 5:34–39) was as much an enemy of God as Saul was (Acts 8:1–3). When Gamaliel said it was difficult to be sure whether Christianity was true or not he was not only being inconsistent with his own position, but also denying the absolute claims of Christ. He was denying that God's truth is clear and inescapable—there is nothing more sure than that Jesus is the only savior of the world and that we need to live by every Word that comes from His mouth (Matt. 4:4). To say, "Maybe Christianity is true" does not mean you have an open mind towards it. This is still a hostile position, though it is subtler. We think that if someone is not cursing Christ then they are not really opposed to Him. However, all unbelievers are hostile to God and want to destroy His truth, though they go about this in many different ways. Some fight against the truth of God violently, others in a more "unnoticed, gentle" way, however, both are committed to total war against God and His purposes. When Christians are ignorant of this, they seriously weaken their ability to glorify Christ in every area of life.

Saul clearly understood that if he did not destroy Christianity, then his system of belief would be destroyed. Christ's goal is nothing less than total conquest of all hearts and minds. Unbelieving systems use violence in order to bring about total conformity, whereas Christ, through the power of the Spirit, changes people's hearts and in this way their minds and actions are brought into willing submission.

Saul not only agreed (consented) to the murder of Stephen, but all his actions were controlled by an intense desire to destroy the church of Christ. Saul so supported the death of Stephen that he used all his time and efforts in an attempt to do the same thing to every Christian. It was due to the efforts of Saul that this persecution became so fierce and cruel. There needs to be some motivating personality behind such a wave of persecution and this was found in Saul.

All the Christians were scattered as a result of Saul's fierceness and zeal. This great persecution against the church appears to have been launched the day Stephen was murdered. Often the ungodly are spurred on by their own acts of wickedness and become more and more bold. It is estimated that there were at least twenty-five thousand believers in Jerusalem at this time and it was most probably all of these that were thrust into the outlying areas because of the persecution. The apostles remained behind, probably because their lives were not directly threatened. They had already been tried by the whole leadership of the nation and been released. It was also easier to make up false charges against those who were not as well known as the apostles. The apostles, nevertheless, demonstrated true courage and faith, as real leaders should. God obviously wanted them to remain in Jerusalem, which was the center of the NT church at this stage. The scattered believers did return to Jerusalem once Saul's motivating zeal to destroy the church was removed (cf. Acts 9:26).

At Pentecost the NT church was empowered not only to reproduce itself, but also to fulfill its mandate from Christ to disciple all the nations and teach them everything Christ had commanded (Matt. 28:18–20). In their attempt to stop the spread of the good news, Saul and his companions actually caused this message to be spread far and wide, as Christians, fleeing for their safety, shared the Gospel wherever they went. It appeared for a moment that Christianity had suffered a great defeat with the "legal" execution of Stephen and then with Saul being empowered to arrest any believer. However, what actually takes place is an explosion in the size of the church and a massive spread of the Gospel (see comments on Acts 2:24 where Satan's plan to destroy Christ turned out to be God's plan to destroy Satan's power). The Pharisees were now fully in support of this persecution (Acts 26:5; Phil. 3:5). It is difficult to know when Gamaliel's advice (Acts 5) was overturned and why, since he was still alive and his prominence and respect appear to have continued until his death.

Acts 8:2

This term "devout men" appears to refer to Jews who had not yet believed in Christ, but were nevertheless, disturbed by the trial and murder of Stephen. This word is not used to describe Christ's disciples anywhere in the NT (Ecclesiastical/Majority Text). These devout Jews separated themselves from this terrible act. The great lamentation could have been because they knew Stephen, or because they were trying to avert the judgment of God that was hanging over the city as a result of Stephen's murder. Their great sorrow could have been for the great sin of their leaders, thus they were not only upset about the death of an innocent man, but also upset by the threat to themselves, their families and their city as a consequence of this injustice. The Jewish Talmud (civil and religious laws) said that there should be no mourning for a criminal that was put to death. This was not observed by these God fearing

Jews who lamented greatly, thus clearly showing their rejection of the council's verdict of guilty brought against Stephen.

Acts 8:3

Here we see a contrast between these God-fearing Jews and Saul who was making havoc with the church. The word used to describe Saul's actions is used to describe what a wild beast does to a body—tearing and ravaging. Saul's desire was to destroy the church (Gal. 1:13), thus he was vicious and cruel and used all his zeal and energy to search out and find Christians. He severely treated any Christian whether man or woman. He was not just stopping the Christians from meeting in public places, but was invading private homes where there were not even any meetings and dragging believers off to prison. Saul knew that there could be no compromise between the two orders—only one could survive and he was determined that it would be the old order. To Saul, the idea of a crucified Messiah was not only impossible, but blasphemy (Deut. 21:23) and therefore, it made no difference whether Jesus deserved to die or not, the fact that He had been crucified disqualified Him from being Messiah (see comments on Acts 5:30). The Jews were looking for a Messiah who would be covered with divine blessing (Isa. 11:2), not divine cursing, thus the crucifixion was a massive stumbling block to zealous Jews (1 Cor. 1:23). After his conversion, Paul showed that a cursed Messiah was at the heart of God's plan of redemption (Gal. 3:13). We, as Saul did, will also fail to recognize the workings of God if we do not submit to *everything* that God has said (Luke 24:25).

Acts 8:4

The power to reproduce itself had come upon the church at Pentecost and as a result of the persecutions, some twenty-five thousand Christians are dispersed throughout the regions surrounding Jerusalem. Satan had hoped to wipe out Christianity through Saul's actions, however this greatly advanced the spread of the new faith, forever making it impossible to wipe it out. The believers were not only scattered, but shared the good news wherever they went and many more were brought into the church of God. Up until that time the message of salvation was confined to Jerusalem and the surrounding areas, however in the scattering we clearly see that God's intention was universal. This message was not just for the

Jews, but also for all people (see Acts 2:17; 11:19–26). It is believed
that this was the major offence of the "new" message in the eyes of
the Jews—that the message of salvation would be freely offered to
Gentiles. Stephen had taught this when he said the sacrificial system
was completed with Christ, thus the temple and Jerusalem were no
longer necessary and also that God could be worshipped anywhere
(a fact already clearly taught in the OT itself).

We are unable to know all the reasons God does something—especially when we are in the midst of turmoil and trouble. At such
times we need to rely upon the Biblical teaching that God is sovereign and everything is controlled by His providence (see *Faith and
Reason*, chapter 6). Those Christians who fled for their lives and left
behind all their possessions were not discouraged but went out
confidently proclaiming the glorious message of the Gospel. It was
not "preachers" in the technical sense that were scattered, but ordinary Christians. Thus, this verse does not refer to preaching in the
technical sense, but to that joyful spreading of the message of salvation that is the privilege of all believers to do. These people, who
were now destitute, did not go out and beg from those whom they
met, but shared the good news with them. Our problems are often
created in our minds and not by our circumstances. When we
understand the truth of God's Word and live our lives in obedience
to it, then it is we who shape the circumstances around us rather
than being crushed and controlled by the situation surrounding us.
Do we believe in the providence of God? Do we believe in the
power of His Holy Spirit? Do we believe in His victory over the
powers of darkness? Do we believe that He completed the work of
redemption? Do we believe that He blesses those who walk in obedience to Him? Then by faith let us confidently do what He has told
us to do, rejoicing in whatever state we find ourselves, working at all
times to glorify His name and advance His Kingdom, praying that
we might be faithful servants until the end of our lives. What else is
there that is more glorious than this work that God has called us to
do? We are Christ's so let us do all things with all our might for His
Kingdom—let us love Him with everything we are and have!

Acts 8:5

This is not the apostle whose name was Philip, but one of the seven
men ordained to oversee the helping of the distribution to the widows (Acts 6:1–5). We are not told the name of the city to which

206

Philip went—it was merely a city in Samaria. In OT times there was a city called Samaria, however this was completely destroyed and when it was eventually rebuilt it was called Sebaste. This city in Samaria might have been the capital city, however, Luke does not think it is important to tell us the city's name. The important thing for Luke is that the Gospel is taken to non-Jews. The Samaritans were a people who were mostly made up of foreigners who had intermarried with Jews and together they had formed their own culture and way of worship. There had been centuries of hatred between the Samaritans and the Jews. Jesus Himself had said that the Samaritans were deceived in their worship (John 4:22).

Jerusalem was at the very center of Jewish worship, yet this is the city that sets out to destroy those who love the Messiah. The Jews despised the Samaritans, yet it is the Samaritans that fully accept the Jewish Messiah through Philip's preaching—Christ can be worshipped anywhere (John 4:21, 23) and no group of people is excluded from God's offer of salvation in Christ. We see the plan unfolding exactly as Christ said it would (Acts 1:8).

Acts 8:6

Masses of people responded to Philip's preaching and embraced the truth. Philip was just one of the many other believers who was sharing about Christ at this stage (cf. verse 4). The Lord in a sovereign way brought about a massive harvest from Philip's preaching, who is *later* called an evangelist (Acts 21:8). This was the first large scale ingathering of people other than Jews into the NT church. The message about Christ had been confirmed amongst the Jews by many signs and wonders (Acts 2:22, 43; 3:6; 5:12–16; 6:8), and now God confirms the truth of Philip's words in the same way amongst the Samaritans—by granting them signs and wonders (see comments on the above passages as well as on Acts 7:36 and John 2:4). The signs performed by Jesus were done to authenticate His teaching and claims (John 10:25, 37, 38, cf. 20:30, 31). The writer of Hebrews says the purpose of Biblical signs served to verify, establish and seal the fact that the message truly was from God (Heb. 2:3, 4, cf. 1 Kings 17:24; 2 Kings 5:14, 15). The massive conversions that happened in Jerusalem through the preaching of the apostles were being repeated in Samaria through the preaching of Philip: the truth of his message being confirmed by signs.

Acts 8:7

Unclean spirits or demons are a very real part of our existence. Many in our day try and deny the existence of such beings, because once the spiritual realm is accepted they find it harder to suppress their knowledge of the existence of God. People cannot protect themselves against demons if they deny the existence of God— which leaves them at the mercy of these spiritual forces.

Casting evil spirits out of people was not a game of entertainment that Christ and His disciples liked to play, but a manifestation of the clash between two kingdoms—Christ's and Satan's. The devil who had had a relatively free hand in the world was finding that the power of Christ was pushing back his influence. Jesus announced that the Kingdom of God had arrived and was in their midst (Matt. 4:17; Mark 1:15). This reality was then manifested to the people when Jesus cast demons out of people (Luke 4:35, 36). Satan's power and influence fell like lightning when Christ's disciples went forth in His power (Luke 10:17, 18). The very reason Jesus came was to destroy the works of the devil (1 John 3:8). Every time a demon was cast out of someone we are shown how great Christ's power is in comparison to Satan's power. It is by the Spirit of God that demons are cast out (Matt. 12:28) and Acts 8:7 clearly shows that there is a distinction between demon possession and illness (see too Mark 1:32, 34; Luke 13:32).

The glorious Gospel is a message of liberation from the power of the kingdom of darkness. Christ came to proclaim the year of liberty (Luke 4:18, 43) because He came in the power God's Kingdom and Satan can do nothing against such awesome power. There is no basis for fearing the demonic realm when we stand by faith in Christ—the *demons* tremble at the name of Jesus (see comments on John 12:31, see also, Mark 1:24, 25, 34; Matt.8:29–33; Luke 4:34; James 2:19).

We are not allowed to try and communicate with those who have died (Deut. 18:10, 11). Those who have died are not free to wander around the earth to either help or attack those who are still alive. When someone dies they go immediately, either to a place of torment or to be with Christ (Luke 16:22, 23, 26–31). When people "communicate" with someone who is dead, they are communicating with demons who know all there is to know about that dead person and can also imitate them. When we forsake God's Word as our only guide and trust in our traditions and ancestors we are opening ourselves up to be deceived by the devil. Those who do such things will be given up by God to believe a lie and they will be at the mercy of the evil spirits (see comments on Acts 16:16, 17). The Scriptures give abundant testimony of Christ's comprehensive power/victory over the kingdom of darkness—we must not be foolish and doubt this. If we doubt we will compromise the truth, but if we stand by faith, we will share in the complete victory of Christ (Mark 3:27; Luke 11:20; John 12:31; Col.2:15; Heb. 2:14).

Acts 8:8

The whole character of the city changed as true deep joy filled the hearts of those who lived there. This joy was a combination of people being healed themselves or having loved ones healed; of being set free from Satan's torment and his demons; of understanding the truth of God's Word and experiencing the effects of spiritual conversion and regeneration.

Acts 8:9–11

Luke goes on to tell of a real deliverance for the whole city and region that were held captive to a man named Simon Magus. This man did amazing things through trickery and through the power of demons. Such men used the power of demons, though they would do things in a "respectable" way so as not to offend the people. It was believed that such people could speak with the dead, change the minds of the gods, make charms for healing, see into the future and read the stars. Simon had captured a massive following in Samaria due to his sorceries, though the Samaritans did not follow him as a sorcerer, but as a great man from God. He obviously had enough understanding of the Samaritan's beliefs to make them think that he was from God. He said the things they wanted to hear and then backed himself up with mighty works and the people were completely deceived and manipulated by him. The Samaritans had been held in the grip of Simon for a very long time. One of the reasons for this was the Samaritans had rejected the full counsel of God, holding to only bits and pieces of God's revelation in the Scriptures. The world was full of such religious impostors and still is today. It is only as we willingly submit to the whole counsel of God and by the Spirit apply it to our lives that we can be assured that we will not follow false teachers.

Acts 8:12

From showing the control that Simon had over these people, Luke says, "But" and introduces the power of the Gospel that had set the people free from their bondage, fear and death. Philip preaches the Kingdom of God, emphasizing the truth that it is God who is the sovereign Lord of the universe and rules over Satan and his demons—it is God's Kingdom that is supreme and to be marveled at. This Kingdom came in the time of Christ and those who believe in Jesus can live in His Kingdom now. The glory, power, and victory of this Kingdom have largely come, however, they have not fully come and we need to be aware of this tension as we live our Christian lives (the now and the not yet). The entrance into this Kingdom is through the name of Jesus Christ. It is only by believing in Him as our Savior that we can be born again, however this message of deliverance is for all people (Matt. 28:19, 20). The wall of separation and hatred between the Samaritans and Jews had been destroyed (John 4:9).

Acts 8:13

Even the great "witch-doctor" himself (Simon) has to admit that the power of Christ is far superior to anything he has ever known. Simon, extremely astonished by the power of the Spirit, makes a profession of faith in Christ. Maybe he was caught up in the excitement of the times and had the faith that Jesus talked about in Luke 8:13, 14, or maybe his actions were sinister from the beginning—realizing that his own influence and power couldn't match this new manifestation of power, he joined himself to Philip, hoping to get such power for himself and gain back the authority and respect that he used to have. He thought Philip knew some powerful spirit that could be manipulated and used for man's own desires. Simon's outward behavior at first gave the impression that he had repented and committed himself to the Lord, however it turns out that his hunger for the power, praise and riches in this world quickly choked his "belief" (it is possible to "believe" and not have true faith, see comments on John 2:23, 24).

Acts 8:14

Acts is not just a jumbled collection of things that happened in the early church, but there is structure and purpose for the whole book. One of the central messages that we must not lose sight of is that

Luke records the foundational spread of the church from the Jews and Israel to the Gentiles and all nations. We need to realize that it was a major transition or change when God's church moved from excluding Gentiles (for the most part), to making Gentiles completely accepted and equal with Jews. This breaking down of the wall that separated Jews and Gentiles was a major change in the emphasis of God's dealings with the world (Eph. 2:14; Gal. 3:28). This was no small change, and the book of Acts clearly shows how difficult it was for the Jews to accept this new development (e.g., Acts 11:2, 3 cf. Gal. 2:12). The apostles were the ones who were ordained by God to lay the foundation for the NT church to build upon (Eph. 2:20; 3:5; Jude 3). Thus each major step of the unfolding plan was clearly sanctioned by apostolic authority. In this way the church could know which foundation was of Christ and which one was not (2 Cor. 11:3, 4; Gal. 1:6, 7). If we fail to appreciate the awesome authority that the apostles had, we will misunderstand Acts and be deceived in our own day. The apostleship was a one time ministry ordained for the purpose of laying the foundations of the NT church—this job was completed by A.D. 70. This means there is no need for apostles in our day. To claim there are people today with authority comparable to the NT apostles' shows a great ignorance about the role and authority the apostles had and also undermines the authority of the completed Scriptures.

Christ had told His apostles not to preach to the Samaritans when He was still on earth (Matt. 10:5, 6). The apostles had not yet gone to the Samaritans, however, from the persecution, Philip had been driven into this area and the Holy Spirit had moved mightily upon both him and the Samaritans and many believed in Christ and were saved—Christ was both their sovereign Lord and Savior. Philip was not acting in rebellion against the leaders of the NT church and these leaders, the apostles, quickly recognized the moving of God among the Samaritans and thus commission Peter and John to authenticate the work of Philip. The apostles came with a specific purpose—which becomes obvious in the next verses.

Acts 8:15–17

Philip, a powerful, miracle working evangelist couldn't pray for the Holy Spirit to be given to the Samaritans. This should surely caution us to look carefully at this situation to understand why the apostles had to come and pray for the Holy Spirit to be given to baptized believers. Some people have jumped to the hasty conclusion that this process is the normal way that things ought to happen—you first believe, then are baptized and then receive the Holy Spirit. We have argued in Acts 2:38 that the norm is that as soon as a person believes in Christ they are not only saved from their sin, but immediately receive the Holy Spirit. In verse 16 the word *only* implies that the two things usually went together—becoming part of the body of Christ and receiving the Holy Spirit. However here we have an exception to this normal practice. In order to make sense of what was going on in this passage we must look at it in its historical setting.

There was deep hatred between the Samaritans and the Jews—racial and religious hatred. To the Jews, the Samaritans were unclean people and therefore the Jews wouldn't even drink from the same cup as them. The Samaritans hated the Jews and rejected their prophets and the whole of the OT except the writings of Moses (Genesis to Deuteronomy). A great healing needed to be done to people's emotions and minds. A good illustration of this racial tension is seen when John wanted to call down the fire of God's judgment upon Samaritan villages because they rejected Christ (Luke 9:54). However, John never suggested this treatment for those Jews who rejected Jesus. On the other hand, the reason the Samaritans rejected Christ was *because* He was going to Jerusalem—if He was going to worship with the Jews, then they wanted nothing to do with Him (Luke 9:53). There was only one basis for true unity between Jew and Samaritan and that was to have the same foundation and ultimate authority—the whole of the OT Scriptures and that additional revelation grounded upon the foundation of the apostolic ministry. The apostolic coming to Samaria was of vital importance to both Jews and Samaritans alike. The NT church was predominantly Jewish at this time and if the Samaritans were to be accepted into the church as equals, it would need to be made very clear to everyone. Thus God delayed the giving of the Holy Spirit (which normally takes place at conversion) and sent His authoritative leaders of the NT church to impart the Spirit to them (John now prayed for the Holy Spirit to fall upon then and not fire from heaven). It would have been easy, given the natural hatred between these two groups, to continue in their separate ways if the Samaritans had received the Holy Spirit when they believed. God from the very beginning made it very clear that there was only one universal church. Since the first leaders of the NT church in Jerusalem were intimately connected to the first great ingathering among the Samaritans there could never be any doubt that the Samaritans were part of the one church of God. At the same time the Samaritans were shown that it was Jewish apostles who were God's appointed leaders of the church and it was only by submitting to their authority that they could be part of Christ's church. By God's wisdom, the unity and authority of the church were clearly established, despite the previous cultural and religious differences.

This delay in believers receiving the Holy Spirit does not teach that this is the normal way things ought to happen, but rather it was a necessary step needed to confirm the new developments as Christ's church expanded across racial and national boundaries. This was a once off event among the Samaritans to make clear for all time what would happen when a Samaritan believed in Christ—they would become full members in the one universal church. From then on, whenever a Samaritan believed in Christ, they would immediately have received the Holy Spirit, without a delay and without needing the apostles to lay hands upon them, since Samaritans had been fully accepted on apostolic authority and the ministry of the Spirit. Apostolic contact and confirmation were vital as this new stage of God's expanding plan unfolded.

The birth of the NT church at Pentecost was confirmed to us by the powerful outpouring of the Holy Spirit and the speaking in tongues of all the disciples. The 3,000 converts did not speak in tongues and there is no NT proof to show that receiving the Holy Spirit had to be accompanied by this sign of speaking in tongues. We are not told that any of the new converts spoke in tongues when they were added to the Jerusalem church after Pentecost (at least 25,000 persons). We are not told by Luke what sign accompanied receiving of the Holy Spirit by the Samaritans—it might have been tongues (some verses *appear* to point us in this direction). The fact that Luke does not think it is important to tell us what sign accompanied this receiving of the Spirit by the Samaritans should make us hesitate to insist it was tongues speaking. In Acts 10 we see another powerful manifestation of the Spirit together with tongues speaking, but what we have there is the next stage in the spread of the Gospel across racial and religious borders. For the Jews to accept Gentiles into the church was an even greater step than accepting Samaritans (cf. Acts 15), thus once again the Lord confirms His acceptance of them by giving them the Holy Spirit—against which no one could argue (10:46, 47; 11:17). The incident in Acts 19:1–4 we will deal with when we come to that passage.

Thus we see that the faith the Samaritans had towards Christ was not inadequate—it was true and sound faith. There was no problem or weakness with Philip's preaching that caused the delay in their receiving the Holy Spirit. Rather it was God Himself that caused the delay to instruct the infant church in the unity and equality of all those who confess the name of Jesus. We must *not* try to use this as a pattern for the Christian life: that is, first believe, then get baptized, and some time later receive the Holy Spirit when you ask for Him. Rather it must be understood in the context of the development of the early church in history as it moved across racial, religious and national boundaries.

Acts 8:18, 19

There appeared to be some external sign that showed the Holy Spirit had been given to those the apostles laid their hands on. We are not told whether there even was a sign, let alone what this sign was. Simon had been following Philip around (verse 13) and seeing the power of God first hand. It is possible that Philip had told him that the miracles were done by the Spirit of God, thus when the apostles came to give the Holy Spirit, Simon was desperate to have the same power. Sticking so close to all that was going on as he was doing, Simon would have known that the apostles were not selling the Holy Spirit—they were merely laying their hands on people and praying. We do not know if the apostles were already aware of Simon's heart and thus had refused to lay hands on him. All we do know is that the normal channels for receiving the Spirit were closed to Simon, yet it does not occur to him that his not receiving the Spirit could be connected to his moral condition. He was desperate for the power he had been witnessing and thus tries to buy it. Like all those who want "power" they are not concerned with righteousness and truth, but with their position of authority and control over other people. Words such as righteousness and truth are only used by such people as a means to maintain power—everything, including justice and truth takes second place to their main objective, which is to retain or increase their power and control in order to promote their own interests. Pilate scoffed at Jesus and the idea of absolute truth. Christ's Kingship and Kingdom rests upon truth (John 18:37). When Pilate responded, "What is truth?" he was saying that truth was nothing in comparison to power. According to Pilate, it was power that was the foundation for kingdoms, not truth.

Simon himself recognized the superior power of God over the power of darkness that he had been using. However, this does not mean that the reason he professed faith in the beginning was all part of his sly plan to get this power. The Scriptures show that it is possible to have a certain sort of faith for a while that ultimately comes to nothing (Matt. 13:6, 7, 21; Luke 8:6, 7, 13, 14). Such people recognize Christ to be the one in whom life and salvation are found and they willingly confess Him for a season, however, before such faith can be established (put down deep roots) or bear fruit, it is choked. Simon had some kind of understanding of the Word and felt something of its divine power, which he eagerly grabbed. His experience was different from those who immediately *reject* Christ and His truth, though his was not true conversion. Simon and people like him, are not only able to deceive others that they are Christians, but often deceive themselves too.

It is this kind of an experience that Hebrews 6:4–6 is talking about, where a person is not regenerated (made a new creation by the power of God), however, the Word brings deep concern and conviction upon them and they actually partake of the great privileges of the Gospel without being converted. The unconverted person professing faith in Christ can:

Be enlightened—that is, come under the glorious preaching of the Gospel and the light of its truth. We must never underestimate the privilege of hearing the message of salvation when it breaks in upon the darkness of this world.

Taste the heavenly gift—it is possible to taste the many blessings of grace that accompany the Gospel, finding true joy and delight in its beauty, yet without being truly converted: "But he who received the seed on stony places, this is he that hears the word, and immediately receives it with joy" (Matt. 13:20).

Become partakers of the Holy Spirit—this does not talk of having the Spirit dwell within them, but rather that they share in some of the gifts of the Spirit, e.g., Matt. 7:22, 23.

Taste the goodness of the Word of God—is to personally experience and know the goodness of God's Word, believing in your heart that it is holy, true and desirable.

Taste the power of the age to come—talks of being a witness of that power of God when He confirmed the ministry of Christ and apostolic authority by signs and wonders (see comments on Acts 8:6).

Hebrews 6 is not saying a true believer can finally fall away from the grace of God because the doctrine of perseverance is clearly taught in Scripture (John 6:37, 39; 10:28, 29; Rom. 8:30, 33–35, 37–39; 1 Cor. 1:8, 9; 2 Cor. 1:21, 22; Phil. 1:6; 1 Pet. 1:4, 5, etc.). Rather, it shows there are many unbelievers who actually have a real share in the blessings of the Gospel when they come under its light and profess to believe in Christ, yet in reality they stubbornly refuse to truly repent. The Israelites who came out of Egypt were all baptized (1 Cor. 10:2), were illumined in their camp by the heavenly light that followed them (Neh. 9:19), fed on heavenly food and drink, which was Christ (1 Cor. 10:3, 4; Ps. 78:13–16, 20), experienced God's mighty works and gracious protection, heard His voice (Ex. 19:19; 20:19; Heb. 12:19), were instructed by His Spirit (Neh. 9:20), yet never entered the promised land because of their rebellion (1 Cor. 10:5).

Demas had been a fellow worker in the Gospel with Paul, yet his profession of faith was shown to be without substance after a season (2 Tim. 4:10). Judas Iscariot professed faith and appeared to be exactly the same as the other apostles and was seen as part of the body. He shared in the same light as they did, preached and more than likely healed many people too (Luke 9:6), yet he was never converted. Hebrews 6 is a perfect description of him. None of the other apostles even suspected that there was anything wrong with Judas' witness and spiritual life (cf. John 13:22, 27–29). Balaam was a man who tasted the goodness of God's Word and power, yet he preferred to continue in rebellion (2 Pet. 2:15, 16; Num. 22). The fact that a person exercises a spiritual gift or is used by God in some way does not prove that that person is saved (Balaam's donkey, after all, revealed God's will to Balaam). We see that it is possible to taste and partake of the light, gifts and goodness of God's Word and power and yet be unconverted.

Hebrews 6 is also a true warning to believers. A warning does not contradict the doctrine of perseverance, since warnings are one of the means God uses to keep believers faithful (God often uses warnings throughout the Bible for this purpose). Finally, Hebrews 6 is not teaching us about the heart of God, but about the heart of man. These verses do not teach that God refuses to forgive those who have tasted of such blessings even if they truly repent, but rather informs us that when such blessings and light are trampled underfoot, that person will never repent. Such turning away is according to the true proverb: "A dog returns to his own vomit," and, "a sow, after washing, to wallowing in the mire" (2 Pet. 2:22). We see that there can be an appearance of being clean, but when a person's inner nature has not been changed they still desire pollution. Nevertheless the solid foundation of God stands, having this seal: "The Lord knows those who are His," and, "Let everyone who names the name of Christ depart from iniquity" (2 Tim. 2:19). They went out from us, but they were not of us; for if they had been of us, they would have continued with us; but they went out that they might be made manifest, that none of them were of us (1 John 2:19). There is only one sure foundation to stand upon with respect to salvation and security and that is apostolic authority, i.e., the whole of the Word of God (1 John 4:6). If we do not hold to this we will be deceived.

Acts 8:20

Gifts of the Spirit come from God and are to be used for the edification of the body of Christ and for the exalting of God's name. It is extreme wickedness for people to think that they can control God's Spirit with the use of money or anything else and thereby use Him to advance their own selfish and evil desires—this is nothing short of blasphemy. Peter pronounces a severe judgment upon Simon, threatening both him and his money with destruction or utter ruin. Hell is a place of complete ruin for all who enter into it. In hell, people eternally experience everything that is the exact opposite of life. Eternal life consists in the abundance of all things (righteousness, joy, peace, fulfillment, love, etc.), whereas eternal ruin consists in the utter poverty with respect to all these things (there is no hope, righteousness, joy, peace, love, trust, unity, etc.). Eternal destruction or ruin does not mean people cease to exist, but that they cease to experience anything worthy of the term *life*.

Simon wanted to buy the Holy Spirit. The way you use your money clearly shows what is really in your heart. Simon obviously had a lot of money, which is not evil in itself, but what money does is give opportunity for the heart to reveal itself.

Acts 8:21

Peter says Simon has no portion of God's gifts or grace, thus excluding him completely from the Christian community. The center of Simon's being (mind, will and character) was corrupt in God's eyes. God looks into our innermost being and nothing is hidden from His eyes (Heb. 4:13). It is madness to think that we can fool God. Paul prays for grace to be with all those who love our Lord Jesus Christ in *sincerity* (Eph. 6:24). We should ever ask the Holy Spirit to reveal where and when we are not sincere—may our hearts always be sensitive before Him in this matter. Simon had revealed his heart to Peter by his actions, however Peter was speaking under the inspiration of the Spirit and this terrifying judgment was made with the authority of God Himself.

Acts 8:22, 23

Peter used very strong language when he denounced Simon, but it was Biblical and his motive was clearly to make Simon face his wickedness and thus repent. Simon had asked to buy the Holy Spirit and so when Peter said repent (or be converted from this wickedness), he was most likely speaking about the depravity of Simon's heart and not merely about his desire to purchase the Spirit of God. It was the request to buy the Holy Spirit that clearly revealed this depravity. Simon appeared content to remain in this state despite having received so much revelation from God (see comments on 8:18, 19 above). He was in a worthless situation, chasing after temporary rewards and present gratification of the flesh. He still wanted fame and fortune in this life—the respect and riches that he used to have (8:9, 10), however, Peter called it all worthless. Everything about Simon was worthless—his heart, desires, past life, and present life all being included.

When Peter said, "if possible" or "if perhaps" he was not talking about God's ability or desire to forgive, but rather pointing to Simon's refusal to repent. Due to the darkness and stubborn rebellion in Simon's heart, Peter very much doubted that sincere repentance would come from him. There is never reluctance on the part of God to forgive true heart felt repentance (1 John 1:9; Rom. 3:24–26).

Simon's whole being was in complete bondage to wickedness, producing nothing but bitterness. Bitterness is an OT term (Deut. 29:18–20; Lam. 3:15), used also in Hebrews 12:15 and does not talk about having enmity or hatred for someone, but refers to a root producing bitter, poisonous fruit that contaminates and destroys everything it comes into contact with. Being bound in iniquity meant Simon was completely given over to Satan. This was a permanent state that he had been in for a long time (there was no back-sliding here, for he had never been released from this state). Simon was just one big bundle of sin—the whole of this bundle consisting only of wickedness. According to Peter, Simon was not just bound by sin, but was made up of nothing else but sin.

Acts 8:24

There is disagreement among commentators as to whether Simon repented or not. Tradition holds that he did not and that he was the source of many heresies. The Scriptural record ends abruptly with respect to Simon and does not explicitly state what happened to him. My opinion is that since he was such a powerful figure in the kingdom of darkness something would have been said about his conversion, thus the abrupt end appears to support the belief that he did not repent. True repentance is a heart felt sorrow for one's sins and not merely a fear of judgment or a fear to lose some outward privilege. King Saul only wanted to escape punishment and hoped that his kingdom wouldn't be lost, but there was never any true repentance, though he talked about his sin and wept (1 Sam. 15:23–25, 30, 31; 24:16; 26:21). To be struck or terrified by the awesome power of God does not mean that there is true repentance, even the devils tremble before God (Jam. 2:19). Pharaoh did not have true repentance, even though he asked Moses to pray for him (Ex. 8:28, 32; 9:28; 10:17). King Jeroboam is another example of half-hearted or false repentance (1 Kings 13:4–6, 33, 34).

It is possible therefore, that Simon, with his understanding of the way the kingdom of darkness worked, feared Peter and John because of their greater power, but never had his heart pierced by the Spirit of God and thus had no realization of his sinfulness. All he appears to have been aware of was a severe judgment pronounced upon him by some other very powerful men. He thought that they were the ones in control of the power and since they had "cursed" him, they should undo the "curse." He did not want to escape from the bondage of sin and death, but only from judgment. Peter had told him to repent (something that no one else could do for him), yet his request is that others would pray for him. It would be wrong to be dogmatic on this point of whether Simon repented or not. The purpose of the Scriptures (and thus of Acts) is not to give us a detailed account of what happened in any given situation, but rather to bring us to repentance and give us a firm understanding of the Lord. It is not detailed historical knowledge that is the aim of Luke, but such knowledge necessary for a right relationship with God—this relationship is called faith.

We see from this section what a fearful thing it is to play with sin— a small seed will mature into a harvest of bitter fruit. Our only hope is to repent and flee to the Lord for His mercy and rely upon Him moment by moment to keep us on the path of righteousness. We must never be intimidated by the power of sin as though we were at its mercy. Sin binds those who are in stubborn rebellion against God. Guilt also produces bondage, but to be bound when Christ has brought redemption is willful madness. Christ broke the power of Satan (Col. 2:14, 15) and the strength of his grip (Heb. 2:14). Satan never was autonomous (a law unto himself, doing exactly what he wanted), but always under the authority of God (Job 1:12; 2:6; Luke 22:31). When the devil is called the ruler of this world (John 12:31; 14:30; 16:11) it does not mean that he has autonomous rule, for these same verses show us that he is 'cast out,' 'judged' and has no power over Christ.

The victory of Christ arises from the cross, for this is the place of supreme sacrifice whereby reconciliation was made between God and man. God can now make a sincere offer to all people that if they believe in Christ they will be saved from their sin (see comments on John 3:16). Christ's victory was both comprehensive and complete and it is by faith in Him that we fully share in this victory over sin, death and the flesh. Reconciliation is something that was accomplished and so we are not to think about it as though it is something still in the future.

Acts 8:25

The apostles did not preach anything different to what Philip had been preaching. They just encouraged and strengthened the people in the same message and then returned to Jerusalem. On their return journey they were talking about Jesus in every city they passed through. Our responsibility is to faithfully make known the truth about Christ wherever we are and wherever we go.

Acts 8:26

The Spirit of the Lord sent a messenger to Philip (cf. verse 29) and this messenger was an angel (see comments on John 1:51, explaining the way God uses angels). God here gives us a look into His sovereign workings. It was the Spirit of God who was working in the heart of this eunuch and it was God's purpose to bring him into the Kingdom. We also learn that God uses means to accomplish His purposes—He uses Philip to preach the Gospel to this man. There is a responsibility upon all Christians to live and proclaim the truth of the Gospel with the view to leading their neighbors to faith and salvation.

Philip is sent to a particular road in the desert. There were two roads to Gaza and Philip goes to the less used one. The word south could also be translated as "noon," thus there are two possibilities: either he had to travel south on the road to Gaza, or he had to be on that road at mid-day. Philip was told to leave a place of great revival and multitudes of people for a lonely deserted desert road.

Acts 8:27

Philip immediately obeyed, despite the apparent strangeness of the command and met an Ethiopian man who was treasurer to the queen of Ethiopia. Obedience is a glorious path to walk upon—we need to believe this! May we always pray that God would enable firstly ourselves, then many others, to obey His Word on earth as it is obeyed in heaven by His angels (Matt. 6:10)—may God gives us hearts that will always obey quickly and sincerely. This Ethiopian man was a very important official. Eunuchs were often entrusted with positions controlling finances and possessions, since more than any other group of people, eunuchs were bound by the present, having no real concern for the future. Such men had no long term goal and hope beyond themselves. They were well looked after and their lifetime was all that really mattered to them. The godly family man is much more concerned with the long-term goal. In the OT a eunuch was prevented from full citizenship (i.e., responsible leadership) due to this natural weakness to be very present oriented (Deut. 23:1–8). The principle we learn from this is that the Kingdom of God is a long-term project and it is only those who have a strong commitment to the future that can be most effective in the present. Such a person is prepared to sacrifice present comfort and resources for the sake of future generations—present investment (time, money, discipline, sacrifice) for future gain is a Kingdom principle and relates to all of life.

The king of Ethiopia was worshipped as a child of the sun and it was beyond his dignity to be involved in the affairs of ruling the nation. This job was done by the queen mother who had the dynastic name of Candace. All the queen mothers were called Candace, just like all the kings of Egypt were called Pharaoh. It was very common to have eunuchs as officials in these kingdoms. This man had attended one of the Jewish religious festivals in Jerusalem and was now on his way home. He worshipped the God of Israel (he could have been a convert to Judaism or a God fearing Gentile) and had purchased a scroll that he was now reading. Only the very wealthy could afford to buy these since there were so few around due to the time and effort required to make these scrolls by hand.

Acts 8:28–30

The Spirit, or authority of God was behind the whole outreach. Religion as usual was continuing in Jerusalem with respect to the old system. There were no Christians in the city except for some of the apostles and the religious leaders probably thought that they had put an end to Christianity. From around 30,000 Christians talking about Christ throughout the city and holding large meetings within the temple area there was now practically no public testimony of Christ. Saul indeed had done a good job as far as the Jewish leaders were concerned, for worshipers could now come, spend some time in Jerusalem and leave without hearing about Jesus Christ. Yet this couldn't stop the spread of the Gospel! The clear message coming out here is that Christ's name will be proclaimed despite the most zealous attempts to prevent this. Oppressive powers have tried to do this from the beginning, however Christ will build His church and there is absolutely nothing that anyone in the whole world can do—the knowledge of the glory of the Lord *will* cover the earth as the water covers the sea (Isa. 11:9; Hab. 2:14). Philip, on hearing this man reading from Isaiah the prophet asked if he understood what he was reading about. The words that Philip used in asking the question show that he expected the man to say he did not understand.

Acts 8:31

In humility the eunuch admits that he does not understand.
Humility should be a characteristic found in all Christians, for a
proud person will not admit they are ignorant and will therefore be
unteachable. God did not send an angel, but an ordinary looking
man on foot. God has given gifts to His church in the form of
teachers. God uses people to do the work of the ministry—God
sent Ananias to Paul and Peter to Cornelius (Acts 9:10ff.; 10:22).
Although we must realize that it is only the Holy Spirit that can
open our eyes and enable us to understand the Word, God has also
ordained certain means through which the Spirit normally works.
Those pastors and teachers and elders called and anointed by the
Lord are real gifts from God to the church and without such people
the body of Christ would not mature and fulfill the ministry given
to her. Some people are waiting for voices from heaven to teach
them, others feel that they have enough knowledge already. There
are some Christians who think that there is no teacher that can tell
them anything that they do not already know. They feel it is pointless to read commentaries, for that only gives you the thoughts of
men. God has given us teachers as well as the Bible in order to lead
us into all truth (Eph. 4:11). Some think that Hebrews 8:11 means
we do not need teachers, but this is not so. This verse is making a
comparison between the knowledge of the Lord that the general
people had in the Old Covenant and the great change that has taken
place in the New Covenant (cf. Acts 2:17, 18), it is not doing away
with teachers.

Acts 8:32–34

Verses 32 and 33 come from the prophet Isaiah. Verse 33 is
extremely difficult to understand and its meaning is much argued
about by commentators. They all do agree, however, that these
verses describe an innocent victim who did not resist those who led
Him down a path of suffering and death. The eunuch realizes this
much and does not ask for a full explanation about the text, but
rather is struck by this suffering servant and wants to know His
identity. The Jews at this time held onto those passages that
described the Messiah as a powerful King who would be far greater
than king David. They did not interpret the Suffering Servant passages from Isaiah (e.g., 52:13–53:12) as referring to their great Messiah king. These concepts appeared to be contradictory to them—a

despised, suffering, victorious, conquering king. They are not contradictory within a Biblical worldview. Self-sacrificing servanthood is the source of real power. This was Christ's example for us to follow. Our minds need to be renewed to understand the Kingdom of God. Some people use 'servanthood' as a way to get power, they think that if they act like a servant for a season, then one day they will not have to do those menial tasks any more because they will have real power. This is not Christ's way! To be in the Kingdom of God is to reign and rule with power over all things on earth, however, the important question is, "What is living in the Kingdom?" What does it mean to "reign"?

We are so controlled by the thinking of this world that we believe to be great and to reign is to have lots of money and lots of people running around us doing exactly what we say (Matt. 20:25–28). Christ says those who are serving the needs of others in accordance with His Word are the truly great people and the ones who are reigning. *Power is service and flows through service.* God channels His power through real servants so that they are able to serve more effectively. The more power they get the more they serve and the more they serve the more power they get. Christ has ultimate power because He is the ultimate servant (John 13:12–17, cf. Matt. 28:18). A servant does not love his own life or seek his own will (Luke 22:42; John 10:11; 15:13; Rom. 5:6–8; Eph. 5:2). He faithfully does what is expected of him not because he hopes to get something out of it, but because he is a servant and knows that it is his duty to do it (Luke 17:10)—this is Kingdom living! It was Jesus who united the Suffering Servant with the Messianic King in His person and life. The Son of Man came not to be served but to serve, and to give His life as a ransom for many (Mark 10:45). Servanthood is not the first step to some other goal, but rather, servanthood is the goal—this is the Kingdom.

Acts 8:35

The whole of the OT is full of Christ and thus it was not difficult for Philip to preach Christ to the eunuch. Jesus Himself had done the same thing on the road to Emmaus where He showed that the Christ was to suffer many things to enter into His glory, "And beginning at Moses and all the Prophets, He explained to them in all the Scriptures the things concerning Himself" (Luke 24:27). Philip probably ended off where Jesus ended off with respect to baptism and teaching the nations everything that He had commanded (Matt. 28:19, 20). Philip preached the glorious good news about God's gracious provision of deliverance from the power and guilt of sin through the life, death and resurrection of Jesus. Christ indeed took upon Himself our sorrow and pain, though He was despised by us and we said that He was suffering for His own sin. He was wounded and crushed by God for our sinful rebellion. Our whole being, along with our relationship with God can be restored because He received the wrath and judgment of God upon His own body (cf. Isa. 53). The wrath of God has been satisfied in the death of Christ and the way of salvation made known to us and it is simple; just believe in the Lord, Jesus Christ and God's promise of forgiveness found in His sacrifice. We need to always refresh our minds about this glorious good news (Eph. 1:6, 7; Col. 1:20). We too often think lightly about the salvation that God has given to us. We think that because it is free it did not cost anyone anything. There is no greater news in the whole world than this message of reconciliation with God—a wonderful gift, though it cost God everything He had. Such amazing love and grace! Such amazing self-sacrifice! May our hearts be filled with adoration, thankfulness and sincere worship, for in Christ we receive the exact opposite of what we deserve.

Acts 8:36

On this desert road they unexpectedly come upon some water so the eunuch asks his teacher if there is anything to prevent him from being baptized?

Acts 8:37

Most textual critics argue that this verse should not be in the Bible since their research shows that in many Greek manuscripts this verse is missing. Most agree though that what the verse teaches is Biblical. The church has a long history of accepting this verse as part of the Bible and it is quoted by some of the earliest Christian writers as belonging to the sacred text of Scripture. All teachers will agree that there needs to be some confession of faith and belief in Christ before an adult convert can be baptized—we have no such profession if this verse is left out of this story, which I admit, does not mean that such a profession couldn't have taken place (J.A. Alexander says the external evidence is equally balanced on the sides of either including and excluding this verse). When deciding whether to accept or reject this verse I have sided with accepting it as original for the following reasons: (*a*) it is idea is Biblical, (*b*) it makes sense in the context and (*c*) the church, for most of its history, has received this verse as authentic.

Acts 8:38

This verse does not help us determine how someone is to be baptized. Whether the person is to be put right under the water (immersion) or just sprinkled. Some have argued that the word "into" shows that they walked into a deep pool of water, however this is a very weak argument since this word "into" can be translated in many different ways. It can just as easily mean that they both went *to* the water (i.e., up to the water's edge) or that they stood up to their ankles in the water. In John 11:38 the same word is used to say that Jesus came *to* Lazarus's grave, *not into it.* There are many more similar examples where the word cannot be translated 'into.' Acts 8:38 cannot be used in the baptism debate in order to settle the mode of baptism. In verse 39 the translation can just as easily be, they came up "from" the water (i.e., came up to the road from the water that was on a lower level), and not that they came up "out of the water."

Acts 8:39

To be "caught away" refers to Philip's sudden removal from that place in obedience to God—he did not resist the new leading of the Spirit, but rather once again obeyed the Lord on earth as He is obeyed in heaven (Matt. 6:10; see comments on Acts 8:27). The emphasis is upon the fact that God was (and always is) directing everything. The text before us does not say that the eunuch did not see Philip any more *because* Philip was caught away in some miraculous way. Rather, the eunuch was no longer aware of Philip *for he* (the eunuch) was consumed with the joy of the Lord and the excitement of his new birth. This is to be our goal: that we would not promote ourselves but so promote the glory and goodness of Christ that we become "invisible" (cf. John 3:30). Jesus is to be the focus of our lives: of all our actions, words and outreaches. We hear nothing more of the eunuch and although tradition tells us he became an evangelist, we have no evidence to support this tradition. We do know that about 300 years later (A.D. 330) Athanasius, bishop of

Alexandria, sent missionaries to this area where the eunuch came from and their efforts were rewarded with converts.

Acts 8:40

Philip's mission with respect to the eunuch was completed, thus the Spirit of God directed him away from this man towards some other people whom the Lord wanted to hear the Gospel. Philip then, without being told to go to any particular city, came upon Azotus as we might come upon someone in the street whom we were not looking for or intending to come across—he merely arrived at Azotus (formally known as Ashdod, 1 Sam. 5:1), though the Lord was directing his steps.

Many good commentators interpret this incident with Philip as a miraculous transporting of him through the air from where he baptized the eunuch to the town of Azotus. Other commentators, equally as good, do not see this as a miraculous transporting of Philip through the air, and this is not because these commentators do not believe in the miraculous—they do believe in miracles, though they do not think that this text clearly talks of such an event.

The following verses are the ones normally used as support by those who believe that Philip was miraculously carried through the air from one place to another:

1 Kings 18:12, however, there is no evidence whatsoever that Elijah ever traveled about like this in the air, though it is very clear that the Spirit of God led and hid him and that is what Obadiah was referring to. Since Elijah was under the direction and guidance of the Spirit, who could predict his next move? When Elijah was taken up to heaven he was clearly visible to Elisha (2 Kings 2:11, 12) and besides, this is really the only way to move by the Spirit from the earth to some place above the earth (cf. Acts 1:9). Being caught up in the air (1 Thes. 4:17) is referring to a similar situation of being taken from earth to a place above the earth and does not talk about traveling around upon the earth. Paul in 2 Corinthians 12:2, 4 cannot tell whether his experience was in body or spirit, however, even *if* it was in body, once again the situation is one of being taken from the earth to a place above the earth and not to a different location upon the earth. In the same way Revelation 12:5, referring to Christ's exaltation and enthronement, depicts movement between the earth and a place above the earth (this happened when Christ

ascended to the right hand of the Father, see comments on Acts 2:33, cf. Ps. 2:9; Rev. 19:15). Ezekiel the prophet talked about being carried through the air by the Spirit, however this was only in vision and not in his physical body (Ezk. 3:12, 14; 8:3; 11:1, 24, etc.). In my mind, none of these texts support the idea that Philip was miraculously carried from one place to another. The only text that I can think of that mentions something on these lines is John 6:21—this sign, however, was to glorify Christ in the sight of the apostles.

With Philip, there does not appear to be any reason for such a miraculous journey to Azotus. He merely passed through the city and continued his journey preaching in each city he came to. If he was transported to the eunuch in this way, i.e., carried to a certain place in order to capture an important moment, then that might have added support to the idea of "miraculous travel," but he wasn't. Something else that weakens this idea of "miraculous travel" is that even if Philip did experience miraculous travel it does not appear to have become a part of the early church's mode of transport; we are not told of it happening even once again. Paul no doubt, on many different occasions, could have done with this kind of help had it been available (cf. 2 Cor. 11:25–27).

What we need to focus upon in this passage is the power of God working in the lives of both those who are saved and those who are being saved. The truly exciting thing is the sovereign working of the Spirit in the Kingdom of God. We see His divine control and directing of Philip's life and we rejoice to see a heart so submitted to the leading of God. Philip's heart was totally dedicated to doing the Lord's will. He said, "Speak Lord, thy servant hears you." We also see in this passage the glorious union that God has ordained—for us to be involved in the work of the ministry with Him. The Spirit was working mightily in the heart of the eunuch to bring him to repentance and He uses Philip to preach the Gospel to him. There is no greater gift than that of eternal life and God had ordained it so that we might have a significant, though mysterious, part to play in His gracious giving of this wonderful gift. May we be inspired by the example of Philip to be people who are aware of the Kingdom of God and His purposes on this earth. May our hearts rise up in adoration of this marvelous and mysterious working of God's Spirit in the world. May we be forever conscious of His working in our own lives and in the lives of those we come across. This working of

the Spirit in the eunuch's heart was not a once off incident, but was
recorded for our instruction, showing us that God is always working! May we go forth in His power and give everything we have to
bring glory to His name and Kingdom. Oh Lord, catch us away to
do your will! May we be found faithful as we labor in the Lord's
vineyard, for the earth is the Lord's and everything in it (Ps. 24:1).
All our striving and all our efforts are to be towards the ultimate
goal: that every knee should bow and every tongue confess that
Jesus Christ is Lord! (Phil. 2:11). He alone is worthy and we are His
servants—there is nothing else for us to do!

Acts 9:1, 2

Saul understood that there could never be any peace between what
he believed and what the Christians believed. He saw the Christian
faith as a dangerous, aggressive opponent against everything that he
held sacred. Saul realized that his beliefs and the Christian's beliefs
were not just two different ideas that could live side by side, since
both claimed to be the *only* way of salvation. Christianity claimed
to be the absolute revelation of God and everything could only be
understood as it was understood in the light of whom Christ
claimed to be. The Christians said that all who did not rely completely and only upon Christ for salvation and all things were self-
deceived and remained under the wrath of God. Saul said that whoever did not go through the OT priesthood, temple sacrifices, circumcision and the many other Jewish traditions that had been
added by the religious leaders over the years, were cursed by God.

Saul realized what a serious threat Christianity was and thus was
not satisfied to merely drive it out of Jerusalem or merely out of
Judah. He wanted to destroy it from the face of the earth. He saw it
as a cancer that had to be removed completely. Saul correctly realized that Christianity had an absolute claim that touched every area
of life. Christianity was called the Way, because it was seen as a
complete way of life. Christianity reveals the only way of salvation
and is the only source for showing how we are to live in every area
of life. Many Christians in our day do not realize this and have
reduced the *Way* to a very limited area of influence. Such a reduced
understanding of the claims of Christ would not have threatened
Saul—he would not have thought it necessary to persecute the
modern church, for it wouldn't have been a threat to his cherished
religious system and way of life. Jesus said that He is the *Way* (John

14:6), thus everything to do with life must focus on Christ and flow out from Him. Every other way of doing things leads only to death.

Stephen knew that there could be no compromise between the two systems and he died for this belief (cf. Acts 7). The truth of God is absolute, touching all of life and there is nothing higher than it, thus it will not tolerate any other system. Any idea, opinion or action that does not come into line with the Word of God is not only wrong but arises out of stubborn, willful rebellion against the truth and will receive the just judgment of God (both now and at the end of time). This is the Christianity that Saul had declared war on and this alone is true Christianity.

Rome had given the High Priest and the Sanhedrin authority to reach into surrounding nations and bring Jews back to Jerusalem and punish them according to Jewish law. Paul asked for and got letters of authorization to exercise this kind of power in Damascus and other foreign cities (Acts 22:5; 26:11). Paul and the Jewish authorities had nothing but hatred and murder in their hearts for the Christians. We are not told what brought about such a massive change from Gamaliel's council of tolerance in Acts 5:39 to this extremely vicious persecution. Jesus had warned His disciples that such a time would come when people like Saul would believe that by killing Christians (Acts 26:10) they were offering service to God (John 16:2).

Damascus was a commercial center and Saul probably feared that if Christianity was allowed to flourish there, then it could easily spread throughout the whole world—infecting all Jews.

Acts 9:3

Saul was a very determined and cruel persecutor who carried out his task with intense energy and zeal. His mind and his will were filled with only one thing—the destruction of all those who called upon the name of Christ. The furthest thing from Saul's mind as he traveled the 300 km to Damascus was that he would become a believer in Jesus. He acted out what was in his heart, ruthlessly destroying the visible manifestation of Christ—His church. With his heart set on murder and with the authority of his nation behind him, Saul boldly approached Damascus like a wild beast that was about to rip apart the flesh of its prey (see comments on Acts 8:3). He had been traveling for about five days and at last he was about to do that which brought him great delight, when the Lord sovereignly changed his heart. As Calvin says, "Christ tied the jaws of the greedy wolf as he was ready to enter the sheepfold." While this conversion was unique in many respects (the blinding light and the voice from heaven), it was not totally unique in that conversion is always a sovereign act of God's grace. Saul is confronted with the glory of God and it completely overwhelms him.

Acts 9:4

To see the Lord is a terrifying experience (cf. Dan. 8:17; 10:8) and all the strength, energy, hatred and pride that had filled Saul's heart was ripped away in one moment. All that man treasures most and all that makes him feel most secure evaporates into nothing in the awesome presence of the Lord of Heaven. This powerful man who was terrorizing the flock of Christ, collapses in a heap on the floor and is unable to move. Christ then speaks, calling Saul by name and asks him to account for his behavior: "Why are you persecuting Me?" To bless one of Christ's children is to bless Him (Matt. 25:40, 45) and to persecute one of His children is to persecute Him. We must never think that we are alone in what we do for the Kingdom of God, for Christ is so united with us that He endures the hardships that we endure in His name. Those sufferings of Christ that are still to be made up by the body (Col. 1:24), show us that Christ endures what we endure. Christ's presence with us is not just a theory, but reality. We find it so difficult to appreciate the union that exists between Jesus and ourselves. We more readily hold to a Christ "out there" than the Christ "in us." We need to see, believe and draw our strength from the reality of our inseparable union with Christ and not think in terms of separation. We can and must distinguish between the Head (Christ) and the body (us), though we must never separate the two. There is a different kind of relationship that you form when you think of Christ as someone "over there," rather than as being in us and we in Him. Even though this union between Christ and the church is a great mystery, it is still intimate and very real (Eph. 5:31, 32). We are one flesh with our Savior and this is our hope of glory. Our strength and vitality come from this relationship, so may we be encouraged to nurture it. In marriage there is a real wholeness and strength that flows out of an intimate union between the husband and wife. However, if a couple is not living within the reality of what marriage should be (an intimate, inseparable union), then they will not have the wholeness and strength that they should have and that is possible from their union. Such people remain legally married though only relate to each other as they would relate to someone "over there" and do not see each other as being one flesh with themselves. These are two completely different marriage relationships that produce completely different fruit. Our personal intimacy with Christ is vital to our effectiveness in the Kingdom. May God by His Spirit enable us to partake of that intimacy that He has given to us.

Acts 9:5

Saul was still able to speak and asks who is speaking to him. The voice answers and says, "Jesus." Saul hated and despised this name, believing that any person who called upon Jesus deserved to die. The Jesus whom Stephen had preached about and had seen standing at the right hand of God, was now confronting Saul. What is said next is repeated in 26:14 and is a purely Biblical explanation of the sinner's rebellion against God. Jesus says, "Why are you kicking against the goads?" A goad was sharp spike that was used to control oxen. To kick against it was foolish, for this would only hurt the ox more and get him nowhere. Saul is here likened to a stubborn ox who is foolishly harming himself and yet continues to kick against the spike. What is said about Saul here is true of every unbeliever— they all foolishly rebel against what they know to be true and by their rebellion only hurt themselves and yet continue to rebel. Saul knew the Scriptures very well and had heard much preaching and teaching about Christ. The truth of who Christ was, was clear and inescapable, yet Saul continued with his violent desire to destroy the church. Even an ox would eventually realize that it was foolish to kick against the goad, but Christ says Saul was more stubborn and foolish than this, for he had not yet stopped kicking against what he knew to be true. Sin and rebellion have the same effect upon every heart! The sinner consciously chooses to walk on a path of self-destruction, despising the light—all who hate God, love death (Prov. 8:36, see too, *Faith and Reason*, chapters 1 to 3).

Saul had one of the hardest hearts around, but it was the power of Christ that turned him to the truth. It is God who pursues sinners and brings them into His fold. Saul was changed from one who violently tried to destroy the church to one who tirelessly laboured to build up the church. All those who hate Christ are like Saul—they hate His church too. When we are converted, we should cry out to the Lord to give us hearts that ceaselessly work for the Kingdom. Paul told us to follow his example because he followed Christ's (1 Cor. 11:1).

Acts 9:6, 7

Whether the beginning of verse 6 should be included in our Bibles or not falls into the textual debate. I am following the KJV and J.A. Alexander who says that he finds it difficult to believe that this would have been purposely added if it did not originally exist in some Greek Text that we no longer have. Added to this, the words fit in very well with the whole flow of the account. Thus I will side with that which has had a very long history within the church from the earliest days and treat the beginning of verse 6 as part of the text. "So he [Paul] trembling and astonished, said, Lord, what do You want me to do? And the Lord said to him … "

Saul was confronted with a real objective manifestation of Christ and not just something in his own mind. The glory of the Lord and the voice was real. Jesus was pursuing Saul and confronting him alone, though there were others with him. There has to be an internal work done by God in a person's heart in order for them to come to a position of faith and submission (Jesus did many signs in front of other stubborn Pharisees and preached powerful sermons and they just scoffed at Him). Those that were with Saul were knocked to the ground, but were able to rise again and although they heard the sound of the Lord's voice, He did not enable them to understand what He was saying (Acts 22:9; 26:14). Saul was humbled and converted. He had until then despised and hated Jesus and committed his whole life to removing the remembrance of Jesus' name. He now says to Jesus, "Lord what do you want me to do to further your cause?" Remember, to do what the Lord says is to further His cause and not to do what He says is to resist His cause. The root of all sin is man wanting to do his own will and not God's will, thus conversion is bringing man back to that place where he says to God, "What do You what me to do?".

If we are truly servants of the Most High we will not live in a way that merely adds Christ onto what we are already doing, but rather we will seek to live for Him and do only what He wants. We have been created so that we might bring glory to Christ's name and Christ has told us how to do this—we are to live by faith, faithfully doing what He has said. We are not told to make sure that we have great results, we are not told to become famous, but we are told to live in faithful obedience to everything Christ has spoken about. The world has this obsession with success and sets a standard that everyone must aim at. The measuring stick by which people are measured as to whether they have attained the expected goal is also supplied by the world. Everyone has bought into this mindset, including Christians and use their time and effort in an attempt to attain this goal. Many Christians drive themselves and their children towards these goals. Yet the world's success is an outward appearance only and emphasises temporary things like popularity, riches or fame. At the centre of this kind of success is the self—my achievements, ambitions and sense of accomplishing something worthwhile. Rather, our focus should be upon a heart and life dedicated to the Lord. That is where our efforts should be aimed, for what is of more value than godliness and faithfulness to Christ? The world, however, cannot measure these things because it sees them as meaningless.

God's goals for us are to change us into the image of His Son, to enable us to have a real deep relationship with Him and to faithfully serve Him in humble obedience. Anything that distracts us from emphasising these or hinders us from moving in this direction is to be cast from us. The prophet told us what God requires of us: to act justly, love mercy and walk humbly with God (Micah 6:8). As far as the world can evaluate, Saul forsook a very promising and successful career and threw it away when he said to Jesus, "You tell me what to do." He was a highly respected Pharisee (Gal. 1:14) who would have had a nice life consisting of, respect from all the leaders of the nation, much comfort, security and ease. Instead of this he became a member of an outcast group of people, having no riches, being despised by his nation, beaten many times, stoned, arrested, imprisoned and finally executed for his faith. Was the apostle Paul successful? He loved the Lord and from when he was converted until he was martyred, his only concern was to be found faithfully loving, obeying and serving the Lord—everything else was worthless (Phil. 3:7, 8). Paul's boast in 2 Timothy 4:7 was that he had been *faithful* to the Lord. His joy was not in his accomplishments, but in his steadfast faithfulness to God's will. We all ought to constantly ask the Lord, "What do you want me to do?" for we are so easily infected by the world's idea of success. To be found faithfully doing that which the Lord wants us to do is to be eternally successful (Matt. 24:45, 46; 25:21). It is not obvious what we must do or what is important in the Lord's mind, thus we need to get our instructions from the Scriptures and not deviate from this wisdom (Isa. 55:8, 9).

Acts 9:8, 9

Paul was now blind and there had been an extremely radical upheaval in his life. His views, affections, direction and purpose had all been completely changed. Paul tells us in Philippians 3:12 that he had been seized or arrested by Christ.

Acts 9:10–14

Ananias was a devout man and highly respected among the Jews in Damascus (Acts 22:12). Paul who had nothing but curses on his lips for Christ, now is continually praying to Him (verse 11). Paul's hatred for and violence against Christ's church was common knowledge and even his purpose for coming to Damascus was known to the Christians. Ananias is understandably fearful. For him to go to Paul in the name of Christ would be like giving himself up to certain imprisonment and probably death.

Acts 9:15, 16

The Lord is patient with us. There are many different situations in our lives where we are not convinced that the Lord actually knows all the facts. We think that His expectations and instructions are strange and thus we resist them, believing that our knowledge of how to do something is better. "I hear what You say, Lord, but there are other things that need to be taken into consideration"—do we not do this all the time? The just shall live by faith—our actions are to be done by faith. We trust God and His Word and live our whole lives in obedience to His instructions, not because we have worked all things out, but because we trust God. There are so many ideas in the world and different ways of doing things that it is impossible to check them all out and discover which is the "right" way. Life never stands still. We do not have the option of stopping everything until we have discovered the right way to do something. We are moved along by our decisions and the fruit of wrong decisions is hardship and unrest. Most of the time it is not clear when you make a decision that it is the wrong one. This only becomes obvious later on when harm has been done, but there is no turning the clock back. It is a true saying that, "Time waits for no one." When we walk according to the Lord's ways it is in opposition to the way the natural man thinks and the way everyone around us is thinking. Often there might be no other people who will support us in what we do, but the just must live by faith—absolute trust in the Word of Christ. "I have set the Lord always before me; Because He is at my right hand I shall not be moved" (Psalm 16:8). The Psalmist also said that when he rests in the Lord he will not fear even though the earth is removed and the mountains (that which is most secure and stable on this earth) are cast into the sea (Ps. 46:2, 3).

The Lord revealed to Ananias the great task that had been placed upon Paul and the great suffering that he would experience. How do we measure success? John the Baptist's ministry got smaller and smaller as he continued to live in poverty in the desert. He was arrested and spent a long time in a dungeon (Matt. 4:12). He even doubted whether Jesus was the Messiah (Matt. 11:3). He was then secretly beheaded and a few of his disciples came and took away his body and buried it (Matt. 14:10–12). Was he successful? Christ called him the greatest prophet in the Bible (Luke 7:28). Jesus did not have many followers at the end of His life. He was humiliated by being executed naked upon a cross. Was He successful? Paul endured much hardship, was severely persecuted, despised, hated, had very few possessions, was imprisoned and finally executed. Was he successful? If we allow the world's concept of success to control our thinking, we will become weary in well doing and will not live by faith in God's Word.

Acts 9:17–19

Ananias obeys the Lord's Words and totally accepts Paul (Saul), calling him "brother." Real Christian maturity and understanding are demonstrated by Ananias. Before salvation all people are haters and persecutors of Christ, but when He brings someone to salvation, that person is made part of Christ's body and family. In Christ all are equal (Gal. 3:28). Paul was saved, I believe, on the road, though he had not yet received the Holy Spirit, but once again, the reason was due to the unique situation. Paul had been a terrible persecutor of the church. So much so that after much time preaching and teaching about Christ, the Jerusalem believers were still afraid of him (Acts 9:26). Yet immediately after his conversion, the

Damascus disciples receive him—why? I believe it was because of the respect Ananias had among the disciples, so that when he told them about the vision from the Lord with respect to Paul and told them that when he prayed for Paul he received his sight and the Holy Spirit fell upon him, there was no doubt in their minds that Paul was a true disciple. The Lord did not need to use Ananias, but the church needed Ananias' testimony and it also shows that the Lord uses people in bringing about the accomplishment of His will. This should encourage us to faithfully minister where we are, knowing that our labor is not in vain (1 Cor. 15:58). It appears as if Ananias also baptized Paul, though we have no evidence that he was an ordained minister in the church and he most certainly was not an apostle (cf. Gal. 1:17, 18).

Acts 9:20

Saul had been given authority to enter all the synagogues and arrest all those who called upon the name of Jesus. Now, after his conversion, he immediately and repeatedly went to the different synagogues in Damascus and instead of dragging Christians out, preached that Christ is the Son of God. There were many synagogues in the city of Damascus, as there were in Jerusalem and which is very similar to our days where many different churches exist within a single city. Saul, knowing what hatred existed among the Jews for all those who called on the name of Jesus, boldly went out and defended this name. The emphasis of Saul's preaching at this time was that the Messiah was Divine—to be the Son of God is to share in the being of God, thus making Him equal with God. Very fresh in Saul's mind was his recent encounter with the glory and power of the Divine Messiah on the Damascus road.

Acts 9:21

This complete change around in Saul leaves his audiences utterly amazed. It was no secret who Saul was and why he had come to Damascus, thus the Jews would have gathered to hear him condemn the Christians and confirm the Jewish faith through words of exhortation from the high priest. Saul's reputation had come ahead of him to Damascus and all knew of his vicious and successful efforts against the church in Jerusalem—he was a destroyer. Saul had come to ruthlessly destroy the church in Damascus too, yet these people find him glorifying that name he previously hated with his whole heart. The Damascus Jews could not believe what was happening, saying, "This cannot be the same Saul whom we were told was coming to drag Christians back to Jerusalem." Saul, one of the most zealous, influential and gifted Jews of his day (Gal. 1:14), had come to believe that Jesus was the Son of God and his savior—this seriously shook the Jewish religious establishment.

Acts 9:22

The ability and gifting of Saul soon manifests itself for the cause of Christ. God had gifted and prepared Saul and he indeed turned out to be a tremendous gift to the church. God does raise up people in history and give them special gifts so that they in turn might bless the whole body of Christ. God gives gifts to His church, but it is wrong to think that this means that to be a gift to the church or for the church to benefit from someone, that person must be alive (i.e., part of the present generation). The church in our day deprives herself of many gifts that God has given throughout the years, by not remembering her history and the great servants of the Lord who have finished their course. Part of this is due to the fact that the modern church fails to realize just how imperfect she is and has a rather high opinion of herself and her gifting. To have a poor understanding of what God has done in the past will leave you in a very weak position. God does not give all the gifts to any one person, or any one church, but rather to many different people and churches. In the same way, God has given gifts throughout the history of the church that together help make up a strong healthy body on earth. To ignore or despise the unique giftings of the past means that you will not build upon them. Many reject the past because it was not perfect, however they are very blind to their own imperfections. What the church needs in order to glorify God in the twentieth century has not been given to the church in this century. God has slowly given us what we need throughout the history of the church. We need to respect and appreciate those who have gone before us and have laboured in the Kingdom of God. It is only by standing upon their shoulders that we are able to advance God's purposes in history. Not to stand consciously upon their shoulders means that we will not even reach up to their ankles (spiritually speaking).

We all have our own unique gifting and calling in God's Kingdom, but there are also some people that God has raised up throughout history who have been exceptionally gifted and God has used them to strengthen His body and glorify His name in a way different to the rest of us. Saul is one of these people and signs of his great gifting and ability were displayed very early when he completely confounded the Jews in Damascus. Saul's understanding of the Scriptures and his reasoning ability left all those who argued against Christ totally bewildered. They could not answer Saul, yet they refused to believe the truth that he was proclaiming and so were left holding onto a position that they knew was hopeless. Saul had clearly shown that their system of belief (which everything else in their lives rested upon) was unable to support them. They knew they were in error and that Saul was standing upon the Scriptures. When they tried to defend their position they found that they just contradicted themselves and were thus fully aware that Saul had thoroughly defeated them. Saul's courage and wisdom in showing that Christ was the central focus throughout the whole of the OT just increased the more he preached and debated. Not only did his own convictions get strengthened but his ability to take apart his opponents' views and expose their weaknesses also increased. Those Jews who said they placed ultimate authority in the Scriptures had nowhere to hide, for it was these Scriptures that Paul used so effectively to prove that Jesus was the Messiah.

Acts 9:23

We saw with Christ, Peter and Stephen that there comes a point when those who oppose the Gospel resort to violence in order to defend their rebellion against the truth. The light of God's Word is clear and cannot be escaped from and its brightness increases as it is applied to every area of unbelieving thought. As the unbeliever tries to defend his position he allows more light to shine upon it, thus exposing its weaknesses even more. Unless repentance comes, the unbeliever is left in a very desperate position of trying to hold together his destroyed world view. It is not people who are able to convict hearts, thus it is foolish to try and kill someone in order to escape from the conviction of sin and rebellion. Conviction is the Holy Spirit is work and it is impossible to escape from Him. Saul couldn't make his words pierce these Jew's hearts, no matter how wise he was, thus to kill Saul would not remove their deep conviction of sin—only repentance could do that.

And after many days, is a long period of time. In 1 Kings 2:38, 39 it
refers to three years. Luke was not trying to give a detailed account
of everything that happened in these early days of the church. No
biblical writer was merely interested in increasing people's knowledge about historical and chronological details, rather they were
motivated by a desire to give such knowledge that is necessary for a
right relationship with God—a true faith relationship. Luke was
not writing a biography of the apostle Paul, but rather telling his
friend Theophilus about the victorious spread of the Gospel from
Jerusalem to the heart of the Gentile world. Acts records the
advancing of the Kingdom of God by exalting the name of Jesus
Christ, through the power of the Spirit—this is the glorious message that Luke is interested in communicating. Our desires and
efforts should all be aimed at this goal also.

We see that after Paul's conversion there was a period of about three
years before he went up to Jerusalem (Gal. 1:17, 18). During these
three years he was in Damascus and Arabia, though neither Paul
nor Luke give us enough details whereby we can know the exact
chronology of how things happened. Luke allows room for these
three years without including the details. In Galatians, Paul's focus
is not upon chronology, but upon the authority of his calling and
therefore he does not give details about those three years either.
Paul's calling, apostleship and therefore authority were all directly
from the Lord Jesus Christ—this is the important point that Paul
was anxious to communicate. To get side-tracked by the lack of
chronological details and thus ignore Paul's authoritative teaching
is a sign of rebellion against the authority of Christ. Luke and Paul
do not contradict one another. Both accounts are accurate, however, both accounts are *incomplete* with respect to historic and
chronological details.

Acts 9:24

The Jews in Damascus somehow got the support of the governor of
Damascus (2 Cor. 11:32) and thus a serious threat was placed upon
Saul's life at that time. However, their evil plot was made known to
Saul as well as the fact that they were watching the gates day and
night. There were many Christians in Damascus, however Saul was
the one they wanted to kill, probably because the impact of his
influence and leadership was recognised as the greatest threat. If the
church is able to recognise God's gifting in a person, how much

more isn't Satan able to recognise it? The great servants of the Lord have often had to endure much suffering, temptation and persecution, though through their faithfulness their impact within the Kingdom, as a result of these, has been even greater. Satan's evil plans, ultimately *always* work against him.

Acts 9:25

Some of the houses were built upon or adjoined to the city wall. We learn from 2 Corinthians 11:33 that this passing through the wall means that they let him down through a window. The people who helped Saul are called "disciples" and probably refers to those who came to believe in Christ due to his preaching.

The Jews in Damascus could not escape from the light of God's truth which Saul had so clearly made known—fully exposing their rebellion. Their solution was to kill the messenger of God, as if this could stop the purposes of God (Rom. 9:19; 2 Chron. 20:6; Dan. 4:35). At this point these Jews identify themselves with the people of Jericho who also could not escape from the truth of who God was, yet continued to fight against Him, thinking that they could defeat God by killing His messengers (Joshua 2:9–11, 15). By fleeing, Saul was resisting the authorities of the city (cf. Rom. 13:1–5), though he was not resisting God. We need to carefully understand what Romans 13 is teaching, for it is not giving absolute power to the state (government). To think that the state can do whatever it wants and everyone merely has to obey is nothing but blasphemy. God alone is absolute and He has not given absolute power to the state. The state is to obey God and where the state acts in violation to the Word of God, we are not obliged by God to obey them. This whole subject will be dealt with in its proper place, however, for now, it is enough to point out that Saul resisted duly appointed authorities, yet he did not resist God (see *Muse Time,* papers 3 and 5, "Romans 13" and "The State," for a brief discussion). There is a time to flee and there is a time to fight. Later on in Acts, even though Paul is warned of the dangers awaiting him in Jerusalem, he still goes there, saying he is prepared to die for Christ (Acts 21:13). Now, in Damascus, it was right for him to flee.

Acts 9:26

Saul repeatedly tried to join the Christians in Jerusalem, however, they brought fear upon themselves. There was no basis for this fear other than their memories of Saul's reputation that was now three years old. Not one Christian had been brought back to Jerusalem from when Saul had originally left and not one Christian had suffered under the hand of Saul since his conversion. It is possible that there was not much communication between Jerusalem and Damascus due to the conflict between Herod and King Aretas of Damascus. The fact that Saul had spent some time in Arabia would also have added to the lack of definite information coming back to Jerusalem about him. Nevertheless, it was Barnabas who did what was right while those who doubted that Saul was a disciple were in the wrong.

Acts 9:27

There is no real proof that Barnabas and Saul knew each other from Tarsus (from before Saul's conversion) as some have tried to argue. Rather when the Scriptures say that Barnabas "took hold of Saul" it was Barnabas who took the initiative and fearlessly investigated Saul's testimony. It was due to Barnabas' strength of character that led him to do this and not due to having had some previous acquaintance with Saul. By going to Saul he would have exposed himself to the danger that was terrifying the Jerusalem church. We are not told the details, however, Barnabas was convinced that Saul was a true believer and thus the church had caused itself much unnecessary fear which in turn had caused them to act in a timid way. We are told that perfect love casts out fear (1 John 4:18) and Barnabas was a man who had the love of Christ in his heart and thus was willing to lay down his life for others (cf. Acts 4:36, 37). Here the Lord uses him in a powerful way to unite the great apostle with the other apostles.

Many people in our day use the excuse that some church or pastor offended them and therefore they are not prepared to go to church again. May the example of the great apostle rebuke such foolishness! Saul had been serving the Lord and as a result of this his life was threatened. He managed to escape and flee to Jerusalem, the Headquarters of the NT church, yet Saul was repeatedly rejected as he tried again and again to join himself to the Jerusalem church. He did not get caught up in self-pity and bitterness and go off discouraged because the church was imperfect. We see Saul's humility and his understanding that he was part of the body of Christ. He knew that he needed to be united to other believers and therefore did not look for an excuse so that he could go off on his own. It is pride that causes us to think more highly of ourselves than we ought to, thus a proud person is easily offended for he thinks, "How dare they treat *me* like that? *I* deserve much better treatment than that." Whereas, what we *deserve* is God's judgment and not some special treatment from others. We are not worthy of even the smallest benefit. Our only worth is from being united to Christ, but this means that we share in Christ's worthiness and not our own. We need to focus upon the mercies and vast benefits that we have received and not upon the much smaller incidents where we think we have been mistreated. We are here to serve Christ and His Kingdom which means that our focus is never to be upon ourselves, but first upon Christ and then upon others and when we have lived our whole lives in this way, we are still unworthy servants who have done only what we ought to have done (Luke 17:10).

Barnabas takes Saul to the apostles, however, it is difficult to tell whether the apostles were aware of Saul's presence in Jerusalem before this. We learn from Gal. 1:18, 19 that Saul only met Peter and James at this time who, according to Luke, represented the whole group—the other apostles were probably not in Jerusalem during the fifteen days while Saul was there. Once again the details are lacking in both Acts and Galatians (see comments on Acts 9:23). Paul, in Galatians, is proving that he did not receive his authority to preach or his message of the Gospel from any human—not even from an apostle. Luke, in Acts, in introducing Paul to Theophilus is showing that Paul had apostolic acceptance. Both passages emphasise the authority of the apostle Paul, though in different ways and neither passage wastes time filling in chronological details that are not crucial to the main arguments.

It is possible that Barnabas took Saul to the apostles because he realised that Saul had been set apart by the Lord to be an apostle—he had seen the Lord and had been give his commission by the Lord (Acts 26:16).

Acts 9:28

Luke shows just how accepted Saul was within the apostolic circle. He was treated as one of them, going in and out with them. We are not told exactly what was done during this time, however, not much could be accomplished in fifteen days. The main reason for going to Jerusalem was to confer with Peter, thus there wouldn't have been much time to do a lot more, so it is easy to understand Saul's statement that he remained unknown to the churches in Judea (Gal. 1:22).

Acts 9:29

Saul did somehow get involved with some Hellenistic Jews (of the same group that had been primarily responsible for the death of Stephen, see comments on Acts 6:9). Saul, knowing only too well their hatred for the message of Christ, boldly proclaims the Gospel and argues with them. Once again, just as happened with Stephen, when these people couldn't answer or escape from the evidence for Christ found in the OT, they decided to kill the one pointing them to the truth. It is possible that Saul thought since he had a Hellenistic background these Jews might listen to him. Once again Saul's life is threatened.

Saul, however, was prepared to lay down his life for the truth—wanting to follow in Stephen's footsteps. In Acts 22:17–21 we are given some more details by Saul himself. He thought that he should remain in Jerusalem because his testimony would be very powerful since everyone knew that he was a former persecutor of the church. The Lord however tells him that there is other work for him to do and that he needs to get out of Jerusalem for the time being. This is the third time that this message has been repeated—that Saul is being sent by the Lord to the Gentiles (cf. Acts 26:17; 9:15; 22:21).

Acts 9:30

Who these brethren were we are not told, but their response to finding out about the threat on Saul's life was to get him away from Jerusalem. Saul readily agreed to go with them because the Lord had confirmed that this was His will. What Saul did in Tarsus we are not told and exactly how long he remained in Tarsus is also difficult to work out. Some commentators say he was there only one year, others two or three years and some think as much as eight or nine years. The sacred text tells us no more about Saul until he is invited by Barnabas to accompany him on a trip to Antioch (Acts 11:25, 26). It appears, according to the Scriptural records, that the great apostle Paul spent ten years (from his conversion until Acts 11) in almost complete obscurity. What we must remember however is that Acts is not a detailed account of everything that was happening in the early church. There was much, much more going on than is recorded in Luke's brief history. There does appear to be some evidence that Saul was very active in his calling during these "quiet" years: e.g., the Judean churches were hearing about Paul's preaching during this time (Gal. 1:23); Paul's great vision recorded in 2 Cor. 12:2–10 also took place during this "obscure" period; It is also possible that some of the hardships that Paul talks about in 2 Cor. 11:22–27 were endured during this period when the sacred book is silent about him: of the three beatings by the Romans, only one is recorded in Acts (16:22). The five Jewish beatings are not recorded at all. Of these three shipwrecks, Acts tells us nothing (see comments on Acts 27:1, 2). It seems most probable that these unrecorded incidents occurred during this "silent" period. Paul tells us in Galatians 1:21 that when he left Jerusalem he went into Syria and Cilicia. In Acts 15:23 we learn that there were Gentile churches in these areas. In Acts 15:41, Paul on his second missionary journey went with Silas to Syria and Cilicia in order to strengthen the churches that were already there (probably started by Paul during those "silent" years).

Acts 9:31

Luke gives a summary statement about the state of the church as he shifts the focus off Saul and onto Peter. It was at this time that God brought about a period of peace for the Christians who used this time to great profit. I do not believe that Luke is trying to make a connection between Saul going to Tarsus and the churches having peace. It was God who brought about this period of rest and this was not done by getting Saul out of the way. Historians suggest that there was much turmoil between the Jews and Romans at this time as well as changes in the Roman leadership and all of this distracted the Jewish attention away from the Christians. Whatever circumstances the Lord used to bring about this peace are not important in Luke's mind and thus we shouldn't be anxious about trying to discover these details.

There were many churches now in this region. The names Judea, Galilee, and Samaria represent the whole of Palestine. Paul also used the plural when talking about the "churches of Judea" (Gal. 1:22; 1 Thes. 2:14) and the plural is also used in Acts 16:5, thus I follow the Ecclesiastical Text that has the plural, rather than the singular, in Acts 9:31. Jesus had laboured tirelessly in these areas and we are now informed that there are churches dotted throughout the whole region. We must never become weary in what we are doing. We only become weary when we walk by sight and not by faith. It is faith that has the courage and the ability to walk in the Light, proclaiming the truth and seeking the Kingdom of God even when there does not appear to be any immediate fruit. God has said that His truth will succeed and accomplish that which He intends (Isa. 55:11, cf. Heb. 4:12; 2 Tim. 3:16). He has told us that the prayer of a righteous man is powerful and effective (Jam. 5:16). It is by faith that we begin this Christian life and it is to be continued in faith, for it is by faith alone that we stand (2 Cor. 1:24). The just must live by faith in the promises of God (1 Cor. 15:58; Heb. 10:38), which means we are not to walk by sight (2 Cor. 5:7; Heb. 11:1). The true seed needs to be sown before there can be any real harvest and usually the sowing and the reaping are separated by quite some time and are done by different people (John 4:35, 37; 1 Cor. 3:5ff.). It is a denial of Scriptural teaching to say the only measure of success is how many people have been saved as a result of a person's labour. Even if many are saved as a result of our efforts, we must never forget those who went before us and did much sowing (John 4:38).

Peace is a wonderful blessing from the Lord and is given to advance the work of the Kingdom. We must never waste such times or think that we will always have such opportunities. Diligent, disciplined and focused efforts are what advance the purposes of God— remember, the days are evil and therefore we ought to make the most of every opportunity to do good (Eph. 5:16). Time is scarce, there is much evil and many distractions, so it is easy to waste valuable time. The only way to not waste this precious gift from God is to know His will and do what He says (Eph. 5:17). If we walk according to our own wisdom we will definitely waste much time, thus we need to see our desperate need to live by every Word that comes from the mouth of God (Matt. 4:4) every moment of our short lives.

Luke tells us that the church was edified. This refers to the spiritual growth and strengthening of those within the church through the preaching and teaching of the Word. A clear manifestation of this spiritual growth in the lives of the Christians was that they walked in the fear of the Lord—not wanting to do anything that would offend the Lord, they brought every thought into line with the mind of Christ (2 Cor. 10:5). This is coming to a position where we actually do not fear what the world thinks of our obedience to

Christ. It is only by the grace and work of the Spirit that we can come to a point where we will stand against the tidal wave of worldly opinion and walk upon a new path that honours the Word of God. Not only does such a life style bring that true deep comfort from the Spirit (that internal peace that the world cannot understand), but such a way of life can have a powerful impact upon those who do not believe. Our comfort is to be looked for from the Holy Spirit and not from worldly standards or worldly opinions about us.

Acts 9:32

During this period of peace, Peter was doing an extensive tour throughout the region, visiting all the churches (Paul makes a note in passing, in 1 Cor. 9:5, that Peter took his wife with him on his missionary journeys). I do not think Luke is being distracted from his main emphasis at this stage. The inclusion of the Gentiles into the church of Christ was one of the biggest obstacles to overcome and I believe Luke has been steadily building his case in support of this inclusion. It is clear that Saul had been saved and commissioned by the Lord to be the apostle to the Gentiles (verse 15). The Lord, though, chose to use Peter to testify about the clear sign of the Lord upon the Gentiles that clearly indicated their complete acceptance into the Kingdom as Gentiles. Peter had already prophesied about the Gentile inclusion into the church in Acts 2:17, where "all flesh" has reference to the whole human race (see too comments on Acts 8:14).

These two recorded miracles done through Peter at the end of the chapter 9 emphasise his apostolic authority and thus confirm his testimony as coming from the throne of God. Therefore, when Peter testified about the Lord's leading to Cornelius and about what he saw, this was sufficient for the Jerusalem council to make an authoritative statement with respect to the Gentile's acceptance and position in the church of Christ (Acts 15:6–11). Peter's authority had been clearly confirmed by God through all the signs that he had performed (see comments on Acts 2:22; 4:30; 8:6, etc.). Luke here recounts two signs in order to establish, for Theophilus (and us), that Peter spoke with the authority of Christ. These signs also happen to closely resemble two miracles that Jesus had done while on earth.

Acts 9:33–35

Peter does not guess about this man's healing. Christ must have communicated His will to Peter in this respect, for Peter does not pray that Jesus would heal him, but tells the paralytic man that he has been healed. It is not Christ's will that every physical weakness must be removed and the apostles did not have the power to heal according to their own wills (see comments on Acts 5:15), thus it would have been presumption to make such a statement without Christ's confirmation. We are told to pray for the sick, yet healing rests upon God's sovereign will and not upon some formula that we manage to discover and use. As Peter speaks the man is healed, thus he says to the man, sort out your bed. In Mark 2:11 Jesus had told the paralytic that He healed to pick his bed up. Both of these secondary commands demonstrate the completeness of the healings as each man received the full use of previously lame limbs. The effect of this miracle in Lydda was that many people came to put their trust in the name of Christ for salvation.

Acts 9:35–43

In the nearby city of Joppa a faithful disciple of Christ dies and Peter is implored to hurry to Joppa. We are not told, but one assumes that they probably were hoping that the Lord would do a miracle through Peter. The early church is thriving (verse 31), it is now a number of years after Pentecost and yet they do not pray for a miracle on their own authority. Those who want to "get back to the early church" where, they tell us, miracles were done whenever they asked, need to explain the "failure" of the Christians in Joppa and Lydda.

Dorcas was a true servant of the Lord who had her focus upon the needs of others. Peter follows Christ's example to a certain degree in clearing the room and in what he says to the corpse (cf. Mark 5:40, 41). As a result of Dorcas' rising from the dead, many more people came to believe in Christ.

Peter then went and stayed with a man who tanned animal skins. Due to Simon's constant contact with the skins of dead animals (prior to tanning that is) he was seen as ceremonially unclean by the Jews. Peter however goes and stays with this man for quite some time. The signs together with this fact are all leading up to chapter 10 where the Gentiles are officially accepted into the church. It was the ceremonial law that would have pronounced Simon unclean, just as it was the ceremonial law that prevented Gentiles, as Gentiles, from being part of the covenant. However, with Christ, the ceremonial law was put out of operation. Thus Luke has mentioned Saul's commission from Christ to the Gentiles. The authority of the leading apostle is once again underlined through signs (as miracles underlined the authority of the prophets Elijah and Elisha, 1 Kings 17:17–24; 2 Kings 4:32–37; 5:14, 15, and of Christ, Acts 2:22). We see Peter's disregard for the ceremonial law when he stayed with Simon and all of this is leading up to Luke's next point (the main point)—Peter's authoritative declaration with respect to the Gentiles. We must be careful not to emphasise that which was merely support for the main point.

Acts 10:1

We have seen Luke cover periods of many years in a few verses, however the importance of this next issue is so great that he spends an extensive amount of time telling and retelling the story (Acts chapters 10, 11, 15). The full acceptance of Gentiles as Gentiles into the body of Christ was one of the most difficult things for the Jewish believers to accept. On the one hand, we have Cornelius as the representative of the Gentiles and on the other hand, we have Peter as the representative of the Jews and apostolic authority. God prepares both representatives separately, without which, the massive gulf between Jews and Gentiles would never have been overcome.

There is a continuous flow from chapter nine to chapter ten. As we have seen above, Luke is not starting a new subject, but has already prepared us for what is coming.

Cornelius held a fairly high position in the Roman army and Centurions, we are told by historians, were the backbone of the army. This tells us something of the kind of man Cornelius was.

Acts 10:2

Due to the workings of God's grace, Cornelius had already been enlightened by the Spirit—he was a believer in the True God. He was still waiting for the Messiah to come, though his devotion to God and his fear for God were truly Biblical. He was not only devoted, but righteous (Acts 10:35) and these terms are not used for those with unregenerate hearts. The Scriptures know nothing of a righteousness without faith. Morality without faith does not exist! Good works are inseparable from true faith, for what does not flow from a purified heart is polluted no matter how "good" it appears to people. Cornelius was a man of faith in the promises of God and even though his understanding was limited to the OT revelation, he had a true relationship with God, just like Abraham, David and the prophets—who all believed in the coming Christ (John 8:56; Acts 2:30, 31; 1 Pet. 1:10, 11). He was not accepted by the Jews because he had not become a Jew—namely, he had not been circumcised, however in God's eyes he was a just man (Rom. 2:28, 29).

As far as the Jews were concerned, Gentiles were always welcome to become full members of the Synagogue, however this was done by the Gentiles becoming "Jews"—that is, being circumcised and submitting to all the ceremonial laws of purification and separation (abstaining from certain foods, etc.). The great shock to the Jews was that this wall of division (the ceremonial law) was removed, so that Jews were accepted as Jews and Gentiles were accepted as Gentiles—both equal in God's sight (Eph. 2:14; Gal. 3:28, 29). This incident was ordained by God, not for showing that Gentiles could be saved, but rather, that they were worthy of *full* covenant membership in the church of God, as Gentiles.

Cornelius' life demonstrated the fruit of conversion—prayer, care for his family's spiritual well being and generosity to others. This is one of those brief summaries of the Christian life (true spiritual devotion to God and practical first principles starting at home and flowing from there out to others). Remember: *The light that shines the farthest, shines the brightest nearest home.* Luke's brief account of Cornelius' life is really a summary of the 10 Commandments—a relationship of devotion towards God and towards man (Matt. 22:36–40; Mark 12:28–33). If there is no grace, there can be no acceptable works. Cornelius' faith was no private affair. He had influenced his whole household (verse 24) and his stand would have been equally as strong in his work place, which would not have been easy—it is not easy to be a Christian in the military.

Generosity is a sign of true love and devotion. Cornelius was generous to all people—there is always someone we can help if we are not self-centred and filled with covetousness and self-pity (covetousness and self-pity are always found together). Paul tells us that to give everything you have to others is worthless if you do not have love (1 Cor. 13:3) and the love he is talking about here is that which flows from a pure heart (1 Tim. 1:5) and a heart is only made pure by faith (Acts 15:9). Without faith it is impossible to please God, no matter how great the world thinks you are (Heb. 11:6). Our faith must be grounded on the promise of God's redemption found in Jesus Christ. The only works that are acceptable to God are the ones that flow out of true faith in Jesus Christ—every other work will receive His wrath. Cornelius' prayers flowed from a righteous heart of faith and were therefore acceptable.

The word used for prayer in this verse means to want, lack, stand in need of, desire, long for, to ask, beg. It is communication with God, though with the emphasis of urgently pleading due to realising one's need.

Cornelius was a saved man and yet prevented from entering into the fullness of the blessings given to the covenant people of God. This must have been a tremendous struggle for him—a matter of great anguish and labor in prayer, which he did constantly. To the Jews, although they respected him highly, he was still an outsider and unworthy of full participation in the visible church of God. Cornelius' groanings probably arose from his knowledge of the Scriptures and such passages like:

Look to Me, and be saved, All you ends of the earth! For I am God, and there is no other (Isa. 45:22).

All nations whom You have made shall come and worship before You, O Lord, and shall glorify Your name (Ps. 86:9).

And it shall come to pass afterward that I will pour out My Spirit on all flesh (Joel 2:28).

I will bless those who bless you, and I will curse him who curses you; and in you all the families of the earth shall be blessed (Gen. 12:3).

Cornelius knew what a glorious privilege it was to be included in the visible church of God and yet he was powerless to bring this about. The Jews were absolutely incapable of accepting a Gentile on equal terms and their traditions had made the massive gulf between them impossible to bridge. For a devout man like Cornelius this produced pure agony of spirit, though he had the character of a Jacob and a Daniel (Gen. 32:25, 28; Dan. 10:12)—persevering and prevailing in prayer. Cornelius was a man who was hungry for the fullness of the relationship God had for him, and he longed for the fulfilment of all the wonderful Messianic promises, thus he would not rest until he had a share in these (both visible and invisible). This is the same deep desire that Jesus likened to eating His flesh and drinking His blood (John 6:53ff.). Satisfaction is not received until the fullness of Christ enters into us and we enter into the fullness of Christ and His Kingdom. The Kingdom of heaven suffers violence and the violent take it by force (Matt. 11:12, see comments on Acts 2:40). Much earnest and untiring energy is required to possess the fullness of the Kingdom. Such blessings are only experienced by those who aren't afraid to challenge the traditions of men with the pure Word of God. They do not count the cost but press in to take all that God has ordained for them. Such burning zeal is a manifestation of a true son of God and the Father hastens to answer such prayers and efforts, for *this* is the Kingdom of God.

Acts 10:3, 4

Cornelius was not earning God's favour, for he had already received that by God's grace and mercy. What we have here is the fruit of a redeemed man—clearly revealing what is in the heart of a righteous person. This was a sweet savour to God who then responds to these requests from Cornelius by sending a "messenger" to tell him what to do. This is all so similar to Daniel (9:3; 10:12, cf. Acts 10:30, 31). Perseverance is a major aspect that we see in the great saints of God—everything we do should flow from this same kind of determined zeal for the full glory of the Lord to be manifested in us and around us.

Some people foolishly try to argue that this passage teaches that Cornelius' devotion, as a pagan, earned him God's favour—this is madness, for we have seen that without faith it is impossible to please God. It is totally unbiblical to think that an unconverted person is capable of doing any kind of works pleasing to God.

Acts 10:5, 6

These are clear detailed instructions given by the angel. God saw it as necessary to manifest an angelic messenger in order to set-up the incident whereby Gentiles would be accepted into the church.

Acts 10:7, 8

Cornelius, not knowing what this man Peter would say to him, immediately dispatches some men to fetch him—he wanted to know and do whatever God would communicate through the apostle. These men he sends were more than likely chosen for this mission because they were close spiritual companions in Cornelius' life. They were not just sent with a message, but Cornelius explained everything to them—they were real friends in the Lord (John 15:15). The soldier that went with is called "devout" and this is the same word used to describe the spiritual state of Cornelius himself. God had promised Cornelius that his great desire was about to be granted—there was a man in Joppa who had an answer for him and his name was Peter. Sending off his friends to find this man, must have been a time of deep expectation, excitement and solemn urgency. He now had to wait for four days (10:30).

Acts 10:9–13

The ceremonial laws consisted of the sacrificial laws (animal sacrifice, etc.), priestly order (priesthood) and temple system and structure of worship. These served as shadows of Christ and pointed to Him, exhorting worshipers to place their faith in the Promised Savior before He actually came. The many ceremonies were signs or symbols of spiritual truths that were fulfilled by Jesus. Included in these ceremonial laws are laws relating to feasts, places of ritual significance, circumcision, clean and unclean animals, food restrictions and laws against mixing (e.g., Lev. 19:1, 2, 19; Deut. 22:9–11).

The nation of Israel was the visible church of God in the OT. This does not mean that everyone in the nation was saved, anymore than we believe that every person in the visible church today is saved. In this unfolding plan of God's redemption the ceremonial laws separated Israel as a nation from all the other nations (Gentiles) and preserved this separation and thus Israel's identity. Without listing all the different laws of separation, but focusing on the one that is in our present passage, we see that Israel was not allowed to eat certain animals that the Lord said were unclean (Lev. 11; 20:22–26; Deut. 14:3–21). These regulations about unclean animals created a barrier between Jews and Gentiles and God, in this way, protected His church from the influences of the pagan nations around them. This was only meant to last for a season, however (Heb. 9:10–12), for God's purposes have always been international in scope—He is the Lord of the whole earth (Ps. 24:1). Thus God's working with the nation of Israel was meant to serve as a type (or picture) of how He would deal with the multinational church of Christ. The many different ceremonial laws not only served to keep Israel separate from the other nations, but also kept them mindful of the holiness of God who was in their midst (Ex. 29:44–46; Num. 5:3; 35:34; Deut. 23:14), and magnified the glorious work of the Messiah who was yet to come.

There is no Biblical evidence to support the idea that the dietary laws were tied into health requirements—they were teaching separation from ungodliness which the international church is to spiritually honor by separating from all the defilements of the flesh (Acts 2:40; 1 Cor. 5:6, 9–11; 15:33; 2 Cor. 6:14–18; 2 Thes. 3:14; Jude 23; Rev. 18:4; Prov. 9:6). God never gave food restrictions to Noah (Gen. 9:3)—in fact quite the opposite is stated, even though there were clean and unclean animals in his day (Gen. 7:2, 8). Abraham was circumcised, though he was not told that he couldn't eat certain animals. It appears that the dietary laws were instituted in order to keep Israel's national identity whilst in the Promised Land. This national separation was a shadow (sign) of the spiritual separation that would be fully realized in Christ's work and the outpouring of the Holy Spirit. With the Spirit of Christ dwelling in us we will never be overcome by the ways of this world (Rom. 8:11; Eph. 1:19). Our separation is to be ethical and is now only between believers and unbelievers. The way believers are to think, talk and behave is opposed in every way to how unbelievers think, talk and behave—this is the *eternal principle* that was being taught by the *temporary* dietary restrictions. (There were no plants that were unclean to the Hebrews. To argue that the dietary laws were for health, one has to ask why no plants were forbidden). I believe that what Peter saw were only unclean animals and God told him to kill one of them and eat it as an act of devotion and service to God.

Acts 10:14

Peter was horrified by such a suggestion. In religious devotion to God he refuses to do what God had said, saying he would become impure if he ate one of those unclean animals. Jesus had already talked about the ending of clean and unclean foods (Mark 7:14–23, esp. verse 19 "thus purifying all foods"). Paul would later clearly teach the same thing (Rom. 14:2, 6, 14, 17, 20, 21; 1 Tim. 4:3–5).

Peter says that which was commonly done by all the heathen, he would have no part in since God's Word set the bounds for what he could and couldn't do in all of life.

Acts 10:15

The ceremonial laws had been instituted by God and therefore, they could only be changed by His authoritative Word. God is saying that all the pictures and signs (in the ceremonial law) that pointed to Christ were fulfilled and thus removed the moment He accomplished His work of satisfaction (Col. 2:16, 17, cf. Heb. 10:1–14). The moment Jesus died on the cross, the priesthood and the ceremonial law could no longer be observed in the way it had been observed up until then—we now observe them in Christ. He now is our Passover Lamb (1 Cor. 5:7), He is our High Priest (Eph. 5:2; Heb. 9:11, 12, 26, 28), He alone cleanses and washes us constantly from sin (Col. 2:14; 1 John 1:9) and from the defilements of this life (John 13:10, cf. Lev. 11:26–28, 31, 40, etc.). God clearly revealed this reality when He ripped the veil in the temple from the top to the bottom at the time of Jesus' death (Matt. 27:50, 51).

Acts 10:16

The Lord repeated this three times so that there could be no doubt as to what He was saying. Peter probably argued with the Lord each time too. God's repetition underlines the importance of this incident.

Acts 10:17

Peter had gone down to Samaria to witness and confirm the Samaritan's acceptance into the church of Jesus Christ (Acts 8:14, 17). He had spent some time with Paul who had told him about his calling to the Gentiles (cf. comments on 9:28). He was prepared to stay with a "ceremonially unclean" man (cf. comments on Acts 9:43). All of this meant that Peter had a pretty good understanding of the shift that had taken place in the NT church with respect to the covenantal separation between Jew and Gentile. However, even Peter couldn't understand the meaning of his vision, for he did not realize that God would totally accept people without the ceremonial law—forever destroying the wall that separated Jews and Gentiles (Eph. 2:11–22; 3:3–6). God had to move in a mighty and unmistakable way in order to show that Gentiles were to be accepted as full members in the church. Peter was disturbed by what he had experienced. This just goes to show how ceremony had replaced reality in the Jewish minds. We need to constantly be on our guard that we do not fall into the same trap, where the reality of the Kingdom of God and the reality of our relationship with Christ are overshadowed by the rituals of our religious lives. Our praying can become a ritual, rather than an intimate time of communication and fellowship with our Lord. Our worship together as a congregation can become a ritual rather than a time of mutual encouragement and feasting upon the Lord in our hearts by faith.

Acts 10:18–21

The Lord now makes the connection between Peter's vision and the Gentiles—a realization that began to grow in Peter's understanding. In order for the Gentiles to be fully accepted into the church, the ceremonial law had to be "put out of gear." The way the Lord showed Peter that this dietary law was no longer binding in the way it used to be, was to tell him to eat previously unclean animals. The reason the animals were no longer unclean was because God had declared them to be clean. The ceremonial law was no longer valid as a standard for determining clean and unclean, thus, diet and circumcision, the two main things that made the Gentiles unclean were now removed.

There has to be a relationship between this vision and its message of Gentiles being accepted into the church—this connection is found in the ceremonial law: it was the ceremonial law that had made the distinction between clean and unclean animals. God clearly told Peter not to think in this way anymore. Peter interprets the dream as God showing him there were no unclean people (verse 28)— God did this by showing him that there were no unclean animals.

The Jews would not eat with Gentiles because Gentiles did not observe these dietary laws. God was saying that there was no longer a basis for keeping separate from Gentiles because diet could no longer make one unclean. All that was needed was faith in Jesus and whoever had this faith was as clean as the next person—nothing else mattered. God does not have two right ways. There is only obedience to His truth and disobedience. To say that we can eat any animal and not receive God's displeasure, but believe that if we observe the dietary laws whenever we can then that's a better way, introduces a two level Christian life—some actions are righteous and others are more righteous.

Acts 10:22

Cornelius' servants tell Peter about him—he was a just man that feared God. They tell Peter that an angel had told Cornelius to send for him. The Lord had just told Peter that He had sent these men and that Peter was not to doubt their story. Peter was to go and preach to the Gentiles. Our consciences are to be controlled by the revelation of God or else we will be tossed about by many futile things. God was moving and all of man's ideas and misunderstandings were being demolished.

Acts 10:23a

Peter's response is to eat with the Gentiles and invite them to spend the night with him—indeed a further breakthrough in Peter's understanding of the Gospel. May we also quickly submit to the revelation of our God and King and not be bound by our traditions and customs. We are not to be afraid of what the world will think of us, our concern should only be to obey the Lord's revelation in every area of life. Oh, help us Lord Jesus!

Acts 10:23b

God was moving His church in a direction that they were sluggish in perceiving and therefore resisting. It is God who builds His church and here we see Him setting things up so as to abundantly confirm Peter's testimony. Peter leaves with the men sent from Cornelius and with some Jews from Joppa (six in number, cf. 11:12), whose testimony would be very useful later.

Acts 10:24

We see Cornelius' faith. God had told him to call Peter and therefore he knew Peter would come, thus he gathers many people. The Spirit had been working not only in the heart of Cornelius, but in the hearts of many close friends and relatives around Cornelius.

Acts 10:25, 26

Cornelius, I believe was very aware of the deep spiritual significance of Peter's visit and being filled with gratitude, greets Peter in the way he thinks such an important servant of the Lord ought to be greeted. Peter, in true godly humility tells Cornelius to get up, saying that he is also merely a man. The glory is to be always completely given to Christ. Peter is one of the most gifted and significant teachers in the history of the church, yet he says, "I am just a man and thus deserve nothing more than any other person." He knew his gifting was from God, thus there was nothing that he could boast about as coming from himself (1 Cor. 4:7). When God anoints great teachers it is for one primary purpose—so that the church might worship, adore and glorify Christ more truly. We ought to show respect to such people, but we ought never to forget that our focus must always be turned to Jesus and teachers should always remember that their primary responsibility is to always turn people's hearts and gazes onto Christ. The whole reason for our own existence and the existence of everything else is so that Christ might be glorified.

Peter says, "Cornelius, let your overflowing gratitude pour upon Christ. What is happening comes totally from His hand and grace. Give Christ the thanks for every good thing, including my coming to your house, for every good gift comes from above." May our hearts forever turn in ever increasing gratefulness to the Lord for His many, many benefits that He gives to us daily. May our lives and actions forever shine forth the pure light and truth of Christ, thus causing many other hearts to rise in thankfulness and gratefulness to God—may we truly be a blessing in word and deed for the glory of Christ. There is no greater purpose in life than this.

Acts 10:27, 28

When the temple curtain in the Holy of Holies was torn in two, that marked the end of the whole Jewish ceremonial system of law—finding its complete realization in Jesus Christ (Col. 2:17). The ceremonial law can be divided into two broad categories:

1). Those laws and regulations that reminded the people of the principles revealed in God's moral law and encouraged the people to obey these principles.

2). Those laws which provided a remedy for breaking the moral law. The moral law shows the righteousness of God, whereas these ceremonial laws showed how one's relationship with God might be restored after violating God's righteous standard—primarily blood atonement, showing the way of salvation. Thus these animal sacrifices ultimately pointed to the only blood sacrifice that can remove moral uncleanness—that is Christ's sacrifice (1 John 1:7; Rom. 3:25; 1 Cor. 6:11; Eph. 1:7; Heb. 1:3; 9:13,14; 10:1; 1 Pet. 1:18, 19; Rev. 1:5; 7:14, etc.).

Converts to *Judaism* (those fully embracing the ceremonial law: circumcision being an absolute necessity) were made equal with Jews in legal and religious matters, however, were never granted full social equality and were always known as proselytes. Now, Cornelius was not even a proselyte (a convert to Judaism), but remained a Gentile. He worshipped the same One and only true God that the Jews worshipped, though he was not accepted into the visible church, due to the fact that he had not submitted to the ceremonial law entirely (see comments on Acts 10:2). He would have participated in the blood sacrifices, but not all the rituals like dietary laws, circumcision, etc.

Peter says the Lord had shown him something (through the vision of unclean animals). Paul taught that all those ceremonies that defined certain things as clean or unclean (for the purpose of separating the covenant people of God from all the other nations) were abolished in Christ (Rom. 14:2, 14, 20; 1 Cor. 8:8; 1 Tim. 4:4; Titus 1:15). Peter, who at first did not understand the vision he had been given (verse 17), comes to the conclusion, in the light of God's subsequent command to go with the Gentiles, that since he was not to call any animal unclean, neither should he call any person unclean. There had to be a connection in Jewish thinking between unclean animals and Gentiles whereby Peter could make this logical conclusion (one of the primary signs that God's people were holy unto Him, was their physical separation from certain animals that God called unclean, Lev. 20:22–26). To be unclean disqualified you from fellowship with God—God alone sets the basis for having a relationship with Him. Due to our slowness to perceive what is clear, God explains emphatically, by giving a vision to His apostle and then clearly pronouncing through the apostle that these changes were God's doing and no invention of man. Only God can change what He has instituted, though the change is merely in outward form and not in principle.

The Jews had focused more upon the outwardness of the rituals rather than the internal spiritual meaning (remember the two divisions within the ceremonial law: we must not confuse them). It appears that the believing Jews could easily see that Christ's blood replaced the animal sacrifices, etc., but they did not quite know how to deal with those rituals/ceremonies that exalted the principles of the moral law—how were they to be observed in the new dispensation? This failure brought about the need for the Jerusalem Counsel in Acts 15 to discuss and make a ruling on the whole issue of circumcision.

In Acts 10 we have a different ceremonial ritual that the new church did not know how to handle, namely, the food laws.

Such laws were given so as to constantly keep before the eyes of the Israelites the fact that their faith related to all of life and that there were clean and unclean "things" in every area of life.

To think that the righteousness that God desires is somehow related to food is to miss God's purpose totally. It is not what enters a person that defiles them, but what comes out of their hearts (Mark 7:15, 19; Rom. 14:17; 1 Cor. 8:8). This outward ordinance of the food laws was made only for the purpose of spiritual instruction— constantly impressing upon the minds of the Jews (a constant reminder) that at every moment of man's existence moral choices have to be made and we either choose good or evil.

Eating is something that needs to be done all the time, thus constantly before the Jewish eye was the principle that they were responsible to act according to God's Word at every moment— choosing the pure and forsaking the impure. The distinction between clean and unclean in these areas came about by the authoritative command of God. Just as food sustained the body, so the Jews were made aware that it was by discriminating between righteousness and unrighteousness in every area that their spiritual lives were nourished and preserved. God's Word alone can determine good and evil. It is not man's appetite, taste, desire or own will that ought to control his actions and tell him what he should do (God's declaration respecting what could and couldn't be eaten shadowed this truth that everything always had to be kept in check with God's authoritative Word). The Jews were bound by God's revelation in all areas, whereas Gentiles freely did whatever they fancied. The fundamental purpose of the dietary laws was to be holy as God is holy (Lev. 11:44). This does not refer to food entering the belly, but rather to living by every Word from God's mouth.

The ceremonial law also had the purpose of preparing people for the coming of Christ—picturing His salvation and Kingdom.

Another important aspect that comes out in Peter's vision is the separation between Jew and Gentile as a result of these food laws. Having such distinct eating habits naturally hindered fellowship. The Jews couldn't touch Gentile food for fear of being defiled or polluted and this fear led to the Jewish custom of refusing to enter a Gentile's house. God's purpose in these laws of separation was to preserve His people from the immorality and idolatry of the Gentiles, though this was a temporary situation, only until Christ came. With Christ comes the fullness of the reality which was always the law's intention—spiritual purity. The actual food laws themselves were symbolic and not based on moral principles, thus it was *lawful* for Gentiles to do what Jews couldn't (Deut. 14:21). On moral issues, there has always only been one standard. Thus there was no moral change in God or His standard of righteousness when He pronounced these foods clean for the Jews.

The physical separation from people and things in the OT pointed to the eternal principle of spiritual separation from every aspect of unbelieving thought and action. The Jews emphasised almost totally the physical aspect and neglected the spiritual aspect, thus the emphasis of the Jewish religion became outward and it ignored the internal corruption (e.g., John 18:28). The outward was always meant to encourage the inward. The time of Jewish/Gentile separation and therefore all those laws that established physical separation had been brought to an end as a result of Christ's perfect sacrifice and the outpouring the Holy Spirit in abundant measure (Eph. 2:14–16; Luke 3:16; Acts 2; Rom. 8:4). The incident of Peter and Cornelius is God's official announcement that the ceremonial laws of separation were no longer valid. The great problem of accepting Gentiles into the church was not that the Jews thought Gentiles couldn't be saved. Rather, what was most difficult for the Jews was that Gentiles could be full covenant members without submitting to the rituals of the ceremonial law.

The outward appearances between the Old Covenant and the New Covenant are different, however the internal spiritual intention has always been the same—spiritual vitality, holiness and living lives that glorify God. With respect to the dietary laws, the spiritual truth that is *eternal* is that God's people are to stay away from impurity.

This is more fully realised in the NT, e.g., "Do not be unequally yoked together with unbelievers. For what fellowship has righteousness with lawlessness? And what communion has light with darkness? And what accord has Christ with Belial? Or what part has a believer with an unbeliever? And what agreement has the temple of God with idols? For you are the temple of the living God. As God has said: "I will dwell in them And walk among them. I will be their God, And they shall be My people. Therefore Come out from among them And be separate, says the Lord. Do not touch what is unclean, And I will receive you. I will be a Father to you, And you shall be My sons and daughters,' Says the Lord Almighty" (2 Cor. 6:14–18). And again: "Do not be deceived: Evil company corrupts good habits. Awake to righteousness, and do not sin" (1 Cor. 15:33, 34).

Peter is told that this is not a racial thing, but a spiritual thing—righteousness is spiritual. *Christianity is universal and transcends all cultures, exalting Christ's ethics* (His every Word) *as binding for all people and all situations* (Matt. 28:20). Our desire should be to associate with those who are righteous and forsake those who refuse to walk in obedience to the truth of God's Word. We are not to seek close intimate relationships and unions with those who are not spiritually pure. As God authoritatively imposed the "shadow" (Col. 2:17), saying do not touch certain kinds of animals, so He removes it, telling Peter not to call those animals unclean any longer. Peter's conclusion was that there was no longer a basis for separation from the Gentiles. This was a hard lesson for the early Jewish NT church to appreciate.

Acts 10:29

Peter is very humble, for he says that the Lord has corrected his understanding with respect to Jews and Gentiles. It is quite possible that Peter has still not realised the full implications of what God had shown him, though a great shift in his thinking had taken place and he admits this to the gathered crowd in Cornelius' house. Peter tells them that he was in their presence due to divine instructions—he was there because God told him to be there. Peter then asks why Cornelius had sent for him. In short we see that Cornelius says his directives were also divine—this meeting was a divinely organized event from beginning to end.

Acts 10:30

Cornelius then begins repeating what we have seen in verse 3 and following. What is significant is that Luke, under inspiration of the Holy Spirit, sees it as necessary to repeat, in such detail, all the steps showing God's divine leading of both Cornelius and Peter, yet, many in the early church still found it extremely difficult to accept the changes that were introduced. The reason for the resistance was from failing to submit fully to the deep spiritual meaning that these laws pointed to, thus they emphasised the outward ritual and tended to ignore God's emphasis on whole hearted devotion and obedience to Him. It is very easy to be deceived into thinking that outward appearance is all that true religion is concerned about. Such outward rituals, on their own, never have and never will have any value in God's eyes. The outward was always only meant to be a reflection of what was in the heart and encourage heartfelt devotion. That is why the prophets said God desires obedience more than sacrifice (1 Sam. 15:22; Isa. 1:11–17; Ps. 51:16, 17; Prov. 21:3; Hos. 6:6; Amos 5:21–27; Micah 6:6–8). Sacrifice, in this context, refers to the outward ritual, whereas obedience reveals the internal state of a sincere heart. It is easy to make outward actions appear holy to the natural eye, however, it is totally impossible to imitate sincerity of heart. So be not fooled, it is the heart that God has *always* been concerned about and not some outward ritual (1 Sam. 16:7; 1 Chron. 28:9; 29:17; 2 Chron. 6:30; 16:9; Ps. 7:9; 44:21; Prov. 15:11; Jer. 17:10; John 2:24, 25; Acts 1:24; 15:8; Rom. 8:27; 1 Cor. 4:5; 1 Thes. 2:4; Heb. 4:13; Rev. 2:23, cf. Luke 18:10–14).

Acts 10:31

As we said in verses 2–4, Cornelius was a man who was already saved. Men overcome with sin and under God's condemnation cannot do anything that will arouse even the slightest pleasure or acceptance in His sight. Only after people have become partakers of God's grace are they in a position to please or honour Him. Every work that does not arise from living faith is dead, wicked rebellion and receives nothing but God's wrath and displeasure. Cornelius' good works were evidence of his faith.

Acts 10:32

God promised that the issues and questions that filled Cornelius' heart (see comments on Acts 10:2) would be addressed by Peter.

Acts 10:33

Cornelius is very grateful that Peter came and that he came so
quickly. The excitement that Cornelius and those gathered with
him had, was not in anticipation of what Peter's wisdom might
have for them, but rather for what God wanted to tell them. Peter
was merely a channel for God's message. Their hearts were hungry
to know *all* that God would reveal to them. Another sure sign of
true faith is when someone wants to know *everything* that God has
said—not just a part. The modern church is full of people who only
want some of who God is and some of what He says. They want to
pick and choose between what they like and dislike with respect to
God's revelation of His will and attributes. God's Word is not the
source of all wisdom and truth for such people, for they have great
confidence and comfort in their own man made doctrines. This
group in Cornelius' house does not yet know what God will reveal,
but their faith is such that whatever it is they are eager to know and
obey. A preacher cannot ask for a better audience. These people did
not need to be entertained, or coaxed into wanting to know God's
truth, they were eager to know it all and came and waited with hungry hearts to soak in everything Peter would tell them. True faith
desires only one food—that is to feast on Christ, and He is the
Word, He is the Truth. Many people are cold towards teaching that
covers the whole counsel of God (Matt. 28:20), enjoying rather that
which does not make them uncomfortable and therefore they stay
focused on isolated sections of God's revelation. Such people are
more interested in pleasing the flesh than pleasing the Lord (Rom.
6:6; 8:13; 13:14; Gal. 5:16–18, 24; 6:14; 1 Pet. 2:11).

Acts 10:34, 35

"*Then Peter opened his mouth*": this phrase is used to introduce a
statement of great importance (cf. Matt. 5:1). The Jews saw themselves as superior to all other nations because God had chosen them
above every other nation. Such a conclusion was based upon tradition and not careful exposition of Scripture which clearly taught
that people from every nation would have Abraham as their father
(Gen. 12:3; 18:18). Peter even preached about this blessing of Abraham in Acts 3:25 without realising the full implications of the
verse—implications that were now beginning to dawn upon him.
We too are guilty of holding to conclusions that have tradition and
familiarity as their foundation, rather than God's revelation.

God is not restricted by any person and He was not restricted by the Jewish misunderstanding about His impartiality. This means that Gentiles were not kept from salvation because the Jews couldn't accept them on an equal basis—Cornelius was saved despite the fact that the Jews would not treat him as such. What God is making very clear for everyone, is the fact that there was to be unity and equality within the visible church, since all people groups are equal in the sight of God. It is not race, nationality or social standing that separates people, but faith, arising from God's grace—which is distributed according to His secret counsel (Acts 13:48; Rom. 8:28; 9:23, 24; 11:5, 6; Eph. 2:8; 2 Thes. 2:13, 14). The Scriptures made it clear from the beginning that Israel's favoured position with God was not due to partiality in God or anything worthy existing in themselves, but due to grace (Deut. 7:7; 10:17; 2 Chron. 19:7; Job 34:19; Rom. 2:11). The responsibility for receiving grace is to walk in grateful obedience to the Lord.

God's messenger (the angel) and Cornelius' messengers had pointed to Cornelius' righteous life. Peter now realises that those things that had appeared so important in the Jewish mind, namely circumcision and the dietary laws, had nothing to do with making a person acceptable to God. These two things were the main cause of Gentile pollution according to the Jews, thus nothing a Gentile ever did could be pleasing in God's sight, since anything an uncircumcised person did was unclean. Peter now realises that this is not so and that God's acceptance arises from God's mercy alone, for there is nothing in us or that we are capable of doing that is worthy of God's love (Titus 3:5, 6). To misunderstand the basis of God's acceptance of us is to distort and diminish God's grace and exalt ourselves in a dangerous way.

Verse 35 does not teach that people are accepted in God's sight because of their good works, but rather that fear of God and righteous living are evidences that someone is accepted by Him. The fear of God is the first sign of having true wisdom (Ps. 111:10; Prov. 9:10) and true wisdom arises only from God's sovereign work of grace in the heart of a person. Until such a work is undertaken by the mercy of God in a person's heart, they are God's enemies, filled with hatred and rebellion (Rom. 5:10; 8:7; Col. 1:20,21; John 3:20; 7:7), always suppressing the truth (Rom. 1:18ff.) and are rightly called "children of wrath" (Eph. 2:3). It is impossible to obtain God's favor without first receiving God's grace and God's grace is an undeserved gift, coming through the merits of Jesus Christ. No one can fear God, work righteousness and be accepted by God without believing the Gospel—in the OT this was belief in the promise of the coming Messiah and in the NT it is belief in the Man, Christ Jesus. In the light of Peter's own vision and instructions from the Holy Spirit and Cornelius' vision and righteous life, Peter realised that, "in Christ Jesus neither circumcision nor uncircumcision has any value, for all that counts is faith working through love" (Gal. 5:6), and "there is neither Greek nor Jew, circumcised nor uncircumcised ... but Christ is all and in all" (Col. 3:11).

To fear God and work righteousness is a summary of the redeemed man's life, for it includes one's duties to both God and man. True devotion, love, trust, reverence and submission to God (i.e., godly fear) will result in right relationships and dealings with people. The redeemed person's righteous works flow from a new heart and a new heart is a gift from God (Ezk. 36:25–27). This fearing God and working righteousness is the summary of the whole Bible. Jesus had summed it up by saying we are to love God with our whole being and our neighbour as ourselves (Matt. 22:37–40, cf. Gal. 5:14; Jam. 2:8, 9). In the OT, Micah summarised God's desire by saying, "He has shown you, O man, what is good; and what does the Lord require of you, but to do justly, to love mercy, and to walk humbly with your God?" (Micah 6:8). May the Lord burn these same goals into our hearts and make them part of our lives in every way. May working righteousness and fearing God, in all our thinking and actions, be more vital to us than the air for our lungs and the beating of our hearts (Job 13:15; Prov. 3:5; 14:34; Luke 22:42).

Acts 10:36

Peter has said that God does not show partiality between Jew and Gentile. He then says that the Word that God sent to the covenant children of Israel was a message of peace and reconciliation with God and this came through Jesus Christ. Jesus is the focus and basis for the restored relationship or peace (Isa. 52:7; Rom. 5:1; Eph. 2:14). Although this message was sent to the covenant sons of Israel first, Jesus, who brought the message, is not only Lord of the Jews, but Lord of all (including the Gentiles, cf. Rom. 10:12), thus this same message of salvation is for them too (Rom. 1:16; 10:12, 13; Eph. 2:17). God's Word of reconciliation is through Christ and is directed to every nation and culture (Rom. 15:8–12). He is the Lord of the universe, which means that every person is accountable to Him. Everyone is responsible to obey Him and live for His glory. Failure to do this receives God's wrath. The Lord of all is also the only Savior of people from every tribe, tongue and nation (Rev. 5:9; Matt. 28:18). Every person needs to be saved from God's wrath (Rom. 3:23). There is only one Word of salvation from God for both Jew and Gentile (John 12:32; 17:2; Acts 4:12; 26:23; 1 Cor. 15:22; 1 John 2:2) and there is only one Lord of every nation, this Man, Jesus Christ.

Acts 10:37

The nature of Christianity from the very first was clarity of message and purpose and openness of actions (cf. John 15:24; 18:20, 21; Luke 24:18; Acts 26:26). From the beginnings with John the Baptist the message about Christ was a movement that attained national proportions and significance. Peter clearly shows that Christ, His message and His life were based firmly in history. Christ took on human flesh, lived in a particular geographical area of the world, at a particular point in history and was known throughout the region. The fiery prophet, John the Baptist, shook the nation so that it might be aroused from sleep and look for the appearing of the Messiah. Cornelius and those in his household were aware of all these facts about Jesus.

Acts 10:38

Cornelius was also aware of God's hand or anointing upon Christ in great power (John 3:34). Here we see the three Persons within the Godhead working together for man's redemption (see *Faith and Reason*, chapter 7). God set Christ apart, marked Him and equipped Him for the great work that He had come to do (Isa. 61:1–3). All that Jesus did was accomplished through the power of the Holy Spirit. The fact that God had blessed Christ with extraordinary abundance of the Spirit was common knowledge in the whole region. Christ, the supreme example, shows us that the Christian life is not merely keeping away from evil. The force and power of God's Kingdom are positive activity—doing good. Our lives are to be characterised by earnestly seeking the good in every way possible in every possible situation. Christ used His anointing for the benefit of others and not for His own advancement (cf.

Simon Magus, Acts 8:18–21). We need the power of the Holy Spirit in our lives in order to do what is good. God alone defines good and evil and this has been revealed in the Scriptures (2 Tim. 3:16, 17).

Kingdom life is ultimately a spiritual battle (Eph. 6:12), though it is clearly manifested in the physical realm. Satan, the commander of the forces of darkness, has both spiritual and human slaves under his control who serve his purposes. Satan's kingdom, from top to bottom is based upon fear, hatred, rebellion, selfishness, deception, laziness, foolishness, etc. Thus to think that it is capable of attaining any long term, united objective is to totally misunderstand the essence of the kingdom of darkness. Any service that is carried out by Satan's oppressed subjects arises from self-seeking or terror and the ultimate goal of each and every one of them, is nothing but a whole-hearted commitment to self-destruction (Prov. 8:36). Although each member within the kingdom of darkness wants to destroy and overthrow God, they *all* finally have the *same* deep-seated desire and belief, namely, that they can and should be "god" themselves—such a kingdom cannot have any significant, long term success! Besides, every member within the kingdom of darkness knows the true God and that they are under His wrath and authority and are doomed to failure in their futile attempt at rebellion against Him (Matt. 8:29, 31; Mark 3:11; Luke 4:34–36, 41; Jam. 2:19; Rom. 1:18, 21, 32; Job 1:12; 2:6; Luke 22:31). The kingdom of darkness is able to destroy, but totally unable to replace what it destroys with a workable alternative.

On the other hand, in the Kingdom of Light, God also has spiritual and human servants who serve Him. This Kingdom, from top to bottom, is characterised by selfless serving of others for the glory of God, carried out in the power of the Spirit and whole-hearted obedience to every Word that comes from the mouth of God. This Kingdom is backed-up by the power and authority of God, thus its victory is assured. The confrontation between the Kingdom of Light and the kingdom of darkness takes place at every single point, for there can never be any agreement between them—darkness hates the light and the light will have nothing to do with darkness (John 3:19, 20; 8:12; Acts 26:18; Rom. 13:12; Eph. 5:8, 11; 1 Thes. 5:5; 1 John 1:5–7; Ps. 119:105; Prov. 6:23; Isa. 8:20). There can only be total conflict between darkness and light.

What is blatantly obvious throughout Scripture is the greatness of God's power in comparison to Satan's and this was so openly manifested in Christ's life that everyone in Judea was made aware of it. Jesus came to liberate those under the power of Satan. Those possessed by demons are held in Satan's tightest grip, yet this grip was easily shattered each and every time by a simple Word from Christ. All of this was abundant proof of who Jesus is (Luke 7:20–22, cf. Isa. 35:5, 6).

Acts 10:39

That which most people only knew from the testimony of others, Peter says the apostles were personal witnesses of all these things. Peter makes a distinction between the whole region and the capital of the region. The leaders of the nation resided in Jerusalem and it was not some wild out of control mob that killed Jesus, but the leaders of the nation. There is quite a contrast between light and darkness in these verses: Jesus was greatly anointed by God (a manifestation of God's great love for Him) and went about doing good to everyone He came across, yet for this He was hated and murdered, *by men.*

Acts 10:40, 41

God not only anointed Christ, but also raised Him from the dead, thus confirming the injustice of His crucifixion. After Christ was raised He appeared to many selected witnesses. Assurance that He rose, not merely as a spirit or phantom, but with a physical body, is confirmed by the fact that He ate and drank with His disciples (Luke 24:41–43; Acts 1:4). He ate and drank for their benefit and not because He needed food—once again we see Christ's kindness in acting for our benefit in a way that helps our weak faith. This *limited* showing of Himself is in line with His emphasis that our relationship with Him is to be one of faith based upon the testimony of witnesses whom He had selected (John 20:29; Acts 1:8). It exalts God's work of grace in people's lives, when those previously filled with hatred, hardness and pollution, accept the apostle's testimony and believe the good new about Jesus, without earth shattering experiences, visions, signs, etc.

Acts 10:42

The responsibility of God's witnesses is to proclaim the whole truth and nothing but the truth—a herald should not say more than he has been authorised to say, nor should he say less. Christ's office of judgment is a vital aspect of His ministry and is inseparable from His office as Savior. Christ's ministry is a two-edged sword inflicting, in the same thrust, either blessing or cursing. There can never be a neutral response to the message about Christ (see comments on Acts 2:2–3). Christ is the only judge appointed by God to judge every person who has ever lived—past, present and future. No one will escape from this judgement, whether living or dead, *everyone* will stand before Christ (John 5:28, 29; Acts 17:31; Rom. 2:16; 14:9; 1 Cor. 4:5; 2 Cor. 5:10; 2 Tim. 4:1; 1 Pet. 4:5). Be not fooled for the Scriptures clearly reveal that there will be a judgment day where every single thing (whether good or evil) will be brought to the light and receive its just reward.

Acts 10:43

All the prophets have one united testimony confirming Jesus Christ as the Messiah. From seeing Christ as Judge we are now thrown back upon Him as the Messiah. We are not merely left staring into the face of a holy Judge, but are immediately shown a merciful Savior. Peter makes an inescapable connection between the One whom all the prophets talked about (the One in whom Cornelius and his household had believed) and the Man, Jesus Christ. It is at this point that the faith of these Gentiles matured from believing in Him *who was to come*, to believing in Jesus *who had come*. Up until then they had known of their need for the Messiah and believed God's promises about Him, but had not identified Him with Jesus (cf. Nathanael, John 1:47–49).

Acts 10:44

It was at this point that God chose to manifest His acceptance of Gentiles as full covenant members on a level equal to Jewish believers—just as He had done previously with the Samaritans (Acts 8:15ff.). In this incident no hands are laid on any of Cornelius's group. This was God's sovereign work and sign, given primarily to the Jewish leadership of the NT church (as we will see in the next chapter).

Acts 10:45, 46

Despite all that Peter had been shown and his interpretation of it, the Jews that accompanied him were astonished that God would manifest such complete acceptance of Gentiles. We have already pointed out how difficult is was for the Jews to accept this massive change and their reaction here merely underlines this. Baptism in the Holy Spirit is not necessarily a sign that conversion had just taken place (cf. Acts 2:4). It is through faith in Words (instruction about God's plan of redemption) that qualifies one for full membership in the church of God—not outward rituals like circumcision and other ceremonial observances (Rom. 10:17; Gal. 3:2).

Acts 10:47, 48

Water baptism serves as an outward sign showing membership within the visible church of God (this is not the main thing it signifies though). The seal of the Holy Spirit was a much higher sign showing full membership within the invisible church of God—coming only from the hand of God. Peter asks how they can refuse the lesser sign to these Gentiles if God has already granted them the greater sign? The answer was obvious—baptism couldn't be refused to them! Cornelius' prayer and deepest longing had been graciously answered by God. Gentiles could now share fully in all the benefits of the covenant community. This is a strong point for showing the great privileges of being united to Christ's *visible* church—being part of a body of believers. Christianity is not meant to be merely a personal thing, for it is a body thing and the blessings and benefits are real and communicated through the different members, one to another.

Acts 11:1

The news taken back to Jerusalem was that Gentiles had become Christians and gained admittance into the covenant community, the church, merely by receiving the Word. "The Word" refers to the message about the completed work of Jesus Christ. The Words Peter had spoken about Jesus were fully embraced by the Gentiles and the term "receiving the Word" implied not only salvation, but full membership within the covenant community of God—it was more than likely this full membership aspect that caused the greatest offence to the Jews. Cornelius was accepted into the visible

church by baptism and confession of faith and not by becoming a
Jew outwardly (Rom. 2:28, 29).

Acts 11:2, 3

"They of the circumcision" here refers to a group of Jews within the
Christian community who argued that you had to be circumcised
in order to be a member of the Christian church. They believed that
crucial to salvation was the observance of Jewish ceremonies and
that there should be no mixing between those who were circumcised and those who were not. They were strongly against Gentiles
not only because they were not circumcised but because they did
not observe the Jewish dietary laws, thus their accusation against
Peter for eating with Gentiles. Once again we see a link to Peter's
vision which showed Peter that neither the uncircumcised person
nor what they ate were to be called unclean. God had removed the
signs of separation between Jews and Gentiles (circumcision and
diet). The fact that these people condemned Peter for *eating* with
Gentiles meant that they would have utterly abhorred him for baptizing them and thus granting them equal status with Jews in the
church of God.

Acts 11:4–13

Peter proceeds to give a step by step account of what took place.
What is significant is his humility and patience with these people.
He was an apostle and had received an amazing and repetitive
vision from the Lord as well as repetitive, direct communication
from the Lord. He had witnessed the amazing out pouring of the
Holy Spirit upon the Gentiles. Yet when he arrives in Jerusalem, he
is not asked to tell what happened but accused of misconduct. His
behavior is challenged and his accusers demand that he account for
his actions—they wanted him to repent and apologise. Peter,
calmly and gently tells them what happened, following Biblical
principles: A soft answer turns away wrath, But a harsh word stirs
up anger (Prov. 15:1). A gentle tongue can break a bone (Prov.
25:15). But the wisdom that is from above is first pure, then peaceable, gentle, willing to yield, full of mercy and good fruits, without
partiality and without hypocrisy (James 3:17). There are times to
rebuke with strong words, though being patient and gentle does
not mean you are weak. Peter here stands very firmly upon the
truth, but he is humble, for he knew what God had to do in his own

life to bring him to this point of fully accepting the Gentiles. He knows that people can only embrace the truth if God works in their hearts by His Spirit, thus there is no basis for pride. How patient isn't God with us? When we compare God's patience towards us and our lack of patience towards others, aren't we like the wicked servant who was forgiven so much and then refused to forgive even a little? (Matt. 18:21–35). Patience is something we have to learn. That is one way we bear with the weaknesses of others and strive for the unity of the body (Rom.1 4:1ff.; 15:1–3; 1 Cor. 9:22; Gal. 6:1, 2; Eph. 4:3; 1 Thes. 5:14). If you are going to address something it must be done with an attitude that demonstrates Godly wisdom, which is, peaceable, gentle, willing to yield and full of mercy (James 3:17). This does not mean compromise with the truth, but it does mean at all times being aware of and dealing with the attitudes and motives of our heart. To be right about something does not mean you can communicate this in any way you please.

Acts 11:14

Does this verse prove that Cornelius and his household were not saved until Peter came and preached to them? I do not believe so. Remember, Peter is defending the salvation of God against false teaching that said salvation was attained through believing in Christ *and* observing the ceremonial law. Peter tells these Jews that God's angel told Cornelius that salvation rested upon believing a message, or words (the good news, cf. Acts 10:22). The word "saved," as used here, carries within it the idea of being saved "in or through something" (i.e., the words spoken by Peter). Salvation for every nation and tribe is offered *through* the "Words," "Name" and "Life" of Christ (Acts 2:21; 4:12; 11:14; 15:1, 11; 16:30, 31; Rom. 5:10; 10:9, 13), not through the ceremonial laws. There is only one way of salvation for Jews and Gentiles—by grace through faith (Eph. 2:8; Gal. 5:6; Acts 15:11) and that is faith in the Name, Words and Life of Christ. This is Peter's message to the accusing Jews. The angels' message supported the fact that salvation was by faith in the Good News of Christ, without any ritual or law.

Cornelius loved the Lord and so did his family, however, he could have no assurance of salvation, for salvation was of the Jews (John 4:22). The Jews were the ones with God's revelation (Rom. 3:1, 2) and had the responsibility of taking the light to the nations, however, they had not been set free from their strong ties to the ceremonial laws and this was a great hindrance. They still demanded full submission to circumcision and other aspects of the ceremonial law if one was to be saved. According to them there was no other way to have salvation other than going through these rituals (cf. Acts 15:1). Although Cornelius had already been saved by the grace of God, he had no authoritative word from the Scriptures to give him assurance (that is, to release him from the obligation of the ceremonial law). Peter says the angel told Cornelius that salvation rested upon faith in some *words*, not in doing some rituals and that he was to get some authoritative words from God's apostle that would give him assurance. The fact that the future tense is used here does not mean that Cornelius was not yet saved. Peter used the future tense in Acts 15:11 though no one would argue from this that he was implying that he, as well as all the other apostles, were not yet saved. Salvation is spoken about in Scripture as past, present and future. Our salvation is something that *has* already taken place (Rom. 8:24; Eph. 2:5, 8; 2 Tim. 1:9, etc.). It is also seen as something presently taking place (Acts 2:47; 1 Cor. 1:18; 15:2; 2 Cor. 2:15; Heb. 7:25). Yet our salvation is also talked about in terms that are futuristic (Matt. 10:22; 24:13; Rom. 13:11; Heb. 1:14).

Peter's argument in Acts 11:14 was for those Jews who demanded ritual observance as a crucial aspect of holiness and thus of salvation. Peter was accused of violating the ceremonial law (verse 3), thus his point was that salvation rested completely in words, i.e., upon the truth about the Person and work of the Man Christ Jesus who came, died and rose from the dead (this is the mystery of the Gospel, Eph. 3:6). Nothing else was needed other than faith in this message (Rom. 10:17; Gal. 3:2, 14; 5:6; Eph. 3:17). God told Cornelius that both he and his household would be saved by words (the Gospel) and not by observing Jewish rituals (Gal. 3:26–29). Peter wanted the Jews to know that this was what God's messenger had said—this was apostolic confirmation for the whole church with respect to God's official declaration about the Gentiles' standing in the Kingdom. God grants full membership and participation in the Kingdom to Gentiles as Gentiles—that is, without submitting to the ceremonial law. This was a radical announcement which many Jews could not accept. However, through this incident, Cornelius was given assurance of his full acceptance and standing in God's church and the Jews' understanding was brought into line with God's mind. Every aspect of salvation rested upon the completed work of Christ and there was nothing that anyone could do to add to this or advance their own standing before God. Salvation is a comprehensive term and refers to more than "justification" and Cornelius and his whole household entered fully into this.

Cornelius was told what he had to do (Acts 10:6) in order to share in the fullness that God has prepared for those who believe—both in this life and in eternity. He had to make the connection between the Man Christ Jesus and the promises of salvation in the Scriptures and he had to be baptized in Christ's Name—the new sign of covenant membership within in the community of believers. Baptism is not crucial for salvation, though it is a necessary sign to show that the covenant member is set apart unto God. This is the new sign of separation between God's covenant community and everyone else. You cannot hope for salvation from God and reject the Man named Jesus who ministered in Israel. Cornelius was very aware of who Jesus was (Acts 10:37), but needed to know that He was the promise that all the prophets had spoken about and that He was the promised One of God that Cornelius had already believed in. Those who were truly hoping for the Messiah and God's promise of salvation believed in Jesus as soon as they were shown that He was the Messiah. Those who rejected Jesus did not want the Messiah, even though they pretended to be looking for Him.

Acts 11:15

The decisive evidence that the Gentiles were now equal with Jews within the church of God was the Holy Spirit pouring out upon them in Cornelius' house. This incident took place at least six years after Pentecost, however, Peter does not say that God has given the Gentiles the Spirit in the same way that He has been giving the Spirit to everyone who has believed. Rather he says what the Gentiles experienced was the same as that event experienced six or seven years ago with the birth of the NT church. Peter draws attention to the incident when *he* received the Spirit (there is no hint anywhere that the 3,000 people who were converted on the day of Pentecost experienced the same manifestation that those first disciples did). Peter is clearly showing that what took place at Pentecost and in Cornelius' house were special events to mark significant stages within the development of the NT church and not common experiences that happened whenever anyone believed. The book of Acts is an unfolding revelation of the birth and growth of the NT church from Jerusalem, to Judea, Samaria and then the uttermost parts of the earth (Acts 1:8). We have seen the Spirit falling upon the Jews (Acts 2), the Samaritans (Acts 8)and now upon the Gentiles (Acts 10). Peter does not just equate the Gentiles with the Samaritans or with the average Jewish believer, but with the apostles in the sense of being equal in the sight of God: "Exactly what we received," Peter says, "they have also received".

Acts 11:16

Peter is quick to show the source of this out-pouring of the Spirit, for he had absolutely nothing to do with this series of events—He was still speaking and the furthest thing from his mind was that there ought to be such a manifestation. Peter did not suggest it, he did not lay hands on anyone and certainly no one in Cornelius' household was even expecting it let alone asking for such a manifestation. He says the Lord baptises with the Holy Spirit, i.e., this was Christ's sovereign work and thus your argument is with God not with me.

Acts 11:17

The equal gift was bestowed upon equal belief. The reason the Holy Spirit was given to Christ's disciples at Pentecost was because they had believed in Christ. Peter here argues that the reason that the Holy Spirit was given to the Gentiles was because they too had believed in Christ. With neither the apostles nor Cornelius must we think that the outpouring of the Holy Spirit coincided with the moment they first believed in Christ. Certainly in the case of the apostles, to think that true conversion only took place at Pentecost does violence to the rest of Scripture and we have already argued that the evidence supports Cornelius' conversion prior to Peter's coming. Once again the emphasis is for salvation and full acceptance in the church due to faith in the message about Christ. We are told that Jewish faith and Gentile faith are equal in God's eyes, thus once again confirming that the ceremonial rituals counted nothing towards gaining acceptance in God's sight (Gal. 3:2; Rom. 4:5). In conclusion to the whole, Peter says, "In the light of all the evidence which clearly shows that this was a divine work of God, should I have opposed God's acceptance of the Gentiles into the church?" All Peter did was preach. The One who imparted the Spirit was God.

Peter did only what God commanded, thus he could have complete confidence that he was right.

God's Word is our final authority, directing our every thought and action and when we are standing upon God's truth that is our greatest defence for all we do. We need to realize that our natural tendency is to look to something other than God's immovable Word to support us in what we are doing. It is not that God's Word is ignored, it is just that we feel more secure if there is some confirmation of God's command from somewhere else. We need to mature to the position where the world's opinions about God's ways do not affect us in the least—where we are not embarrassed about God's will and ways; are not threatened by the ungodly's rejection of God's Word; and that we do not apologise for being different. We must not be afraid of being hated for the sake of the truth (Mark 13:13; John 15:19; 17:14). Evil people hate the light (John 3:19, 20) and our calling is to be light and expose the works of darkness (Matt. 5:14; Eph. 5:11).

Acts 11:18

If God's authority is recognised as the ultimate authority then there is a possibility for unity (God's truth is the only basis for unity). When people have a sincere heart that is willing to submit to God's revelation, they will embrace the truth when it is shown to them. We are all ignorant in many areas and have our own ideas about what God's truth is with respect to many issues. Thus, when confronted with the truth, it is only pride that prevents us from admitting to our errors and changing our views. Only God has perfect knowledge about everything, whereas we should be constantly learning and bringing our minds more and more into line with true knowledge—change is to be expected and there is nothing wrong with this as long as we have an immovable standard that we are bringing everything into line with. "When a man who is honestly mistaken hears the truth, he will either quit being mistaken, or cease being honest".

It is difficult to tell whether the "circumcision group" fully submitted to the authority of God, though they do appear to have been included among those who glorified God. The reason for my doubt however, is due to the fact that this whole issue kept on flaring up (15:1, 5, 24; 21:20; Gal. 2:12; 5:1–3, etc.). It is possible, however, that though they glorified God their understanding was still very limited. Maybe they were comfortable that God had accepted this one group of Gentiles without the ceremonial law, but their bondage to the shadows (Col. 2:17; Heb. 8:5; 10:1), meant they rejected the Cornelius incident as God's sign showing His acceptance for *all* Gentiles who believe in Christ. They could have bowed to the sign as something that couldn't be argued with, but seen it as only for that particular occasion. So, when many Gentiles started coming into the Kingdom and this same sign was not being repeated each time, they rejected those Gentiles and once again demanded submission to the ceremonial law. This further confirms that the experience in Cornelius' house was *not* an everyday occurrence, for if the same sign accompanied every Gentile conversion, there could have been no argument about accepting Gentiles without the ceremonial law.

Luke's point in this is not to give us a detailed history of the "circumcision group," but to reveal the faulty understanding of those who still believed that the shadows (the ceremonial law) were important in the sight of God.

The Scriptures command people to repent (Luke 24:46, 47; Acts 3:19; 17:30; 26:20, etc.), however, as the believers realize and confess here, repentance is not something that originates within man's heart. Repentance is a gift from God and consists in a change of heart, mind and will on the part of the sinner. There is a radical change in the way the former rebel now sees God, himself, sin and righteousness, but this change is brought about by the working of God within his heart—it is a gift from God (cf. Acts 3:26; 5:31; 2 Tim. 2:25; Ps. 80:3). Repentance, forgiveness of sin and eternal life are gifts from God.

What do the Scriptures say about man's heart?

"The heart is deceitful above all things, And desperately wicked; Who can know it?" (Jer. 17:9). "Keep your heart with all diligence, For out of it spring the issues of life" (Prov. 4:23). "Can the Ethiopian change his skin or the leopard its spots? Then may you also do good who are accustomed to do evil" (Jer. 13:23). "Brood of vipers! How can you, being evil, speak good things? For out of the abundance of the heart the mouth speaks. A good man out of the good treasure of his heart brings forth good things, and an evil man out of the evil treasure brings forth evil things" (Matt. 12:34, 35). "For from within, out of the heart of men, proceed evil thoughts, adulteries, fornications, murders, thefts, covetousness, wickedness, deceit, lewdness, an evil eye, blasphemy, pride, foolishness. All these evil things come from within and defile a man" (Mark 7:21–23).

It is in the light of these above verses that we can understand and appreciate the significance of the following verses (Jer. 31:18, 31–33; Ezk. 11:19; 36:25–38; Zec. 12:10)—what a glorious message the Gospel is!

Repentance is man's duty, however it is only possible when he is moved by the supernatural grace of God. Repentance does not exist until God gives it. Repentance and faith are both gifts from God and cannot be separated—they exist at all times together. It is foolish to argue that one precedes the other or that one can exist prior to the other. Repentance is having a godly view of the wickedness of sin, whereas faith is fleeing to Christ to take hold of His remedy for sin. The Gentiles had been *given repentance* and for this, these Jews glorify God.

Acts 11:19

Luke now picks up were he left off in Acts 8:4, however, this period of ministry in Antioch by Barnabas and Saul takes place about eight or nine years *after* the death of Stephen and the dispersion brought about by Saul's persecution. Luke's point is to demonstrate the spread of the Gospel going far beyond the boarders of Judea and Samaria (Acts 1:8). Through the persecuted church God had spread the message of Christ far and wide, multiplying the church in the process. Initially, these persecuted Jews only evangelised other Jews in these different areas.

Acts 11:20

Antioch was a large and important city within this region and Luke's attention now focuses on the development of the church there. In the context of this section it is best to see Luke's distinction between "Jews" and "Hellenists" as the Jewish/Greek distinction (i.e., Jew/Gentile). Thus, we see Jewish Christians from within the church beginning to evangelise Gentiles. Luke gives us no indication as to when this outreach to the Gentiles took place in relation to Cornelius and Peter's account of it in Jerusalem. Once again Luke is not interested in giving details about what happened exactly when, but rather showing that the Gospel is for the whole world—

Jew and Gentile alike. How these evangelists came to the understanding that the Gospel was for non-Jews we are not told, however,
what is clear is that within the flow of God's unfolding plan, they
were absolutely right.

Acts 11:21, 22

Many Gentiles were swept into the church by the power of the lord
and the calm response of the Jerusalem *leaders* probably means that
the question about admitting Gentiles into the church was a settled
matter in their minds. Thus, it is probably safe to conclude that
Peter had already delivered His address found in 11:1–18 by the
time the news of the Gentile conversions came to the attention of
the Jerusalem leaders (11:22). It is very interesting to notice the
emphasis placed upon the Lordship of Christ in verses 20 and 21
(occurring three times). The heart of the Gospel is that Jesus is lord
and the early evangelists made this the thrust of their preaching.
Christ is Lord of heaven and earth; all authority belongs to Him; He
expects complete obedience to His every Word from everyone; and
His Word relates to every area of life. Any concept of "Lordship"
that does not have, at least, these above points, fails to grasp who
Christ is and what He expects from us. Here in Antioch the Gentiles, through God's working, readily respond to this news about
Christ the lord, the only savior of humanity. It was God who had
opened up this door and this is the key for achieving success in His
Kingdom. If God does not open the doors, for whatever we might
seek to do for Him, we must not foolishly beat against closed doors
in frustration. Everything in God's Kingdom is ordered and controlled by Him, thus we need to bring all our thoughts and actions
into line with His revelation (the Scriptures), then in an attitude of
patient, prayerful, trusting devotion, rely upon Him to open and
close doors and direct our affairs (Prov. 3:5, 6; 1 Pet. 5:6, 7).

The Jerusalem church dispatched Barnabas to travel throughout
that whole area, ending up in Antioch. It is possible that there were
no apostles in Jerusalem at the time and that is why Barnabas was
sent (Peter and John had been sent to the Samaritan revival, 8:14).
What was desperately needed among these new converts was sound
teaching and grounding in the apostolic tradition and Barnabas
was well equipped for this task, providing great encouragement
because he was a great teacher (see comments on Acts 4:36). The
church in those days and no less in our own times, desperately

needs to be instructed in the full counsel of God (i.e., the apostolic tradition), which is preserved for us in the Scriptures. To the degree that we do not base all our thinking upon the immovable revelation found in the Bible, to that degree we are not following the apostolic tradition—not to follow the apostolic tradition is to be greatly deceived. The church's responsibility is to build upon the foundation that has already been laid by the apostles (Eph. 2:20). What we need is not more apostles, but hearts that will submit to and follow what has already been revealed so that we might achieve the maturity Christ intends (Eph. 4:13–16). To ignore the full revelation found in the Bible and seek "revelation" from some other source in order to become mature and discover the "deep things" of God is, at best, to be totally confused.

While the significance of Antioch would have been perceived by the leaders of the church in Jerusalem, there is no way that they could have realised God's intentions for that city. In time, Antioch became the centre of missions outreach in the early church and took over the role of leadership held by Jerusalem after Jerusalem was destroyed in A.D. 70.

Acts 11:23

It was the grace of God that was moving in Antioch and made these believers a part of the true church of God—Barnabas did not do anything to sanction or confirm their faith. These Gentiles were full members of Christ's body the moment they believed the preaching of the Gospel. Barnabas merely went to help these new believers and confirm, for the Jerusalem leaders, that what was happening was indeed from God.

Barnabas' generous heart was filled with joy at seeing the workings of God among these Gentiles and immediately he exhorts them to remain true to their lord. This start had been real and wonderful, though the cry of this godly man's heart is that they would persevere and produce long term fruit for the Kingdom (such exhortation to new Christians was foremost in Paul's heart too, Acts 13:43; 14:22, cf. John 8:31). Barnabas encouraged them to have whole hearted commitment and single minded dedication in the service of Christ. The lord wants our whole being to follow Him with the utmost determination and focus. This is the nature of true discipleship, which will not only exalt, but manifest the glorious Kingdom of God. Those who love the Lord desire this kind of dedication not only from themselves, but from everyone who names the name of the Lord. Does not your heart groan for Christ's name and King-dom to be exalted? Do not you long to see many people persevering with whole hearted devotion in the things of the Lord? We need to encourage one another to do this.

Acts 11:24

The qualities of this man Barnabas are comparable to those of Stephen (Acts 6:5). Luke tells us that he was a *good* man, which has reference to both his ability and his character. He had a big heart that wanted the best for other believers and he would use his own talents and efforts to help motivate and encourage them in attain-ing this. He took the time to be helpful where he could. He was a humble devoted disciple of Christ who did not come to conclusions about people based upon speculations. Some people like to read evil and malice into the actions and words of others, but our views should be based upon firm clear facts, without which we should make no conclusions. Barnabas had a pure love for the Lord and thus could truly rejoice in the Lord's working among others even though he was not involved in those workings. He was an upright, devoted disciple whose gentleness and gifting made him a very effective servant in the Kingdom.

Barnabas' character and capabilities flowed from his relationship of devoted fellowship with God and this relationship arose from God's gracious gift of faith. We need to be people who have faith in God, yet those who have great faith are the first to admit that their faith comes from the goodness of God. Being filled with the Holy Spirit is what made Barnabas such a strong, stable, gentle person with lots of love for other believers and inspired him to serve the Lord with such single minded, self-sacrificing dedication. We are to thank the Lord for Barnabas, but must immediately recognise Christ as the *only* source for these qualities that Barnabas had in such abun-dance.

Many people had come to know the Lord before Barnabas came, yet many more were added through the ministry of Barnabas. We are to rejoice in the truth *and* wherever God is working. It is only those who have an exalted opinion of themselves and think that nothing happens in God's Kingdom without their direct involve-ment that cannot rejoice in or recognise God's working in the lives of others. Barnabas' desire was to exalt the Kingdom of God, not himself. He wanted people to be totally dependent upon Jesus and he used his abilities to achieve this end. Many preachers use their gifting to exalt themselves and make people dependent upon them.

Acts 11:25, 26

It appears as though Barnabas decided on his own that the situation required the services of Saul. Once again we get an insight into the character of Barnabas and see his pure love for the Lord and His Kingdom—it would have been obvious to Barnabas that Saul was his superior, yet he was not threatened to call him into this situation. Barnabas was not out to make a name for himself, for his single-minded desire was to advance Christ's Kingdom and whatever would help toward that goal, Barnabas would do—even if it meant making himself obscure in comparison to someone else. Foolish competitive thoughts would never have entered the mind of Barnabas or Saul when considering strategy in advancing the Kingdom and Paul himself ridiculed such childishness (1 Cor. 3:3–7).

It was now about eight years maybe nine, since Barnabas had introduced Saul to the apostles (Acts 9:27). We are not told how Barnabas knew where to look for Saul. The job was now too big for Barnabas to cope with on his own and the best man to help was Saul, the apostle to the Gentiles. For a whole year they laboured together teaching these new believers in the full counsel of God. The church continued to grow rapidly in Antioch and the Scriptures tell us that they taught a "great many people".

So effective and comprehensive was this teaching and so mightily was the Spirit working in the hearts of the disciples that their behavior clearly manifested Christ. They became known as the followers of Christ because they were distinct from the rest of the people in the city. A Christian is a disciple of Christ and a disciple is so completely dedicated to his master that he reflects his virtues and does everything for the master's honour and glory. This is the highest complement a disciple can receive—that he acts like his master. The dedication, graciousness and wisdom of Barnabas and Paul had produced much fruit in the lives of the believers in Antioch—students and teachers were real disciples, or Christians. May we too be called Christians because we think and act in accordance with the full counsel of God found in the Scriptures.

Acts 11:27

The NT prophet was the same as the OT prophet in the sense that both received direct revelation from God and then communicated this to others. They spoke by divine inspiration and would predict, or declare things that could only be known by divine revelation, such as, future events; God's will with respect to His Kingdom; His reproof for the rebellious; His comfort for the afflicted; His plan of salvation and His work of restoration. A prophet received divine knowledge as a result of *direct, personal revelation* from God. Whatever the content of this revelation might have been the distinctive characteristic was that the message was a direct communication from God to the prophet. It was through prophecy that God made known *new* revelation to His church, thus prophecy is essentially receiving divine knowledge by immediate special revelation from God. Prophets were necessary for the establishment of the NT church on the earth, for believers needed to know the will of God in the days before the Scriptures were completed. Revelation through prophecy, however, was merely a temporary measure in God's plan. The revelation necessary for the well-being of God's church, He has preserved in the Scriptures and thus no further revelation is required in our day in order to lead us to maturity (2 Tim. 3:16, 17). God did not preserve every prophetic utterance that was ever made, but those which have been preserved are a *complete revelation* and thus do not need to be added to in any way. The way God now communicates His will to us and directs us is by the working of the Holy Spirit through the Scriptures. The Holy Spirit does not give direct revelation any more, for the way He communicates with us is through the written Word—enlightening our understanding and quickening our conscience to perceive what has already been revealed. We do not need more special or supernatural revelation, because this foundation was laid by the apostles and prophets and does not need to be re-laid or improved upon (Eph. 2:20; 3:5).

Although in the history of the church, preachers and teachers of God's truth have been called "prophets," the Bible nowhere calls someone a prophet other than those few individuals who received special revelation directly (or immediately) from God. Prophets were *infallible* interpreters of the OT and inspired, *authoritative* preachers of divine truth. In the Biblical sense, the office of prophet ceased when God's special revelation ceased—by A.D. 70 with the destruction of Jerusalem. *To argue that since there were prophets in the NT we ought to have prophets today, is a very weak argument, similar to saying that since an infant receives its food in a certain way, that is the only way it can be nourished for all time.* The first Christians did not have the completed Scriptures and they were spread over a very wide and ever increasing geographical area, yet they needed to know God's will about every issue, thus God provided for their need through the prophetic gifts. Any one prophet only ever saw and understood a small part of God's whole will (1 Cor. 13:9), whereas believers now have God's complete revelation gathered in one book and instantly available to provide answers for every situation we will face in life (2 Tim. 3:16, 17). To long for the "nourishment" that the infant church received is a sign of our own childishness, confusion and laziness in studying God's revelation (2 Tim. 2:15). Many today want a "quick fix" answer to pop into their head or they merely use the Scriptures as some magic scroll, waiting for answers to "jump" off the page as they read. The Kingdom of God is not advanced in this way!

Why these prophets came to Antioch we are not told, though the NT prophets appear to have had a roving ministry. It would be safe to assume that the Lord had led them to Antioch, which is a very interesting illustration showing that no one person who received direct revelation from God received the whole picture. Why did not the Spirit reveal the famine to Paul or Barnabas? They were both prophets in their own right (Acts 13:1), yet God brought other prophets to Antioch and revealed the coming famine to them instead. No single prophet received all of God's revelation, thus we need to realize that the position we are now in (every believer having the completed Scriptures at their fingertips and the abundance of the Holy Spirit poured upon the church), is one of *immense* wealth. May our hearts be filled with deep thanks and reverence for what we have been given and may we press on to attain that maturity God wants for us.

Acts 11:28

This famine that the prophet predicted took place during the reign of the Roman Emperor Claudius, who ruled from A.D. 41–54. This famine is confirmed by secular historians (Josephus and Suetonius), though we do not need their confirmation in order to believe Luke's account. Whether the prophet meant that the famine would affect the whole world or just the known world (i.e., the Roman

Empire) is debated. We do know for sure that the whole of the
Roman Empire was affected and that Judea in particular was hard
hit by shortages caused by persistent droughts. Josephus says that
many people died in Judea because they were unable to buy food,
due to its high price during famine conditions.

Acts 11:29

Why the church in Antioch immediately decided to collect funds
for the church in Jerusalem we are not told. As in all famines, some
areas are harder hit than others for various reasons and possibly
Jerusalem was going to be much harder hit than Antioch. The historian and commentator, F.F. Bruce, says that the Jerusalem church
in the time of the apostles suffered chronic poverty. This might
have been brought about due to the persecution of Christians by
the authorities in Jerusalem. The Jews rightly understood that all of
life was religious, thus, when someone became a Christian, their
rejection was from all of life—family, work, home, inheritance, etc.
(remember, to be rejected by the Jewish leadership disqualified you
in all of life, making you a complete outcast in society, cf. John
9:22). If the church in Jerusalem was already very poor, then it
would have been obvious to the Christians in Antioch that when
the famine arrived, this poor church would be in serious trouble.
The poverty of the Jerusalem church could explain why the believers in Antioch immediately started gathering help for those in
Jerusalem, even though the effects of the famine were going to be
felt throughout the whole Empire. Christians are exhorted to care
for the poor and especially those in the household of God (Gal.
6:10).

The prophet said that the famine was coming and the church in
Antioch started their process of collecting aid for the Jerusalem
church. It appears that this collection covered quite a period of
time, whereby the Christians each committed themselves (*voluntarily*) to putting aside a little each month or week for their brethren in
Jerusalem. Each person freely decided to give what they were able:
this was no enforced tax! These were totally personal decisions with
respect to what each person's ability entailed. We too are expected
to act in the same way. We are not to neglect our primary responsibilities (1 Tim. 5:8; Mark 7:9–13), but we are all expected to give
according to our ability. God prospers us so that we can give. The
whole decision rests upon our own judgement, but we are expected

to judge righteously. The Gentile church had a desire to give to the Jewish church and part of their motivation was to show appreciation for the spiritual gifts that had come from Jerusalem to Antioch (cf. Rom. 15:26, 27).

Acts 11:30

Luke confirms that what the Christians in Antioch had purposed in their hearts, they actually did. They entrusted Barnabas and Saul with the task of delivering their contribution to the suffering church. We ought to be concerned with the affairs and situations of other Christians around the world and especially concerned for those who are suffering. We are one body and our thinking has to be renewed in this area of identifying with all who call on the name of the Lord in *sincerity*. We must hold to the unity of the faith and manifest this to the world by our genuine concern for other believers (1 Cor. 10:17; 12:20, 25).

Barnabas and Saul gave the gift to the elders of the Christian church in Jerusalem, not to the non-Christian Jewish elders in the city. This was about twelve years after Pentecost, so the church was well established in the sense of organisation. It appears best not to equate the elders with the apostles as some commentators do (cf. Acts 15:6). The apostles were probably not in Jerusalem and thus the contribution was given to the elders. This is the first time that we are told about "elders" in the book of Acts and yet Luke does not tell us anything about them, i.e., describe the term. His "silence" is probably due to the fact that since the early Christian gatherings were modelled on the Jewish synagogue, the structure and leadership were known to the people of that day. Every organisation needs office bearers that can act on behalf of and represent the mind of the body. With the passing of the apostles, elders now have the responsibility of leading the local groups of believers wherever they gather, though we need to pay close attention to the specific qualifications needed to be an elder (1 Tim. 3:1–7; Titus 1:5–9)—structure and order are very important. God raises up leaders and we recognise them by very practical everyday signs.

Acts 12:1

Now about that time: much debate exists as to how these events relate to Barnabas' and Saul's visit to Antioch. Once again Luke is not concerned about the details that would give us an exact understanding of these chronological events. This does not mean that what is written here is inaccurate, but rather that the message Luke wanted to communicate does not *require* a detailed understanding of how all the incidents connected with each other. Even though there might be many questions raised in our minds about the exact timing of one event in relation to another, such knowledge is of no real significance to Luke's message—everything he says is perfectly correct and complete for his intention; which is to show the spread and growth of the church.

We are not told when the famine hit Judea the hardest. We are not told by Luke that the famine had already started before the relief was delivered—the relief could have been sent out before the famine conditions had arrived. The actions of the church in Antioch were based upon faith in the prophetic Word of God and not upon some visual observation of famine conditions. In many instances it is not possible to arrive at definite conclusions, even using other historical sources to fill in what we do not know from Luke—there are still too many details we just do not know. Thus, it seems best to maintain that Luke *has* recounted these events in chronological order even though he leaves out many details. The events happened in the following way: once the relief was collected it was carried by Barnabas and Saul for delivery to the elders in Judea (11:30), however, while on this relief mission, Herod's persecutions (12:2,3) and death (verse 23) occurred, after which, having completed the delivery, Barnabas and Saul returned to Antioch (verse 25).

This king was Herod Agrippa I, the grandson of Herod the Great (Matt. 2:1), who had the children of Bethlehem murdered (Matt. 2:16). Agrippa was educated in Rome where he became friends with two future emperors (Caligula and Claudius), who when in power placed under the rule of Agrippa territories that equalled those ruled by Herod the Great (see comments on Acts 4:27). Agrippa I, was a very powerful king and retained political favor with his subjects by making sure that he strictly obeyed the Jewish laws when among the Jewish leadership. The Jewish authorities saw Agrippa as one of them and even gave him the honour of publicly reading a passage from the law during the Feast of Tabernacles celebrations—he was a shrewd politician. It is not clear why the king suddenly began this ruthless abuse of church members, though his courage to persecute did increase when he saw that his actions pleased the Jews (verse 3). It is quite possible that Herod's desire for

Jewish approval is what lead him, from the beginning, to attack the church, but we cannot be certain.

Acts 12:2

James was the first apostle to be killed for the cause of the Gospel. Luke is very brief in his account of James' martyrdom. Up until now no civil authority had taken such drastic steps against the apostles of the NT church. In mentioning James' death, Luke reveals the ruthlessness behind this outbreak of violence against the church, which could very well have been a determined effort to wipe-out the church. There is no evidence that Herod had personally clashed with these leaders or whether they had challenged his morality (e.g., Matt. 14:4, 5—Agrippa's uncle, Antipas, was the Herod who had John the Baptist beheaded, Matt. 14:10). This outburst could have been mere political expediency, that is, he might have decided to persecute this small group of people for some personal or political gain even though he personally knew little about their beliefs. His character was such that he would have persecuted anyone, as long as it advanced his political ambitions. This was yet another attempt by Satan to destroy the NT church. The whole church rests upon the foundation that the apostles laid (Eph. 2:19, 20), thus to remove them before this foundation was complete would have retarded the church for all time. Since the execution of Christ there had not been a united assault upon the church by the Civil and religious authorities—now there is complete agreement between these two powerful bodies and humanly speaking, there is nothing to stop Herod from succeeding.

Acts 12:3

Herod's wickedness is strengthened by the Jewish response to his murdering of James and his evil efforts become bolder, arresting Peter, the most prominent of the apostles. It is interesting that Herod had now arrested two out of the three apostles who were closest to Christ while He was ministering in the flesh (Matt. 17:1; 26:37; Mark 5:37; Luke 8:51). Even if Herod was ignorant about the full implications of his actions, Satan certainly was not and Herod was acting in line with his father, the devil (John 8:44). Peter was arrested just before the feast of Unleavened Bread or the Passover. The Passover sacrifice and meal was followed by seven days where no leaven (yeast) in any form was allowed to be eaten or even be in people's homes (Ex. 12:6, 8, 18–20; Deut. 16:3, 4, 6, 8). This was to remind the Jews of their deliverance from Egyptian bondage and more importantly, was meant to remind them how important sincerity and truth were in their relationship with God (1 Cor. 5:7, 8).

Acts 12:4

Thus, in order not to disturb the religious celebrations and offend the Jews, Peter is kept in prison until he can be brought to trial. This religious "sensitivity" arose from nothing but a formal ritual and was totally divorced from sincere heart-felt righteousness. Herod, maybe aware of previous "strange" happenings when the apostles were held in jail (Acts 5:18, 19), assigns heavy security to detain Peter.

We are immediately struck by the providence of God working in two completely different ways—James is murdered and Peter is delivered. Both men were apostles, both men were close friends of Christ, both experienced captivity and injustice, yet one was killed and the other freed in a miraculous way. We cannot understand the purposes of God and why He does what He does. It is necessary therefore to have our minds renewed so that we do not look upon Peter's escape as greater than James' death—i.e., one where God was in control and one where He wasn't. Job had said, "Even if God kills me, yet I will still trust Him" (Job 13:15). The writer to the Hebrews tells us that some of God's people, by faith, escaped death by the sword, while others, by *faith*, were killed with the sword (Heb. 11:34, 37). God's divine providence is a mystery that He does not have to explain to us. Our responsibility is to rest in God's sovereign will and always act in obedience to His Word, praying, "Not my will but your will be done Lord" (Matt. 26:39). Our sense of security, assurance, well-being and victory is not to be based upon our immediate outward circumstances but upon the accomplished work of Christ and His victory over the powers of darkness (see comments on Acts 2:24, 33). It is our relationship with God that is of ultimate value and nothing is to be compared to it (Gen. 15:1). Life and death on this earth fade into insignificance when compared to this eternal relationship.

Acts 12:5

God's sovereign control of all things does not mean fatalism (whatever happens must just be accepted mindlessly). We do not know

God's secret counsel that orders all things, though we are expected by God to always live in a way that glorifies Him. We do this by always walking in obedience to His commandments and seeking to exalt His righteousness and justice in every area of life. Our responsibility is to always act according to God's revealed will for us, even though the details of every situation will unfold according to God's secret workings. Thus the church was not to say, well, Peter is in jail, this is God's will so that is that. They knew God was sovereignly in control, yet their responsibility was not to guess about God's secret ordering of the outcome, but to respond to every circumstance according to the light of Scripture. God has revealed that life is precious and to be preserved (unless the person has committed a capital crime—which is also defined by God) and that righteousness and justice (defined by God) are to be sought after. The way one seeks to live according to these principles also has to be done with wisdom within the *particular* context that one finds oneself in.

Thus, the Jerusalem church, a despised and rejected group of people (by both the Roman and Jewish communities), had no official platform and authority whereby they could appeal to a lawful authority on behalf of Peter. Peter's imprisonment was unjust, however, there was nothing more the church could do other than pray. This was their *particular* context and they responded accordingly, but it is poor Biblical reasoning to say that this is the only legitimate response open to the church if someone is put into jail today. Prayer is always the first and most important aspect of our lives and responsibilities. However, it is not always the only thing we ought to do. Paul, who prayed without ceasing (1 Thes. 5:17), also made appeals to appropriate authorities to receive their protection or intervention, etc. (Acts 23:12–24; 25:11; 28:17ff.). We are to seek justice and righteousness in every area of life by wisely using every available channel. An oppressed underground church will not respond to different situations in the same way that a strong, free, influential church will. Yet, both are expected to glorify Christ in their different situations with godly wisdom, e.g., Elijah hid from king Ahab, while Jeremiah stayed in the city. We must not be foolish and think that every circumstance ought to be responded to in the same way, yet there is always only one goal—to seek first the Kingdom of God and His righteousness.

The church, being one body, constantly intercedes for Peter during this feast period. All Christians are in the same battle and the physical assault upon one for the sake of the Gospel is an assault upon them all. Peter's life was in real danger and the whole church was concerned for his safety, as if their own lives were threatened. With James already dead, the situation must have appeared helpless, yet the church faithfully stood with Peter, earnestly, or constantly pleading his case before the throne of God. In all likelihood they acted in the exact same way with respect to James and they are now prepared to pray for Peter until such time that he is delivered or killed. Their responsibility was to seek for justice in every way they were able to, acting at all times with wisdom, according to God's revealed will, while leaving the outcome to God's secret providence. We are not rendered helpless in such situations. We are not out of the spiritual battle ever! Even if there is nothing we can do physically we can still be in the centre of the battle in prayer and we ought to be. Prayer plays a significant part in God's purposes and He has graciously made a way for our involvement in the affairs of His Kingdom no matter who or where we are. Our hearts are often too cold to feel for other believers or the things of the Kingdom as we ought. May the Lord by His Spirit enable us to rise up and enter into the heat of the battle (Rom. 12:12; 2 Cor. 10:3–5; Eph. 6:10–18; Col. 4:2; 1 Pet. 4:7).

Acts 12:6

Peter's response to these extreme circumstances, arose from his complete trust in God's Word, where we are promised that He will never leave us nor forsake us (Deut. 31:6; Matt. 28:20; Heb. 13:5, 6). He had probably been in custody for a week (the duration of the feast), and this was Peter's last night before his "trial" and execution. By killing Peter, Herod was hoping to gain more support from the Jewish people and there was not any doubt as to how the "trial" would turn out, he was merely going through the motions so as to make things appear legal and just.

God gives His beloved sleep (Ps. 127:2) and Peter committed his case to Him who judges righteously (1 Pet. 2:23). "I lie down and sleep; I awake, for the Lord sustains me. I will not be afraid of ten thousand people who have set themselves against me on every side" (Ps. 3:5, 6). "The Lord is my light and my salvation; whom shall I fear? The Lord is the strength of my life; of whom shall I be afraid? … Though an army encamps against me, my heart shall not fear; though war should rise against me, even then I will be confident"

(Ps. 27:1, 3). "I will both lie down in peace, and sleep; for You alone, O Lord, make me dwell in safety" (Ps. 4:8). "When you lie down, you will not be afraid; yes, you will lie down and your sleep will be sweet" (Prov. 3:24). "In God (I will praise His word), In God I have put my trust; I will not fear. What can mortal man do to me?" (Ps. 56:4).

A squad of soldiers was four men and there were four squads assigned by Herod to specifically guard Peter. There were obviously other guards in the rest of the jail, but these were Peter's special guards. Two soldiers were chained to Peter and the other two guarded his particular dungeon door in some way. We do not know if they were inside or outside Peter's dungeon. The fact that four squads were assigned to Peter alone, meant there would be regular changes and therefore the soldiers would always be fresh and alert—this was maximum security.

Acts 12:7–10

The Lord's hand is not too short to assist those who trust in Him:

"Is anything too hard for the Lord?" (Gen. 18:14). "Yes, again and again they tempted God and limited the Holy One of Israel" (Ps. 78:41). " … Is My hand shortened at all that it cannot redeem? Or have I no power to deliver? Indeed with My rebuke I dry up the sea, I make the rivers a wilderness … " (Isa. 50:2). "Behold, the Lord's hand is not shortened, that it cannot save; nor His ear heavy, that it cannot hear" (Isa. 59:1). But Jesus looked at them and said to them, "With men this is impossible, but with God all things are possible" (Matt. 19:26). "For with God nothing will be impossible" (Luke 1:37).

According to Luke, Peter's deliverance is miraculous. God does not use some human helper, but an angelic messenger (see comments on John 1:51). Either the guards were all asleep or the Lord somehow prevented them from seeing what was taking place. We must never doubt the Lord's ability to deliver, for that is the basis of our peace and confidence—the Lord is abundantly able to deliver from anything if He so desires. We are to act according to His Word in every situation we find ourselves, though having total trust in *whatever* God ultimately causes to happen. Our only desire should be like Paul's who said, "I hope that in nothing I shall be ashamed, but with all boldness, as always, so now also Christ will be magnified in my body, whether by life or by death. For to me, to live is Christ, and to die is gain" (Phil. 1:20, 21).

God could have delivered Peter in an instant. Peter could have woken up in the house where the other Christian's were praying, yet God chose to show us the different stages so that we might see many miracles happening one after another and thus have our faith strengthened—the light, the chains falling off, the "blindness" of the guards and the opening of secure gates. The whole experience for Peter was so amazing that he thought he was seeing a vision. We must not underestimate the power and ability of the messengers who watch over us and minister to our needs in obedience to God's command (Heb. 1:14). The last gate was an extremely heavy iron one that required a number of men to open and close it, however, it unbolts, opens, closes and bolts again "automatically." All the guards are still in place, all the doors are secure and nothing is suspected, yet Peter is now on the streets of Jerusalem. The angel departs from Peter as suddenly as he had appeared. The Scriptures teach that God commissions His angels to guard and serve us (Ps. 91:11). Jesus warns against despising little children (as insignificant or irrelevant) since God's estimation of them is immense (Matt. 18:10). Nowhere do the Scriptures tell us that we have one *specific* guardian angel that has the responsibility of watching over us, rather, all of God's angels have been commissioned by Him to protect every believer. To say that we each have one particular angel who watches over us is to say more than God has revealed and therefore it is foolish.

Acts 12:11

The suddenness of the angel's appearing, the speed that Peter had been led from the dungeon to the street and the miraculous nature of the whole happening had left Peter in a daze. When he had gathered his thoughts together he realised that he was not dreaming or seeing a vision but that the Lord had actually delivered him from certain death. We see that Peter's death was not only desired by the Jewish leaders but by the common people also. This confirms the fact that Peter would have certainly been executed in the morning, for no one could resist the united intentions of Herod and the whole Jewish community—no one, that is, except God. If God is for us who can be against us? (Rom.8:31). No matter who unites against us, their efforts will be worthless! (Num. 14:9; Ps. 46:1–3).

Acts 12:12

Despite the hardships, the church continued to gather together in small groups whenever they could. This underlines the importance of Christians coming together for mutual encouragement, prayer and teaching (Heb. 10:25). Mary was the mother of John Mark, the author of the second Gospel (see too Col. 4:10; 2 Tim. 4:11; Philemon 24; 1 Pet. 5:13). Peter, probably after considering where he was in the city, decided Mary's house was the closest regular meeting place to him. Peter, probably at this time decided upon his strategy, which was to tell the Christians he was free, but since the whole Jewish community would be after him, he would go into hiding to avoid recapture or endangering other believers.

Acts 12:13, 14

In the midst of this serious situation, Luke preserves some humorous details about what took place when Peter came to Mary's house, which was very large and grand (having a forecourt and gate onto the street). The girl's response to hearing Peter's voice is very realistic and we probably know a number of people, if not ourselves too, who might react in this way to a similar situation. Whether this prayer meeting was a regular one or a special one organized for Peter, we do not know. Nor do we know if they were praying for his deliverance or merely that he would have the courage to glorify Christ whatever happened to him—either way they wanted *Christ* to be exalted.

Acts 12:15

The people within the house said that the girl was "crazy." In other words, it was absolutely impossible for Peter to have escaped from prison. It does seem likely, based upon their reaction, that they were not praying for Peter's deliverance from jail. They might have been praying that he would receive a fair hearing or that he would face death with courage. It is not clear what they meant by saying that it was Peter's angel outside. There was an unbiblical idea believed in those days that a guardian angel could assume the appearance of the one they protected and this is what they might have meant. Or they might have thought that Peter had already been killed and it was his spirit that had come to the house, however it is not possible to be sure what they meant. All we know for certain from these statements is that they were convinced that it was impossible for Peter to be the one knocking on the door.

Acts 12:16, 17

There is nothing wrong in being astonished by God's workings, even if God does what you are specifically praying for.

There must have been quite some noise from these people—shouts of joy, astonishment and praising God. Peter quickly silenced them, probably because he wanted to be on his way as soon as possible and not knowing what was going on at the prison, silence would be safest. He did not know if his absence had already been discovered and a search was already underway for him. If it was, then loud celebrations in the middle of the night would attract unnecessary attention. We are always to act wisely within our own particular situation and a hasty exit out of Jerusalem, before daylight, was extremely wise in this particular situation. One must never presume upon the protection of God, for it is surely putting Him to the test when you unnecessarily expose yourself to danger (Matt. 4:7).

Peter tells them about the miracle—so that Christ's name might be exalted and then wants them to tell James, the Lord's brother (see comments on Acts 1:14). James was seen as one of the pillars in the Jerusalem church (Gal. 2:9). "Brethren" possible represents the other leaders of the church, but indirectly would include the rest of the body in Jerusalem.

We have no historical records telling us where Peter went. It is generally accepted that he left Jerusalem, but there is no real evidence to show where he settled, probably because he became an itinerant missionary (cf. 1 Cor. 9:5) and travelled much, though he did return to Jerusalem again (Acts 15:7–11).

Acts 12:18

As the light of the day entered the cell where Peter had been held it was discovered that his chains were empty. What utter horror must have gripped the hearts of the guards for they well knew what Roman law stipulated for such a situation—the guards received the punishment that their prisoner was going to receive if he escaped. Thus it is easy to imagine the shouts and commotion (stir or disturbance) that must have erupted as the guards frantically started to look for the prisoner in utter shock, terror, disbelief and distrust of one another. This commotion included the desperate shouts and rushing around as well as the mental and emotional horror of the guards, knowing that if Peter was not found they would face possible death.

Acts 12:19

Herod, being informed, ordered a thorough search to be made for Peter. When Peter was not found he interrogated the guards. Herod would have been aware of the apostles' previous miraculous escape from jail. This awareness is the most likely explanation for the extremely heavy security that Peter was placed under. It certainly must have been obvious to Herod as he examined the guards that there was no massive conspiracy among them to free Peter. It would have needed a conspiracy for Peter to have escaped from two chains, two guards he was chained to, gone through two guarded doors or posts, and then through the massive iron gate that locked the whole prison. After examining the guards it would have been obvious that a conspiracy was ruled out and that only a miraculous intervention could have released Peter. However, the implications of accepting this were too great for Herod. It would mean admitting that he had murdered James. He would have had to oppose his political support base (the Jews) and tell them that Jesus Christ was God and Savior. He would have had to identify himself with the despised, persecuted, poor minority Christian group and face the uprising of the Jews. This uprising would have cost him his rulership (for Rome wanted rulers who could keep the peace, especially in Palestine). For Herod, Peter's miraculous release was unacceptable, both philosophically and practically. To have released the guards without punishment would have been admitting to the miraculous, thus Herod, in order to reject the miraculous possibility, had to treat the escape as a conspiracy and therefore he punished the guards. He was probably also trying to save some of the favor from the Jews who would have been very disappointed when Peter was not executed.

The Greek word merely says the guards were "led away," which can refer to being led to execution or imprisonment. The almost unanimous interpretation by commentators is that these guards were executed. Those in rebellion against God will go to extreme lengths in their useless attempts to suppress the truth.

How many guards were executed we do not know. What we can be sure about is that Peter, during his week of imprisonment, would have shared the Gospel with his guards. So for them to have died without Christ they would have only themselves to blame—their own wilful, foolish rebellion against the truth. Belief in Christ removes the sting of death (1 Cor. 15:55). Thus, while Herod's actions were tyrannical and wickedly unjust, the *tragedy* in this story would have been if the guards rejected the offer of the Gospel and died in their sin—without Christ, without hope and without God (Eph. 2:12).

Herod then went down to Caesarea, a predominantly Gentile city, where he remained until his death. The Jewish historian Josephus tells us that Herod went to celebrate the games being held in Caesarea in honour of the Roman Emperor.

Acts 12:20

These two great cities were dependent upon Galilee for their food supplies. For some reason that we do not know about, Herod had become very hostile in his mind towards these people. Being aware that they had offended Agrippa and that they were dependant upon food from his region for survival, they sent a delegation to try and reconcile the relationship. Representatives of the cities managed to make contact with Blastus, who was the officer in charge of Herod's bed-chamber. This was not someone who made the king's bed, but a person of considerable influence with the king. He was probably a high ranking security officer and advisor to the king. Kings were very vulnerable when they slept thus one of the most important offices in the kingdom would have gone to the one in charge of the bed-chamber. The way they made Blastus their friend was probably through bribery (it is wicked for those in authority to receive bribes because it perverts their ability to make just judgements, Ex. 23:8; Deut. 16:19; 1 Sam. 12:3; Amos 5:12). It appears as though their "intercession" to the king was made through Blastus and in this way peace was restored.

Acts 12:21, 22

At an appointed day during these grand celebrations, Herod was to address the delegation from Tyre and Sidon, making an official statement of reconciliation and mutual co-operation. Due to the positive nature of Herod's speech it was a very grand and festive occasion. The delegation, filled with relief and gratitude resort to flattery in an attempt to further strengthen their bond with Herod. Their ultimate hope for security and well-being was placed in man, thus they were not afraid to sin against God in order to secure the favor of powerful people.

Many people in our own days prefer to look to rich and powerful people for the solution to their every need. Their hope is in what they can see, rather than in the Kingdom of God and His righteousness. Their principles of behavior are determined by whatever will gain them favor with the rich and powerful. As far as they can see, God's eternal unchanging truth is irrelevant to their immediate goals and needs. They cannot stand by faith in God's revealed will. They will not walk by faith in what He has promised and commanded. Hope of success, for them, comes from "befriending" those who have power and money and they are prepared to compromise God's eternal truth and principles if necessary in order to obtain their desired benefits.

Acts 12:22

Herod, puffed up with his own self-importance and grandeur, was enjoying the praises of the crowd. He was not ashamed of the blasphemous honour being showered upon him, but was rather enjoying it. Herod's philosophy of governing was to accommodate everyone's ideologies and religions, chopping and changing his moral principles according to the people he was with. It is possible that he was caught in a difficult position, for here he was addressing a Gentile audience and it was these Gentiles that were bestowing upon him these divine titles. This was not uncommon for Gentiles to do and it was common for Roman leaders to be equated with divinity. Now for Herod to have rebuked this crowd he would have had to explain that such honour should not be given to a man, thus indirectly calling into question Caesar's acceptance of this kind of praise. This whole festival was in celebration of Caesar and thus it is very possible that this incident could have been very politically sensitive. Herod, we know, was anxious to remain in good favor with the Roman authorities as well as the Jewish people—the reason for this being that he loved to be in power. Thus, together with the fact of his enjoying such praise, the thought of making a political statement against Caesar by refusing this praise would weaken rather than strengthen his political position. Herod's pride and also his

love for power above the truth of God led to his foolish acceptance
of such blasphemy.

Acts 12:23

God immediately dispatches an angel to strike down this foolish
man, very clearly exposing the frailty and weakness of human flesh
(Jer. 17:5). The kind of death God brought upon Herod was one
that greatly humiliated him. The higher someone exalts themselves
the lower they will be brought down by God (Prov. 16:5, 18). Herod
was reduced from proudly strutting around and "speaking like a
god," to a position of a vile, stinking, rotting, worm-filled body
where all he could utter were cries of pain and helplessness.

The flattery that the crowd gave to Herod was empty and worthless,
for they despised him while they spoke—history tells us that there
were great *celebrations* in Caesarea upon the death of Agrippa
(which occurred in A.D. 44). Josephus says that after Herod was
struck down he lived for five days in intense pain and rotting of
body before he died. He thought he was god, yet the lowly worm
killed him! There are other examples recorded in history where
people's bodies were eaten by worms *before* they died (Lenski).

We need to be aware of how wicked it is to take any honour due to
God for ourselves. It is also a foolish thing to believe the flattery
people might pour upon us, because the flatterer is seeking his own
benefit when he flatters someone and his words of praise are forgotten or cast off as meaningless the moment he attains his purposes.

Acts 12:24

It is God who is building and protecting His church and this sentence sums up Luke's whole purpose for writing Acts—to show the
spread and growth of God's Word and Kingdom. How can mere
men put an end to the purposes of God? As history has so often
shown, persecution actually spreads and multiplies the church—
China being an amazing example of this. The "great, powerful"
political leader dies and his hopes of destroying the church die with
him, whereas the church is boosted rather than retarded by his
efforts.

Acts 12:25

For Luke to place this verse here, following on from 11:30, is best explained by seeing the whole story between these two verses as having taken place while Barnabas and Saul were on their mission of delivering the aid to the church in Judea. Luke is now going to focus upon the ministry of Paul and the major missionary outreaches to the Gentiles, as the Gospel continues its amazing spread and of which we are still a part.

Acts 13:1

Luke now focuses his attention upon the work that the risen Christ was doing through His body in Antioch and more particularly through the apostle Paul (Saul). The church in Antioch had been instructed by Barnabas and Saul for some years and it had developed into a mature body of believers. Other leadership had either been attracted to the city or was raised up under the ministry of Barnabas and Saul. Luke names five leaders whom he describes as prophets and teachers, however, he does not tell us which of them were prophets and which of them were teachers. Some say that each of them filled both functions. The making of leaders is Christ's work and we need to trust that He will do it in our own church. Strong, godly, mature leadership means being able to do much in the way of advancing the Lord's name and Kingdom—which should be our greatest desire.

We know who Barnabas and Saul are, however, we do not know anything about the other three leaders except what Luke tells us here. Niger is Latin for dark-coloured or black, thus he might have been an African or an Arab, though there is no certainty of this. Lucius was from Africa and Manaen was brought up in the home of Herod the Great and thus was the foster brother of Herod Antipas. Antipas was the tetrarch of Galilee and Peraea from 4 B.C. until A.D. 39—the one who murdered John the Baptist and whom we read about during the life of Christ (Matt. 14:3–10; Luke 3:1; 13:31, 32; 23:7–12). Antipas is not to be confused with Agrippa who died in chapter 12. We see quite a variety of races, nationalities and social standings among these five leaders. Paul who was educated in the religious heart of the Jewish nation (where Christ was despised) and Manaen who was raised in the political heart of the nation (where Christ was also despised), are now united and at the heart of Christ's evangelistic outreach to the Gentile world.

Acts 13:2, 3

These five leaders were in their offices of ministering and fasting, probably together with the rest of the congregation. Fasting is not seen in the NT as a regular part of the Christian's service, rather it is employed at times of crisis or when special direction is needed from God. Fasting has no value in and of itself and there is no Scripture that has prescribed it—there is no religious value in merely abstaining from food. A practical application of the concept would be to eat very simply (which is more the Biblical understanding of the fast) and then use the time saved in prayer and the food saved for sharing with others. Isaiah the prophet tells us what a real fast is (Isa. 58:4–14)—sacrificing one's own will, while seeking to obey and glorify the Lord's will. God wants people to "afflict" themselves with heart felt repentance and then walk in righteousness (that is a Godly "fast"), which will result in joyful *feasting* (Zech. 8:16–19).

Barnabas and Saul were called, commissioned and sent by the Holy Spirit. By the laying on of hands, the church did not appoint these two to any office or impart any spiritual gift upon them. It was merely a sign of showing their goodwill and support for the two missionaries and a public recognition of God's calling upon them. The church merely entrusted them into God's hands, commending them to His grace for the work He had called them to do (cf. Acts 14:26; 15:40). The church showed their unified commitment to the Kingdom of God and His purposes by agreeing to release these two very gifted men to go and minister to others. It was no small sacrifice on their part to release teachers of this quality. Though we see God's bountiful provision in raising up others to continue with the work in Antioch in the absence of Barnabas and Saul. Having the backing of this godly congregation must have brought much comfort to Barnabas and Saul when facing the many dangers and hardships of missionary work. Having the support of a church behind you for this kind of outreach is vital.

Acts 13:4

Once again it is made very clear that this major outreach into the Gentile world was completely God's doing—this was not some idea formulated in a Gentile church (Antioch). These missionaries were acting under the commandment of God. Paul was very quick to tell the Galatian church that his calling and office was not from men but from Christ alone (Gal. 1:1). Since God was sending them, they had the full backing of God.

Acts 13:5

It was less than a day's journey by ship to Cyprus, which was governed by Rome. On reaching the east coast they went to the town of Salamis and preached in their synagogues. Their strategy was to preach first to the Jews (cf. Rom. 1:16), though knowing that in the synagogues there would also be many Gentile "God-fearers" and thus they would have an immediate and convenient contact point with the Gentiles. John Mark was ministering with them and it seems best to understand this as practical training for the ministry under Barnabas and Saul, while himself doing some amount of ministering. This was an excellent Bible School and a better one couldn't be wished for—even in our day. It appears that Saul saw John Mark as an important part of the team and mission, thus his great disappointment when John abandoned the mission (verse 13, cf. 15:38).

Acts 13:6, 7

Luke, once again is not giving a detailed account of what happened, but rather highlighting some points that he feels best show the glorious spread of Christ through the Gentile world. The missionary team then make a 100 mile journey across the island to the main city Paphos. One assumes that they would have ministered along the way if there was opportunity. In this city there was a Jewish sorcerer who probably disguised himself as a "prophet" and thus he is called a false prophet by Luke. This sorcerer had assumed a position of significant standing within the court of the Roman ruler of Cyprus. The proconsul was under the Roman senate, which gave him absolute military and judicial authority and he had employed the services of this deceiver. We are told that the proconsul was an intelligent man, meaning he was thoughtful and able to apply his mind and grasp or understand a situation. This is probably why he was deceived by the sorcerer who paraded himself as one having great philosophical and religious answers.

News of Barnabas and Saul came to the attention of the proconsul/ governor and he earnestly sought to hear the teaching they were proclaiming. Modern leaders, for the most part, are so proud and satisfied with their own "great wisdom" that they do not realize their desperate need for true knowledge. This Roman leader was very aware of his need and thus immediately wants to hear everything that Barnabas and Saul have to say.

Acts 13:8

The deceiver, Elymas (also known as Bar-Jesus, verse 6), realised that he stood to lose his privileged position with all its riches, fame and luxury that went along with it. Thus we see him, with all his might, trying to undermine the truth and distract the governor's attention away from it. Satan opposes the truth at every opportunity and we need to realize that he constantly tries to distract us from following the truth also. That is why it is so foolish and dangerous to be satisfied with tradition and personal feelings as the basis for confirming that you are living according to the truth. The only way to really know is to bring every thought into line with the Word of God and do everything for the glory of His Kingdom. We need to be ruthless in our desire to know and do the truth, for it does not come naturally and there will be deception and opposition waiting round every corner. We need to realize our total dependence upon the grace, power and revelation of God. To be self-confident in any area will open us up for deception.

Acts 13:9

His Hebrew name Saul, is now changed for his Greek name Paul, which he retains throughout the rest of the book. Here we catch a glimpse into the heart of Paul and his zeal for the truth, though more importantly, we see the Lord's zeal for His truth (cf. Ps. 69:9; John 2:17). Paul, filled with the Holy Spirit and thus consumed by the purposes of God, refuses to tolerate such opposition to the truth. This sorcerer was a destroyer of people's souls and a vicious opponent of the True God—openly and blatantly contradicting the truth and calling it error.

Acts 13:10, 11

Paul assumes the full authority of his apostolic office and speaks with the absolute authority of God, completely exposing the perversity and wickedness in the sorcerer's heart. This is not Paul's accusation and condemnation but the Lord's, thus the same condemnation stands for all time. Though pronounced through the mouth of Paul in Cyprus to Elymas, it applies to all who will oppose the truth and purposes of God—this is ultimately revelation of the heart of God! God does not look lightly upon sin and rebellion against His ways. He is a consuming fire and will not allow people to mock Him or trifle with Him (Deut. 4:24). God is zealous for His own glory, truth and purposes. May we not be fooled or allow others to fool themselves in believing that just because God does not immediately judge (Rom. 9:22; 2 Pet. 3:4, 9), He is unconcerned about wickedness. Paul did not say to this sorcerer, "Well you believe differently to the way I do and we are all entitled to believe anything we want, so let's just leave it at that." Not to submit to the truth of God is to oppose Him and to oppose Him is to stand in the same position that Elymas was standing in. We desperately need to realize how violently opposed to each other light and darkness are—there never has been and never will be any peace between them!

Elymas opposed everything that could be called truth and righteousness. He knew he was opposing the truth and Paul asks him if he is ever going to stop perverting it. It was God's gracious work to bring Paul and Barnabas to preach to this Roman ruler, yet Elymas was frantically trying to prevent the grace from reaching the ruler. The Lord's way is very simple and straight: we are sinners and stand under His judgement, but if we believe in the name of Christ we will be saved. Many try to complicate and deflect people from this truth. What about those cults and "churches" that deflect people's attention away from the saving grace found in the Person of Jesus Christ alone? Do they not stand with Elymas and receive from God the same evaluation? They do! The exact way God will judge each act of rebellion against Him is not up to us to prescribe—this is in God's Sovereign and secret will. What we need to believe is that God is the same and He does judge, both now and on that last day. God does delay judgment according to His mercy, but sometimes we fail to recognise His judgment and thus think He hasn't judged.

God then reduces Elymas to a physical state that is comparable with his spiritual state, yet even here we see God's mercy, for he is told that it will only be for a time (not for the rest of his life).

Acts 13:12

The proconsul believed in Christ. There is no reason to doubt that this was true faith. He was astonished at the way the Lord taught—

both the method and content. The truth and the power of Christ
are united and complement one another. We are responsible for
proclaiming the truth, but the manifestation of the power is in
God's hand. Often we restrict God to the limits of our own minds,
expectations and preconceived ideas, thus we do not recognise His
power working in our midst. At other times we do not know His
truth and thus do not proclaim His full counsel and that is why we
do not see the power. When we understand the truth and thus
God's purposes in His Kingdom, we will recognise His powerful
working in our midst. When our hearts are consumed by His Kingdom and our every breath is breathed for the glory of His name;
when our hearts are zealous for the truth of God and we stand
against all lies and deception and all perversion of the truth, then
we too will be astonished by the teaching and power of Christ.

Acts 13:13

With the evangelism in Cyprus at an end, Paul and his party set out
for the south coast of Asia Minor. Perga was not right on the coast,
but some miles inland, however, in Paul's day it could be reached by
boat, sailing up the Cestrus river. Luke's brevity might be the reason
no mention is made about what evangelism took place in Perga. On
the other hand it is possible that they did not evangelise in Perga at
this time, though they did on their return (14:25). Luke is also very
brief about John leaving the missionary team. We know that Paul
saw this as deserting his post (15:38) and as a great character weakness. Paul was determined not to rely upon John again. There are
many different opinions about why John left them (this is *not* the
apostle John, but the cousin of Barnabas, John Mark, see comments
on 13:5). It could have been that the rigours and dangers of missionary travel were too much for John to face (cf. 2 Cor. 11:26) and
his nerve failed him—though every suggestion rests only upon
speculation.

Acts 13:14

This is not the same Antioch that Barnabas and Paul had left from
(13:1, which was in Syria), but another city by the same name
(which was in Pisidia). All the travelling on the main land was done
in modern day Turkey. In fact, the Antioch of 13:1 was also in modern day Turkey. The great light of the Gospel was brought to these
areas so early after Christ. Ephesus was also in this same region and

Christ warned that church in Revelation 2:5 that unless they repented He would remove the light of the truth. This whole region is now under the dominion of Islam—modern Turkey is the largest unreached nation for Christ in the world!

Acts 13:15

We see something of what the worship service was like in the synagogues. The leadership kept structure and order in the services. Specific passages were read, first, one from the five books of Moses (the law) and then another one taken from the prophets. The important part of the service was the sermon (exposition of the Word) and opportunity was usually given to visiting Rabbis to address the local congregation. Paul was quick to respond to such an opportunity—the leadership not realising that things would not be the same after this sermon.

Acts 13:16

The Jews came together in the synagogue not only for worship, but also to meet friends and catch up on the latest news. Thus, if there was a pause in the service they would all begin talking to one another about family or business or the like. The speaker therefore had to gain their attention and restore order before he was able to deliver his sermon. It is of interest to note the different customs within the synagogue worship among the Jews in different parts of the world, e.g., Paul here stands to deliver his teaching, whereas Jesus, in Israel, sat down to teach (Luke 4:20, 21). Where there are no specific commands on how something ought to be done, we need to be slow to judge others, thinking that our way of doing things shows greater reverence for the Lord than their way.

Paul acknowledges the Jews and Gentiles in his opening, saying, "Men of Israel and you who fear God, listen to me." The implication is that they were about to hear something that was *very* different to the sermons they usually heard. This is the first recorded sermon that we have of the apostle Paul and it is more than likely an abbreviation of the actual sermon, though Luke would have preserved the main points. The sermon is very similar to those we have already seen in Acts given by Peter (2:14–36; 3:12–26) and Stephen (7:2–53).

Acts 13:17

Paul gives an historical account of Israel's relationship with the Lord, though the emphasis throughout Paul's address is upon the sovereignty of God. Israel's calling, nationhood and preservation were God's doing and this He did for His own glorious purposes. God did not choose Israel because she was a mighty people (Deut. 7:6, 7) and nor did her righteousness attract God's attention (Deut. 9:5). From beginning to end it was all God's doing—the unfolding of God's eternal plan that finds its ultimate realization in the Person of Christ. Despite the harsh conditions in Egyptian bondage, God multiplied them beyond human expectation and turned them into a nation (Acts 7:17). Despite their continued stubborn rebellion against the truth of God and against Moses in Egypt, God delivered them in a most powerful way (Ezk. 20:6–9, see comments on Acts 7:25–29). It was God's arm that brought them out, despite their foolishness.

Acts 13:18

Despite all that the Lord had done for the nation and all that they had seen as God overthrew the nation of Egypt; despite the awesome manifestation of His presence on Mount Sinai; despite God's miraculous provision for the children of Israel in the wilderness—food, water, protection and clothing (Ex. 16:35; 17:6, 8–13; Deut. 8:4; 29:5), they still walked in rebellion—idolatry, disobedience and much murmuring (Acts 7:42–45; Ex. 14:12; 16:3; 17:3; Num. 11:5; 14:2, 22; 16:13, 4). It is a common thing, even in our day, that those who have lived under oppression and slavery do not want to assume the maturity needed to live in freedom. They prefer the "security" of an oppressive ruler. Paul is not saying that God took care of the children of Israel in the wilderness for forty years, but that He put up with (endured) their rebellion. God disciplined them, to be sure, but the reason He preserved them, despite their wickedness, was for His own plans. The great hope of the Jews was that they were "Jewish"—this was their security and boldness before God, whereas Paul is showing that from the beginning, the nation has been characterised by rebellion. Paul is removing any basis for boasting, or having any confidence in the flesh.

Acts 13:19

God gave Israel the land, it was not Israel's own power, righteousness and wisdom that conquered Canaan.

Acts 13:20

Some translations say there were 450 years before the period of the Judges, because 450 years is too long a period for the Judges in their chronological time frame. The Ecclesiastical Greek text has the 450 years referring to the time the Judges ruled and I believe this is the most reliable text. If you add all the periods of the judges and all the times of oppression from Cushan (Judg. 3:8) up to and including Samuel, it is 450 years. This period was a time of persistently turning away from the Lord and it is summed up as the time when "everyone did what was right in his own eyes" (Judg. 21:25). God, graciously kept delivering Israel from those He had sent to oppress them for their rebellion against Him. After the deliverance, Israel kept turning back to their own ways and forsaking the ways of the Lord—this continued for 450 years (a very long time).

Acts 13:21

Israel's rebellion knew no bounds. They rejected God as their King and asked for a man to be their king instead (1 Sam. 8:5–22). God gave them their wish, which they had to live with for forty years. Samuel warned them that their king would be oppressive and demand an excessive 10 percent tax (1 Sam. 8:15). What word should we use for those modern leaders that demand taxes far in excess of this *oppressive* 10 percent? This is the only place where we are told in the Scriptures how long Saul's reign was. Many commentators reject this as far too long since it does not fit into their "organized" understanding of Biblical chronology. The 450 years for the time that the Judges ruled is also rejected as far too long. People are quick to start amending the Bible and giving reasons why mistakes were made in the Scriptures, though they stubbornly refuse to admit that their understanding of the given chronology could be wrong.

Acts 13:22

It was God who deposed the rebellious Saul and raised up David in his place. Saul had refused to submit to the Word of the Lord and placed his own will and desires above those of the Lord (1 Sam. 15:11, 19, 22, 23, 35). Samuel the prophet was directed by God to anoint David as king. The people had chosen Saul, but David, was specially chosen by God. Outwardly, even to the prophet Samuel, others appeared more suitable to lead Israel (1 Sam. 16:6, 7, 12). Remember Saul was someone who was very tall and had all the outward appearances of a great king (1 Sam. 9:2). God's praise for David was meant to make us focus upon the One who would come from David. Everyone knew that David failed the Lord badly by committing adultery and having Uriah murdered, thus one automatically looks beyond David when God says, "he will do all My will." Yes David was a man who had a soft heart towards God and found his assurance in the grace of God (Ps. 51:1), but that which was promised to David pointed far beyond David (cf. Ps. 89:20–29)—"His seed I will make to endure forever, and his throne as the days of heaven" (verse 29). The truth is, disaster came upon David's house and everything according to human appearances looked lost. The Psalmist writing this Psalm couldn't reconcile God's promises to David with what he saw happening around him thus he said, "Lord, where are Your former lovingkindnesses, which You swore to David in Your truth"? (verse 49).

The prophet Ezekiel prophesied about the overthrow of the kingly line and looked to the one who had always been expected and who had always been the only true King—the Messiah. It is to Him that the Davidic line had always pointed (Ezk. 21:27) and it is to Him that God wants us to direct all our attention and hope. In Him alone is there any hope. In Him alone can we find righteousness and peace. The people longed for the times of David, yet the end of David's reign was disruption and ruin—David himself being trapped by the bondage of sin. What we need is someone far greater than David. Someone who will completely accomplish everything God desires and demands.

Acts 13:23

Sin and bondage are our lot and it was the same for Israel. The greatest figures in the nation's history, those to whom everyone looked back upon as fathers of the faith, all failed dismally. Even good examples are not enough for us to succeed—much more is needed! Israel's whole history had been one of failure due to her sinful ways. Even when there is great love for God as in the case of

David, there is no escaping from the reality of sin—that is why the starting place is to be saved from our sin. We need to be saved from the guilt, condemnation and the power of sin and no man, politician, king, riches or government can do that. This is our most desperate and vital need. We need a savior and Jesus is the only savior that exists. He is the One promised from the foundation of the world—He is the seed of David, the one whom David believed in to be saved. This is Paul's message—you can only trust the promise of God, which is found in Jesus Christ.

Acts 13:24

The fact that John was a prophet is not even a matter for debate as far as Paul is concerned and most of the people in Israel held to the same opinion: all the people "counted John to have been a prophet indeed" (Mark 11:32, cf. Matt. 21:26, 32; Luke 20:6). Actually the people in the nation thought so highly of John many believed he might even have been the Messiah (Luke 3:15). The ministry of John was a clear fulfilment of prophecy (Isa. 40:3; Mal. 3:1). The religious leaders in the nation of Israel rejected John because he exposed their hypocrisy (Matt. 3:7). Nevertheless, John's preaching and baptism were from heaven (Luke 20:4), thus to reject his message and call was to reject God (Luke 7:30). This message of God that John preached to his nation was rejected by many because it clearly showed that being a Jew (a descendent of Abraham) was not enough to gain acceptance before God. The proud religious leaders were highly offended by the idea that they were sinners who needed to repent and be washed (Mark 11:31; Luke 7:30). John's message however was meant for *all* the people of Israel because *all* of them were sinners needing forgiveness and deliverance from their sin. This is the same starting place for our own day—everyone needs to repent. People have not changed and they still deny personal accountability with respect to their sin before God. Nevertheless, our guilt is something we cannot escape from, because it arises from rebellion that is aimed directly at God—all sin is first and foremost an assault against God and His absolute rule.

Acts 13:25

Paul had been showing the historic references to Christ in the prophets. Now he shows prophetic confirmation of Christ given by a contemporary prophet. This highly esteemed prophet, John the

Baptist, clearly and repeatedly said the Messiah was coming and
then identified Jesus as the Messiah. Paul says that John's ministry
was only meant to be temporary—giving way to Him who would
come after. John was the first prophet that God sent to Israel in over
400 years and he made a significant impact upon the whole nation.
It was due to their great ignorance of God's revelation that people
thought John might be the Messiah. Paul uses John's stature as a
prophet in Israel to exalt the name of Christ and to confirm that
Jesus is the Messiah. The term, "the One who comes" clearly
referred to the Messiah in Jewish thinking. Preparing for the coming of Christ was the essence of John's ministry, which was indeed
an exalted calling (Matt. 11:9, 11; Luke 1:15–17, 76; John 5:35), yet
John says you cannoteven begin to make a comparison between
himself and Christ. John illustrated this by finding the lowest
ranked servant in a household, then selecting the most menial task
that this servant performed (taking the sandals off the master's feet
and washing his feet) and said he was unworthy of doing even this
for the One coming after him.

Acts 13:26

Paul acknowledges his awareness of the two distinct groups listening to him—Jews and Gentiles. Paul was the one who had the message of salvation and God had sent him to proclaim it to these
people. In Paul's first recorded sermon, while on the first official
missionary trip to the Gentiles, he makes it very clear that salvation
in Christ is offered equally to both Jew and Gentile. He first names
the two groups and then joins them together saying, "To *you* the
word of this salvation has been sent" (I follow the Ecclesiastical Text
here which has "to you" and not "to us"). There is a possibility that
Paul is exhorting his audience in Antioch not to reject Christ as
those in Jerusalem had done.

Acts 13:27

The people of Jerusalem and those leaders thought to be the most
spiritually enlightened, all dismally failed to recognise Jesus as the
Messiah. They did not only fail to understand Christ, but they
totally failed to understand the prophets who clearly revealed the
Messiah. Every week the prophets were read to the people in their
synagogues and thus every week they were brought face to face with
God's inescapable revelation about Jesus. Yet, when Jesus appeared

they rejected Him. Thus, it is plain that to reject Christ means you haven't understood the message of the Scriptures—it is all about Christ (Luke 24:27). They not only failed to recognise Christ, but failed to realize that by condemning Christ, they were fulfilling the prophecies that were read ever week. They did not understand the prophecies and were doing the very things the prophets had predicted. The condemnation, suffering and death of the Messiah was clearly revealed. That is why Jesus rebuked his disciples on the road to Emmaus when they were so discouraged by His death. Jesus said, "O foolish ones, and slow of heart to believe in all that the prophets have spoken! Ought not the Christ to have suffered these things and to enter into His glory?" (Luke 24:25, 26, cf. Luke 18:31–33). The people in Jerusalem were the ones who caused the Messiah's suffering that was predicted by Isaiah (Isa. 52:13–53:12—this is the same passage that the Ethiopian eunuch was reading and Philip said it spoke of Jesus, Acts 8:35).

It was not just the religious leaders that were guilty of Christ's death—it required the majority consent of every group and class in the city to bring it about. Pilate would never have conceded to the pressure of the religious leaders to put Christ to death if it was not for the support they had from the people (Matt. 27:24). However, may we never rise up with proud accusations against the people of Jerusalem, because *our* sin and rebellion is just as much to blame for Christ's condemnation on the cross as were their calls for His crucifixion. Romans 4:25 shows that our sins were the proper cause of Christ's death. The sin of the city of Jerusalem and its leaders was reprehensible and they were all held accountable before God. Yet all sin is reprehensible to God and will receive His just judgement.

Acts 13:28

The innocence of Christ is of vital importance if He is to be our substitute. The religious leaders had diligently searched for some kind of evidence to convict Christ of sin, but had been unable to come up with anything (Matt. 26:59, 60). The Holy Spirit, through Paul, reveals the depths of the wickedness in the hearts of those involved in Christ's murder. It was all done with the appearance of legality, yet the whole thing was completely lawless and immoral, since there was no legal case. Both the religious leaders and Pilate knew there was no evidence to convict Christ of anything, let alone of a capital crime. When Pilate asked them to explain what evil

Christ had done, all they could say was, "Crucify Him!" (Matt.
27:23). When God's Word is forsaken as the standard for all of life
then justice will never prevail: the Jews knew Christ was innocent,
yet He was standing in the way of their wills, thus murder, in this
instance, was what was best for the nation (John 11:50). Pilate knew
that Christ was innocent (Matt. 27:18, 19; Luke 23:14, 15; John
19:4), yet in order to secure his own political position, the murder
of an innocent Man was authorised (Matt. 27:24; John 19:12, 13,
16). Those who think it is possible to have justice in a society without complete submission to the Word of God are deceived.

Acts 13:29

Those who fulfilled their wicked desires by murdering Christ, actually fulfilled everything that had been ordained and predicted by
God. To hang on a tree was to be accursed by God (Deut. 21:23, cf.
Gal. 3:13). Paul says Jesus was hung on a tree in order to fulfill
everything God said would happen to the Messiah. God is always in
absolute control of even the smallest details and yet this does not
excuse the guilt of those who do wicked things (see comments on
Acts 2:23; 4:28). Christ was not only crucified and accursed by God,
but He died and was buried.

Christ was sent from the Father because of His love for us, yet we
cannot separate God's love from His holiness. Sin is more wicked
and offensive to God's Person and character than we could ever
appreciate and His justice is real justice. Sin has to be dealt with in a
just way, it cannotjust be ignored. Only in this light can we understand the great emphasis the NT writers place upon the cross of
Christ. Sin has to receive the judgment of God and every sin will
receive His wrath. When we believe in Christ our sin is transferred
onto Him—Jesus bore the wrath of God for this sin on the cross
(Matt. 26:28; Mark 10:45; 2 Cor. 5:21; 1 Pet. 2:24; 1 John 2:2; 4:10).
If we do not believe in Christ, then our sin remains on us and we
bear the wrath of God in our own bodies—which is nothing less
than eternal torment and separation from God. The death of Christ
is a fundamental pillar in the message of God's gracious redemption.

Acts 13:30

If the death of Christ is one of the pillars of the Gospel, then the resurrection is *the* central pillar in our salvation. The resurrection of

Christ is inescapable proof of His Deity (Acts 17:31; Rom. 1:4). It was none other than God who raised Christ from the dead, a Divine act showing God's Divine ruling on the matter. God's ruling was that Christ's suffering on the cross had perfectly satisfied the requirements of justice with respect to sin. The resurrection completes the atonement, showing God's full acceptance of Christ's substitutionary offering for us. Paul tells us that Jesus "was delivered up because of our sins, and was raised because of our justification" (Rom. 4:25). The resurrection of Christ is a miracle whereby God declares us righteous and worthy of eternal life. We are guaranteed to rise from the dead because Jesus did (1 Cor. 15:20–23; 2 Cor. 4:14). The Christian's hope with respect to Christ's resurrection is not only for the future, it also speaks of our rising above the bondage of sin in this life to a life of righteousness (Rom. 6:1–11). Without the resurrection of Christ there can be no salvation from sin and no hope for eternal life. What wonderful news the Gospel is! What wisdom we see in God! What a decisive victory over sin, death and Satan. Hallelujah, Christ is risen!

Acts 13:31

We have accounts of Jesus appearing on ten different occasions to His disciples after His resurrection, covering a period of forty days (Acts 1:3). On one of these occasions over 500 people saw Jesus at the same time (1 Cor. 15:6), thus there was a multitude of eyewitnesses to the fact of Christ's resurrection. Jesus appeared to those who knew Him very well and it was these very people who were now testifying in Jerusalem and beyond about what they had witnessed. Christ's resurrection was not some dark mystery done in a corner, rather there were hundreds and hundreds of eye witnesses, thus we do not have to rely upon the testimony of only one person, e.g., like the Mormons who have to rely upon the testimony of one man, Joseph Smith, who was the only person who saw and could "translate" the *supposed* golden tablets. If people could look upon the very Word of God (Jesus Christ), why couldn't others look upon the golden tablets of Joseph Smith? How could these be more "holy" than Christ, who is a revelation of the brightness of God's glory and the express image of His Person? (Heb. 1:3, see too 2 Cor. 4:6; Col. 1:15). John says, about Christ, "That which was from the beginning, which we have heard, which we have seen with our eyes, which we have looked upon, and our hands have handled, concerning the Word of life" (1 John 1:1), yet Joseph Smith said if anyone other than himself looked upon the golden tablets they would be struck dead. The stone tablets Moses received were written by the finger of God (Ex. 34:1), yet despite this, many others saw them and they remained with the people of God for hundreds of years. It is deceivers who do not want others to see too much and so they surround things in secrecy.

Acts 13:32

The good news Paul is talking about was nothing new, but had a long established history among God's people and was in total agreement with everything God had previously said. This message was in fact the glorious fulfillment of the promise given to the fathers of the faith with respect to the coming of the Messiah.

Acts 13:33

The fathers had longed for and patiently waited for the time of the promise, yet it was their children that lived to see the fulfillment. This fulfillment was a historical event that had happened and now stood for all time. Paul's announcement was that the Messiah had come. This raising up of Christ is not referring to the resurrection, but to God bringing the promised Savior into the world (Deut. 18:15, 18; Acts 3:22; 7:37). The early church said the second Psalm was clearly referring to the Messiah and it was for the purpose of redemption that God "raised up" or "brought forth" or "brought into being as a Man" His Son (Ps. 2:7, cf. Heb. 1:5; 5:5). This raising of Christ, which is declared with formal authority by the King of the universe, is a fundamental law with respect to the workings of God's Kingdom (Ps. 2:7). The nation had longed for the fulfillment of this promise and now Paul had the unspeakable joy of testifying that all had been accomplished through the life of Christ. Whatever idea or religion does not have its beginning and ending focused upon Christ, it is in error. There is nothing more glorious and more central in the Kingdom of heaven than Jesus Christ—whoever tries to diminish this glory or centrality is an enemy of God and Christ.

Christ's throne is equal in authority to God's and His Person and work is the fundamental law or essence of God's Kingdom. The Messiah came at a definite time in history, yet His relationship with the Father is from everlasting and they both have the same standards and goals. God promised to raise up Someone who would save us from our sin and who would be our glorious King with universal dominion—this long standing promise, which the fathers eagerly looked for, Paul told his audience it had been completely fulfilled in their day through Christ. God raised up Christ to fulfill all His promises and to accomplish all His purposes, thus everything about the Kingdom must be understood in the light of what Christ did and of who Christ is.

Acts 13:34–37

The raising of Christ from the dead fulfilled the promise made with respect to David. These promises couldn't have been realized without the resurrection of the crucified Messiah. Isaiah talks of "the sure mercies of David," which he equates with the everlasting covenant (Isa. 55:3). This is a promise that God would establish the seed of David and his kingdom forever (2 Sam. 7:16; Ps. 89:3, 4). The prophet said that these mercies promised to David were sure, that is, they would *most certainly* be accomplished. It was very obvious that someone far greater than David was being talked about and this is confirmed by Psalms 16:10, which couldn't refer to David, because his body had rotted in the grave (i.e., saw corruption). What use is the promise of an everlasting Kingdom to the people of God if they have no personal share in this Kingdom? Thus the hope is that we might be a part of and share in God's glorious, *everlasting* Kingdom—this is what God promised His people from the beginning.

The prophets said the basis for a share in the "sure mercies of David" depended upon One who was far greater than David—*requiring Someone who would not see corruption.* The whole hope rested upon this necessity, thus every Jew and God fearer should have been looking for the workings of God that would fulfill this requirement.

God's holiness reveals how terrible and serious sin is and unless sin is removed there can be no salvation. God's justice demands that sin must be judged (Deut. 27:26; Gal. 3:10, 13), for the consequence of sin, God says, is death (Rom. 5:12; 6:23). To think that all God needs to do is pronounce our forgiveness and sin has been dealt with, is to greatly pollute the righteousness and justice of God. God's grace and His righteousness cannot be separated from each other. It is the purity of God's law, the unchanging nature of His holiness, the eternal standard of justice and the reality of His wrath against sin that requires sin to be dealt with in a righteous way. To think it is possible to ignore the penalty required for violating the law of God is to turn the law into a meaningless oddity. Peace with God is obtained only upon the basis of prefect righteousness.

What sinful people need is a perfectly sinless substitute, someone who obeyed every detail of God's law. It is God's grace that has made it possible for us to be saved from our sin—there never has been a necessity upon God to save sinners. There is however, only one possible way of being reconciled to God and that is by a legal provision made according to the wisdom of God, which fully satisfies His justice (see comments on John 1:17). This is what the whole of the Jewish ceremonial law proclaimed every day.

Christ perfectly obeyed the whole law of God. He was an innocent man who was by "legal" action condemned to die. In His death, the full wrath of God was poured out upon Him, for He was dying in the place of sinners. He fully endured the penalty for sin and then He rose from the grave in the same body He suffered in, proving His sinlessness and God's complete acceptance of what He had done. The legal work had been completed—now sinners could be reconciled to God without violating His holiness or justice and without making a mockery out of His law. All of this is implied in the statement that Christ did not see corruption.

Acts 13:38

There is only one basis for the forgiveness of sins and it is a thoroughly legal basis, finding fulfillment only in Jesus Christ (Mark 10:45; Col. 1:14; Titus 2:14). It is impossible to find forgiveness in any other way than that way graciously provided by God (Rom. 3:24). It is the height of foolish, arrogant rebellion that despises the salvation offered in Christ. He alone perfectly obeyed God. He took our sin upon Himself and endured the wrath of God against sin, thus fully satisfying the requirements of justice (Rom. 3:25, 26; 1 John 4:10). Christ alone could pay for the sin of others and then rise from the dead, demonstrating the total acceptance of His sacrifice before God. It is only when we believe in Christ that all the necessary legal transactions can take place. It is only by complete dependence upon God's promise and provision that we can be reconciled to Him (Rom. 5:8–11; 2 Cor. 5:18–20). For it is only here that we can exchange our sinfulness for Christ's perfect obedience and God can declare us justified (Rom. 5:19; 1 Pet. 2:24). All of this is a legal transaction that takes place in the High Court of God, where Christ's righteousness is accounted ours by the Supreme Judge and our sin receives its full reward in Christ (2 Cor. 5:21). No one other than Jesus Christ could have satisfied these legal requirements and therefore there is no salvation outside of Christ (1 Tim. 2:5; Acts 4:12).

Acts 13:39

The law was never designed to be the means for reconciling us to God. The Jews foolishly thought they could use the law to secure their justification. The law, however, reveals our sin, pointing us to Christ as the only way of salvation, for "if there had been a law given which could have given life, truly righteousness would have been by the law" (Gal. 3:21). Paul in Antioch is saying to these people that their only hope of being reconciled to God and thus escaping from the wrath of God that rested upon them, was by believing in Christ.

Acts 13:40, 41

Paul then, by repeating the warning of the prophets, confirms that outside of Christ there is no salvation. Jerusalem, for the most part had rejected this offer of salvation. Paul quotes Habakkuk, though the disaster hanging over the heads of those to whom Habakkuk spoke was oppression by Babylon (Hab. 1:5). Paul's warning is far more serious than this, for the disaster he is speaking about is the consequence of rejecting God's provision of reconciliation found in Christ—which is nothing less than eternal damnation. Many in Habakkuk's day despised the Word of God and rejected His warning and many in our day do the same with Paul's warning. Do not be a foolish despiser, for our gracious and loving God has provided a glorious deliverer for all those who will receive His merciful offer.

Acts 13:42

Following the Ecclesiastical Greek Text, my translation of this verse is, "And departing from the synagogue of the Jews, the Gentiles begged [Paul and Barnabas] to speak these words to them until the next Sabbath." It is not clear whether Luke is making a distinction between the God-fearers and the Gentiles or if these two terms refer to the same group of people. It appears as though Paul and Barnabas left the synagogue service straight after the sermon, whereas the meeting was only officially disbanded in the next verse. Thus, it is difficult to know what relationship these Gentiles had with the synagogue, nevertheless, they were profoundly influenced by the teaching of Paul with respect to the basis of salvation.

Acts 13:43

After the meeting was officially ended, many others (Jews and devout proselytes) followed Paul and Barnabas—this appears to be a different group to that mentioned in verse 42. Devout proselytes were full converts to Judaism, which means they would have been circumcised and they were very often zealous for the Jewish traditions. These people had responded favorably to the message of salvation by grace through faith in Jesus Christ. The most difficult thing for those steeped in Judaism would be to continue trusting that faith alone was sufficient for their salvation. Works salvation was such a major part of Judaism that their own natural tendency and the pressure from their leaders would entice them to return to the old ways of salvation by works (Gal. 1:6,7; 3:1–3). The message that salvation is by grace through faith can be received with much joy, but this does not prove true conversion. Even the perverse Herod, "gladly" listened to the preaching of John the Baptist (Mark 6:20) and the nation of Israel, for the most part, rejoiced in the light that John brought (John 5:35), yet in the end completely rejected the One John pointed to. Only perseverance in the truth of God is proof of conversion (Matt. 3:8; 7:20; 13:5, 6, 20, 21; 21:43; Luke 3:9), though our firm assurance comes from the Holy Spirit who sheds the love of God abroad in our hearts (Rom. 5:5). It is from this sincere love that we confidently proclaim "Abba Father," being fully convinced that we are His children (Gal. 4:6; Rom. 8:15). Many of the people Paul had been preaching to responded joyfully to the truth that forgiveness and justification came through faith in Christ, yet this is not merely the starting place for Christianity, but the only basis for the *whole* walk. Thus Paul and Barnabas exhorted them to constantly remain in and totally rely upon the grace of God (Rom. 11:6; Gal. 5:4; Heb. 13:9). We too must never forget how dependent we are upon God's grace for everything we need to do in this life.

Acts 13:44

Paul and Barnabas were obviously very busy the whole week teaching among the Gentiles (see verse 42) and thus almost the whole city came together to listen to the new teaching. The attraction for the Gentiles was that they could become full members of the covenant without becoming Jews, but merely by having faith in Jesus Christ. This gathering must have been in some suitable location because the synagogue wouldn't have been large enough to hold this amount of people.

Acts 13:45

The success Paul and Barnabas were having made the Jewish leaders very jealous. People react against the Gospel for many different reasons and it is not always easy to know what is motivating them—here it was envy and jealousy. It is only perverse thinking that leads to jealously in this kind of a situation, for only the working of God's Spirit can cause people's hearts to respond to the truth. Thus, if the truth is being proclaimed and many people are responding to it we ought to rejoice no matter whom God is using to accomplish His purposes (1 Cor. 3:7). When people become jealous it is because they think they have the ability to change people's hearts and therefore they want some of the glory for themselves. What motivates such people is glorifying themselves rather than glorifying God. Success in God's Kingdom is faithfully living by and proclaiming His truth in every area of life and not by how people respond to our message (cf. John 6:66). We need to be faithful to our responsibilities and leave the outworkings to God's secret counsel.

These Jewish leaders despised the message of salvation by faith in Jesus, and thus spoke blasphemous words against it, probably by viciously attacking the Person of Christ. The Jews took great pride in their religious rituals and the thought that the Gentiles could now be equal with them in God's eyes, without these rituals, was very offensive and so they jealously tried to guard their previous privileged position. These leaders probably felt that they had earned and thus deserved a special place in God's Kingdom, yet now Paul was saying they had to share this with those whom they greatly despised. Salvation by grace alone, which means we are unable to do anything to earn God's favor, is an offensive doctrine to those people who want to claim some personal credit for their standing in the Kingdom.

Acts 13:46

The response of Paul and Barnabas was to clearly state the truth of God's Word—this manifested their boldness and readiness to apply the light of God in the midst of that hostile situation. We should not hold back or become silent when God's truth is fiercely opposed, but rather we ought to cry out to the Lord for more courage to make known His truth in the difficult situation (cf. Acts 4:29). It is one thing to know the truth of God, but quite another thing to declare it in a hostile environment, yet this is a characteristic that distinguishes those who are consumed by zeal for God's truth (Jer. 20:9). Strong opposition against the truth should receive an even stronger and clearer declaration of the truth. Like those godly men before him, Paul too was unafraid of the faces of men and the opposition they might throw against him (1 Thes. 2:2–6). Such boldness arises from the Spirit of God and is a distinctive mark found among those Luke tells us about in Acts (cf. Acts 4:13). We, as God's people, have a responsibility to Him and to our society to be the light (Matt. 5:13, 14). We are not to bend and bow to the threats and terrors of those who hate the truth and light (cf. 1 Kings 22:24–28; Jer. 26:8,12–14). May we cast ourselves upon Christ and know His enabling as we seek to proclaim, by word and deed, the unshakeable truth of our Lord and King. May our love and zeal for God's will and our hatred for all that opposes Him give us great courage to witness for the light and against the darkness, not fearing the "greatness" or numbers of those who despise us. May nothing distract us from this and may we trust whole–heartedly in Him whom we serve (Isa. 50:7; Jer. 1:8,17–19; Ezk. 2:6, 7; 3:8; Micah 3:8; Acts 7:51–56).

In God's plan, it was Israel that was to be the light bearers to the rest of the world, yet the light bearer himself must first receive the light—this was God's ordained order for spreading His light throughout the whole world (Acts 3:26; Rom. 1:16; 2:9, 10, cf. Matt. 28:19; Acts 1:8). Since these Jews rejected the Gospel of Christ they had disqualified themselves from both having the light themselves and taking it to others. It was a great privilege to have been a Jew, because they were born into a people who had been given the oracles of God (Rom. 3:2). The whole foundation for the history of redemption was laid and worked out in Israel and among the Jews—an amazing privilege and blessing (Rom. 9:4, 5). However, Paul says to these Jews that in rejecting the Word of salvation, they were judging themselves unworthy of eternal life (cf. Matt. 22:2–5, 8). They despised the privileged position God had given to them and blasphemed Him who was the very reason for their existence. These Jews, by their conduct, condemned themselves, though in their own minds they believed they were most worthy of eternal life. Filled with selfishness they did not want others to share in the light they *thought* they had and being filled with pride they thought they did not need Christ. However, without Christ, Jew and Gentile alike are full of perversion and deserving of God's wrath (cf. Eph. 2:1–3).

There are consequences for rejecting the light of God's truth and those who despise it will have it removed far from them. These people had not rejected religion in and of itself, for they were an extremely religious people, yet they had rejected the truth of God. This ought to be a sober warning for us, for we too can run after our own man-made religious traditions and pride ourselves in our efforts, while we are actually at war with the purposes of God. We need to constantly be reminded how totally dependent we are upon the revelation of God found in the Scriptures and by the grace of God we need to be forever watchful that we bring every thought into captivity to the mind of Christ (2 Cor. 10:5). We must be terrified to walk according to our own wisdom, for by doing this we will be despising and rejecting the wisdom of God. Those who continue to behave in such a way will have the light of God's truth removed from their midst and how great the darkness will then be.

This hardness of heart on the part of the Jews meant that the Holy Spirit was turning Paul and Barnabas to the Gentiles. They said, "We are being turned" (which is in the passive voice), the reason being that Luke is once again showing that the inclusion of the Gentiles into the church as equals, was God's doing and not due to the ideas of some "radical" apostle like Paul. Paul was certainly not hoping to win a popularity contest by saying such a thing, but this was in accordance with God's revelation and therefore he was bound to be faithful to the truth no matter what these hard-hearted people thought of him. Until the church in our day loves the truth in the way that the apostle Paul did, we will not glorify Christ as we ought to do. Paul couldn't have said something more offensive to his kinsmen, yet he did not flinch from his responsibility to be a faithful witness about God's truth (1 Thes. 2:4). Until the truth of

God burns in our hearts like this we will continue to fear the faces of men and thus compromise the truth.

Acts 13:47

Paul and Barnabas had boldly declared that they were being turned to the Gentiles and it is natural to assume that this was due to the work of the Holy Spirit in their hearts. The purpose of Luke's account is to show that it was God guiding His apostles (whether Peter or Paul) in this evangelistic thrust to the Gentiles. Often we fail to notice how the Spirit guided the apostles. It is true that the apostles had a unique office and with this came special revelation directly from God for the purpose of completing the Scriptures and establishing the foundation of the NT church. Once God had revealed everything necessary for us to know, that special revelation given independently of the Scriptures, ceased. God by His sovereign control, has preserved the Scriptures for us and now in them we have everything we need in order to accomplish every good work (2 Tim. 3:16, 17). The Holy Spirit is function is to enable us to understand what has been preserved in the Bible and not to give us new revelation independent of the Scriptures (see comments on Acts 11:27; 15:6 and John 14:26). We have seen that even with the apostles, their guidance was often according to what had already been written (e.g., the case of choosing an apostle to replace Judas, Acts 1:20).

Paul now in Acts 13:47 says that the justification for their going to the Gentiles was because of God's clear command to them found in Isaiah 49:6. Paul and Barnabas were being turned to the Gentiles by the Holy Spirit helping them understand what had been written— no new revelation was guiding them at this point. The passage in Isaiah is talking about the Messiah whose salvation extends to the ends of the earth, clearly showing that from the beginning, God's salvation for the Jews was only the first small step in a much grander goal of bringing salvation to the ends of the earth. The old man Simeon said the same things when he saw baby Jesus in the temple, "For my eyes have seen Your salvation which You have prepared in the sight of all peoples, a light to bring revelation to the Gentiles, and the glory of Your people Israel" (Luke 2:30–32). Israel was supposed to spread the light of salvation to the ends of the earth (Isa. 42:6; 60:1–3). Paul says that there is a long-standing command from the Lord, the force of which is still binding and therefore he is going to obey the Lord. It is the Messiah who is the light and savior of all people, yet Paul is not distorting the text by saying that this command has been given to him and Barnabas. It always has been God's plan that the true Israel of God should take His light and salvation to the uttermost parts of the world. The Messiah gathers around Him a redeemed community who then share in His ministry to the nations (1 Pet. 2:9). Christ is the light of the world (John 8:12), yet we too are called to be light (Matt. 5:14, 16, see too comments on John 9:5). The body and the Head (Eph. 1:22; 4:15; Col. 1:18) together proclaim the message of salvation to the ends of the earth. While the Head *alone* is the basis of salvation, the body has the privilege and responsibility to proclaim this message throughout the whole world (Matt. 28:18, 19).

Acts 13:48

When the truth of God is proclaimed boldly and clearly there are only two possible responses: joy or anger. Paul had said that forgiveness of sin and salvation was received through believing in the Man, Christ Jesus. This meant that Gentiles could become full covenant members without observing the ceremonial law since all that the ceremonial law pointed to was fulfilled in Christ. The Gentiles could now share in all the privileges previously reserved only for Jews and their response to this message was amazing. The Jewish leadership, however, argued strongly against Paul's teaching and tried to refute it, thus it must have been an anxious time for the Gentiles as this debate raged on. Paul's quoting of Isaiah completely destroyed the Jewish arguments. The Biblical debate was over (though the battle would continue in other ways) and it was very obvious that Paul's teaching was God's truth. The Gentile's acceptance of this was total and their joy was openly manifested. How did these Gentiles "glorify" the Word of the Lord? They glorified God's Word by acknowledging it to be true—to acknowledge the truth glorifies God (see comments on John 9:24).

We are told that almost the whole city came out this Sabbath (verse 44), most of whom would have been Gentiles. Here (verse 48) we are told that the Gentiles gladly believed what Paul was saying—the implication is that all the Gentiles who were listening to Paul had this positive response, yet only as many as had been appointed to eternal life believed. We see that it is possible to have a positive reaction to Christ and the message of salvation, yet not be a true believer (see comments on Acts 13:43 and 8:19). Many try to avoid the clear teaching of this passage by saying that as many as believed were appointed to eternal life, or they try to change the meaning of the word "ordained." However, every time this word is used in the NT it refers to the exertion of force upon an individual from somewhere outside of himself. It certainly never refers to a personal internal decision arising from an individual. In this verse the word is in the passive voice, which further rules out any personal disposition or action coming from those who believed. Their believing was something that had been ordained in eternity and was awaiting that specifically appointed day when they would actually believe. These people believed (had faith) because they have been elected by the eternal counsel of God. The only way to escape from God's predestination in this verse is to *pervert* what is very clear. The mystery has already been presented in verse 46 where those who reject the Gospel, judge themselves unworthy of eternal life. The absolute sovereignty of God cannot be compromised even for one moment of time and this applies to God's absolute sovereignty with respect to salvation. The Bible does not apologize for this fact, yet nor does it excuse people from their own, real, personal guilt for not believing (see comments on John 3:16). While it appears to us that our believing was the moment we were saved, nevertheless it is far different from God's perspective, for it is only those who have been enrolled in the Book of Life that believe—this is what Luke is saying. God's election rests in God's secret counsel and it is not for us to know who is and who isn't elected. Our responsibility is to bringing much glory to God—we glorify Him by testifying about the truth in word and deed. We are to speak about Christ and live like Him. God has ordained that through these two means (preaching and godly-living), those ordained to eternal life will be saved (1 Cor. 1:21, 23, 24; 2 Cor. 6:7; 2 Tim. 4:2; Matt. 28:19, 20, and Matt. 5:16; Eph. 2:10; 5:8; Phil.2:15; 1 Tim. 2:9,10; Heb. 10:24; 1 Pet. 2:12; 3:1, 16). It is foolish to say that since we do not know who is elected we do not have to fulfill these God given responsibilities!

The only way to be true to the Scriptures is to hold *both* of these clear Biblical teachings as true (God's sovereign predestination and human responsibility), even though we are unable, with our limited ability, to show how they fit together. To suppress the truth of God's predestination unto eternal life because of some personal prejudice is nothing but foolish rebellion against the clear teaching of Scripture. Either God's Word is the ultimate authority or something else is (i.e., our minds), but once we have named our ultimate authority then we have to live consistently upon that basis. If someone wants to pick and choose what they will accept from the Bible, then everyone can do the same and you cannot denounce those who reject Christ's Divinity, or the Trinity or the validity of the commandments—everyone becomes their own ultimate authority and the Scriptures become irrelevant.

Acts 13:49

The Word about Christ was carried into the whole region. This was most likely accomplished through the efforts of those who had believed, sharing the truths of the Gospel wherever they went.

Acts 13:50

The Jewish leaders couldn't tolerate the success nor prevent its spread by Biblical arguments, so they resort to persecution. This was a Gentile region and the leaders of the city were Gentiles. Many of the wives of these leaders had become devout converts to Judaism (the historian Josephus tells us that in the city of Damascus almost all the Gentile women had been converted to Judaism). There were usually many more female converts to Judaism than male. The Jewish leaders managed to stir up these women who persuaded the leaders of the city to persecute Paul and Barnabas and expel them from the region. It seems likely that the persecution was aimed at all who believed, though only the foreigners could really be expelled.

Acts 13:51

This symbol was for those who had denounced and rejected the Gospel—a most serious warning instituted by Christ (Matt. 10:14; Mark 6:11; Luke 9:5; 10:11). It denoted the utter defilement of the region, so much so that the dust itself was polluted and total pollution calls for God's total destruction (Gen. 15:16; Joshua 6:21; Dan. 8:23; Matt. 23:32–35; 1 Thes. 2:16). The severity of the sign shows how serious it is to rise up and condemn the Word of God. To utterly reject the gracious offer of the Gospel makes one fit for extermination. We should not think it is a small thing when people openly pour contempt upon God's Word—it is a serious offence in God's eyes!

Acts 13:52

True faith finds its full satisfaction in Christ and not in outward circumstances. Thus, despite the climate of persecution, the converts who remained in Antioch were full of joy due to the real living relationship they had with Christ. Being filled with the Holy Spirit was a condition that persistently remained among these disciples—an exhortation common to Paul (Eph. 5:18), since this is the Kingdom (Rom. 14:17).

Acts 14:1

Not being discouraged by the persecution, Paul and Barnabas traveled about 160 km to the city of Iconium (the modern name of this city is Konya, regarded as the fourth largest city in Turkey today). Once again the two missionaries started their evangelizing in the synagogue and met with great success, for many believed from among both Jews and Gentiles—the Lord again adding to His church.

Acts 14:2

God's call to repentance and faith in Jesus Christ is not a suggestion, but a command. This verse actually says the "*disobedient* Jews stirred up the Gentiles." God expects and deserves obedience to His every Word from every person in the world. All people have sinned and come short of His glory (Rom.3:23). God is holy (Isa. 6:3; Rev. 4:8) and will not tolerate even the slightest evil (Isa. 59:2; Hab. 1:13; Rom. 1:18; Heb. 2:2, 3). Many people foolishly ask, "How can God send people to hell?" However, the question really is, "How can such a holy God save people from hell and let them dwell with Him?" In God's wisdom, He is able to be merciful while not destroying His justice (see comments on John 1:17). Through Christ, the obstacles facing every sinner, arising from their guilt and the law, are ready to be taken out of the way. This means that from *God's side* there is nothing preventing the sinner from responding to the Gospel (see comments on John 3:16). Thus God is not only able to make a sincere offer of the Gospel to every person, but He can command every person to repent and believe in Christ (Acts 17:30)—a command, which if disobeyed, results in personal guilt since it is willful disobedience. Paul had preached the Gospel and many had obeyed the call to repentance, however, those who were disobedient, fought against the message of salvation. Often those who are disobedient to the heavenly calling are not satisfied with merely rejecting the call, but seek to war against it and even destroy the Gospel if it were possible. This manifests the extreme perversity in the hearts of the disobedient, who react with hatred and violence against God's message of merciful deliverance from their bondage to sin and death.

These disobedient Jews, in violation of the law of God that they claimed to love so much, poisoned the minds of other Gentiles by bearing false witness against the Christians (cf. Ex. 20:16). This slander and speaking evil was directed against all those who had believed in Christ, not only against Paul and Barnabas.

Acts 14:3

As a result of this verbal persecution, Paul and Barnabas stayed for a considerable time in the area, strengthening the new converts and making sure that a firm foundation was laid for this new congregation. The boldness of the preaching refers to them not holding anything back, but faithfully declaring the whole counsel of God. The persecution was coming from those within the OT church who rejected the full counsel of God, though they loved the outward show of being religious. This can be seen in our days too, for where the church has become worldly, it persecutes those who stand upon the Word of God alone. Do we shrink back and avoid those issues and statements in God's Word that are unpopular in our days? Is our zeal for the truth of God and His glory, or is it for the praises of men? If you desire to be popular in an age of apostasy, then you will never proclaim the Word of God boldly. If you are anxious about what people think of you, you will compromise the truth and thus offend God. We are going to offend someone, either God or those who hate the light (John 3:19, 20). The Light of God's truth will cause offence (Jer. 15:10; Matt. 10:34; Luke 12:51–53) and true disciples will be hated (John 15:18–20), but this does not give us the right to ignore anything God has revealed.

Luke's emphasis is upon the growth and strengthening of the NT church despite the difficulties. The disciples were totally dependent upon the Lord and this is a point we cannot overemphasize.

God once again confirmed the truthfulness of this "new" message by granting signs. The disobedient Jews were strongly opposing the message of grace in Christ and their position in the community, as the recognized "authorities" with respect to the Scriptures, would have made it very difficult to evangelize. The Lord, therefore, graciously confirmed the "new" message in miraculous ways. Another very important reason for the Lord doing signs among the Gentiles was to show the Jerusalem church that it was God's will to fully accept Gentiles as Gentiles (cf. Acts 15:12). These signs confirmed that salvation was by grace through faith and not by observing some religious ceremonies, thus establishing the authority of the Gospel (John 20:30, 31).

Acts 14:4

Was Barnabas an apostle of Christ? The word "apostle" is used in the NT in two ways. One way refers to those who were specifically appointed by Christ to be witnesses of the resurrection. There were special qualifications for this office (see comments on Acts 1:21) and there is no evidence that Barnabas was ever included in this group. The other way the word is used is to refer to those who were sent by a church to fulfill some special task or service (John 13:16; Rom. 16:7; 2 Cor. 8:23; Phil. 2:25). Translators of the Bible recognized the different uses of the word and the same Greek word is translated by different English words, depending on the context. The word *elder* is the same, for it can refer to someone who is mature or to an office in the church, so too with the word *deacon*, which refers to someone who is being a servant or to an office in the church. We cannot automatically assume that a word means exactly the same thing every time it is used—we must distinguish between the function and the office. Paul and Barnabas were both "apostles" sent out by the church in Antioch (Acts 13:3, 4), yet only Paul was an apostle of Christ (Gal. 1:1).

Acts 14:5–7

Violent persecution now raises its head and somehow being made aware of this, Paul and Barnabas were able to escape from the city. This was a united effort between the Jews and Gentiles to insult and stone the missionaries. The rulers of both groups were behind the mob action. There is a time to flee, for we must not needlessly give away our lives. The church had been planted and established and there were still many other cities that had not heard the Gospel. They left Iconium in victory and moved on to claim similar victories in other cities. Paul was now becoming very accustomed to fleeing from persecution (Acts 9:23–25, 29, 30; 13:50) and he was beginning to appreciate the Lord's Words about suffering for Him (Acts 9:16).

Acts 14:8

Luke clearly wants to impress us with the hopelessness of this man's condition by expressing it in three different ways: without strength in his feet, crippled from the womb, and had never walked.

Acts 14:9, 10

By God's gracious working, the message of the Gospel captured the cripple man's heart and the Spirit revealed this to Paul. Paul was preaching forgiveness of sins in the name of Jesus Christ, thus the message was about eternal salvation. The exact form of this word translated as "healed" is used nine times in the NT excluding the reference in this verse. In every instance except one, it refers to salvation unto eternal life (Matt. 19:25: Mark 10:26; Luke 18:26; Acts 4:12; 15:1,11; 2 Thes. 2:10; 1 Tim. 2:4). The one exception refers to saving one's physical life from physical death (Acts 27:31). However, in Acts 14:9 the translators prefer to use the word "healed" rather than "saved"—saw his faith to be healed. This is probably because Paul immediately heals the man. Yet it is quite possible that Paul does what Jesus did in order to demonstrate the power of Christ's name to forgive sins (Matt. 9:5, 6). In the midst of preaching that these people need to be saved from their sins by faith in Jesus Christ, Paul commands a crippled man to stand up. The authority behind such a visible manifestation of healing a cripple was obvious and couldn't be denied, whereas to merely pronounce someone forgiven did not carry the same kind of weight in these people's minds. Among these pagans, God used the sign to establish the authority of the message that forgiveness was found only in Christ (John 14:6; Acts 4:12; 1 Tim. 2:5; 1 John 5:11, 12).

Acts 14:11–13

The cripple submitted to the Gospel message, but the rest of the city certainly didn't. This is a good example showing how all religious beliefs outside of Christ are just different manifestations of rebellion against the truth and very far from a sincere desire to discover and submit to the truth. How could these people think and do this after Paul's sermon exalting Jesus Christ? Rebellion against the truth can take many forms: there can be angry persecution of the messengers or worship of the messengers—both are perverted responses to the inescapable truth of God's Word and both reject it, though in quite different ways. Paul and Barnabas, unable to understand the local language, were unaware of what was taking place until things had progressed to an advanced stage.

Acts 14:14

Paul and Barnabas were somehow made aware of what was taking place and reacted in the strongest possible way. Ripping one's garment was a sign of experiencing great grief or pain and this is what the apostles felt when they saw the terrible blasphemy around them. They were horrified and deeply pierced by the divine adoration and worship the city was wanting to give them. Quite a different response to that of Herod Agrippa (Acts 12:22, 23). They courageously ran right into the middle of this frenzied religious mob, disrupting the proceedings. It appears that the city was already in the process of fulfilling a religious ceremony honouring these two gods (Barnabas and Paul). To disrupt a zealous religious ceremony is to seriously risk one's life, yet the apostles were in the midst of the proceedings doing just that. When the glory and honour of God captures your heart, how can you do less? When Paul was later warned about the chains and tribulations awaiting him, he responded, "But none of these things move me; nor do I count my life dear to myself, so that I may finish my race with joy, and the ministry which I received from the Lord Jesus, to testify to the Gospel of the grace of God" (Acts 20:24). On another occasion he said, "I am ready not only to be bound, but also to die at Jerusalem for the name of the Lord Jesus" (Acts 21:13, see too Phil. 1:20). This is Kingdom understanding and is summed up in Revelation 12:11 where the Christian, because of the grace and completed work of Christ, stands boldly in God's presence—this is the only and eternal basis of our acceptance with God. However, because of this foundation, the Christian resists all that is of the devil, boldly proclaiming the truth. This does not mean giving the "Christian smile" at the appropriate times, but *standing* for the truth, even when to do so threatens one's life. We will never proclaim the full counsel of God boldly if we fear for our lives and we will always fear for our lives if our hearts do not burn with zeal for the glory of God. If we have a distorted understanding of the King and His

Kingdom, then the "word of our testimony" will also be distorted. We should always be ready to defend the glory of God, by proclaiming the truth and refusing to accept any honour that is due to God alone.

Acts 14:15

The question implies rebuke and dismay at behavior that is extremely foolish. The apostles were not wanting to know the reasons for this "worship service," rather they were saying, "Since you have no basis whatsoever to justify your actions, why are you doing these things?" Paul and Barnabas cry out that they are humans just like the rest of the crowd and proof of this was that they endure the same "passions" or "affections" that all people do. What they mean is that their bodies were made from the same mortal substance and they endured the same physical suffering and limitations as everyone else, thus how could divine honour be given to them? They experienced the same changes, ups and downs, disappointments, discouragements, frustrations, sorrows, hardships, etc., that all people endured. Whereas gods were supposed to be above these "mortal" things.

Paul says, "If you are impressed by the miracle then believe our words. We are calling on you to turn from these useless idols to the true and living God." It took great boldness to tell this zealous mob that their religious beliefs and practices were vain. Paul says, "We have come to tell you to stop this foolish behavior of sacrificing to idols." He tells them that their so called gods were not real, meaning that they were unable to do anything to help those who worship them and therefore they would always disappoint. The very reason the apostles came preaching was to get these people to turn away from this kind of "worship," yet here they are incited to greater acts of idolatry. Christ's preachers are saying that these idols have no personal existence and are therefore unable to do anything, thus they should turn from this vain practice and worship the *living* God who created the universe. Paul tells us in 1 Cor.8:4 that idols are nothing in the world, i.e., they have no real existence. Paul merely compares the true God with these idols as the prophets of old had done (Ps. 115:3–8; 135:15–18; Isa. 44:9–20). It is a stubborn, deceived heart that worships a dead idol instead of the living God (see *Faith and Reason,* chapters 3 and 4). Any man-made image of God, whether carved out of wood or merely held in people's minds, is non-existent. There is only one God (1 Cor. 8:4) and we know Him by what He has revealed to us of Himself—the final and clearest revelation being preserved for us in the Scriptures.

Paul and Barnabas, though speaking to people who were not acquainted with the Scriptures, were still able to challenge them with the inescapable truth of God. No one can escape from the knowledge of the true God, for every person is made in the image of God and lives in the universe that God created. Paul tells us very clearly that the true God's eternal power and divine nature are clearly seen in that which He has made (Rom. 1:20). Thus, these idolatrous pagans are challenged to act appropriately towards the truth that they know, rather than distorting it and trying to suppress it (Rom. 1:18).

Acts 14:16

This does not mean that God's righteous standard was not applicable to the Gentile nations. God's holy law is eternally binding upon all people and all are held accountable to this one standard. However, God's plan of redemption involved raising up one people and instructing them in His truth and then through them, to bring the Messiah into the world. Until such time that the Messiah had come and accomplished redemption for the whole world (John 3:16), God's focus was upon the nation of Israel whom He constantly kept in check. It was to them that He gave His revelation and it was to them primarily that He sent His prophets to instruct, rebuke and exhort. It was due to this focus that the apostles say God "allowed the other nations to walk in their own ways." Some Gentile nations did receive some prophetic witness (e.g., Jonah in Nineveh) however this was the exception—the central focus was upon those whom God had called out to be His special possession. God was not being "unfair" (whatever this is supposed to mean?) when He did not *focus* on the Gentile nations in the way He did upon Israel, for He did not leave the Gentiles totally without any witness of the True God (verse 17). Remember, it was as a result of hardness of heart and rebellion against the truth that led the Gentiles to where they found themselves. All people groups were/are direct descendants of Noah, "a preacher of righteousness" (2 Pet. 2:5). It was only by wilfully suppressing this great heritage that they ended up living in darkness and ignorance (see also comments on Acts 17:30).

Acts 14:17

Even though the specific prophetic witness was not given, it did not mean that people were no longer accountable to God, for God has never left Himself without a witness. There is absolutely no excuse for the pretended ignorance of God we see in so many people. The witness of God in creation and nature is very clear, even to those "lost" tribes in the Amazon jungle, thus according to Scripture, there is no excuse for those who refuse to worship the true God and refuse to forsake their sin and rebellion. It is the *kindness* of God that such people are rebelling against. While abundantly benefiting from His bountiful kindness, people call God unfair and harsh and hate Him. Sin perverts the truth wherever it is found, whether in God's gracious provisions for life, the gracious message of the Gospel, or the gracious healing of this cripple man, all is perverted and turned upside down. Idolaters want to worship their own wills and minds, which can change as quickly as the wind—from worship to stoning in a very short time (cf. Matt. 21:8–11; 27:23).

God gives rain, fruitful seasons and fills people with both food and joy. When you walk down the street and see people laughing and children having fun, this is an inescapable manifestation of the goodness of God. The apostles say nothing about the miracle, rather the much clearer and more obvious manifestation of God is pointed to. Surely those who chase after miracles in our day are *blind* to the presence of God that inescapably confronts every person all the time. May the Lord open our eyes to appreciate and recognise His bountiful goodness that we exist in (Acts 17:28). Why do we thank the Lord when we eat a meal? Because the food we are about to eat is a glorious manifestation of God's goodness, for which we should be immensely grateful.

Acts 14:18

Only with great difficulty were the apostles able to stop the idolatrous service from progressing, but they did succeed. A great moral victory for the True God.

Acts 14:19

An amazing verse! These were religious Jews who prided themselves in worshipping the one and only true God and prayed the "Shema Israel" every time they met together in the synagogue (Deut. 6:4).

Yet, we see that they have more in common with the idolatrous pagans who worshipped many gods, than with Paul and Barnabas who worshipped the one and only True God. The reason being, that both the people from Lystra and the Jews from Antioch and Iconium were idolatrous—that is, worshipping a god created by their own minds. If we do not submit to the whole of God's revelation and bring all our thoughts into line with what the Scriptures say about God, man, sin, redemption, justification, law, Christ, etc., then we will fall into idolatry. You are either thinking about and worshipping the true God in the way He has told us to, or you are, in some way, worshipping and serving something that God has created (Rom. 1:25), which is idolatry. Therefore the importance of having an eternal, immovable standard by which to check everything we do, cannot be overestimated (Isa. 8:20).

These Jews had great influence and managed to persuade the city to stone Paul, basing the whole case, as usual, upon lies and slander (cf. Acts 14:2). Stoning was not merely a Jewish punishment, but something with a long standing history among the Greeks too (Kittel). We do not know why only Paul was stoned, but, being the chief speaker, he was the one who had probably caused them the most offence. They would not allow a corpse to remain in the city limits and so dragged the body out of the gate, though they left his body exposed (no burial), as a further act of judgement. Paul's judgment does not appear to have arisen from a proper trial, but from the rantings of an angry mob. Paul tells us in 2 Corinthians 11:25 that once he was stoned. The fact that those who stoned Paul thought him to be dead, certainly gives the impression that he was well battered and did not merely receive one blow to the head. Those Jews who had pursued him from Antioch and Iconium wouldn't have left him for dead if there was any doubt in their minds.

Acts 14:20

Luke does not tell us that Paul was dead. What we have here is the manifestation of the incredible grace of God in difficult circumstances rather than a miracle. Paul would, not long after this, tell the Galatians that his body bore the marks of the Lord Jesus (Gal. 6:17). What we see in Paul is an amazing example of courage and determination to fulfill the divine calling upon his life. The very next day he sets out for Derbe, which was about sixty km away (2 Cor. 4:9, 10). All indications are that they used their normal means of transport—walking. Let us magnify the grace and strength of God (2 Cor. 12:9) and pray that we too might receive from the Lord such single minded determination and toughness to finish our course (John 4:34; Luke 9:51; 1 Cor. 9:24–27; Phil. 3:13, 14; 2 Tim. 4:7; Heb. 12:1, 2).

Acts 14:21

They not only evangelised that city but discipled them, which would have meant grounding them in the foundational principles of the faith and setting up some kind of structure whereby these believes would have been able to persevere and grow together after the apostles left. Luke is once again brief in his account of what happened, yet his focus of showing the spread of the Gospel among the Gentiles does not require him to say more than this. Despite the great opposition and hardships they faced in these other cities, Paul and Barnabas are not afraid to return to them. We see here the hearts of true shepherds, where their concern for the wellbeing of the sheep far out–weighs their concern for their own lives (see comments on John 10:11–18, see too 1 Pet. 5:1–4).

Acts 14:22

They were not looking for trouble and it would appear best to understand their return trip as having a vastly different focus to their first visit. They were now going to move among the circle of believers and strengthen them, rather than evangelising in the streets. Thus, the danger of upsetting those who had previously been upset was not so great. They strengthened the believers through instruction and mutual fellowship. They exhorted them to continue in the simplicity of salvation by grace through faith, for they were surrounded by paganism and the perversion of the Jewish teaching of salvation by works of the law (see comments on Acts 13:43). These new believers were in difficult situations, however, Paul and Barnabas explain that persecution and suffering are to be expected by all believers. The "many" tribulations refers to both the amount and the variety that come across the Christian's path. The apostles are not talking about the road to salvation when they talk about entering into the Kingdom of God through suffering. When we are born again through faith in Christ we enter into the Kingdom (John 3:5), yet all Christians, including the apostles (note the "*we*"), have to walk a path of suffering that leads to that ultimate and glorious state where suffering will be no more—here called the "Kingdom of God" (cf. 1 Cor. 6:9, 10; 15:50; Gal. 5:21; Eph. 5:5; Jam. 2:5, with Matt. 5:10; 19:25; 25:34; Luke 12:32; 2 Tim. 4:8; 1 Pet. 1:3–5, 9; Rev. 21:7). The Kingdom of God is a present reality as well as a glorious future hope. While we live in the Kingdom we are changed more and more into the image of Christ by the path we walk in this life, always looking toward that glorious and final hope.

The world is in hostile rebellion against the Lord of the universe— the mindset of the world hates the Light (John 3:19) and suppresses the truth in unrighteousness (Rom.1:18ff.). The Light of Christ exposes such behavior (John 3:20), thus when Christians shine this light (Matt. 5:14), they too will experience the hostility of a world in revolt against Christ (Isa. 53:3; John 15:18, 19; 2 Tim. 3:12). This is the clear and repeated testimony of Scripture, although we cannot understand fully why God has ordained suffering to be a vital part of discipleship and growth into Christian maturity (Ps. 34:19; John 16:33; 2 Cor. 4:8–11; 1 Thes. 3:3). Our supreme example, the Great Shepherd of God's flock, suffered and entered into His glory (Luke 24:26; Phil. 2:6–11; 1 Pet. 1:11), and the same path has been ordained for us who follow Him (Rom. 8:36; Phil. 1:29; 1 Pet. 2:21). There will be no sharing in Christ's glory if we do not share in His suffering (Matt. 10:38; 16:24; 2 Thes. 1:4, 5; 2 Tim. 2:12a).

The sufferings of Christ's saints are somehow linked with *His* sufferings, showing the closeness of the union between Christ and His body (Col. 1:18). The NT clearly sees the sufferings of God's people as the sufferings of Christ (Acts 9:4; 2 Cor. 1:5; Phil. 3:10; Col. 1:24; 1 Pet. 4:13)—this is the only path to glory, thus we must not be amazed, wearied or discouraged by it (2 Tim. 1:8; 1 Pet. 4:12–16). Our sufferings do not in any way add to the accomplished work of Christ with respect to His atoning for our sin and reconciling us to God, nevertheless, there is a sense whereby our sufferings fill up the quota of Christ's suffering in the overall plan of God. The sufferings the godly experience in this life do not just refer to external persecution and difficulties, but also includes the weakness of our imperfect nature (Rom. 7:7–24; 8:23; 1 Cor. 15:53, 54; 2 Cor. 5:4).

The suffering we endure is nothing to be compared to the glory that shall be revealed in us (Rom. 8:18). The glorious victory is far greater than the temporary suffering that we might have to endure and this is something we must never lose sight of. Our minds need to be renewed so that we understand the sovereign purposes of God in every aspect of our lives and His ultimate goal is to bring us to perfection and to give us this glorious Kingdom. We have both the glorious eternal hope and the real present comfort of Christ in our sufferings (Matt. 28:20; John 14:18–23; 2 Cor. 1:5; 2 Tim. 4:16, 17). We need this message today, just as much as these early Christians did.

Acts 14:23

The churches were also strengthened by setting up a leadership structure. There are many questions that arise due to Luke's brief account and because these people were such new converts. It is possible that those from Antioch and Iconium had a certain amount of understanding due to being instructed in the synagogues prior to conversion, however, in Lystra there does not appear to have been any such foundation, thus it seems as though they went from idolatrous pagans to church leaders in a few months. It does not seem wise to try and prove one's own particular view of "ordination" from this text, since no specifics are given. The primitive church was facing very real practical difficulties in these cities: the missionaries couldn't hang around any longer; the chances of being able to send a mature leader to these people were none existent; and all the converts were young in the Lord. Leaders needed to be ordained if this work was going to be preserved. Did God move in a miraculous way and raise up leaders in a very short period of time? Or were leaders ordained whose *maturity* specifications were not able to be tested as one would do in more "normal" circumstances, but due to the urgent need and difficult situation some kind of leadership had to be put in place? One feels that the rigid structures of many modern churches would have meant leaving some of these early groups without any leadership whatsoever. Rather than trying to force upon this verse our own particular understanding of what it takes to make a leader, we should use it to keep us aware of the real difficulties facing believers in a society where there is not a strong Biblical heritage. Great wisdom and flexibility is required in these awkward situations and often mission societies, judging from a distance, are unable to appreciate what is the right thing to do at these times. Christ builds His church by His grace and power and we need to beware lest we find ourselves trusting in structures and man-made rules rather than upon Him—misplaced dependence is not a small threat to the church in our day!

There is no spiritual merit in fasting other than helping us focus on our total dependence upon Christ and enabling us to find more time to pray. This was a most serious situation facing these new churches and they all cast themselves upon the Lord. These new churches had a structure and leadership, they would receive apostolic counsel and letters and had great hope in God's grace and divine faithfulness. This is all we need in our own day too: leaders who love the Lord, who submit to the absolute authority of God's revealed will (found in the Scriptures) and have total dependence upon the grace and provision of Christ to bring us all to maturity and glorify His name.

Acts 14:24–26

The church in Antioch had graciously given up Paul and Barnabas so that they could take the Gospel to the Gentiles. The Lord had accomplished much through these two servants, yet all glory must be given to the grace of God. It is difficult to determine how long this first missionary trip had been and suggestions range from one to two years, but it is impossible to be sure. While all glory belongs to God we need to realize that His grace works through people— God extends His Kingdom through the labours of His faithful servants, however it is His Grace that is working (1 Cor. 3:9; 2 Cor. 6:1). Paul and Barnabas had been committed to the grace of God, had laboured in this grace and totally depended upon this grace and thus accomplished much for the Lord.

Acts 14:27

The whole church was anxious to hear about these exploits of grace whereby a door of faith had been opened to the Gentiles. The only entrance into the Kingdom of God is through the "door of faith." This is the glorious news of the Gospel: we are saved by faith in Christ and not by observing any rituals or OT ceremonies. Moreover, Gentile churches had been established for the very first time and there had been a massive influx of Gentiles into the church of God. The tide had now changed and Gentile believers were becoming more numerous than Jewish believers. This would threaten many Jewish believers and give rise to the problems dealt with in the next chapter. However, this dangerous, first time launch into the "unknown" Gentile world, had been a tremendous success and both the senders and those who were sent rejoice together in the goodness of God. The Holy Spirit had ultimately sent, directed and prospered this journey since it was all in perfect accordance with God's eternal decree.

Acts 14:28

Paul and Barnabas probably assumed their teaching positions once again in the Antioch church, which once again highlights how much of a sacrifice it was for this church to release these two gifted men to go and bless others. The Antioch church still needed to learn much, thus Paul and Barnabas stayed for a long time instructing them. The church in Antioch had understood its responsibility to missions and they sacrificially gave of their own in order to be faithful to this calling. Desiring to extend the Kingdom of God should burn in the hearts of all believers. Let us pray that God, by His grace, would enable us to be faithful in this way too—sacrificially giving to extend the light of the Gospel.

Acts 15:1

Paul and Barnabas had faced many difficult situations before and overcome massive obstacles, but these had all been from those who had hated Christ and His church. What they now faced was a conflict from within the church itself that was more dangerous than anything that they had faced up until then. We have many Christians in our day who say doctrine is irrelevant and all that one needs is to know Jesus Christ and if everyone just did this, there would be no problems. It is doctrine that divides, we are told. Such a view, however, arises from incredible ignorance! Here in Acts 15 we have two groups that believed in Christ, yet their different beliefs about Christ and His work would either preserve or destroy the church. This whole matter was doctrinal and the only way to solve it was with sound Biblical *doctrine*. Those who scoff at doctrine in the name of "spiritual maturity" are either greatly deceived or wilfully trying to destroy the church of Christ and we should expose their foolish or wicked intentions for what they are. Doctrine is merely that which God in His wisdom deemed necessary to reveal to us and without which we would be unable to glorify Him or function in this world as we ought to. God has told us about Himself, Christ, man, sin, redemption, the Holy Spirit, His Kingdom, His Triune nature and much, much more. If we do not think God's thoughts after Him with respect to all that He has revealed, we will not be able to think truly about anything and we endanger ourselves for we will have no way of knowing whether we have eternal life or not. To be mistaken about the basis of salvation is to make the biggest mistake that can be made and for which there are *eternal* consequences.

We are not told who these "teachers" were who had come down from Jerusalem, though they were connected to the believers there and used this as a means to support their teaching and open doors for them to teach. Their message, however, was not sanctioned by the apostles or the Jerusalem church (Acts 15:24). These men were attacking the very foundation of the Christian faith. Their message did not deny Jesus Christ nor did it oppose Gentiles coming into the church, but they taught that faith in Christ was not enough. Something extra had to be added to what Jesus had done in order for someone to be made righteous before God. They said people needed to believe in Jesus, however, in order to be saved they *also* had to be circumcised and observe the other ceremonial aspects of Moses' law—faith was not enough on its own. The idea that something must be added to the completed work of Christ, or that there is something we need to contribute toward our salvation is blasphemy and attacks the very foundations of Christianity. It is doctrine that is needed to stand strong in the face of the many deceptive ideas that roam around in the world. We cannot rely upon our feelings, or the appearance of those who speak to us, or their credentials—everything has to be brought into line with the Scriptures and evaluated in that way. These men who were troubling the church in Antioch came from the mother church of Christianity—Jerusalem. They sat under the teaching of James and the apostles and their credentials were that they had been sent by James (which was not true). By appearance everything seemed to be in order, but when their message is evaluated by true doctrine it is found to be a complete perversion of God's revelation.

Is salvation a joint exercise between God and man? Is the basis of man's salvation partly what God has done and partly what we do by our good works? Is there something we do that pleases God and moves Him to contribute His share, adding it to what we have accomplished so that together we have enough to earn salvation? No, never! God has revealed that we can contribute absolutely nothing towards our salvation—the whole, from beginning to end, is God's gracious gift. God's grace is His favor towards us which is manifested by His actions of establishing a personal relationship with us. These actions involve Christ becoming a substitute for sinners and also giving to His people the gift of faith (Eph. 2:8) which involves both our heart and mind—there is a relational trust or assurance in God's provision, but there are also specific truths that our faith rests upon. Saving faith consists in God's mercy towards us. It is a firm assurance of God's goodness towards us in Christ, which is sealed in our hearts by the Holy Spirit. It is a belief that Jesus Christ, by His life, death and resurrection, has done *everything* necessary for salvation and we do nothing to deserve God's gift of eternal life. To suggest that what Christ has done is defective or not enough, even in the slightest way is to condemn oneself, for eternal life is attained only through the merits of Christ. If we want to contribute our own merit towards this then we stand alone, without Christ and therefore, without hope. There is no merit on our part for exercising the gift of faith we receive from God. The saving power is in Christ alone not in the faith. Faith is a relational response of trust in the Person of Christ, yet it is God who quickens our dead hearts so that we are able to have this relationship consisting of trust and obedience towards everything Christ is and says (Eph. 2:1; Col. 2:13). Resting upon Christ's righteousness by faith is the only way to be justified by God (John 1:12; Rom. 3:28; 5:1). To pervert this truth and claim that we have to do something, no matter how small, in order to complete Christ's work is to condemn yourself to eternal damnation. Many who oppose the truth of God, do so while acting as dedicated servants of the Gospel and we cannotevaluate them by feelings or appearances (Isa. 8:20).

Acts 15:2

Paul and Barnabas certainly saw the seriousness of this new teaching and would not for one moment compromise with it, but fiercely resisted it. It is not pleasant or easy to be involved in these kinds of controversies, yet to fail in courage at a time like this or to desire the praises of men above the praises of God is foolish. We are to seek for unity and peace in the church, but not when the truth of God is under attack. The battle here had to do with man's salvation, received as a free gift from God. These deceptive teachers were not even being faithful to the ceremonies of Moses, but perverting them too. The ceremonial law (which included circumcision) was meant to lead people to Christ so that they might believe in Him and be saved by faith, whereas they were saying salvation rested to a large extent upon fulfilling the demands of the ceremonial law—in other words, you earned your salvation through obedience. True Christian teaching does not deny that the Christian is to be obedient to God's moral law (this is different to the ceremonial law), but this obedience is a result of God's gracious gift of salvation, whereas these false teachers were saying that obedience to Moses was necessary to earning salvation—there is a massive difference between these two positions (one says that good works are a consequence of receiving the free gift of salvation, the other says you cannot earn salvation without good works). Salvation by grace was under attack, not just the basis of Gentile salvation.

The leadership in Antioch decided that the only way to settle this issue was to bring it before the apostles in Jerusalem and obtain a ruling with apostolic authority that would settle the matter for all time (though it is not impossible that those who came from Jerusalem also agreed that the matter be settled in this way). It must be added that Jerusalem was not the head of all the churches in some kind of organisational way. They went to Jerusalem because they needed a unified declaration from the church sanctioned with apostolic authority.

Acts 15:3

The delegation going to Jerusalem was escorted by the rest of the Antioch church for a certain distance before they said goodbye—showing, I believe, that church's awareness of how serious the issue was. The delegation from Antioch take the opportunity to recount the great things God was doing among the Gentiles to the churches in the areas they were passing through (Phoenicia, which is modern day Lebanon and Samaria). The great rejoicing among these churches must have been a great encouragement to Paul and Barnabas as they prepared for the Jerusalem debate. It is possible that these churches were also aware of the issue and thus they would have been very concerned too, if the whole of the ceremonial law of Moses needed to be obeyed by Christians. The testimony by Paul and Barnabas of God's mighty works among the Gentiles, without the ceremonies of Moses was strong evidence supporting those who believed the ceremonial laws were no longer binding.

Acts 15:4

The whole Jerusalem church gathered to hear the delegation from Antioch who shared about the work among the Gentiles.

Acts 15:5

No sooner had Paul and Barnabas finished sharing about the power and glory of God moving among the Gentiles, than a group of Pharisees, who believed in Christ, added their opinions. Their understanding of circumcision before they were saved was wrong and they merely imported this wrong understanding into the church. This should be a warning to us about the danger of presuming that we understand things. We need to always base out thinking upon the Scriptures. The areas where we are liable to make the biggest mistakes are where we think the answer is so obvious we do not need Scriptural confirmation. These Pharisees who had come to faith in Christ thought that the subject of keeping the ceremonial law of Moses was so obvious and clear that they did not need to have their thinking renewed when they were born again— they were making a fatal mistake. Our minds need to be renewed about every aspect of life and unless we diligently do this we too will make terrible mistakes. We have the Scriptures which are sufficient and clear; we have the Holy Spirit in abundance who enables us to understand them, thus it is only stubbornness, laziness or wilful ignorance that keeps us ignorant. May we strive by the grace of God to glorify Him and advance His Kingdom by bringing every thought into obedience to Christ (2 Cor. 10:5).

Acts 15:6

We see here that the *apostles* appealed to God's revelation as the basis for their authoritative declaration. They did not merely ask God to give them a prophecy to settle the matter. This shows us the direction God was moving His church. God's previous revelation, whether by sign or Word, was to serve more and more as the ultimate authority when deciding on all matters of doctrine and practice, slowly replacing God's direct, personal and specific revelation given to His servants (see comments on Acts 11:27 and 13:47). The revelation that was considered by the apostles has been recorded and preserved for us in the Scriptures. This should be a warning to those who look for easy "solutions" in our day, believing that the Lord will somehow show them the answer to their problems even though they remain ignorant of God's recorded and completed revelation. The revelation the apostles had at their disposal was still very incomplete, yet it was sufficient to overcome one of the most serious challenges that was brought against the Gospel of Christ. Until we see the revelation of God in the Scriptures as the ultimate authority for all of life and rely upon the Holy Spirit who enables us to understand what has been written, we will neither know nor follow the apostolic tradition (2 Tim. 2:15; 3:16, 17, compare Col. 2:3 with 2 Cor. 10:5). The apostles were appealing to past revelation to settle a very current debate. It is a serious failing not to recognise the greatness of divine wisdom (as we find it preserved in Scripture) and submit to it (1 Pet. 3:15)—we can be ready and confident because God has given us all we need to answer every question.

Acts 15:7

Luke does not record the details about what was said in this debate. He only records the three main speeches that settled the argument. Peter says the fundamental issue had already been settled some time before (some think as long as ten years before) when he had addressed the Jerusalem leadership on this very subject about the basis of Gentile acceptance before God (Acts 11:2–18). Peter uses the word for Gentiles that was commonly used among the Jews and carried the idea of religious and moral inferiority. He says it was he who took the news about Jesus Christ to these "inferior" people according to the sovereign ordering of *God*. Through Peter's preaching, the "inferior" Gentiles connected God's promised Messiah with the Galilaean, Jesus Christ and believed in Him.

Acts 15:8

It was not Peter or the apostles that testified about what had taken place in the hearts of the Gentiles, but God, from whom nothing is hidden—He is the one who passes judgement. God, who sees into the depths of people's hearts, acknowledged them or showed His approval of them. This approval is equal to the approval that God showed towards the apostles themselves—both were given the Holy Spirit (see comments on Acts 11:15, 17). If God had fully accepted Gentiles as Gentiles, then how could mere men impose other conditions upon them that needed to be fulfilled before salvation could be obtained? As we saw earlier (Acts 15:2), the place these Pharisees gave to the ceremonies of Moses perverted them. It must never be forgotten that salvation has always (even in the OT), only been through faith in the promises of God and not by our observance of some ritual or obedience to some set of laws. Ultimately the controversy was not between Jews and Gentiles, but about the basis of justification.

Acts 15:9

The great dividing line between Christianity and other religions is their different concepts of purity. Christianity requires purity of heart whereas others focus upon outward appearances, so when someone's outward actions line up with what a particular religion has specified, then that person is deemed holy. Only a pure heart is acceptable to God (Ps. 24:4; 73:1; Matt. 5:8; 1 Tim. 1:5; 2 Tim. 2:22), but this is not achieved by fulfilling some religious ceremonies. Only God can take care of the impurities of the heart (Ezk. 36:25–27). Before the coming of Christ and the abundant outpouring of the Holy Spirit, the ceremonies of the OT served to strengthen and assist the faith of those who had believed in God's promises—it was their faith, though, that had constituted them righteous in God's sight (Rom. 3:22; 4:13; 9:30–32; 10:6–10; Gal. 5:5; Phil. 3:9; Heb. 11). The ceremonies contributed absolutely nothing towards their *justification* before God (Heb. 7:19a). However, neither is faith some kind of work that merits God's forgiveness and it certainly has nothing in it that can make us clean. Faith is merely that relational response of complete trust in the promises of God, where we receive the cleanness of Christ. God, in His righteous wisdom and power has made it possible to place the perfect obedience of Jesus into our account. God opens our hearts to respond to His truth and gives us repentance (Acts 5:31; 11:18; 16:14; Phil. 1:29; 2 Tim. 2:25, 26). He also gives us the gift of faith (Eph. 2:8, 9), whereby we believe that the righteousness of Christ is accounted as ours and thus we are declared justified in the Supreme Court of heaven. God is the author and finisher of our faith! (Heb. 12:2).

The covenant is eternal, but the outward sign of the covenant is not the covenant. The sign merely signifies what the covenant is. The sign of circumcision spoke of God's grace and His cleansing power. Christ is the ultimate manifestation of God's grace and power to make absolutely pure. The power is not in the sign, but in Christ, thus with the coming of Christ there was a need to change the sign.

But changing the outward sign does not change the covenant. Both the sign and that which is signified are eternally established in the Person of Jesus Christ. The eternal sign of the everlasting covenant is in Christ's flesh, i.e., in His circumcision. Thus to argue as these Pharisees did, that the sign of the eternal covenant (Gen. 17:13) was to be made in sinful man's flesh for all time is to be greatly mistaken. God ratifies the sign of the eternal covenant with Himself and marks it in His own flesh (cf. Gen. 15:17). The ceremonies of Moses are not done away with in Christ, but find their eternal fulfilment in Him. Thus we do not do away with blood atonement, the priesthood, the temple, circumcision, etc., for all find their fulfilment and eternal significance in Christ. The true spiritual significance of circumcision finds its realization in the "cutting off of Christ," i.e., His death. Paul clearly substitutes the OT sign of circumcision with the NT sign of baptism (Col. 2:11, 12). The sign had to change because the one (circumcision) looked forward to the coming of Christ, whereas, the other (baptism), signifies that He has come, thus only one of them could remain. It is the same covenant, the difference being that what was anticipated in the OT has been fulfilled by Christ, thus the glory of the New Covenant far excels the Older Covenant (see the book of Hebrews).

According to Peter, God sees no difference between these "inferior" Gentiles and the Jews. Both receive forgiveness upon the same basis. It is a heart issue, thus it is God's work for He alone can purify hearts. Hearts are not purified by outward actions or by any other activities that people are capable of doing. For our hearts to be made pure, God has to sovereignly put Christ's merits into our account and give us the gift of faith, whereby we are able to relate to God and His promises in complete trust and hope. The gift of faith is the relational connection (some use the term, "channel") that unites us with God. Grace is God's attitude of favor towards us (which is unmerited), but as a result of this favor we enter into an intimate union or relationship with Him. Faith in God is the ultimate relational gift from Him and thus faith is, ultimate relationship—in the true sense. Everyone has some kind of relationship that is ultimate in their eyes and from where they gain their source of hope, instruction and authority. A person's ultimate relationship is their God! True faith in the living God is a relationship of surrendered trust in the character and promises of God (Rom. 1:17; Gal. 3:11).

Acts 15:10

The debate was about the basis of justification. Was one justified as a result of obeying the law or was one justified by grace? These Pharisees were tempting God by despising and resisting His provision, calling it inadequate and believing they were able to earn favor with God by their behaviour. They rejected God's clear revelation stating that acceptance before Him was by grace and added their own conditions. When the law of God is used *un*lawfully then it becomes a burden—the law is good when it is used lawfully (Rom. 7:12; 1 Tim. 1:8). When people are told that their acceptance before God is determined by their obedience to the whole law of Moses then it becomes a burden too heavy for any one to carry. This is what Jesus said the religious leaders in His day were doing (Matt. 23:4). As we have already said, salvation has always been by God's grace, through faith, yet this clear teaching had been perverted in the OT days and they were now trying to pervert it in the NT days. Peter called it dangerous rebellion against the plain instructions of the Lord.

Acts 15:11

It is through grace alone that both Jews and Gentiles receive salvation—both are equal in this respect and both need to believe in Christ alone to be accepted by God (Rom. 3:21; Gal. 3:21, 22).

Acts 15:12

Paul and Barnabas reinforce what Peter has said, namely, that God granted full acceptance to the Gentiles they preached to, by doing many signs and wonders among them. The signs were God's inescapable revelation to the church that He accepted Gentiles into His presence by faith alone without circumcision or any other outward activity. The whole of salvation, from beginning to end always has been and always will be by grace through faith. No one could reject the evidence that confirmed Peter and Paul's teaching that denied that the observance of the Mosaic law formed the basis of justification. God had confirmed their message with His sovereign power and these same signs stand for all time as proof of this inescapable fact—we are saved by grace through faith and not by any works of the law. Do not despise the law because these people used it in a perverse way. The law has a vital role to play and we need to know, from God's revelation, what that is lest we fall into another kind of error.

Acts 15:13

James was highly respected in the Jerusalem church and carried much authority, yet, he submitted his observations to the evaluation of the rest of the church.

Acts 15:14, 15

What God had done among the Gentiles was not some new invention of Peter or Paul, but something planned and predicted from the earliest days. James is saying to the Jews, "Relax, this is of God and in complete agreement with His Word." He says all the prophets agree (e.g., Isa. 11:10) and then he goes on to quote from Amos 9:11 and 12 as confirmation of his statement.

Acts 15:16–18

David's throne and kingdom were promised to be eternal (2 Sam. 7:12, 13, 16; Ps. 89:4, 29, 36, 37; 132:11, 12), however, they were so broken down that they appeared to no longer exist. This was merely preparing the way for the Messiah to burst upon the scene and fulfill what no man was able to do. Christ is the promised Seed of David and it is His Kingdom and Reign that was pictured in David's (Isa. 9:7; 11:1–3; Matt. 22:42). With the restoration of the Kingdom rule of the Messiah, there would also be a great ingathering of Gentiles into the Kingdom. James says that what Peter and Paul had experienced was confirmed by the Scriptures and this was the crucial basis for James giving his total support to Gentiles coming into the Kingdom as Gentiles. Our experience of what we think God is doing must never be separated from authoritative confirmation from the Scriptures. James was thoroughly convinced by the revelation of God manifesting Himself through the working of the apostles among the Gentiles because it agreed with what God said through the prophets (Isa. 49:8). This fully agrees with the other predictions of Christ's rule over the whole earth (e.g., Ps. 2; 110, see comments on Acts 2:30, 33).

Acts 15:19

James says to insist upon circumcision for the Gentiles is a hindrance. He says we should not trouble the Gentiles and in saying this he agrees with Peter that the route these Judaizers were suggesting was a yoke too heavy to be carried (see comments on Acts 15:1 and 2 where we saw that the Pharisees rejected salvation by faith alone and therefore perverted the use of the law).

Acts 15:20

Many interpret these restrictions as ceremonial laws that were necessary at that time to maintain the unity of the church between Jews and Gentiles. Fornication, however, is not ceremonial. Even if you try to restrict the meaning of "fornication" to who can and cannot marry, how can you call that ceremonial (Lev. 18:1–30; 20:19–21)? Are we now free to marry our father's wife? Others see James' commands as a mixture of moral (fornication) and ceremonial (the other three), the reason for giving them though is the same as above—to keep the unity of the church. But is seems strange indeed that Judaizers would be satisfied to have table fellowship with the Gentiles, if only they did not eat idolatrous meat, or meat that had been strangled or meat with the blood in (there being practically no difference between the last two when interpreted in this way). Was not circumcision and the other multitudes of dietary laws close to the hearts of such people (Lev. 11:1–47)? Why would the Jews have been satisfied with these few requirements James is supposed to have singled out as necessary? If these few were necessary, then why not the rest of Leviticus 11? Would the Jews have been happy with the Gentiles eating pork, just as long as the blood was properly removed? James does not tell the Gentiles to only observe these requirements in the presence of Jews, but merely says that it is *necessary* that they observe these commands.

Paul clearly had no problem in Galatians 2 with Gentiles living like Gentiles (remember the context was eating), i.e., he did not care what they ate and he did not rebuke them for being insensitive when the Judaizers came, saying that they should have been more careful about what they ate. Peter was rebuked because he knew the truth with respect to all food (Mark 7:19; Acts 10) and thus freely ate what the Gentiles ate, yet when the Jews came he feared their criticism of him for eating such foods and so withdrew from the Gentiles (Gal. 2:11ff., especially verse 14)—the issue here was eating. Do we have a difference of opinion between Paul and James? Never!

It would have been extremely dangerous for James to have said, "You do not need to practice circumcision (one ceremonial law), but you do need to observe these other ceremonial laws." Judaizers were not only wanting to use *circumcision* as a necessary requirement for salvation, but were demanding the observance of *all* Moses' laws—i.e., all the ceremonial laws.

The clear, inescapable statement coming from the council was that Moses' laws could do nothing to earn salvation, yet those who are saved by the grace and power of God are renewed so that they will not walk in the ways of the old nature. It is the law of God that instructs us about the path of righteousness, which our new hearts, empowered by the Holy Spirit and totally dependant on Christ, long to walk in. Salvation and fruit, or faith and works are inseparable and if the Jews wanted proof that the Gentiles were really saved they were *not* to watch how well the Gentiles observed the ceremonial law, but rather they were to look at the lives of the Gentiles— were they morally upright in their way of life? (Matt. 7:16; 12:33)— the Scriptures allow no other test for us to determine true conversion.

Idolatrous worship and fornication were sins that the covenant people of God were constantly warned about in the OT (Ex. 34:15; Num. 25:1ff.; Deut. 32:17; Ps. 106:34–40; Prov. 2:16, 19; 5:3, 4; 6:24ff.; 31:3; Jer. 5:7, 8; 7:9; Ezk. 18:5, 6; 20:30, 31; Hos. 4:2, etc.). In the NT these continued to pose a serious threat to those Gentiles who had come to believe in Christ. Their whole background was steeped in such practices and they continued to live in communities where their old friends and their relatives were totally committed to such wickedness. The whole of life is religious and a culture is a manifestation of a people's religious beliefs. Thus, when living in a pagan culture, there is a real and constant threat that those who have turned away from paganism will be sucked back into such activities. *Throughout* the NT the people of God are warned to stay away from fornication and idols (1 Cor. 5:11; 6:13, 18; 7:2; 10:8, 20– 22; 2 Cor. 12:21; Gal. 5:19; Eph. 5:3; Col. 3:5; 1 Thes. 4:3; Heb. 12:16; Rev. 2:14, 20). In the light of this, why do some think it would be strange for James to warn the Gentiles about these moral pollutions? Fornication covers all sexual immorality and can even include other perverse behaviour. The only context for sexuality is in marriage—a covenant relationship between one man and one woman. Any sexual activity *whatsoever*, outside of this God defined boundary, is perversion.

The Greek word translated as "strangled" could be translated as "throttled, suffocated, or smothered" (TDNT 6:456; Thayers) and comes from the root word that means "to choke." Translators and commentators immediately connect this word with the laws forbidding the eating of animals that were not slaughtered properly, thus resulting in people eating blood (Lev. 17:13, 14; Deut. 12:16, 23). When the Greek translation of the OT (called the Septuagint) talks about animals that somehow died without the blood having been properly drained or animals that were ripped up by other animals, it uses completely different words (Lev. 17:15). The word that we have in Acts 15:20 is not used in the OT (Septuagint), thus there is no straightforward connection to tie Acts 15:20 with those OT passages. The "translations" that say, "the meat of strangled animals" are not translating the Greek but telling us what they think the verse means, because in the Greek only the word "strangled" appears; there is nothing about "meat" or "animals." There is nothing about eating anywhere in the verse either, but this is supplied by commentators in order to help them explain what they think the verse means.

A much more satisfactory solution is arrived at when we see the two words, "strangle" and "blood" as connected to the moral rather than the ceremonial law (all we have in the Greek are these two words joined with "and the"). We have seen that we cannotlook in the Greek translation of the OT in order to find out how to use this word, because the word James uses does not appear in the OT. It does appear in the NT in connection with strangling, drowning, suffocating and choking (TDNT 6:456). One of the most well known incidents is Christ's teaching about the sowing of the seed in the different types of soil (Matt. 13:7, 22). The cares for this world, riches and other desires (Mark 4:19), along with the pleasures of life (Luke 8:14) all choke the word and life in the believer. Calvin uses a similar phrase when talking of those who "choke the pure doctrine of salvation revealed to them in the law and the Gospel" (Acts 16:17, p.109). It was a serious moral issue Christ was pointing to when He said that you cannot serve God and the riches of this world (Matt. 6:24, 25; Luke 16:13–15). The danger of being distracted from serving the Lord and His Kingdom by the attractions and cares of the world are very real and serious and this chokes and strangles the source of our Christian life. This is not merely a NT concern (Joshua 7:20, 21; Jer. 4:3; Ps. 52:7; 62:10; Prov. 11:28; 23:5, etc.), though the NT concern is certainly massive (Mark 10:24; Luke 12:15–21; 14:26, 33; 17:32; 18:24; 21:34; Phil. 2:20, 21; 1 Tim. 6:9–11, 17; 2 Tim. 4:10; 1 John 2:15, 16; Jude 11, etc.). We need to beware lest we are strangled (choked, smothered) by the enticements of this world—its philosophy of life (Col. 2:8) and many promises of "rewards" (worldly fame, power, and riches). It is possible Simon Magus was choked in this way (see comments on Acts 8:13, 18, 19). James clearly warned those he wrote to in his epistle about these same obstacles (James 4:1–12, especially verse 4). To warn believers to avoid being choked is not only Biblically sound, but very necessary.

It is certainly *not* "far fetched" to equate the word "blood" with violence and murder as Stott believes (*The Message of Acts: The Spirit, the Church and the World*, p. 249). Machen certainly accepted it as possible (*The Origin of Paul's Religion*, p. 88). "Blood" is used in this way in the Apocrypha (Wisdom of Solomon 14:25). The NT clearly uses it in this way many times, referring to Christ's death (Matt. 27:4, 6, 8, 24, 25; Acts 5:28) as well as to the murder or killing of Christ's servants (Matt. 23:30, 35; Luke 11:50, 51; Acts 22:20; Rev. 3:15; 6:10; 16:6; 17:6; 18:24; 19:2). Murder and the violence that leads to murder are both included in the term "blood" (cf. Matt. 5:21–22; the greater naturally includes the lesser, see also Hos. 4:2) and such behavior is not to be named among those who call themselves by the name of Christ. To say this to Christians is not stating the obvious. One of the qualifications for leadership in the church is that the leader is not to be a violent person (1 Tim. 3:3). If James is accused of stating the overly obvious fact that Christians shouldn't be involved in this kind of behaviour, then we must accuse Paul of stating something even more obvious with respect to leadership qualifications (cf. where Paul also appears to be stating the obvious Rom. 13:13; 1 Cor. 6:9, 10; Gal. 5:19–21; Eph. 4:31; 5:3; Col. 3:5–9). Why say these things if there was no danger that *Christians* might have become entangled with such practices? Christians do need to be warned!

The crucial issue of salvation by faith alone, without the works of the law, was settled once and for all by the apostles and elders of the early church. James, however, was anxious to quickly show that this did not remove the believer's responsibility to walk according to the

moral law of God. The teaching of justification by faith alone
should not lead the saved person to ignore the moral law of God.
This was clearly James' burden in his epistle (James 1:19–27; 2:14,
17, 18, 22, 24). Acts 15:20 was not an attempt to repeat the *whole*
moral law that God required the Gentiles to obey. The most important and relevant issues were raised, though the main message is
consistent with James' teaching, namely, that faith without works is
dead. The whole law did not need to be repeated to make this point
clear. In a similar way, when Jesus only stated some commandments to the rich young ruler, are we free to conclude that Jesus
released him from his responsibility to all the other laws? (Luke
18:18–20). Certainly not! Different contexts always require the
emphasising of different laws, but this shouldn't lead us to the foolish conclusion that what is not stated is now done away with.

James highlighted moral issues and not dietary issues, thus Paul
was not contradicting them or changing them when he wrote his
instructions about when and when not to eat (Rom. 14; 1 Cor. 8;
9:19ff.). Paul did not refer to the Jerusalem council in these passages
because the Jerusalem council had not given any ruling on such
matters—the council's stipulations had nothing to do with diet or
unity between believers with respect to "table" fellowship. Paul was
not changing or modifying the ruling of the Jerusalem council, thus
we can avoid all those thorny issues that are normally raised about
why Paul did not mention the council's ruling, or to whom was the
council's ruling applicable and for how long, etc. The Jerusalem
council's ruling is applicable for all time and Paul's writings fully
support it to the smallest detail (see also comments on Acts 16:4).

Acts 15:21

James was not giving some unheard of standard to the Gentiles to
observe. The moral requirements of the law were not something
totally new for their influence had been around for a very long time
and it was still possible to find out what the law said, since it was
read every Sabbath in the synagogues. It was not difficult for the
Gentile believers to be further instructed about their responsibilities so that they might walk worthy of the gracious salvation they
had been given. The Judaizers wanted to place a restriction upon
the Gentiles with respect to entering the Kingdom. James totally
rejected this and showed that once in the Kingdom, as a result of

God's abundant grace, the necessary fruit is to walk in newness of life (Rom. 6:4–7); this light is the revealed will of God.

Acts 15:22

True theology had been preserved and what was needed now was a wise strategy to mend the damage that had been done. We are not told what happened to the Judaizers who argued for the necessity of circumcision. They either would have had to repent of their position or they would have been standing against apostolic truth and thus standing against Christ. To have a distorted view with respect to salvation is to fail to enter the Kingdom (Gal. 5:1–4). If you try to contribute anything towards your acceptance before God you are despising the completed work of Christ and are greatly deceived concerning God's holiness—our finest works are nothing but refuse when they are used as a basis for acceptance in God's sight (Phil. 3:6, see comments on John 1:47). Would the apostles and elders of the Jerusalem church have tolerated rebellion against the authority of God's revealed will? Never! This is as much as we can say with respect to these Judaizers and what became of them—Luke does not tell us since his focus was revealing the eternal truth about the basis of salvation, rather than giving us a detailed history full of interesting trivia. The same problem would continue to raise its head in the church, however, we cannot prove that it was this same group who continue to stir up trouble. As we know, some errors keep manifesting themselves at different times in the history of the church even though there is no official connection between the groups that hold to these views. There is one common cause for these errors though—refusal to live by every Word that proceeds from the mouth of God (Matt. 4:4).

The whole church was involved in sorting out this matter. They all agreed with the ruling and on how best to communicate it to those Christians who had been offended by the perverse teaching. They wanted to make sure that there could be no doubt in the Gentiles' minds with respect to the basis of salvation and they wanted to leave no door open for other Judaizers to deny that the ruling had apostolic authority and carried the unanimous agreement of the whole Jerusalem church. Paul and Barnabas had been the ones who "fiercely" opposed the Judaizers when they came to Antioch, and the Antioch church had chosen them to represent the Gentiles at the Jerusalem Council (verse 2), thus it would have been possible, if they had only returned with a letter, for the Judaizers to challenged the legitimacy of the letter, i.e., suggesting that it was merely expressing the opinions of Paul and Barnabas. The Jerusalem church, with great wisdom, was going to make sure that such a charge could never be made against this ruling. They would send with the letter, highly respected and influential members of the Jerusalem church, who would be able to explain the full intention of the letter. The message was no different to what Paul taught (the relationship between salvation by grace through faith alone and the redeemed person's responsibility to walk in the light of God's law-word), but doing it in this way would establish it as the official doctrine of the *whole* church in a way that it couldn't be denied.

Acts 15:23

The letter comes from everyone in the church at Jerusalem—apostles, elders and the brethren. They address the Gentiles as brethren showing the unity of the body of Christ. There was no discrimination between the churches no matter what their national or religious background—all who believe in Christ stand upon the same level and need to realize that their acceptance is due to grace not race. The word, "greetings" tells them to rejoice or wishes them joy. No greater joy can be found than the good news that salvation rests upon the merits of Christ alone and not upon anything we are expected to do. To believe that salvation is dependant upon our striving to fulfill certain requirements is a burden too heavy for us to carry and destroys any possibility of true joy. Understanding the basis of salvation ought to give us a deep constant joy that no outward circumstances can quench.

Acts 15:24

We do not know whether these Judaizers had any positions of authority within the church, i.e., if they were recognised teachers or not. What is clear is that they were from Jerusalem and that their teaching destroyed the peace of the Gentile believers—for if there were certain laws that had to be observed in order to attain salvation, then you could never be sure that you were accepted in God's sight. On this basis, those who have a sensitive heart will always be full of doubt and in great turmoil about their eternal well-being. Only those who have a *hard* heart feel confident before God when relying upon their own good works. The letter admits that the teaching of these Judaizers had turned the whole being of these Gentiles upside-down. The Ecclesiastical Greek text mentions the false teaching that was being propounded—that the Gentiles would need to be circumcised and keep Moses' law before they could be saved. It is clear that this teaching was not from the Jerusalem church. The Judaizers were on their own mission and acting under their own authority. The Jerusalem church had not changed its understanding, but is merely clarifying what it had always believed. The Judaizers were not repeating teaching that they had heard from the leaders of the Jerusalem church and they certainly were not sent by the church to proclaim that message—the Judaizers were misrepresenting the mother church.

Acts 15:25, 26

We see the very high esteem the rest of the church had for Barnabas and Paul, calling them beloved and recognising their single-minded dedication for the Kingdom of God and their immense courage. They risked their lives for the name of Christ—meaning for Christ's honour, and cause (Acts 9:23–25, 29; 14:19; 1 Cor. 15:30, see too Paul's words about physical danger Acts 20:24). We too need to be prepared to stand by our beliefs with courage and zeal. The truth about Christ and His will is more important than life itself and we need to pray for God's strength to always help us choose the eternal option. There may come a time for us where life and truth cannot both be preserved and to preserve the one means the loss of the other—may we have the courage and wisdom to make the right choice at such times and choose truth above life, rather than life above truth.

Acts 15:27

The letter was brief, though Judas and Silas would be able to explain any unclear areas, since they fully understood the spirit and intent of the letter. Once again we are made aware of how serious the apostles, leaders and other members of the church treated this matter. They made absolutely sure that there could be no chance of misunderstanding the basis of salvation—by grace *alone*. In our day many believers are extremely casual and even slothful when it comes to discovering the truth in this area, thinking man's works and God's works *together* form the basis of salvation. This is a dam-

nable error and the apostles' strong stand here shows how determined they were to correct this wicked teaching.

Acts 15:28

This shows the authority that the apostles had—that they are linked
with the Holy Spirit. Inspiration is certainly implied by such bold
language. The apostles were very much aware of the unique authority God had given them for laying the foundations for the NT
church, though included in the "us" are others in the Jerusalem
church. Those who have the Spirit dwelling in them and are walking in submission to God, immediately recognise His truth and
support it, thus the rest of the church immediately recognises the
authority of God's truth. The ultimate authority here was the Holy
Spirit and the letter merely shows how the whole church was led by
His revelation to adopt these conclusions. We are now led by the
Holy Spirit using the Scriptures and thus we can also be confident
in what we do when we (relying upon the illumination of the
Spirit), check all our actions and thoughts by the Word of God.

The only burden to be placed upon all believers for all time is their
responsibility, through the enabling of the Holy Spirit, to walk
according to the light of God's revealed law-word. The letter states
that the observance of these things was necessary or indispensable
for their "well-being" (verse 29). There can be no escaping from the
compulsory sense of this word "necessary" (Abbott-Smith; Thayer).
If these rules were all or mostly ceremonial, merely to be observed
for the unity of the body at that time, then why use such strong language, especially when Paul would later totally overturn this ruling
(Rom. 14:14; 1 Cor. 10:25)? The only way to do justice to the strong
language of the letter is to understand these stipulations as moral
and thus absolutely necessary and eternally binding on all people,
including those who have been saved by grace (see comments on
verse 20 above).

Acts 15:29

The letter says "idol sacrifice" as opposed to "idol pollution" which
we see in verse 20, yet they are both saying the same thing. They
were to carefully guard against these things and if they did, their
beings (the wholeness of who they were), would be well. There is a
great sense of well-being in doing what we ought to do and great
frustration in living according to our own selfish desires and ambi-

tions. Walking in the light of God's Word brings health and vitality to the whole of our being. God desires His people to practice the right things and with His gracious salvation comes His empowering to work out our salvation with fear and trembling (Phil. 2:12; Eph. 2:10). It is possible to see these four stipulations as a summary of the entire law—covering the first and second tables of the law. The first table is summed up as loving the Lord with all your heart, soul, mind and strength and the second table as loving your neighbour as yourself (Matt. 22:36–40; Mark 12:30, 31). The final word is "farewell" or "be made strong"—a common way to end off a letter in those days.

Acts 15:30, 31

The entire church is gathered together in Antioch when the epistle from the mother church was read. The whole church had been unsettled and anxiously awaiting the decision from the Jerusalem meeting and their response was one of joy and gladness. The church was greatly comforted and encouraged when they heard that their faith was not in vain and their standing before God was secure in Christ alone, without the works of the law. The teaching of the Judaizers had been overthrown and the teaching of Paul established as the truth.

Acts 15:32, 33

Judas and Silas, who were recognised prophets, further encouraged and strengthened the faith of the church by their preaching and teaching, expounding the glorious message that *hearts are purified by faith* (Acts 15:9). Their prophetic office enabled them to speak with authority about the Lord's will and doctrine. Maybe they filled out even more what James briefly said: that the gathering of the Gentiles was something clearly taught in the prophets (Acts 15:15). Such clear, abundant, authoritative teaching would have really fixed and established these believers in their faith, for they would have been absolutely sure what God's mind was on the whole matter. The only basis for having assurance and confidence about anything we believe is attained by standing self-consciously upon the unshakeable Word of God.

These prophets were in no hurry to leave, however, eventually when their time was up the parting showed the great love and unity that now existed between them. In a bigger picture it shows the great unity that existed between the respective churches—the predominantly Gentile church in Antioch and the Jewish church in Jerusalem. Luke has certainly dealt a death blow to any ideas suggesting the law was necessary for salvation or that there were different ways of salvation for the Jews and the Gentiles. What we have here is one way of salvation and a complete equality of standing within the Kingdom for all those whose hearts have been purified by faith in Jesus Christ.

Acts 15:34

It appears as though some copyists thought they needed to explain why Silas was around in Antioch when Paul set out on his next missionary journey (verse 40). The Ecclesiastical text supports the fact that this verse isn't original. The most simple explanation for Silas' presence in Antioch later, is that Paul sent a message to Silas to come back to Antioch and join him for the journey.

Acts 15:35

Paul and Barnabas were extremely active in exercising their callings. The church in every age is in great need of good, comprehensive teaching and we see how blessed this church of Antioch was because there were many gifted men labouring in this way. They were also declaring the good news or evangelising. Every believer should be using his own particular circumstances and giftings to make known the good news found in Christ. This does not mean that every person is to stand upon the street corners and preach to those passing by, but we are to all ask God to help us keep His Kingdom and the glorious message of salvation at the centre of all we do. It is only as we rely totally upon the grace and enabling of Christ that we will be able to fulfill our respective callings. There needs to be a gracious urgency about our lives and relationships—graciousness because only the Spirit can open people's eyes to see His truth and an urgency because we believe how serious it is to walk in stubborn rebellion against God. Those who reject the gracious message of salvation will spend eternity in hell. May we walk in *wisdom, fear and total dependence* upon Christ—we will fail if any of these are absent from our Christian life.

Acts 15:36

We see here the great love and concern Paul had for those whom he brought to the knowledge of the faith. He thought nothing of his own safety and comfort, but rather desired to examine the well-being and spiritual growth of his children in the Lord. We see this same concern in Paul's epistles where he expressed his heart-felt desire and longing to fellowship with these converts and see them grow into maturity (Rom. 1:11; Gal. 4:19; Phil. 1:8; 4:1; Col. 2:1–3; 1 Thes. 2:8; 2 Tim. 1:3, 4). Many accuse Paul of being a hard person, yet here we see real tenderness in his sincere longing to see these new believers—a wonderful glimpse into the heart and character of this great man. Paul was very much aware of the great need Christians have for receiving persistent sound instruction. There is much in the world to challenge the faith of even strong believers, thus we can understand why Paul is anxious to discover how these "babes" in Christ were doing.

Acts 15:37, 38

Barnabas is in agreement with Paul regarding the principle of visiting these new churches, however, with respect to who should accompany them there is no agreement. Barnabas, who was related to Mark (Col. 4:10), wanted to give the young man another try at mission work. Paul believed that Mark's desertion in Pamphylia had seriously threatened the whole mission and he was not prepared to risk this next mission by taking such an unreliable helper (cf. Acts 13:13).

Acts 15:39

This was not wrath or great anger (1 Cor. 13:5), but irritation. There was no clear moral truth that was being violated by either Paul or Barnabas. Rather, it was a judgment call—was Mark mature enough for this journey? One said yes, the other said no. There was no rank (authority) to settle the decision (neither Paul nor Barnabas saw themselves as greater than the other) and neither of them is criticised by the Spirit. Much has been written on supporting either Paul or Barnabas, yet the "evidence" that is produced is equally as strong for both of them. However, since we do not have any Scriptural statement with respect to Mark's original desertion or who was at fault for this split now, we have to guess what the different motives and thoughts of Paul and Barnabas might have been and then make our ruling on that, which is not solid ground. The Scriptures are not afraid to point out faults, no matter who the culprit is, thus its silence here and the lack of evidence to help us to make a judgement, should make us very cautious in placing blame on either of them. Rather, it seems to me that there is not only one way to view a split of this nature—many immediately call it bad, but this is not necessarily the case.

What appears from the passage is that the unity of the believers was not threatened and the work was not hindered. What separated was their working together, but their relationship was not destroyed. The way the two groups went into different areas to minister appears to show that their strategy was planned together. There is a time where separation is a legitimate option. There was no binding covenant stating Paul and Barnabas had to work together for the rest of their lives. They both had their own reasons and felt very strongly about taking, or not taking Mark, thus, what we are to learn from this is that there is not only one way to accomplish a task. If people feel very strongly that they cannot go along with the strategy of someone else (we are not talking about a moral problem), then the best thing to do is to agree to separate. What is of vital moral importance is that there is mutual honour and respect maintained between the separated parties for at such times it is so easy for slander, pride (self-righteousness) and other things, unworthy of Christian conduct, to creep in. We see only a real, sincere and meaningful unity between Paul, Barnabas and Mark after this (1 Cor. 9:6; Col. 4:10; Paul recommends Mark to the church and speaks of him as useful, 2 Tim. 4:11 and as a fellow labourer, Philemon 24). God leads in mysterious ways and often it takes a disagreement like this in order to expand the work in a way that would never have entered into the minds of God's people otherwise. Though they felt very strongly about their own positions, they openly discussed their differences and decided the best thing to do was separate. We are not to be crunchy and disagreeable (making issues where there are none), but rather always seek the unity of the body. However, if we are mature people we should be able to respect the views of others and not be threatened if they disagree with our views (we are not talking about holding to false doctrine or having immoral views—there was no room to respect the views of the Judaizers). The work of the Kingdom is vast and extremely diverse and no one person is able to comprehend it all. So when you have people who are totally committed to the purposes of God and have a history of self-sacrificial service for God, if differences of opinion on issues like this arise, we need to respect these differences. The mature response to conflicting opinions that cannot be reconciled, is to seek to labor independently of one another, though united in heart, spirit, purpose and relationship.

Moreover, such times of disagreement are good for evaluating your own foundation and making sure that you are not in the wrong. In the family, if there is a strategy disagreement between husband and wife or parents and children, there is a God ordained authority structure that can overrule and expect submission where a moral issue is not at stake. But if there is no authority structure and it is impossible to agree over something vital to your working together, then work separately. There is no need to bring the church in to mediate on such matters. You can maintain the unity of Christ's body by separating in the manner of Paul and Barnabas—separation is not bad in and of itself. If you maintain godly principles with respect to your relationships, then God's Kingdom will be glorified through it all. As is clear from the rest of Acts, God was certainly behind the next phase of partners in Paul's life as he fulfilled the missionary tasks God gave him to do. God was also as involved in Barnabas' life, however, since Luke is focusing on Paul we do not hear anything more about Barnabas after he leaves with Mark for Cyprus.

Acts 15:40, 41

We now, in God's providence, have *two* teams out on the mission field, strengthening the churches. Silas was a great preacher and a Roman citizen (Acts 16:37), which was a great benefit on these travels. We mustn't read too much into the fact that Luke tells us of the Antioch church only commending Paul and Silas to the Lord for their journey. The silence about Barnabas and Mark should not lead us to assume that the church was not fully behind their trip. Rather, since Luke now focuses exclusively on Paul, it should not be strange to us that Luke, who has left out so many other details, does not see it as necessary to include any further details about Barnabas and Mark. On this second missionary journey, Paul would do far more than he initially intended, taking the Gospel not only to Asia Minor, but also into Europe.

Acts 16:1, 2

In this region Paul meets a young man who was a disciple and
whom Paul later called his son in the Lord (1 Tim. 1:2; 2 Tim. 1:2;
2:1; 1 Cor. 4:17, cf. Gal. 4:19). The most obvious way to explain this
is to say he was converted to the Christian faith on Paul's first missionary journey to this area (Acts 14:19–21). Timothy had been
grounded on the Scriptures from his earliest days, because his
mother and grandmother were Jewish (2 Tim. 1:5; 3:15), though
his father was Greek. In Paul's absence, Timothy had gained a very
good reputation among the believers in these parts. It was obvious
to the believers that God's hand was upon Timothy and this was
also immediately obvious to Paul. The faithfulness of his mother
and grandmother played a major part in the preparation of this
young man for the work that God had ordained for him to do. The
Word of God is the basis for making us mature and wise beyond
our age (Ps. 119:98–101). In our days, people are seen as wise
"beyond their age" because we live in a time where maturity is not
highly valued. Immaturity is the philosophy of our day, because the
goal of our day is to "achieve" a way of life where responsibilities are
reduced to the bare minimum—freedom to do whatever you want
whenever you want to, is held up as the ultimate success. Thus,
when you find someone who knows God's Word, what God expects
of him and zealously does this, by the power of the Spirit, he will
outshine his elders for maturity and wisdom. Timothy had been
born again by the Spirit of God, he had a great understanding of the
Scriptures and God's hand was upon him preparing him for this
task. When God raises up someone it is obvious to other believers
and this is a vital ingredient to confirm that one is called into this
kind of service—other wise, godly people acknowledging God's
gifting in that person's life. Remember, if the gifting is God's then
there is no room for boasting. The gifting comes from God and is
given for the purpose of advancing God's Kingdom, and this is
done when that gift is used to edify Christ's body (Eph. 4:12, 16; 2
Cor. 12:19). Edification flows from humble, selfless service, not
from dominating people's lives and trying to demonstrate your
"power and importance" (Mark 10:42, 43; Luke 22:25; 1 Pet. 5:3).

Acts 16:3

Paul wanted to take Timothy with him on his journey; however,
they were going to be ministering to many Jewish people who did

not believe in Christ. The Jews throughout that region knew about Timothy's family, primarily because it had been a mixed marriage. They would have greatly resented the fact that this Greek man was married to a Jewish lady. As we have seen time and again, outward ceremonies were central to these peoples' religion, while the heart, if it had any significance, was a very low priority. Paul knew this. So in order to be able to share the news about Christ with these unbelieving Jews, Paul was going to make Timothy acceptable to them. Timothy was a very valuable companion since he was well acquainted with both the Jewish and Gentile ways of life and so could relate to both easily. Paul was not changing his position with respect to circumcision, but he was merely being sensitive to the culture (fundamental beliefs) of those to whom he was wanting to minister. Not wanting to cause any unnecessary offence and have them close the door to the Gospel, Paul set about to make his team culturally acceptable to the people they wanted to reach. Timothy's circumcision was not to gain acceptance before God, but to gain acceptance from the unbelieving Jews who would have correctly assumed that since his father was a Greek, he would not have been circumcised. The Jews would have refused to have fellowship with an uncircumcised person and would have even shunned Paul for having a close association with someone like Timothy. Timothy was not circumcised to appease those Jews who had come to believe in Christ, because this would have destroyed the message of salvation by grace through faith alone. With Titus, Paul refused to circumcise him (Gal. 2:3–5), because in his case it was being demanded as a necessary condition for salvation. The difference between the circumcision demanded by the Judaizers and this circumcising of Timothy are vast, and it is only those who are extremely dull to Spiritual truth who criticise Paul for what he did in Timothy's case. For Paul, circumcision was a matter of indifference (1 Cor. 7:19; Gal. 5:6; 6:15), unless people were using it as a basis for gaining God's acceptance, whereupon he would strongly condemn such ideas. To have some hope in the merits of circumcision, meant, according to Paul, that you could not be saved by grace but were obliged to keep the whole law as the only way to please God (Gal. 5:3, 4; Rom. 2:25). The law is always the basis of acceptance before God: perfect obedience is the only standard God will accept. We either try in our own efforts to perfectly obey the law of God and have this as the basis of our salvation, or we have Christ's perfect obedience imputed to us. We can only receive Christ's righteousness (obedience) through faith (Eph. 2:8).

Paul was acting in line with his teaching on evangelism where he said that he becomes all things to all men so that he might win them to Christ (1 Cor. 9:19–23). We see also the single minded zeal in Timothy's heart, for he would do anything to advance the purposes of the Kingdom. His circumcision was merely a practical tool to help the missionaries accomplish their goals. This same principle can be copied today in a thousand different ways, all depending on the culture you are wanting to reach. Paul says we can change our appearance and behavior to blend into different cultures and thus have a greater influence among them, as long as we do not violate God's moral law and the doctrine of salvation by grace through faith alone. Hudson Taylor was a missionary who went China in 1866. He grew his hair and dressed as the Chinese and was able to have a far greater impact than those who refused to make their outward appearance acceptable to the Chinese. He was criticised by other missionaries in China for doing this, though.

Acts 16:4

They would not have delivered these "decrees/resolutions" without also giving the background to the Jerusalem council. So in the midst of circumcising Timothy, they were clearly teaching that *salvation* was by grace through faith alone. These churches were obliged to submit to the decrees—they were not negotiable! Paul's insistence here that the Jerusalem council's commands were binding, supports the interpretation given earlier (15:20), that they were moral laws and not ceremonial or dietary. Moreover, it would be very strange for Paul to take such a strong stand here, enforcing ceremonial, dietary laws, since a little while later, when dealing with dietary issues, he gives a different ruling (Rom. 14:2, 17; 1 Cor. 8:4, 8; 10:25; Titus 1:15). The reason Paul "ignored" the Jerusalem council's decrees when he was dealing with dietary matters, was because they had not dealt with such matters.

Acts 16:5

Every time the letter from Jerusalem is talked about we are told that the churches were strengthened and established (15:32, 41; 16:5). A strong church is one that is saved by faith and walks in obedience to the law-word of God by the power of the Spirit. We need to be exhorted to put aside those things that cause us to stumble and that hinder the Kingdom from being magnified through our lives (Heb. 12:1). True strength rests upon godliness—knowing and doing what is right. Only God can tell us what is right and wrong and only He can empower us to walk in accordance with His revelation. A strong church fully understands the connection between grace and law—it wants to live by every Word that comes from the mouth of God, yet it also knows how desperately it needs God's grace to do this. We are not only saved by God's grace, but live our whole lives by His grace. Any church that ignores either of these aspects will be a weak, irrelevant church. God also greatly increased the number of believers in these churches that were strong and grounded on the truth.

Acts 16:6

It appeared natural to the missionaries to move west into Asia and reach the big cities, e.g., Colosse and Ephesus. We do not know how, but the Holy Spirit forbade them from preaching in Asia. God's sovereign ordering had planned how the spread of Christianity should be and it was not the right time for these Asian cities to hear the message of Christ. Things have not changed even for our days; Christ is still the one in charge of the Gospel and the spread of Christianity.

Acts 16:7

The missionaries, with two prophets (Paul and Silas), still did not know where they were supposed to go, thus in their opinion, the wisest course appeared to be to head north into the highly populated area of Bithynia along the coast of the Black Sea. They had probably covered something like 200 km before; once again the Spirit stops them from reaching their intended destination. On this second occasion we are not given the details as to how this message was communicated to them either.

Acts 16:8

A very brief verse, though what they did was to change direction again and travel west towards the Aegean Sea, covering a distance probably close on 400 km. There were far quicker and easier ways to get to Troas than the way they had come. Why did the Lord have his missionaries wander around in these harsh, dangerous conditions for 600 km? We are not told specifically, however we do know that God's leading is never without purpose and significance. God alone knows the whole of the picture and He knows what is needed in the lives of each of His children to accomplish the goals He has ordained (Isa. 46:10). We often forget that God never stops working in the lives of any of his saints, conforming them all, more and more into the image of Christ. Thus the Spirit was at all times working as much in Paul's life as He was working in the lives of those whom Paul would teach. So in such circumstances we need to learn patience, perseverance and trust in the workings of God. Is God in sovereign control or not? We need to trust His working of all things, knowing that all is for our good and His glory. God did not allow the Gospel to be taken into the province of Bithynia, for once again all things move according to the plan of God. It is note-worthy that this area later became a stronghold of the Christian Faith and the famous church Councils of Nicaea (A.D. 325) and Chalcedon (A.D. 451) were held here. The Lord is not in a frantic rush. All things are made beautiful in His time (Ecc. 3:11), we are to walk by faith in His Word, trusting in His timing.

Acts 16:9, 10

God leads by closing and opening doors. This was now a clear opening showing that the Lord wanted them to preach in Europe (Greece). Though going into Europe was not part of Paul's plans when he set out on this missionary journey, they are all now convinced that this opening was from the Lord. It appears to have been some kind of vision, though there was no direct communication from the Lord as in Peter's case (Acts 10:13ff.). We all have many plans and desires, however we are the Lord's servants and ulti-mately it is only His will that counts (Prov. 16:9; 20:24). May we not struggle against the working of God in our lives as He changes us more and more into Christ's image and prepares us more and more for the tasks He has ordained for us.

Guidance is usually not merely a straight forward yes or no. At times there are very obvious closed doors to the plans we might seek to accomplish. We should not fight against these and murmur in our hearts. The missionaries knew they were supposed to be on this journey and so when one door closed they aimed at another one—"being in the way, the Lord led them" (Gen. 24:27). These men had a great zeal to advance the Gospel and knew that the whole world was Christ's field, so did not stumble when God prevented them from going into one particular part of His field. They were sure they were called to evangelise and there were so many other places to reach and other doors to try. They did not sit down and say let's not move until we get a "word" from the Lord. God's guidance is both negative and positive—prohibition and permission. When one route is closed, another one is opened, but if we give up we will not find the open one. Perseverance is often the means God expects us to use in order to accomplish great things for Him. We see the missionaries using their minds to determine the best next option available to them and also discussing the vision in order to discover if this was really the Lord's will for them. We need to rely upon other godly people when we are trying to make major decisions. Guidance is not purely subjective (within a person's heart), for God gives us wise counsellors to discuss our moves with (Prov. 11:14; 13:10; 15:22; 19:20; 20:18; 24:6, cf. Acts 15:6). You need to have others who are mature in the Lord who can think and pray about the Lord's possible direction for you, especially when you are facing major decisions. A necessary part of guidance is being able to discuss all the details, giving enough time to respected counsellors to think and wrestle with the options in the light of God's Word. Others can see things from a different perspective and give advice about things you do not know. All of these factors are obvious in the guidance of the missionary team (who finally end up in Greece) and should instruct us with respect to our own guidance. Through the guidance of the Spirit, the team planted the Christian faith in Philippi, Thessalonica, Berea, Athens and Corinth and who can even begin to calculate the significance of this? The Lord does know better—this is the lesson we need to learn! When things do not work out exactly as we have planned them, we are not to become despondent. We must use all the aids God has given to assist us in determining His will for us, but even after we have decided upon a particular path, we must not think that we know exactly how everything will work out. We still have to walk by faith. "Trust in the Lord with all your heart, and lean not on your own understanding" (Prov. 3:5).

Acts 16:11, 12

We are not told why Philippi was selected as the city where they would "begin" their evangelism. They do not appear to have stopped in Neapolis, but carried straight on to their destination of Philippi. This city had been made into a strong military post by Rome in order to protect the empire. It was also a colony and many Romans lived there. Being a colony meant that Philippi was governed by Roman law and the city's administration was modelled after Rome. Roman citizens were protected under Roman law from being whipped and could appeal if they were arrested (these were powerful privileges and liberties in those days). Philippi was treated like an extension of Italy, which made it very attractive for Romans to live there, which in turn made the city into a strong outpost for the empire. Luke calls Philippi the "first" or "leading" city. Thessalonica was the capital of Macedonia, thus it seems best to think that Luke was talking about the rank and dignity of Philippi, since its educational facilities were very good and its economy very vibrant.

For the first few days the missionaries do not appear to have had much success. Even after travelling such a long way and having God's clear leading into Macedonia, they still needed much patience and trust in the Lord's timing.

Acts 16:13

There was no synagogue in this city; all that existed was a place where people would gather to pray and this was some distance outside the city. On this particular Sabbath some women had gathered to pray, so the missionaries joined them and began talking about the Gospel. They had travelled such a long way to address this small "insignificant" group of people—God's ways are so very different from the way we think He should work things. If God had brought them all this distance, surely they could have expected a response to the Gospel similar to the one in Samaria (Acts 8:6). Here there were not even multitudes to listen, let alone turn to the Lord. We need to remember that we are called to persistent, consistent, faithful service of God, but the fruit and the impact our lives have are in God's secret counsel and we are not to be concerned about such issues. We are to be doing and saying that which God has told *us*, because that is our whole responsibility. We are not to be guided by emotions, circumstances or feelings, but by diligent obedience to every Word that comes from God's mouth. We are servants in His Kingdom and accounted as sheep for the slaughter and thus we must not exalt ourselves more highly than we should (Rom. 8:36; 12:3). If we have this mindset, then we will not become despondent and discouraged—we are to live selflessly, walking by faith in the Word of God (Rom. 1:17), seeking His glory in everything (Matt. 5:15, 16; 1 Cor. 10:31; Col. 3:17, 23; 1 Pet. 4:11).

Acts 16:14

The lady we are now introduced to comes from a city in Asia. The missionaries had been forbidden to preach the word in Asia (Acts 16:6), had travelled hundreds of miles and their first convert is an Asian. The first convert in Europe is an Asian woman. Lydia traded in purple linen, which would have made her a very wealthy person. Such linen was worn by kings and dignitaries and was extremely expensive to buy. Lydia had somehow come to believe in Israel's God. Paul was preaching about Christ to all the ladies present, however, as far as we know only one of them responded to his message. Why? Here we are let into the secret of how salvation works every time the Word is preached to people. It is God alone who is able to open people's hearts and minds to the Gospel (cf. Luke 24:45). We know that the Lord gives us faith (Eph. 2:8), He gives repentance (Acts 5:31; 11:18; 2 Tim. 2:25) and He turns people away from iniquity (Acts 3:26). It is God who has to deal with our hearts (Ezk. 36:26) so that we can turn to Him (Zech. 12:10). All preaching, even that of the apostle Paul, is ineffective without the inward call of God coming to peoples' hearts. The mind and the heart are inseparable and when God opens the heart this includes all the other faculties like our ears, eyes and mind (Deut. 29:4). The same words from Paul that made no impression upon other people, deeply moved Lydia's heart. The work of the Spirit is to give us a deep reverence and love for the Word of God. Those who claim to have no need for the "cold letter" of the Word and claim the Spirit as their guide without the Word are greatly deceived. We are confronted here with the working of God's electing grace which is not open for our scrutiny and judgment (Acts 2:39, 47; 13:48; Rom. 8:30; 2 Thes. 2:13, 14). This is part of God's eternally set plan of ordering all things (see comments on Acts 2:23; 4:28). Everyone's heart is not only closed, but hostile to God and His truth and it is only by His divine working that our hearts can be made receptive to eternal truth. The opening of one's heart is, as the Greek tense shows, a once for all incident performed by God. God opened Lydia's heart, which enabled her to understand Paul and respond to the salvation call.

Acts 16:15

Who is included in this term, "household"? How do we answer this question? There are two possible approaches to finding an answer:

1). We assume continuity between the OT and the NT, or

2). We assume that there is a great break between the two Testaments.

Once you have chosen an assumption you need to demonstrate that it can be used consistently to understand and interpret the rest of Scripture. My assumption is that there is no great break between the Testaments, because there is much in the NT that cannot be understood unless it is explained by the OT. If we claim there is a massive break between the Testaments, then there is no justification for using the OT in this way. We must not view the NT as something totally new with massive changes so that what is done in the NT has no recognisable relation to anything in the OT. One of the most basic principles of interpreting Scripture is seeing the continuity of the whole Bible. God has only one plan of redemption and He has unfolded this to us in stages. There is one revelation of God and one essential covenant that runs from the beginning of Genesis to the end of Revelation. There were times when the outward appearance of this one covenant differed, but the essentials have always been the same. Unless we assume continuity between the two Testaments then much in the NT will be meaningless. When Galatians 3:29 tells us that we are "Abraham's offspring" and "heirs according to the promise," if we do not understand these terms as the OT explains them, they can mean anything we wish. Philippians 3:3 tells the Christian that he is the "true circumcision" and Romans 15:8 tells us that Christ came to confirm the promises given to the fathers (Booth, *Children of the Promise*, p.21). When the NT calls Christ our Great High Priest (Heb. 5:10) or the Lamb of God (John 1:29), or the Lion of the tribe of Judah, or the Root of David (Rev. 5:5), unless these terms carry a consistent meaning from OT to NT then we will have no basis for giving them meaning—you can make them mean anything. Likewise the Lord's Supper celebrated in the NT is to be understood in the context of the OT Passover meal (Luke 22:15–20; 1 Cor. 5:7–8; 10:16–17).

God relates to us by means of His covenant and circumcision was ordained by God to be the sign of the covenant (Gen. 17:11). God determines the "mark" He wants to use upon those that have a special relationship with Him. Paul clearly tells us that circumcision signified and sealed the faith that Abraham already had (Rom. 4:11). God's calling and ownership is comprehensive and when we believe in Him every aspect of our existence comes under His authority. Everything Abraham did or thought was now to be brought into line with God's will. Everything Abraham owned belonged to God and was to be used for God's glory. This is how the covenant operates, thus when Abraham received the sign of the covenant, God said, "Your son Isaac, who has not yet been born, must be marked with the sign of the covenant." Abraham had received the sign after believing, yet his child would receive it before. Did this mean that the way of salvation was different for Isaac than it was for Abraham? No, never! Salvation has always only been by faith. Isaac would need his own personal trust in God, just as Abraham had. However, despite not yet having that, he was given the covenant sign, showing his full participation in God's covenant blessings. The covenant sign is primarily God's message to us—a message of favor and promise of good will, etc. (see comments on Acts 22:16). Just because we see life as disjointed parts does not mean God does. God relates to His creation only in terms of covenant and the terms of this covenant are determined by Him. God's claims are upon individuals, households and nations. Those who argue for "believer's baptism" only in the NT, do violence to the continuity between the Old and New Testaments. But if you take this line then you must be consistent and say if the NT does not clearly and specifically explain something then we cannot come to a conclusion about that issue. The argument says that since there is no specific statement in the NT saying, someone's infant was baptized, there is no Biblical basis for doing so. Surely, in the light that a believer's children were automatically given the covenant sign in the OT, if the NT does not specifically show that there was a change in God's Kingdom in this regard, then when the NT merely says Lydia believed and she was baptized and her household, it is far more natural to assume her children were included. How could there be such a drastic change with the Covenant Keeping God without Him also clearly explaining this change? i.e., that households were no longer brought into the covenant when the head of the house was. If the Bible does not show that there is a change, then we have to assume continuity and when we assume continuity with Acts 16:15 and 1 Cor. 1:16, etc., we *naturally* conclude that not everyone had saving faith that was baptized, but all entered into the privileges of the covenant and thus received the sign of the covenant.

The rejection of infant baptism is based upon an assumption of discontinuity between the Testaments, but if this is true, then how do we define incest? Where is the NT passage showing us all the relationships that would be incestuous if marriage took place? Is bestiality wrong in the NT age? The NT names and condemns other sexual perversions, but not bestiality—does this silence in the NT mean the OT prohibition is no longer binding? To assume discontinuity between the Testaments leaves you in a real mess, so what Christians do is, based upon their own authority, pick and choose what is still binding from the OT. However, if this is done, you no longer have an absolute word from God.

The *sign* of the covenant in the NT is not circumcision, but baptism. There has been a clear change, made by Scripture. Though the outward sign was changed, what the sign stood for hasn't changed, it still shows that a covenant relationship exists between God and His people. Paul says to the Colossians, you were circumcised in Christ with "Christ's own circumcision, when you were buried with Him in your baptism" (Col. 2:11, 12, Moffatt Translation). Paul clearly saw a connection between circumcision and baptism. Are we to assume continuity or discontinuity with the sign of God's covenant? Every argument that is brought against infant baptism is brought against OT infant circumcision too—not many realize this. The questions are: (1) who will tell us the meaning of the sign of baptism? And (2) is there continuity or discontinuity between the Testaments? To be able to place God's mark upon our children is a glorious sign of God's graciousness towards us, our children, our churches and our society. There is no other basis for relating to God other than through the covenant and it is God who reveals the terms and the sign of His covenant (see too, comments on Acts 2:38).

Hospitality is a Christian virtue which Lydia sincerely demonstrates. The Scriptures place a great emphasis upon being hospitable (Rom. 12:13; 16:2; 1 Tim. 3:2; 5:10; Heb. 13:2; 1 Pet. 4:9).

Acts 16:16

The missionaries were based at Lydia's house and continued to go to the "place of prayer" where they had first met Lydia. It appears best to think that this was not the only outreach activity the missionaries were involved in, since they were accused of trying to convert Romans (verse 21) and teaching customs opposed to "normal" Roman belief. In other words, their teaching was known by these accusers who did not attend this "place of prayer," so one assumes this knowledge arose from the other evangelistic efforts of Paul and Silas (see verse 40).

In Philippi there was a young slave girl who had a spirit of divination and many people consulted her to find out about the future. This was a very profitable business for those who owned her, for there were many foolish people who sought her "wisdom." Remember, she was possessed by a demonic spirit and demons are liars and deceivers who have one primary intention and that is to destroy people. They use great subtlety to entrap the foolish by mixing a certain amount of truth with their predictions. Satan's power is grounded in sin and rebellion. Demons are far stronger and wiser than humans and therefore the only protection people have against them is from God. Satan's power is nothing in comparison to God's power, however, when people walk in rebellion against God they alienate themselves from God's protection and are thus fully vulnerable to the power of the demonic world. It is in this way that Satan's power arises out of sin and rebellion, for when people rebel against God they open themselves up to demonic power and deception, which is far greater than mere humans are able to withstand in their own strength and wisdom.

Consulting such people to find out about the future is strongly forbidden in the Bible (Lev. 19:26; Deut. 18:10–12)—it is an abomination. When people look to divination and such things they are entrusting themselves to the demonic realm to provide their protection, wisdom and hope—which is a path to self-destruction. All of God's commandments are for our good and protection, for He alone is the source of truth, help and salvation, thus, to look anywhere else for these is to open oneself up for total deception. The frightening thing about deception is that you do not think you are deceived, but when God is rejected as the only source of truth, then there is no basis by which you can distinguish between right and wrong or whether you are believing a lie or not. How can you trust the words of a witch-doctor or diviner? They are under the control of the father of lies (John 8:44), the ultimate deceiver. Demons can make themselves look like and talk like anyone they want. When people think they are talking to their dead ancestors they are actually talking to demons and demons are wanting to destroy individuals, families and cultures, thus any advice they give will always be towards that end (see comments on Acts 8:7). Demons do not want people to look to and trust Christ, thus to take demonic advice and act upon it is to open one's self up to more of their deception and ultimately, self-destruction. When people reject God's truth, He hands them over to believe lies (1 Kings 22:18–22; 2 Thes. 2:11, 12)—this is a terrifying judgement! God wants us to look to Him alone for everything we need and if He has not told us about some aspect of the future or whatever, we are still to walk by faith, trusting in His promises and protection. There is no safer way to live!

Acts 16:17

What this demon possessed girl was saying was perfectly correct. She was bringing attention to the missionaries and exalting their message. Why would Satan do this? We are not to think for one moment that Satan was doing this for anything other than evil ends. Calling people's attention to the missionaries, saying their message was from the Most High God and revealed the way of salvation, was Satan's way of *assaulting* the Gospel. Whatever Satan does is an act of total war against God and His Kingdom, whether it comes in the form of violent, aggressive assault or open, enthusiastic praise. It is important to be aware of the craftiness of the devil (the destroyer), who uses a great variety of tactics to undermine the truth of God and destroy people. To think that we are able to stand against the schemes and subtlety of the devil without total dependence upon Christ, means we are already greatly deceived. Demons can also "predict" the future by using terms that could be interpreted in many different ways, thus fooling people that the diviner is able to give counsel regarding the future. They might even have some access to knowledge about future events.

What we see manifested here is a common tactic of the devil who knows that sometimes it is best to parade himself like an angel of light in order to accomplish his destructive work (2 Cor. 11:14). Many times, people who are full of perversity and false doctrine, will not merely go on their own and start a work, but will seek to associate themselves with a legitimate work and then from that position undermine the Gospel. Satan knows that he is no match for the power and wisdom of God, yet due to his self-deception and pride he still seeks to overthrow the work of God. On this occasion the devil's plan was to be identified in the minds of the Philippians (through this slave girl), as supporting the missionaries' work. From this position Satan would be able to hinder both those who responded to the Gospel and those who didn't. Not every one in the city would have agreed with divination, even as in our days, some people dabble in this and others don't. Those who did not dabble in divination would not have thought very much of this girl and would have avoided her, as we would avoid such people in our own day. Now, by connecting herself to the missionaries, those people who rejected her activities would have rejected the missionaries, thinking that they were of the same spirit—thus, she became a stumbling block preventing them from responding to the Gospel. Now on the other hand, those who did respond to the Gospel would have been vulnerable to the "teaching" of this demon possessed girl and open to her practices, since they too would have believed her to be of the same spirit with the missionaries.

Acts 16:18

Paul was grieved by this girl and not deceived for one moment, yet one wonders why he waited so long before doing what he did? The most obvious reason was that he was waiting on the timing of the Lord, who knew what was best for advancing His Kingdom. This girl was respected by many people in the city and probably despised by many also. Thus what we see here is the wisdom and power of God against the wisdom and power of the devil (there is no real contest though). By waiting for many days, it meant that many people would have witnessed the demon possessed girl's actions which would have been a great talking point in the city by both those who liked and disliked her. Thus, in God's perfect timing the effect of casting out the demon would have been of far greater impact than if it had of happened the moment Paul laid eyes on the girl. By waiting, those who came to believe in the Gospel would have seen that her behavior was unacceptable to the Christian faith and this would have strengthened them to resist other such people, whereas those who despised this girl would have been made more open to the message of the Gospel. Both groups would have been made aware of the superior power of the God the missionaries preached about. In the delay, Satan's exposure was much greater and grander. Paul, walking in obedience to God, though being grieved from the first day, patiently waited upon the Lord and trusted in His timing. We too can learn from this that we need to be patient and always seek to make the greatest impact for the Kingdom of God in all that we do. We need to pray for wisdom and rely upon the Lord to guide us so that we not only fight the battles He has given us to fight, but that we fight them according to His timing. Our own strength can accomplish nothing so may we look to Him at all times. It is also possible that the Lord made Paul delay casting out this demon since this would end his time of ministry in that city. But ultimately we will never be able to understand all the reasons that God has for His actions and timing, for such things are beyond our limitations— the just shall walk by faith, not demanding an explanation about every detail they do not understand.

Many people think man's limited knowledge means there are many areas of life where we do not have clear guidance from God telling us what we ought to do. Such a position is, however, rebellion disguised as ignorance. God's Word speaks to all of life, and thus, every action He *requires* from us in all these areas, has been revealed to us (2 Tim. 3:16, 17). The vast amount that we are ignorant about, has nothing to do with how we *ought* to act and think at any give time in order to fulfill our responsibility before God and glorify His name.

Our ignorance is about: God's secret counsel; eternal purposes; many historical details; why certain things happen in the way they do; much about the future, etc., however, this ignorance is never to be used as an excuse for us not *acting* as we ought to act—as individuals, families, churches and nations. All of our respective responsibilities have been revealed to us and to be ignorant of them does not "prove" God hasn't revealed such, but rather shows our refusal to bring every thought captive to the mind of Christ and live by every Word coming from God's mouth (2 Cor. 10:5; Matt. 4:4).

In the name of Jesus Christ: this refers to Christ's authority most certainly, however it includes who Christ is, that is, what He has revealed about Himself. When we pray according to the name of Christ, it is praying according to His revealed will. Thus, the authority to cast out this demon came from who Christ is and we know who He is because He has revealed Himself to us. It is only as we stand upon this Christ that we stand in His power. If we think about Christ according to our own imaginations then we are not standing upon the authority of Christ. When we bring our thoughts into line with Christ's revelation and use that as the basis for all we do, only then we can be confident that we have His authority backing us. To go forward with our own ideas about any aspect of life is to walk in our own name and rely upon our own strength. To try and accomplish anything on this basis is foolish, for it has no foundation and so, no matter how "grand," it will collapse (Matt. 7:24–27).

The term, "in that hour" is used in a variety of ways in the NT, but it is used here to refer to that very instant when Paul commanded the demon to leave (cf. other passages where the exact same Greek term is used, Mark 13:11; Luke 2:38; 20:19; Acts 22:13). There was no resistance from the demon. There is no reason to fear the demonic realm when we stand in Christ by faith. Fear arises from unbelief and sin (which is the source of Satan's power) and fear stifles the pure and free preaching of the Gospel.

Acts 16:19

With the casting out of the spirit, the income that this girl gained by divination was also cast out. Those who owned the girl and benefited greatly from her being possessed were extremely angry. The market place was where all the main activities of the city took place, including where the magistrates sat to hear cases and pass judgement. Paul and Silas were brought into this "market court." Those who *love* money will pervert truth and righteousness in order to increase their money (1 Tim. 6:10). This is true for businessmen, individuals and politicians. People will use the language of justice, truth, seeking the benefit of others, etc., in order to disguise their motives and hide the fact that all they are interested in is increasing their own wealth and attaining their own personal ambitions.

Acts 16:20, 21

These men give a show of great patriotism for the city of Philippi, saying the whole city is being disturbed by Paul and Silas. The truth is, these men could care about nothing other than themselves and they want revenge against Paul for removing their source of wealth. The demon was their treasure and when it was cast out their treasure was lost. Dabbling in divination and witchcraft was the real destroyer of the city, for to play with demonic forces, in any way, is to promote destruction, chaos and death.

There is no conclusive proof to show that evangelising of Romans by Jews was illegal (F.F. Bruce, nicnt). Dr. RJ Rushdoony has pointed out that the clash between Rome and Christianity was not "religious" from the Roman perspective, but political (*The One and the Many*, pg.94). For Rome, their ultimate authority, source of law and hope was found in Caesar, whereas for the Christian these were found in Christ. Inseparable from the Christian message is the absolute Lordship of Christ over every aspect of life and for Rome, such teaching amounted to treason. It was not illegal in Roman law to believe in any number of gods. Later the Christians were accused by Rome of being atheists, but this was because they did not give Caesar divine honour—to deny Caesar this honour was to deny god, according to Roman thinking. In the passage before us it is difficult to know what these accusations were based upon, though the Philippians must have realised the total claims of Christ presented in the Gospel message. The accusers do not mention the demon possessed slave girl and their financial loss as a result of her being set free from that oppression—their love of money was what was really motivating them and not their love for Roman law and customs. We need to be able to see through such deceptive nonsense in our own day too, where people for their own selfish ambitions, use terms which will gain them the support of others.

Due to the trouble in Rome itself, the emperor Claudius had expelled all Jews from that city as trouble makers (cf. Acts 18:2), thus within the Roman world there was a strong prejudice against Jews. To be identified as a Jew was almost enough to "prove" that you were a troublemaker. The accusers of the missionaries therefore make sure the magistrates know Paul and Silas are Jews.

Acts 16:22

It is easy to get a mob uprising, especially if it is against a minority group. Slogans and false information are enough to excite a mob to rioting and violence. As soon as everyone hears the accusations, they are all angered and convinced that these men are guilty and deserve to be punished. The excitement of the mob convinced the magistrates that the charges were correct. It is a very dangerous mistake to listen to only one side of a story and make a judgment on that. You can be absolutely convinced of someone's guilt and wrong doing, until you hear their side of the story, thus we are warned in Proverbs, "The first one to plead his cause seems right, until his neighbour comes and examines him" (18:17). This pre-caution needs to be burned deep into our hearts and become an inseparable part of how we live. We must be slow to judge and be quick to find out both sides of the story if we are going to judge. These magistrates would have saved themselves a lot of anxiety if they had followed this simple procedure and being judges, their neglect of this was inexcusable. Their judgment was based upon prejudice and fear of the mob and had nothing what so ever to do with justice. The magistrates ripped the clothes off of Paul and Silas and had them beaten with rods—usually upon the bare back. Jewish law limited the amount of strokes someone could be beaten (maximum being forty, Deut. 25:2, 3), however, Roman law had no such limit and thus they were beaten with *many* stripes. In 2 Corinthians 11:25, Paul tells us that he was beaten on three different occasions with rods. He was also beaten by the Jews on five different occasions, receiving thirty nine stripes each time (2 Cor. 11:24). The reason the Jews gave thirty nine stripes was so as to be sure not to go past forty and thus violate God's law—this exemplifies the hypocrisy of the Jews in the case of beating Paul for they were careful not to break the law of God, yet they were thrashing God's anointed messenger.

Acts 16:23, 24

According to the magistrates, the thrashing was not enough, so they cast them into prison, probably wanting Paul and Silas to really feel the pain and discomfort of the beating. If they had been let go right after the beating, then their friends would have taken then, washed their wounds and made them as comfortable as possible. However, they were cast into the innermost cell which was dark, damp, dirty and cold. Here their feet were secured in the stocks, which was a wooden contraption that would stretch the legs wide apart and then clamp the feet in this position—an extremely uncomfortable ordeal. Not only were they left in this uncomfortable, joint aching position, but they would have been in tremendous pain due to the beatings. Their bodies would have been a mass of intense agony.

Acts 16:25

The missionaries had been in this agonising and sorry position for some hours when Luke picks up the story again, yet we find them worshipping the Lord. The other prisoners, would have seen the condition Paul and Silas were in when they were placed in the inner cell and they would also have known what it was like to be in that cell, thus they are amazed when they hear the prayers and songs coming from these missionaries. Not cursing, but praising their God for who He was and for what He had done and would still do. This verse should pierce all of our hearts when we compare ourselves and see how quickly we become disgruntled and despondent, whereas Paul and Silas, despite their harsh conditions, were a million miles away from despondency and discouragement.

Acts 16:26, 27

This earthquake did not destroy the prison in any way, but merely released all the doors and the chains fell off the prisoners—a supernatural work of God. When the guard awoke, he did not find a destroyed jail, but merely all the doors open. There would have been no explanation for such an occurrence and he would have been accused of letting everyone go, so he judged it far better to kill himself right then. It was dark and all he saw were open prison doors, thus the logical conclusion was that everyone had run away.

Acts 16:28

Why no one had run away we do not know. What we can assume is that it was God's intention that none of them escape and in the light of the praying and singing and then the shaking of the jail's foundations, when the doors all opened and the chains fell off everyone, they were too awed and fear struck to move. How Paul knew what the guard was about to do, again we do not know, however he calls to him not to harm himself. Paul is not vengeful towards this jailer, but merciful, desiring his well-being.

Acts 16:29, 30

The jailer, rushing into the innermost cell with a light, seeing that
no one had escaped, is overcome with awe, fear and relief, thus his
body begins to tremble. It is the Holy Spirit working in his heart
that enables him to perceive not only his own need for salvation,
but that Paul and Silas can instruct him on how to receive it. The
jailer finds himself falling down at the feet of the missionaries, but
this is not an act of worship—his strength was drained as a result of
his shock at what had happened and it also shows his helplessness,
indebtedness to and awe of these two men. After bringing them out
of their cell, the first thing he wants to know is how he can be saved
from his sin and he addresses them as superiors—sirs, or masters.
This is true conviction of the Holy Spirit, showing the sinner his
desperate need for forgiveness and to be delivered from the wrath
of God.

Acts 16:31

Paul's response is the Gospel in a nutshell—salvation is obtained by
believing in Jesus. The only way to be saved from God's eternal
judgment upon sin is to have total trust and confidence in God's
provision and promise of salvation found in the completed work of
His Son. We are not saved because we have faith, but because we
believe in Him who alone is able to save. Salvation requires a sure
and clear knowledge of who Jesus is and this knowledge is found in
the Gospel and we are enabled to understand this revelation by the
working of the Holy Spirit. God looks to save households, for families play a vital role in the Kingdom of God. The jailer's family
would not be saved by his faith, for each person has to believe in the
Lord Jesus for themselves, but what Paul says is that this glorious
offer of salvation is for everyone—old and young alike.

Acts 16:32–34

The missionaries then had opportunity to share the Gospel with
the jailer's whole household and in a glorious move of the Spirit, his
whole family is brought to saving faith. The jailer, from harshly
treating Paul and Silas, is now mercifully serving them and ministering to their needs—their wounds and hunger. The whole household is baptized, receiving the mark of the covenant (see comments
on Acts 16:15) and the jailer is filled with great joy because of his
own and his family's salvation. A short while before this he was in

utter despair and suicide seemed like the only option, now he was overcome with joy. He was but a moment away from eternal separation from God and his family, yet now he had eternal union with God and his family. A little while before the family were almost without a father in a hostile environment (the Roman authorities would not have looked kindly upon the family of a man who allowed all his prisoners to escape), now they stood in the security of God's heavenly family. What glorious and radical changes the Gospel brings. It is only hardness of heart and wilful blindness that causes people to resist such a wonderful gift from God. The foolishness and sinfulness of people is most clearly seen in their rejection and despising of the gracious offer of salvation found in Christ.

Acts 16:35, 36

The magistrates had probably judged that the lashing and the discomfort of the stocks was an adequate punishment for these troublemakers. Their suggestion was that they should now leave the city peacefully, that is, not stir up any more trouble. By the way the magistrates responded the day before, with the very swift punishment, it does appear that they were afraid of civil unrest. The reason that they now wanted to get Paul and Silas out of the city first thing the next morning could have been based upon the desire to remove the possibility of more trouble. Rome had ordered all Jewish "troublemakers" to leave Rome, thus these magistrates probably thought it would be wise to remove such men from their city and their beating was a clear enough warning that they shouldn't return.

Acts 16:37

There was a law structure in this place and Paul knew it and appealed to it, showing where the magistrates had violated Roman law. Roman citizens were exempt from imprisonment and public beatings unless properly convicted in a court of law. Paul was born a Roman citizen (Acts 22:28). These magistrates had severely beaten Paul and Silas before many witnesses and then imprisoned them without a trial. This meant that the magistrates, according to Roman law, had committed a crime—by violating the rights of Paul and Silas, they had violated Roman law. This was a serious offence. Paul was not going to allow these magistrates to get off so lightly and wanted them to acknowledge their wrong doing and apologise by personally releasing the men they had treated unjustly. It seems likely that Paul was not on a personal errand here, but seeking the advancement of the Kingdom of God in Philippi. The people of the city would have known about the beating and imprisonment and then the way these men had been released. Thus, the message of the Gospel could not be dismissed on the basis that the magistrates had beaten those who proclaimed it, for the magistrates had apologised to these preachers. By Paul's actions, the believers in Philippi were left in a much more secure position than they would have been if he had of just quietly left town. In extreme cases where there is no course open for appeal, we are to bear our circumstances with patience, receiving them from the hand of God (Matt.5:39), however, this does not mean we shouldn't ever appeal. If there is no possibility of justice, then we are to just slide out of the situation as quickly and quietly as possible (Matt. 5:25, 26, 41), but if some sort of justice is possible we are to appeal to those laws, as Paul does here and did again (Acts 22:24, 25; 25:11; 28:19). We do not know what Paul had with him to prove his Roman citizenship, however, if you lied about being a Roman citizen and were found out you would be executed.

Acts 16:38, 39

The magistrates were terrified when they heard this message—their own death sentences were staring them in the face. With great fear and humility they quickly came to the prison and escorted the prisoners to freedom. While leading them out of the prison, the magistrates were asking a favor of Paul and Silas. The magistrates had no authority to throw a Roman citizen out of a Roman city, but here the magistrates were saying to the missionaries, "For your own safety and the peace of the city would you not consider leaving the city?" They were not commanding the missionaries, but seeking a favor from them. Not only did Paul and Silas leave the prison as honourable Romans but the magistrates' actions show that the missionaries' *teaching* was not condemned either.

Acts 16:40

Paul and Silas, being guided by the Holy Spirit, agree that it is best for them to move on. Their work in Philippi was complete and there were many other cities to visit. All that remained for them to do was encourage the new church that they would leave behind. It is possible that others had come to believe in the Lord, though Luke has only told us about Lydia, the Philippian jailer and their families. While, "the brethren" might only refer to these believers, it could quite naturally include others. Paul and Silas, still in much physical discomfort and probably not having slept, are anxious to strengthen the brethren and are totally indifferent to their own needs. What was expected from this new church, was maturity. Something we find hard to understand in our days where immaturity is accepted as normal. In every area of life we see how people seek to escape from maturity and responsibility. Right from training our children, it is very obvious that maturity is not taught or expected and this affects every area of society—immature people cannot produce mature actions or thinking (see *Muse Time,* papers 7 and 9). It is only by the grace of God that we are able to assume our responsibilities and labor maturely in the Kingdom of God, so let us cast ourselves upon Him and walk worthy of the high calling we have in Christ (Eph. 4:1; Col. 1:10; 1 Thes. 2:12; 4:1). True freedom is growing up into the fullness of the stature of Christ (Eph. 4:13) and this means assuming our full responsibilities under God. The church many times caters to this immaturity and allows Christians to remain in their immature states. True Christianity is a vibrant, living, dynamic force that transforms and matures people, bringing them more and more into the image of Christ. We are to be gracious and patient and kind, but not with perpetual immaturity. Perpetual immaturity has nothing to do with the Kingdom of God and certainly does not come from the Spirit of God. Those who are comfortable with immaturity must not deceive themselves into thinking that God is not concerned about maturity.

Acts 17:1, 2

Thessalonica was the capital of Macedonia and Paul continues his strategy of going to the major centres. Thessalonica was an important trading city, being accessed by land and sea and was therefore a significant hub for spreading the Gospel far and wide. Ultimately we have to realize that this was the Holy Spirit is strategy, though we must not make it into some kind of Scriptural rule for modern evangelism. The Lord has given specific gifts and callings to each Christian and there are many other aspects involved in leading people to evangelise in either a major city or a remote village. Too much of modern evangelism and Christian work is motivated by the glamour of travelling to "exotic" places. Travel in Paul's day was extremely hard and dangerous. Remember the missionaries had just been released from jail and were in a pretty battered state physically, yet set out on another difficult and long journey—a walk, somewhere in the region of from Mutare to Marondera (about 200 km).

If there was a synagogue, Paul would start his ministry there. Paul was a man of faith, yet we see that his Christianity was totally reasonable. For Paul the Scriptures spoke with ultimate authority and thus he had a solid standard to challenge the thinking of those he encountered. Only the Scriptures can provide the unshakeable answers to life's many questions. These answers are clear and thus we shouldn't apologise for them, or think that we are able, with our own reasoning, to supply better answers to those who ask questions. We are to start our reasoning from the foundation of the Bible and lead everyone to the conclusions found in its pages.

Acts 17:3

Paul does what Jesus Himself had done—shows the necessity of His suffering, death and resurrection (Luke 9:22). As we have seen elsewhere, the Messiah's suffering and death was something the Jews were unable to grasp (see comments on Acts 8:32–34). This was God's glorious plan of atonement and it was necessary in the sense that God had explained His plan long before it happened. Paul is now relating historical facts to the Scriptures and showing that Christ and Christ alone fulfils all the prophecies and requirements exactly. The only way to deny Christ is to reject the clear teaching of the Scriptures. The seriousness of sin required the death of the Messiah, something the Jews of Paul's day and people in our own day do not appreciate. Sin's penalty has to be paid and Christ alone is able to pay for the sins of others. His rising from the dead was the necessary proof to show that Christ had accomplished His work and that it had been fully accepted by the Father. The resurrection plays a vital part in our redemption and this is the Christ that saves us, the Jesus who lived, suffered, died and rose again at a particular time in history. It is the Jesus who perfectly obeyed the law of God and completely fulfilled the OT Scriptures that spoke about the promised Messiah. There was only one possible conclusion for Paul—this Jesus whom he was preaching about was the Messiah.

Acts 17:4

Some Jews were persuaded about the truth of Paul's doctrine, though many Gentiles embraced it and this included many prominent ladies of the city—leading citizens. Whether Paul and Silas withdrew from the synagogue at this time we do not know, however, these new converts clearly identified themselves with the missionaries in some way.

Acts 17:5

This is not surprising and we should not be shocked by such behaviour. Those who profess to be seeking the truth, to worship the true God and claim to be labouring for Him ought to embrace Jesus Christ—He is the express image of the true God. To reject Christ means that your labor in God's name was never motivated by a love for Him, but by some self-seeking perverse objective. The behavior of these Jews shows that they were always suppressers of the truth—even when they claimed to be promoters of the true God. They were trying to make converts to their own perverse religion and they had been working hard for this among the Gentiles (cf. Matt. 23:15). Many people throughout the ages have used this same method to accomplish their goals (politicians included)—pay some rogues to cause chaos or assault those whom you do not want around. Here we have a mob attacking the house where Paul and Silas were staying. It is easy to excite a mob into action and once started it takes on a life of its own and is totally without reason. When mobs begin their violence they have already made their conclusions, passed judgment and proceed to carry out the "necessary" sanctions or judgement. The Jewish leaders knew that they had no legal case against Paul and Silas, so their only hope was to manipulate the legal system in order to get a ruling in their favour. Such people are not concerned about justice, bur merely use the system to achieve their own desires. Our ultimate hope is not to be in a good constitution, or legal system, but in the grace of God turning people from their sin and rebellion to willing obedience to His truth. While we should never ignore our responsibility to draft good constitutions and have good legal systems, our hope must always be in Christ's work of redemption and on-going sanctification in the lives of His people. Godly morality and justice will only arise out of a people's true faith, not out of documents, since those who try to manipulate and pervert the clear evidence with respect to God (Rom. 1:18ff.), will manipulate and pervert a constitution no matter how good it is.

Acts 17:6, 7

The missionaries were not in the house that the mob descended upon so they dragged out the owner of the house and some other believers who happened to be there. They were taken to the rulers of the city and serious charges were brought against them. The crowd claimed these believers were causing social upheaval that was revolutionary. Jason was accused of harbouring Jewish troublemakers who had stirred up much social strife in other Roman cities. More serious was the charge that these Jews were proclaiming a rival emperor to Caesar—this rival King had been accused of sedition before a Roman judge (Luke 23:2). Thus, the mob argued, it was obvious that this movement was totally unacceptable and should be dealt with swiftly and firmly. The announcing of another King threatened the foundations of the Roman Empire. The Roman emperors of this time had made it illegal for astrologers or any other kind of fortune teller to make predictions about the state or the emperor's well-being (F.F. Bruce, Acts, p.325). The accusation from this crowd was that Paul's preaching violated Caesar's decree. Paul had told the Thessalonians about great social and political upheaval that was to come upon the nation of Israel and thus the Roman Empire (2 Thes. 2:3–8, especially verses 5,6). Though he was not referring to Caesar, it was easy for those who despised his message to twist what he was saying. It was true that Paul's message had troubled the whole world, for darkness will always be disturbed when light is introduced (see comments on Acts 16:20, 21). True preaching of the Gospel message will bring about drastic changes in every aspect of society.

Acts 17:8, 9

The charge brought against Jason and the other new Christians was that they befriended and welcomed such nation destroyers into their midst. The magistrates do not care that Paul and Silas are not given an opportunity to defend themselves—they are strangers and play no significant role in the political lives of these leaders. It was not justice that these leaders were anxious to secure, but favor from those who had a say on their political futures. It is impossible for a magistrate to give a just ruling by listening to only one side of a dispute (see comments on Acts 16:22). Besides, the rulers and the people of the city did not want any trouble with Rome, who might take away their status of being a free city (though they were under Roman authority they were not directly ruled by Rome). These Jews who are angry with Paul know how to manipulate the leaders—get the crowd angry and on your side and the leaders will do what you want. The decision of the leaders was to cast Paul and Silas out of the city and the way to ensure this was to take security from Jason and the other believers. They placed some kind of claim upon their property and money so that if there was more turmoil in the city or if Paul and Silas did not leave, then their property would be confiscated. The responsibility was placed upon the Christians to make sure peace prevailed in the city. This bond upon Jason and the other believers appears to have been in force for a long time and kept Paul from returning personally to that city. Paul later would write to them saying how he longed to return and visit them, however, Satan prevented him (1 Thes.2:18). It is best to take the reference to "Satan" as applying to those who prevented Paul from returning, namely, the civil authorities and possibly also those Jews who had caused the uproar in the beginning. Paul did, however, send Timothy in his place to encourage the believers in Thessalonica (1 Thes. 3:2.3), since he was not included in this legal ban.

Acts 17:10

Paul and the rest of the team, after being dispatched from Thessalonica, make their way to Berea, which was about 100 km away. Upon arrival, they immediately begin evangelising again in a synagogue.

Acts 17:11

Fair-minded, means that they were "open-minded," not in the sense that they would accept anything that people said, but that they were open to God's truth. Their ultimate authority was the Word of God and they had a sincere desire to know all of God's revelation to them. This also shows that Paul's message was not some new religion, but rested firmly upon the OT. The Scriptures that the Bereans went to search were the OT Scriptures since the NT had not yet been written. God does not leave us to be tossed about by every new idea, for He has given us a comprehensive and complete revelation (we now have far more than the Bereans had). If we bring all our thoughts, plans and doctrines to the light of the Scriptures with "open minds" as the Bereans, we will bring much glory to the Kingdom of God. Many people do not want to know what God has said and others merely want to use the Scriptures to support their own preconceived ideas—neither of these are "noble" in the way the Bereans were. Our prayer should be that God, by His Spirit, would so work in our hearts that we would "receive His Word with eagerness." It is a noble thing to be totally bound to the authority of God's revelation, not trusting human wisdom and understanding that is not guided by the Scriptures. Why does Christ's church find it so difficult to live their lives in total subjection to every Word from God's mouth? Surely it is a sign of the subtlety of sin that still remains in the believer's heart. What is the rational basis for rejecting or ignoring the wisdom from Him who is the source of *all* the treasures of wisdom and knowledge? (Col. 2:3). The truth is, it is not rational! Sin and rebellion are irrational—they do not make sense! It is only the power of the Holy Spirit that can release us into the liberty of total obedience, where we long to know and do all that God has said. May we cast ourselves upon the Lord in desperation and helplessness as we realize that we are unable to bring this about in our strength—it is God's work!

What made these people accept Paul's message? The authority of the OT was the standard that confirmed Paul's message as God's message. Answers are not found by a simplistic casual "dip" into the Bible. There are very few "instant answers," rather, God expects us to diligently search His Word on a regular basis in order to establish His truth on particular issues. Such a diligent study of God's Word has been so neglected by many Christians that they do not even believe God has given revelation concerning many issues, let alone believing they are able to discover what this revelation is.

Each of us is individually responsible to make sure that what we are being taught is the truth. While God will judge those who teach wrong doctrine (Jam.3:1), He will in no way excuse those who follow such teachers. All believers have access to the Word of God and have the Holy Spirit and thus ignorance, at the end of the day, is totally their own fault. It is either a sign of wilful blindness or laziness, resulting in neglecting one's responsibilities. We are God's servants and He has told us what He expects from us and we have all of this contained in the Scriptures. Good teachers are a great benefit to the church, however, bad teachers cannot be used as an excuse if we do not do what God has told us to do. The Bible is not complicated in its basic message and each verse has only one true meaning. Whether an individual or a group of people search out a matter, there is only one message from the Bible that everyone, if they are searching correctly, should arrive at. God has not designed the Scriptures to mean different things for different people, since the meaning of any particular passage is *one* and not many. Thus when someone receives a message from the Scriptures that is not clear and obvious to other believers reading that same text, it is usually because that person is trying to make the Scriptures mean something that they don't.

Acts 17:12

Not everyone in Berea believed, but many Jews did, together with many prominent Greek women and men—these were leading figures and families in the Berean society.

Acts 17:13–15

The Jews from Thessalonica were determined to try and prevent Paul's message from being preached anywhere else. Once again they use deceptive means to incite the crowds to violence. Many people still seek to achieve their goals by causing social chaos. Ultimately, it is fairly easy to spread false rumours about people who are not given the opportunity to defend themselves. Paul being the one singled out by the Jews from Thessalonica is escorted by other believers out of harms way and into a ship. Since Timothy and Silas were not threatened they stayed behind with the new Berean believers and were obviously able to instruct them further in the doctrines of Christ. Other believers from Berea escorted Paul all the way to Athens: a sign of their love, respect and gratitude for his courage in bringing the Gospel to them. On his arrival in Athens, Paul for some unknown reason believes that Timothy and Silas should come and join him immediately. This message was probably sent back with those Bereans who had escorted him to Athens. According to 1 Thes. 3:1–6 it appears as though Timothy and Silas did come to join Paul as requested, yet once again the Lord has not seen fit to give us a detailed account of their movements, since the message He wanted to give us did not require this.

Acts 17:16

Paul is in a city that was the centre of human philosophy and wisdom. Athens was the home of all the world famous philosophers, whose thoughts and ideas still impact our own day, men like Socrates, Plato, Aristotle and many others—these men left behind schools that continued in their footsteps. Athens was a city that prided itself in its intellectual attainments. Paul was not ignorant about these different philosophical ideas. Tarsus, the city Paul was from, was also known for its philosophical schools. Paul had been an excellent student, studying under the famous Gamaliel (Acts 22:3; Gal. 1:14). He had studied Greek culture and philosophy and had read widely in Greek literature. Paul, being thoroughly schooled in the Scriptures and also having a deep grasp of Greek philosophy was the perfect man for a showdown between the best in humanist thinking and the Word of God.

Paul's spirit is disturbed by the idolatry in this pagan city. He would not have been disturbed if these folk were just ignorant of the truth, because then they would have merely been acting according to what they could see. He was disturbed because knowledge about the True God is inescapable and it requires a massive effort to try and suppress what is obvious (Rom. 1:18–24). The multitude of idols that were in this city shows us just how much effort they were prepared to exert in order to try and escape their responsibility to worship the True God. Paul was greatly disturbed by the sight of a city overwhelmed by countless idols. Today, many Christians wouldn't think further than the beauty of these crafted idols, failing to realize the consequences of such idolatry.

Paul was provoked to a Godly jealousy. Remember it was not Jews who were worshipping idols here, but pagans and yet Paul was greatly angered by what he saw. God is a Jealous God (Ex. 34:14). He is the only True God (Deut. 4:35, 39; Isa. 44:6, 8) and Lord of heaven above and earth beneath (1 Chron. 29:11; 2 Chron. 20:6; Dan. 4:35). It is due to these inescapable facts that He forbids any form of idolatry (Ex. 20:3–5; Isa. 42:8)—even among pagans! God demands total allegiance and worship from every person on the earth, for we are all His very own possession (Ps. 24:1). The word used here for Paul's strong reaction to the idolatry is the same one used in the Greek translation of the OT for God's reaction to the children of Israel when they followed strange gods (Num. 16:30;

Deut. 9:8,22; 32:16, 21; Judges 2:12). Paul was repulsed to see people giving man made idols the glory and honour due to God. Our minds need to be renewed so that we too see *all* peoples and nations as belonging to God and accountable to obey His every Word. Paul's response arose from his love and commitment to God and His glory. Paul was thinking God's thoughts after Him. We see a similar reaction in Acts 14:14 when the people of Lystra wanted to sacrifice to him and Barnabas. Paul would not tolerate any kind of idolatry (Rom. 1:21; Gal. 4:8; 1 Cor. 12:2).

Christ has been highly exalted by God (Acts 2:33; Eph. 1:20–23; Phil. 2:9; 1 Pet. 3:22) and all authority in heaven and earth has been given to Him (Matt. 28:18) and this is for one purpose: so that every knee should bow and every tongue confess that Jesus Christ is Lord (Phil. 2:10, 11). Being Lord (Acts 2:36; Rom. 14:9; 1 Cor. 15:27; Heb. 2:8; Rev. 11:15), all nations are expected to come and live in willing subjection to every Word of Christ (Matt. 28:19, 20; Ps. 2:10–12; 22:27, 28). We too should be grieved when Christ is not glorified in any way. We ought to earnestly search out what will glorify God in every area of life and then boldly work towards this goal by word and deed. An individual, family, church, nation, etc., glorifies God by doing everything in the way God has revealed (Matt. 4:4; John 14:23; 2 Cor. 10:5). To live in willing, joyful obedience to everything Christ has said is the ultimate glorification of Christ's Lordship by the people of God. This should burn in our hearts and spur us on through hardships and disappointments, knowing that our labor is not in vain in the Lord. May our sights always be fixed upon this goal: the glory of our Lord and Savior, Jesus Christ and may this be the motivation for all our sacrifice and labour. We exist for Him (Col. 1:16) and may we always rejoice in God's graciousness for giving us life, salvation and the privilege of labouring in His Kingdom. Paul was provoked, because the earth is the Lord's and every creature ought to worship Him, but this city had exchanged the glory of the incorruptible God for idols (Rom. 1:23).

Acts 17:17

Godly anger should lead us into action and Paul therefore gets moving to address the great need in Athens. He starts, as is his custom, with those who profess to be worshipping the True God, however, Paul did not restrict his outreach to only the Jews and God-fearing Gentiles. He also went into the heart of the city, which was not only the central market, but also where the philosophers met to debate and other people met for various reasons. He went there every day and reasoned with the people of Athens, as he reasoned with those who met in the synagogue on the Sabbath. Christianity is very reasonable and can be shown to be the only world view that can account for life as we know it and make sense out of it. Paul would not have been debating about the possibility that Jesus had come and died, but rather that without faith in Jesus' work and resurrection, people would remain under the wrath of God and be controlled by foolish reasoning and darkened minds (1 Cor. 1:18ff.; 2 Cor. 4:4; Eph. 4:18; 1 Tim. 6:5). Paul boldly proclaimed the truth and showed that what these people were holding in its place was worthless and foolish.

Acts 17:18

The two different philosophical schools that Paul ran into in the market place were the Epicureans and the Stoics. These were contrasting philosophical positions that were trying to explain the meaning and purpose of life. The Epicureans said that we can only know what we can learn from our senses. If there was something beyond our senses then it was meaningless to us as knowledge. Thus they denied the possibility of life after death and said there was no need to fear death since we were merely composed of a mass of atoms that dispersed into infinite space at our death. The Epicureans said that pleasure was the goal of life and the perfect life was one free from pain, disturbing passions and superstitious fears. They did not deny the existence of gods, but said they paid no attention to the affairs of people and did not punish disobedient behaviour, thus humans were free to pursue pleasure and satisfaction as life's ultimate goals (Prov. 21:17).

Very simply, the Stoics, while agreeing with the Epicureans that knowledge was only possible through the human senses, believed that mankind's goal was to totally subject himself to whatever happens in life. For the Stoic philosopher, God is identified with the world, thus whatever happens in life is a manifestation of God, so man's greatest goal is to live in harmony with whatever happens. While the Christian believes in the sovereignty of God and that whatever happens is in accordance with God's will, God is not identified with nature and the course of life. God is personal and separate from what happens and His being is never to be identified with what He has created. God has revealed how a Christian should respond to the different situations in life. So while the Christian receives what comes his way as coming because God ordained it, this does not mean that we are to do nothing about it, e.g., if we are in a society where there is no justice, we have a responsibility to work for Godly justice, rather than merely accept things as they are. For the Stoic, happiness is found when he is able to accept and leave everything as he finds it—submission to the unavoidable fate that governs all things.

These different philosophers entered into an extended period of debate with Paul and were insulting his teachings. They called him a "seed-picker," meaning he was a worthless person who picked up scraps in the market place. They were saying that his views were not sound and rational and did not make up a comprehensive world and life view. Paul did not try and make his message appeal to these people. He would not submit his message to their standard of "wisdom" in order to gain their acceptance. All he had, they claimed, were little bits and pieces of meaningless cast-offs (what other people had thrown away). Others accused Paul of promoting foreign gods, which meant they rejected his ideas as foolish and unacceptable (1 Cor. 1:18). Some commentators have suggested that it is possible the Athenians thought Paul was talking about two different gods, one called Jesus and another called Anastasis (the Greek word for resurrection). Paul was not afraid or embarrassed to proclaim what these people needed to hear, even if they mocked and despised him. Paul emphasised man's dilemma: that we are sinners standing under the wrath of God, in desperate need to be reconciled to Him. People are dead in their sins until such time that they are made alive and renewed by the power of God's Spirit so that they might begin living in newness of life in the Kingdom of God (Rom. 4:25; Eph. 2:1, 5; 5:6; Col. 1:13; 2:13; 3:6; 2 Cor. 5:20). The resurrection of Jesus from the dead is clear proof that we can be delivered from sin and death and be assured of our own resurrection unto eternal life. Such preaching is offensive to the natural man and he takes even more offence when he is told that Jesus is the *only one* who can save him from his sins.

Acts 17:19–21

Paul was not on trial, though this might have been a preliminary inquiry to see if formal charges should be laid against him—none ever were. Some people who had heard his teaching and found it to be new and fascinating, asked him to address the very learned group who were considered as experts and leaders of the city in the areas of religion and morals. Those who heard him would have been mostly experts, together with many common folk who were also very intrigued to hear this "new" teaching. In all likelihood they were wanting a fuller explanation of Paul's teaching for he spoke of many things that they had never heard of before. This great occasion, from a human perspective, was most likely, brought about by curiosity more than anything else. Luke clearly tells us that the Athenians were prepared to spend their time talking about or listening to new ideas. This shows their rejection of their real responsibilities, which they replaced with some easy pastime. They wasted much time because of their refusal to work (Prov. 14:23; 21:25). They were after sensationalism rather than sound knowledge (2 Tim. 3:7). The church in our day is very influenced by this kind of thinking: always looking for something new. Some Christians are offended by the way God has made life to be and are forever expecting incredibly exciting events to fill their day-to-day lives—this to them is proof of having a relationship with God. Contrary to this, the back-bone of God's Kingdom is diligent, self-sacrificing hard work, day in and day out. We have all the knowledge we need in the Scriptures. Our task is to apply ourselves, by the grace of God, to finding out what we ought to do and then do it cheerfully for God's glory. Our joy and contentment should be in doing what advances God's Kingdom, not in pleasing our own appetites for excitement, constant change and frivolous debate.

Acts 17:22

All people are religious and Paul points this out to his hearers. No person can escape from the knowledge of the True God—they know Him, His Works and the reality of right and wrong (Rom. 1:19; 2:15). People try to escape from this knowledge in many different ways and one way is to worship idols. Paul says, "You fear the deities" (gods, spirits), thus you have numerous idols, however, this is not a compliment (F.F. Bruce tells us that it was forbidden to use complimentary speech when addressing the Areopagus court). Other translations have, "You are very superstitious." Superstition does not rest upon a solid foundation or reasonable thought, but upon irrational feelings. Paul was addressing his audience with respect, however, he was very straight in his evaluation of what he saw. He was not about to praise them for what they were doing. He certainly was not about to say that their religious devotion was good and all they needed to do was add Jesus to this devotion. Paul made it clear from the outset that their devotion, though intense, was misplaced. Religious zeal is an abomination unless it is in accordance with truth—which is found in the triune God alone.

There is never any justification for getting angry or abusive towards people in such situations, even when they totally reject what you have to say. It is not our own truth and reputations that we are to be worried about. To get upset and angry when defending and proclaiming the Christian faith reveals a great weakness in you. It is the Spirit alone that can open people's eyes and ears and the best way to get people to at least listen to you is not by ranting and raving and spitting in their faces, but by a calm, clear, strong and respectful presentation of the truth (1 Pet. 3:15). If we present the truth of God with anger and frustration, we are trampling over that same truth we claim to be trying to defend. There is no justification for this in God's eyes (2 Tim. 2:24–26). What you want is for people to remember the inescapable truth of your words and not your abusive manners. Paul, though extremely disturbed in his spirit by what he had seen in the city, speaks with calmness and respect, though unashamedly standing upon God's revelation alone. If a person cannot control their tongue then they are extremely dangerous (Jam. 3:5, 6) and controlling one's tongue includes your words as well as your tone—both what you say and *how* you say it.

These people did not know the OT Scriptures, however that did not mean Paul had to change his message. He continued to preach the God of the Bible without apology, as the Creator, sustainer and judge of all things. He did not try to argue with these philosophers about the possibility that such a God exists. Paul was not intimidated by the fact that these people did not accept the Scriptures as God's authoritative Word. He did not try and find a basis of "authority" that both he and the philosophers could agree upon and then from there try and prove that Jesus came and died on the cross. Paul proclaimed reality as God had revealed it and their acceptance or rejection of this did not in any way diminish the authority of the Scriptures. Moreover, Paul knew that the knowledge of the True God was inescapable because the Athenians, like everyone else, were made by God and lived in His creation (Rom.

1:18ff.). Thus, he could tell them, with absolute authority, about God's claims upon their lives and about their need for Jesus Christ. Whether people agree with this or not does not change the fact that this is *reality* and whoever denies it is standing in deception and darkness. Our confidence that the Scriptures are true should not be based upon how many people accept its truths. Rather, our confidence rests upon this one eternal, unshakeable fact: that Christ and His Word are the only foundation for truth in a world full of sin and rebellion against the truth. Without Christ, people have no basis for saying some things are just and others are unjust. If we do not start our thinking with the Scriptures then our understanding of God, mankind, the world, sin, justice, etc., will be distorted and we will not be able to account for the way we find things in this world, or be able to explain the purpose of life or find true fulfilment in what we do.

The people Paul was addressing were highly intelligent in worldly standards, yet we know, from other passages in Scripture how Paul viewed their thinking—they were alienated from God and enemies in their minds towards Him (Col. 1:21). Paul said the wisdom of this world has been made foolish by God (1 Cor. 1:20, 27; 3:18–20); unbelievers walked in the vanity of their minds and were darkened in their understanding because of their ignorance and hardened hearts (Eph. 4:17–24); and unbelievers, in professing themselves to be wise, became fools (Rom. 1:21, 22). When we, as Paul did, stand firmly upon the truth of God's Word (Col. 2:3), we need not fear anyone, no matter how intellectual they are.

Acts 17:23

Paul says that he had carefully searched out and scrutinised the "religious objects" in Athens until he had found something suitable for his purposes. The ancient world often made alters to unknown gods, either to appease their wrath or to thank them for their help in those situations when something occurred for which they had no explanation. Paul does not say, the little bit the Athenians claimed to know about this unknown god was correct and now all he was going to do was increase their knowledge about him. Paul chose this particular altar because it was an excellent example of the Athenians' bankrupt philosophy. The Athenians, in having this altar, were acknowledging that even after their multitudes of idols and different deities, they were religiously unsatisfied and unsure. They acknowledged the reality of yet another god though at the same time claimed that nothing could be known about this god. While claiming that nothing could be known about this god, they were also claiming to know enough about him to be sure that he wanted an altar to be made in his honour. How could they know that this unknown god would tolerate their worship of other gods? How could they know that this unknown god wanted the kind of worship and recognition that they gave to him? How could they be sure he did not merely want to be left alone? They were claiming to worship what they did not know (cf. John 4:22) and in doing so, openly acknowledged their own ignorance.

Unbelievers try to suppress their knowledge of the True God in many different ways and the Athenians were claiming ignorance as their justification for their refusal to bow to God's sovereign demands. Due to their refusal to acknowledge the True God, the Athenians suppressed the inescapable knowledge about Him (Rom.1:18ff.), though to ease their consciences they pretended to be acknowledging Him by making an altar for Him—their ignorance is clearly immoral. Paul says, "This God whom you are aware of and yet ignorant of, I proclaim to you." Paul is going to challenge them to repent of their wilful ignorance. In this he also shows, with apostolic authority, that full knowledge of the True God requires God's own revelation of Himself and does not come from man's imagination and feelings. Paul, authoritatively and without apology, claims to have access to this special revelation.

Acts 17:24

How do you preach about the True God to a people who do not acknowledge the authority of the Scriptures? You preach the truth as it has been revealed in the Scriptures—you tell them about the only True God and His demands upon them. There is no other source of truth, thus Paul, standing upon this foundation preaches to them from the OT. He does not say this is what he is doing, but that is exactly what he does (Nestle's Greek NT has twenty-two OT references that Paul is alluding to in this section from verse 24–32). Paul speaks with absolute authority and does not apologise for it (see how Christ did the same, in my comments on John 8:14).

Paul starts with the fact that the True God made the whole world and everything in it. The world and its orderliness did not come about by some mindless force, or worse still, by accident, but was made and arranged by a Personal God. Such a God has sovereign right over all that He made, because it all belongs to Him (Col. 1:16; Ps. 24:1). For Paul, the fact that God is the Creator, automatically necessitates His Lordship. The Greeks believed that matter was eternal, but Paul says, no, it had a definite beginning, coming from the power of God, who alone is eternal and uncreated. Paul here shows that God was not to be identified with His creation. God made all things and owns all things, yet He is totally separate from all things. The Stoic philosophers identified god with creation (See comments on verse 18). Paul here excludes all other gods, proclaiming there is only one God. Everything else has come into being through this one God and is subject to His authority. Paul, impressing upon them the nature, size and glory of this one God, points out how foolish it was to think that such a God could be contained in structures made by men's hands. Even for the Christian, many times our concept of God is too small and restricting. Our God is the Creator and Lord of the universe and He is intimately related to and concerned about those who love Him. It is this God we are to look to, trust in and rest upon.

The pagans felt they had a certain amount of control over their gods since they were the ones who made and kept the gods' houses. The gods, therefore, were dependent upon the worshipers to a certain degree. The God that Paul preached, on the other hand, cannotbe manipulated in any way by people—He stands sovereign and independent. He is Lord of heaven and earth, not some small temple or tract of land somewhere.

Acts 17:25

It is easy to see how the pagans tried to manipulate their gods, believing that both the worshipers and the one who was worshipped depended upon each other. The True God, however, is perfectly sufficient in and by Himself. He is perfect in every way and this means that He needs nothing from those whom He has created. He did not make us because He needed our worship. The pagans believed they sustained their gods to a certain degree, but Paul says it is utterly foolish to think like this about the True God (Ps. 50:10–12). Everything in the world is totally dependent upon God, not only for its beginning, but also for its continuance (Col. 1:17; Heb. 1:3). God not only created all things, but He alone continues to uphold all things by His own power. Paul is showing these people the foolishness of their thinking with regards to idols and temples.

It is God who gives us life, breath and all things. This is reality and ultimate truth. Everything has only one source, thus having multiple gods, all doing and giving different things, is cast aside by Paul in one stroke. Do we believe that God gives us all we need and do we receive what we have as from His hand? Where does our ultimate trust rest for what we need in this life? Is it in God and His truth? We need to know God's truth and then live according to that by faith, not relying upon our own understanding and wisdom. The just must live by faith in the Word of God (Matt. 4:4; Rom. 1:17). We are to look to Him and totally rely upon Him for all things. If we do this, we must never think that we are now somehow supporting God by our devotion. Some people think that God is lucky to have them in His Kingdom. There is no place for pride in God's Kingdom, because we not only have nothing to offer God, but are totally unable to even sustain ourselves. The God who needs nothing is the only source for everything. Let us worship this God in sincerity and whole hearted devotion.

Acts 17:26

Paul is very far from trying to debate with these philosophers whether such a God as he preached, actually exists. Not only was the reality of the True God assumed as the basis for all of Paul's statements, but Paul claimed that these intelligent people couldn't escape from the knowledge of God, thus he preached as though he was speaking to people who already knew the truths of what he was saying. These people had knowledge of the truth through the natural revelation that surrounded them, however, due to their sin and rebellion they were suppressing this knowledge and in doing so made their thinking futile (Rom. 1:18, 21).

The Athenians were a very proud people, claiming that their direct ancestors were the founders of the Greek nation. They believed they were superior, not only to all other races of people, but also to all other Greeks who had a slightly different ancestry. Paul shows the foolishness of such pride since the whole of the human race descends from the same ancestor. Paul does not mention the OT, yet quotes its teaching with authority and without apology—all people are God's handiwork and descend from Adam. The Greeks called all other races barbarians, however, Paul destroyed this unfounded pride, for no race or people in and of itself, is superior to any other race or people. Such a statement would have been very painful and offensive to these Athenians. How much do not we need this same understanding in our day where each race is filled with deep pride. In God's Kingdom the basis of association and unity rests upon faith, righteousness and truth and there is no justification whatsoever for feeling superior to someone else because you are of a different race to them. Only extremely foolish and ignorant people hold to the notion of racial superiority—there is no Biblical justification for such beliefs. Paul says that not only do we all come from the same source, and have the same sinful nature, but we are all controlled by the same providence of God. God has ordained each nation's boundaries (geographical location) and historical times or dates—God brings them into being and removes them. Moreover, every race or people group needs Christ just as much as any other.

Acts 17:27

Paul says God's providential control of history was designed to bring them to repentance—this clear manifestation of God's goodness should lead people to Him (Rom. 2:4; 2 Pet. 3:9). Paul's argument is that God's control and ordering of all things is obvious and a clear manifestation of His graciousness. Thus, when people refuse to come to God it is because they have blinded themselves. God's providential control and ordering of nations' histories should lead people to seek Him. All nations, no matter where they are on the geographical map, have the opportunity of coming to know God, for all peoples are confronted with the inescapable revelation of God's eternal power and providential control of creation (Rom. 1:19, 20). However, due to mankind's hatred of the truth, he suppresses it, making himself blind and ignorant (Rom. 1:18, 21–23; Eph. 4:17, 18).

Paul has clearly told us elsewhere that the unbeliever does not seek after God (Rom. 3:11, 12, cf. Ps. 14:2, 3). He is not contradicting this position now in the Areopagus speech. The words he uses (verse 27) are difficult to translate into English, but what I believe Paul is showing is how the unbeliever seeks to "satisfy" his religious desires. "If perhaps you might grope for Him and find Him"—the wording here shows that this is an extremely doubtful possibility. Seeking after the True God is actually a none-existent possibility, however, Paul is saying, "As if it were possible to find God in this way?" You do not find the True God by groping around in the darkness, yet this is how the Athenians approached the whole subject. The mere fact that they were groping, meant that they were not looking for the True God. Due to the unbeliever's moral condition, all he can do is stumble around in the darkness and Paul wants to know how you can possibly find God in this way? Thus, these highly intelligent, religiously zealous people are being told that the way they went about seeking for God was nothing but groping around in utter darkness—rather like a blind, ignorant person stumbling around trying to find something he denied existed. In other words, the Athenians' religious achievements, which they were so proud of, were nothing but ignorant guesses and blind stumblings in the darkness. Paul is not praising the Athenians for their religious fervour as though it was a sign of their sincerity in seeking after the True God. Paul is saying that on the one hand there is no excuse for not seeking after the True God, yet despite this awareness of the truth, they merely grope around in the darkness—this groping is one of the ways they try and suppress the truth in unrighteousness (Rom. 1:18).

The fault for this groping in the darkness is not God's, but man's wilful suppression and perversion of what is very clear. Paul shows this at the end of verse 27 when he says God is not difficult to find, however, the unbeliever is nothing but a blind, stumbling fool— and that, because he wants to be. The truth is, God is so near to us that He is inescapable (Paul is talking here of the most intimate closeness possible), thus what this highlights, is the moral pollution of sin and its effect upon the unbeliever's heart. Deep down in the unbeliever's heart he knows the True God and he has to base a certain amount of his thinking upon this reality, however, at the same time he suppresses this awareness and tries to substitute it with some vain ideas of his own. God is not far from any person in the world, yet when it comes to the True God, people talk and act as though it was impossible to know anything about Him.

Acts 17:28

Paul now supports his last statement with this assertion, showing just how close to us God is. Paul is not talking about our mystical union with Christ, but rather showing our utter dependence upon God for everything. Every aspect of our existence is totally dependent upon God's sustaining power and providence—all things are upheld by the power of His Word and in Him all things consist (Heb. 1:3; Col. 1:17). Paul, very knowledgeable in Greek literature, is not appealing to the pagan poets to support the theological reality that we are totally dependent upon God—this dependence is an undebatable and inescapable fact. What Paul is doing is showing the inability of the unbeliever to suppress this truth. These poets confirm Paul's argument, that even in the very act of suppressing the truth, they show they are aware of it. Such quotes are clear evidence of the unbeliever's deep awareness of the truth and of his guilt for trying to pervert this truth he cannot escape from. Despite making such perceptive statements, these people continued to grope around in the darkness with respect to the True God. They also condemned themselves, for their statements showed both their knowledge of the truth and also their suppression of this truth in unrighteousness and this is the point Paul was anxious to push home. No matter how much the unbeliever tries to escape from the truth he cannot suppress it completely, thus his words and actions will often reveal his awareness of this truth in his heart of hearts.

When people say there is a difference between "right" and "wrong," they are testifying to the reality of the True God (Rom. 2:15), even though they probably reject God's definition of right and wrong.

Acts 17:29

Paul continues to evaluate the Athenians' philosophy of life and to expose it as woefully inadequate. He says, "Though you will agree that we are the offspring of God, nevertheless, you then make idols out of different things and give these objects divine honours" (17:29 paraphrased). Paul asks, how can a cold, lifeless object that has been made by a person, be worshipped as man's maker, protector and provider? God's image is found in His creative works and man is the preeminent one among these (Gen. 1:27). God alone can show His image in this way and therefore we are forbidden by Him from trying to image Him by making any kind of idol (Ex. 20:4). If we are God's offspring (imaging Him), then how, Paul wants to know, can we call these idols, made of stone and precious metals, god? How can we make our god out of something that has itself been created by God? As God's offspring, surely intelligent people cannotseriously believe that a metallic idol bears any resemblance to God? These idols cannoteven do justice to who man is, how much less to the creator of the universe? (Isa. 40:18–20; 44:9ff.). This is a devastating critique of the Athenian's position and there is no chance of recovery. What they need to do is repent of their foolish suppression and perversion of the truth. Paul, without apology is telling them, in the light of God's revelation, that their concepts of God are immoral and they ought not to think of Him in that way. Paul is preaching to pagans, yet he is talking to them about the Creator of all things and rebuking their *idolatry*. All people are responsible to give God the honour and respect that He deserves and all who do not are without excuse.

Every philosophy or view of life, other than Christianity, will have internal contradictions. People are unable to fully suppress the knowledge of God that surrounds them and indwells them. Thus, while they might vigorously deny the existence of the God that Paul preached, in order to live in this world they have to live according to much of His truth. The unbelievers' actions and words will constantly reveal his utter dependence upon God, even while he might be in the process of denying his dependence. There is one truth, there is one God and there is only one view of life that can be consistently followed in this world. We mustn't apologise for the Christian faith and we mustn't think that unbelievers know nothing about its truth—they are working very hard trying to suppress this truth. Our responsibility is to testify about the truth, with meekness and fear, for it is the truth that is sharper than any two edged sword (Heb. 4:12) and it is the truth that the Holy Spirit uses to convict people of sin, righteousness and judgment (John 16:8).

Acts 17:30

It is wrong to think about God in any way other than according to truth. God alone is able to reveal Himself and tell us what He is like, thus the only way people are allowed to think about Him is in line with His revelation of Himself—this alone is truth. To have any other kinds of thoughts about God is proof of extreme wickedness and suppression of the truth. The revelation of the True God is inescapable (Rom. 1:18ff.), thus, to have vain thoughts about Him shows wilful blindness, arising from your moral perversion and this is inexcusably sinful.

Paul has been showing the Athenians that their way of worshipping God was perverse and then calls such worship a "time of ignorance." Paul does not excuse the Athenians by saying they were ignorant, because if he did that he would be contradicting what is written in other parts of the Bible. This ignorance is inexcusable. The same word is used in Eph. 4:18; 1 Pet. 1:14; Acts 3:17 and is also used as equivalent for "sin" in the Greek translation of the OT. Paul talked of his former life when persecuting the church as a time of ignorance (1 Tim. 1:13), yet he in no way excused his guilt, calling himself the "chief of sinners" because of his actions in this matter (1 Tim. 1:15, cf. 1 Cor. 15:9).

Paul says something very similar in Acts 14:16, 17 (see comments) and there we have shown that this "ignorance" arises from a wilful suppression of the truth. Here in Acts 17:30, Paul is not saying that God is unconcerned about the Gentile's past sins or that He ignored these sins in a way that they were not accountable for them. When God's chosen people walked in sin, God sent them prophets and preachers of righteousness who called on the people to repent and be reconciled to God. When God "overlooked" the sins of the Gentiles it was not that He did not condemn them for their sin (for all sin is worthy of condemnation), but that He did not immediately send people to them calling on them to repent. God's focus in the time of the OT was *primarily* upon Israel and therefore He was constantly pointing out her shortcomings and exhorting her to walk in the light of His truth, while appearing to ignore the wicked ways of the Gentiles.

The Athenians had never before been confronted by a preacher of righteousness sent from the True God. Paul's explanation for this was because God had previously overlooked their rebellion. The reason God planned things to work out as they had done in history, with His focus being upon Israel, is hidden in His secret counsel and we have no right to demand an explanation from Him or find fault with His plan. Now, however, God was sending His preachers into all the world because all the world was expected to bow to Jesus Christ and walk in His truth. The message of the Gospel is to be proclaimed to every tribe, nation and person—all are to bring their thoughts into line with God's Word (Matt. 28:19, 20). It is through Christ, the Great Prophet, that this call of repentance goes to everyone. All people must now submit to the clear and authoritative revelation of God that has been fully revealed in Christ. There is no justification for any kind of idolatry, anywhere in the world. The prophetic message had gone out previously into all of Israel, but now God had sent it into the whole world: the message is, repent and embrace righteousness (Titus 2:11, 12)—which is found in Christ alone (Rom. 3:21ff.). It is only God who is able to bring us to and keep us on the right path and if He does not graciously do this, we will be forever lost (Eph. 2:8). Failure to repent, however, is due to stubborn rebellion against God.

Acts 17:31

Why should these Athenian's repent? Because God's judgment is inescapable, coming and applicable to the whole world—no one will be exempt. The day for this judgment has been fixed in the heavenlies and was therefore going to happen. By calling on the Athenians to repent, Paul was highlighting their guilt and sin. By warning them of the coming judgement, Paul was saying that they were morally accountable for their actions and false views of God—which were deserving of His wrath. The message of the Gospel is the same for every person in the world, Jew or Gentile, rich or poor, leaders or slaves—all have sinned and come short of the glory of God, are under His wrath and therefore need to repent if they are to escape His judgement.

The day of God's judgment was clearly proclaimed throughout the OT (e.g., Ps. 9:8; 96:10, 13; 98:9, etc.) and widely taught in the NT also (Acts 10:42; Rom. 2:5, 16; 2 Tim. 4:1, 8). Paul now repeats what Jesus Himself had taught, that judgment rested in the Son's hand (John 5:22–29). Paul, however, does not mention Christ's name, but merely says this authority had been given to a Man. This Person had been designated by God as the only one able to carry out the awesome task of perfect, righteous judgement.

Christ the Man, had earned this authority by His self-sacrificial life and perfect obedience to the will of the Father. After His resurrection, Jesus proclaimed that *all* authority in heaven and in earth had been given to Him (Matt. 28:18). Many hundreds of years before Christ came, Daniel saw Him ascending to the right hand of the Father where "to Him was given dominion and glory and a kingdom, that all peoples, nations, and languages should serve Him" (Dan. 7:14). This was completely fulfilled in Acts 1:9 (see too comments on Acts 2:33).

The standard of judgment is known—God's righteousness. The day of judgment has been ordained in God's secret counsel and is inescapable. The Person who will do the actual judging has also been ordained by God. All of these are fixed and unmoveable. All the necessary requirements for such a judgment to take place are eternally secured in God's providence. This is one of the certainties of life—everyone will stand before the Righteous Judge and everything that they have done will be evaluated by the righteousness of God. Nothing will remain hidden, nothing will be covered up and no one will be able to twist the facts. Perfect justice will be measured out and people will receive exactly what they deserve from this Man who has been appointed by God—"Vengeance is mine, I will repay says the Lord" (Rom. 12:19).

Paul is not here trying to prove the resurrection, but rather stating it as a fact with absolute authority (see too, Rom. 1:4). Paul is using the resurrection as proof that Jesus has the qualifications and authority to fulfill His role as judge. Christ's resurrection is proof of God's perfect justice in the world and that it will be according to this same justice that Jesus will judge every person and nation. There is absolute security in the fact that our universe is run according to principles of unchanging justice. Christ's resurrection proves that He is without sin, thus though He received the wrath for sin in our place, ultimately death and hell could not hold Him (Acts 2:24) and therefore cannottouch those who are His (1 Cor. 15:55–57; Heb. 2:14, 15).

The resurrection is the final seal showing God's Divine acceptance of Christ's teaching, life and authority. Jesus had claimed to be the one who would judge all people. Paul says proof that Jesus is indeed qualified to do this is seen in the fact that He rose from the dead. God assures us that Jesus is the Judge by raising Him from the dead. The resurrection of Jesus is the heart of the Gospel message giving a message of blessing and hope to those who believe and a message of death and condemnation to those who do not believe. It is only in the resurrection of Christ that we can hope for eternal life—if Christ did not rise from the grave then our faith would be useless (1 Cor. 15:14). Because He rose, those who believe in Him have a strong confirmation that they also will be raised from the grave. Because He rose, those who do not believe in Him have a strong confirmation that they will be found wanting before the Righteous Judge and condemned. The resurrection is proof of the great dividing line between those who are saved and those who are lost. The resurrection is inescapably clear proof of the coming judgement!

Acts 17:32

The idea of someone rising from the dead was nonsense to these philosophical people. One of their gods, Apollo, is reported to have "said" that once a person dies there is no resurrection. Paul, aware of this, preached the truth without apology or compromise—here the mocking and sneering was very open, yet it did not deter Paul. We are not to try and change the message of the Gospel because people scoff at different aspects of its message. People can call the Gospel foolish if they want (1 Cor.1:18), nevertheless, it alone is the eternal truth and foundation of all knowledge. Scoffing at the message of salvation found in Christ is proof of a stubborn, rebellious heart that refuses to repent and take heed of the warning of coming judgement. The warning is a sign of God's graciousness in reaching out to sinners (John 3:17; Rom. 2:4) and should not be treated lightly (2 Cor. 6:2; Heb. 3:15). The fact that the day of judgment was still coming, meant that the present time was a period of grace and salvation—there was still time to repent and thus escape the wrath of judgment day. People need salvation because they are sinners and deserve punishment, but when this is pointed out to them they will, more often than not, despise and mock you. It is God who grants repentance and therefore it is foolish to try and win people to Christ on their own terms. Christ demands total surrender which requires a total change of your most fundamental beliefs about God, man, sin, judgement, what is the basis for truth and authority, what is the source of all knowledge, etc. Only the Holy Spirit can do this in a person's heart, so trying to get an unbeliever to agree with unimportant details is a waste of time if his "first beliefs" (see *Faith and Reason*, chapters 1 to 3) are not changed. People interpret the details by their first beliefs and if these are not sound then their conclusion about everything else cannot be right.

Acts 17:33, 34

With the disruption and outburst of scoffing, Paul departs from the Areopagus. There was still some interest among the crowd and some were even converted. One was a very significant person, apparently one of the twelve judges of the Athenian Court—Dionysius. Not much is known about the lady that is named. Church tradition tells us that Dionysius became the first Bishop of the church in Athens. There appear to have been only a few converts in Athens, however, this does not mean Paul's visit and efforts were a failure. It is God who is working all things according to His purposes and whether many or few are converted, our responsibility to bear witness to the truth remains the same. Paul had presented a comprehensive picture of God and His truth—He is Creator, Law-giver, Judge and Savior. Paul did not leave out the message of the cross in this message, because the cross is inseparable from the resurrection (Rom. 8:34). Whether Jew or Gentile, their needs are the same. Whether Jew or Gentile, the message is the same—God, the Creator of the universe, demands sole and complete worship from every creature and complete obedience to His every Word. Anything less than this will receive the righteous judgment of Christ. Proof that Christ has the authority to carry out this judgment is clearly seen in the fact that God raised Him from the dead. No more proof is needed as nothing could be clearer. If you reject this clear proof you will not accept anything else, because your first beliefs are perverting the truth which is inescapably clear and obvious.

Acts 18:1

Corinth was a very vibrant commercial city, being ideally situated to serve as a link for the sea routes to the west and east and for the land routes to the north and south (F.F. Bruce). It was also a city of great moral perversity, as is made clear from historical evidence and Paul's letters to the Corinthians.

Acts 18:2

We are not told about the conversion of Aquila and his wife Priscilla, thus we do not know if they were already believers when they met Paul, so it is best to leave this issue unsettled. We do know that they became very strong, knowledgeable and influential people in the Kingdom of God after this time with Paul. Aquila and Priscilla had been staying in Rome at the time when the Emperor, Claudius expelled all Jews from that city. The Roman historian of that time, Suetonius, tell us that Caesar banished the Jews from Rome because they were "indulging in constant riots at the instigation of Chrestus" (F. F. Bruce). Many assume that this is a reference to the trouble that arose between the Christians and the Jews over Christ's claims of being the Messiah. It is not really possible to be absolutely sure what was creating the disturbance among the Jews in Rome, nevertheless it was large enough to bring about their expulsion. When Paul arrived in Corinth, we are told that he came to Aquila and Priscilla. This does not prove that they were believers, though they might have been.

Acts 18:3

Priscilla and Aquila were tentmakers or workers of leather. The main type of cloth they worked with was made from goats hair and was good for making waterproof shelters like coats, curtains or small travelling tents. To support his missionary endeavours Paul needed to earn a living, thus he worked very hard. He did receive some support from the Philippian church (Phil. 4:14, 15), however, this was obviously not enough to fully support him and not wanting to be a burden to the Corinthians, he laboured to keep himself (2 Cor. 11:8, 9). Paul taught that those who labor in the work of preaching and teaching the Word of God, should be supported by that work (Gal. 6:6; 1 Cor. 9:4–14; 1 Tim. 5:17, 18, cf. Matt. 10:10). However, in these early days Paul did not demand this right. Paul's desire was to spread the Gospel and he did not want to hinder this in any way. Thus, where he thought he might have been a burden or where false accusations might have been thrown at him about his motive for preaching, he would rather earn his support in a way other than from struggling or immature converts (1 Thes. 2:9; 2 Thes. 3:8; 2 Cor. 11:7–9).

Acts 18:4

The truth of God is very reasonable and is to be addressed to the whole of a person, thus their mind is not to be left out. Much of modern Christianity has left out the importance of the mind and has merely appealed to people's emotions. Christianity, however, is the only philosophy of life that can account for and make sense out of the whole of life—it is the only comprehensive world view that exists. All other world views contradict themselves when they seek to apply their espoused beliefs to the real world situations they find themselves in. The Gospel of Christ must not be reduced to merely an emotional appeal, but must be shown to be the only rational basis for living in this world. Sin and rebellion are not merely emotional attitudes, but arise from conscious moral decisions made by people and these "rational" decisions (they are really irrational), need to be challenged and exposed for what they are—foolishness! (1 Cor. 1:19, 20; Ps. 10:13; 14:1). Sin is a moral choice supported by reasoned arguments and the truth needs to tear down these "supports" (2 Cor. 10:5). Paul was busy doing just that, every Sabbath in the Synagogue.

Acts 18:5

I am once again following the Ecclesiastical Text here. I do not believe that this verse says that Paul was given extra courage and zeal to preach the Gospel *because* Silas and Timothy had arrived. Rather, I believe it teaches that when Silas and Timothy arrived, they found Paul in a certain state, namely, constrained by the Holy Spirit, or seized in his spirit, solemnly declaring that the Christ is Jesus (the same word is used in 2 Corinthians 5:14 where the love of Christ exerted a continual pressure upon Paul to proclaim the good news). The Jews would have agreed on the need for a Messiah and that such a person was prophesied in the Scriptures, Paul however, was showing them that the Messiah is Jesus. This truth has to capture our hearts with an unmoveable zeal, just as Paul was captured. We must think and talk about Christ, believing that He alone is the source of all wisdom and truth (Col. 2:3), that He alone is the source of salvation and that if people do not believe in Him then they cannot be saved. If people do not embrace Christ by faith and seek forgiveness for their sins in His completed work on the cross, then they will spend eternity in hell (Ps. 2:12; Matt. 25:41; John 3:18, 36; 8:24; 16:8; Acts 4:12; 1 Thes. 1:10; 5:9; Heb. 2:3; Rev. 6:16, 17). Christ is not merely one of the many options available to people to fulfill their religious desires—He is the only one who can deliver sinners from the wrath of God. There is only one basis for salvation and that is Christ and Him alone.

Acts 18:6

The Jews united and rose up to resist and overthrow this teaching Paul was giving. Their blasphemy was directed against Christ and their strong resistance was against Paul, thus there was nothing he could do. Paul shaking his garments is a symbolical act showing two things, firstly, that he did not want to be contaminated with their stubborn rebellion against God (similar to shaking the dust off ones feet in Matt. 10:14 and Acts 13:51). Secondly, it testified to the fact that Paul could not be held responsible for their condemnation. Those who refuse to believe in Christ destroy themselves and therefore their blood rests upon their own heads—to reject the Gospel is to commit suicide in the ultimate sense. Paul is alluding to the passage in Ezk. 33:1–5 and says in the light of his testimony to them, he is now guiltless of the judgment that would come upon them—they alone would be blamed for their destruction. What hope can there be for those who ridicule and forcibly drive out of their midst the only remedy there is for their serious condition?

God has laid a charge upon us to testify to the truth and spread the good news of the Gospel to those we meet. In our evangelism, we ought to be motivated by love for the Lord, compassion for those who are dead in their trespasses and sins and awareness of our responsibility before God to warn sinners about the consequences of their rebellion (2 Cor. 5:14; Rom. 9:1–4; Ezk. 3:18). May the Holy Spirit work in our hearts that we too might find ourselves *constrained* to share the good news with others. May He make us aware of our responsibility to point the lost to Christ and enable us to do this in humility, motivated by deep compassion and love for those we share with.

God will not, however, constantly strive with man's hardness of heart and rebellion (Gen. 6:3), for there comes a time when they will no longer have access to the means of grace to repent (see comments on John 7:34). If people do not respond appropriately to the light they receive, then that light will be removed from their presence (cf. Rev. 2:5, see too Prov. 29:1; Zech. 7:11–14). We are to seek the Lord while He may be found (Isa. 55:6). We are not to think it is a sign of great Christian virtue to constantly strive with those who blaspheme and abuse the Gospel. There comes a time when such people are to be left to themselves and their destruction. If we have proclaimed the truth to them, we have done our duty and they alone bear the guilt for their eternal death. The great apostle says his efforts in Corinth would now be spent on the Gentiles (see comments on Acts 13:46).

Acts 18:7

Paul moved from the synagogue into a house, which happened to be next door to the synagogue. Paul, continuing to preach so close to the synagogue, angered the Jewish leadership greatly. This house belonged to a person who was a God-fearer and had probably come to believe in Christ through the ministry of Paul. His house now became Paul's preaching point and many people, both Jews and Gentiles, continued coming to hear him.

Acts 18:8

Crispus, the ruler of the synagogue, together with his household came to believe in Christ (see comments on Acts 16:15, 31–34). This probably further angered the Jewish leaders, but it would have encouraged the Gentiles and other Jews who had come to believe in Christ. There were also a great number of other people coming to faith in Christ which gave rise to a situation whereby Paul's life was endangered by those who hated the Gospel and resented his labours.

Acts 18:9–11

Paul had been harassed wherever he has preached boldly in the name of Christ and here in Corinth his preaching was no different. Everyone needs encouragement in their labours for the Lord and Paul was no exception. Paul had endured much persecution and danger on this journey already: in Philippi he had been beaten with rods and jailed and in Thessalonica and Berea he had been rushed out of the city to avoid problems. Remember on his first missionary journey a violent attempt was made upon Paul's life in Iconium (Acts 14:5) and he was then stoned and left for dead in Lystra (Acts 14:19). I do not believe Paul was afraid for his life in Corinth and therefore Jesus said these words to him. Paul's words in 1 Corinthians 2:3 refer to his feeling of inadequacy for the task that lay before him. He did not come to the Corinthians in self-confidence, but rather was very aware of his own inability to fulfill the task God had given him to do. Paul was not afraid of any man, yet needed to be encouraged by the Lord that fruit *would* come from his efforts. Jesus tells him that He has many people in this city and thus Paul must keep on preaching so that they will come to repentance. The Lord tells Paul that despite the opposition and threats that would come his way, he was to remain in Corinth. Jesus confirms to Paul His promises to protect and stand with us in all that we do for the glory of God. We need to be reminded about these promises from the Lord often and stand upon them as we boldly make known the truth in our dark generation (Ps. 23:4). Fear will hinder us from standing where Christ stands (see comments on John 12:26). If we are proclaiming the cause of heaven, we have no reason to be afraid. When we proclaim the Word of God boldly, the power to bring about results does not depend upon our eloquence, but on the power of the Spirit (1 Cor. 2:4).

God had purposed to use Paul as the one through whom many would come into the Kingdom, so the Lord tells him that the plans and schemes of the enemy would not be able to hinder him in any way. Paul is encouraged that his efforts for the Lord in Corinth would succeed and bring much glory to God. There were many people living in Corinth who had been ordained, in eternity, to believe the message of the Gospel and be saved. In this city of extreme vice, whose reputation was known throughout the known world as a city where sexual morality hardly existed, the Lord was going to save many people. The Lord does often encourage us by success, however, we shouldn't be overcome if our efforts do not see immediate rewards. All that we must be concerned about is that we are found faithfully doing what the Lord has told us to do. How much fruit comes from our efforts is not to be our concern—this rests in God's hands. What Jesus told Paul, namely, not to be afraid, to speak, not to keep silent and that He would be with him, are truths that we can stand upon too. May we not be fearful and may our hands not become weary as we look to Christ for all we need to glorify Him and finish the course He has given us to run.

Paul then remained in Corinth for eighteen months, giving intense instruction to these new converts. Even after this we see, through Paul's letter to the Corinthian church, that there were still many problems among these believers. It can be a long, laborious and often frustrating task to instruct the people of God in the Lord's ways. However, when we depend upon the grace of God and seek His Kingdom in all we do, we will not only succeed in our efforts but find our labor very rewarding. Christ is to be the focus at all times. In Him we must begin, continue and end.

Acts 18:12

Gallio was the son of a famous public speaker who also taught others to speak publicly. Gallio's brother was the famous Stoic philosopher/statesman, Seneca—who instructed the young Nero Caesar, the Roman emperor. Nero later, after his reign had turned into a ruthless tyranny, forced both Seneca and Gallio to commit suicide. A tyrant is afraid of and threatened by everyone.

At the time of this incident in Acts, Gallio was new in office. History tells us that Gallio was a man who sought to uphold truth and justice and he was a very likeable, tolerant and kind person. His philosopher brother, Seneca, spoke highly of him saying, no one is as pleasant to one person as Gallio is to everyone.

The Jews, in great unity, rose up and accused Paul before Gallio as he sat in the judgment seat (this was a raised platform from where he would judge cases).

Acts 18:13

The Jewish religion had been made legal in the Roman empire, thus Jews were free to worship in their own way—Judaism was an authorised religion. These Jews who were accusing Paul were saying that he was preaching a religion that was in violation of the Jewish religion and was therefore in violation of Roman law. The Jews rejected Jesus as the Messiah and thus said Paul's religion was not Jewish. Since he taught people to worship God in a way different to the accepted Jewish way, he could not receive the same freedom, privileges and protection that the Jews had. They were not asking Gallio to judge according to Jewish law, but according to Roman law and find Paul's doctrine to be an unauthorised religion within the Roman empire. These Jews were presuming that if they came with a united voice saying Paul's doctrine was not authentic Judaism, then Gallio would accept their word about this, ban Paul's doctrine and prosecute him according to Roman law.

Acts 18:14, 15

Gallio, however, took offence at this invasion of his court, realising that it was not a simple matter to get drawn into the finer details of these different religious arguments. He saw this as a waste of his time and a distraction from his many pressing duties. Gallio totally rejected these charges even before Paul defended himself. He said that if Paul had committed something immorally wicked and unjust or had violated someone's rights, then he would most gladly have judged the case. However, Gallio said no legal or moral wrong had been done, but rather what they had brought to him was a disagreement better handled within the synagogue by the Jews themselves.

Gallio, in great ignorance, rejects God's law, seeing it as irrelevant to the purposes of justice. Gallio was someone who had a high regard for justice and yet he rejected the only sure foundation there is for real justice to flourish. Although he did not act unjustly in this particular incident, he was sinning by despising God's law and restricting its use to a very small and insignificant area of life. If man makes himself the final authority when it comes to making laws, then he can change those laws as and when it suits him. This means that whoever has the greatest power and ability to influence the law making process is in a position to manipulate things for his own ends. When people reject God's law and authority they are living in rebellion against Him and therefore it is foolish to think that such people can be trusted. It is extremely naive to believe that those who reject God's Word for all of life will put in its place a law system that seeks to establish truth and justice. Good intentions are not enough, for there is only one basis for true justice to triumph and that is to make all our laws and decisions according to God's Word. Justice does not arise by speaking about justice, but by acting and thinking in line with God's justice. God's justice is defined by Him and any action that is not in submission to His revelation cannot produce true, long-term justice. The concepts of justice, even from "good" and "sincere" people, are filled with the seeds of injustice. Thus no matter how high the ideals of a society might be, if they allow man's wisdom to be the source of their law and justice, they *will* reap a mass of injustice in time. To seek to live by words other than those that proceed from the mouth of God is a journey to self destruction. To try and build a just social order apart from God and His law will ultimately reap a state of lawlessness.

Despite having said this, it is far better to have a Gallio ruling you than a Nero. Gallio was desiring to rule by a form of justice and truth, whereas Nero cared absolutely nothing about such terms, seeking only his own pleasure and doing whatever his passions desired.

Acts 18:16

This was not a violent driving out from the "court room," rather, Gallio was making it very plain that he wanted nothing more to do with this kind of uproar and would not hear any further arguments on this case. The Jews' accusations against Paul had been thrown out of court and that ruling was final!

Acts 18:17

This is a difficult verse and poses many problems to commentators. Firstly because some translations merely say, "Then they all turned on Sosthenes." Other translations say, "Then all the Greeks took Sosthenes." The debate is whether it was the Jews who beat up Sosthenes or whether it was the Greeks? I follow as a rule the Ecclesiastical text of the Greek NT and thus believe that it was the Greeks who beat the Jewish leader of the synagogue, who was probably the main spokesperson laying the charges against Paul. This outbreak of violence shows the racial tension that existed between the Jews and Greeks. Remember there had been recent turmoil in the Roman Empire which many blamed upon the Jews and even the Emperor himself believed this and had the Jews banished from Rome (Acts 18:2). It appears as though the Greeks in Corinth did not take kindly to this recent uproar and after Gallio dismissed the case so quickly and strongly their anger boiled over into violence. They saw Sosthenes as the ring leader and wanted to show their own disapproval of the Jews' actions, however, the Greeks' actions were also wrong and cannot be justified.

The next difficulty about this verse is to think that Gallio would allow such an unlawful act of violence to take place not only before his eyes, but at the very place where he sat to administer justice. The historical evidence is that he was a man who was concerned about the rule of law and justice and yet after wisely dismissing the case brought against Paul, he appears to turn a blind eye to an act of brutal injustice (mob "justice"). The Ecclesiastical text has a slightly different word here to the other texts and the meaning appears to do more justice to what we know about Gallio. The other texts have the word *melw*, which means Gallio took no notice of this injustice, whereas the Ecclesiastical text has *mellw*, which translates to mean Gallio did not *intend, purpose, design* or *have in mind* this violent outburst against Sosthenes. We are not told whether Gallio had left the judgment area or not, before this violence broke out, but would he have tolerated such disrespect for his office if he had been present? To turn a blind eye towards acts of injustice would have undermined his office as judge. What we know of his character does not support this kind of indifference towards injustice. It appears that Luke's statement at the end of verse 17 is an attempt so show that Gallio was not accountable for the injustice that took place in his court over this matter.

It certainly appears as though Gallio's ruling on Paul's doctrine had far reaching implications for the spreading of the Christian faith. Wherever these missionaries went in the Roman empire they would receive the same protection as the Jews, since their faith was a "legal religion" as far as Rome was concerned. It is very probable that other Roman judges would have heard about Gallio's ruling and taken that as a precedent. Such a ruling Paul would have mentioned to others as he moved around the Empire and this probably played a major role in preventing a serious conflict between Rome and the Christian religion in these early days. Maybe this is why Paul later appealed to Caesar in order to get a just ruling with respect to what he was teaching, when the judge, Festus, was more concerned about pleasing the Jews than making a just judgment (Acts 25:9, 10). The Lord had promised Paul that nothing would happen to him whilst in Corinth and he had held onto this by faith even in the midst of what seemed like a dangerous situation. A great victory had been wrought for the church in Greece through Gallio's ruling and the church began to increase throughout this area.

Acts 18:18

Paul, now protected by Roman law, remained some time in Corinth, strengthening the church and preaching the Gospel. In all, we know Paul stayed eighteen months in Corinth (Acts 18:11), and these "many days" are included in this period. Paul is now joined by Priscilla and Aquila who become very influential people in the early church and close friends of Paul (Acts 18:26; Rom. 16:3; 1 Cor. 16:19).

I do not think this was a Nazarite vow. Vows were common among the Jews (e.g., Gen. 28:20; 1 Sam. 1:11; 2 Sam. 15:7) and although they are not commanded by God, the Word does say that if you make a vow then you are bound to fulfill it (Num. 30:2; Deut. 23:21–23; Eccl. 5:4), thus one is warned against making rash vows (Prov. 20:25). Vows were made either as a way of giving thanks for God's past protection, healing, blessings, etc., or as a petition for His future protection, help, blessings, etc. Whether this was the end of Paul's vow or the beginning is debated since it is believed that one's hair was shaved sometimes at the beginning of a vow and other times at the end. Paul was merely acting in a way he was accustomed to and this expression of gratitude and devotion to God was in line with his Jewish culture and traditions. A vow reveals a person's realization of complete dependence upon the will of God. Vows are only to be made to God and are to be governed by His revelation. It is rebellion to vow what is contrary to our calling and not within our power to keep, i.e., to vow to remain celibate when God has not given that gift, is to tempt Him. We are not to vow to people, but rather our yes must be yes and our no must be no (Matt. 5:37; James 5:12)—our words must have integrity. All we need to know in order to please God has been revealed to us in the whole of the Bible and our greatest service is to walk according to this revelation. There is no need to make all kinds of vows in order to please God—He hasn't commanded them. Simple obedience to His every Word (to what He *has* commanded) is what He wants. Vowing does not enhance your acceptance or standing before God, however, if you feel you really want to make a vow, make it carefully and make sure you keep it or else you will receive God's displeasure, for God *has* commanded us to keep what we voluntarily vow to Him. If a person made a vow today, there is no Biblical rule that says they would need to shave their head.

Acts 18:19

Paul had been forbidden by the Holy Spirit from going to Asia (and thus Ephesus) in Acts 16:6. However, now the timing is right as far as God is concerned, and so Paul can at last reach this major city with the Gospel. Priscilla and Aquila remained in the city of Ephesus when Paul continued on to Jerusalem. This verse does not say that only Paul went into the synagogue to reason with the people there. The contrast is between those who remained in Ephesus and Paul who was not going to remain. Priscilla and Aquila were very much involved in the work of establishing a church in this city and that was the reason they were left there.

Acts 18:20, 21

Paul's message was well received by the Jews in Ephesus and they wanted him to stay and teach them more, however, there was a sense of urgency upon Paul to get to Jerusalem. I do not believe that Paul's urgency to get to Jerusalem was connected to the ceremonial law and his desire to keep this. I believe it was a feast that Paul wanted to be in time for, however, Paul's desire was to meet with those who would be coming to Jerusalem at that time—probably other apostles and recognised leaders of the church. Luke is very brief about these details, but the rest of the NT certainly does not give you the impression that Paul was one who emphasised the importance of the ceremonial observance of the law after Christ.

Paul, knowing God was in total control of his movements, tells
these people that he would return to them again, if the Lord
allowed (cf. James 4:15). Our desires and every decision should be
submitted to the sovereign working of God in our lives: "A man's
heart plans his way, but the Lord directs his steps" (Prov. 16:9, see
too 3:5, 6; 19:21; 20:24; Jer. 10:23).

Acts 18:22

It is believed by most commentators that Paul's "going up" was to
Jerusalem, as this was the common way of referring to the "holy
city." Luke is extremely brief, only saying that Paul greeted the
church in Jerusalem and then passed on to Antioch, the church that
had sent him out on these missionary journeys (Acts 15:40). It is
possible that this verse supports our view as to why Paul wanted to
attend the feast, namely, so he might meet as many people as possible in Jerusalem and testify on how the Lord was working among
the Gentiles. The last time Paul had been in Jerusalem was to sort
out the "Gentile question" where he met with the apostles and
elders (Acts 15:6). Paul on his missionary journey after this great
conference, had instructed the Gentile churches about the Jerusalem ruling (Acts 16:4) and it does not seem far fetched that he
wanted to share with the Jerusalem leadership how these decrees
were received by the Gentiles. The feast was the best chance of finding many of these leaders together in the same place.

Acts 18:23

It appears as though Paul once again spent some time ministering
to the church in Antioch (Some think that Paul could have stayed as
long as six months in Antioch before he set out again). Paul was
ever anxious to see how his "children in the Lord" were doing and
longed to impart more instruction to them—Paul had founded
these churches (Acts 13 and 14). He sets out taking the same route
that he had done on the previous journey (Acts 16:1–6). Paul
strengthens these churches by further instructing them in the truth
of God and challenging them to act out their faith or practice it.
Christianity is a way of life, lived according to the truth of God, thus
our responsibility is to know the truth and do it. Luke deals very
quickly with what was a very long and exhausting venture by Paul
and we should not miss Paul's zeal, energy, determination and self-
denying effort in labouring for the Lord.

Acts 18:24

Alexandria was a significant centre for Greek and Hebrew learning, having a highly respected university and some say, the greatest library of its day. Apollos, a man of Jewish descent, who was very well trained in the knowledge of the Scriptures and in his ability to communicate the truth, came to Ephesus. The Bible tells us he was "mighty in the Scriptures." What a wonderful thing to have said about yourself. May the Lord by His Spirit enable us to know and love the Scriptures as well as show their great wisdom to others. The mightiness of Apollos was also due to his ability to refute all those who opposed the light of God's truth and wisdom.

Acts 18:25

Apollos was instructed in the way of the Lord. This refers to his doctrine, faith, confession and life (Lenski). He was full of zeal to teach and make known the glorious message of Christ. Although we see that Apollos knew only the baptism of John, we know that John the Baptist clearly taught about Christ and even identified Him, saying this is the Lamb of God that will take away the sin of the world (John 1:29). John exalted Christ throughout his ministry (John 3:28, 30) and so true disciples of John would have had true doctrine with respect to the coming of the Messiah and that sins could only be forgiven by believing in Him. Apollos taught these truths, *exactly.* You can have a true understanding about Christ and the basis of salvation without having an exhaustive understanding of Christ. Just because you do not know everything does not mean that you cannotknow some things *exactly.* If what you know is perfectly correct and you only speak about these limited things, you cannot be faulted.

Acts 18:26

Aquila and Priscilla, heard Apollos preaching in the synagogue and somehow detected that he was not preaching the full message of Christ. Paul had lived in their house in Corinth for eighteen months and thus they would have been well grounded in the full apostolic message of the cross. The humility of Apollos is very evident: he allows a tentmaker and his wife to teach him doctrine. He could have claimed to be much more educated and eloquent than them, but his love for the truth meant he was prepared to learn. We should be the same. Our most intense desire ought to be to grow in our knowledge of the truth so that we might bring more glory to God. Thus, we shouldn't be threatened by learning something we were ignorant about. The greatest glory we can bring to Christ is through knowing the truth, not pretending to know the truth or wishing we did know the truth.

Some texts place Priscilla before Aquila and it is believed that this together with other references where Priscilla is named before her husband (Acts 18:18; Rom. 16:3; 2 Tim. 4:19), show that she was more gifted in teaching than he was. The Ecclesiastical text has Aquila first in Acts 18:26. Not too much should be made about the order of the names, however, it cannot be avoided that Priscilla taught doctrine to Apollos and got him to understand *the way* more *exactly.* To only know the baptism of John, meant that Apollos did not know anything about Christ's atoning death, resurrection, ascension to the right hand of power, the coming of the Holy Spirit, baptism in the name of the Father, Son and Holy Spirit, or apostolic authority. This was not some small amount of instruction coming from Priscilla and Aquila, but deep and crucial doctrines. Nor can we try and make this out to be a time of discussion over a cup of coffee where theological issues were raised. The reason Apollos was taken aside was to instruct him more exactly in the Christian doctrines. Teaching was at the forefront of Aquila's and Priscilla's minds. It is not possible to escape from the role played by Priscilla in *teaching* this dynamic young man who would have a significant impact upon the early church.

How does this relate to 1 Timothy 2:11, 12? I believe that Paul is talking here about positions of authority within the institutional church. A woman must not be allowed to assume the offices of ruling and teaching, that is, women cannot become ruling or teaching elders. Paul's words are not an absolute statement saying a woman can never teach a man anything. Paul is talking about official positions of authority within the institutional church. Priscilla did not assume a position of authority over Apollos when she was teaching him.

Acts 18:27, 28

The believers in Ephesus sent Apollos on his way with good references and going into Achaia we know that he went to Corinth, the capital city. Paul tells the Corinthians in his letter to them that he planted the church and Apollos watered it (1 Cor. 3:6). Here in Acts we are told how Apollos greatly helped these churches. It seems possible that the Jews in Corinth and other cities in Achaia were unsettling the new believers, however, Apollos, with his mighty grasp of the Scriptures, was able to refute these people showing that Jesus is the Christ. It is a wonderful comfort to have the authority of the Word as your foundation and then see how it applies to all of life and how it can silence the critics. May we pray that the Lord would give us a desire to know His Word as well as the ability to understand and apply it. We need to be able to "vigorously" show why the Scriptural position is the only sure foundation to stand upon for everything in this life—for personal, family and national blessings (Deut. 28).

Acts 19:1

Paul eventually returns to Ephesus, which he had promised to do if the Lord allowed (Acts 18:21). Apollos had already left for Corinth. We are told that Paul then came across some people who Luke calls disciples. The word "disciple" is not used in Acts as exclusively referring to Christians (BAGD, Kittel). When we look closely at this passage I believe we see that these twelve people were not true believers in Jesus Christ and I believe that they were far more ignorant than Apollos had been with respect to the teaching of the Christian religion.

Acts 19:2

Paul, in his discussions with these people, must have perceived their lack of true faith, though Luke is very brief on the smaller details of this incident. Paul graciously investigated their faith once he realised their ignorance, asking them doctrinal questions. Some Christians have tried to use this passage as proof that people can first believe in Christ and then later only receive the Holy Spirit. It is a poor translation that makes Paul ask if they had received the Holy Spirit, *since* they believed. What he actually asks is if they received the Holy Spirit *when* they believed. We have shown before that it is impossible to be a Christian without the Holy Spirit (see comments on Acts 2:38). Paul, trying to find out the basis of their faith asks them something that is a fundamental belief of the Christian religion, namely, whether they had received the Holy Spirit at the moment they believed? It is possible that they had all been talking about believing in the Messiah, thus initially Paul might have thought that they had faith in Christ. True faith in Christ and receiving the Holy Spirit are inseparable and so when Paul suspected a problem in their faith, he asked them a basic doctrinal question.

Their response to Paul's question was as amazing as it was honest— they had not even heard that there was a Holy Spirit. It is difficult to know what they meant. If these people were Jews one finds it very difficult to believe that they had never heard of the Holy Spirit, since the OT Scriptures teach about Him. What is possible is that their answer is to be seen in the context of the question: Paul asked if they had received the Spirit, thus in the context of them personally receiving the Spirit, they had never even heard that there was a Spirit to receive.

Acts 19:3

It is obvious what Paul's next question had to be. If they knew nothing about the Holy Spirit then they couldn't have known much about the Messiah, thus, whose disciples were they? To be baptized in someone's name means that you are their disciple. It does not mean that you become the follower of a man, i.e., those who were "baptized into Moses" (1 Cor. 10:1 ,2), followed Moses' teaching, nevertheless, it is clear that they were ultimately following God. These disciples who were baptized into John the Baptist, would have been followers of his teaching, though, since he was a prophet, it was God they were really seeking to follow. To be baptized into John's baptism meant to submit, through baptism, to the doctrine that he taught. Whether these disciples had personally heard John teaching and been baptized by him, or whether they had been instructed by other disciples of John, we do not know. It does appear that they had only heard some of John's teaching, though the little they knew they believed and followed. Thus they were standing somewhere at the very beginning of the path leading to Christ, without knowing Christ. I think the evidence appears to show that they had not heard John himself teaching, but some fragments of his teaching from his disciples. Ephesus was a long way from Israel and how many steps or stages it had taken for the message to arrive in Ephesus, we do not know, however, John's full message had not been preserved along the way.

Acts 19:4

John's doctrine emphasised repentance and bringing one's life and heart into conformity to God's moral standards. He exhorted the people to turn from their sin and rebellion and do that which is right in God's eyes. It appears as though this is the part of John's message that these disciples in Ephesus had heard and taken hold of. John, however, taught that his ministry was merely to prepare the way for someone else. The power to cleanse and deliver from the bondage of sin was to be found in the Messiah who was coming after John—this was his message. It is easy to talk about sin and man's bondage to it, but this is almost a waste of time if you do not also show them where to find forgiveness and the power for change. Paul says to these disciples that John indeed did call for a change of heart, however, he always told the people to believe in the one who was coming after him, that is, in Jesus Christ. This was the great principle and emphasis of John's teaching, however, it was the part of his message that these disciples were ignorant about. They knew not the Messiahship of Christ, or His teaching, miracles, death on the cross, resurrection, ascension or His giving of the Holy Spirit to His church. The baptism that these disciples had undergone was into part of John's message—signifying their pledge to live in a moral way. It is instructive to us to notice that on discovering these disciples' total ignorance about the Holy Spirit, Paul does not begin teaching a course on the Holy Spirit, but instructs them about Jesus Christ. This passage does not give the basis for a so called "second blessing," but the necessity of true faith in the Lord, Jesus Christ.

Acts 19:5

We were not told that Apollos was baptized again, although John's baptism was the only one he knew (Acts 18:25). The difference being, I believe, was that Apollos knew John's whole message and had actually believed in the Messiah he had spoken about. Apollos had a true understanding about the significance the Messiah played with respect to salvation, even though his understanding was limited as to the full extent of the Messiah's work. He had been baptized into the full teaching of John, which clearly pointed to the Messiah, and therefore it was adequate. It appears as though all of Christ's disciples were probably baptized by John, but were not re-baptized when they came to follow Christ. These disciples in Ephesus, however, needed to trust in the Messiah and commit themselves to Him, thus they needed to be re-baptized into His Name or teaching. If you separate John the Baptist's teaching from Christ, you have a perversion of the truth.

Acts 19:6, 7

This is the fourth incident in Acts where we see the Holy Spirit poured out upon some people. The first was upon the Jews (Acts 2:4), the second upon the Samaritans (Acts 8:15), the third upon the Gentiles (Acts 10:44) and the fourth upon this group of John's disciples in Ephesus. As we have seen before, the outpourings of the Spirit were to show clearly that that particular group of people were incorporated into the body of Christ. What happened here in Ephesus was what happened in Samaria—the apostles laid hands on the people in order for them to receive the Holy Spirit. Why was it necessary for this kind of manifestation to be given to these Twelve disciples in Ephesus? We do not have here a pattern of what ought to happen when we come to faith in Christ. Speaking in other tongues is not the Scriptural proof that people have received the Holy Spirit. The 3,000 who believed and were baptized at Pentecost did not speak in tongues (Acts 2:41), nor did the Ethiopian Eunuch (Acts 8:38, 39), Paul (Acts 9:18), Lydia and her household (Acts 16:15), or the Philippian Jailer and his household (Acts 16:33). You do not have to speak in tongues in order to prove that you have been filled with the Holy Spirit (cf. Acts 4:8; 7:55; 13:9). It is not possible to prove the modern theory that says, in the NT, being filled with the Holy Spirit results in speaking in tongues. This passage is supporting the teaching that when people *believe* in the Lord, Jesus Christ, they receive the fullness of the Spirit—this is the very question Paul had asked first: "Did you receive the Holy Spirit *when* you believed?" To be baptized into the name of Christ is to be baptized into the Holy Spirit (Matt. 28:19). The reason these Ephesian disciples did not have the Holy Spirit was not because they lacked information about Him, but because they knew not Jesus Christ. This was not a second experience, but a first experience of Christ and the Holy Spirit. The new birth is a spiritual baptism, which is the Christian experience.

Through this gracious manifestation from the Lord, there can never be any doubt as to the direction and goal of John's ministry. Despite John's clear emphasis upon exalting Christ, people who called themselves John's disciples, still found John as the fulfilment of his own message. The fact that these disciples could still be so ignorant about Christ and the emphasis of John's ministry some twenty five or thirty years after his death shows how stubborn people's hearts can be. Jesus Christ is the only source of life and all things. We do not have much information from history about the size of the movement that still followed John's teachings, but it does appear that the Holy Spirit thought it needful to clearly show them the only way to be included in the family of God—through faith in Christ's completed work. This text shows that the last OT prophet (John the Baptist) pointed to Jesus Christ as the only basis for salvation. Thus what we see here is, once again, a message telling the Jews that a moral life and following the prophets was not enough to gain them access into heaven—they needed faith in Jesus Christ. People must either accept the One all the prophets (including John) clearly pointed to, or stop fooling themselves that they are disciples of the prophets (Luke 24:27). There is no other way to be accepted in God's sight, other than to stand by faith in Jesus Christ: God has clearly revealed this fact for anyone who has eyes to see.

Acts 19:8

Paul had been well received by the Jews in Ephesus during his first brief visit (Acts 18:20) and upon his return, he was given great liberty to expound the Gospel of the Kingdom in the synagogue. True preaching and teaching has to be associated with boldness—this is true not just for Paul's day, but for our days too. The mindset of the world has always been opposed to the truth of God, thus in whatever age we live, the full counsel of God will be offensive to the natural man. In every age, some aspects of God's truth will be more readily accepted than other aspects and the great temptation is to major on the things that give the least offence. Paul, fully aware of the offence of the cross (Rom. 9:33; 1 Cor. 1:18; Gal. 5:11), spent his time explaining the inescapable claims of Christ, fully supporting his position with OT Scriptures. As a result of Paul's bold uncompromising presentation of Christ's claims, many people were being persuaded.

Paul was speaking about the Kingdom of God—this includes everything about the life and work of Christ: His incarnation (John 1:14); message; miracles; death; resurrection; exaltation to the right hand of God; and His coming again to judge the living and the dead (Acts 10:42). Paul would have told his hearers that salvation could only be found in Jesus Christ (Luke 24:45–47; Acts 4:12; 1 Tim. 2:5; Heb. 2:3; 1 John 5:11, 12). The Kingdom came with Christ and all those who believe in Him, actually live in His Kingdom now. While all believers are longing for the fullness of the Kingdom, which will arrive when Christ returns to execute the final judgement, they already share in the reality of His Kingdom. The Kingdom of God is the only unshakeable foundation to stand upon (Heb. 12:28). In our days it is vital to have something which is stable, because everything around us is being severely shaken (Heb. 12:26, 27). The glorious message of the Kingdom is none other than the glorious message about Christ and what He has done for us (cf. Acts 20:24, 25). This is the message Paul preached for three months. The message of the Kingdom of God is the most rational philosophy of life in the whole world—this is because God made all things and controls all things and thus He alone can explain why things are as they are, how they ought to be and what we need to do.

Acts 19:9

It seems best to translate this verse as saying that these people "began to harden themselves" rather than that they "were hardened" (Lenski). There can be no neutral response to the message of the Kingdom. People will either humbly bow to the truth or they *will* harden themselves against it—there is no other option available to them (see comments on John 7:33,34; 12:40 and Acts 7:42, 43). It is totally unnatural to resist the truth and the unbeliever's heart convicts him for suppressing what he knows to be true. This stance produces real guilt and sooner or later, the unbeliever will resort to anger and/or violence in his vain attempt to escape from the discomfort of God's light (cf. Acts 6:10; 7:54; 9:22, 23, 29). Here in the synagogue at Ephesus, those who were disobedient to the truth and refused to change, started to publicly slander the Gospel. Luke calls it *The Way,* because it is the only way of salvation and the path of Christian discipleship. Christianity is a way of life—it is not a small something we add to our already established way of doing things, but a *totally new* way of thinking and living in every possible area of life. *The Way* encompasses everything!

It appears as though the outbursts within the synagogue against Paul's teaching were so disruptive that he was unable to continue teaching in that place. The Gospel message is a free offer of salvation to people who don't, in and of themselves, deserve it. You cannot force people to receive the truth and repent, thus if people have heard the truth and begin to revile it, then the only course open to the preacher of truth is to leave the foolish in their own sin and darkness. It is also wise to remove the new converts from such company, lest they become confused by the stupidity of man's "wisdom" (1 Cor. 1:20, 25). Those who hate the truth, also do not want others to embrace it and so they will oppose it with scorn, ridicule and slander. God does not expect us to continue striving with such people to accept the truth of the Gospel, rather the godly response is to have nothing more to do with them, leaving them in their wilful ignorance and self-imposed darkness (Matt. 10:14, 15; Luke 10:9–13; Acts 13:51; 18:6).

Paul found another location where he could continue instructing those who desired to know more about Christ and His Way. There is no real justification for trying to fill in the details about the "school of Tyrannus," since the only *facts* we have about these matters is what Luke tells us. Those translations that say Paul was "disputing" daily with those who followed the Way are unfortunate. What Paul was doing was delivering lectures or sermons (Kittel)— carefully and consistently expounding the whole counsel of God and clearly demonstrating how perfectly *reasonable* it is.

Acts 19:10

Paul spent two years in this location at the school of Tyrannus, systematically expounding God's Word. We see quite an amazing consequence of Paul's focused, diligent labours, for Luke says what Paul did in Ephesus resulted in the whole province of Asia being evangelised. The seven churches that Jesus speaks to at the beginning of Revelation are all in Asia and probably came into being during this period when Paul was in Ephesus. From Ephesus, the Gospel message went out, reaching every Jew and Greek in Asia. While Paul remained in one place, many of those he impacted went far and wide into the surrounding regions proclaiming the good news about Christ. Both Jews and Greeks could freely come into this meeting place, whereas when Paul was meeting in the synagogue the Gentiles would have had many reservations about attending. Through Paul's faithful, consistent lecturing for two years, a whole province heard the Gospel—the human part in this was Paul's determination and self-sacrifice in bringing people to a mature understanding about the Kingdom (1 Cor. 14:20; 15:10; Eph. 4:13; Phil. 3:8; Col. 1:28, 29; 2:2).

The modern church is afraid of learning too much doctrine and has no real desire to grow into the full maturity of understanding in all that Christ has revealed. It is only those who know their God that will be strong and do exploits for Him (Dan. 11:32; John 17:3). We know God by grace through faith, however, inseparable from this true knowing of God is having a solid grasp of all that He has revealed about Himself. The only reason we can know God in the first place is because He wanted to reveal Himself to us, thus it is our responsibility to know God to the extent that He has revealed Himself—no more and no less. If we truly love God we will serve Him with our whole being, but we are to serve Him in the way He has told us to. The way we serve God is by having God-honouring relationships with Him and all of His creation—the only way to do this is to live by every Word that proceeds from the mouth of God and by bringing every thought captive to the mind of Christ. The clearest and most authoritative revelation we have about God's character and purposes is in the Scriptures.

Faithful preaching will reach places that the preacher himself could never have gone. We have, in the modern church, reduced the Gospel message of the Kingdom to a very narrow area and today, that is what our evangelism proclaims. Paul preached the *Way*, referring to a whole new way of living. Christianity is a way of life touching every part of our existence. The reason we are to repent and believe in Christ is so that we can live in His Kingdom and manifest His Kingdom rule in our personal, family and national lives—for His glory. When people are systematically taught the full wisdom of God that has been revealed to us in the Scriptures and apply it to every aspect of their lives, they in turn will be equipped to do effective evangelism. The Christian message should consume the whole of our life, thus there is an urgent need for believers to grow in the grace and knowledge of our Lord (2 Pet. 3:18).

The goal of evangelism should be to get people to serve God by seeking to establish His Kingdom rule wherever they find themselves. Having been made a new creation by God, the believer is to live in terms of God's Word, submitting totally to the Savior-King and seeking through His grace to manifest the new creation in every area of life. This new creation is not merely limited to the hearts of people. The fall of mankind did not only effect hearts, but every aspect of life and it is comprehensive redemption that Jesus Christ has accomplished for us. We must not limit evangelism to conversion even though this is the starting place. Our emphasis should always be to get the convert to see the extent of God's Kingdom and calling and therefore the extent of his responsibility to glorify God by seeking to apply eternal truth to ever sphere of life. The changing of people's hearts is the first step in God's plan to change the whole of society, thus Biblical evangelism challenges the modern man to be reformed in every area of his thinking and living, calling on him to serve the Lord with all his heart, soul, mind and being (Matt. 22:35–40). We are saved to serve the Lord of this world, who has told us what will and will not glorify Him in every aspect of this life in the world. Man is not the centre of all things. Man's ideas and goals are not to be our guiding principles. God made all things for His glory and we find our purpose for our existence when we serve the Creator and seek His will and glory in all things in this world. True faith is concerned about actively reforming all those things that do not submit totally to every Word that God has spoken. We are born again to serve God's Kingdom and exalt His truth in every area of life and thought. We are saved to serve in God's Kingdom and this means implementing the principles of the King's rule in every part of His domain. Remember, the earth is the Lord's and everything in it (Ps. 24:1). Every thought and every action in every aspect of life is to be lived for the glory of God, which means it must be done in accordance with His revealed will. This is the foundation and goal of Biblical evangelism and the only way to accomplish this is through in-depth systematic instruction in the whole of God's Word. This is what Paul was doing in Ephesus and the results were significant and far reaching. True evangelism is done when we truly glorify God by doing everything according to His will and wisdom—in every area of life.

Acts 19:11, 12

Luke is careful to tell us that these happenings were unusual, even for an apostle they were far from the typical way people were healed. He calls these miracles "special," meaning that they were not common in the way in which they were performed. Cloth that had come into contact with Paul was taken to people who were sick or possessed by evil spirits and they were healed and delivered. Luke makes it very clear that the healing power was God's and that Paul was merely an instrument. The people being healed were probably from outside of Ephesus and could not be brought to Paul. We saw in verse 10 how the whole of Asia heard the Word of the Lord as a result of Paul's efforts and these signs would have greatly assisted the spread of Paul's teaching. The use of some cloth that had been with Paul was not magical or superstitious (though there was much of this in Asia), but rather the reason for this unusual method was so that the glory for the healing would go to God. A direct connection was established between Paul, His teaching and the healed person. There is nothing stopping God from healing from a distance, remember Jesus healed the nobleman's son in this way (John 4:50–53). However, among a people who are filled with superstition and trust in the magical arts of the occult, if there was no direct and clear connection between those being healed and the message of Christ, then the glory would be given to many other sources. The apostles and Jesus Himself, were always careful that people were aware who was responsible for their healing (see comments on John 5:6; Acts 3:4).

God used signs as a way of confirming the authority or credentials of the one who did the signs and Paul's credentials of apostleship were certainly confirmed in this way, as Paul himself argues (Rom. 15:19; 2 Cor. 12:12). It is Christ and His Word that are to be honoured and God graciously gave signs as a way of exalting and confirming His messengers (see comments on John 2:4; 5:6, 36; Acts 2:22, 43; 3:6; 4:30; 5:12–16; 6:8; 7:36; 8:6; 14:3; 15:12, see too Heb. 2:3, 4), so that people would believe the message and be saved (John 20:30, 31). Signs in the Scriptures were always to authenticate the messenger and thus the Word that he brought (1 Kings 17:24; John 10:24, 25; Acts 2:22). Signs marked the great periods in history where God was giving us revelation, for this was the way He accredited His messengers. The powerful and extensive manifestation of such signs, through Christ and under the authority of the apostles, was due to the abundance of revelation given to the church at that time. The signs of God are inseparable from His giving of new revelation. We believe that the revelation that God intended us to have is now complete and needs no additions, thus the signs that accompany the giving of revelation have also come to an end.

Those who are saved (the just), are to live by faith, that is, obeying and trusting every Word that has come from the mouth of God

(Matt. 4:4; Rom. 1:17). We are to walk in the Spirit, i.e., in the power of the Holy Spirit (Gal. 5:25) and we are also to have the Word of God dwell in us richly (Col. 3:16), which means obeying the Word. Thus, it is clear that a Christian is someone who obeys the Word in the power of the Spirit. The focus of the saints from the beginning of time has been upon obedience to the revealed will of God. God did many signs through Moses (Acts 7:36) so that the people would obey the Word that came from his mouth. Moses spoke of another prophet who was to come and he emphasised that everyone was to *listen* to Him (Acts 7:37)—all of the signs were for one ultimate purpose and that was so the children of Israel would receive the "living oracles" from God (Acts 7:38). The signs all confirmed the Word that was given and that Word remains for all time and is to be our light for today (Rom. 15:4; 1 Cor. 10:11; 2 Tim. 3:16:17). Our responsibility is now to preach and teach that Word that has been revealed through the apostles and prophets, applying it to our own lives and all of life around us. We do not forever need new signs to reconfirm, again and again, the eternal Word of God that is preserved for us in the Bible. The power to heal did not rest upon the discretion of the apostles, for there were times when healings did not take place (2 Cor. 12:7–9; Gal. 4:13; 1 Tim. 5:23; 2 Tim. 4:20 and Phil. 2:26, 27 where the great distress that Paul was feeling was because there was no absolute guarantee that Epaphroditus would be healed). True faith is living in submission to the purposes of God, in obedience to His Word, even in the face of hardship, sickness, loss, discouragement and disappointment. The Lord we serve is greater than us and our understanding of how things ought to be working out around us. Faith manifests itself by obedience and trust and it is not a formula whereby if we "conjure" up enough of it we can organize all the details of our lives by getting God to act according to our expectations and desires. If we fail to understand the significance of the signs in the Bible we will fail to grasp the absolute *authority* and *sufficiency* of the Scriptures. This will remove our foundation and thus destroy our ability to be effective within the Kingdom. You cannot undermine the *authority* and *sufficiency* of Scripture without reaping disaster. The Westminster Confession of Faith puts these two concepts together saying, "The whole counsel of God concerning all things necessary for His own glory, man's salvation, faith and life, is either expressly set down in Scripture, or by good and necessary consequence may be deduced from Scripture: unto which nothing at any time is to be added,

whether by new revelations of the Spirit, or traditions of men ... "
(1:6).

Acts 19:13

To deliver people from evil spirits is a Divine work, no less supernatural than a miraculous healing. Such authority was a manifestation that the Kingdom of God had come into the midst of people
(Matt. 12:28). It is God and God alone who determines when
demons are to be driven out of people (see Acts 16:16–18 where
only after some days did Paul cast out the demon). With Christ and
the apostles, through the special authority they had from God, they
could manifest this divine function. This is not a function open to
every Christian—either in the NT church or today. Such specific
Divine communication from God to individuals to command
demons to leave people ceased with the apostolic age. God continues to deliver people from the oppression of Satan and sin, but this
is according to God's sovereign, secret plan and timing. Christians
today cannot command demons to leave people any more than
they can change peoples' hearts or command miracles. Our responsibility in the face of all rebellion, whether demons are present or
not, is to proclaim the good news about Jesus. God, then, through
this Word will bring about salvation and deliverance according to
His Divine prerogative. *All* who live in rebellion against God are
under the authority of Satan (2 Cor. 4:4; Eph. 2:2), not just those
possessed by demons.

The coming, ministry, death and resurrection of Christ was all for
the purpose of overthrowing the authority of Satan's Kingdom (see
comments on John 12:31). The power of Satan and his hosts has
been destroyed by Christ and they can only do what God allows
them to do (Col. 2:15; Heb. 2:14; 1 John 3:8; Rev. 12:9–11)—we
overcome them by the blood of the Lamb and the Word of our testimony. As we stand by faith in Christ, walking in obedience to His
Word, it is the power of God that protects us and gives us the victory over all the powers of darkness. Repentance, faith and obedience to Christ is the way we are delivered and protected from
Satan's oppression (2 Cor. 2:10, 11; Eph. 4:27; 6:11–18; 2 Tim. 2:25,
26; Jam. 4:7; 1 Pet. 5:7–9). It is only when we stand in Christ that we
can partake of His victory, might and protection.

Jewish exorcists were not uncommon in those days though they
often used magical formulas to drive demons out of people. Per-

haps these exorcists had witnessed Paul commanding demons to leave people in the name of Jesus, or maybe merely heard about his success. Thinking Christ's name could be used like a magical formula, these exorcists began commanding demons to leave people in Christ's name. How exorcism normally worked for those who did not have true faith is difficult to know, maybe the whole thing was merely a deceptive game played by the demons, giving people the impression that the demon had left. What authority can there be over demons other than God's authority and God's authority cannot be used by those who do not know Him? There is much we haven't been told about demons and perhaps I have already done too much speculating. What is clear though, is that Christ's victory over this whole realm of darkness is comprehensive and victory for us is assured when we stand by faith in Him. We have nothing to fear!

Acts 19:14–17

We see here the consequences of seeking to use God's name and power for one's own ends. We also see that demonic power is superhuman, though not miraculous (it is greater than human power, but does not even begin to compare with God's power). The evil spirit exposes the fact that these seven men had no basis or authority for what they were saying: "Christ and Paul have authority, but on what are *you* standing?" For one man (with an evil spirit) to overpower and utterly humiliate seven men shows the power of demons, yet what strikes everyone in Ephesus is the power of Christ that so easily casts out demons. The city was confronted with the reality of the risen Lord who rules over every aspect of heaven and earth—His power was very obviously real.

Acts 19:18–20

The impact of this incident with the demon was powerful for the Kingdom of God and many people saw their need for Christ and salvation. Ephesus was a leading city in the magical arts, but the power of God brings many people to repentance and to a realization that involvement in the kingdom of darkness in any way was utterly foolish. The power of spells and the occult is usually closely tied to its secrecy, thus when these people came and confessed, telling their deeds it seems likely that it included exposing these secrets, thus removing the "power" of these spells. The amount of literature that was brought to be burned was massive. The impact of Christ upon the city of Ephesus was incredible, affecting everyone who lived there in some way and would have made a profound change to every area of life. We are told that a piece of silver was equivalent to a days wages. If this is correct then we have a total in excess of 160 years of wages. With such violence against the kingdom of darkness and its ways the Word of the Lord prevailed mightily. May the Lord work in our days to bring cities and nations to such whole hearted dedication to the Word of God and such rejection of all that is not from His Word. The conversion we ought to be praying for is for people to confess and forsake their sins (Prov. 28:13) and then embrace a whole new way of living— according to the mind of Christ, as revealed in the Scriptures (Matt. 28:20; 2 Cor. 10:5). It is the Word of God that must prevail if we are to experience success in our personal, family and national lives. Let us earnestly seek the Lord for this.

Acts 19:21

In the light of what follows, with respect to whether Paul should go up to Jerusalem or not, we need to understand this "purposing in the Spirit," to be divine guidance and instruction from the Spirit to Paul (see Acts 20:23; 21:4, 11, 12). We see clearly from Acts 23:11 that it was God's will for Paul to eventually go on to Rome after having testified to the truth in Jerusalem. The whole of Paul's life was lived in submission to the purposes of God and he did whatever the Holy Spirit showed him to do. Hardships, danger and death are not signs that we have missed God's leading. We are to walk by faith in the clear revelation of God, not counting our lives dear unto ourselves and not seeking a path that will benefit us alone (Acts 20:24). All our plans are to be determined by God and done for His glory. What should be foremost in our hearts and minds, is knowing that, as Christ's servants, we are to see ourselves as sheep for the slaughter (Rom. 8:36; 2 Cor. 4:11). Paul's desire was to benefit other believers and churches, even to the detriment of his own safety and well-being and we see him imitating Christ who when He set His face to go to Jerusalem, could not be distracted (Luke 9:51, cf. Isa. 50:5–9). Paul wanted to see the church in Rome, so that he could impart a spiritual gift to them and so that they could encourage each other (Rom. 1:11, 12). We know that Paul's ultimate vision was upon the unreached land of Spain and that his passing through Rome would be while on his way to Spain (Rom. 15:24, 28), which as Bruce tells us, was the most westerly outpost of Roman civilisation in Europe. This was Paul's desire, however, we do not know if he ever reached Spain with the Gospel. We do know that before Paul got to Rome, he preached the Gospel in Illyricum, which is modern day Yugoslavia (Rom. 15:19).

Acts 19:22

Paul, wanting to encourage and strengthen the churches he had planted, planned another trip to Macedonia and Achaia—the main cities of these respective areas being Philippi and Corinth. There was another reason for his proposed visit to these areas just before he went to Jerusalem and that was to gather a free-will offering from these churches for the poverty-stricken saints in Jerusalem (1 Cor. 16:1–4; 2 Cor. 8:2–4; 9:3–7; Rom. 15:25–28). After dispatching his close companions, Paul remained in Ephesus for a season. In all, the time Paul spent in Ephesus was three years (Acts 20:31) and although very little detail is given, we know that it was an extremely difficult time for him (1 Cor. 15:32; 16:8, 9; 2 Cor. 1:8, 9).

Acts 19:23

Christianity is a world and life view, touching the whole of our existence here on earth. "The Way," refers to living our lives in submission to God's truth. God has revealed how we ought to live in every area of our lives (2 Tim. 3:16, 17) and by bringing our thoughts and actions into line with Him is the only way to please Him (Matt. 4:4; John 14:15; 2 Cor. 10:5). There is only one way to God and only one way to glorify God—that is to believe in Christ for salvation and to have His Words direct us completely. This kind of living will have an impact upon everyday life, because it will be in conflict with the "wisdom" of this world. The teaching of the Way, will create a commotion when it confronts practices and thinking that are in rebellion against God's truth. It is only by compromising the full implications of Christ's message (Matt. 28:19, 20) that we can be at peace with this world's mindset (Rom. 8:7; James 4:4).

Acts 19:24–28

Every practice or job that arises from cultic thinking is threatened by the full counsel of God. This obviously includes all false religions, but it includes more than that. Many times we fail to realize that everyone acts in the way they do and believes the things they do because of religious commitments. The foundational pillars in everyone's thinking are held to with *religious convictions* and this includes the evolutionist, who holds to his starting principles, not because of scientific evidence, but because of religious devotion/commitment. The only True God, who has revealed Himself in the Bible, does not just speak to a small religious part of our lives, but touches everything in life. Thus when we talk about "cultic beliefs" we mustn't just think of those narrowly defined religious cults, for it includes everything that does not submit to the mind of God (see *Muse Time*, paper 21). For example, the modern concept of the state is cultic and when you start to apply God's truth to the cult-state you will receive the same reaction that Paul experienced in Ephesus. Those who obtain their wealth from "state-craft" will react like Demetrius and his fellow workers when God's truth evaluates their practices and defines what is and isn't legitimate. When you challenge the legitimacy of peoples' religious foundations and threaten their livelihood (which rests upon these foundations) then you will experience their wrath, for these two things are at the core of who people are.

The effects of grass-roots reformation within the hearts of people should have an impact upon everyday life. We must not think that the hope of the Gospel rests in bringing about external legislation, but rather it rests in the power of internal regeneration, where people's hearts reject all that is not pure and promote all that is pure—as defined by God's Word. Paul, in Asia, had expounded the full counsel of God and the converts, who had been born again and persuaded to bring their lives into line with God's authoritative Word, turned away from impure activities. Paul's evangelism was not an appeal to the emotions, but a persuasive, reasoned presentation of the truth. The Holy Spirit is the Spirit of truth and when He opens people's minds to Christ, He does this *with* the truth, not in spite of the truth. Thus, Paul spent his time reasoning with and persuading people about the truth of the Way (Acts 18:4, 13; 19:8, 9, 26). We too need to be able to give a reasoned defence of our faith (1 Pet. 3:15). Biblical faith is not a leap into the unknown, but rather it is standing upon the only foundation that can make sense out of life—true faith is reasonable. When the just live by faith (Rom. 1:17), they apply the whole of God's Word to the whole of life—bringing every thought and action into line with the mind of Christ.

Acts 19:29–32

It appears as though the silversmiths incited people in the streets, until there was great confusion in the whole city. It is easy to incite mobs, who get caught up in the excitement though they know very little about the real facts (see verse 32). Paul immediately wants to come to the aid of his companions and probably also was hoping for an opportunity to present the Gospel to this crowd. Paul's friends, some of whom had prominent positions within the city, persuaded him not to risk his life in the midst of this frenzied mob. We see Paul's humility here, as he receives this counsel as from the Lord, whereas later on when people strenuously tried to persuade him not to go to Jerusalem, he did not heed their counsel (Acts 21:4, 12).

Acts 19:33, 34

It was the Jews who put forward Alexander and it seems best to see him as someone who did not believe in Christ. He was going to make sure that the Jews were distinguished from the Christians in the minds of the Ephesians. The Jews were ready to denounce Paul and stand with these pagans against the Way—something that had been done before (see comments on Acts 14:19). The mob, after perceiving that he was a Jew, knew that he was not a worshiper of Diana and so they would not let him speak. For two hours they kept their captives and chanted themselves into a frenzy. The temple of Diana was so large and splendid that it was regarded as one of the seven wonders of the world in its day. The magnificence and beauty of Diana's temple is long gone and all that is left are some stones showing where it once stood and one has to try and imagine its grandeur. You can shout slogans for as long as you like, but whatever is not grounded upon Christ and His immovable Word will come to ruin. Why should we waste our time and effort upon that which refuses to bow to the authority of God's revelation? Whether we are trying to build a family or a nation, it is utterly worthless to do it in a way that does not honour God, because God will not honour man's work, no matter how impressive we might think it is (Ps. 127:1). In the history of the world, many nations and civilisations, far greater than our own nation, have ceased to exist. All that remains of them, if anything, are overgrown, tumbled down ruins, because they refused to humble themselves under the hand of God (Matt. 23:11; James 4:10; 1 Pet. 5:5, 6), or give true honour to the Son and trust in Him (Ps. 2:12). Anything people do that does not have Christ as its focus and foundation is ultimately worthless.

Acts 19:35–41

The town clerk, who was probably equivalent to our modern city mayor, or even a government minister, manages to quieten the crowd. He says no one will dispute the fact that Ephesus was the guardian city of the goddess Diana—his implication being that Diana's supreme position was immovable. It is believed that Diana was originally a meteorite that fell from the sky (verse 35) and that from there the Ephesians filled out the details of what this goddess looked like. It is not usually the facts that are in dispute, but rather its the interpretation of the facts where great differences arise. Remember, everyone interprets every fact they come across in this world according to their "first beliefs" and people hold to these beliefs with religious zeal (see *Faith and Reason*, chapters 1 to 3). The meteorite was a fact, yet the Ephesians interpreted it as proof that god had come to dwell with them and wanted their worship, whereas in reality, what they were worshipping was a dead stone that had neither eyes nor ears and was unable to help them in any way (Deut. 4:28; Ps. 115:4–7; 135:15, 16; Isa. 44:9, 13–19; 45:20; 46:7).

This Ephesian leader said that their interpretation of the facts about Diana were irrefutable and therefore it did not matter what Paul and his companions taught, thus why do something foolish—i.e., act lawlessly towards these Christians? He says, according to Roman law these people had not done anything wrong. He goes on to say that if someone has a legitimate case against them, then there were appropriate channels to redress grievances which would be judged according to the Roman judicial system. He then condemns the crowd's behavior as being in violation of Roman law and dismisses the crowd—who left willingly.

Luke's point in recording this incident was to show that each time the Christian faith was brought to trial by mobs and there was a proper judicial system that could evaluate the charges, Christianity was cleared of all charges. Luke shows that Rome had no case against the Christian faith or Paul—Gallio dismissed the charges brought against Paul in Corinth (Acts 18:15, 16), Paul had the support of many of the city officials in Ephesus (Acts 19:31) and finally the clerk in Ephesus said there was no justification for the mob's behaviour, since there were no legitimate charges (Acts 19:40, 41). This meant that the Christian faith could continue spreading unopposed by the authorities in these regions. It is only Satanicly inspired prejudice that reacts against a true presentation of the Christian religion, but it is this reaction that is shown to be clearly immoral and not the Christian faith.

Acts 20:1

Paul did not leave Ephesus because of the uproar. Luke is merely using the uproar as the time frame for when Paul left the city. Word was sent out to all the believers in the city, who then gathered for a farewell service with Paul. Having encouraged these disciples to remain steadfast in the faith, he set out upon his planned trip.

Acts 20:2

Luke does not specify which areas Paul went through. Some think that this was when he went as far a Illyricum (Rom. 15:19, which is modern Yugoslavia). We know that Paul, many years later, sent Titus to Dalmatia (2 Tim. 4:10) which is southern Illyricum, presumably to follow up Christians that Paul had earlier brought to the faith. Paul then ended up in Greece and stayed three months in Corinth. Paul's relationship with Corinth is an interesting one. After he had left Corinth the first time (Acts 18:18) and settled in Ephesus, he wrote a number of letters to the Corinthians. The first letter he wrote no longer exists. Paul tells us about this letter in the second letter he wrote (1 Cor. 5:9), thus, what we call First Corinthians, we could in our discussion, call letter "B." The first letter, letter "A" was in response to reports Paul had received about what was happening in the church. It appears as though the Corinthians responded to letter "A" with their own letter and Paul's answer to them is letter "B," what we call First Corinthians. In letter "B" Paul was able to clear up misunderstandings of his first letter (cf. 5:10, 11) and deal with other problems that had been raised in one way or another.

The problems in Corinth continued to increase until, it appears, Paul made a special visit to them to sort things out. This however, did not work either and Paul's authority was rejected, whereupon he had to leave, having accomplished nothing. Paul talks about this visit in 2 Corimthians 2:1, calling it his painful visit, or sorrowful visit. Paul, not wanting to leave the situation as it was, decided to write a very stinging letter which Titus delivered to the Corinthian church. This letter, which no longer exists, can be called letter "C" (Paul talks about it in 2 Corinthians 2:3, 4). The church in Corinth responded wonderfully to this strong letter and thus Paul, full of joy, writes Second Corinthians, or letter "D," which was written after he had left Ephesus and sometime before he arrived in Corinth for his third visit (i.e., the visit of Acts 20:2).

Luke briefly tells us that Paul "had gone over that region." Some commentators think that this could have covered a period of eighteen months. The NIV says, he "finally" arrived in Greece, implying a long period of time had elapsed since leaving Ephesus. There is much we need to know about Christ and His Kingdom and great encouragement comes to us when we are instructed in the full counsel of God. Paul took every opportunity to give as much teaching as he could, knowing that the churches' strength depended upon knowing the truth. There were many things that were vital for these Christians to know and do if they were to glorify Christ, thus Paul would not skimp on the teaching or apologise for it ("encouraging them with *many* words"). During Paul's stay of three months in Corinth he wrote the book of Romans.

Acts 20:3

It is believed that Paul was wanting to be in Jerusalem in time for the Passover Feast. It appears as though there were many other Jews who would have been making this same voyage to Jerusalem—Jews who hated Paul and his doctrine. Somehow, Paul got wind of a plot against his life and since he refused to sail afterwards, most people conclude that those who wanted to kill him would have been on the same ship and the chances to kill him and dispose of his body overboard would have been very much in their favour. Paul wisely delayed his plans and went back into Macedonia, planning to be in Jerusalem for Pentecost instead (Acts 20:16).

Acts 20:4, 5

The group that accompanied Paul could have been representatives from some of the churches that had contributed towards the offering for the poor saints in Jerusalem (Rom. 15:25–28; 1 Cor. 16:1–4;

2 Cor. 8:1–5). It is also possible that these people were going with Paul to the "mother" church as representatives of the newly founded Gentile churches. Such meetings, Paul saw as vital for strengthening Jewish-Gentile relations within Christ's body.

Acts 20:6, 7

Luke, who is travelling with Paul now, supplies us with details about the timing of many of the steps of the journey back to Jerusalem. They stayed seven days in Troas, the last day being a Sunday (the first day of the week), which made it very convenient for the church to gather together and hold a farewell service for Paul. You cannot prove from Luke's writings that "breaking of bread" refers to the celebration of the Lord's Supper (see comments on Acts 2:42). Sundays were not days of rest, but normal working days and thus it appears best to see the believers coming together *after* their day's work. Thus this meeting probably got going in the evening and being Paul's last day with them, it is very logical that they decided to eat together as well. Paul did not merely preach, for the word used includes the idea of discussing and debating. There must have been many questions that these believers wanted answered and Paul was very well qualified to address these issues. It seems an easy thing to me, to remain in discussion with the apostle Paul for many hours on end. The sense in this verse is that this was not the church's normal practice, but an exception because Paul was present with them.

Acts 20:8, 9

We must not try and make too much out of Luke's details with respect to the lights. Nor must we find fault either with Paul's long discussion or with Eutychus falling asleep. He was a "young man," meaning he was neither a child nor an adult (it is a vague term, though the use of a different word in verse 12 places him between nine and fourteen). It is an interesting use of "young man" and I think our own day has exalted immaturity, which has had a disastrous effect upon our young people. This young man, being overcome with sleep, found it impossible to stay awake and thus fell to his death. This was quite a tragic moment in the midst of this significant last meeting with Paul.

Acts 20:10

Paul imitates the great prophets of old who stretched themselves
out upon dead boys and God brought them back to life (1 Kings
17:21; 2 Kings 4:34, 35). Paul does not say, no wait you are mistaken
the young man is not dead, but rather, he announces that his life
has *returned* to him. This was a glorious raising of the dead and was
ordained by God to underline Paul's authority so that these believers would embrace his teaching (see comments on Acts 4:30; 19:11,
12). This sign was not to glorify Paul, but to strengthen the church
and in this way glorify God. No doubt could have remained in the
minds of these believers as to their need to take heed to everything
Paul had taught them. God graciously confirms the authority of
His servants for our benefit so that we might know that they spoke
with divine authority. We glorify God by bringing our thoughts and
actions into line with all the Words that have been preserved for us
in the Scriptures.

Acts 20:11

It is very possible to be so caught up in discussion and talking that
you forget to eat. Now with this unexpected break and the relief
that came with the miracle, it was natural to notice one's hunger
and therefore they stopped to eat. The discussion continued, with
no one wanting to go home, right until daybreak. Paul was not
worried about himself and his needs, but always longed to serve the
needs of the believers and so thought nothing of staying up the
whole night teaching them on the things of the Lord. The believers,
hungry to grow in the knowledge of the Lord, were also prepared to
sacrifice sleep for the sake of God's Kingdom. We must point out
again that this was a unique situation, for we do not read that such
all night services were done in those places where Paul remained
and instructed new believes for any length of time. There will
always be some zealous and misguided Christians who think that
you have here a pattern for how we ought to do things on a regular
basis and that this is the way to receive God's anointing.

Acts 20:12

The great comfort that the believers experienced was obviously due
to seeing Eutychus alive and well, however, inseparable from this
would have been the real comfort one attains in knowing that you
are standing upon the authority of God's immovable Word. The

wonderful teaching that Paul had given them for the last twelve or so hours, confirmed by God's authoritative sign, would have given them tremendous confidence and comfort for the future. Despite Paul's departure and that they might never see him again, they had the living Word of God and the indwelling Holy Spirit and this was a foundation that couldn't be moved. On this foundation, one person can face all the hosts of darkness and overcome them. We need to find our comfort in the place where real comfort is found—in Christ and His Word. May we stand upon the promises of God no matter how threatening the outward circumstances might appear to be. We are to love the truth, proclaim the truth and find our rest in the truth. Though the earth be removed, we will not fear (Ps. 46:2). Our comfort is in knowing and doing everything that Christ has commanded (John 14:23).

Acts 20:13–15

Much can be said about the historical details of all these places, both before Paul's time and after his time, but surely this is not Luke's intention. Luke, in giving the details of their movement towards Jerusalem, is showing how Paul had set his intentions firmly on getting to Jerusalem, allowing nothing to get in the way.

Acts 20:16

We see the reason for Paul's haste is because he wants to be in Jerusalem for the Jewish Feast of Pentecost. These feasts were always great opportunities to meet many believers and reach out to many unbelievers. Paul was someone who was very aware of the preciousness of time and actually how little of it we have to labor for the Kingdom. It is possible that he feared if he got into Ephesus again, he would be delayed and miss the great opportunities in Jerusalem brought about by the feast. There would be many needs in the congregation at Ephesus, since Paul had been away from them for quite some time (about two years had elapsed since Acts 20:1) and ministering to these needs would have meant a long delay.

Acts 20:17

There was some kind of a delay in the journey at Miletus, whether intentional or unintentional on Paul's part we do not know, however, it gave him an opportunity to have one last meeting with the Ephesian elders. The *elders* were the official leaders of the church, whom Paul later calls *overseers* or *bishops* in verse 28, clearly equating the terms.

Acts 20:18

We see in Paul's speech, the tender love he had for these people. This is the only speech recorded in Acts where Paul addresses Christians. Paul had spent three years with these people and thus appeals to those things that they clearly knew to be true. He is not trying to exalt himself, but challenging them to labor for the flock as Paul himself had laboured—selfless dedication in serving the needs of others. Faithful leaders are a vital ingredient if the church is going to be strong and vibrant for the Lord. Paul was not asking them to do anything that he had not done himself. He says to these men, "As you saw and were benefited by my labours for you, you ought to labor for those under your care." We need to realize how our own good works spur others on to accomplish good works too. We can challenge and inspire others by our faithfulness and diligence for the Kingdom, so that they go and do likewise, thus our efforts can be multiplied many times more than we dreamt possible. Paul says that from the very first day until the last day, he had not sought to please himself or benefit himself—the whole time he was in Asia he spent in serving the needs of others. This was done openly and clearly in the sight of all these leaders. Paul is not writing to some mission organisation 5,000 miles away, telling them how hard he had worked, but says to those who had full view of his life, every day for three years, "You know that this is true".

Acts 20:19

Here we see three qualifications for true servants of God—humility, tears and trials. Humility is a fundamental pillar in God's Kingdom, as Christ so abundantly demonstrated (see comments on John 13:1–17). Augustine said that to follow Christ's way, the first most important things was humility, the second most important thing was humility and the third most important thing was humility. Paul had served the Lord in the office Christ had called him to and although he was one of the most significant apostles, he served with lowliness of mind, thinking more highly of those whom he served than he thought of himself. Paul would relate to and labor for the lowest of the low, seeking their good above his own. Paul was prepared to serve everyone he came into contact with and there was nothing he wouldn't do for them. You cannot labor in this way if your opinion of yourself is too high. Servant-hood is the sign of greatness in the Kingdom of God. Paul did not think that he was qualified for his calling and responsibilities (1 Cor. 2:3, 4), however he was faithful to all that Christ gave him to do, knowing that it was the Lord who was labouring in him (1 Cor. 2:5). Nor did Paul turn away from the reproach of the cross. If you see yourself as a lowly servant then you will not care what people think about you, because you are Christ's servant and can be used in any way He sees fit. Paul understood this and later said, we are accounted as sheep for the slaughter (Rom. 8:36). Paul neither trusted in himself and his abilities nor laboured for himself and his glory.

Paul's tears were not for himself, but for those whom he laboured amongst and for those of his own people, the Jews, who continued in stubborn rebellion against the truth of Christ (Acts 20:31; Rom. 9:1–3; 2 Cor. 2:4; 11:28, 29; Phil. 3:18; Ps. 119:136). Paul earnestly desired that Christians would come to maturity in Christ, for their own good and God's glory and he would agonise in prayer and labor towards this end (Gal. 4:19; Eph. 1:16ff.; Col. 1:9ff.).

There was much opposition to Paul's teaching, from both Jews and Gentiles, however, here he focuses upon the trials that came to him from the Jews while he was labouring in Ephesus. These Jews hated Paul because he told them that unless they believed in Christ they were damned to hell, just like any other Gentile in the world. These Jews were full of self-righteousness, thus when Paul said that all the Jewish customs and laws that they kept contributed nothing towards their acceptance before God, they wanted to destroy him. He said it was only by trusting in the merits of Jesus Christ that people could be accepted in God's sight, for even the very best efforts and works of men were nothing but filthy rags and refuse (Isa. 64:6; Phil. 3:8, see comments on John 1:47). To say this to self-righteous people, who pride themselves in their own works, is like teasing a mad bull. Paul faced the trials of people opposing his work, slandering his name, misrepresenting his doctrine and seeking to kill him. If we stand and proclaim the full counsel of God in our day, we will be hated by those who hate Christ (Matt. 5:11, 12; John 15:20, 21; 16:3). Paul's time of labor among the Ephesians was very tough and it was only because Paul was prepared to sacrifice his life for the benefit of others that he was he able to succeeded in his calling—this is the only way to succeed in any calling in the Kingdom (whether you are called to be a mechanic or a pastor).

Acts 20:20

Paul was not ashamed of anything found in the Word of God and not counting his life as dear to himself (Acts 20:24), he was able to proclaim the full counsel of God. There is much preaching in our days, but one is very aware of the fact that so often the church has shaped her message according to what will be accepted by the world and church traditions. What is needful however, are often those truths that are being ignored because of their unpopularity. We must not shrink or draw back from those truths that are particularly needful in our day. A pastor or teacher is not to want merely to tickle the ears of those he watches over, he is not to appeal to their desires or seek to exalt his own popularity. He is to exhort, rebuke and encourage, seeking at all times the real welfare of his people, trusting that it is the Lord who knows what is best for the flock and not the flock themselves. The church needs the whole counsel of God for their spiritual development and it is the whole of God's Word that provides this completeness (2 Tim. 3:16, 17). That is why, I believe, expository preaching should play such a major role in the life of the church, because it is a great temptation to steer away from teachings that are offensive to the natural man. However, if you are constantly working your way, as a preacher, through complete books of the Bible you are more likely to cover all that needs to be covered than if you are jumping around each week finding different texts to preach on. The temptation is to shrink back from proclaiming those things that can cause you to be despised and persecuted. Oh, how desperately we need fearless, sound teachers and leaders in the church today!

Paul instructed both in big public gatherings and in the groups that met in the houses—house churches. I do not see this as referring to house to house visitation. Such visitation has become one of the most expected things a pastor has to do. I do not believe that this is a Biblical picture of the responsibilities of the pastor. Fellowship and visitation is a *ministry* of the church and it is the congregation who are called on to be ministers in this way. The office of deacon is more involved in this kind of work, but the main *focus* of the pastor and elders is to be prayer and the ministry of the Word (Acts 6:4). Ultimately it is through sound preaching that the flock will come to maturity, however, it requires much time and study to provide solid food for the flock. If pastors are spending their time going from house to house, they will not be able to feed the sheep with solid food, which will result in them being needed even more by the sheep, which means even less time to prepare and so the problems worsen. Sound preaching will equip the church for the work of the ministry (Eph. 4:12) and part of this *ministry* required of the flock is to build up one another in the most holy faith (Rom. 14:19; 15:2; 1 Cor. 10:23, 24; Eph. 4:16, 29; 1 Thes. 5:11; Jude 20). I believe what we see in Acts 2:42ff., is body ministry, one to another, flowing out of sound apostolic instruction. Paul used every opportunity that availed itself in order to instruct those under his care in the full counsel of God. He did not apologise for God's Word and did not shrink back from declaring it all. May the Lord grant us the grace to imitate Paul as he imitated Christ, for he was not ashamed of the Gospel of Christ (Rom. 1:16, see too 2 Tim. 1:8).

Acts 20:21

The message Paul preached was the same for both Jews and Greeks, since *all* people are sinners and have come short of the glory of God. Paul makes an important distinction, saying people need to *repent* towards God and have *faith* in Jesus Christ. Repentance and faith cannot be separated, however, we must not think that they refer to the same thing. We must not try and give to these two activities an order, saying one has to come before the other, since the one automatically implies the other. While both repentance and faith are activities that humans have to exercise, neither of them can exist unless God grants them. We believe, because we have begun to repent and we repent, because we have begun to believe and both depend upon the gracious working of God in our lives (Acts 5:31; 11:18; 2 Tim. 2:25; Eph. 2:8). Nevertheless, the responsibility is still upon people to repent and have faith and thus we are to call on them to do that. Both repentance and faith are graces that flow out of a heart that has been made alive from the dead by God's sovereign working (Eph. 2:1,5; Col. 2:13). If God did not first regenerate us, giving us new hearts, we would be incapable of repenting or having faith. Repentance and faith, while being absolutely necessary if we are to be saved, contribute absolutely nothing towards making us acceptable in God's eyes. If you do not repent and believe in Jesus, you cannot be justified, however, the only basis for our justification is the righteousness of Christ which is imputed to us and which we receive through faith alone (see comments on John 12:32, 33).

Repentance has its basis in the holiness of God's righteous character (and the law is a revelation of God's character). Repentance is an acknowledgement of His purity and a realization that we are corrupted in every part of our being. It involves seeing the wickedness of our sin and fearing God's righteous judgment that rests upon us. Repentance involves a sincere desire to walk in the light of God's Word; to bring every thought and action into obedience to Him; to deny ourselves and put to death the works of the flesh. Repentance includes a real sorrow for our sin accompanied by real dread of the consequences for our rebellion. For repentance, however, to be of any real value, it must be accompanied by faith, because knowing about our wickedness and the righteousness of God leaves us in a desperate situation, for together with the awareness of our sin, comes the realization that we are unable to change our situation (Rom. 7:14–24). Knowing how we ought to live is not enough, we also need the power of God to enable us to walk according to His truth and His gracious provision so that our sin and guilt can be forgiven (Rom. 7:25ff.). We desperately need both grace and truth, for it is only through His grace that we can have assurance that we have been freely adopted by God into His family and are fully accepted in His eyes (see comments on John 1:18). It is in Christ that God has promised to forgive all our sins, thus faith is a firm and sure knowledge of God's favor towards us, founded on the truth of a free promise given in Christ, and revealed to our minds and sealed in our hearts by the Holy Spirit (Calvin, *Institutes*, 3:2:7). Faith is a relational connection that unites us to Christ and through which we partake of His righteousness and share in His Spiritual life. Without Christ, God's holiness and righteous demands are nothing but a terror to us (Ps. 15; 24:3, 4; 76:7; 90:11; Matt. 5:48; 2 Cor. 6:17; 7:1), however, when we stand by faith in the completed work of Jesus we can come into the presence of God with boldness and delight in His holy requirements. We need both mercy and truth, inseparably united and constantly before our eyes. We present this picture to the world by calling on people to repent towards God and have faith in Jesus Christ. Unless we know about the mercy in Christ, the knowledge of the truth (i.e., God's holiness) is too much for us to bear. It is a terrifying thing to fall into the hands of the living God, for He is a consuming fire and a righteous Judge (Ex. 24:17; Num. 11:1; Deut. 4:24; Ps. 50:6; 96:13; Heb. 10:31; 12:29; 2 Thes. 1:8; 2 Tim. 4:1, 8). It is only in Christ that we learn of the Father's favor towards us and that everything we need for salvation has been provided for us in Jesus (2 Tim. 1:9; Titus 3:3–7; 1 John 4:9, 10). As Calvin says, "By the sacrifice of his death he has purged our sins; he has suffered the punishment that he might acquit us; he has made us clean by his blood; by his obedience he has appeased the Father's wrath; by his resurrection he has purchased righteousness for us" (Comm. On Acts). As faith cannot be separated from repentance, so too, Christ's salvation cannot be separated from His Lordship (John 14:15; Matt. 28:19, 20).

Acts 20:22, 23

God had clearly revealed His will to Paul who had fully embraced it as his own. Not to have obeyed God here would have been an act of stubborn rebellion on Paul's part. He was not being forced to do something he did not want to do, but rather, was explaining the reason for the course he was taking. Many in our day try to attribute to the working of the Spirit strange ideas that spring solely from their own minds. Unless our understanding about all things, as well as all of our reasoning and acting, have their foundation and boundaries set by the Scriptures, then we will be led astray by our own delusion, claiming it is the leading of the Spirit. It is foolish to give to the Spirit a role that God never intended and the Spirit was never meant to speak with absolute authority independently of the revelation of God and in our situation that revelation is the Bible (see comments on John 14:26; 16:13).

Paul admits that he does not fully know what awaits him in Jerusalem. What he does know however, is that he is going to endure much difficulty and suffering for the purposes of God. As Paul had been moving on his way to Jerusalem, in a number of the cities he went through, there was a consistent message from the Spirit saying, that at the very least, imprisonment was awaiting him. It was God's plan for Paul to go to Jerusalem and be chained and it was God who was leading him and giving him the grace to face this ordeal, because through it all, God's Kingdom would be glorified. Paul was merely an obedient servant doing what his Master wanted him to do. Paul not only had a strong conviction from the Spirit, but also a strong confidence in God's sovereign working. Paul did not know what would come of his obedience, nor did he know the details of what would happen to him, nevertheless, he was not distracted from his course by this. All he needed to know he knew, namely, that he was to be an obedient servant testifying to the truth of God and Christ and proceed to Jerusalem. The results of Paul's obedience he left in God's hands and did not concern himself with them, but rather concerned himself with his responsibilities, which were to be found faithful no matter what. If we faithfully do our work in the Kingdom for the glory of God and in submission to His revelation, then we do not have to concern ourselves with the results of our efforts. God alone knows what is best and alone is able to work all things for His good (Rom. 8:28). We could never even begin to understand what would bring the most glory to God or what was the best for His Kingdom, thus our greatest contribution to the Kingdom is to walk by faith, submitting totally and quickly, to every Word from God (Matt. 4:4; 6:10; Rom. 1:17).

Acts 20:24

The tribulation which awaited Paul he accounted as nothing. The importance of Paul's own safety and comfort he saw as meaningless in the context of God's glory and purposes. This was a characteristic of Christ and can be seen in the lives of all the great saints of God throughout the ages. They believed that their responsibility to stand for and testify to the truth was more valuable than life itself, thus they would cheerfully lay down their lives so that God's truth might be exalted and His purposes fulfilled. Paul valued the course he had been given to follow, higher than life itself because of his love for God. Paul found his significance and purpose in God's will for him and his life had meaning only if he was living in accordance with what God wanted. To live for his own desires and labor for his own benefit alone was meaningless for Paul. He knew he had a course to run and as God's servant he would do nothing else, because he knew that true joy was found in selflessly serving the King so that He might be glorified.

Many in our world are caught up with the desire to find self fulfilment and joy, however, they seek it by focusing upon themselves and so never attain it (Mark 8:35). The only way to find real joy and satisfaction in this life is to totally deny ourselves and see the Kingdom as more precious than our lives. Paul testified on many occasions that he was prepared to sacrifice everything, even his life, if this was required by Christ (Acts 21:13; 2 Cor. 4:8–12; 6:4–10; 12:10; Phil. 1:20, 21; 2:17; 3:8; Col. 1:24).

We have all been given our own course to follow for God in this life and the only way to finish it, with joy, is to make sure that our focus is at all times upon doing everything in accordance with God's revelation and for His glory. If that path leads to our death, then true joy is attained in death and in such a situation to seek to preserve our life would mean not completing our course. The testimony of Paul at the end of his life was that he had fought the good fight, he had finished the race and he had kept the faith (2 Tim. 4:7). Paul liked to talk about the Christian life as a race that is to be run with discipline, enduring difficulties and hardships (1 Cor. 9:24; Heb. 12:1). If we have the wrong idea of what the Christian life should be like we will be offended by the difficulties and we will not know where true joy is to be found. Although the world constantly tries to tell us where true joy is to be found, it does not know, so do not be deceived and spend the little time you have chasing the wind.

Faithfulness is of immense value in our lives and learning to be faithful, in whatever we do, is worth more than much gold, for such a person will abound in the blessings of God (Prov. 28:20). The Scriptures also lament that a faithful man is so hard to find (Prov. 20:6), yet authority and responsibility in the Kingdom of God will flow to the faithful people (Neh. 7:2). The Scriptures tell us that it is possible to lay down our lives with joy, knowing that we have lived our whole life, faithfully serving our Great Lord. There will be no regrets when our time is up, if we have served God with our whole being. We are to make the most of every opportunity that comes across our path, seeking to glorify Christ by doing all things according to His will and for His glory (Isa. 50:5–7). Joy is attained when we realize (that is, accomplish) the purpose for which we were created. We were created to selflessly expend ourselves in the service of our King—this alone is real joy for the faithful servant. It is God's will that must be done at all times, because His name alone is worthy of being glorified and we exist for God's glory (Matt. 6:13; Luke 22:42). Danger for the Christian is not when all kinds of obstacles or people threaten us because of our faithful witness about Christ, but rather, danger is when we seek to follow our wills instead of God's will.

Paul says his ministry was to proclaim the Good News about the free, undeserved favor and love of God extended to all people, who deserve nothing but God's condemnation—this is the Gospel of the grace of God. To proclaim this message effectively, one has to be a servant, whose only desire is to glorify the name of Christ by selflessly doing everything for His Kingdom.

Acts 20:25

The Kingdom is the reign of God through the Messiah. Although Paul would no longer be present with the Ephesians, the reigning Messiah would be with them and it was His Kingdom that they were serving. All authority in heaven and on earth belongs to Christ (see comments on John 12:31) and He promised He would always be present with His servants as they labor for Him on earth, though they are to teach every nation everything He has commanded (Matt. 28:20). Luke said that repentance and forgiveness of sins was to be proclaimed to all nations (Luke 24:47). As we saw in Acts 20:21, repentance relates to God's holy character and His commandments, thus to preach repentance to the nations is the same as teaching them everything that Christ has commanded (Matt. 28:20). Which is the same as proclaiming Christ's Lordship over every area of life (Ps. 103:19) and mankind's responsibility to live by every Word that proceeds from the mouth of God (Matt. 4:4). Paul preached the message of the Kingdom, calling upon everyone to submit to the reign of the King (see too comments on Acts 1:3). Paul was now bidding farewell to this region—he had probably spent about 7 or 8 years ministering in these parts (Bruce) and even though he did not know what the future held for him, he was confident that he had completed his work here and so believed that they would see his face no more. Paul had plans to visit other unreached areas, faithfully following the commission God had given him (Acts 13:47; 22:21).

Acts 20:26, 27

Paul is calling upon these Ephesian leaders to bear witness to the fact that he had faithfully fulfilled his responsibilities amongst them. Paul says that if any people whom he had instructed proved to be unfaithful, *he* could not be held accountable. Anyone who continued to live in guilt and condemnation would have only themselves to blame, since Paul had clearly and unashamedly pro-

claimed the whole counsel of God. Paul did not fear the consequences of preaching the full counsel of God, nor did he seek to
peach a popular message so as to gain a massive following. He did
not shun from proclaiming those truths that are offensive to the
natural man, nor did he water them down so as to make them
acceptable to those who despised the light. If you listened to Paul,
you either loved him or you hated him, but whatever it was, you
could not go away claiming ignorance as to who God is or what He
demanded from you. There are some doctrines and teachings in the
Scriptures that will particularly infuriate the enemies of God and
Paul did not avoid speaking about these. There are also some truths
that those who profess faith in Christ do not want to hear, yet God's
faithful servant will not be afraid of anything revealed in the Scriptures. Paul calls on these elders to testify to the fact that he had
clearly presented everything they needed to know to thoroughly
equip them for every good work (2 Tim. 3:16, 17). The message
that elders are to proclaim is God's message, not their own, thus
they do not have the right to emphasise what they like and ignore
or hardly touch those things they do not personally like. A leader's
responsibility before God is to declare His whole counsel, without
apology and without change and not rely upon foolish, human wisdom to try to determine what is needful for people to hear. To do
less than this is to fail in one's calling as a leader in the church of
God.

Paul, echoing the prophet Ezekiel, says he will be clean from the
blood of everyone he had spoken to (Ezk. 3:18–21; 33:1–9)—he
had been faithful to declare the whole of God's will for the whole of
their lives. The only way to achieve such a goal is if you see yourself
as the Lord's minister, faithfully and selflessly serving His purposes.
Those who are serving themselves, will not proclaim the whole
counsel of God, because to do so runs totally opposite to the way
the natural man thinks. Paul, not caring for his own safety or reputation, boldly declared every doctrine and every truth. Paul tells
these leaders that he held back nothing that was "profitable" (verse
20), preached "repentance towards God and faith towards the Lord,
Jesus Christ" (verse 21), testified of the "Gospel of the grace of God"
(verse 24), proclaimed the "Kingdom of God" (verse 25), and the
"whole counsel of God" (verse 27)—all of these overlapping and
complimenting each other and sealing the comprehensive nature of

Paul's ministry. It is only God's grace and power that can enable us to fulfill this high calling (see Acts 4:18, 29).

It is a heavy responsibility to assume the position of instructing people in the Word of God, for to be negligent in some way towards the whole counsel of God means God will require the blood of those who go astray at your hands. Whoever walks contrary to the will of God is first and foremost personally guilty for their rebellion, however, teachers who did not present the whole of the truth before the eyes of these wayward people will also have "blood" upon their hands. This is not a light matter and it is not a small thing to be called to proclaim the full counsel of God (Jam.3:1). Christians are exhorted to pray for those holding such positions of authority and responsibility, since they are accountable for more than just themselves (Rom. 15:30; Eph. 6:19, 20; Col. 4:3, 4; 1 Thes. 5:25; 2 Thes. 3:1; Heb. 13:18).

Acts 20:28

Paul has highlighted his example and doctrine to serve as an example to these Ephesian elders. They were to lead the flock of God and Paul's instruction to them starts with telling them to watch over themselves. A shepherd has to watch over himself as well as those under his oversight (1 Cor. 9:27)—Paul said he "buffets" his body, though the body is not evil, rather it is the vehicle through which sin and death are able to assault us and we overcome these powers of darkness by making our body the slave of righteousness. This is a fight and we ought not to become weary because of the battle, but realize that even the apostle Paul had to fight. We are to always be looking to Christ to supply our every need for overcoming the law of sin and death. Paul exhorted Timothy to take heed to himself and to doctrine (1 Tim. 4:16). Here, Paul has been talking about his example and his doctrine, thus we see how important these things are in God's Kingdom—pure life and pure teaching. This also applies to the rest of the flock and all Christians need to know *true doctrine*. A preacher cannot preach the *whole* counsel of God with power if he is not bringing his own life into submission to the same. Thus we see that the primary reason for taking heed to yourself as a leader, is so that you can better serve and take care of the Lord's flock.

It is the Holy Spirit, according to Paul, that appoints overseers in the church. This is not a calling that people can take unto themselves. It is important to note that Luke called these leaders first "elders" (verse 17) and now he calls them "overseers." Both Paul and Peter use the terms "elder" and "overseer" interchangeably (1 Tim. 3:1–7; Titus 1:6–9; 1 Pet. 5:1–4)—they mean the same thing and are not to be thought of as two different offices within the church. Thus the terms; bishop, elder, presbyter and overseer all refer to one office. An elder is to take diligent care of God's flock, which includes their protection, ruling and feeding—all of these functions must be understood when the Scriptures talk about "shepherding" the church of God.

The blood of God is a phrase that has ancient support and acceptance in the church. This refers obviously to Christ (Heb. 9:14) who is both human and Divine and it is His blood that has bought redemption for us. It was the whole of Christ's life that secured our redemption, because His obedience to the Father in the flesh was needed to put right Adam's disobedience. However it is not wrong to see the sacrificial death of Christ as having the power to blot out all sins, thus Luke sums up the whole of what Christ did in the terms "the blood of God." Christ has two natures (human and Divine), however He is only one Person and the unity between His natures is such that it is not improper to apply the property of the one nature to the other. So here we see that the Holy Spirit has no problem in mentioning Christ's blood (from His human nature) while referring to Him as God (His Divine nature)—for it was the blood of Him who is God. It must always be maintained that although Christ has two natures, He is only one Person.

The care and price that the Lord places upon His church is beyond measure and question—giving His own blood for it. Thus, if this is the value that God has for what is His, how should the shepherds watch over the flock? How can they fear the faces of men, when God places such a value upon the protection, teaching and feeding of His flock? Dare we dilute the message He has given us to proclaim? God loves His flock with an infinite love and what they need to know, He has revealed in the Scriptures, thus for shepherds to refuse to proclaim the whole counsel of God is an act of rebellion against God's wisdom. What more could the Spirit have said to spur shepherds on to faithfully care for the flock than that God's blood was given for it. Remember Christ's strong condemnation upon hirelings (see comments on John 10:11–13). A hireling has no real relationship with Christ and so cannot care for that which

Christ cares for and places very little value upon that which Christ purchased with such a high price—His blood. If Christ gave His blood for His sheep, it is but a very small thing for an elder to lay down his life for the sheep. Not to live in such a self-sacrificial way for the flock of God is a sure sign of being a hireling. Elders are but servants looking after what belongs to their Lord and it is no small thing if shepherds betray such an important trust of looking after God's flock.

Acts 20:29, 30

Paul warns these elders that the enemies of Christ will come from without and within the church and seek to destroy the sheep. Were such attacks going to arise because Paul was now out of the way? While Paul was an imposing and strong theologian I do not think his time in Ephesus was without this kind of opposition. He talks about the opposition to His teaching as being life threatening and like fighting with wild beasts (1 Cor. 15:32; 2 Cor. 1:8). Paul risked his life by consistently and diligently exposing error and upholding the truth. This responsibility had fallen heavily upon Paul when he had been in Ephesus, but with his departure he was making these elders aware that this responsibility was now theirs. Paul's insights might have been prophetic with him seeing specific instances of deception and destruction that were coming, however, the warning that error will challenge the light is a sure thing and therefore, his warning is for all generations and to all elders. Being an elder is not to be taken lightly and nor should the sheep take for granted good elders. It is a sign of great blessing to have leaders who are equipped to expose the darkness and point out error, not fearing for their own welfare and not worried what a rebellious world thinks about them (Matt. 10:22; 24:9).

It is madness to play down how serious the threat of error is. Those who are in rebellion against the truth are called "ravenous wolves." Error violently and viciously destroys those who embrace it. Even when error presents itself as peaceable and only seeking what is best for people, it is still ruthlessly destructive. Unless we realize there is only one absolute truth and everything that disagrees with that is violently opposed to the truth and seeking to replace it, then we will not appreciate the life and death struggle we are in. All views are not equal.

Some people assault the truth while making it very clear that they want nothing to do with it, whereas, others try to overturn the truth by identifying themselves with it. Thus Paul talks of attacks from without and attacks from within the church. In the final analysis however, both kinds of attacks have the same objective—to utterly destroy the truth. There are many similar warnings throughout the Scriptures against opponents of the truth (2 Pet. 2:1–3, 17, 18; 3:16; 2 Cor. 11:13–15). Those opponents who arise from within the church will sooner or later be revealed for who they are by their lives and/or their doctrine. If we are casual about identifying false teaching and false teachers then we will be risking our own destinies. God has given us an objective standard whereby we are able to test every teaching and action (Isa. 8:20; Matt. 7:15–20; 2 Tim. 3:16, 17), thus God says through the prophet Jeremiah, "he who has My Word, let him speak My Word faithfully" (Jer. 23:28). Our own ideas, divorced from the Word of God, bring only death and it is rebellious fools who seek to exalt human wisdom above God's truth. It is immoral to say it will be well with those who despise the Word of God and stubbornly walk according to their own imagination. There will be no peace when nations walk contrary to the mind of Christ and for teachers to ignore such blatant rebellion and ask for God to bless them is itself rebellion and makes these teachers ravenous wolves. Every path does not lead to God and to encourage people to walk on a false path or to ignore their error leads to eternal destruction and thus Paul uses very strong words to refer to those who propagate error in the church. Ignorant sheep mistake such wolves as one of themselves and therefore Paul exhorts the elders to be on guard to protect the flock. Pure doctrine, holy living and being on the constant lookout for wolves (eternal watchfulness) are the marks of Christ's shepherds.

Unity is not the goal, but unity *of the faith* is (Eph. 4:13), that is, we need to bring all our thinking into line with the revelation God has given to us in the Scriptures for it is here alone that we will find true unity. Many people think that we need to get all the churches united, though they seek to do this by watering down the truth to a level where most people can agree. This, however, is unity based upon the "wisdom" of men, which is actually a path leading to destruction. Unity cannot be separated from truth, just as grace and truth cannot be separated. To be patient and long suffering does not mean forsaking truth, but that we show graciousness as we seek to make known and lead people to the *truth*. Christ is gracious, yet He will never allow compromise. Christ's love cannot be divorced from righteousness, or His mercy separated from His truth. Those who proclaim a message other than Christ's, are wanting people to follow them instead of Christ—this is not innocent, but ruthlessly destructive. Pride and self-centredness have eternal consequences and can affect many people.

Acts 20:31

Paul says the only way to accomplish this task is if the elders demonstrate the same selfless concern for the flock that Paul had manifested. It is not just the elders that need to be on the alert, but the flock also needs to be constantly warned to be vigilant. Paul never stopped warning the people of God to bring all their thinking and living into line with the truth. Paul kept the truth constantly before their eyes and challenged them to apply it to their own lives. He did this with tears, which does not mean he was always crying when he was speaking, but that his whole ministry was motivated by a deep heartfelt concern for their wellbeing. Night and day means that Paul never ceased from his responsibility to watch, warn and instruct—it was constant. This had been Paul's example for three years: an example which should inspire and encourage these elders who witnessed it, to continue in the same sacrificial way, seeking the eternal welfare of their flocks rather than their own ease and comfort.

Acts 20:32

With Paul leaving, he commends these believers into the care of God: God, His Word and His Grace cannot be separated. Paul tells us that the Gospel is the power of God (Rom. 1:16; 1 Cor. 1:18) and it is the gracious working of God through His Word that accomplishes His purposes in our lives. This was not something new that Paul was introducing, rather, he was encouraging these elders by reminding them where their focus should be. Paul would no longer be with them, but God would and it was always and only God's Power, Word and Grace that had preserved them in the past, thus there was no need to fear the future. The whole of our Christian life is to be one of total dependence upon the workings of God in our lives. Their hope, as our hope, is to rest upon an immovable foundation—the gracious power of God's Word. This Word is living and active or powerful (Heb. 4:12)—not merely a collection of good, moral principles (1 Thes. 1:5). As Christians believe and obey the Word by God's gracious power, they will be strengthened and built up in the Lord. This means being conformed more and more to the image of Christ so that the whole of our Christian life becomes one of mature obedience.

When we know and love the truth with our whole heart, the wolves will be unable to disrupt the flock of God. While we stand by the grace and power of God, having faith in His ability to keep us unto the end, we must never forget that one of the means God uses in making us overcomers, is His Word. It is the Word that has revealed to us who God is, what He has done for us, what the truth is, how to spot error, what sin is, how to be saved, etc. It is through knowing God's truth and having that mould our lives, that we are built up spiritually. We are kept by the power of God through faith (1 Pet. 1:5). Our hope is in a sure Word and in the power of God. Paul tells these elders of the Christian's inheritance which belongs to all the sons of God—and this is God's own work (Phil. 1:6; 1 Thes. 5:24). If we are going to be strong in the Lord then we must not place trust in ourselves, but in the gracious power of God working through His Word. We are to take hold of Him, cast aside our own wisdom and desires and live wholly for His glory. Those who have faith in Christ become heirs to the throne of God and become part of His massive family, being united to all those who are sanctified. When we stand by faith in Jesus, God looks upon us as completely sanctified, though at the same time He is constantly working in us to sanctify us more and more.

Sin can no longer have dominion over us (Rom. 6:11, 14). This means that because of the power of the Holy Spirit and resurrection life of Christ working in us, sin can no longer dominate us. That which sin has to offer cannot control us because our motivating desires are no longer in the firm grasp of sin. There is a greater power than sin working in us and thus Paul can speak with confidence to all Christians, telling them about their inheritance. This is not wishful thinking on Paul's part, because it is based upon God's own revelation which not only tells us of His purposes but also about His power to accomplish the task (2 Cor. 3:18; 5:17; 1 Thes. 4:3; 2 Thes. 1:11, 12; 1 Pet. 5:10). Spiritual progress is God's will for our lives and there is one immovable foundation and that is Christ (Eph. 2:20)—the only hope for anything in this life is Christ's Word and the power of His grace. If we do not cast ourselves upon Him we will strive in our own futile power and wisdom to accomplish a Divine calling which will cause nothing but frustration and failure. The Word of God's grace has been preserved for us in the Scriptures and the power of God remains with His Word today in the same way as it did in Paul's day. One of our biggest obstacles is wanting some "physical" proof or sign before we will whole-heartedly follow every Word of God, but this is nothing but lack of faith. We are to live by faith. We do not walk by sight (2 Cor. 5:7), but by total trust in what Christ has said (Rom. 1:17), for here is our victory: "whatever is born of God overcomes the world. And this is the victory that has overcome the world—our faith" (1 John 5:4). "Therefore since we are surrounded by so great a cloud of witnesses, let us lay aside every weight, and the sin which so easily ensnares us, and let us run with endurance the race that is set before us, looking unto Jesus, the author and finisher of our faith, who for the joy that was set before Him endured the cross, despising the shame, and has sat down at the right hand of the throne of God" (Heb. 12:1, 2). We are heirs to all that Christ received from the Father, thus, we should live in a way that is worthy of this high calling (Eph. 4:1; Col. 1:10; 1 Thes. 2:12).

Acts 20:33

Paul had worked among some very wealthy people, yet his motivation for the work he did was never to gain some of their riches. Paul did not condemn riches and nor did he covet them. Covetousness relates to both internal desire and outward actions. Any desiring of or taking of, in an unlawful way, that which belongs to our neighbour, is condemned by the law of God. The sole motivating drive in the life of Paul was to labor so that he might benefit others and glorify the name of Christ—he never thought about enriching himself (1 Cor. 10:24, 33; 2 Cor. 5:14, 15). Unfortunately, for many people, in Paul's day and in our day, it is self-centred gain that plays the biggest part in their deciding how and where they will "labor for the Lord." At one stage in Paul's life, out of the many people he knew who were working in the name of the Lord, he only knew of one person who would seek the benefit of the sheep above their own benefit (Phil. 2:19–21). Paul had no desire to live like any of the rich Ephesians, rather he was content with whatever state the Lord saw fit to give him (Phil. 4:11). To feed and warn the flock of God is a calling from God and thus one must do it without thought for material reward. You cannot be effective for the Lord if your heart is set on riches and comfort. The great prophet Samuel, at the end of his long ministry in Israel asked the people to tell him when he had taken a bribe or defrauded someone (1 Sam. 12:3–5)—his judgment had not been for his own benefit, but was righteous judgment for the glory of God. It is only those who are not seeking to enrich themselves at the expense of others that are able to act in this way and it is a vital qualification for elders: "Shepherd the flock of God … not under compulsion, but because you are willing, as God wants you to be; not greedy for money, but eager to serve" (1 Pet. 5:2). As soon as a person is enticed by the riches or praises of this world, they will not be able to declare the full counsel of God and thus they will not be seeking what is best for others—serving their own interests, rather than the interests of others. It is only the whole truth of God that can benefit people and to keep any of this truth from them, for whatever reason, is to harm them. Paul did not labor among the Ephesians because he wanted fancy clothes or other riches, thus he could fearlessly and unashamedly state this in the midst of people who knew him well. (See also 2 Cor. 7:2.)

Acts 20:34

Paul, for his own particular reasons, makes an exception to the very well established Biblical principle that those who labor in the Word, ought to be supported by the Word (1 Cor. 9:14; 1 Tim. 5:17). When people receive spiritual things from someone, they ought to respond by giving them physical things (Luke 10:7; Rom. 15:27; Gal. 6:6; 1 Cor. 9:11; 1 Tim. 5:18). This is the Biblical principle, however, while it is Paul's right to be treated in this way, he can refuse it if he so chooses. Paul believed there were other concerns that justified him refusing any help. He did explain his reasons to the Corinthians and Thessalonians (1 Cor. 9; 1 Thes. 2:9; 2 Thes. 3:8, 9). His practical situation also made it possible that without neglecting any other responsibilities, he could refuse what was rightfully his and still obtain what he needed to live. He had no family responsibilities thus he could easily work very long hours—preaching as well as working for his own physical needs. While establishing the churches in the Gentile world, Paul did not want there to be even the slightest chance that he could be accused of seeking to benefit himself by taking advantage of ignorant people.

He also wanted his example of self-sacrificial work for the benefit of others to be embraced by those he taught, since that is how the Kingdom of God functions. Paul's single focus was to advance the Kingdom of God, thus he would put away his rights if he believed that it would advance the work of the Lord in the lives of those he was ministering to. Paul was driven by his love for Christ and his realization that he was a lowly servant, rather than by his rights (cf. Luke 17:7–10). Paul never asked for or expected anything from the churches he started, however, he did accept the gifts sent to him by the Philippian church while he was in Thessalonica (Phil. 2:25; 4:16–18), thus he was not totally against receiving from these churches (see too 2 Cor. 11:8, 9). Nevertheless, Paul worked extremely hard with his own hands when he was not preaching so he could earn enough to support himself and others who were ministering with him, thus the ministry that flowed from Paul was never a burden upon those he ministered to (2 Cor. 12:14).

Acts 20:35

Paul says his example of Kingdom life was to set the standard for the Ephesians—labouring hard for the benefit of others, namely, the weak. This refers to the spiritually weak (Rom. 15:1), the sick and those, who for some *legitimate* reason, couldn't support themselves (cf. 2 Thes. 3:10–12). Christians are not to think "rights," but "sacrifice." Paul was very far from being a wealthy man, yet his thoughts were still about how he could help others more. The ministry he had undertaken was already a massive sacrifice, yet he was constantly thinking of ways to sacrifice more so he could be a greater blessing to those around him. Paul knew that he was saved by grace alone, however, he also wanted the Lord to say to him, "Well done, good and faithful servant," thus he would pour everything he had into the Kingdom. The way we live so often reveals that we do not really believe in the eternal aspect of our existence. Paul did not have riches though he was sacrificing so much, nevertheless, he still said, "I want to give more, thus what must I do in order to be able to do so?" He truly believed the saying of Christ, "It is more blessed to be giving than to be receiving." It is not wrong to receive, if your mindset is one of doing everything within your power so that you can be a giver. We need to exhaust every opportunity that comes our way and use every gifting so that God's Kingdom can be advanced. We exist for Him and His purposes. There is nothing that we have for ourselves—our strength, time, resources and giftings are given to us so that we can glorify God. The Lord expects us to fully utilise for Him, everything we have (Matt. 25:14–30).

As I have said above, the key to this kind of life is to be thinking "sacrifice," not "rights." We are to redeem the time we have so that its use brings the greatest benefit to God's Kingdom. Not every person can give the same amount of money into the Kingdom work, however, every person is capable of making the same sacrifice. This is something that is between each individual and God, for it is God alone that knows our hearts and the details of our lives. He knows if you are seeking in all sincerity to be a giver. Paul did not say, well if I happen to have something over after I have done everything I want to do, then I will be a giver. He truly believed Christ's Words that real happiness and completeness is found in being givers and so Paul lived his whole life in a totally sacrificial way so that he could be a giver. Paul gave out of his lack—this manifests Christ's Kingdom (cf. Mark 12:44). Has not God freely given us all things? (Rom. 8:32; 1 Cor. 2:12; Rev. 21:7). We are to be givers with our resources, our time and our patience so that others may benefit and the Kingdom advanced.

Remember, it is only in Christ that we can find the desire and strength to live like this (see comments on John 1:16), yet this does not release us from the responsibility of embracing what Christ has for us. It is only stubborn foolishness that prevents us from receiving from Christ all that we need to glorify Him fully (1 Cor. 15:10). Do you believe that it is more blessed to give than to receive? If so, then demonstrate it by your works (James 2:17–26). It is our actions that reveal what we really believe to be true.

Acts 20:36–38

Prayer is a vital ingredient for success in the Kingdom. Whatever we do or teach, if it is going to bear fruit in the Kingdom, it needs to be undergirded by prayer. The outward form or position one assumes while praying can take on many different forms, however, what is crucial is to rest totally upon Christ's completed work, in humility of spirit (Ps. 34:18; 51:17; Isa. 57:15; Matt. 5:3). Both Paul and the elders needed God's grace if they were going to complete the work He still had for them. Prayer plays a vital part in our tapping into the resources that have been made available to us in Christ.

There was a deep and sincere bond between these elders and the apostle and all felt real pain over the news that they would never see each other again in this life. Those who try to deny the real human emotions one feels in this life when you are parted from people you dearly love are deceived by a false spirituality. While our emotions are to be kept under control, we must not try to totally suppress or deny them. The elders here were filled with "deep distress" (mentally and spiritually) and openly wept as they said goodbye. Paul, throughout his ministry had stood unbending upon the truth of God and made it fully known to these people. Those who love Christ and His truth will whole-heartedly love such teachers. May the Lord make us like Paul, who did not want the praises or love of those who did not love the whole of Christ's Word. Let people curse us if they so desire, but we should not be distracted by such people, who by their lives curse Christ every day too. We ought to glorify Christ and desire to be loved by those who want to live by every Word from God's mouth (Matt. 4:4) and who want to bring every thought captive to the mind of Christ (2 Cor. 10:5). Any "love" that does not arise from and rest totally upon the truth of God, is not worthy of being called "love," so do not seek after it.

Acts 21:1–4

Luke fills in again some of the travelling details. In Tyre there was a seven day wait while the ship's cargo was unloaded. The ship had made good time so this delay did not hinder Paul's hopes of being in Jerusalem for Pentecost (Acts 20:16). Paul and his party naturally sought to find the believers in the city and spent this time with them. We do not have much information about the beginning of this church in Tyre or about Paul's previous connections with them, if any. We do, however, have references to the Word being preached in these areas (Acts 11:19; 15:3). The time is spent, presumably, in instruction and mutual encouragement—undoubtedly, a great time of spiritual feasting for the Tyre Christians. Some believers in Tyre, through the revelation of the Holy Spirit, saw what awaited Paul in Jerusalem, but this was as far as the revelation went. Their natural response to this revelation was to think that it was a warning for Paul not to go up to Jerusalem. The revelation they had seen was true, however, their application of that revelation to the situation was wrong and so Paul does not listen to them. Prophets only see little bits and pieces of the whole picture (1 Cor. 13:9, 12). It was the Holy Spirit that was leading Paul to Jerusalem (Acts 20:22, see too comments on Acts 19:21). Others along the way had also seen, through the Spirit, the trouble that awaited Paul (Acts 20:23). To be aware of even certain danger when pursuing a particular path, does not mean that you are on the wrong path and therefore need to change direction. Christ is the most obvious example of someone facing the danger head on, however, there are many other examples, e.g., Daniel who ended up in the lion's den; Daniel's three friends who ended up in the furnace; and many others who suffered for being lone voices in a perverse generation (Dan. 3; 6; Matt. 5:11, 12; 21:35; 23:31). Paul used these warnings to prepare himself for what would happen to him in Jerusalem. These verses also show how totally committed Paul was to the cause of Christ, not fearing what might happen to himself. His single desire was to faithfully walk the path God had ordained for him and complete his course (2 Tim. 4:7), and if this meant chains, persecution or even death, so be it. Like Christ, Paul had firmly set his face to go to Jerusalem and nothing could distract him from that path (cf. Luke 9:51; 12:50).

Acts 21:5, 6

There is an obvious bond established between the Tyre Christians and the visitors. They commit themselves and each other in prayer to the Lord's keeping and resume their different callings and responsibilities in the Kingdom.

Acts 21:7, 8

Even when there is a brief stop over in a city, Paul and his companions seek out the Christians, showing that the church of Christ is one body no matter where they are and even if they have never met before. When people believe in Christ and love His truth, they will want to fellowship together and encourage one another in the Lord's ways.

Philip was a very well known figure in the early church, being one of the seven chosen by the apostles to oversee the administration of helping those in need (Acts 6:3–6). Later, Philip had great success as a missionary in Samaria and ended up in Caesarea (Acts 8:5, 6, 35, 40). Twenty years have elapsed since Acts 8:40 and Philip is still in Caesarea and it seems probable that Paul and his friends headed straight to Philip's house because he was so well known and established in that area.

Acts 21:9

Philip had four unmarried daughters who prophesied. Such gifts had been promised as a sign to the church, marking the great visitation promised by the Lord, when He would abundantly pour His Spirit upon the church (Joel 2:28ff.; Acts 2:17, 18). These gifts were only meant to serve for a season, as a temporary measure until the Scriptures had been completed (see comments on Acts 11:27). A question that immediately comes to mind is how these girls would have exercised their gifts in the church? We do not believe that the Holy Spirit would contradict Himself and allow these girls to do something in the church which He had forbidden somewhere else (cf. 1 Cor. 14:34, 35). Thus, the usual interpretation is that these girls did not exercise their gifts *within* the institutional church, but in private. My understanding of these passages is that the daughters of Philip were free to exercise their gifts within the church, because making known the will of the Lord with respect to some truth or even predicting an event, does not grant the one who brings the revelation authority over the hearers. To have authority over the flock of God is a specific office and calling from God. Thus it is not immoral for a woman to teach a man something (see comments on Acts 18:26). What Paul forbids, is for a woman to assume the authoritative position of ruling or teaching in the church (1 Tim. 2:12. I also believe 1 Cor. 14:34, 35 is connected to this kind of authority function). To have great understanding about something and pass on your knowledge to someone else, does not give you authority over that person. Authority within the church is an office that comes from God and is only to be given to qualified men. Having and imparting knowledge does not give you authority over those you are instructing. If we do not keep this firmly fixed in our minds then we will be unable to make sense of the Scriptures (Isa. 8:3; Ex. 15:20; Judges 4:4; 2 Kings 22:14; Luke 2:36–38; Acts 18:26; 21:9; 1 Cor. 11:5; 14:34, 35; 1 Tim. 2:12). An elder, on the other hand has knowledge and an authoritative office from God, qualifying him to rule and teach in the church. When prophets were given divine revelation from God, which they were to impart to others, this did not necessarily place them in an authoritative office over people in the church. While it was possible for a prophet to have a position of authority over the flock of God, such authority was something added to the prophetic gift and not a necessary part of it. Paul refused to listen to the prophets' counsel that he should not go up to Jerusalem. Although they had received divine revelation about Paul's future in Jerusalem (Acts 21:4), they still had no authority over him, thus Paul's refusal to listen to them, did not contradict the revelation or authority of the Holy Spirit. When prophetesses received divine revelation from God and imparted it to the church, this in no way gave them an authoritative position over the church and therefore, their prophesying in the church did not contradict Paul's instructions to the Corinthians or to Timothy—where women are excluded from assuming *authoritative* positions of teaching or ruling in the church. This does not make men superior to women. It is merely the order in God's authority structure. It is the same in marriage—men and women are equal, though for the purpose of authority and structure, the man is the head of the home. Those philosophies and cultures that treat women as inferior to men are perverse. Equality, however, does *not* mean both are able to or should do the same things—this too is perverse. God made fundamental differences in the make-up of men and women and their roles and responsibilities cannot be changed at will, without society-destroying consequences. When God forbids something it is not to cheat people out of something that is good and satisfying, but to protect them from that which is a violation of how life has been designed to function. It is only when men and women operate within the boundaries God has set, that we can bring glory to Him and harmony, progress and satisfaction to ourselves.

Acts 21:10, 11

This prophet, Agabus, was probably the same person who predicted the coming famine in Acts 11:27, 28. His warning is at the end of a very long line of warnings that had come to Paul ever since he had set out to return to Jerusalem. This time the prophet uses a very graphic illustration about what awaits Paul—he would be bound so that his movements would no longer be as free as they had been in the past. The prophet does not predict Paul's death and nor does he tell Paul not to go to Jerusalem. Some have challenged the preciseness of the prophecy, since it was the Romans who bound Paul (Acts 21:33; 22:25), not the Jews and the Jews did not hand him over to the Gentiles, but the Gentiles had to rescue Paul from the Jews (Acts 21:30–33). However, is the prophecy wrong? Was it not due to the violent resistance of the Jews against Paul, that in a real sense, delivered him into the hands of the Romans? The Romans would never have touched him if the Jews had not created the uproar (Acts 21:27–31, 35) and did not the Jews make it clear that, at the very least, this man deserved to be kept in bonds? (Acts 22:22–24). It was indeed the actions of the Jews that delivered Paul into Roman bonds and kept him there—Agabus was perfectly correct and Paul agrees with him (Acts 28:17). We must not force a preciseness onto predictive prophecy that the Scriptures do not support. Was Malachi's prophecy fulfilled? Malachi said Elijah would return (Mal. 4:5). Jesus said he did return, though the disciples understood that Jesus was talking about John the Baptist (Matt. 17:11–13).

Acts 21:12, 13

It was not Agabus but those who accompanied Paul and others in Philip's house in Caesarea who pleaded with Paul not to go to Jerusalem. Once again the warning is misinterpreted and a meaning given to it that God had not intended (see comments on Acts 21:4). Those persuading Paul not to go to Jerusalem included, among others, Luke, the author of Acts, Timothy and probably even Philip and his daughters. They believed certain danger faced Paul and wanting to preserve both his life and his vital ministry for the early church, they earnestly tried to protect him. Paul knew what awaited him, but he also knew the Lord's will for him and thus nothing could distract him from that path. It is likely that those trying to protect Paul would have used very convincing reasons when trying to persuade him to avoid Jerusalem. Paul was not against taking counsel from other Christians, however, in this instance their counsel was not in line with the will of God that had been revealed to him. Paul casts himself totally upon the sovereign leading and authority of God and puts aside anything or anyone who would speak a different word from God. We ought to hold to the Scriptures in the same way, seeing them as the final authority for everything in life (2 Tim. 3:16, 17). The Scriptures are God breathed, perfectly complete and preserved by the power of God. The Westminster Confession of Faith, chapter 1, section 6, says, "The whole counsel of God concerning all things necessary for His own glory, man's salvation, faith and life, is either expressly set down in Scripture, or by good and necessary consequence may be deduced from Scripture: unto which nothing at any time is to be added, whether by new revelations of the Spirit or traditions of men ..." (2 Tim. 3:15–17: Gal. 1:8, 9; 2 Thes. 2:2).

It is obvious from Paul's response that it is not possible to serve the Lord properly unless we are prepared to lose our lives for His sake. God's truth and purposes should be more highly esteemed than anything else in this life and fullness of life is only found when we live whole-heartedly for Christ. This does not mean it was easy for Paul to lay down his life in this way. His actions were not determined by his emotions, since he clearly tells these friends that they were breaking his heart. The course he knew he had to walk for Christ was clear, however, the concern of his friends was tearing at his emotions and softening his determination, thus he asked them to stop. Paul's friends were being guided by emotions and whereas Paul too is deeply touched by emotion, he brought them into line with the revealed will of God and faithfully continued with his responsibilities. To die for the name of Christ is a high honour indeed. Paul does not think he is going to die in Jerusalem, but is rather telling them that he is prepared, not only to suffer bonds, but to die also. How can darkness withstand such zealous advancing of God's truth?

Acts 21:14

When Paul's friends realised that Paul was convinced that he was acting according to God's divine will, they stopped opposing him and also found their rest in the sovereign purposes of God. It seems likely that although they were of a different opinion, they submitted to the apostolic authority of Paul, believing that Paul's determination to go to Jerusalem, despite what awaited him, was now sufficient proof that he was being led by divine revelation. Everyone's submission to the will of the Lord in this matter should exhort us to bring all our emotions and personal desires into line with what God wants and has ordained for us.

Acts 21:15–17

For the last stage of the journey, Luke just records some brief facts. We are not told how this group of believers felt as they approached Jerusalem, but surely they must have wondered what exactly awaited them in the light of all the prophetic warnings they had received. The disciple Mnason, who accompanied them, could quite possibly have come to believe in Christ when the Holy Spirit was poured out at Pentecost in Acts 2. This disciple lived in Jerusalem and was going to be the host to Paul's group of believers. Paul and his companions had been well received by the believers in every city they passed through and Jerusalem was no different. There was real oneness and unity in the early church.

Acts 21:18–20a

James was recognised as one of the pillars of the Jerusalem church, having great respect from all the Christians. James was seen as the main leader among the Jewish believers and Paul as the main leader among the Gentile believers. Paul was very aware of the difficulty of bringing these two bodies together and did much to demonstrate unity between the two—the offering Paul had brought was one of the ways he hoped to cement this unity, showing the Gentiles' gratefulness and indebtedness to the Jews (Rom. 15:27, 31). James and the elders in Jerusalem rejoiced in what God had done through Paul. They were not jealous but overjoyed that the Lord's name was being exalted and His Kingdom extended. True fruit in the Kingdom comes from the working of God alone, thus it is very immature and foolish to be jealous of someone God is using to advance His purposes. If Christians' hearts are truly seeking the Kingdom of God they will recognise and rejoice in whatever the Lord is doing through others.

Acts 21:20b–23

The Jerusalem leadership faced a very real problem. Many Jews who had truly believed in Christ had been told that Paul was opposed to the Jewish *customs* (verse 21). This was a lie being spread by those who hated Paul and Christ, however, it did create a real problem for the Jewish believers in Jerusalem. They saw this supposed position of Paul as assaulting the Jews' Jewishness and also as opening the door for totally lawless living. The Jerusalem elders wanted these lies to be silenced by actions rather than words, thus they ask Paul to participate in some of the ceremonial rituals that were still being practised in Jerusalem.

We must not despise any aspect of the law, including those ceremonial aspects that have now been fulfilled in Christ. Although the ceremonial aspects of the law were only shadows of something better that was coming, you cannot despise the shadow without also despising Christ. The unbelieving Jews were not keepers, but opponents of the law (Gal. 6:13; 1 Thes. 2:15). They had perverted the true meaning of the law by substituting their own ideas in its place and it was these man-made laws that they zealously protected. Thus, when Jews were born from above and given new hearts by the Spirit of God they would see the whole law of God in a completely different way. Those who came to Christ in Jerusalem had great zeal for the law because for the first time in their lives they understood the meaning of these laws and thus the significance of their own actions. Their hearts could readily see the Messiah pictured in the ceremonies and understand God's plan to accomplish redemption through Him. Although to continue using these shadows after the coming of Christ was a sign of immaturity, these Jews who now believed in Christ were not using them as the basis for being *accepted* in God's sight. They believed in the work of Christ for salvation, however, had lived their whole lives in at least some kind of outward conformity to these laws and now felt great zeal for them when looking at them with enlightened eyes. These laws which were inseparable from Jewish culture and traditions now took on new meaning and they saw the significance of being Jewish, in a much deeper way. It was because of their immaturity, that they were hanging onto the ceremonial shadows with great zeal.

The Gospel is both revolutionary and not revolutionary (see comments on Acts 2:46). Some things in life require radical and immediate change, whereas, God in His patience allows us to grow in maturity and have our minds slowly renewed with respect to other things in life. It is a Biblical principle to conform ourselves to different cultures for the purpose of extending Christ's Kingdom, so long as we do not violate the moral law of God or compromise salvation by grace alone (see comments on Acts 16:3). Paul knew the freedom he had in Christ and thus could bring his actions into line with different cultures without compromising his faith or violating his conscience (Acts 23:1; 24:16; 2 Tim. 1:3). What there was in Jerusalem at this time was a vast number of Jews who had come to believe in Christ, however, they were also very immature and the church elders were faced with a real problem that required great wisdom to resolve. You cannot trust in your obedience to the law to be the basis of your salvation and these Jewish believers were not saying this. However, while they did not say everyone (including Gentiles) had to observe the ceremonies of Moses in order to be saved, there was a very strong desire amongst them to preserve their

"Jewishness"—which they tied closely to the observance of the ceremonial law. These Jews were not equating Jewishness with being a Christian, but rather, as well as being Christians they wanted to preserve their Jewish culture (which had been formed by the law of Moses. A people's culture is shaped by their religious beliefs). God, at this stage, had not forbidden the practice of the ceremonial system, even though it had found its fulfilment in Christ's completed work (His life, death and resurrection). As long as people did not think that their observance of the Mosaic ceremonies was the basis for being accepted by God, it was not unlawful to use the ceremonies as a reminder of what Christ had done. Although hanging onto these ceremonies was not the mature thing to do, it was not *unlawful*. God would Himself bring a complete end, once and for all time, to the possibility of observing the sacrificial ceremonies of Moses. He did this in A.D. 70 when the Romans totally destroyed Jerusalem and the temple, forever ending the whole way of worship that rested upon the ceremonial law. Until God brought about this end, the apostles did not have the liberty to condemn the observance of the old order, as long as Christ was acknowledged as the focus and substance of the ceremonies. What the apostles could and did condemn was when people thought their salvation depended upon fulfilling the ceremonies, rather than trusting in Christ alone.

When Paul said that he became as under the law to the Jews (1 Cor. 9:20), he had to be referring to those Jews who observed the ceremonies of Moses, with Jerusalem being the centre of this whole system of worship. It does appear as though the great tension in this incident in Acts was a matter of cultural identity and preservation. The rumours that Paul was seeking to destroy the Jews' Jewishness was resented by the Jews in Jerusalem who believed in Christ. Paul's teaching was not wrong; James and the elders in Jerusalem did not believe that Paul's doctrine was wrong; Moreover, it would be wrong to assume that the Jerusalem leadership had failed to explain the basis of salvation correctly to these people in Jerusalem. In the light of Acts 15 and the ruling that took place then and the fact that the Scriptures show that these people truly did believe in Christ, their understanding about salvation had to be correct. They could never have been saved if they were trusting in the Mosaic ceremonies and the temple to justify them. Paul would never have tolerated this for one moment (Acts 4:12). Even if the apostles and the Jerusalem leadership were supporting such heresy (which they were not), Paul would not have been afraid to rebuke them all as he had rebuked Peter (Gal. 2:11–17, see too Gal. 1:8, 9). These Jewish converts had not equated the ceremonial law with being Christian, but rather they had equated the ceremonial law with being Jewish and the rumours that Paul was forbidding the Jews to follow the ceremonial laws was interpreted as an attack upon their Jewishness. Paul was not in any way against being Jewish, but was striving to bring unity between Jews and Gentiles in Christ, for there was nothing left to separate people when they stood by faith in Christ (Eph. 2:14–16). Paul was not against circumcision as such (1 Cor. 7:18), but against the claims that circumcision was a necessary requirement for reconciliation with God (Gal. 5:2–6). These Jewish believes were immature in their understanding of the freedom that had come through Christ, however, their tying together the ceremonial law and being Jewish was not *immoral*. God was going to bring an end to the whole OT sacrificial system in due time, but things at this stage were in a transitional period between what had been and what had now come. The basis of salvation, however, was not in a transitional stage (if one did not believe in the Person and completed work of Christ alone as the basis for salvation, then they couldn't be saved). It was the shadows or visible signs pointing to the Messiah's work that were in the process of being removed. Thus, for the sake of these weaker brethren, Paul was prepared to be involved in some ceremonies that had served their purpose and were therefore no longer binding upon him. He was quite willing to follow certain regulations while among the Jews, which he was unconcerned about whilst among the Gentiles—it made no difference to Paul whether he observed them or not. We have to try and understand this incident in its historical times and not interpret it in the light of our own times. Once we correctly understand what the real issue was and thus how Paul and the Jerusalem elders dealt with this problem, we will be able to apply the same principles to our own very different situations.

We must make a distinction between how to gain the favor of men and how to gain the favor of God, because there is a massive difference between the two. The favor of God can only be obtained through faith in the completed work of Christ upon the cross, whereas knowing how to gain the favor of men will vary greatly from culture to culture. In gaining the favor of men, we are talking about an acceptance based upon how you conform to their cultural and traditional norms. This does not mean ignoring, in any way, the moral issues that are clearly revealed in the Word of God. When Paul said he was not under the law to the Gentiles, this did not mean the was now free to steal and commit adultery. There can be no debate whether we should or shouldn't obey God's moral requirements—every culture and person is absolutely bound by them for all time and there can be no turning to the right or to the left (Deut. 5:31, 32; 17:19, 20; 28:14; Joshua 1:7; 2 Kings 22:2; Matt. 28:19, 20). Thus we cannot compromise the moral law of God in an attempt to gain the favor of some person or people group—to do so is madness.

While all cultural groups are to submit to God's moral requirements in every area of their lives, this does not mean that all cultures ought to, or will become one. There still remains great scope for expressing cultural diversity within the bounds of God's moral law. The great difficulty facing us all is to be able to evaluate our own cultures by the light of the Scriptures and bring about the necessary changes so that the whole of our existence brings glory to God. We mustn't close off any compartments or areas in life to the truth of God, but rather let His light penetrate and reform everything. We can all fall into the pit of allowing our sentimental feelings to blind us towards many of the long standing, ungodly beliefs and activities in our cultures and thus fail to bring these areas into true submission to the mind of Christ. Preferring tradition to God's truth is a symptom of a dying culture and civilisation. We must also be able to conform ourselves to other people's cultures and customs in order to reach them for Christ, being able to discern the difference between moral and traditional norms of behaviour. We are at all times to seek the unity of the faith, which is conformity to the image of Christ, and should put aside anything that hinders this goal. Our zeal should be for the Kingdom of God and His standard of righteousness, not our own ideas or customs. When we know the truth we will also know the glorious liberty of the sons of God (Rom. 8:21).

Acts 21:24

It seems best to understand that these four Jerusalem men had taken a Nazarite vow and that Paul was being asked to pay for the expenses involved in completing this vow. At the end of the specified period of the vow their heads would be shaved and certain offerings would be offered in the temple. It was not uncommon for someone else to cover these expenses. The expenses were fairly substantial as each person had to offer (together with their hair) a male lamb, a female lamb, a ram, a basket of unleavened bread, a grain offering and a drink offering (Num. 6:14, 15). Paul, who had been away in Gentile lands needed to undergo some kind of "purification" in order to become ceremonially clean before he would be allowed to pay for the offerings. This purification period for Paul lasted for one week and entailed being sprinkled a couple of times by the priests with water. The Jerusalem leadership said that if Paul accommodated himself to doing this then it would be obvious that the stories circulating about Paul were nothing but rumours. Due to their immaturity, the Jewish believers in Jerusalem thought that to ignore the ceremonial aspects of the Mosaic law was an assault upon being Jewish and would also lead to total lawlessness. Paul was not lawless by any means, however, the Jerusalem leadership believed that the only way to show that Paul was neither anti-Jew nor anti-Law, would be for him to publicly show his involvement in some ceremonial rituals. In the minds of the Jewish converts there was no distinction made between the ceremonial and moral aspects in the law (both were God's law) and so, the church leaders tell Paul that his involvement in the Nazarite vows would put to rest the concern that Paul was opposed to God's law. Rather it would demonstrate that he had respect for the law, was careful not to violate it and walked by rule, that is, lived in submission to its precepts. No one here was promoting salvation by obeying the law, but rather confirming the Biblical understanding that if we are truly born from above and love Jesus Christ, we will obey the commandments of God (John 14:15; 15:14). Paul was not an opponent of the law but a guardian of the law (Rom. 3:31; 7:12, 14; 12:2; 1 Tim. 1:8) and the Jerusalem leadership knew this and determined that the best way to get the whole Jerusalem church to realize this, was for Paul to follow their suggestion (see comments on Acts 21:20b–23).

Acts 21:25

There are not two different ways that Jews and Gentiles are to be saved and there are not two different requirements of behavior once they are saved. There is one way of salvation and there is one eternal moral standard that is binding upon both Jews and Gentiles. The reality is, there is no longer a distinction within the Kingdom between Jews and Gentiles (Eph. 2:14–18). The only distinction that exists now is between those who believe in Christ and those who do not—between covenant keepers and covenant breakers. The Jerusalem leadership was quick to acknowledge that what they were asking Paul to do was not binding upon all believers, but was designed to put to rest the Jews' fears that Paul wanted to destroy their Jewishness. The list of "requirements" for the Gentiles has been explained in Acts 15:20.

Acts 21:26

Paul went with the men who had made the vow to inform the priests when they would be coming with the Nazarite offerings. They needed to give the priests fair warning so the necessary arrangements could be made and so that the priests would be ready to make the sacrifices when the vow was finished.

Acts 21:27–29

Paul's fiercest enemies were the Jews who rejected the Gospel and lived outside of Israel. Remember at Corinth, the Jews had brought him to the judgment seat (Acts 18:12) and plotted against him (Acts 20:3). It was the Jews from Asia (probably Ephesus) who now stirred up the mob to assault Paul. They had earlier seen Paul with someone they knew to be a Gentile (Trophimus). Now these Asian Jews saw Paul in the temple with four men they did not know and thus assumed that either they were also Gentiles or that Paul had earlier brought Trophimus into the temple. It was not the Jewish believers who were accusing Paul, but the Jews who rejected the Messiah. Their charge was that he was against "the people," that is, against the chosen people of God. Paul was being accused of tearing down the privileged position God had granted to the Jews. He was also accused of being against the law of God and against the temple. Paul heard very much the same kind of accusations brought against Stephen before he was murdered (Acts 6:13, 14). The ceremonial law showed how sinners were to be reconciled to God. Paul taught that these ceremonial aspects of the law had found their fulfilment in the completed work of the Messiah. Paul was not against these laws in any way, but rather showed that they were merely shadows of that which had now come in its fullness. Paul taught that what was needed to be reconciled to God, was to believe in the completed work of the Messiah, thus it was through faith in Jesus Christ that one fully realised the meaning and purpose of the ceremonial law (see comments on Acts 6:13, 14). The ceremonial law only had significance and value when its relationship with Christ was maintained. As soon as it was separated from Christ, it became a dead, worthless religious ritual. Paul was not against the law or the temple, but pointing to their true meaning and thus, their true glory. It was not Paul's doing that Christ's work was the focus and fulfilment of the ceremonial law, but God's and so these accusations were against the Lord of the universe. To reject Christ meant that you neither understood nor cared about the true intention of the ceremonial law, this meant that you were not reconciled to God and thus never knew God. Only an enemy of God would seek to overthrow the message about Christ in the name of upholding the ceremonial law, which is what Paul's accusers were doing. Paul faithfully stood by the message of his Lord, no matter what people wanted to do to him.

It is never the truth that angry mobs are seeking to exalt or protect. The reality here is that Paul was showing respect to the Jewish customs and the requirements of the temple by being made ritually clean when he was pounced upon and treated as someone who utterly despised the temple. This mob assumes, without any facts whatsoever, that Paul had defiled the temple by bringing Gentiles into the inner court. It was a capital crime for Gentiles to enter this area and Roman law allowed this sentence to be carried out even if the offender was a Roman citizen. Gentiles were not permitted to go any further than the outer courts. Profaning the holy place was something that would raise intense emotional feelings in any Jew. Paul realised, in the midst of the violent mob, that this was what the Holy Spirit had been preparing him for (Acts 20:22, 23; 21:4, 10, 11).

Acts 21:30

The commotion of this violent mob quickly attracted the attention of many others, upsetting the whole city. Paul's accusers were now joined by the rest of the city and they dragged him out of the temple. The doors that were shut were those separating the inner from the outer court. The temple guards were afraid of the violence spreading into the inner court, though it is also possible that they wanted to make sure Paul's blood couldn't be spilled in this sacred area, since that would defile the temple (2 Kings 11:15, 16). Some see the "closing of the temple doors" not merely as an historical detail, but as carrying a message of its own, namely, here the Gospel is cast out of and excluded from the place it should have been most welcome and by closing its doors, the temple seals its own doom, that was not far off (the destruction of A.D. 70 was close).

Acts 21:31–36

The mob was not dragging Paul off to have him stoned, they were trying to beat him to death right there. Luke does not tell us about the effect of this beating upon Paul's body, but we must not treat it as a small thing. It would have taken some time for the Roman commander to realize what was happening and then mobilise his troops and get to this scene. In that time Paul would have received many blows. The Scriptures are very clear: they were trying to kill him and so they would have been hitting him accordingly. It was only when the soldiers arrived on the scene that the mob stopped beating Paul. The commander had Paul bound with two chains and this signaled the end of Paul's way of life and ministry up to that point. Ahead of him was the long road of imprisonment, which Paul probably would have called a "prison ministry." Paul knew this and was prepared to walk on this path, knowing that His Lord was in sovereign control of everything and that he would be presented with opportunities to preach the Gospel to people he would never otherwise have reached. God's will always has purpose. The challenge is to be found faithfully serving the Lord when we do not know exactly what His purpose is—godly living with contentment.

The commander who had literally saved Paul's life, asked the crowd what Paul had done, but, as is usual with mob violence, they did not even know why they were killing him—people gave conflicting answers (cf. Acts 19:32). Paul was led to the barracks, though the anger and force of the crowed was such that the soldiers needed to carry Paul in order to protect him. Paul's opinion was held by a minority in Jerusalem, whereas the majority strongly against him, but was this "proof" that Paul's position was wrong? Only the Scriptures can provide the standard for determining right and wrong—the "voice of the people" can never serve in this way.

As Paul was taken out of the mob's reach and they realised that they would not be able to kill him, they started to cry out, "Away with him!," meaning, put him to death. Not far from this very spot, some twenty seven years before, another angry mob had said these same word about Christ (John 19:15). One wonders what personal knowledge Paul had of that fateful day when Christ was condemned to death. Now, however, it was Paul's turn to feel what it was like to be unjustly hated and despised. Undeterred by this rejection, Paul still wanted an opportunity to preach Christ to these people. We must testify to the truth even if people want to kill us for it and we must not be deterred by their resentment and hatred they have for us because we told them the truth. Though our actions must always be motivated by true love and manifest graciousness in the way we proclaim the truth.

Acts 21:37

Paul must have looked a sorry sight: having been severely assaulted by a violent mob, then chained and man-handled by the soldiers. His body and face were at least bruised, though probably also bleeding, his clothes most likely torn and his hair wildly ruffled. Apparently, Paul's stature and looks were not very impressive to begin with (2 Cor. 10:10), but now he looked even worse. The Roman commander was sure that Paul was a very dangerous criminal or revolutionary. Paul, then shocks the commander by addressing him in very educated Greek.

Acts 21:38

The commander, unable to get any answer from the mob about who Paul was, had arrived at his own conclusions on this matter. Paul had been bound with two heavy chains because the commander thought he was a known Egyptian revolutionary. Apparently (according to Josephus), this Egyptian had claimed to be a prophet and had gathered a following of people whom he led into the wilderness, promising them that at his word, the walls of Jerusalem would fall down and then they would defeat the Romans. The Romans, however, had attacked this band of people, killing and capturing some, though the Egyptian had escaped. It is possible that this Roman commander thought Paul was this false prophet who had returned to Jerusalem and the Jews were angry with him because of his previous deception. This might explain why two heavy chains had immediately been placed upon Paul. It seems that the Egyptian was not able to speak Greek, thus as soon as Paul began speaking Greek, the commander realised Paul was not this revolutionary.

Acts 21:39, 40

Despite all the violence, hatred and rejection directed towards Paul from his fellow countrymen, his heartfelt desire was still that they might come to faith in Christ (Rom. 9:3; 10:1). The commander granted Paul permission to address the mob, probably hoping that through this he might be able to work out why the mob wanted to kill Paul. Paul, on the other hand, wanted an opportunity to proclaim Christ to them. By speaking in the Jews' own language, Paul managed to secure even more of their attention and demonstrated his Jewishness, which he was going to explain in greater detail.

Acts 22:1–3

Paul begins his speech in very polite and affectionate terms, calling his fellow countrymen, "brothers and fathers." Paul is about to defend his actions with God's revelation. Paul was accused of being against the Jews, God's law and the temple (Acts 21:28). His response shows just how baseless their accusations were. It was obvious, in the light of Paul's history, that he was one of the most highly qualified people in Jerusalem with respect to understanding and interpreting the law of God and there was no conflict between his faith in Christ and the law of God. Paul had studied under Gamaliel, the most eminent and respected teacher of that time (Acts 5:34) and mastered the "exactness" of the law. Paul, himself, had an impressive reputation among the Jews before his conversion to Christ and had been a shining example of what his accusers believed a Jew should be like (Gal. 1:14; Phil. 3:5, 6) and now, Paul emphasises all the things that had shown him to be an exemplary Jew (2 Cor. 11:22). Paul's conversion to Christ was not due to being ignorant about the law, but was a result of God's sovereign work in his life.

Acts 22:4, 5

The proof of Paul's zeal to preserve the Jewish traditions was demonstrated by his violent destruction of anything that differed from these traditions. He did not want to destroy only the leadership of the church, but everyone who called upon the name of Christ, believing they should all be executed. The history of Paul's pre-conversion life was known by the highest and most respected leaders of the Jewish community and could be easily checked out and confirmed by the High Priest and Sanhedrin.

Acts 22:6–11

This is the second time Paul's conversion account is given in Acts (see comments on Acts 9) and it will be repeated once again (Acts 26). The natural response from someone who has truly seen the Lord, is "What shall I do, Lord?" Such a person does not want to be led by their own ideas and goals, but wants to serve the Lord by doing everything according to His will. To see Christ is to know that your life is not your own, but has been bought with a price and thus, should be lived for the glory of God.

Acts 22:12–15

Paul shows that he was not introduced to Christ by a Gentile, but by a Jew who was highly respected in the Jewish community as someone who zealously observed the law. Paul is emphasising that the true meaning of the law is not in any way against Christ. He then lays out his apostolic credentials—his calling came directly from Christ and he also saw the Lord—a vital qualification in order to be an apostle (see comments on Acts 1:21). Paul would know the Lord's will by receiving special revelation that he would then pass on to the whole church. God completed the Scriptures under the oversight of the unique gift of apostolic authority. The only foundation, which we as Christ's church can build upon, is that which has already been laid (1 Cor. 3:10, 11; Eph. 2:20; Jude 3; Rev. 21:14).

Acts 22:16

The only way sins are washed away is with the blood of Christ. Baptism does not wash away sin, because water cannot purify sin. It is God who washes us with Christ's blood and He does this by the working of the Holy Spirit is hidden power. The outward sign of baptism is given to us by God because of our own weakness, confirming to us God's bountiful promises of forgiveness and thus strengthening our faith. Through the sign of baptism we are better able to receive the promise that God washes our sin away by the blood of Christ. While baptism itself does not wash away any sins, it does represent, to our dull senses, the washing away of sins. There are three things that baptism signifies to us: It speaks of our being united to God and of our intimate fellowship with Him; it tells us that our defilement has been totally removed, for we couldn't have fellowship with God if we had any sin; and it is a seal of the righteousness that comes through faith. Water is universally seen as a "cleaning agent" thus God in His wisdom decided to use this known sign to represent the internal cleansing of God upon a repentant heart. The sign of baptism is God's mark upon the person showing that they are "holy" or "set apart" unto the Lord. The sign is God's gift to us and not our "gift" or profession to Him. The sign confirms the testimony of God to our own hearts—baptism bears witness to ourselves, not to other people. It is a sign of God's promise of righteousness that comes through faith. Primarily, baptism is not a sign of anything we do, but a sign of what God does in our hearts through the power of the Holy Spirit with the blood of Christ. It is a sign of God's gracious work—a work that we are incapable of doing or even contributing towards. Baptism is a confirmatory sign of God's promise to forgive us and reckon us righteous when we totally trust Christ's work on our behalf. The sign of baptism helps us trust in God's gracious gift of salvation. Infants look back to the sign of the promise given to them. Parents should point to their children's baptism explaining to them that God has graciously made them share in the many blessings of the covenant and that He will cleanse them from all sin if they trust in His promises. It is a sign of God's gracious work of washing away our defilement, which is applied to us through faith (see too comments on Acts 2:38; 16:15).

Acts 22:17–21

Paul once again shows that he was not an opponent of the temple, using it as a place of prayer and it was here that God once again spoke to him and revealed his calling to preach to the Gentiles. Paul shows that the mob's fight was against God and not Paul. They were angry with Paul because of Paul's ministry to the Gentiles, however, it was God who had revealed what Paul had to do. Although Paul was prepared to lay down his life for the Lord, the time was not right and Christ told him to leave Jerusalem, for there was much other work to be done among the Gentiles. Paul did not apologise for the form in which this revelation came, nor did he expect God to personally appear and repeat this revelation to satisfy the mob. What Paul knew was that God had spoken and that once God had said it, it was beyond question and authoritative for all time (see comments on John 8:14). Many people today feel that for Christ's Words to be authoritative, He has to somehow personally "speak" to them in some way and give them some kind of individual confirmation. Paul, unashamedly tells this mob about the divine, authoritative, revelation that came to *him alone* and says this is the absolute truth binding upon all people. God has revealed all He wanted to reveal and He has preserved it for us in the Scriptures and now, through the Holy Spirit, enables us to understand and apply this one truth to our lives and societies. When we bow ourselves to Christ and do what He has told us to do (2 Tim. 3:16, 17), then we perceive the authority of that which has been revealed (John 7:17). God never intended to and thus does not keep "confirming" His truth according to the demands and expectations of those who are in rebellion against Him (Matt. 12:39; 16:4, see comments on John 14:9). Many signs have already been given to us and abundantly confirmed the authority of the revelation we now have (see comments on John 5:36; Acts 4:30; 5:15; 19:11, 12).

Acts 22:22, 23

These people had their own preconceived ideas and their own ultimate authority (which was not the revelation of God) and they judged Paul's words with their standard. They would not bow themselves to the authority of Christ's Words and thus sought to destroy anyone who challenged them with the truth. These people in their pride thought that their own wisdom and efforts had made them eternally superior to all other people and thus it was offensive to think that Gentiles could be accepted into the Kingdom as equals with them. They would have all people become Jews in order to be accepted by God. They trusted in their works, rather than the grace of God for salvation and thus became very angry when Paul showed that their basis for salvation was wrong (Rom.10:3; Phil.3:9). When you touch someone's religious "security" they become mindless with rage. However, there is only one basis for salvation: the completed work of Christ and there can never be any compromise with this message even if people hate it so much they want to kill us. Every person has to submit to Christ and everything He has revealed about salvation and life or else they will not be accepted by Him. If people do not come before God standing in Christ, they will remain under His wrath for eternity!

Acts 22:24–29

The commander was still ignorant as to the real reasons for the uproar thus, as far as he could see, the only way for him to get the information he wanted, was through torture. While it was legal under Roman law to "question" others in this way, it was illegal to interrogate a Roman citizen like this—Romans couldn't be whipped until they had had a fair trial. The authorities were disturbed by the news that Paul was a Roman citizen, fearing the possible repercussions that could come their way because of their hasty actions. Paul's citizenship is seen to be superior to the commander's since he had been born a Roman and had not bought his citizenship (that is, paid a bribe for it).

Acts 22:30

The commander decided that since Paul had offended Jewish religious customs, the only way to find out what was going on was to bring Paul before the Sanhedrin.

Acts 23:1, 2

Here we see the boldness of a righteous man (Prov. 28:1; Isa. 26:3, 4). Standing alone against this formidable host of enemies, Paul is ashamed of nothing and looking his accusers in the eyes, he is ready to proclaim the full counsel of God in Christ Jesus (Rom. 1:16; 2 Tim. 1:8, 12; 1 Pet. 4:16). Paul says his present doctrine and life style left him with a clear conscience before the God of Israel (for a discussion on conscience see comments on Acts 24:16). He said elsewhere, "For our boasting is this: our conscience testifies that we conducted ourselves in the world in simplicity and godly sincerity" (2 Cor. 1:12). The high priest who saw Paul as a blasphemer and a perverter of the Jewish religion, could not control his anger and thus violates the judicial process and orders Paul to be assaulted. There comes a time when the only way to hold onto a false ideology is by resorting to lawlessness and violence.

Acts 23:3

The law states that you cannot beat a man unless his guilt has been proven in a just court of law (Deut. 25:2), yet Paul was struck after his opening statement, showing that the high priest had already judged Paul to be guilty, even before he had heard his side of the story. Paul said the high priest might look acceptable from the outside, however, inside he was corrupt and rotten. He then pronounced a prophetic judgment upon Ananias (see comments on verse 5 below). You cannot pretend to be zealous for one aspect of the law and yet totally ignore another aspect without exposing your hypocrisy.

Acts 23:4

The perversion of the rest of the Sanhedrin is seen in that there is no attempt on their part to challenge the actions of the high priest. Some remained silent in the face of the high priest's injustice, while others rebuked Paul.

Acts 23:5

There are many different views as to what Paul meant in this verse and many suggestions as to why he said he did not know who the high priest was. In trying to understand what Paul meant we need to remember that he was intimately familiar with these kinds of proceedings—he was on "home ground" so to speak. Paul, before his conversion to Christ, had been an active participant, many times, in similar gatherings, thus he fully understood the procedures and protocol, which makes it virtually impossible to believe that he did not understand the inner workings of such a political gathering. Paul knew exactly who Ananias was and neither corrects himself for what he said nor apologises for it. There is no apology here, thus, if Paul sinned and did not apologise to the offended person, how could he, a little later, say to Felix that he always strives to have a conscience without offence toward God and men? (Acts 24:16). Paul was standing upon Christ's promise that when the apostles would be brought before rulers in this manner, they would be given the words to say by the Holy Spirit (Luke 12:11, 12). Paul, with apostolic authority, had spoken the Word of God into this situation, prophetically declaring the coming judgment of God upon Ananias. A prophecy that was fulfilled in A.D. 66 when Ananias was murdered by militant Jews as the war against Rome started.

Paul's response was, "I did not know, brothers, that he is high priest." J. A. Alexander says that the past and the present tenses used here by Paul, show that his previous ignorance about Ananias had not been removed and was still present as he spoke. In other words, he is saying, "I did not know (and I do not now know) that he is the High Priest" (Alexander, Acts pg.788). Paul's challenge to the whole gathering being that, not only was this man who called himself "high priest" acting in violation of God's law by having Paul struck on the mouth, but his very title was a violation of God's law. Ananias was standing as the supreme judge on matters pertaining to God's law, however, the mere fact that he called himself "high priest" was a flagrant violation of the law. Paul says, "If we are talking about being true to the law of God, then I do not understand how this man can be called, God's high priest".

Paul is touching the nerve-centre of the Jewish religion, because it was the high priest who made atonement for the sins of the people on the day of atonement—he alone was allowed to go into the holy of holies with the blood to make atonement for the whole nation (Ex. 30:10; Lev. 16). God was very strict with respect to the details about making atonement and will never tolerate any inventions from men (Lev. 10:1, 2). Not to follow God's instructions implicitly in this respect will result in His judgment and no atonement being made for the nation. To deny the legitimacy of Ananias was to expose these Jews' greatest need (atonement) and leave them without hope. There could be no atonement without a high priest and a high priest had to measure up to the detailed requirements that God had laid down. The purpose of God in this was to drive all people to the only true and eternal High Priest, the Messiah (Heb. 2:17; 4:14–16; 8:1; 9:24–28; 10:10–12). The absence of a high priest who was a descendant of Aaron should have made these Jews flee to God and thus to Christ, but instead of doing this, they made their own plan and thus mocked God's law.

Paul accepted the ceremonial aspects that were in accordance with the law of God, as long as the worshipers saw that the reality of these things was Christ, however, he would not tolerate anything that ignored Christ or deviated from the express revelation God had given. Thus Paul could go along with the Nazarite vows (see comments on Acts 21:20–23) and other ceremonies, accept the legitimacy of the Sanhedrin (who were the civil power in Israel under Roman oversight), however, under no circumstances could he acknowledge the legitimacy and authority of this so called "high priest." He shows that he was not carried away by a fit of passion, but was very much in control and aware of the full counsel of God by saying, "Indeed, it is written, you shall not speak evil of the ruler of your people" (quoting Ex. 22:28). The implication here is that Paul had not violated this law from God, but rather, had said what he had said about Ananias in full awareness of it. Once again Paul is denying the legitimacy of Ananias' office and challenging these people to think about these things. He says, "You reconcile Ananias' office with the law of God and then we can talk about whether I have violated Exodus 22:28. Indeed, it is impossible for this man to be *God's* high priest".

The office of high priest was of heavenly origin (Heb. 5:4) and all who held it were to be descendants of Aaron (Ex. 27:21; 28:1; 29:9, 29, 44; 40:12–15; Num. 17:8; 18:7; 25:13; 1 Chron. 23:13). An unbroken line descending from Aaron continued until 171 B.C., with the last of these priests coming from Zadok (who served David and then Solomon). The prophet Ezekiel, greatly praised the faithfulness of the Zadok priests (Ezk. 44:15; 48:11), taking no notice of any priests besides them. The high priest office from 171 B.C. until the destruction of the temple in A.D. 70 was controlled and manipulated by political figures for political ends and bribery played a major part in the appointments (see comments on Acts 4:5, 6). You cannot make a high priest of God by *political* appointment.

The high priest, under Roman rule, assumed a political position of administering the internal affairs of the Jewish nation. He was also the unquestioned spokesman and representative of the nation to both the provincial governor and the Roman emperor (Bruce, *New Testament History*, pp. 62, 63). This is interesting because Paul does not deny Ananias' political authority, but denies that he is "God's high priest." Yet, nor does he apologise for what he said to this *political* authority (Rom. 13:1).

Many Christians express a pagan rather than a Biblical understanding when they insist that you cannot challenge the actions of political leaders with the light of God's Word. What does Exodus 22:28 mean? Many commentators say the verse should be translated as follows: "You should not revile your gods (i.e., judges) nor curse a ruler of your people" (cf. Ps. 82:6; John 10:34). The word translated "revile" means to "regard or treat as exceedingly vile, to curse, to vilify, to revile" (Parkhurst). The word translated "curse" is to curse greatly. Both these words (revile and curse) are very extreme actions and cannot be equated with judging according to God's truth. We are told to judge righteously (John 7:24). We are not at liberty to judge according to our own standards or pronounce curses upon people in positions of authority, because we must bring all things into submission to the Lord—including how we respond to lawless rulers. Our conduct and humility must be like the arch-angel Michael's who said to Satan, "The Lord rebuke you"

(Jude 9). We are to bring all things, including every political idea and action, into the light of God's Word, rebuking what is out of line and praising that which is in line with the Lord's revelation. Paul brought Ananias' behavior to the light of God's law, exposing its hypocrisy and his judgment was spoken with the authority of a prophet. Paul was not merely expressing his own opinion or unable to control his anger, but speaking as God's divine messenger.

Political leaders are God's servants and are fully accountable to His revelation. When we challenge lawlessness in high places with God's truth, we are representing God who has told us to be salt and light in this world (Matt. 5:13–16). David challenged the unrighteous behavior of king Saul by resisting his authority—if a king wants to kill you and you flee from him, you are despising his command and resisting his will (1 Sam. 23 and 24). Nathan rebuked the unrighteousness of David (2 Sam. 12:7). Elijah told king Ahab that it was his sin that brought trouble upon Israel (1 Kings 18:18), then later he rebuked king Ahaziah and resisted his commands (2 Kings 1:9–16). John the Baptist rebuked Herod's unrighteous behavior (Matt. 14:1–5) and Christ called king Herod a "fox," referring to his unrighteous ways (Luke 13:32). Stephen rebuked and openly exposed the sinfulness of the Sanhedrin (a political body, Acts 7:51–53). In none of the above examples did these faithful saints, "revile" their rulers and thus violate Ex. 22:28. It is clear that to rebuke one's leaders with the truth of God's Word is a necessary part of our calling, for the earth is the Lords and everything in it (Ps. 24:1) and thus all things and people are accountable to Him.

Finally, we need to note that neither Christ nor Paul turned the other cheek when they were hit in the face, rather, both rebuked the lawlessness of those who hit them (John 18:22, 23). Did Christ neglect His own principles? When Christ gave the command to turn the other cheek (Matt. 5:38, 39), He was not forbidding us to challenge unrighteous behaviour, but rather exhorting us to respond to injustice according to His law and not according to our own principles of retaliation and vengeance. What Paul said to Ananias, the judge, did not contradict what he had said to the Corinthians (1 Cor. 4:12). We are to act justly at all times, not taking the law into our own hands, yet we are still to uphold God's eternal standard of justice that applies to all people and all areas of life. We are to bring the light of God's Word to bear upon every situation we might find ourselves in (Lev. 24:22) and this is what Paul did in Acts 23:3, 5. There is One God, one law and one standard of righteousness that all nations, leaders and individuals are accountable to and when the very least person stands upon the Word of God, he has authority to challenge the most powerful leader or nation in the world.

Acts 23:6

Paul has been criticised by some commentators for what he did here, however, he did nothing unlawful or deceptive. The Sanhedrin which was judging Paul, was made up of two factions that hated each other. Their "unity" until now was brought about by their hatred for Paul, or in other words, their hatred for the Gospel. In warring against Christ, they put aside the hatred they had for one another. It was obvious to Paul that a fair trial and justice were the furthest things from the minds of these judges. Paul shows that he was not against the Jewish people, law or temple, but still saw himself as a Pharisee. He was claiming that what he believed and the way he was living had in no way disqualified him from being a Pharisee. Paul was on trial for his Christian beliefs and at the heart of Christianity is the doctrine of the resurrection (Acts 4:2; 13;34; 17:18, 31, 32; 26:6–8, 23; 28:20; 1 Cor. 15, see comments on John 14:18, 19). The resurrection is only absurd to those who do not know God's Word and deny His power (Mark 12:18–27, cf. Acts 26:25). Paul believed, with the Pharisees, in the great hope of the resurrection, without which there could be no hope (1 Cor. 15:16, 17).

Christ could have divided the forces as Paul did (John 18:23), however, He didn't, because He came to die and make atonement for our sin—this was His primary mission and everything else was determined according to this ultimate goal. We must never simplistically say that because Jesus did not do something in this life then we shouldn't do that thing. We must never forget that Christ had a primary responsibility to fulfill and many other good works and activities (e.g., like preaching to Gentiles) had to wait until reconciliation with God had been accomplished through His death on the cross (see comments on John 13:37). It is the whole counsel of God that is to show us what to do, not merely the life of our Savior. There is an order in the spread and growth of the Kingdom and there are certain foundations that need to be laid first, before others activities and emphases are possible (Mark 4:28).

Acts 23:7, 8

Paul, in a sense, was suggesting to the Pharisees in the Sanhedrin
that if he was condemned for preaching about the resurrection of
Christ, then they would be destroying one of the fundamental characteristics of the Pharisaic party—belief in the resurrection. The
Pharisees saw the threat to their own position and thus stood with
Paul, igniting the age old conflict that had raged between the Saducees and the Pharisees. This question about the resurrection, then
brought to the surface all the other disputes between these two rival
groups and thus the whole meeting was thrown into chaos. We are
to be as wise as serpents and harmless as doves when we deal with
those who are trying to destroy the Gospel (Matt. 10:16).

The Saducees said there was only real meaning and significance in
this life. They believed God controlled the affairs in this world,
however, all the rewards and blessings were received in this life,
since there was nothing but a meaningless shadowy "existence"
after it. Thus they saw peace and prosperity on earth as a sign of
God's blessing and hardships and suffering as proof of God's judgement. However, this cannotbe an absolute rule for there is more to
life than this life. The Psalmist struggled when he compared the
prosperity of the wicked with his own hardships (Ps. 73:3ff.), until
he realised the eternal purposes of God in the midst of his troubles
(Ps. 73:22ff.). If you do not believe in the bodily resurrection and
the reality of the spiritual realm, then everything has to happen
here on earth and death becomes a terror and suffering brings great
anguish. The fundamental reason the bodily resurrection is
rejected, is because people have an inadequate understanding of
God's power.

Acts 23:9, 10

The Pharisees, from wanting to kill Paul, were now defending his
position. The commander, fearing for Paul's life, once again rescues
him from a violent mob. There was no chance of arriving at a conclusion as to Paul's supposed "crime" in such an atmosphere.

Acts 23:11

As Christ had told Paul that he was to be the apostle to the Gentiles,
so here he is confirming that he will yet represent God in this
capacity in the capital of the Gentile world—Rome. There is no

proof that Paul was downcast at this time and the term, "Be of good cheer" is a standard greeting assuring the hearer of God's approval and involvement. It would be better to see this as God graciously encouraging Paul for the delay of two years that faced him before he would be sent to Rome and also to help him face everything else that he would endure on his way to Rome. Paul was going to spend the next two years in Roman custody in Caesarea. The Lord is always present with us to strengthen us in our difficulties. Even when God does not remove us from a difficult situation, we need to be aware of His care and perfect plan of glorifying His name through our lives. We must always trust in His Word and not let our security depend upon our circumstances. Our confidence must arise from knowing that God is indeed the Sovereign, Almighty Lord of the universe in control of every detail of our lives and intimately concerned about us.

Acts 23:12–15

A massive conspiracy now unfolds between over forty zealous Jews and the top officials of the nation. It is a simple plan—get Paul to be moved from the barracks to the council chamber under the pretence of wanting another hearing. He would not be heavily guarded as he moved through the narrow streets, thus it would have been fairly simple to ambush and murder him. The self exalted "protectors of the God's law" agree to this murderous plan.

Acts 23:16–22

Luke tells us nothing about Paul's family, except this little diversion here. There are so many details that our minds would have liked him to include, e.g., telling us about the relationship that existed between Paul, his sister and her family; about how his nephew found out about the conspiracy; how he was able to see Paul so easily; and why the commander so readily believed the boy. God's providence over all these things is evident (Isa. 54:17) and surely this is Luke's point, thus he merely sketches the barest outline of the details. We are to trust that the Lord is in control of the details of our lives also, knowing that nothing can happen to us except what is according to His sovereign purposes for our lives and we know that His purposes for us are for our good (Jer. 29:11; Rom. 8:28). It seems best to understand the end of verse 21 to mean that those lying in wait were waiting to hear whether the commander would agree to the request from the Sanhedrin to bring Paul for further questioning. I do not think that the conspiracy included trying to get the commander involved in the murder. We ought not to fear death, but nor should we throw our lives away unnecessarily. The Lord uses many different means to protect us and we need to make use of them—with wisdom.

Acts 23:23, 24

The life of Paul was under serious threat in Jerusalem and this commander did not want to be held responsible for the death of a Roman citizen whom he was supposed to be guarding. With an extremely heavy military escort, Paul was transported to Caesarea which was a predominantly Gentile city, thus the threat of murder by Jewish zealots was greatly lessened. Moreover, Paul would then become the responsibility of the governor, thus relieving the commander of this burden. The escort leaves that same night, so that by the morning, Paul was far away from Jerusalem. One cannot help wondering whether these zealots managed to get released from their vow before they starved to death.

Acts 23:25–30

The commander explains a brief history of Paul's case. He exalts himself by saying that he saved Paul who was about to be murdered by the Jews, knowing he was a Roman citizen—which is not true. He does not say anything about putting Paul in chains and almost flogging him. The commander gives his opinion of Paul, saying that he had done nothing worthy of death. He then shows that even the Jews had no real case against Paul since they were wanting to murder him rather than deal with him through the legal channels. The Lord, by his great mercy, had made the commander paint Paul in a very favourable light. Paul's accusers would now need to make the trip to Caesarea in order to make their case against him.

Acts 23:31–35

Once Paul was a safe distance from Jerusalem, the threat on his life was greatly lessened and so the bulk of the soldiers returned home. Felix wanted to make sure that Paul fell under his jurisdiction before he would judge his case. History tells us that Felix was a cruel, greedy and excessive ruler (we will see that Paul's continued imprisonment was due to Felix's greed, Acts 24:26). The Roman historian Tacitus (A.D. c. 55–117) says of Felix that he "exercised the power of a king with the mind [disposition] of a slave" (Bruce). Paul cannot find his hope for the future in the goodness of men, but must, as always, rest totally upon the providence and faithfulness of God. Our lives and our futures are secure in the Lord. However, our personal peace and thus effectiveness in His Kingdom is determined, to a large degree, by how strongly we believe this truth.

It is hard to understand why such a dynamic and energetic evangelist and teacher would be confined by God in this way. From our perspective we think Paul's effectiveness would have been far greater had he been able to continue with his missionary journeys into the far corners of the Gentile world. God's ways, however, are not our ways and His thoughts are not our thoughts (Isa. 55:8, 9; Rom. 11:33–36). The just must at all times live by faith (Rom. 1:17; Heb. 10:38), trusting in God's Word (Matt. 4:4) and in who God is (Heb. 11:6). Our circumstances will be different to Paul's circumstances, however, the requirement to glorify the Lord is still the same—for all people, for all time. What is best for us is that which God has ordained. Our responsibility is to whole-heartedly serve Christ in an attitude of humble submission to His every Word, living a life of godliness, contentment and seeking His glory in all things.

Acts 24:1–4

The Jewish leadership bring with them someone who was a very good public speaker and was probably also a lawyer. This man leads the charge against Paul, starting his attack in the traditionally accepted way, in the pagan world, for such procedures to begin. The judge was complimented in an attempt to gain his favour, but here Tertullus heaps up the flattery and nonsense. Even if such flattery was the common way of starting off such proceedings, it does not justify its perversity. Our words at all times, no matter the company, are to express the truth. This does not mean that we cannot be wise and polite, as Paul is (verse 10), but it does mean that we cannot lie about the facts and thus flatter the judge. Such behavior is a form of bribery, where you "give" the judge something so that he feels indebted to rule in your favour. Everything we say is said before God and ought to reflect His wisdom and truth (Matt. 5:37; James 5:12). The danger with great eloquence, is that it is capable of moving people through emotion rather than by faithfulness to the facts.

Eloquence, together with the truth, is a powerful weapon that can be used for the good, however, eloquence without the truth, is dangerous and destructive. In this instance the Jewish leadership resorted to eloquence and flattery because the truth was not on their side.

Felix had been extremely brutal in putting down any uprisings and the historians, Josephus and Tacitus, both paint Felix as a cruel, ferocious, oppressive, greedy tyrant. No person with integrity who loved true peace and justice could have even *thought* about Felix in these terms, let alone praise him out loud. Rather all lovers of justice would have been deeply horrified by the rule of this man.

Acts 24:5

Tertullus says the peace that Felix was striving to maintain was severely threatened by Paul who was notorious throughout the whole world, causing dissension wherever he went. Although much trouble did follow Paul (Acts 13:45, 50; 14:2–5; 16:20–23, 37; 17:5), when he was brought before Roman judges and judged fairly, he was found not guilty (cf. Acts 18:12–16). Tertullus cites no facts to support his accusations, but is rather appealing to emotional generalisations. Rome was very aware of the trouble among the Jews throughout the empire (cf. Acts 18:2) and so to point to Paul as the cause of these many disturbances (in the light of what had happened in Jerusalem) had an appearance of validity. Since Paul's accusers before Felix were the most powerful, respected and influential leaders in Israel, they were counting on Felix accepting their word as fact. In a sense they were saying, "As the leaders of Israel, we love peace and submit totally to Roman rule, despising those who are creating disturbances throughout the empire and being Jews, we have inside information about the identity of these troublemakers and Paul is a ringleader of these pests."

Tying Paul to the Nazarenes was identifying him with Jesus of Nazareth (Acts 22:8) who had been executed by a Roman judge—this case would have been well known to Felix. According to the "evidence" brought against Paul, the sect, of which he was one of the chiefs, had been condemned by Rome (with the crucifixion of Christ) and was also totally rejected by the Jewish leadership as being outside mainstream Judaism (as these official Jewish leaders were testifying). Paul was presented as an enemy of the Roman Empire and the Jewish nation and if he had not been a Roman citi-

zen, his fate would have been sealed by this trial (if not before)—
once again we *see* the providence of God.

Acts 24:6–9

If you remember how anxious Pontius Pilate was to avoid an
uproar in Jerusalem (Matt. 27:24), we can appreciate how Felix too
would have dreaded such a happening. Felix knew that the Jewish
temple was at the heart of the Jewish nation and any defiling of it
would cause tremendous upheaval. The Romans had recognised
this early on and had given the Jews the authority to personally protect the sanctity of their temple (see comments on Acts 7:58). Tertullus was both warning Felix of the potential danger to the peace of
Jerusalem because of Paul and also reminding him that the Jews
had authority to deal with cases related to profaning the temple.
The implication in these words is also that it was lawful Jewish
authorities that had apprehended Paul and not an out of control
mob that knew nothing about the situation (cf. Acts 21:33, 34).

Many translations now have the rest of verse 6 through to the
beginning of verse 8 as a footnote and are in some doubt about
whether it should be included in the Scriptures or not. I am persuaded that this section should be accepted as part of God's Word
and will comment upon it accordingly.

Tertullus says that the Roman authority in Jerusalem had not only
interfered where he had no authority to, but had also used excessive
force. The Jews on the other hand, wanted to handle this matter in
their own way, according to their own law and so were appealing to
be allowed to judge the case. They knew they had no case that could
stand up in a Roman court and so were trying to get Paul back into
their custody, where he could be murdered. Tertullus mentions
nothing about the trial before the Sanhedrin where the Pharisees
said Paul had not done anything worthy of death (Acts 23:9). He
ends off by saying that it would be easy to verify these facts through
the commander in Jerusalem. The top officials of Israel then all
agree that these are the facts as they happened.

Acts 24:10–13

Paul does not flatter Felix, but merely acknowledges that he was
happy that someone who was familiar with the situation in Israel
was judging the matter. It is hard to know exactly what Paul had in

mind when he said this. He could have meant that Felix knew about the Jews and Judaism and had some perception about the lack of integrity in the Sanhedrin, thus Paul was more than satisfied that Felix was judging because he wouldn't allow these charlatans to pull the wool over his eyes. Tertullus' opening remarks were an attempt to blind the judge's eyes, whereas, Paul encourages Felix to focus upon justice, by judging the facts with his eyes open.

Paul says that during his brief time in Jerusalem, which had not been enough time for him to cause an uprising, he had not even addressed a large crowd in the temple area, in a synagogue or in the city—actually he had not even argued with anyone. Paul says that there was absolutely no evidence to support the charges brought against him. He says "I came to Jerusalem to worship, not riot and the facts easily prove this".

Acts 24:14

Paul was identified as a ringleader of the sect known as the Nazarenes by Tertullus. Paul does not deny this, but readily admits that indeed he does worship the eternal God in this way—he was not ashamed to be identified as a Christian. In a sense, a wonderful platform was given to the Christian faith to present an official explanation about its beliefs. Since Paul was acknowledged by all to be one of the pre-eminent leaders of this sect, he was able to speak authoritatively for all Christians with respect to their religious commitments. Paul says the Christian faith was a continuation of the faith held by all the patriarchs in the Scriptures. The way Paul worshipped God was no different to the way Abraham, Isaac and Jacob had worshipped—they were worshipping the same God according to the same revelation. Christianity believes in the whole of the Scriptures—the Law and the Prophets was a common way of referring to all that God had revealed in the Scriptures and Paul says Christianity fully accepted everything in them, thus showing it was not a new religion worshipping a new god. Can the modern church say what Paul said? Far too many Christians do not really want to know what the Law and the Prophets have said and there is a much too simplistic use of the OT in the church today. The Jewish religion was protected by Roman law as a legitimate religion and since Christianity believed everything contained in the Jewish Scriptures, they were a legitimate "sect".

Acts 24:15

Paul says his hope is in the promises of God (the implication being, those promises clearly revealed in the Law and the Prophets). Paul says his hope is the same hope that *they* expect. Some think the "they" refers to his accusers, however, this is not only wrong, for his accusers did not have such a hope, but also ignores the context. The context here points to all those saints of God who were used to compile the Law and the Prophets. The hope that these people had written about and were still waiting for, was what Paul was also looking for. And what is this hope? A hope in the righteous judgment of God through the resurrection, resulting in eternal blessing or eternal damnation. Paul, in stating that the whole of the Scriptures testified to the fact of the bodily resurrection, relegated the Sadducees to a sect outside mainstream Judaism, since they did not believe in the resurrection of the dead (Acts 23:8), yet all the Law and the Prophets clearly spoke about this (Matt. 22:32; Acts 3:24, 26). It is a fundamental doctrine in the Christian religion that both the just *and* the unjust will be raised and receive their due reward. We are not merely waiting for the resurrection of the just—it is a heretical belief that says the unjust merely cease to exist. Everyone is going to live for eternity and the only question is in what state will each person spend eternity? Jesus taught that everyone will come before His judgment seat (Matt. 25:31–46). He said elsewhere that all the dead would be raised and judged—those who have done good, to the resurrection of life, and those who have done evil, to the resurrection of death (John 5:28, 29, see too Rev. 20:11–15). Paul confronts, not only Felix, but also his accusers, with the eternal consequences of rebelling against God. The resurrection is the foundation of the Gospel (see comments on John 14:18, 19) and the only way to be declared righteous by God is to believe in Christ—there is no other way to attain this. Everyone will be resurrected—those who are righteous will live in eternal blessedness with God and those who are not righteous will live in eternal torment, being separated from God (see comments on John 6:68). This is reality and this hope ought to give us great confidence and motivation to live our whole lives to His glory.

Acts 24:16

In the light of the inescapable judgment of God (verse 15), where He will evaluate and reward accordingly, both the just and the unjust, Paul says he strives to have a conscience without offence towards God and men. Our conscience is our moral reason and it is important to understand its role in guiding us. Martin Luther is instructive in this respect. When he was told to repent for his teachings he said, "I cannot and will not recant anything, for to go against conscience is neither right nor safe." Just before he said these words, he said something vital, showing he had a sound understanding about the role and place of conscience. He said, "My conscience is captive to the Word of God." Our conscience is not the ultimate authority for determining what is right or wrong. Thus while it is foolish to go against what our conscience will allow, we cannot blame our conscience when we act in a wrong way. We are always responsible to make sure our conscience has been informed by the truth of God's Word. Our conscience does not make us act: we act either in accordance with our conscience or in violation of it, but our conscience does not force us to act. Thus each of us is responsible to make sure that his conscience has been correctly informed, for only then can you be certain that your actions are right. Each person's conscience needs to be instructed by a perfect rule or standard and only one such standard exists—the revelation of God, preserved for us in the Scriptures. Luther said his conscience was captive to God's Word, meaning his absolute authority was not found in the pope, the traditions of the church or in his own feelings of right and wrong, but in the Scriptures. His conscience had been instructed by eternal truth and thus he said it was madness to violate a conscience that had been informed by Scripture.

We can only have a conscience without offence to God and man (as Paul claimed), if we are living by every Word that proceeds from the mouth of God and bringing every thought captive to the mind of Christ (Matt. 4:4; 2 Cor. 10:5). We cannot guess at what is right and wrong and we must not presume that we know what is right and wrong. A sound rule for life is to never act until you are certain that what you are doing is right. Certainty comes from knowing and obeying God's Word (2 Tim. 3:15–17). Our minds and consciences do not naturally lead us in the right way, thus total dependence upon the Lord and His revelation is the only way to find certainty in what we do. Having certainty about your actions is vital when you realize the awesome nature of the final judgement, where people will give account to God for their every word and action (Matt. 12:36; Rom. 14:12; 1 Pet. 4:5).

Acts 24:17–21

Paul says he had come with gifts from the Gentile churches for the needy believers in Jerusalem. His motive was not to start trouble of any sort, but to assist Jewish Christians who were struggling. Contrary to what Tertullus had implied while speaking on behalf of the Sanhedrin (cf. Acts 24:6), it was actually Asian Jews who had apprehended Paul in the temple and not temple authorities or members of the Sanhedrin. Paul says that when these Asian Jews assaulted him, he had already gone through the required purification rites specified by the temple authorities. The charges against Paul included defiling the temple, but why, he asks, would someone who had come to defile the temple go through the whole purification process? Moreover, Paul says, those who were apparently witnesses to his defiling of the temple were not even there to give evidence against him. Moreover, Paul was not even in a crowd, let alone creating a disturbance within the temple, but privately and peaceably fulfilling his purification rites. It was unacceptable in Roman law, to be accused of something without witnesses being present in the court. The absence of witnesses pointed to the lack of evidence on the part of Paul's accusers. Paul was exposing the glaring defects of the Sanhedrin's case against him—defects which Felix would have clearly seen.

Paul continues by revealing more details left out by Tertullus, who had not mentioned Paul's trial before the Sanhedrin and that no charges had been brought against him (Acts 23:7, 9). Paul tells the governor to ask the "distinguished" leaders of the Jewish nation, who were present, whether they had discovered anything worthy of civil punishment when he had stood before them. He then quickly adds that the only accusation the council might have against Paul was that he believed in the resurrection of the dead. Paul is saying that the Sanhedrin merely had some false charges against him which would not stand the test of a court trial. The real reason for wanting to kill him was because of theological differences. Paul once again is able to emphasis one of the fundamental pillars of the Christian religion—the resurrection (1 Cor. 15:16, 17, see too comments on John 14:18–20). If I am on trial for this, Paul says, then most of the Jews in the world should be put on trial, including many members of the Sanhedrin. Do you see why they wanted to murder rather than put Paul on trial? Corrupt leaders can never follow the path of true justice and still attain their perverted goals. They will give the impression that they are after justice, but manipulate the facts according to their own wicked desires.

Acts 24:22

It was obvious that there were no legitimate charges against Paul. Felix knew much about the faith that Paul held to, he knew how the Jews despised this "new" teaching and clearly saw that the charges against Paul were trumped up. He should have dropped all charges and freed Paul immediately, however, Felix was a politician—more concerned about his privileged position of power and comfort than justice. He knew how powerful Paul's accusers were and thus did not want to offend them too much and so delayed things with the excuse that he needed to see the Roman commander before he could rule on the details of the case.

Acts 24:23

Probably to ease his conscience for not releasing Paul, Felix allows Paul to have unlimited access to his friends, food and other things that they might bring him. This was where Philip lived (Acts 21:8) as well as a strong Christian community, thus Paul's ministry would have continued amongst them. For all we know, Luke probably also stayed in the area and remained in contact with Paul.

Acts 24:24, 25

Felix and his third wife (Drusilla) were inquisitive about the message Paul preached and so had him preach to them. It is noteworthy that Drusilla's father, Herod Agrippa I, killed James, the brother of John, with the sword (Acts 12:2). Her uncle, Herod Antipas, beheaded John the Baptist (Mark 6:16ff.) and her great-grandfather, Herod the Great, tried to murder Christ (Matt. 2:16). What Felix and his wife saw as an interesting and entertaining way to pass the time, turned into a very personal and disturbing challenge. It would have been foolish to think a sermon from Paul could have been any different to this. No matter how important and influential people are, they still need to hear the Gospel of Christ. Whoever we come across, we are to seek an opportunity to challenge them with the truth of God's claims upon their lives. Whether they bow to the

Lord or not, has nothing to do with us, our responsibility is to faithfully make known the full counsel of God. Paul's life and comfort were in the hands of the governor, yet this in no way influences his preaching of the Gospel. Today, too many preachers want to tickle the ears of corrupt leaders and those in rebellion against God, rather than challenge their sin. These preachers are themselves offended by the offence of the Gospel and seek to remove everything that will upset those in rebellion against God's truth (Luke 9:26; Rom. 1:16; 9:33; 2 Tim. 1:8). Paul would not compromise the Christ's truth, no matter what hardships might come upon him as a result.

Paul boldly proclaimed that righteousness that has been revealed to us in the Law of God—the one and only eternal standard that will judge all people and all nations. The Spirit was here in abundant measure taking the truth that Paul proclaimed and driving it deep into the hearts and consciences of Felix and Drusilla (John 16:8). Paul, after presenting the righteous standard of the law, shows its demand that people bring their lives into line with the law—this is self-control. We are to live by every Word that proceeds from the mouth of God and bring every thought captive to the mind of Christ (Matt. 4:4; 2 Cor. 10:5). Finally Paul tells of God's fearful judgment that awaits all those whose lives have not gained mastery over their unrighteous passions. Without Christ, the demands of God are nothing but a terror to all people, because each person's heart condemns them in the light of God's righteous standard and yet they remain helplessly unable to do anything about their condition. Or to put it another way: they continue refusing to embrace the only way of escape there is—faith in Christ's completed work of redemption upon the cross. It is only through faith in Christ that we can be made just in God's sight and empowered to live a life of self-control (Gal. 5:22–26). Felix stubbornly refuses the salvation offered in Christ and dismisses Paul from his presence. Everyone who resists God, does so because of the hardness of their own heart, which is constantly fighting against the truth (Rom. 1:18ff.) and trying to make the world function according to their own unrighteous principles.

Acts 24:26, 27

Here we see that it was ultimately Felix's greed that kept Paul in prison for two long years after he should have been released. Felix knew that Paul was one of the most prominent, loved and respected leaders in the Christian church in the Gentile world. Many of these churches were very rich and Felix, knowing that Paul had brought a significant gift to the Jerusalem church from the Gentile churches, was hoping to receive a substantial bribe from them for Paul's release. Felix would have done very well in modern politics, for he was someone who used his office to enrich himself by corrupt means and sought to stay in favor with other influential people who might be useful for his own ambitions and well-being. Josephus tells us that Felix had killed, imprisoned and looted the houses of some Jews when there had been a clash between them and some Syrians. It appears that the Roman Emperor, in order to keep peace in the region, was forced to withdraw Felix and replace him. Felix, still thinking that being in favor with the powerful Jews in the Jerusalem leadership would be of benefit to him, left Paul in prison. This ploy did not help Felix's cause, because Josephus informs us that when the new governor, Festus, arrived in Caesarea, the Jews went to Rome and condemned Felix before the Emperor, Nero. It was only because Felix's brother was highly esteemed by Nero and pleaded for Felix, that Felix escaped punishment (*Antiquities* 20:8:9; *Wars* 2:13).

Acts 25:1–6

Festus, wanting to visit the famous city of Jerusalem as well as wanting to become familiar with the Jews and their leadership, immediately journeyed to the holy city. We see how offensive Paul was to the Jewish leadership, that they straight away mention him to Festus. Remember, it has been two years since the last trial when the Jews accused Paul before Felix (Acts 24:1). Ananias (Acts 23:2) had been replaced as high priest, his successor had been murdered and now a third high priest was on the throne (Ishmael). This request was a very shrewd move by the Jewish leadership, because they probably knew how little Festus knew about things in Israel, but he would have been informed about the influence the Jewish leadership had in the politics of the region. The Jews, therefore, were hoping that he would be wanting to make a good impression with them and thus they put forward their request. The Jewish leadership was in rebellion against the Lord, but understood one thing very clearly, namely, that Paul's message was a very serious threat to their man-made religious system. While the Sanhedrin claimed to be serving the Living God, they were living in rebellion and serving themselves in the name of God by refusing to bring their thoughts and actions into line with His clear revelation in the Scriptures. Once again we see that it is not the rule of law and justice that these leaders wanted, for they intended to murder Paul, *not* give him a fair trial. The Lord in His sovereignty protected Paul through Festus refusing to do this favor for the Jewish leadership (Prov. 21:1).

Acts 25:7, 8

The Jews brought serious complaints, though they had no evidence to support these accusations. They had had two years after Felix to put together their facts and gather their evidence and yet, at the outset of the retrial, the evidence is non-existent. These so called champions of God's law (the Jewish leadership) were not placing themselves under God's law, for the law said that if the accusations brought by Paul's accusers were false, then they should receive the same punishment they were hoping he would receive (Deut. 19:16–19). One of the fundamentals of God's law is the forbidding of bearing false accusations against someone (Ex. 20:16; 23:1–8; Lev. 19:16). Moreover, anyone who has a sensitive heart before God, would be severely convicted for being a false witness, for God deals severely with slanderers (Ps. 15:1–4; 101:5–8; Prov. 10:18). Paul's accusers were hard hearted rebels and Paul easily refuted them.

Acts 25:9

The supreme court and powerhouse of the nation of Israel was the Sanhedrin and it was these influential men that were strongly condemning Paul. Festus was totally ignorant about the real issue in this case, however, he wanted to be on good terms with the Sanhedrin, which he probably thought would make his governing far easier. Festus was very naÔve and the Sanhedrin was prepared to take full advantage of him. This was a serious blunder by Festus: Paul had been tried by the Sanhedrin in Jerusalem and no charges had been brought against him; he had been tried before Felix and found not guilty; he had been tried before Festus and it was obvious that there was no evidence so support the accusations, however, Festus thinks that he can obtain justice by perverting justice. That is, he was trying to win the favor of the Jewish leadership by playing games with an innocent man's life and liberty.

Acts 25:10

Paul says he is being held by Roman authority, according to Roman law and it is here that he ought to be judged. For Festus to have denied this would have called into question the legitimacy of the trial underway and would have meant that he had no authority to hold Paul, who could have walked out of the proceedings. Paul had been tried in the Sanhedrin and the Jews had now twice brought charges against Paul in Caesarea without any evidence. Paul is asking Festus what the point was to take him to Jerusalem for trial when Festus himself had just witnessed the absolute lack of evidence to support the Jewish accusations. Yes, it might have been legitimate if there was some solid evidence that had been brought by the Jews and that needed to be looked at in Jerusalem in order to make a ruling, however there was nothing. Festus knew this was true and Paul challenges him with this fact. The book of Acts bears witness to the struggles and victory of the Gospel in a world that is hostile to and separated from Christ. The *triumph* of the Good News in this environment is the work of God Himself and reporting this fact is very obvious in Luke's writings.

Acts 25:11

Paul quickly adds that he was not against the due process of law or justice being measured out, however, there was no evidence against him and thus not even Festus could justly make a gift out of Paul, meaning giving a gift to the Jews by sending Paul back to Jerusalem (this is what the text actually says). Paul, no longer confident that Festus would make a just, impartial decision with respect to his case, had no alternative but to remove it from Festus' hands by appealing his case to Caesar, which was a right of every Roman citizen. Paul's appeal reveals how serious the threat against his life was because of the ignorance, injustice and softness of Festus. It is instructive to realize that Nero was Caesar at this time and in the light of Nero's reputation as an extremely wicked and lawless Emperor, why would Paul trust his welfare into the hands of such a judge? We know from history that the first 5 years of Nero's reign, under the influence of Seneca and Burrus, were looked upon as a golden age (see *Muse Time*, paper 3). Bruce tells us that in A.D. 59 there was nothing that gave warning of what would happen in A.D. 64 and 65—which was when the terror of Nero's wickedness was fully unleashed (Acts, p.454).

Acts 25:12–22

The previous governor, Felix, was married to Drusilla (Acts 24:24), the daughter of Herod Agrippa whose death is recorded in Acts 12:23. King Agrippa of Acts 25:13, was the son of Herod Agrippa (from Acts 12), being just seventeen when his father died (though he was now at least thirty years old). Bernice was king Agrippa's younger sister, though Drusilla was the youngest of Herod's three children (Agrippa, Bernice and Drusilla). Agrippa and Bernice were involved in an incestuous relationship—a brother and sister may not live together as husband and wife (Lev. 18:9; Deut. 27:22). Agrippa had been given the responsibility by Rome to appoint the high priests in Jerusalem, so he was a very influential person on the Jewish political scene. Was this not a clear sign of God's judgment upon the nation of Israel, who were in a position where a man living in incest was the one who appointed their high priests? (see comments on Acts 23:5). Agrippa's kingdom was not over the province where Festus was governor, but was over an area north and north-east of it.

Acts 25:23–27

Who would have thought that Paul would next be presented with such an audience of influential people: the governor, the king, at least five high ranking military commanders in the Roman army and all the prominent people of the city of Caesarea. The Lord has His reasons for wanting the apostle Paul to address this gathering, though we know of no fruit that came from it. Nevertheless, we must remember that when the Gospel is preached, some people come to repentance while others are left under greater condemnation for hardening their hearts to the Good News—both of these fall under the sovereign working of God and glorify His name, exalting His mercy and His justice.

Festus says that the Jews were wanting Paul dead, but then adds that he had found nothing worthy of death in Paul. Luke tells Theophilus (Acts 1:1) about yet another high ranking Roman ruler, who, in an official capacity, found Paul innocent of all charges brought against him—Gallio (Acts 18:14–16), Felix and now Festus.

Festus, it appears, is in a tight spot because of his refusal to declare Paul innocent and release him. In wanting to use Paul as a bartering chip to win favor with the Jews, Paul had appealed to Caesar which

now meant that Festus had to explain what the charges were against
Paul. Festus knew that there was no case against Paul and he also
knew that any Roman official could easily see this. The fact that this
case was now going to be tried by the Emperor exposed the foolishness of the governor. He was thus desperate for someone, among
the prominent audience, to give him some ideas as to how he could
explain the problem and charges to Caesar in a way that would protect him from being exposed. When you play games with justice
you will find yourself in a deep hole for such behavior has a way of
creating a violent backlash. Justice is at the very core of God's heart
and to trample upon it is a game played by fools, seeking destruction. Festus says that it is absurd to send someone to be tried by
Caesar, but not specify any charges against the person. If there were
no charges, Paul should have been immediately released, however,
when Festus had the chance to let justice prevail, he had refused to
follow that path. Nor does he now explain to these important
guests why Paul appealed to Caesar—Paul appealed because Festus
perverted justice by wanting to put a man, whom *he* had found
innocent, back on trial, merely so he could buy favor for himself
from the Jewish leadership (Deut.16:19). God will not long tolerate
unjust judges or leaders, who use their positions of authority to
benefit themselves.

Acts 26:1–3

King Agrippa II gives Paul the opportunity to speak for himself.
Paul is very polite in the way he addresses the king, however, he is
not flattering him but telling us something very important. Luke
too was anxious to record Paul's words because they are a brilliant
and inescapable defence of the Christian message and its truthfulness. The Lord had brought Agrippa and a very prominent delegation to listen to Paul and Paul, full of the Holy Spirit and boldness,
lays out his own defence and the defence of the Christian religion
for all time. Paul shows that the Jews' charges against him had absolutely no substance to them whatsoever. In a sense, this speech was
the final nail in the coffin with respect to the Jewish claims that
Christianity was a perversion of the law and the prophets. Agrippa
was extremely well acquainted with the Jewish Scriptures and customs, as well as being very familiar with the history and affairs of
Palestine. Rome looked to him for counsel with respect to the Jewish religion and had given him the authority to appoint the high

priests. Thus, Agrippa had significant standing in both the Roman
and the Jewish realms and Paul was thankful for the king's knowledge and authority.

Acts 26:4, 5

Paul's life, from the very beginning, was an open book that everyone in Jerusalem had witnessed. His zeal and dedication to the
Pharisaic party was without question and it would have been
extremely difficult, if not impossible, to find someone more zealous
and qualified than Paul. His knowledge and single minded dedication to the beliefs and traditions of the Pharisees were exemplary
and couldn't be called into question by anyone. Paul had had a long
history of dedicated obedience to the minute details of the strictest
sect in the Jewish nation. Paul's father was a Pharisee and thus from
his earliest memories until his conversion, Paul's life was lived in
strict obedience to the ideals of the Pharisaic party (Phil. 3:5, 6).
Paul was careful to underline the fact that both his learning and his
practice were unquestionable as far as the Pharisees were concerned
and many people still living in Jerusalem could testify to this fact.
He wanted Agrippa to know that he had not introduced some new
religious beliefs, whether from the pagan world or from the imagination of his own mind, but that his doctrine was in total agreement with the Jewish Scriptures. Paul was a man not only grounded
and learned in the Scriptures, but also whole-heartedly committed
to bringing his every action into line with what they said.

Acts 26:6–8

The Pharisees believed in the resurrection and Paul says this has
been the hope from the very beginning in Israel—all the patriarchs
had their faith focused upon this great promise from God. If there
is no resurrection, then the faith of Abraham, Isaac and Jacob was
all meaningless. Paul says that this hope has been the dominating
belief for every one of the twelve tribes of Israel throughout their
history. He says that the most basic reason for Israel's service and
dedication to the ways of God, rested upon their belief in God's
promise of the resurrection. Paul says, "King Agrippa, I stand
accused by the Jews because I believe in and preach about this
hope".

We know that the Saducees did not believe in the resurrection (see
comments on Acts 23:7, 8), however, I do not think Paul is merely

speaking to those who held to the Saducean philosophy. It is possible that Agrippa was more inclined to the Saducees way of thinking (it was always Saducees that were appointed as high priest by him), but we have no evidence to prove this. We do know that even the Pharisees, who believed in the resurrection, denied that Jesus had been raised from the dead. Ultimately, Paul was hated by the Jews because he proclaimed that *Jesus* had been raised from the dead (Acts 25:19). This is the great stumbling block for all those who refuse to bow to Christ, thus Paul challenged their unbelief by asking why it seems incredible that God raised Jesus. While not mentioning His name, it is obvious that Paul was not merely talking in general terms about the resurrection but specifically referring to Christ. Why is it so hard for people to believe that Christ was raised from the dead by the Creator and upholder of the universe? Paul says it is a contradiction to claim to believe in the resurrection, but then deny the specific resurrection of Christ, which clearly fulfilled God's promise and was supported with inescapable proofs. The whole basis for having a resurrection hope rests firmly upon the reality of Christ's bodily resurrection from His tomb in Jerusalem. The hope of Israel from the beginning, was not in the *idea* of a resurrection, but in the actual resurrection of Him whom God said would rise from the dead and be the first fruits of every other resurrection. This is not an argument in order to prove the resurrection, rather Paul is using the inescapable fact of Christ's resurrection to prove that He is the Messiah, the promise of God and the hope of all Israel. If Jesus Christ did not rise from the dead, then there is no such thing as a resurrection for anyone.

Acts 26:9–11

Paul says, even I, an exemplary student in Pharisaic doctrine and believing in the resurrection, refused to accept the fact of Christ's resurrection. He shows that believing in Christ was not something that came easily to him, for in the beginning he was filled with violence and hatred for Christ. Paul (before his conversion) was convinced in his own mind that he had a moral duty to oppose, in every way possible, with whatever resources he could gather, the claims that Jesus was the Messiah. Paul's opposition to Christ, in every possible way, is ultimately how every unbeliever acts towards Him (obviously with varying degrees of effort and understanding, yet they all want to dethrone Him nonetheless). To stand against the name of Jesus, is to oppose everything He said and is—Savior, Messiah, Lord, Prophet, Priest, King, etc. If some area of life is not being brought into submission to God's Word, then it is opposing the name of Christ. Paul tried to make people deny Christ in some way and thus blaspheme—to deny that Jesus is the Messiah, or Lord of the universe and that His will is to be done in every area of life is to blaspheme Him. Paul tells Agrippa that he was more violently opposed to the name of Christ than his accusers now are and no one could question the fact that Paul had been consumed by violent hatred for anyone who believed in Christ—"being exceedingly enraged against them".

Acts 26:12–15

Paul had the full backing of the Jewish leadership, who had granted him authority to do whatever he felt compelled to do to those who called on the name of Christ. There was no doubt in the minds of the Sanhedrin that Paul was the man who could exterminate Christianity from the face of the earth and they whole-heartedly wanted just that. It was in this state of intense hatred for Christ that Paul's conversion took place—the exterminator of Christianity becomes the greatest defender and promoter of Christ's cause. Paul, the most terrifying weapon the Jews could launch against the church of Jesus Christ, we see is under the total control of God's ordering. Whom or what is there to fear? Every person in this world is as much under the controlling hand of God as Paul was. The only thing to fear is fear itself, because if we are consumed by fear it is because we have no faith and no understanding about the reality of who Christ is. The Lord's will, will be accomplished in our lives (John 10:29; Eph. 1:11) and in this world and nothing is able to prevent it (2 Chron. 20:6; Dan. 4:35; Acts 5:39).

Paul's urgency to get to Damascus and silence the Christians is seen by the fact that he was travelling in the mid-day heat rather than resting at this time and waiting for the day to become cooler. However, the sun at its brightest was outshone by the light of Christ's glory. The fact that it was mid-day made it easy to compare Christ's glory with the sun's brightest light. It is hard for us to imagine something more brilliant than the sun, however, the brightness of the noon sun turned suddenly dull in comparison to the glory of Christ that shone around Paul and his party. A hardened group of Christ's persecutors were Paul's companions and these men were also overcome by the intensity of Christ's glory and would have later testified to the sudden conversion of Paul from a violent hater to a devoted lover of Christ. This was a manifestation of the power and working of the Sovereign Lord upon one of the hardest hearts in Israel.

The Jesus whom Paul refused to believe had risen from the dead was now confronting him with the glory of God. Paul's persecution of Christ's followers was the same as persecuting Christ Himself. Jesus says Paul is fighting against something that is inescapable—He is the Messiah. To "kick against the goad" is an expression that comes from training oxen to pull a plough or wagon. If a farmer harnessed an untrained ox up to his plough, the animal would try to kick the plough and free itself. Thus, to counter this, the farmer would hold a long sharp pole just behind the ox's back legs so that when it tried to kick the plough, it kicked the sharp goad and so eventually submitted to the reality of pulling the plough. Paul was only hurting himself by fighting against something that is indestructibly real—Christ *is* the resurrected Messiah and Lord of the universe and there is nothing that anyone can do to change that. We either submit to Christ or we perish. There is no other option (Jam. 4:12). To live in rebellion against the reality of Christ's Lordship is utterly foolish: it is a path leading to self destruction if you attempt to resist the Divine will of God and the Divine will of God has been clearly revealed to us in the Person of Jesus Christ. Kiss the Son lest He becomes angry with you (Ps. 2).

Acts 26:16

Paul's conversion to Christ is clearly seen in this incident, however, I think Paul is wanting to emphasis his *commission* to Agrippa—that is, his God appointed, apostolic authority to both Jews and Gentiles. Paul's calling is comparable to the callings of the OT prophets, e.g., Isaiah, Jeremiah, Ezekiel and Amos (Isa. 6:9; Jer. 1:5, 7; 7:2; Ezk. 2:3, 4; Amos 7:15). In all likelihood, these "important" people listening to Paul would have thought very little, if anything, of him. They were there because of Agrippa—it was the king's presence that had made this gathering attractive to the officials of Caesarea. Paul was merely an interesting oddity who was practically irrelevant as far as this gathering was concerned—he had no recognisable standing or office. However, we are struck by the immense authority that Paul had been give by God. When a Jew thought about awesome prophetic authority, they thought, Isaiah, Jeremiah and Ezekiel. Now Agrippa, who was very familiar with the Scriptures, was being confronted with a commission that was equal to the biggest and most respected names in the Jewish nation. Even as God's prophets of old were to take the Lord's Word to both Israel and Gentile nations, Paul received the same calling—to Jews and Gentiles. So often the great prophets of God were despised by those they were sent to (e.g., 2 Chron. 36:15, 16; Jer. 7:25, 26; Ezk. 3:7) and Paul received the same kind of treatment. That is why God said that He would deliver Paul from the hands of all those he was sent to—they would want to harm him because of their rebellion against God's truth. Where there is hardness against the Lord, those who bring God's Light into that situation (Eph. 5:11, 13), will be hated and opposed (John 3:19, 20; 15:20, 21; Rom. 1:32). Remember, all of Christ's disciples are meant to be light and salt (Matt. 5:13–16), applying the truth to every area of life (see *Muse Time*, paper 22, "Dualism").

Agrippa would have known that Jesus had been crucified, yet here Paul is clearly confirming His resurrection and exalting the hope of all Israel (Acts 26:6–8). Jesus had died a condemned criminal, however, His resurrection proves His absolute innocence. Paul, the persecutor, had become the servant of the one whose name he had tried to remove from the face of the earth—submitting completely to Christ's every command. Paul now did everything Christ told him to do, which included being a witness for the risen and glorified Lord of the universe—Paul had been thrust into the ministry by Christ (1 Tim. 1:12), who also instructed him (Gal. 1:12). It was the divine purposes of God that had qualified and commissioned Paul for the tasks that he had been faithfully carrying out and for which the Jews wanted to kill him, i.e., for preaching salvation to the Gentiles through the Gospel (see Acts 14:19; 26:20, 21; 2 Cor. 11:24; Eph. 3:6; 1 Thes. 2:15, 16). Proclaiming to the Gentiles forgiveness of sins through the Messiah was God's plan from the very beginning (Luke 24:44–47). Persecution of God's messengers is a recurring picture throughout the Scriptures—the people of God consistently despised those whom God sent to them (Matt. 21:35, 36; 23:29–31, 34, 35; Acts 7:51, 52) and Paul was no exception. Paul unashamedly tells Agrippa that he was a divinely appointed prophet of God and his message was in complete agreement with all the prophets who had come before him.

Acts 26:17

Paul was fiercely opposed by both Jews and Gentiles, yet this never influenced Paul's witness for Christ. He never feared to go where Christ wanted him to go and he never compromised the message Christ wanted him to proclaim. We learn what the basis was for Paul's uncompromising boldness—he rested totally upon the Word that Christ had spoken to him when he was commissioned. Jesus did not say no trouble would come Paul's way, actually the opposite was the case, for Jesus, through Ananias, showed Paul how much he would have to suffer for Christ (Acts 9:16, see too, comments on John 15:18–21). What Christ promised Paul was that he would be kept and sustained *through* the trouble. Nothing would be able to prevent him from fulfilling the work God had given him to do. Martin Luther (1483–1546) had the same understanding for his own life: when friends confessed their fears about his well-being, Luther said that he was invincible until he had completed the work God wanted him to do. Paul lived in the reality of God's sovereign control over the details of life and thus could faithfully and boldly declare the truth amidst people who utterly despised the truth and wanted to destroy anyone who brought it to their attention. No one can separate us from the love of God or pluck us from His hand (Rom. 8:35, 39; John 10:28, 29), because He is in sovereign control of all the details in life (Deut. 4:39; 10:14; 1 Sam. 2:6–8; 2 Chron. 20:6; Ps. 135:5, 6; Isa. 33:22; Dan. 4:3, 17, 35; John 19:11; Jam. 4:12; Rev. 19:6, etc.). Our focus and desire, like Paul's, should be to complete the course that Christ had given us to run (2 Tim. 4:7, cf. Heb. 12:1). It is only those who truly know their God that are able to boldly and effectively stand against the wickedness in their own days (Dan. 11:32).

Acts 26:18

Paul was commissioned by the Messiah and therefore he would do the Messiah's work—open the eyes of the blind, turning them from darkness to light (Isa. 29:18; 35:5; 42:6, 7). The work of the Messiah is constantly advancing through the labours of *all* His true servants (see comments on Acts 13:47). It is the work of the Holy Spirit to open the eyes of those who are living in darkness, however, it is the privilege of Christ's messengers to proclaim the good news and see the working of the Spirit in the lives of those they speak to. We are all called to labor in the Lord's Kingdom, however, we must never forget that when people come to repentance it is God alone who grants this increase (1 Cor. 3:6). The commission of Christ is always accompanied by His power. It is never the eloquence or wisdom of the preacher that enables someone to see the truth, but always and only the working of the Holy Spirit in their heart. The preacher must present the wisdom of God to the unbeliever and he needs to study and prepare himself in order to do this properly (1 Pet. 3:15), however, he must never forget that success comes *entirely* from the Lord.

All who know not Christ are blind, sitting in darkness and under the power of Satan (2 Cor. 4:4). It was to such people that Paul was to boldly proclaim the message of Christ, knowing that the Lord has His own who would have their eyes opened by the Holy Spirit (Ps. 33:12; Matt. 11:27; Acts 13:48; Rom. 8:28–30), so that they could discern spiritual things (John 3:3; 1 Cor. 2:14). The same Spirit that worked through Paul works through us (Eph. 3:20; Phil. 2:13; Col. 1:29), thus may we not become discouraged by the magnitude of the task or if there is little response (2 Cor. 4:1; Gal. 6:9; Jam. 5:7, 8). The work is the Lord's and things always work out exactly as He planned them (Isa. 46:10, 11; Jer. 1:4, 5; Acts 2:23; 22:14; Eph. 1:5, 11; 2 Tim. 1:9). All we ought to be concerned about is whether we are faithfully representing Christ in our lives and by the message we bring in His name (2 Cor. 10:5; Eph. 4:1; Col. 1:10). There are only two kingdoms and ultimately two leaders within these kingdoms and every person in this world is serving either one or the other—there is never a possibility of neutrality (see *Faith and Reason*, chapters 1 to 3).

When we are released by the power of God from the kingdom of darkness into the glorious liberty of Christ's Kingdom (Col. 1:12–14; 1 Pet. 2:9), we are adopted into God's family and partake of all the benefits that accompany being a child of God. Satan's bondage touches every aspect of a person's being and existence, however, God's liberty delivers us from this bondage in every part of our being and existence (2 Cor. 5:17). Paul was told by Christ to proclaim to the Gentiles the message of attaining full covenantal standing within the Kingdom of God through faith in Him alone. To obtain full forgiveness for sin and share in the full inheritance of those who are sanctified, you have to embrace Christ by faith, trusting completely in His Words (John 15:3) and in His completed Work upon the cross for us. There is no other doorway that gives a person entrance into the family of God (John 10:9; Acts 4:12). Those who have been justified, have peace with God (Rom. 5:1) and can come before Him with boldness and full assurance (Heb. 10:19, 22), knowing that they are totally accepted by Him. What a glorious message this is for sinful rebels who are ensnared by the dominion of Satan and thus living under the terror of God's wrath. There is a way of escape, "Believe on the Lord Jesus Christ and you will be saved" (Acts 16:31). When God justifies us, He forgives our sin and restores us to a position of Divine favor in His presence which includes an eternal inheritance in His Kingdom.

Acts 26:19

Paul was not disobedient to the heavenly vision. What was this vision? It was the Word or instructions from Christ! We must not think that somehow the Words that Paul obeyed carried more authority than other Words that have come from Christ's mouth. There are only two possible responses to everything Christ has revealed—obedience or disobedience. Jews and Gentiles alike wanted to stop Paul from proclaiming the Good News, however, he could say after many years of service that he had been obedient in the face of many trials and hardships. All believers have been called with a holy calling (2 Tim. 1:9) and given a commission to serve the Living God (John 15:16; 1 Thes. 1:9; Heb. 9:14). He has revealed what we ought to be doing wherever we find ourselves in this life (2 Tim. 3:16, 17). He who lacks wisdom in the area of serving the Lord, needs to find it in Christ (Col. 2:3; Jam. 1:5), pursuing after the truth and searching for it as for hidden treasure (Prov. 2:4; 3:13–18; 4:7, etc.). There is no basis for pleading ignorance at the end of our lives when we have wasted our time and talents. This was nearing the end of Paul's life and yet he could boldly say, "I was not disobedient to the heavenly vision." By God's grace, may we be able to say this at the end of our lives. We have a King to serve, advancing His Kingdom purposes—that is why we exist (see comments on John 15:1–17). May we not foolishly despise the heavenly vision, but cast the whole of our being into that which Christ has told us to do, for His glory.

Acts 26:20

Paul does not give a step by step account of how he carried out his commission. He did first proclaim the Gospel in Damascus and later in Jerusalem, but he is giving a broad summary of faithfully fulfilling his commission to the Jews and Gentiles. Christ had sent him to both Jews and Gentiles and he tells us that he went to every Jewish region and to the Gentiles where he made known his Master's message. Every person and thus every people group in the whole world are sinners and need to repent and turn to God (Luke 24:47). To repent means to have a complete change in one's conscious life—this touches everything including our will and affections. There is to be a complete turning away from ourselves and a returning to God. Paul adds, by way of clarification, lest there be any misunderstanding, that repentance means turning to God. We must not think that turning to God has some merit in itself so that we earn His forgiveness through repentance (see comments on Acts 20:21). The Larger Catechism tells us that "Repentance unto life is a saving grace" (Q 76). While true repentance cannot exist without faith, we must make a distinction between them. Repentance entails a forsaking of ourselves and turning to God, a putting away our old way of life and putting on a new one. To paraphrase Calvin: repentance can be defined as a true turning of our life to God, flowing from a pure and serious fear of Him and incorporated in this is the putting to death of our flesh and the old man and being quickened by the Spirit (*Institutes* 3:3:5). To repent of any sin means having a complete change around in life and going in the opposite direction and actually practising the opposite of sin. For example, Paul says in Ephesians 4:28 that it is not enough to just stop stealing, but that the repentant thief should now work so that he is able to give to those in need. Sin is a life of active opposition against the will of God, whereas true repentance is assuming a life of actively serving God in the way He has said. The sinner, being fully aware "not only of the danger, but also of the filthiness and odiousness of his sins, as contrary to the holy nature, and righteous law of God; and upon the apprehension of His mercy in Christ to such as are penitent, so grieves for, and hates his sins, as to turn from them all unto God, purposing and endeavouring to walk with Him in all the ways of His commandments" (Westminster Confession 15:2).

Inseparable from conversion is moral fruit manifested through the life of the convert. James tells us that proof of our justification is seen by what we do (Jam. 2:14–26). We are not only to profess that we have repented, but we are to live a life of repentance—our profession and our living must be in agreement. Living to the glory of

God is living in submission to every Word that proceeds from His mouth (Matt. 4:4). As the Larger Catechism says, the repentant person purposes and endeavours to constantly walk with God in all the ways of new obedience (Q 76), which means in all the ways of His commandments. "Works befitting repentance," as Paul calls them, are works done in submission to God's revelation (2 Tim. 3:16, 17) and not those works that are done in the name of God, but have their origin in the "wisdom of men." We are saved by grace through faith, however, we are saved so we might advance God's Kingdom in the way He has ordained (Eph. 2:8–10). We are saved to bear fruit (John 15:8, 16).

Acts 26:21

The Jews had tried to kill Paul in Jerusalem because he boldly preached salvation through faith in Christ alone and also because of his missionary zeal which touched numerous Jews and Gentiles. Paul was in trouble for doing what God had told him to do (Matt. 5:10–12; John 15:18–21). He was not afraid, however, to be hated, despised and ridiculed for what he believed, because God's truth and glory burned in his heart—"the zeal of thy house has eaten me up" (Psalm 69:9).

Acts 26:22

Paul attributes all his amazing achievements to the enabling of the Lord and it is only because of the Lord that Paul is able to continue standing. The only reason we can and do keep standing in and serving the Lord is because of His help and it is vital that we acknowledge this and praise Him for it. In a sense Paul was saying that he was holding his ground and would not compromise the truth that he was entrusted with, but declare it boldly to both the highest and the lowest in society. He was not ashamed of what he believed, but owned up to it, even in the midst of the most hostile opponents of the truth. Paul's message was completely in line with everything the prophets had said before him, and with what Moses had said (Moses being the greatest law-giver in Israel's history is singled out in a way that would greatly impact any Jew). Paul was challenging, with the whole weight of the Scriptures, the deceptive claim that he was anti-Jewish or trying to introduce unbiblical ideas in the name of the God of Israel. Rather, he claims to have taught nothing but what the whole of the OT Scriptures spoke about. How could he be accused of apostasy or blasphemy in the light of this? Everything Paul did and taught could be justified by comparing it to what the prophets had said would happen.

Acts 26:23

Even if one did not want to believe Paul's testimony of his commission by God, no one could find fault with Paul's message if they honestly compared it to the Scriptures. As Jesus had expounded the OT Scriptures concerning Himself to the disciples on the road to Emmaus (Luke 24:25, 26), Paul had done the same thing throughout his ministry. The Messiah was to suffer in order to be our savior (Ps. 16:10; Ps. 22; Isa. 53:3–11). The Jews could not accept a suffering Messiah and so were suppressing the testimony of the prophets that said the Messiah would indeed die. The Messiah would not only die but be the first to rise from the dead, meaning, the first to get a *resurrection* body. Many other people were raised from the dead by the power of God, though I do not believe these assumed their final resurrection bodies. Rather, they still await, like the rest of us, their resurrection bodies (see comments on John 11:25, 26 and compare Matt. 27:52, 53 which is too brief to prove a point one way or the other). What is very certain is that Christ has received His resurrection body already and that this abundantly proves that we too will receive ours (1 Cor. 15:20–23; Col. 1:18; Rev. 1:5). Christ is the Lord of the whole earth and God's plan from the beginning was that all people would glorify Him, thus the message of the Gospel is meant for all people (Isa. 2:2–5; 11:10; 42:6; 49:6; 52:10; 60:3; Ps. 22:27; 98:2, 3; 117:1, 2; Amos 9:11, 12; Micah 4:1, 2)—Christ expects all people to walk in His Light (John 8:12; Rom. 14:11; Phil. 2:10). Christ had fulfilled what the Scriptures had foretold and Paul was merely someone who drew attention to this fulfilment. To condemn his teaching or ministry would be to condemn Moses and the prophets—something a true Jew couldn't do and something even Rome would not do.

Acts 26:24, 25

Was Festus' Greek philosophy clashing with the doctrine of the resurrection (cf. Acts 17:32), or was he trying to escape from the searching light of the Gospel which Paul was preaching? It is difficult to know what the real reason was for Festus' outburst, but to call someone out of their mind is an attempt to overrule everything they have said without having to come up with a reasonable argument to support your claims. It is a common tactic by unbelievers to try and evade the truth by calling those who proclaim it mad or their reasoning foolish (John 10:20; 1 Cor. 1:18). Paul replies by showing respect to Festus' office but not necessarily to the man within the office. We must not be personally offended by the attacks of those whose minds are captivated by darkness, but nor should we be intimidated by them. Nothing can overturn the truth of God and it alone provides an eternally immovable foundation from which to begin all our thinking. It is this foundation that must form the basis of our determining between truth and error, what is reasonable or unreasonable and what is sane and what is insane. Paul says his words are truth and because they are truth they are inescapably *reasonable*. Christianity alone provides a world and life view that is internally consistent (i.e., does not contradict itself) and can account for reason (a reasonable God created all things and controls them. He gave people the ability to reason and has revealed His will to them in a way that they can think His thoughts after Him about the creation around them and thus make sense out of life and have purpose in this world).

Acts 26:26–28

The truth of what Paul was saying was well known (cf. Acts 10:37). Someone of Agrippa's background and standing would have been very familiar with both the Scriptures and the history of Christ's life. Paul had inescapably tied Christ to the OT Scriptures, thus Agrippa was placed in an awkward situation. Agrippa professed to be a Jew who respected the Jewish religion, so when Paul asked him if he believed the prophets, it was the same as asking if he accepted the Divine authority of the Scriptures. Every professing Jew would answer this with a yes and so Paul answers it for Agrippa. Paul's argument was inescapable and Agrippa couldn't refute it, but nor would he bow to it (showing that Agrippa, like the Jews who were accusing Paul, did not in practice submit to the authority of the Scriptures, though they *professed* submission very loudly). It is not possible to honour the prophets and Moses if you refuse to believe in Jesus and this is the dilemma that Agrippa was confronted with. To admit the authority of the prophets in this context would have necessitated believing in the truth of the Gospel—something Agrippa was not prepared to do. Thus with great subtlety he escapes from giving a direct answer by saying that it is not possible for someone to become a Christian after such a brief explanation of its beliefs, i.e., "Do you think that I could be persuaded to believe with such a little explanation?" The unbelieving heart has many schemes whereby it seeks to hide from the penetrating light of God's searching truth, but this is nothing but self-deception. The truth cannot be successfully suppressed (Rom. 1:18–23).

Acts 26:29

Whether with a short or a long explanation of the Christian faith, Paul says it makes no difference, his desire is the same for everyone who hears him—that they might be saved (Rom. 10:1). There was nothing about his own life or faith that Paul was ashamed about, but rather he wanted all people to come to that same place he was at with respect to his relationship with Christ. He just did not want them to be in chains and prison like he was. Paul was not angry or vengeful, but truly desired what was best for others, even if they had not treated him in the best way.

Acts 26:30–32

Once again it was obvious to all concerned, including the high ranking officials of Rome, that Paul, the representative of the Christian faith, was innocent and that all the charges against him and his teachings were groundless. However, once an appeal was made to the Emperor, no one else had the authority to pass official judgment on that case, thus Paul couldn't be released. Paul was now on his way to Rome, according to God's purposes and timing and for His glory.

Acts 27:1, 2

Luke gives us some very detailed narrative about the journey to Rome. The reasons for this are most likely to show God's providence in bringing Paul to Rome and also, by describing the drama of the journey, we can appreciate Paul's total trust in God's providence. It is only if we know nothing about how perilous sea travel is (and even more so in those days) that we can remain unmoved by what Luke describes. This account also helps us appreciate Paul's zeal and endurance in doing so much travelling on his missionary journeys. He was actually shipwrecked three times in his life *before* this incident and on one occasion he spent a day and a night in the

ocean before being rescued (2 Cor. 11:25). A shipwreck is not
something you get used to and Paul's calmness and taking charge in
many ways reveals his leadership qualities and his rest in the Lord's
will, whatever that might mean for him. Most of this narrative
makes gripping reading on its own and does not require further
comment, though I will touch on some verses that I think need a
little further explanation and application.

Acts 27:3–8

True Christianity should make us likeable people (Prov. 3:3, 4; Luke
2:52). When we are despised by people we must be sure that it is
because of Christ and His truth rather than because we have an
abrasive and offensive nature. The dog that bites everyone who
comes near to him will not have any "friends" and neither will an
unlovable person (Prov. 18:24). The commander of the Roman
guard both likes and trusts Paul and so allows him to visit some
Christians in the city while the ship was in harbour.

Acts 27:9–19

From around mid September until the first few weeks into Novem-
ber was an extremely dangerous time to be at sea. Luke notes that
the "Fast" was already past, meaning the Jewish Day of Atonement,
thus it was probably into October already (Bruce). Paul's opinion
that they would be taking an unnecessary risk to sail now was based
upon sound human understanding of sailing and weather conditions and Paul was a very seasoned traveller. He later speaks with
divine revelation about what would happen (verse 22), but here, it
was an opinion made in the light of the facts that were available to
every person who cared to look.

Acts 27:20

This violent storm did not stop for many days and nights and the
psychological strain of living in these kinds of conditions is tremendous. There is no way to find relief from the hardship and danger
that is facing you in such a situation. Hour after hour you are tossed
around until you are overcome with exhaustion and despair. Luke
says, "all hope that we would be saved was finally given up." It is a
mature faith that can trust Christ in such circumstances and maintain a deep joy in the Lord. Too often our sense of well-being and
joy is based upon what is happening to us—if it is something we

like then we feel on top of the world and are full of joy, however, if it is something we do not like, then we lose the joy of the Lord (Phil. 3:1; 4:4). Our joy in the Lord is to be based upon who He is and for what He has done and continues to do for us: He loves us (Jer. 31:3; 1 John 4:19); has redeemed us (John 3:16; Gal. 3:13); made us His children and heirs to His throne in Christ (John 1:12; Rom. 8:16, 17; Gal. 4:5; 1 John 3:1); no one can pluck us out of His hand (John 10:28, 29; 2 Tim. 1:12); not a hair from our head can fall out without His ordering of it (Luke 12:7); and all things in our lives work out for His glory and our good (Rom. 8:28; 1 Pet. 1:7). To *know* this, is to know joy!

Acts 27:21

It had been foolish to set sail at this time of year and Paul reminds them that they had taken a gamble against all sound judgement, and lost (verse 10). Not only was the ship going to be destroyed, but the cargo lost as well as everyone's possessions who were on board. I am sure Paul was quite angry because of such foolish behaviour. No one has the right to risk other people's lives and property without their consent and to do so is immoral. We are to be diligent and careful to protect the life and property of others.

Acts 27:22–29

Paul is quick to acknowledge whose property he is and whom he lives for. He also wanted God to get all the praise when all the lives were spared. In the midst of a situation where there was no hope whatsoever, Paul confidently trusted totally in the Word of God. It was not possible to get even the slightest support from any human source to confirm what God had revealed, yet Paul is prepared to stand upon the truth as immovable. We are always so quick to find "good" reasons why we shouldn't totally believe what God has said and it is often because we think that what God says just does not make sense to our particular situation. We argue that it would be fine for another era or that it is fine for other people, but not for us, well not right now anyway. Paul wouldn't tolerate such foolishness and unashamedly takes his stand upon the rock of Christ's Word. Jesus graciously confirms His earlier message to Paul (Acts 23:11). It appears as though Paul had been praying for the lives of all on the ship and the angel brings a reply that God had heard and granted this request (Jam. 5:16). Ultimately our well-being is always in the hand of God and not in our perception of what is happening around us. We need to be wise and walk in the way God has revealed, but our security is always to be in God's purposes, whatever they might be.

Acts 27:30–32

These sailors had rejected Paul's words and were out to save their own lives, without concern for the other passengers. If we live only for ourselves and not for God and His purposes, then such behavior is the most logical—save yourself and do not care about anyone else. Christ has taught a far more glorious path (John 15:13). The Centurion this time quickly obeys what Paul says and keeps everyone together.

Acts 27:33–44

No one had wanted to eat in such conditions, with the threat of death hanging over their heads, but now Paul insists that they are going to need some strength if they are going to survive. Swimming to safety in a stormy sea is no easy task. Paul was not celebrating the Lord's Supper with these unbelievers, but merely having a normal meal and thanking the Lord for it (see comments on Acts 2:42).

A Roman soldier could forfeit his life if he lost a prisoner and thus these soldiers wanted to kill all the prisoners so that none could escape. Paul's friendship with the commander of the soldiers was the means used by God to save Paul. Through Paul, God spared 276 lives from the ship.

Acts 28:1–6

The conditions were far from comfortable, yet Paul does not complain, rather we see him serving others by collecting wood for the fire. While doing this he is bitten by a snake. The natives of the island are horrified, knowing that Paul is now going to die—they obviously knew, through experience, that the viper was poisonous. Paul hardly pays any attention to the snake, knowing whose Word he had believed. The locals' conclusion that Paul was an evil man quickly changed when the snake bite had no effect upon him. We tend to interpret situations in life as good or terrible, yet Paul saw every situation as God working out His purposes and this incident opened up a wonderful opportunity to evangelise the people on Malta. Just think about the route God had lead Paul to evangelise these people, beginning with being beaten up in Jerusalem in the temple area (Acts 21:30, 31), then the attempted murders, the unjust judges, the long wait in jail, the shipwreck, the near murder by the soldiers and now the snake bite. The Lord's ways are not our ways and everything the Lord ordains has a specific purpose. May we learn to submit our lives to His sovereign plan and serve Him with joy in it, even when we do not understand all the details about it.

Acts 28:7–11

The Lord graciously allows Paul to have a massive impact upon the people of Malta, healing many, many people. We are not told of any locals coming to know the Lord, but this does not mean none did. Paul ministered among them for three months until it was safe to sail again. Because of Paul's labours among the island people, this group of 276 destitute people were given everything they needed to complete the journey to Rome.

Acts 28:12–15

Finally they arrive in Italy and find some believers in the port city. There appears to have been a week's delay in this city (probably the Centurion had official business to do) and Paul was allowed to stay with the Christians who lived there. Christians from Rome now heard that Paul was on his way to them and went to escort him into the city—a sign of their love and respect for Paul. It had been about three years since Paul had written his letter to Rome and expressed how much he wanted to see them (Rom. 1:10, 11). Paul was greatly encouraged by this show of love and support. The giants in the faith need to be encouraged too, though Paul's primary focus was on how he could encourage the brethren in Rome. Paul thanked God for his safe arrival in Rome and fulfilling his great desire to meet the Roman Christians (Rom. 15:23, 24). It is the Lord who gives us the desires of our heart, if we immerse ourselves in Him, seeking first His Kingdom and righteousness (Ps. 37:4; Matt. 6:33).

Acts 28:16

Paul was once again granted great freedoms in comparison to other prisoners, though we are not informed why. It might be safe to assume that his friendship with Julius and what had transpired during the voyage had something to do with it, though. Many people would come to Paul in his house over the next two years and each Roman guard would have heard every word of Paul's conversation with those who came to him and Paul would also have spoken personally to these guards about the Gospel. Many commentators think that it was through this kind of exposure to the Gospel that the whole palace guard came to know why Paul was in chains (Phil. 1:13).

Acts 28:17–19

Paul allows himself no time to recover from the six month ordeal he had just endured while travelling from Israel to Rome. There is urgent business to get done—proclaiming the Kingdom of God in Rome. As was Paul's custom, he first wanted to preach to the Jews (Acts 13:5, 46; 18:6; Rom. 1:16), but he probably also wanted to explain about his imprisonment so that his message wouldn't be rejected because of his bonds. To these leaders, Paul maintains his innocence with respect to the Jewish religion and customs and also towards Roman law (cf. Acts 25:8). Paul's authority for saying that he had not done anything against the Jewish customs was that he was acting in line with the revelation God had given with respect to all their customs. He was not suggesting that he was living in a way that would please the religious establishment of his day and all their man-made customs and perversions of the truth. Paul does indirectly expose the injustice of the Jewish and the Roman authorities, for neither had any case against him, yet he still was forced to appeal to Caesar in order to try and secure justice. He does make it clear though, that he holds no grudges against any of his accusers and that he does not intend to use political means to get his own back. His purpose for appealing to Caesar was not to bring legal cases against his accusers, but to protect himself from their injustice (murder). Paul could have brought charges against both the Jewish leadership and against the Roman authorities that had handled his case, yet he doesn't.

I believe Paul's name had been adequately cleared from any wrongdoing already (e.g., Acts 26:31, 32) and so he did not need to pursue any legal means to do this. The fact that Paul does not do anything about the injustice he endured does not mean that we are never allowed to make perverse leaders and judges accountable for their actions. Paul's time was limited, like all of us and we all need great wisdom to know how best to utilise the limited resources we have at our disposal. We need to constantly ask ourselves how we can make the most out of our limited time, finances and ability in the Kingdom of God. The amount of good things a person could do are far greater than, for example, the amount of time they have to do them, thus we all have to carefully choose and do the things that will have the *greatest* impact for the glory of God—we cannotdo everything! People will expect us to do everything, thus it is vital to realize our limitations and that if we are going to do worthwhile work for the Kingdom, we need to focus and be selective about how to spend our limited resources. The starting place for any long term change in the direction of justice is salvation and Paul knew this and therefore, the thrust of his efforts were to establish the right foundations. Others, after him, could build upon these foundation, but if the foundations are not in place it is pointless trying to build structures that will secure justice and peace for everyone. Usually we need to be evangelising as well as exposing injustice and seeking change by instructing people about the full counsel of God—which touches every area of life. I believe it was Francis Schaeffer who said the devil never allows us the luxury of fighting on only one battle front. This is true, though we must remember that we will not be able to fight in any meaningful way if we spread ourselves too thin—we cannotfight all the battles, for no one has either the time or the gifting to do this. We need to be able to read the signs of the times and pick those battles that are most needed in our day and that will be most beneficial for those who follow us, to build upon. This requires selflessness, humility and Godly wisdom (James 1:5).

Acts 28:20

The Jews clearly knew that the "hope of Israel" was the Messiah. Paul was hated by his nation because he proclaimed that the Messiah was Jesus and what this meant in their everyday lives. In essence he taught that the Jewish traditions, law and temple could offer no hope without Christ. The only security available for everyone is found in knowing Christ in a personal way. Not to know Christ means it is impossible for you to have assurance of salvation in your heart and thus you can never rest in the household of God as only a true child of His can rest. There is no hope whatsoever outside of Christ and all the saints and fathers of the Jewish religion found their hope in the Messiah. Hope is not to be found in a messiah created in our own minds, but in the Christ revealed to us in the Person of Jesus. Abraham, David and the prophets all found their assurance and hope in Christ (John 8:56; Acts 2:29–31; 1 Pet. 1:9). Paul was pointing out that he was the one standing in full agreement with the whole history of the Jewish nation and it was due to this faithfulness that he was in bonds. Each successive generation easily recognises how previous generations persecuted those who proclaimed God's truth, however, they then persecute those who proclaim the truth in their own generation (Luke 11:48).

Acts 28:21, 22

It was probably due to practical reasons that the Jewish leaders in Rome had not been informed about Paul, because we know how the leaders in Jerusalem hated him. If letters had been sent on the ship that Paul left on, they would have been lost when the ship sank. The ship Paul had been on, had risked the weather conditions and thus was well ahead of any other ships carrying people or messages to Rome about Paul—this is just a guess though as to why they had not had an official word about Paul. What these leaders had heard was negative reports about the Christian message. One does wonder how the Roman church, described by Paul as very vibrant (Rom. 1:8), could be so unknown by these Jewish leaders in Rome. It is possible that they were buying time until they had some information from Jerusalem and thus pretended ignorance. It does appear as though Paul's reputation preceded him, for these leaders gathered at short notice when he called for them.

Acts 28:23

For a brief consideration of the Kingdom see comments on Acts 1:3. The evidence throughout the whole of the Scriptures inescapably points to Jesus Christ and Paul spends the whole day pointing them to this evidence. Jesus had pretty much done the same thing after His resurrection on the Emmaus road (Luke 24:27). Paul's zeal and energy is once again evidenced by him being able to continue for such an extended period of time. It also says much about his gifting and knowledge of the Scriptures for him to be able to hold an audience for this long.

Acts 28:24, 25

Truth in the Scriptures is very clear and the connection between what the prophets said and the Person and Life of Jesus Christ is also very obvious (Acts 10:43). Paul's hearers had not merely had a few allusions from the OT Scriptures tied to Christ, but had had a detailed explanation from numerous passages showing that Jesus was the Messiah and this had continued for the whole day. The wilful resistance that Paul encountered, despite the inescapable evidence he presented from God's Word, lead him to quote from Isaiah, exposing his nation's stubborn refusal to bow to the revelation of God. To reject the truth in the Scriptures and to reject Jesus Christ, is a total denial of the Living God.

Acts 28:26, 27

We are to bring all our thoughts, beliefs and reasoning into submission to the revelation that was given by God and is now preserved for us by Him in the Scriptures. The root of every problem comes about when people and nations refuse to submit to every Word from the mouth of God (Matt. 4:4). The problem that Isaiah pointed out and that Paul emphasises is not that these people did not have access to the truth, but that they refused to bow to it. They refused to give the truth access into their lives by stubbornly blocking it out. Paul quotes from Isaiah 6:9,10 where the prophet was to proclaim the truth of God, but he was also told that his hearers would harden themselves against this truth. Paul is telling his audience that even as they look back upon what Isaiah said and acknowledge how clear and true his words were to that generation, so too, Paul's words were as clear and true, but also rejected by those listening to him. Paul, with apostolic authority, says his own generation was as hard-hearted as Isaiah's generation. While salvation rests in the sovereign ordering of God we must never ignore the reality of the deliberate suppression of the truth by those who are not saved—they know the truth, yet refuse to repent (Rom. 1:18–20).

Acts 28:28–31

The glorious message about the Messiah, the hope of Israel from the beginning, was rejected by Israel and thus this message would be proclaimed to the Gentiles and the Gentiles would believe in the Messiah. Christ came to bring salvation to all people groups—"But as many as received him, to them gave he power to become the sons of God, even to them that believe on his name" (John 1:12).

Acts is not a history lesson about the apostle Paul and thus we mustn't expect it to tell us everything about Paul. Luke's purpose was to show the preaching of the Gospel and the spread of Christianity from Jerusalem to the "capital" of the world (Rome). We can only guess as to why it took so long for Paul's case to come before Caesar, but this was not important to Luke. What was important was that Paul was powerfully and without hindrance preaching the Kingdom of God and everything that concerned the Lord Jesus Christ (there was nothing illegal about the Christian faith). This too is to be the focus of all that we live for— that the Lord's will be done and that His Kingdom come on earth as it is in heaven.

There are different opinions about what happened to Paul after these two years, but that does not really have anything to do with the text of Acts. Paul was a very faithful, fearless servant of the Lord, whose heartbeat was to make known the glorious message of salvation in Jesus Christ and exalt His Kingdom. May we be challenged and inspired to imitate Paul even as he imitated Christ (1 Cor. 11:1).

The conclusion of Acts, after all the hindrances, persecutions, imprisonments and martyrdoms, is that the Gospel cannot be stopped. Christ's work will continue and success is assured! Nothing shall be able to prevent the victorious advancement of Christ's power, working through His elected servants, in the whole of His Kingdom (Matt. 16:18, see comments on John 12:31; 14:13, 14; Acts 2:24; 5:27, 28). To God alone belongs all power, honour and glory—Amen! (1 Tim. 1:17; Rev. 5:12, 13).

ABOUT THE AUTHOR

Derek Carlsen, a native Zimbabwean, was a resident in that country until he was called to be the pastor of the Church of Christian Liberty in Arlington Heights, Illinois. He is also the Director of Reason of Hope Ministries in Zimbabwe, a ministry focused upon printing and distributing Christian literature in southern Africa. He received his theological training through George Whitefiled College, Cape Town, South Africa (L.Th. 1992) and Whitefield Theological Seminary, Lakeland, Florida, USA (M.Miss. 1999 and D.Miss. 2001). Derek served as a pastor in Zimbabwe for ten years and was also involved in running a Christian school in that country together with his wife Elise. Derek has written three commentaries so far: *Faith and Courage: A Commentary on Acts; That You May Believe: A Commentary on John's Gospel; Grace and Law: A Commentary on Galatians* (which is yet to be printed). Derek and Elise have been blessed with three children.

BIBLIOGRAPHY

Alexander, J. A. *Commentary on the Acts of the Apostles.* 2 vols. Minneapolis: Klock And Klock Christian Publishers, 1980.

Anderson, James. *What the Bible Teaches, Acts.* Kilmarnock: John Ritchie, Ltd., 1992.

Bahnsen, Greg L. "Socrates or Christ: The Reformation of Christian Apologetics," in *Foundations of Christian Scholarship,* Ed. Gary North. Vallecito, CA: Ross House Books, 1979.

"The Encounter of Jerusalem with Athens," in *Ashland Theological Bulletin.* XIII:1 (Spring, 1980)

Barclay, William. *The Acts of the Apostles.* The Daily Study Bible Series. Edinburgh: St. Andrew Press, 1955.

Barnes, Albert. *Notes, Explanatory and Practical, on the New Testament: Acts of the Apostles.* London: Partridge and Oakey, 1850.

Brown, David. "Acts of the Apostles," in *Commentary, Critical and Explanatory, on the Old and New Testaments,* by Jamieson, Fausset, and Brown. London: William Collins, Sons and Co., Ltd., no date.

Bruce, F. F. *The Book of the Acts, Revised,* The New International Commentary on the New Testament. Grand Rapids: Eerdmans Publishing Co., 1988.

"The Acts of the Apostles," in *The New Bible Commentary: Revised.* Eds. Guthrie, Motyer, Stibbs, and Wiseman. Downers Grove, IL: InterVarsity Press, 1970.

Paul: Apostle of the Free Spirit. Revised. Carlisle: Paternoster Publishing, 1980. US Title: *Paul: Apostle of the Heart Set Free.* Grand Rapids: Eerdmans Publishing Co., 1977.

The Speeches in the Acts of the Apostles. London: Tyndale Press, 1942.

Calvin, John. *Commentary upon The Acts of the Apostles.* 2 vols. Trans. C. Fetherstone. 1585. Ed. H. Beveridge. Reprint. Baker Book House, 1993.

Conybeare, W. J. and J. S. Howson. *The Life and Epistles of St. Paul.* New Edition. Grand Rapids: Eerdmans Publishing Co., 1964.

Farrar, F. W. *The Early Days of Christianity*. New York: Cassell, Petter, Galpin and Co., 1884.

Ferris, T. P. and G. H. C. Macgregor. "The Acts of the Apostles," in *The Interpreter's Bible, Volume 9*. Nashville: Abingdon Press, 1954.

Gempf, Conrad. "Acts," in *New Bible Commentary, 21st Century Edition*. Eds. Wenham, Motyer, Carson, and France. Downers Grove, IL: InterVarsity Press, 1994.

Henry, Matthew. "Acts of the Apostles," in *Acts to Revelation*, Volume 6 of *Matthew Henry's Commentary on the Whole Bible*. 6 vols. McLean, VA: MacDonald Publishing Co., no date.

Josephus, Flavius. "The Antiquities of the Jews and The Wars of the Jews," in the *Life and Works of Flavius Josephus*. Trans. William Whiston. Philadelphia: The John C. Winston Company, no date.

Kistemaker, Simon. *New Testament Commentary: Exposition of the Acts of the Apostles*. Grand Rapids: Baker Book House, 1990.

Lenski, R. C. H. *The Interpretation of the Acts of the Apostles*. Minneapolis: Augsburg Publishing House, 1961.

Machen, J. Gresham. *The Origin of Paul's Religion*. Grand Rapids: Eerdmans Publishing Co., 1965.

Martin, Ralph P. *Acts*. Scripture Union Bible Study Books. Grand Rapids: Eerdmans Publishing Co., 1967.

Oetting, Walter. *The Church of the Catacombs, the Early Church from the Apostles to A.D. 250*. St. Louis: Concordia Publishing House, 1970.

Stott, John R. W. *The Message of Acts*. Second Edition. The Bible Speaks Today. Downers Grove, IL: InterVarsity Press, 1991.

Stonehouse, N. B. *Paul Before the Areopagus: and Other New Testament Studies*. London: Tyndale Press, 1957.

Vaughan, Curtis. *Acts: A Study Guide Commentary*. Grand Rapids: Zondervan Publishing House, 1974, 1979.

Vos, Geerhardus. *Redemptive History and Biblical Perspective*. Philadelphia: Presbyterian and Reformed Publishing Co., 1980.